T0330405

Harvard Studies in Business History · *49*

Published with the support of the Harvard Business School
Edited by Thomas K. McCraw
Isidor Straus Professor of Business History
Graduate School of Business Administration
George F. Baker Foundation
Harvard University

The Emergence of Modern Business Enterprise in France, 1800–1930

MICHAEL STEPHEN SMITH

HARVARD UNIVERSITY PRESS
Cambridge, Massachusetts, and London, England   2006

Library of Congress Cataloging-in-Publication Data

Smith, Michael Stephen, 1944–
    The emergence of modern business enterprise in France, 1800–1930 /
Michael Stephen Smith.
      p. cm.—(Harvard studies in business history ; 49)
    Includes bibliographical references and index.
    ISBN 0–674–01939–3 (alk. paper)
    1. Industrialization—France—History. 2. Industries—France—
History. 3. Capitalism—France—History. 4. Business enterprises—
France—History. I. Series.
HC275.S64   2005
338.944'009'034—dc22   2005050231

To my wife, Carol,
and to the memory of our beloved daughter, Laura

Contents

Acknowledgments   *ix*

Prologue   *1*

Introduction: Laying the Foundations for Modern Capitalism in France, 1500–1800   *11*

I   From Merchant Capitalism to Finance Capitalism

   1   Continuity and Change in Merchant Capitalism, 1800–1840s   *33*

   2   The Revolution in Banking and Transportation, 1850s–1870s   *67*

   3   The New World of Financial and Commercial Capitalism, 1870s–1900s   *96*

II   The Flowering of Industrial Capitalism

   4   Textile Capitalism   *131*

   5   The Capitalism of Coal   *161*

   6   The Capitalism of Iron and Steel   *177*

   7   Hardware, Machinery, and Construction   *198*

8   The Capitalism of Chemicals   *219*

9   The Capitalism of Glass, Paper, and Print   *237*

10   Industrial Capitalism and Consumer Goods   *265*

11   The New World of Industrial Capitalism   *295*

III   The Second Industrial Revolution and the Beginnings of Managerial Capitalism, 1880s–1930s

12   Big Steel   *333*

13   The Electrical Industry   *372*

14   The Automobile and Its Allies   *400*

15   Chemicals and Materials   *432*

16   The New World of Managerial Capitalism   *461*

Conclusion: France on the Verge   *483*

Notes   *495*

Index   *561*

Acknowledgments

After working on this book for more than fifteen years, I welcome the opportunity to finally acknowledge all those who have offered me aid and support, although I do so at the risk of inadvertently omitting names that deserve mention. I first want to thank the staffs of the libraries and archives I have used: the Thomas Cooper Library of the University of South Carolina, the Baker and Widener Libraries of Harvard University, the Bodleian Library of Oxford University, the Library of Congress, the Bibliothèque Nationale, the Archives Nationales (including the Archives du Monde du Travail in Roubaix), and the Archives Historiques du Crédit Lyonnais. I particularly want to thank Jo Cottingham and the intrepid interlibrary loan service at Thomas Cooper Library; Roger Nougaret, Conservateur of the Crédit Lyonnais archives; and Armell Le Goff, Conservateur en Chef du Patrimoine, Archives du Monde du Travail. For their help in securing microfilm copies of many French doctoral dissertations, I thank Catherine Vervacke and the staff of the Atelier National de Reproduction des Thèses at the Université de Lille.

The section on Air Liquide in Chapter 15 was first published in longer form as "Product Innovation and the Growth of the Large Firm: The Case of Air Liquide, 1902–1930," in *Essays in Economic and Business History,* 17 (1999), 49–61. I thank the journal's editor, Michael V. Namorato, for permission to include that material in the present work.

Fellow historians on both sides of the Atlantic have contributed in various ways to the researching and writing of this book. These include, in France, Louis Bergeron, Maurice Lévy-Leboyer, and Patrick Fridenson, and, in the United States, Mansel Blackford, the late Rondo Cameron, Alfred D. Chandler, Jr., William Childs, Edmund Clignan, the late Edward Whiting Fox, Christopher Johnson, William Keylor, Bruce Kogut, Richard Kuisel, James Laux, Michael Namorato, Edwin Perkins, Donald Reid, and Mira Wilkins. I also thank Patrick Maney and Peter Becker, the present and immediate past chairs respectively of the University of South Carolina Department of History, who provided both financial and moral support for this project over many years.

I owe an incalculable debt to Thomas McCraw who, in his dual role as editor of *The Business History Review* and editor of the Harvard Studies in Business History, took an active interest in this book at an early stage, strongly supported its publication, and repeatedly offered much-needed advice and encouragement. Also offering crucial support at the Harvard University Press early on was Jeff Kehoe, former associate editor for history and social sciences. The readers' reports for the press, one anonymous and one by Michael Miller, provided invaluable guidance and constructive criticism as well as much encouragement. Any omissions and errors that remain in the book—along with the failure to follow sound advice—should be attributed solely to the author.

I owe thanks to many others at Harvard University Press, especially Kathleen McDermott and her assistant, Kathi Drummy. Barbara Goodhouse at Westchester Book Services ably shepherded the book through copyediting, indexing, and production.

Lastly I want to thank Carol for her many substantive contributions to this project but mostly for a lifetime of love and support in both times of joy and times of sadness. Our daughter, Laura, did not live to see the completion of this book, the writing of which spanned much of her adult life. Yet she too contributed to it in untold ways. It is to Carol and Laura, the most important people in my life, that I have dedicated the book.

The Emergence of Modern Business
Enterprise in France, 1800–1930

Prologue

This book tells the story of how French business became modern—how, in the course of the nineteenth and early twentieth centuries, France left behind the world of small-scale, merchant-dominated capitalism and entered the new world of large-scale, industrial capitalism. In the process, it traces the rise of the scores of businesses that collectively defined the commercial and industrial economies of modern France. It especially seeks to explain how and why France acquired the roster of large corporate enterprises that would come to dominate France's domestic economy and project French economic influence throughout Europe and the world over the course of the twentieth century.

Underlying this book is extensive research in various primary sources, including the annual reports of major companies and other materials deposited in the Archives Nationales, the credit reports on companies in the Crédit Lyonnais archives, and jury reports for the Paris expositions of 1878, 1889, and 1900. But, given its breadth, the book depends also on secondary sources, starting with the company profiles published by the business journalist Julien Turgan in the nineteenth century and the studies by economic geographers such as Raoul Blanchard, Claude Prêcheur, and Michel Laferrère, who mapped the development of French industry in the twentieth century. It draws on earlier contributions to French business history by American scholars, especially David Landes, Rondo Cameron, Charles Freedeman, James Laux, Michael Miller, and Donald Reid. Even more, it depends on the work of French historians, from the pioneering studies by Bertrand Gille, Claude Fohlen, Jean Lambert-Dansette, Pierre Léon, Jean Bouvier, and Maurice Lévy-Leboyer in the 1950s and 1960s, when business history interested few academic historians in France and centered mainly on banking history, to the great outpouring of company and industry histories published in the past thirty years by what in effect has been the first full generation of French business historians. Without this newly created corpus of secondary literature, a work of synthesis like this could not have been written.

While much of this book's basic information comes from the work of French historians, it derives much of its conceptual framework from the work of the eminent American business historian, Alfred D. Chandler, Jr., especially his two masterworks, *The Visible Hand* and *Scale and Scope*.[1] Like Chandler's work, this book is a kind of collective biography (of companies, not people). It constructs a history of French business from the bottom up, from the experiences of hundreds of firms, especially those that emerged as the leaders in their respective sectors of the French economy in the course of the nineteenth and early twentieth centuries. Also like Chandler's work, this book finds the central theme of modern business history in increasing organizational complexity and especially in the rise of "big business." In Part III it argues that the same forces that were giving rise to a new kind of very large, very complex business organization in the United States, Germany, and Great Britain between 1880 and 1930 were also at work in France, and that for France, no less than for the other advanced industrial nations, the early twentieth century represented the "seedtime" for modern managerial capitalism.

While this book finds much in common between the way business evolved in France and in the other major industrial countries, it is also sensitive to what has been distinctive and idiosyncratic in French economic and business development. At the same time that it stresses the importance of technological innovation and market dynamics in the rise of large-scale industrial enterprise (as does Chandler), it emphasizes the pivotal role of the French state and the abiding and pervasive influence of French bankers and financiers. Moreover, by its very subject matter, the book takes a position on—and seeks to make a contribution to—the long-running debate over the relative success and failure of French economic development in the nineteenth and twentieth centuries, a debate that antedates and transcends Chandler's reconfiguration of business history. To understand how the book relates to that debate, we must look briefly at the historiography of the past fifty years.

Assessing French Economic Development

For decades, the study of the economic and business development of France in the nineteenth and twentieth centuries has been dominated by a dispute between two schools of thought, optimist and pessimist. The pessimist school, established as a kind of orthodoxy in the years after World War II and long associated with the American economic historian David Landes, views the story of French economic development from 1800 to the mid-1900s as a failed (or at least incomplete or "retarded") case of British-style industrialization. Implicit in the pessimist argument is the assumption that, because France had achieved rough economic parity with Britain by the end of the eighteenth century, it was in a position to match the growth and development of the British economy stride for stride in the nineteenth century. That this did not happen—that instead there was a growing disparity between the total value of French and British production as the nineteenth century progessed, with British GNP exceeding French GNP by 50 percent at the beginning of the twentieth century—was seen as less a matter of exceptional British achievement than a matter of French failure. Under the influence of this pessimist orthodoxy, economic historians on both sides of the Atlantic devoted much of their time and effort between the late 1940s and the early 1970s to identifying the factors—social, political, and cultural as well as economic—that might explain why France had fallen behind Britain and could not subsequently catch up.[2]

The pessimist school arose at a time when what seemed to require explanation was France's chronically poor economic performance in the first half of the twentieth century and the apparent slowness of its economic recovery immediately after World War II. But the subsequent "thirty glorious years" of high-speed growth (really about twenty years, from the early 1950s to the early 1970s) seemed to render obsolete the pessimists' preoccupation with the sources of French backwardness and focused attention instead on the possible hidden strengths in the French approach to economic development that might account for the country's postwar economic resurgence. Accordingly, in the 1970s a revisionist school arose that took a much more optimistic view of French economic performance in the nineteenth century. Especially influential was a book by Patrick O'Brien and Caglar Keyder that reinterpreted the macroeconomic data to show that, in terms of per capita output, France had never really fallen behind the British. Apparently it did not matter that France had not developed large-scale industrial enterprise as much as the British or Germans, because France's small-scale craft-based system of production turned out to be just as efficient and gave the French a standard of living comparable to that of its more industrialized neighbors. The French path to economic modernity was different, the revisionists asserted, but not necessarily inferior.[3] As the notion of France's separate path caught on in the 1980s, France became something of a "poster child" for critics of mass production, mass consumption, and corporate giantism who were promoting ecologically cleaner, more worker-friendly models of economic development.[4]

But the argument was not over. "Anti-revisionists" soon produced new figures on French per capita output and per capita growth that disputed the revisionists' optimistic view of French macroeconomic development. Indeed, a comprehensive comparative study of the French and British economies on the eve of World War I, published in 1997 by the French econometrician Jean-Pierre Dormois, appears to have fully rehabilitated the pessimist view of France's economic performance and to have delivered a fatal blow to the notion that France followed a "different but equal" path to the twentieth century (by showing inter alia that French industrial production per capita and total output per capita were at best only two-thirds of British per capita output throughout the nineteenth century).[5]

Yet even as the pessimists were counterattacking by reworking and reinterpreting macroeconomic data, the temporary ascendancy of revisionism led to—or at least was accompanied by—new interest in business history among aspiring professional historians in France. The resulting surge in firm-level research demonstrated that French industry was much more expansive and technologically advanced in the nineteenth and twentieth centuries than once thought. It has also documented the emergence of a number of French firms that compare favorably in size and competitiveness to their British or German counterparts—even when the sectors to which they belong remained comparatively small. So, in the final analysis, perhaps the revisionists had not been too bold—as their quantitatively oriented critics held—but rather too timid. Rather than following a special path, perhaps France did participate in the mainstream development of large-scale industrial enterprise.[6]

Embracing this "post-revisionist" conception of French business history, this book argues against the "special path" interpretation of French economic development and in favor of the French experience being simply a variation on what occurred in the other leading industrialized countries. Above all, it views the story of French economic development over the past two centuries as one of considerable achievement. What else could it be, considering that in the year 2000 a medium-sized country like France, with a population of 58.7 million (twentieth largest among all nations), possessed the world's fourth largest economy and played host to some of the world's leading commercial and industrial firms? From the perspective of the present day, what seems important is not that France initially industrialized more slowly than Great Britain and was overtaken by Germany in the late nineteenth century, but that France remained among the four or five leading economic powers in the world throughout the nineteenth century and was in a position, once it got beyond the disasters of 1914–1945, to catch up with and even surpass the other economic powers of Europe in the second half of the twentieth century. It is with an eye to France's eventual success in the late twentieth century that this book tells the story of the modernization of French business from 1800 to 1930.

Some Preliminary Considerations

Before proceeding further, there are some issues of definition and interpretation as well as some areas of potential misunderstanding that warrant further discussion.

Defining Business and Capitalism

Over the years, the word "capitalism" has been imbued with multiple meanings, and its usage has long been surrounded by controversy. Some have used the term very broadly, as a virtual synonym for the economic, social, and political order based on private property and free enterprise that came to dominate western Europe and America in modern times. Capitalism is used in this sense, especially by Marxists, in contrast to "feudalism" (the agrarian-aristocratic economic and political system of the Middle Ages, out of which capitalism supposedly sprang), and it is used by Marxists and American conservatives alike in contrast to "communism" and other "command economies" of the twentieth century. At the other extreme, the renowned French historian Fernand Braudel gave capitalism a very narrow functional meaning, reserving it for the monopolistic, high-profit international trade that emerged in Europe in the early modern period.[7]

This study follows Braudel in using capitalism in a functional sense— as a sub-category of the broader term "business"—but it does not construe the word as narrowly as Braudel. If "business" can be defined as the various activities associated with producing and selling goods and services in a market for a profit, "capitalism" can be defined as those business activities that involve utilizing pre-existing wealth ("capital") in a sufficiently rational and systematic way and on a sufficient scale to allow the accumulation of additional capital. In other words, all capitalists are businessmen (or women), but not all businessmen are necessarily capitalists, a term best reserved for the big operators and the high rollers. In truth, however, we need not adhere to this distinction too closely. Because we are looking mostly at the rise of the large enterprises that came to dominate the French economy and polity in the nineteenth and twentieth centuries, the terms "business" and "capitalism"—and "business enterprise" and "capitalist enterprise"—tend to be used interchangeably in the pages that follow.

The Question of Entrepreneurship

In writing any history of business or capitalism, it is hard to avoid the concept of "entrepreneurship." In the long debate over France's economic performance, the pessimists were strongly influenced by Joseph Schumpeter's definition of entrepreneurship as mold-breaking innovation that involves the "creative destruction" of both institutions and enterprises in the cause of moving the economic system to a more productive level. For the pessimists, it was ultimately a deficiency in Schumpeterian entrepreneurship that doomed France to economic decline or backwardness in the nineteenth and early twentieth centuries, and accordingly they devoted a great deal of effort to discovering the reasons for this deficiency. This study, by contrast, is much less concerned with the "problem of entrepreneurship" in general or with a lack of Schumpeterian entrepreneurship in particular. To be sure, in the chapters that follow, there are plenty of things that qualify as entrepreneurial failure, either in the conventional sense (bad management of a specific enterprise) or in the Schumpeterian sense (failure to innovate). But these examples are more than balanced by many instances of entrepreneurial success of both kinds. Even if (as some would argue) the French socioeconomic system encouraged and rewarded entrepreneurs less than, say, the British and American systems did, there is little evidence of a systemic shortage of entrepreneurs and entrepreneurship in the period 1800–1930. It is perhaps true that France produced fewer world-class, home-grown entrepreneurs than it needed in these years, but by then France was an open society that allowed foreigners of talent and ambition to participate fully in its economic life. Indeed, as we shall see, France regularly received infusions of entrepreneurial talent from outside (much as the United States did then and is doing now). In short, the position here is that, when the full record of French business activity is taken into account, questions about systemic deficiencies in entrepreneurship and chronic entrepreneurial failure in France become moot.

Critical Periods in French Business History:
1880s–1920s versus 1945–1975
While arguing against the prevalence of entrepreneurial failure in modern France, this book also challenges how scholars have conventionally defined the critical periods in France's recent economic and business history. It is generally agreed that the recent convergence in economic output between France and its neighbors Britain and Germany, and the emergence of a number of French firms as world leaders in their respective industries over the past two or three decades, could not have occurred without the "thirty glorious years" of high-speed growth after World War II. But what was behind that growth spurt, and does it by itself account for France's subsequent economic and business successes?

It has long been accepted—perhaps because of the ascendancy of the pessimist orthodoxy concerning the state of the French economy prior to 1940—that the sources of the thirty glorious years were to be found in the recent past, in a cluster of shocks and innovations that began with military defeat in 1940 and continued with wartime and postwar experiments in economic planning, the postwar population explosion, and Marshall Plan aid. In other words, it was new attitudes, new policies, new mouths to feed, and an influx of outside capital and expertise in the late 1940s and early 1950s (rather than anything that had happened before 1940) that accounted for France's success in the late twentieth century.[8] Likewise, the merging of the French economy into a larger continental economy through the formation of the European Economic Community is often seen as the chief cause for the emergence of larger, more competitive French industrial firms after 1960.[9] Certainly all these things made a difference, but do they provide a sufficient explanation for what happened?

The message of the Chandlerian literature is that national economic success since 1945 has been less the product of short-term capital flows and government policies than the product of the steady accretion of technological and organizational capabilities by a country's leading companies over many decades. This is perhaps truest for the United States where, as Chandler has shown, the firms that introduced the new technologies of the Third Industrial Revolution, and thereby dominated the world economy after 1945, did so on the basis of corporate resources and capacities acquired in the half-century or so prior to 1945. However, recent research has shown that the economic successes of many other countries in the late twentieth century were similarly grounded in the earlier development of their leading companies.[10] It is the contention of this book that the same can be said for France.

The success of French capitalism and the emergence of French firms as European and even global leaders in the second half of the twentieth century rested on organizational foundations put in place as early as the nineteenth century but particularly during the Second Industrial Revolution (1880s–1920s). No amount of tinkering with domestic economic policy, no amount of state economic planning, no amount of outside capital investment, and no amount of European economic integration could have generated the postwar economic miracle if France had not already possessed a high level of technological, entrepreneurial, and organizational expertise, as well as an array of large business enterprises (either private or state-owned) that could serve as the vehicles for the development and application of new technologies. In other words, the economic breakthrough of 1945–1975 and the subsequent success of big French companies depended on the prior development of a modern system of industrial enterprise in France. Seen in this context, the period 1800–1930, and especially 1880–1930, represents a "critical period" in the modern economic and business history of France comparable to the period 1945–1975. To understand how France attained the position it occupied at the end of the twentieth century, one must take both periods into account. Of course, one of the principal purposes of this book is to provide the thick description of French business development that will demonstrate the validity of this assertion.

Plan of the Book

The story of how the modern French business system emerged between 1800 and 1930 is presented here as a drama in three acts. Part I describes the maturation of French commercial and finance capitalism in the nineteenth century. In particular, it explores how various French merchants, merchant bankers, and entrepreneurs transformed France's commercial infrastructure by renovating France's transportation and banking systems and by creating modern forms of enterprise in distribution and retailing. Merchant capitalists also provided much of the impetus for the creation of mechanized production of manufactured goods. These efforts are explored in Part II, which describes the "flowering" of industrial capitalism over a broad front in the nineteenth century. These simultaneous developments in commerce and industry in turn provided the prerequisites for the Second Industrial Revolution and the great economic expansion of 1890–1930—the subject of Part III—which ushered in the era of big business and managerial capitalism in France and thereby put French business on the course it would follow through the rest of the twentieth century.

Before launching into the history of French business in the nineteenth century, we must take note of where France stood at the end of the eighteenth century. It need hardly be said that France—unlike the United States—was not a new country in 1800. By then the French state (and in many ways the French nation) had been in existence for over a thousand years, and capitalist enterprise had been developing in France—and interacting with the French monarchy and French society—for hundreds of years. Moreover, at the end of the eighteenth century the French Revolution fundamentally changed the legal framework under which capitalist enterprise would operate in the years ahead. To provide a foundation for our examination of French business development in modern times, the introductory chapter summarizes the legacies of the early modern era.

Laying the Foundations for Modern Capitalism in France, 1500–1800

The chapters that follow trace in some detail how the great edifice of modern business enterprise took shape in France over the course of the nineteenth and early twentieth centuries. This introduction briefly describes how the foundation for that edifice was slowly put in place over the 300 years that stretched from the end of the Hundred Years' War to the time of the French Revolution. It first looks at three crucial contributions of the early modern era: (1) the creation by the kings of France of a large territorial state and a strong central government committed to achieving "national" economic prowess, in part through the promotion of private enterprise in trade and manufacturing; (2) the development of interregional trade and the introduction of the institutions of merchant capitalism into France's predominantly agrarian economy; and (3) the emergence of a kind of "proto-industrial" capitalism that would subsequently give rise to full-fledged industrial capitalism. This chapter then considers the impact of the French Revolution, in particular how the reforms of the Revolutionary era helped to create a pro-business legal environment and to make France "safe for capitalism." It concludes with a brief description of the new framework for business enterprise that emerged in the wake of the Revolution and the Napoleonic Empire.

Creating France: From Royal Domain to Nation-State

The creation of what for all intents and purposes was already a modern nation-state on the eve of the French Revolution was the great achievement of the long line of French monarchs stretching from Hugh Capet, Count of Paris in the tenth century, through the Valois kings of the sixteenth century to the Bourbon monarchs of the seventeenth and eighteenth centuries. To be sure, this achievement was somewhat inadvertent. The early kings of France were aiming not to "create France" but only to survive and, if possible, to expand their personal territorial holdings, and their success in this endeavor was by no means foreordained. The political history of the French monarchy in the Middle Ages is a story of recurring cycles of territorial expansion and contraction. It was not until the English were driven out and the lands of the dukes of Burgundy reabsorbed during the reigns of Charles VII and Louis XI in the fifteenth century that France attained (permanently, it turned out) anything approaching its modern territorial configuration. The rounding out of what are today considered France's "natural boundaries" came only under the Bourbon kings in the seventeenth and eighteenth centuries. However, from 1500 onward, the kings of France controlled the largest contiguous territory in Europe. As the various natural and man-made barriers to communication within this territory were lifted (a process that began to accelerate with the building of royal roads in the seventeenth and eighteenth centuries), it came to form the largest "national" market on the Continent, which in itself provided an enormous stimulus to capitalist enterprise.

As they acquired more territory, the kings of France gradually put in place the governmental institutions necessary for the functioning of a modern state and a modern economy. Foremost among these institutions was the French legal system. History books have long emphasized the arbitrary nature of monarchical rule in France, especially in the era of divine-right royal absolutism under the Bourbons. But, as recent scholarship has emphasized, royal absolutism was more propaganda than reality, even in the age of Louis XIV.[1] Bourbon France, it turns out, was as much a nation of laws as Hanoverian Britain. From the twelfth century on, the French kings sought to extend their authority in recently conquered lands by setting up law courts that offered people royal justice that was more evenhanded than the feudal justice meted out by local lords. These courts in turn became the vehicles for the creation and spread of a distinctly French system of law.

France actually had two systems of law: the customary law of the feudal North, which was gradually written down by royal clerks starting in the fifteenth century, and the written law employed in southern France since the days of the Roman Empire. These two systems were eventually merged and codified in a series of *grandes ordonnances* issued by Louis XIV and his successors. The Ordinance of 1667, for example, authorized the creation of a code of civil procedure, and later ordinances codified criminal and commercial procedure and maritime and testamentary law. These ordinances were supplemented by legal commentaries that in effect gave France an embryonic system of common law by the late eighteenth century.[2] By modern standards, this system was riddled with inconsistencies and injustices, notably the absence of equal standing of all citizens before the law, variations in the law from province to province, and the omnipresence of special rights and privileges. Yet, even before these flaws were addressed by the reforms of the French Revolution and by the definitive (re)codification under Napoleon, French law provided a viable framework for the workings of a civil society and a capitalist economy. Businessmen could enter into contracts enforceable at law, civil suits could be settled, and crime could be prosecuted. Most importantly, the rights of property owners were reasonably secure.

In addition to a legal system, the monarchs of early modern France put in place three other elements of government that were indispensable for the effective functioning of a capitalist economy:

1. *A system for defending the realm and for maintaining domestic order.* From earliest times, war was the principal vocation of French kings. The Valois and Bourbon monarchs converted the feudal army of the Middle Ages into a standing professional army in the late fifteenth and early sixteenth centuries, and they subsequently added a navy in the seventeenth century. These forces shielded France from the depredations of foreign invaders for over 300 years, from the end of the Hundred Years' War to the onset of the wars of the French Revolution in the 1790s. The resulting domestic tranquillity was further enhanced by the crown's success in eliminating private armies and in utilizing its army as an internal police force.

2. *Fiscal and monetary systems.* To support their professional army and navy, the French monarchs collected a variety of direct and indirect taxes from their subjects. As a necessary ingredient in its fiscal system, the crown created a national currency based on the *livre* (the French pound) and fostered the monetization of the French economy.

3. *A pro-growth national economic policy.* As early as the 1480s and especially by the 1600s, advisers to the French kings realized that

the military strength of the monarchy depended on the underlying strength of what we would call the national economy. In the 1660s, Louis XIV's great controller-general of finances, Jean-Baptiste Colbert, came to believe that managing trade flows—buying less from foreign suppliers and selling more to foreign customers—held the key to maximizing national wealth. To achieve a more favorable balance of trade, Colbert and his successors instituted the various economic policies that historians later grouped under the term "mercantilism." These measures included a systematic policy of import substitution through the state-supported transfer of foreign industries to French soil (such as Dutch papermaking and Venetian glassmaking), as well as the state-sponsored buildup of the French merchant marine and the acquisition of overseas colonies, especially among the sugar-growing islands of the Caribbean, to give France a share of the burgeoning Atlantic trade and a stake in the production of the new colonial goods. As it embarked on the promotion of domestic industry and foreign trade, the government of France thus played an increasingly important role in nurturing the development of merchant and industrial capitalism, the twin pillars on which the modern business system of France would eventually rest.

The Rise of Merchant Capitalism

Agriculture dominated the French economy from its beginnings until the twentieth century, and maintaining the health of the agricultural system—and extracting a surplus from it in the form of taxes—remained the central concern of French monarchs from the Middle Ages to the eighteenth century. Therefore, developments on the land and in rural society—the growing of crops and the raising of livestock, the struggle by peasant farmers to shake off the constraints of serfdom, the gradual commercialization of agriculture—have long been, and will continue to be, of great interest to economic and social historians of early modern France. This book, however, gives little attention to agriculture simply because the rise of modern business enterprise in France depended less on what was happening on the land and in the agrarian villages than on what was happening in the towns, where trade and industry developed, and along the rivers and coastlines, where interregional and international commerce arose.

As Fernand Braudel emphasized, first in *The Wheels of Commerce* and then in *The Identity of France,* local and regional trade had become well established in the agrarian heartland of France by the end of the Middle Ages thanks to the emergence of hundreds of market towns. Initially peasant farmers exchanged their produce with one another and with itinerant peddlers on weekly market days in these towns. In time these towns came to play host to resident shopkeepers *(commerçants),* who in turn came to depend on wholesale merchants *(négociants)* who supplied them with an array of manufactures, both domestic and imported. Among the wholesale merchants, the ones who really mattered in Braudel's estimation, because they alone accumulated great wealth, were the *grands négociants,* who organized long-distance trade in goods of high value, like fine cloth and spices.[3]

To the extent that France participated in this highest level of merchant capitalism (and Braudel thought France was long deficient in this area), it developed less in the agrarian heartland—the earliest area to be incorporated into the French monarchy—than on the periphery, in areas that remained outside the control of the French kings until the fifteenth century or even later. For example, it was found in Bordeaux, which emerged as a center for the international trade in wine during the Middle Ages, and in the Breton port of Saint-Malo, long a center of the coasting trade between France and the Iberian Peninsula (both of these port cities were permanently incorporated into the French kingdom only at the end of the fifteenth century). More importantly, high-level merchant capitalism was found in the towns and cities in eastern France that became involved in the overland trade in spices, cloth, and precious metals between Italy and the Low Countries. Foremost among these was Lyon.

In the late Middle Ages, Lyon was emerging as an important European trade center, largely due to the gradual colonization of the French economy by Italian merchants. In the 1460s, the Medicis of Florence moved the headquarters of their transalpine operations from Geneva to Lyon, and the French king, Louis XI (whose government was becoming ever more dependent on loans from the Medicis and other Italian bankers), granted Lyon the right to hold four annual fairs. Soon Lyon had become the official port of entry for silks and spices coming into France from Italy and the chief port of egress for French woolens heading for the Mediterranean. While a small group of Italian merchants continued to control Lyon's long-distance trade, a population of native French merchants arose to distribute to the rest of France the goods brought to Lyon by the Italians. Eventually the Lyon merchants took over the importation of silk, and, with lavish support from Colbert in the 1660s, Lyon emerged as Europe's leading center for the production of, and trade in, silk cloth. As discussed below, Lyon remained France's second city, and a leading center for commerce and manufacturing, into the twentieth century. In the seventeenth century, however, the center of gravity for long-distance trade in Europe shifted from the overland corridor between Italy and the Low Countries to the Mediterranean and Atlantic seaboards, and increasingly French seaports displaced Lyon as the principal incubators for merchant capitalism in France.[4]

The modern development of France's maritime commerce began in the Mediterranean in the sixteenth century. The ancient port of Marseille, at best a junior partner of Venice and Genoa in the spice trade of the late Middle Ages, came under the control of the French crown in 1481 and soon became the principal beneficiary of the reassertion of French power in the Mediterranean. In 1535, François I defied the Pope and the Christian sensibilities of his fellow European monarchs by concluding a treaty of friendship with the Ottoman sultan in Constantinople. When the Turks broke the Venetian stranglehold on Mediterranean shipping later in the century, the Marseillais took control of the trade between France and the ports of the eastern Mediterranean. By the eighteenth century, Marseillais merchants dominated the coasting trade of the Ottoman Empire, earning handsome profits that in turn underwrote their entry into the even more lucrative Atlantic trade.[5]

The French played at best a minor role in the first wave of overseas exploration and colonization in the sixteenth century. Only after the English entered the race for New World colonies and a share of the Atlantic trade in the early 1600s did the Bourbon monarchs of France make their move. Under the direction first of Richelieu and Mazarin and later Colbert, the French government subsidized the building of an oceangoing merchant fleet, launched a navy, and began acquiring colonies in North America, the Indian Ocean, and (most importantly) the Caribbean. France captured Martinique in 1635 and Guadeloupe in 1659, and over the next thirty years it gained control of the biggest prize of all, Saint-Domingue (Hispaniola). Soon plantations to cultivate sugar cane were established, and a spirited trade in African slaves followed. Initially Colbert granted exclusive control of the Antilles trade to a privileged company, but protests from France's leading Atlantic ports ended this arrangement (access to this trade, however, remained the exclusive preserve of French merchants and ships until the mid-nineteenth century). Meanwhile, another privileged trading company, the French East India Company, developed a burgeoning trade with India and China through its newly created home port, Lorient (from "Orient"), on the coast of Brittany.

The eighteenth century proved to be, in the estimation of Paul Butel, the "golden age" of France's foreign commerce, which grew at a rate that exceeded even that of English commerce over the course of the century, thanks largely to the rapid and continuous expansion of the Antilles trade. Of the dozen ports granted letters patent to trade with the Caribbean islands in 1717, Bordeaux came to control the largest share of that trade and as a consequence experienced the fastest growth of any French city in the eighteenth century (its population rose from 45,000 in 1700 to 110,000 by 1789). Already a cosmopolitan city of merchant capitalists in 1700, thanks to the wine trade, Bordeaux attracted even more merchants from all over Europe in the course of the 1700s to oversee the redistribution of its colonial imports (87 percent of the sugar that entered Bordeaux from the French Antilles was re-exported). The transatlantic segment of that trade, meanwhile, remained in the hands of a wealthy coterie of French merchants and shipowners.[6]

The rise of the Atlantic trade—like the overland spice trade in eastern France before it—served as a catalyst for the development of subsidiary trades through much of the French hinterland. Behind every great port merchant stood dozens of smaller merchants who oversaw the production of various goods for the maritime and colonial markets. For example, much of western France, especially in the triangle defined by Brest, Nantes, and Rouen, was mobilized in the eighteenth century to supply sailcloth for the Atlantic merchant fleet and for the French navy as well as shoddy cotton and linen cloth for the colonies. The only comparable "pole of attraction" for merchant capitalism in France was found in the capital, Paris, and at the nearby royal court at Versailles (much of northern France—turned into a unified free trade zone by Colbert—was organized by the cloth merchants of Paris to supply this market). Thanks to the colonial trade and the Paris trade—as well as the Levant trade of Marseille, the silk trade of Lyon, and the commercial activities of dozens of smaller cities in all parts of the country—France possessed a sophisticated, multilevel commercial economy that supported a large and diverse population of merchant capitalists by the end of the eighteenth century. The demands of this commercial economy—especially the colonial trade—also stimulated the development of merchant-manufacturing, an incipient form of industrial capitalism, over the course of the eighteenth century.

The Beginnings of Industrial Capitalism

In this book, the term "industrial capitalism" refers principally to manufacturing enterprises that employ powered machinery and large numbers of semiskilled wage workers in a factory setting. The rise of mechanized industrial enterprise in France depended to a great extent on the importation and application of new technologies from Great Britain—especially steam engines, machines for spinning and weaving cotton, and coal-based techniques for refining iron—although the French also made important contributions to the new industrial technology (including the Leblanc soda process and the Robert papermaking machine). Technology transfer and the rise of mechanized manufacturing in France from the late eighteenth century to the late nineteenth century is addressed more fully in Part II. Here it must simply be noted that these later developments did not arise in a vacuum but rested on foundations put in place earlier.

In the seventeenth and early eighteenth centuries, France witnessed the emergence of what might be called "proto-industrial capitalism," in which large, complex enterprises arose on the basis of traditional unmechanized production methods by more efficiently organizing the existing pool of native-born artisans and by recruiting additional artisans from abroad. The founders of these enterprises, known as *marchands fabricants* (merchant-manufacturers), were drawn from the ranks of both merchants and master craftsmen. In some cases the merchant-manufacturers worked within the guild system in the cities, subcontracting with master craftsmen for the labor of their journeymen, and in some cases the merchant-manufacturers circumvented the guilds by "putting out" work to non-guild rural workers. The latter strategy was especially common in the textile trades, which could draw on a large pool of spinners and weavers willing to work for low wages in the countryside. To assure quality and to curb embezzlement of materials—both of which were hard to do in the putting out system—some merchant-manufacturers brought their workers together under their direct supervision in "proto-factories." More often than not, merchant-manufacturers combined these various practices, employing outworkers for phases of production requiring less skill (spinning yarn, smelting iron ore) while employing urban craftsmen and factory workers for crucial preparatory and finishing work.

A number of the new proto-industrial enterprises were set up with the aid and support of the French crown as part of its efforts to foster a favorable balance of trade through import substitution. Some of the founders of these enterprises were foreigners recruited to bring in crucial technology previously unavailable to the French and to develop entirely new industries on French soil. Whether of foreign or domestic origin, many of these enterprises were granted the status of "royal manufactories," which typically entailed direct subsidies or coveted privileges, such as exemption from certain taxes, protective duties, freedom from visits by royal inspectors, the use of the royal seal as a trademark, and even a monopoly in producing their specialty in a region or in the nation as a whole.

In the seventeenth century, the Bourbon government turned to merchant-manufacturers rather than to the established guild-based woolens manufacturers to expand the production of fine woolen and worsted cloth in France and to reduce French dependence on foreign sources of these goods. In 1646 three Paris merchants, with royal backing, started making Dutch-style wool cloth in the newly annexed city of Sedan in northeastern France (Sedan was chosen because, as the only Calvinist-majority city in the region, it provided a receptive environment for the Calvinist artisans recruited in Holland). Once launched, the Sedan woolens industry grew steadily through the eighteenth century under the direction of a small group of merchant-manufacturers who coordinated the work of thousands of spinners and weavers in the villages surrounding Sedan with the dyeing and finishing work carried out by skilled artisans in large workshops in the city itself. Four of these enterprises became royal manufactories and enjoyed extensive government support.[7] Meanwhile, under the auspices of Colbert, the Dutch cloth merchant Jesse van Robais set up a large woolens manufacturing enterprise in Abbeville in Normandy that also combined a factory-based finishing operation with extensive rural outwork in spinning and weaving.[8] Similar merchant-run proto-industrial woolens manufacturing enterprises were set up, with various forms of royal support, elsewhere in Normandy as well as in Picardy, Champagne, and Languedoc.

By the mid-eighteenth century, important proto-industrial enterprises were also emerging in cotton manufacturing. Under the patronage of Madame de Pompadour, Rouen merchants founded a factory-based cotton manufactory at Darnetal in 1646, which was soon superseded by the enterprise set up at Saint-Sever by the English technician John Holker. In 1760, a German immigrant technician, Christophe Oberkampf, founded what would become the largest textile manufactory in pre-Revolution France at Jouy-en-Josas to supply printed "Indian" cloth to the nearby court of Versailles and to the Paris market (see Chapter 4).

Proto-industrial enterprises also began appearing in metallurgy. Because the royal army and navy provided the only sizable, concentrated market for iron and steel in France, these enterprises depended on royal favor even more than textiles did. The largest French metallurgical undertaking of the mid-eighteenth century was founded by a former timber merchant, Badaud de la Chaussade, who won contracts to supply anchors and other hardware to the French navy and to France's greatest trading company, the Compagnie des Indes, thanks to his friendship with Maurepas, Louis XV's secretary of state for the navy. Starting with France's largest iron forge, Guérigny, Badaud put together an industrial empire that included ten iron smelters, 35–40 forges, four anchor plants, and various warehouses and entrepôts located at dozens of sites in the central Loire Valley and that employed over 2,000 workers at the height of its operations in the 1770s. A similar enterprise, combining various smelters and forges with extensive timber holdings, had been founded in Alsace in 1684 by the Strasbourg banker, Jean Dietrich, and it continued to operate under the control of Dietrich's grandson on the eve of the French Revolution. A third large ironmaking complex was founded at Hayange in Lorraine by the Wendel family. In the 1780s, Ignace de Wendel took over direction of the royal cannon factories at Indret and Ruelle, and in 1785 he joined with the English ironmaster, William Wilkinson, to launch at Le Creusot in Burgundy the first French forge to use coke (partially combusted coal) to smelt and refine iron in the English manner. While the proto-industrial enterprises in metallurgy that clung to traditional technology eventually disappeared, those that made the transition from charcoal-based to coal- and coke-based smelting and refining usually survived. A few of them, including Hayange and Le Creusot, went on to rank among the leading French industrial enterprises of the nineteenth and twentieth centuries.[9]

Of all the proto-industrial enterprises set up under the Bourbons, the one with the greatest staying-power was the royal glassworks of Saint-Gobain. Today its direct descendant remains one of the largest industrial firms in France. The origins of Saint-Gobain lay in Colbert's determination to end the monarchy's dependence on foreign sources for the plate glass mirrors that figured so prominently in the interior decoration of the new palace of Versailles. In 1665, with Colbert's backing, a group of royal officials launched a company to make Venetian-style plate glass for mirrors, using artisans brought in from Venice, at glassworks at Tourlaville in Normandy and at Reuilly near Paris. In 1688, a rival company began producing plate glass with a new rolling process *(laminage)*, instead of the traditional glass-blowing techniques, at a new works at Saint-Gobain in the forests north of Paris. In 1695, the Tourlaville-Reuilly and Saint-Gobain companies merged, only to fail five years later as a result of the economic downturn that accompanied the outbreak of the War of the Spanish Succession. However, the enterprise was soon relaunched as a royal manufactory by a group of Protestant financiers who had an exclusive contract to supply plate glass to Parisian mirror-makers. Thereafter Saint-Gobain grew steadily, and it continued to generate handsome profits for the Swiss bankers and French aristocrats who owned and managed it until the outbreak of the French Revolution.[10]

For the most part, manufacturing technology in France remained on the eve of the French Revolution what it had been at the outset of the eighteenth century. However, thanks to strong government support and the efforts of a dynamic group of merchant-manufacturers, as well as the efforts of an increasingly influential corps of growth-oriented state industrial inspectors, large-scale manufacturing enterprises had begun to appear in France ("large-scale" in comparison to traditional artisanal enterprises). As evident in the case of Saint-Gobain, the launching of these new enterprises often involved the active participation of merchant bankers and financiers. The emergence of a powerful community of bankers and financiers in France, especially in Paris, provided yet another foundation stone for the future development of France's capitalist economy.

Banking and Finance

The great French banking historian Jean Bouvier argued that banking and finance represented separate and distinct occupations in early modern France even though bankers and financiers formed a single socioeconomic class. By Bouvier's definition, banking involved raising and dispensing funds for the private sector, while finance involved raising and dispensing funds for the public sector, the state. More specifically, banking meant "merchant banking"—receiving funds and making payments for merchants, buying and selling currencies, and loaning money at interest, mainly on a short-term basis to finance commercial operations. In all these areas, the bill of exchange was the principal tool of banking, serving simultaneously as a means of payment and as an instrument of credit.[11]

By the early eighteenth century, the rise of joint-stock banks capable of mobilizing large amounts of capital for commercial and industrial ventures, as well as for government finance, was well advanced in Holland and England (reflected in the founding of the Bank of Amsterdam and the Bank of England), but in France it was delayed by the disastrous failure of John Law's schemes to recast state finances in 1718–1720. Indeed, after the collapse of Law's Banque Royale in 1720, no similar bank appeared again in France until the 1780s, and even then it was called a "caisse," not a "banque." Consequently, throughout the eighteenth century, merchant banking remained mostly a sideline of the merchants themselves, with retired merchants bankrolling the operations of younger merchants from their own families or from their local circle of acquaintances. To the extent that there were specialists in banking in eighteenth-century France, they were drawn disproportionately from the ranks of outsiders (especially Protestants and Jews) and foreigners (Italians, Dutch, and Germans), reflecting the air of disrepute that surrounded moneylending and money-dealing in an aristocratic Catholic society in the aftermath of the Law debacle.

While the growth of trade necessarily stimulated the growth of merchant banking in France during the 1700s, the financial needs of the private sector were increasingly overshadowed by the formidable financial needs of the French state. The government loan business, of course, had long been important in France inasmuch as the monarchy's penchant for making war repeatedly overwhelmed the capacity of the state's fiscal system to provide the necessary funds. But this business took on new dimensions in the mid-eighteenth century when the expense of a new round of wars, added to the expense of servicing the debts left from the wars of Louis XIV, led to chronic and growing budget deficits. A large part of the problem lay in the highly regressive nature of the tax system, wherein the richest subjects were exempt from paying the most important taxes. Another problem was structural: From the time of Henry IV in the early 1600s, collecting royal taxes had been in the hands of venal officeholders, including the "tax-farmers" who collected the indirect taxes and treated their offices more as private profit-making enterprises than as public charges. The monarchy increasingly lived hand-to-mouth, borrowing more and more funds from its own financial officers and from foreign financiers. This situation had a positive long-term consequence: The foreign financiers— especially the Protestant financiers from Geneva and other Swiss cities who flocked to France in the course of the eighteenth century to service the growing royal debt—went on to found the Bank of France and to launch France's modern banking system after 1800 (see Chapter 1). But the more immediate consequence of the French financial crisis was the calling of the Estates-General and the outbreak of the French Revolution in 1789. Before it ran its course, the Revolution brought down the entire financial system of the French monarchy and ruined most of the financiers associated with it.[12]

The French Revolution: Making France "Safe for Capitalism"

Although many of the elements of a modern capitalist system were already in place in France by the late eighteenth century—at least in embryonic form—a number of impediments to the full development of that system remained. These included an aristocratic value system that denigrated business activity and relegated businessmen to second-class status; a monarchical government that claimed the power to act arbitrarily and absolutely by divine right and that continued to focus its energies on the pursuit of dynastic glory through increasingly expensive wars; a jerry-built architecture of privilege that continued to restrict enterprise in commerce and industry; and an unfair, regressive tax system that penalized productive investment and discouraged domestic commerce and consumption. It was the outbreak of the Revolution in 1789 that made it possible to remove these impediments through the comprehensive reform of French law and government and thereby opened the way for the emergence of a more "business friendly" political and economic order.

The main contribution of the French Revolution to France's economic and business development can be found in the sweeping reform of France's governmental and political institutions between 1789 and 1791. These reforms were based on the liberal principles set forth in the Declaration of the Rights of Man and the Citizen, written in August 1789 as the preamble to the constitution that eventually went into effect in the summer of 1791. The essential clause in the Declaration proclaimed that all Frenchmen (and it was *men* whose rights were being declared) were "free and equal in rights." Not only did this end the separate legal status of aristocrats, but it also made possible the elimination of all manner of other long-established privileges. For example, the guild system, which had been abolished by Turgot in 1775—only to be reinstated after his fall from power—was definitively ended by the Allard Law in February 1791. Henceforth all adult men, at least in theory, were free to enter all occupations. The special status and privileges of royal manufactories were likewise abolished, along with the trade monopoly of the Compagnie des Indes and Marseille's privileged position in the Levant trade. The power of chambers of commerce to regulate trade in French ports and of state inspectors to dictate how manufacturers operated was severely curtailed. "Free enterprise" was to be the order of the day, at least for French citizens operating on French soil, in French waters, and in French colonies. Such freedom, however, was not extended to foreigners: The Revolution reaffirmed the exclusive right of French merchants to trade with the French colonies and likewise restricted the coasting trade and maritime commerce into and out of French ports to French vessels. Loans at interest—long prohibited in theory if not in practice because of the Catholic Church's ban on usury—were legalized in October 1789. With the abolition of the whole structure of seigneurial rights and duties, restrictions on the free use of private property were largely ended (though the state retained ownership of subsoil rights and the right to grant concessions for mining). The one great exception to the doctrine of free enterprise was embodied in the Le Chapelier Law of 1791, which, by prohibiting all unauthorized associations, effectively outlawed labor unions and strikes and gave employers a decisive advantage in their relations with their workers. Along with the provision in the Constitution of 1791 that restricted voting and office-holding to substantial taxpayers (so-called active citizens), the Le Chapelier Law continues to be "Exhibit A" for those arguing that the French Revolution was at bottom and at heart a "bourgeois" revolution—a revolution by and for the capitalists.

The reformers of the early Revolution also acted to end restrictions on domestic trade and to create a legally unified national market by eliminating the various internal customs duties and with them the omnipresent barriers and tollbooths operated by tax-farmers. Toward the same end, the reformers created a uniform national system of weights and measures (the metric system). To be sure, many restrictions on commerce and industry were reinstated in response to the war and civil war that consumed and radicalized the Revolution after 1792. For example, the free domestic trade in grain that had been reestablished in 1789 was rescinded in the face of wartime shortages in 1792. Still, on balance, the reforms adopted in the early years of the Revolution gave France a more open and unfettered market economy and cleared the way for the fuller development of capitalist enterprise in the years ahead.

Just as important as the measures that directly or indirectly promoted capitalist enterprise were the broader reforms of the French government. The primary goal of the leaders of the French Revolution was less the promotion of capitalism than the ending of arbitrary government and, even more, the rationalization of government (which, among other things, entailed solving the fiscal crisis that brought on the Revolution in the first place). Ultimately, the reform of government did as much to improve the environment for business in France as the overt economic reforms did. In 1789, the Constituent Assembly swept away the multiple layers of offices and jurisdictions that had accumulated since the Middle Ages and began to rebuild the French government from top to bottom, following the principle of separation of powers that had been enshrined in the Constitution of the United States two years before. A new territorial unit, the department, became the basis for all executive, legislative, and judicial governmental functions. The king still headed the executive branch of the government (at least until his overthrow in 1792), but his powers were defined and circumscribed by law, and all expenditures were to be spelled out in an annual budget approved by an independent legislature, elected not by all adult men but, as mentioned above, by "active citizens" who paid substantial taxes. The legislature had sole authority to enact laws, as the constitution denied the king even a suspensive veto. The tax system was rebuilt on the basis of a limited number of direct and indirect taxes to be paid by all citizens on an equal basis, irrespective of social status. The old system of royal law courts, run by a self-perpetuating corps of aristocratic judges who owned their offices, was abolished, and a new system of courts was created, first with elected judges and later with judges selected by the executive on the basis of legal training and experience. Most importantly, courts were to decide cases on the basis of a single, unified law code that applied equally to all parts of France and to all citizens regardless of birth or wealth. The creation of this new law code, which derived from and extended the codification begun under the Bourbons, was not completed until the reign of Napoleon Bonaparte, and thus came to bear his name.

As the structure of the new governmental system took shape, the leaders of the Revolution continued to fight over where ultimate authority over that system would lie. France lurched from a limited constitutional monarchy run by property owners in 1791, to an ostensibly democratic republic in 1793, to government by committee under the Directory in 1795, and on to the military dictatorship of Napoleon Bonaparte after 1800. In the process, the highly decentralized system set up under the Constitution of 1791 gave way after 1793, largely in response to the pressures of war, to a highly centralized system that, in the eyes of Alexis de Tocqueville, returned France to the governmental traditions of the Bourbon monarchy. Yet even as France moved from one constitution to another (it had had four by the time Napoleon replaced the Republic with an empire in 1804), and even as ultimate power was gradually reconcentrated in the executive, there remained a strong commitment to rational government and to government that recognized and upheld the basic civil rights and civil equality of all French citizens. This newfound governmental rationality and evenhandedness would prove to be as important for the future expansion of the French business system as the specifically pro-business policies put in place in the Revolutionary era.

The reforms of the French Revolution, of course, came at a high price in terms of human suffering and damage to the French economy. Most of this damage resulted from the war between Revolutionary France and monarchical Europe that began in 1792 and continued almost without break for the next ten years (and, after a short break in 1802–1805, resumed for another ten years). The continuous warfare not only diverted resources and energies from peaceful pursuits; it also subjected the French economy and French enterprise to enormous collateral damage. This damage included the disruption of foreign and domestic commerce, severe inflation, and the depreciation of the French currency (the last also sprang from an ill-conceived attempt to solve France's long-standing financial crisis through the issuance of a new paper money, the *assignat*). Of longer-term consequence was England's definitive triumph over France at sea, which caused France to lose overseas colonies and much of its share of the Atlantic trade and brought on the subsequent decline of France's Atlantic ports. Many economic historians also blame the Revolutionary wars for the interruption of French contact with English industry at a crucial point in the evolution of manufacturing technology. For some, this put French industry a generation behind British industry by 1815 and permanently handicapped France's industrial development. Others, however, point out that the wartime blockade did not totally cut off technology transfer and, in fact, gave France's infant cotton industry a crucial respite from British competition and allowed it to progress in 1800–1815 more than it would have in peacetime.[13]

Whatever the nature and extent of the wartime damage to the French economy, its impact on the development of the capitalist system in France was ultimately outweighed by the long-term positive effects of the Revolutionary reforms. The French Revolution may not have been a bourgeois revolution, since it was neither planned nor carried out by capitalists, but in the end it served to make France "safe for capitalism" in a way that would not have occurred—or at least not as quickly—had the Ancien Régime persisted. The Revolution thus stands as an indispensable prerequisite for the rise of modern business enterprise in France in the nineteenth and twentieth centuries.

After the Revolution: The New Framework for Capitalism in France in the Nineteenth Century

In addition to the Revolutionary reforms and the short-term effects of two decades of warfare, the period 1789–1815 left behind a host of new conditions and circumstances that profoundly affected the economic and business development of France in the nineteenth century. To complete our examination of the foundations of modern capitalism in France and to set the stage for the story of French business development that will unfold in Parts I and II, we need to identify and briefly characterize the most important of these conditions and circumstances.

Geography and Demography

In accounting for why some countries prosper and others do not, geography matters, as David Landes has recently reminded us.[14] After 1815, the size and location of France's territory and the natural and human resources contained within its boundaries both promoted and constrained economic development. Having lost most of its overseas colonies by the end of the eighteenth century, France expanded to encompass much of western continental Europe between 1800 and 1814. But the final defeat of Napoleon and the destruction of his empire in 1814–1815 forced the *grande nation* back into its prewar borders. For the next fifty years, the economic life of France centered on exploiting the resources within those borders and was inevitably molded by the nature of those resources.

France has always been blessed with a moderate climate, abundant water, and some of the world's most fertile farmland. These resources continued to foster the growth of French agriculture in the nineteenth century even though control of the land by peasant proprietors reluctant to change their ways—one of the chief legacies of the French Revolution—tended to slow the rate of that growth. Meanwhile, France's endowment of mineral resources presented both problems and opportunities for industrial development. On the one hand, France possessed abundant deposits of iron ore and bauxite (the ore for aluminum). On the other hand, France was deficient in coal—the *non plus ultra* mineral resource of the industrial age—and entirely lacking in copper, tin, and petroleum. Coping with these deficiencies—finding either alternative sources of necessary raw materials or ways to do without them—would be a concern for both the French government and French capitalists in the nineteenth and twentieth centuries. Indeed, the search for vital raw materials provided a major stimulus to efforts to project French power and influence abroad through both foreign direct investment and the acquisition of new overseas colonies.

In addition to the constraints of geography, French government and business leaders had to deal with another economic constraint during the nineteenth and twentieth centuries, slow population growth. Although France participated in the population explosion that engulfed Europe in the mid-eighteenth century, it experienced a leveling off of population growth after 1850 that was unique in the developed world. By the 1890s, many French politicians and intellectuals had come to fear "depopulation," and stimulating the French birthrate became a matter of public policy during and after World War I. We now know that France was simply the first country to experience the demographic "climacteric" that would become commonplace for all industrialized countries in the twentieth century. Moreover, we know that France's decline in population growth occurred for the same reasons as elsewhere—mainly because free men and women wanted to maximize their economic well-being by limiting the size of their families (although family limitation was particularly encouraged in France by the Napoleonic law on equal inheritance). In any event, the decline in the population growth rate emerged as a major constraint on French economic growth in the late nineteenth century, affecting both the supply of labor and domestic demand for manufactures, especially mass-produced consumer goods. This problem was made all the worse by the simultaneous slackening in the rate of urban growth as French peasants resisted joining the rush to the cities that characterized the rest of western Europe at the end of the nineteenth century (partially the result of their success in defending traditional agriculture through the reimposition of protective tariffs).[15]

A Strong State with Contested Politics

Government and politics were just as important as geographical and demographic conditions in determining the nature of economic and business development in France in the nineteenth century. As Alexis de Tocqueville famously noted, following a brief experiment in decentralized government in 1791–1792, the French Revolution and even more the Napoleonic Empire resumed and completed the drive toward centralized authority in France that dated back to the late Middle Ages. Although the French state lacked the military power to impose its will on its neighbors after 1815, it proved highly effective in organizing and dominating the domestic affairs of France through the nineteenth and twentieth centuries. In addition to establishing and enforcing the "ground rules" for private economic activity—including the reforms that "made France safe for capitalism"—the Paris-centered French government played a continuing role in planning and managing the development of the French economy, especially in matters of infrastructure. This was seen in, among other things, the planning, financing, and regulation of the railroads and state control of all forms of telecommunications. A particularly important contribution of the post-Revolutionary state was the creation of a corps of professional engineers trained in the newly formed *grandes écoles*—the Ecole Polytechnique, the Ecole des Mines, and the Ecole des Ponts et Chaussées. These state engineers would play a central role in developing and applying the new industrial technologies and in founding and managing the new enterprises in transportation, mining, and metallurgy in the nineteenth century.

However well-meaning and constructive, the efforts of state administrators and engineers to promote French economic development were caught up in and subordinated to the continuing contest for political power and the continuing quest for a stable political order in the nineteenth century. After 1815, a new political superstructure sat atop the administrative apparatus of the French state, and control of that superstructure remained an open question. The government of the restored Bourbon monarch, Louis XVIII, was founded on constitutional principles, but it was far from democratic. Many questioned its legitimacy. Some sought a return to the republican system of 1792–1800; others yearned for the glory and stability of the Napoleonic Empire. In short, the French Revolution was not over. In 1830, the people of Paris again overthrew the Bourbon king, and eighteen years later his successor, the "Citizen King" Louis-Philippe, was similarly deposed. The ultimate nature of the French government was not determined until the closing decades of the nineteenth century when a democratic, parliamentary republic—the Third Republic—finally took root. Meanwhile, political strife and turmoil affected the development of capitalist enterprise and the pace of industrialization in France in myriad ways. Moreover, even when another revolution was not in the offing, politics of the mundane sort affected all areas of French economic development, from the building of the railroads to the promotion (or restriction) of foreign trade, as we will see especially in Chapter 11.

Great Power Rivalries

Along with continuing conflict on domestic issues, the nineteenth century also brought a continuation of the centuries-old rivalries among the European powers and a recurrence of the warfare that inevitably accompanied those rivalries. In the aftermath of the great bloodletting of 1792–1815, France enjoyed a period of relative peace under the restored monarchy. But with the return of a Bonaparte to power after 1848, the French government again sought to assert its military power abroad, and a series of short but nasty wars followed, starting with the Crimean adventure in 1853 and culminating in the disastrous confrontation with Prussia in 1870. Defeat in the Franco-Prussian War resulted in a new foreign military occupation and the loss of Alsace-Lorraine, which had serious economic consequences, especially for the iron and steel industries. The subsequent armed peace spawned an accelerated race for colonies and rising expenditures on armies and navies, eventually leading to the outbreak of the greatest war in European history in 1914. That war had an enormous impact on all facets of French national life, including business and industry, as we will see in Part III.

In sum, the French people continued to grapple with immense political challenges, international as well as internal, in the century following the Revolution and the Napoleonic Empire. Yet this did not prevent them from simultaneously addressing the even larger challenges posed by industrialization and the need to modernize their system of business enterprise. We now turn to the story of how those challenges were met.

PART ONE

FROM MERCHANT CAPITALISM
TO FINANCE CAPITALISM

The emergence of modern business enterprise in France began with two simultaneous and interconnected developments in the nineteenth century. First, there was the transition from traditional commercial capitalism and merchant banking to a modern system of commerce based on the all-weather, all-season system of rapid transportation provided by railroads and steamships and a modern financial system centered on the operations of large joint-stock investment and deposit banks. Second, there was the rise of large-scale manufacturing in factories employing water- or steam-powered machinery. Part II examines the latter in some detail. Part I deals with the former.

The modernization of commerce, transportation, and banking in nineteenth-century France unfolded in three chronological stages, each of which will be treated in a single chapter.

1. *1800–1840s.* The French Revolution and the Napoleonic Empire brought a new generation of merchant capitalists to the fore in France. Many, perhaps most, of these men were quite content to do business according to the established traditions of merchant capitalism. Some, however, realized that they and France could not prosper or even survive in the new economic environment emerging after 1800 without expanding and modernizing France's commercial infrastructure, its system of banking and credit, and its transportation system. Chapter 1 introduces this new generation of merchant capitalists and chronicles what they did to begin this process of modernization.

2. *1850s–1870s.* By the early 1840s, the leaders of both business

and government in France were convinced that national economic development depended on the building of a national rail system, and in 1842 the National Assembly approved a plan for accomplishing this through a joint effort of the public and private sectors. But France's leading merchant bankers soon realized that they could not raise the capital needed for their part of this project through the existing banking structures. With construction of the rail system stymied in the early 1850s, a cohort of "Saint-Simonian" bankers, supported by the government of Louis-Napoleon Bonaparte, founded a new kind of joint-stock investment bank, the Crédit Mobilier, that not only mobilized unprecedented amounts of capital for building railroads but also quickly led to the creation of a whole phalanx of new joint-stock banks that transformed France's financial landscape. Chapter 2 tells the story of this dual revolution in banking and transportation in the 1850s and 1860s.

3. *1870s–1900.* While the private bankers *(la haute banque)* continued to run the Banque de France, preside over the new rail and steam navigation companies, and play a major role in international government finance in the last quarter of the nineteenth century, France's new joint-stock banks extended their reach by setting up networks of branch banks at home and by undertaking a wide range of industrial investments and financial operations abroad, and local and regional banks played an increasingly important role in financing domestic trade and industry. At the same time, the new national rail system made possible the development of a more modern system of distribution and marketing that included a more efficient system of wholesale trade and novel forms of large-scale retail enterprise, especially the great department stores in Paris and France's first chain stores in the provinces. Chapter 3 surveys these developments to convey a picture of the new world of financial and commercial capitalism that was taking form in France by the end of the nineteenth century.

CHAPTER ONE

Continuity and Change in Merchant Capitalism, 1800–1840s

A curious blend of tradition and innovation characterized the world of French merchant capitalism in the first half of the nineteenth century. It was certainly a world in expansion: The value of France's national product and foreign trade doubled between 1815 and 1850, and the number of merchants in France rose 50 percent in the same period, from 900,000 to 1.4 million.[1] Yet growth in the merchant population and in the volume of trade did not seem to alter the organization and conduct of merchant capitalism in any fundamental way, perhaps because the underlying conditions of trade had not changed that much.

In 1800 France possessed a relatively good network of roads—some dating back to Roman times—which facilitated the movement of mail and small parcels and travel by coach for the wealthy. Some rivers—notably the Seine, Marne, and Saône—supported inland transport of bulkier goods, as did the coasting trade along the Atlantic seaboard and in the Mediterranean. But this hardly constituted a national system of all-season, all-weather transportation. By modern standards, travel and transport remained slow, erratic, and expensive.

Trade—whether local or long-distance—remained what it had been since medieval times: a personal process carried on by myriad individual merchants, partnerships, or family firms, all arranged in a pyramidal hierarchy. At the bottom of the pyramid were thousands of petty retailers *(commerçants),* who sold a variety of goods in small quantities to a restricted clientele, normally the populace of a single village or urban neighborhood. Above them was a much smaller population of wholesale merchants *(négociants)*, who acted as middlemen between producers of raw materials, makers of finished goods, and retailers and who often took the lead in setting up the networks of home workers still responsible for most manufacturing, especially in the textile industry.

At the apex of the pyramid was a relative handful of *grands négociants*, who organized and financed interregional and international trade in certain commodities of high value such as metals, fine cloth, sugar, and spices, as well as grain and flour in times of scarcity. Yet even the great international merchant houses were small, rudimentary organizations by modern standards. In the 1820s, the richest merchant banker in Paris, James de Rothschild, needed only thirteen salaried employees (eight clerks, one messenger, one porter, one coachman, and two security guards) to keep his business running smoothly. Another major Paris merchant house, that of the Mallet family, employed twenty.[2] However, small payrolls and simple organization did not limit the span of interests of these firms, which typically combined commodities trading and merchant banking with currency speculation, government finance, industrial investment, and whatever else promised a profit. Like their forebears in earlier centuries, French merchant capitalists remained generalists—jacks-of-all-trades—at the outset of the nineteenth century.

Even though the pace and structure of commerce and banking and the profile and practices of the typical French merchant capitalist seemed little changed in the early 1800s from the previous century, a crucial but subtle transformation of the world of French merchant capitalism was under way. This involved a substantial turnover and renewal in personnel due in particular to the arrival of Protestant and Jewish merchant families from elsewhere in Europe, especially from Switzerland and Germany. (Once established in France, these families continued to play an important role in the economic life of the country down to the twentieth century.) Joining with established families to form a new merchant elite, they also set out consciously to remake France's economic and business system to keep it abreast of developments in Britain and elsewhere in Europe. This modernizing drive was manifested in three ways: (1) the renovation of banking and finance, starting with the founding of the Banque de France in 1800 and continuing with the launching of other joint-stock banks to provide much needed short-term commercial credit through the discounting and rediscounting of commercial paper—initiatives that were sufficiently successful, according to Bertrand Gille, to allow French banking "to pass from a primitive structure to one that approached our own system of banking" in the period 1815–1848[3]; (2) efforts to improve support services for the commercial economy, reflected in the founding of joint-stock companies to offer marine, fire, and life insurance; and (3) recognition of the need for a national system of speedy, all-season transportation of people and goods, and the first efforts to provide this through improved sailcraft, steamboats, canals, and France's first railroads.

The rise of the new merchant elite and its efforts to modernize French commerce, banking, and transportation were manifested in dozens of seaports and scores of inland cities and towns, but for the sake of clarity and brevity let us restrict our discussion to what was happening in France's six largest commercial centers: Paris, Lyon, Marseille, and the principal Atlantic ports, Le Havre, Bordeaux, and Nantes. Even within this restricted group, however, contributions were by no means equal. Although the surge in colonial trade seemed to put Marseille and the Atlantic ports at the forefront of French merchant capitalism at the end of the eighteenth century, these cities suffered substantial economic losses during the Revolution and the Napoleonic Empire, as did Lyon. Consequently, after 1815 the leading merchants of these cities focused more on repairing the damage and recovering lost trade than on wide-ranging innovation. By contrast, the events of the Revolution and Napoleonic era generally served to enhance the primacy of Paris in trade and finance, and the new merchant banking families that came to the fore there after 1789 clearly played the leading role in renovating the French business system not only in 1815–1850 but throughout the nineteenth century. To fully appreciate their achievements, however, we must view them against the backdrop of the more limited achievements in the provincial trade centers. Therefore, our discussion begins with them.

Retrenchment and Renewal in Provincial France

In the eighteenth century, France enjoyed unprecedented commercial expansion led by the spectacular growth in trade between France's ports and its colonies in the Caribbean and the Indian Ocean. According to Dale Tomich, France's colonial trade increased tenfold between 1716 and 1787 and "was in large measure responsible for propelling French foreign trade to a level comparable with that of England by the end of the century."[4] Over nine-tenths of this trade was funneled through the ports of Bordeaux, Nantes, and Le Havre on the Atlantic and Marseille on the Mediterranean, so those four cities (along with Lyon) stood at the heart of French merchant capitalism on the eve of the Revolution.

France's colonial trade was soon undermined, however, by three events: the outbreak of war with England in 1793; the subsequent British occupation of Guadeloupe and Martinique in the Caribbean and the Ile-de-France (Mauritius) in the Indian Ocean; and even more the slave revolt on Saint-Domingue (Haiti), which culminated in that colony's independence. The value of France's sugar production fell from some 103,000 tons in 1791 (39 percent of world production) to virtually nothing in 1814, and it recovered only to 39,000 tons (10 percent of world production) in 1818–1819 after the French had reoccupied Martinique and Guadeloupe.[5] France's lucrative slave trade was similarly decimated in 1793–1815, and the outlawing of the international slave trade in 1814, along with the outlawing of slave trading within French territories in 1818, made it unlikely that this business would ever recover. For France's four great port cities, the challenge after 1815 was to salvage and rebuild what remained of the colonial trade or, alternatively, to find new niches in the international trade system that was taking shape in the early nineteenth century. Despite the destruction and losses of the previous two decades, all four cities retained significant resources in capital and entrepreneurial expertise, but how they utilized those resources and how each contributed to the future development of French trade and finance varied with their individual circumstances and opportunities.

Bordeaux

Bordeaux emerged as a major port in the late Middle Ages by exporting the wines of the Gironde and the grain and foodstuffs of the Garonne and Dordogne valleys to England and northern Europe. Although the volume of Bordelais wine exports did not increase appreciably over the course of the eighteenth century, the growing reputation (and thus price) of those wines gave the merchants of Bordeaux the financial resources to move into the potentially more lucrative trade with the French Antilles. By setting up their own version of a triangular trade in the Atlantic, exchanging wines and foodstuffs in northern Europe for manufactures that were coveted in the islands, the Bordelais turned their city into an entrepôt for sugar, indigo, and other tropical products which were then distributed not so much in France but in the rest of Europe by the Dutch and German merchants who had long been coming to Bordeaux for wine. To further enhance their profits, the Bordelais eventually added black slaves from West Africa to their export mix, although this trade never became as important for Bordeaux as for Nantes.[6]

The loss of Saint-Domingue and the blockade of French ports during the Revolution and Empire largely destroyed Bordeaux's colonial trade, or at least the role of Bordelais shipowners in that trade. In truth, just as neutral ships continued to carry Bordeaux wine to its usual customers in most of the years from 1793 to 1814, neutrals maintained Bordeaux's role as a sugar entrepôt, with Americans bringing sugar to Bordeaux from various sources in the Caribbean and other neutrals— mostly Danes and Germans—transferring the sugar to northern Europe. Then, after 1815, sugar production in the remaining French colonies gradually recovered, despite the loss of Saint-Domingue, and Bordeaux shipowners captured a respectable share of this reconstituted colonial trade.[7] But Bordeaux never again served as Europe's principal sugar entrepôt as it had before 1789 (that role passed to the British). And, because of its peripheral location in the Southwest, far from France's largest cities, Bordeaux was not in a position to supply sugar to the French market. Consequently, the merchants who set out to rebuild Bordeaux's fortunes after 1815 looked less to the trade in colonial sugar than to the wine trade and to a new business, the importing of exotic staples from Africa, Asia, and the South Pacific.

Although the volume of wine production in the Gironde remained stable in the first half of the nineteenth century, the growing reputation and lucrativeness of Bordeaux's *grand cru* wines attracted new merchants to Bordeaux after 1815. The most successful of these newcomers intermarried with the established *négociant* families that had come to Bordeaux in the previous century, primarily from Britain and Germany. The result was the consolidation of a close-knit community of family firms that continued to dominate the wine trade into the twentieth century and, because of their wealth and connections, sometimes played a role in French business beyond Bordeaux. These families included the Johnstons, a Scottish family that came to Bordeaux by way of Ireland in the 1730s. By the early 1800s, the Johnstons had gone beyond selling "first growth" wines to running a general import-export house that also dealt in tea, copper, cacao, indigo, coffee, tobacco, and other commodities, and they had become the acknowledged leaders of a growing Anglo-Irish community in Bordeaux that included notable wine brokers such as the Bartons and Lawtons. Other leading families came from the Continent, including the Schÿlers and Cruses from Hamburg, the Bethmanns from Frankfurt, and the de Luzes from Switzerland. Although Herman Cruse was the largest-volume wine dealer in Bordeaux by the 1840s, the most famous wine exporting firm in the city then (as now) was Barton et Guestier, founded in 1802 when a French sea captain, Daniel Guestier, teamed up with Hugh Barton to send Bordeaux wines to London during a lull in the Anglo-French war.[8]

While some Bordeaux *négociants* concentrated on the wine trade after 1815, others compensated for the decline of the Antilles trade by opening new trade routes to South America, Asia, and Africa. For example, Daniel Guestier, in addition to dealing in wine with Hugh Barton, helped to establish Bordeaux as France's leading port of entry for pepper, indigo, and spices by regularly sending ships to India and the East Indies, while the Bordeaux cloth and wine merchant Pierre Balguerie-Stuttenberg pioneered France's trade with Brazil and Southeast Asia in the decade after 1815. Following in the footsteps of these early pioneers, a new generation of Bordeaux *armateurs* had even greater success in long-distance trade with three-masted clipper ships from 1830 to 1880. Most notable in this group were Casimir Le Quellec and Antoine-Dominique Bordes, who became the leading French importers of Chilean copper and nitrates, and Hubert Prom and Hilaire Maurel, who developed a varied trade with West Africa that eventually made Bordeaux a center for the production of tropical oils.[9]

In addition, a few of Bordeaux's leading merchants formed joint-stock companies to undertake larger ventures beyond trade and shipping. In 1818, Pierre Balguerie-Stuttenberg, Daniel Guestier, and William Johnston won government authorization to create a joint-stock bank on the model of the Banque de France to provide local merchants with a wider array of financial services than those provided by existing private banks. The same group set out to improve Bordeaux's transport facilities by forming a company to build the first bridge over the Garonne. The reach and resources of the Bordeaux merchant community remained limited, however. When it came to projects of national and international scope—the building of the rail system, the launching of transoceanic steam navigation—the leading Bordeaux merchant capitalists either chose not to participate or were simply muscled aside by more aggressive capitalists from elsewhere, including, ironically, Emile and Isaac Pereire, who came out of the Sephardic Jewish community of Bordeaux but made their marks as entrepreneurs and financiers in Paris, not in Bordeaux.

Nantes

While the Bordeaux merchants moved beyond the colonial trade in the early nineteenth century, the merchants of Nantes sought to recapture the prosperity of the previous century by rebuilding their trade in sugar, and even in slaves, with the French colonies in the Caribbean and Indian Ocean. Although the slave trade was outlawed after 1814, slavery remained legal in the French colonies until 1848 and the build-up of sugar production on Martinique and Guadeloupe in the Caribbean, and even more on Réunion (Bourbon) in the Indian Ocean, to compensate for the loss of Saint-Domingue, created a strong incentive to continue the slave trade illicitly. Although it is impossible to determine exact numbers, Dale Tomich has estimated that between 152,000 and 237,000 slaves were brought into the French colonies from 1815 to 1833, with Nantes ships supplying 47 percent of these.[10] This renewed slave trade may have yielded good profits for a few Nantes shipowners, but it lasted scarcely fifteen years, and it seems not to have produced any great new fortunes or to have catapulted any new families into the city's merchant elite. Of far greater long-term significance were the efforts of Nantes merchants to rebuild the other side of the old colonial trade, the importation of sugar.

In the 1780s, Nantes had imported 55,000–60,000 tons of cane sugar each year, second only to Bordeaux. Those imports collapsed following the slave revolt on Saint-Domingue and the British occupation of Martinique and Guadeloupe in the 1790s, and many of the city's largest commercial houses were ruined. However, unlike Bordeaux, which had depended on selling sugar outside of France (and had little hope of recapturing that trade from the British after 1815), Nantes had always sold most of its sugar within France. With the domestic market reserved to French suppliers by high customs duties after 1815, Nantes merchants could reasonably hope to rebuild their sugar business as trade with the colonies resumed. Nantes concentrated particularly on developing good relations with the sugar planters of Réunion. As the output of Réunion plantations soared between 1820 and 1860, so too did the fortunes of the Nantes sugar importers. In 1835, Nantes imported only 10,000 tons of sugar, well below the levels brought into Le Havre, Marseille, and Bordeaux. By 1845, its imports had risen to 18,600 tons (75 percent from Réunion), and by 1866 to

66,000 tons, finally surpassing the level of the 1780s and making Nantes France's largest sugar port.[11] The Nantes shipbuilding industry, which had been France's largest in the eighteenth century, also enjoyed a limited revival by producing the clipper ships used on the trade routes to the South Atlantic, Indian, and Pacific oceans.

Yet even if the recovery of the sugar trade and shipbuilding restored a measure of Nantes' pre-1789 prosperity in the 1840s and 1850s, neither provided a strong base for long-term development. The steady rise of the domestic beet sugar industry in France from the 1840s onward constrained the growth of cane sugar imports, and the shift from sail to steam limited the prospects of a shipbuilding industry that remained dedicated to sailcraft (Saint-Nazaire, at the mouth of the Loire River downstream from Nantes, would become a leading center for the construction of steamships, but this would be the work of Paris capitalists, not the Nantais). With the coming of the railroads, Le Havre proved to be much better situated than Nantes to serve Paris and the emerging industrial centers of northern and eastern France, and Nantes saw the volume of ship traffic in the port decline after 1835.[12] Although the city eventually produced a few major firms in sugar refining, food processing, and canning, the merchant capitalists of Nantes found themselves playing a diminishing role in the economic life of the country as the nineteenth century wore on.[13]

Le Havre

Founded as a naval base on the tidal flats at the mouth of the Seine River in 1517, Le Havre de Grâce continued to be dominated by the French navy well into the nineteenth century (the city's walls and fortifications were torn down only in the 1850s). At the same time, Le Havre developed as a commercial port, first as a center for cod fishing and then for the Antilles trade. By the 1780s, Le Havre was France's fourth largest sugar port, after Bordeaux, Nantes, and Marseille, but this trade had to be rebuilt from scratch after twenty years of almost continuous blockade by the British from 1793 to 1814. In the 1820s, Le Havre briefly rose to first place among French ports in sugar imports and also participated in the revival of the slave trade, but the old colonial trade was soon overshadowed by new interests.

In contrast to Nantes and Bordeaux, Le Havre was ideally situated to play an important role in the new maritime economy of the nineteenth century, particularly as a port of entry for British goods bound for French markets and as a conduit for people and goods moving between continental Europe and the Americas. The steady expansion in both the coastal trade with other European ports and the *long cours* trade with the Americas brought a fivefold increase in the tonnage of shipping entering and leaving Le Havre between 1825 and 1846 (from 473,000 tons to 1.6 million tons). The majority of the ships operating directly between Le Havre and the British and American ports sailed under British or American flags, but Havrais shipowners played a significant role in the coasting trade. They also had some success in establishing steamer service to Rotterdam and the Baltic ports and greater success in setting up regular service to the ports of Central and South America with clipper ships.

As domestic and foreign shipping companies established Le Havre's connections to America and the rest of Europe, it became France's leading port of entry for a variety of goods, including British coal, Brazilian coffee, and especially American cotton. Le Havre also became a major point of departure for Europeans emigrating to the New World.[14] All this shipping and mercantile activity in turn stimulated the development of shipbuilding, banking, and insurance. In some cases, local capitalists launched the new enterprises in these areas (for example, Augustin Normand and the Mazeline brothers in shipbuilding). But to a large extent outsiders—especially Paris houses and their agents—played the dominant role in developing the commercial economy of Le Havre. The Hottinguers of Paris (and Zurich), for example, were the key players in the cotton trade, along with representatives of the cotton manufacturers of Mulhouse such as the Roederers and Siegfrieds. The Banque du Havre, founded in 1837 to discount commercial paper and to issue banknotes for local circulation, was governed by regents drawn from the ranks of local businessmen, but it depended on financial backing from "the most considerable houses of Paris, Holland, Switzerland, and Germany."[15] Similarly, when the largest private bank in Le Havre, the Banque Dubois, failed in 1848, it was relaunched as the Crédit Commerciale du Havre with the backing of nineteen Paris bankers. In marine insurance, local companies founded by old Le Havre families were displaced in the 1830s and 1840s by Paris- and London-based insurance companies. In short, as Le Havre emerged as France's foremost Atlantic port and second largest port overall after Marseille, it increasingly was colonized by capitalists headquartered elsewhere, especially in Paris and Alsace.[16] By contrast, Marseille and Lyon played a role in trade and finance in the early nineteenth century somewhat more independent of the French capital.

Marseille

The ancient port city of Marseille, founded around 600 B.C. by Greeks from Phocaea, had long served as France's main connection to the Mediterranean world and the Levant. When trade with France's Caribbean colonies was opened to all French ports in 1719, Marseille began to import sugar from Saint-Domingue and also entered the Atlantic slave trade, but it never became as dependent on sugar and slaves as did the leading Atlantic ports. On the eve of the French Revolution, Marseille ranked third in the Antilles trade, after Bordeaux and Nantes, but that trade accounted for only 11 percent of the port's traffic, versus 67 percent for the Mediterranean and Levant trade. Like most other French ports, Marseille was virtually shut down for most of the period 1793–1814—partly by the wartime blockade, partly because it was subjected to the Reign of Terror in 1793–1794 by the Revolutionary government in Paris for opposing the overthrow of the monarchy. In the process, much of the commercial elite of the city was either physically exterminated or ruined financially.[17]

Like other French ports, Marseille recovered slowly in the two decades after the fall of Napoleon as its merchants went about reestablishing trade links with the Levant and the Antilles and as its shipowners made tentative moves into new areas such as the Indian Ocean, Africa, and South America. By the early 1830s, the value of imports and exports through Marseille was double that in 1792, but this was mainly due to price inflation; the number and tonnage of ships entering and leaving the port remained below the 1792 level. However, the next thirty years were much more expansive, with both the value of Marseille's commerce and the tonnage of its shipping tripling by 1860. This upswing was due in part to Marseille's role in the French conquest of North Africa, which began with the expedition to Algiers in 1830, but it also stemmed from the port's changing economic position.

Marseille benefited from the development of various industries in its hinterland (woolens in Languedoc, silk in the Lyonnais, iron and coal in the southern Massif), for which it served as port of entry or exit. Just as important, Marseille itself industrialized, becoming a center for the milling and re-export of Russian wheat as well as for sugar refining. Its imports of cane sugar grew steadily from 12,000 tons in 1820 to over 55,000 tons in 1860 (second only to Nantes) as it grew to be the principal supplier of refined sugar to much of the Mediterranean world. Marseille also developed as a center for soapmaking, based on the importation of oil seeds from the tropics (for Marseille's role in the French sugar and vegetable oil industries, see Chapter 10).

Meanwhile, Marseille's shipping business developed at a somewhat slower pace. Despite a heavy tax on goods imported in foreign ships (the *surtaxe de pavillon*) and the restriction of the coasting trade to domestic carriers, French ports were more open to foreign shippers after 1815 than under the mercantilistic policies of the Ancien Régime, so much of the rising volume of goods coming into or leaving Marseille in the first half of the nineteenth century was carried in non-French ships. Thus the size of the merchant fleet based in Marseille remained largely static both in numbers and tonnage from the 1780s to the 1830s. Moreover, the Marseillais were slow to move into steam navigation. Steamboats first came to Marseille in 1818, but they were Italian, not French. The Bazin brothers finally launched the first home-owned steamships in Marseille in 1831, but the French government's decision to build and operate its own fleet of steamers in the Mediterranean in the late 1830s limited the development of private steamship companies in Marseille. Only in the 1840s, when private companies introduced a second generation of steamships with screw propellers and iron hulls (which were clearly superior to the state's first generation steamships), did the balance shift from public to private ownership. By 1845 Marseille's steam fleet had grown to sixty ships (thirty-nine privately owned and twenty-one state owned), second only to Le Havre's.[18]

In 1850 the glory days for the port of Marseille and its merchant fleet still lay ahead, but the foundations for that future glory had already been laid with the emergence of the family firms that would direct the development of the Marseille shipping industry—and much of the rest of the city's economic development—over the next century. The great majority of these firms date from after 1800. Almost none of the great families of *négociants* and *armateurs* of the late eighteenth century continued in trade and shipping in the nineteenth century, in part because they followed the age-old practice of converting commercial wealth into landed wealth (and aristocratic status), and in part because they were ruined (or killed) during the Reign of Terror in 1793–1794. Three of the leading merchant families of nineteenth-century Marseille—the Rostands, Fraissinets, and Bergasses—had taken up residence in the city before 1789 but rose to prominence in trade and shipping only after 1815. Alexis and Bruno-Xavier Rostand, sons of a Marseille cloth merchant, established themselves as *négociants-armateurs* in the 1820s and 1830s. The descendants of Alexis moved into journalism and letters (including his great-grandson, Edmond, who gained international fame as the author of *Cyrano de Bergerac*), but Bruno's sons continued in commerce or moved into local industry (the eldest son, Albert Rostand, was a founder of the Messageries Maritimes Steamship Company). Meanwhile, in 1836 Marc-Constantin Fraissinet founded a shipping company specializing in the coasting trade that his sons and grandsons built into one of the leading steam navigation firms in France (the Fraissinets' big break came in 1854–1855, when they made a killing transporting troops and war matériel to the Crimea).[19] Henry-Joachim Bergasse, scion of a Lyon merchant family, came to Marseille in 1775 to set up a wine export business. After 1815, his son Henry was a leader in the rebuilding of Marseille's trade with the French colonies, and his grandson Henry Bergasse II played a prominent role in numerous Marseille business ventures, including the Saint Louis Sugar Refining Company (see Chapter 10).[20]

The founders of three other leading merchant family enterprises in nineteenth-century Marseille—the Pastrés, Bazins, and Fabres—were newcomers to the city as of 1800. Jean-François Pastré was a merchant-tanner who entered the Marseille shipping business in the tumultuous era of the Revolution and Empire and married Marie-Eugénie Gauthier of a *négociant* family that had long been prominent in the Antilles trade. After the death of Jean-François, Marie carried on the business as Veuve Pastré in association with her four sons, especially Jean-Baptiste Pastré, who established the firm's dominant position in Franco-Egyptian trade from the 1830s onward.[21] The Bazins were a Huguenot family from Blois that had gone into exile in Holland, where Joseph-Charles Bazin served as secretary to the Prince of Orange in the mid-eighteenth century. His son, Charles-Samuel Bazin, set up a banking house in Paris in the early 1790s, was ruined by the Terror, and then joined a brother in Marseille in 1806. The sons of these brothers, Charles and Auguste Bazin, launched Marseille's first steamship company in 1831 and set up regular steamer service from Marseille to Italy and Algiers in the 1840s. Augustin-Félix Fabre, a sea captain from La Ciotat with long experience sailing to Cayenne and other South American ports, came to Marseille in 1816 to set up his own shipping business and merchant house, which his sons carried on. It was his grandson Cyprien Fabre, however, who elevated the family to the merchant elite of the city through his success in the African trade and as founder of a leading steam navigation company.[22]

Throughout the nineteenth century, the great merchant families of Marseille remained generalists who combined the management of shipping companies with various commercial and industrial ventures. Charles Bazin, for example, got into flour milling, salt making, and shipbuilding (he was one of the founders of the Forges et Chantiers de la Méditerranée). In the 1830s, several of the leading merchants of the city founded the Banque de Marseille to discount commercial paper and to issue banknotes to offset the constant drain of specie to other commercial centers. Other merchants founded private banks, including the Zafiropoulos, Zarifi, and Rodocanachi families, who came to Marseille from Greece in the 1820s to oversee the Black Sea wheat trade. Later in the century, Henry Bergasse and Cyprien Fabre also added banking to their wide range of interests.

Despite the breadth of their activities and the inherently cosmopolitan nature of their businesses, however, the leading businessmen of Marseille were reluctant to move beyond the framework of traditional merchant capitalism. While pursuing ventures in shipping, banking, commerce, and industry through proprietary or family firms, they only occasionally organized or participated in limited-liability companies to undertake larger-scale enterprises. Ultimately, the task of building Marseille into a world-class trade center—through the expansion of the port, the creation of large-scale steam navigation companies, and the mobilization of capital and credit—depended on outside money and leadership. Like the merchants of the Atlantic ports, the merchants of Marseille played an important regional role, but they tended to take a backseat to Paris-based capitalists in the renovation of the national system of commerce and banking in nineteenth-century France.

Lyon

In the High Middle Ages, Lyon played host to a cosmopolitan community of merchant capitalists who grew rich on the trade in Levantine and Italian goods coming over the Alps via Geneva (which is upstream from Lyon on the Rhône) or up the Rhône Valley from Marseille and the other ports of Provence. From the sixteenth century onward, the Lyonnais turned more and more to silk, first as middlemen in the importation of Italian and Oriental silk cloth and then, after Colbert brought silkworms and silkworkers to France in the late 1600s, as the dominant manufacturers and exporters of silk cloth in continental Europe. In the 1790s, Lyon's silk business was disrupted by the French Revolution, especially in 1793–1794, when Lyon, more than Nantes or Marseille, was subjected to a brutal reign of terror by the Revolutionary armies dispatched from Paris. However, silk production soon recovered and expanded steadily throughout the first half of the nineteenth century in response to strong demand from the British and Americans. Chapter 4 looks more closely at the silk industry of Lyon, especially the extent to which it gave rise to factory-based, mechanized manufacturing, and later chapters examine Lyon's role in the rise of industrial capitalism in coal, iron, and chemicals. What is of interest here is how Lyon continued to develop as a center of international trade, finance, and interregional transport in the first half of the nineteenth century.[23]

Although much of the trade between the Mediterranean world and northern Europe had shifted from overland routes to the high seas between 1500 and 1800, the continental blockade during the reign of Napoleon I served to briefly reestablish Lyon as the fulcrum of trade between Italy and southern France and the rest of Europe. For example, the woolen cloth of Languedoc that had previously reached foreign markets by sea through Marseille could only move northward by land routes through Lyon in the years 1803–1814 when Marseille was closed. Accordingly, the era of the First Empire witnessed a surge in new freight and commission businesses in Lyon. Many of the most prominent Lyonnais merchant families of the nineteenth century, such as the Gallines and Bonnardels, got their start in haulage and freight between 1800 and 1815 and worked hard to preserve Lyon's position as a shipping and transportation center after 1815.

The years of the Bourbon Restoration, 1815–1830, brought continued growth in both water-borne and overland freight and passenger transport in the Saône-Rhône corridor. Paris capitalists set up express coach service between Lyon and the capital, and Lyonnais capitalists such as Oscar Galline launched coach service to Marseille in competition with the boatmen who had long dominated the carrying trade in the lower Rhône Valley. However, both land and water transportation through and around Lyon remained slow and expensive, so merchants moving goods between Italy and northern Europe increasingly shifted their operations from the Saône-Rhône to the Rhine corridor. To meet this competition and to restore their position in international trade, the Lyonnais turned to a new technology, the steamboat. Although steamboats had first appeared on the Saône as early as 1783, regular steamer service was not set up until the early 1830s when, at the instigation of the American consul, Edward Church (a friend of Robert Fulton), a group of Lyonnais merchants founded two joint-stock companies to operate steamboats on the Saône and Rhône, respectively. By 1839, there were at least eleven companies operating riverboats upstream and downstream from Lyon, and by 1851 the politician Jules Dufaure could boast to the National Assembly that "since 1845 the navigation of the Rhône has become the largest and most active industry in France."[24]

As things turned out, however, the golden age of steam navigation on the Saône and Rhône lasted a scant ten years, as steam locomotives supplanted steamboats as the principal means of moving people and goods across the French isthmus. As we will see in the next chapter, the building of the Paris-Lyon and Lyon-Marseille railroads and their subsequent merger into the Paris-Lyon-Méditerranée were mostly the work of Paris-based capitalists seeking to construct an international rail transportation system. But Lyon men and money were involved in creating both the regional railroads that fed into the national system and the related commercial infrastructure. Oscar Galline, for example, was a major backer of the Lyon-Geneva railroad, and Jean-Jacques Breittmayer managed the expanded port facilities built in Marseille to accommodate the railroads.

In addition to participating in the development of modern steam-based transportation services in southeastern France, Lyonnais capitalists also joined the movement to expand commercial credit through the creation of new joint-stock banks. Lyon had long had many private merchant bankers who financed the silk trade by means of letters of credit and bills of exchange. The historically low level of discount rates on commercial paper in Lyon compared to discount rates elsewhere attested to the efficiency of this system of finance, and local bankers were not eager to change it. Efforts after 1815 to found a joint-stock bank that would discount paper and also issue banknotes on the model of the Banque de France were repeatedly blocked by the local bankers working through the Lyon Chamber of Commerce. Eventually, however, this resistance to financial innovation was overcome through the efforts of Adrien Delahante, scion of a prominent family of royal financial officers, who came to Lyon in 1832 as *receveur-général* for the department of the Rhône and thereafter took a leading role in the economic development of the region. In 1835, Delahante succeeded in bringing together some of the leading merchants and bankers of Lyon to found the Banque de Lyon, a joint-stock bank that augmented the local money supply by issuing banknotes and greatly expanded the local discount business.[25] Although the Banque de Lyon was merged into the Banque de France in 1848, its success between 1835 and 1847 paved the way for Lyonnais bankers to make significant contributions to the expansion of the French banking system later on, most notably through the founding of the Crédit Lyonnais in 1863 and the Société Générale in 1864 (see the next chapter).

Overall, it is fair to say that the merchant communities of the leading provincial trade centers in France, reinvigorated by the infusion of new blood after 1789, undertook limited modernization of the commercial and financial infrastructures of their respective cities in the period 1815–1850. But only rarely did they look beyond their local or regional circumstances to address the renovation of the national business system of France as a whole. That task was taken on mainly by the merchant capitalists of Paris.

Paris and the Remaking of French Merchant Capitalism

As the capital of France, and as its largest city and largest consumer market, Paris had been a center of trade, manufacture, and banking since the Middle Ages. Indeed, commercial finance in France had already become centralized in Paris by the early eighteenth century inasmuch as only "paper on Paris" was accepted for discount in all other French cities. This was reinforced after 1800, when the city became, in essence, the capital of continental Europe in the era of the Napoleonic Empire. The fall of Napoleon in 1814, and even more the contraction of France to its antebellum borders, inevitably deflated the city's importance, but only somewhat. Paris remained the largest city on the Continent, and, in contrast to the retrenchment and stagnation that characterized the economic life of much of provincial France, it continued to grow and to exhibit economic dynamism throughout the first half of the nineteenth century. It was in those years that a new merchant banking elite—the *haute banque parisienne*—came fully into its own in the capital. Acting collectively through informal syndicates and more formally through joint-stock companies, these men started to lay the foundations for France's modern business system by investing in new industrial technology, developing new banking institutions, and overhauling the country's commercial and transportation infrastructure. The remainder of this chapter looks more closely at who these merchant bankers were and how they began to modernize French commerce and finance even as they continued to play the role of traditional merchant capitalists (their equally important role in the launching of industrial capitalism will, of course, be treated at length in Part II).

The Emergence of the Haute Banque

Paris had always been a magnet for the rich and for those who aspired to be rich, but the influx of the wealthy and their acolytes accelerated in the course of the eighteenth century as the French monarchy's ever-growing need for new money attracted financiers (or their agents) from all over France and Europe. In spite of the upheaval of the Revolution and the danger it posed for the conspicuously affluent, at least during the Reign of Terror, this influx continued into the 1790s. This was due in part to the end of religious persecution and the extension of full civil rights to non-Catholics in France, which attracted Protestants—especially the descendants of the Huguenots who had fled France after the revocation of the Edict of Nantes in 1685—as well as Jews, to whom post-Revolutionary France offered a much more welcoming environment than was available anywhere else in continental Europe. But opportunism was also a factor: There were fortunes to be made in supplying France's armies and in speculating in currency and public lands at a time when many of the established bankers and financiers had withdrawn from the scene (or had been forcibly and permanently removed with the aid of the guillotine). This influx was further stimulated and facilitated in the Napoleonic era by France's annexation of much of western Europe. And after 1815 bankers and bill brokers continued to be drawn to Paris because of the city's peculiar position in the system of international payments. According to Jean Bouvier, "Paris was at the hinge of two complementary disequilibria in foreign exchange" wherein, as a net creditor of the British and Americans, Paris accumulated paper written on London that the Germans and Belgians (chronic net debtors of the British) needed to cover what they owed in London.[26] In any case, as early as 1800 and even more by the 1820s and 1830s, it was becoming evident that a new merchant banking establishment was taking shape in Paris, comprised of the most agile holdovers from the pre-1789 banking elite and the most successful newcomers.

Whether newcomers or holdovers, what distinguished members of the *haute banque* was not so much the quantity of their assets as how they employed them. In essence, the *haute banque* consisted of the men who financed Napoleon Bonaparte's coup d'état in 1799, then founded the Banque de France in 1800 and continued to control it throughout the nineteenth century by monopolizing chairs on its board of regents. While pursuing the various businesses long associated with merchant capitalism, the members of the *haute banque* also dominated government finance in France and much of western Europe in the first half of the nineteenth century and took the lead in transferring the new industrial technology from Britain to France by launching ventures in mining, metallurgy, textile manufacture, and transportation (canals and railroads)—usually through limited-liability joint-stock companies. In short, it was the members of the *haute banque parisienne*, more than anyone else, who orchestrated French economic development and the modernization of French business practices in the nineteenth century.

The *haute banque* represented not so much a single, cohesive ingroup as a collection of overlapping family networks differentiated by religious affiliation and regional origins. The most important network was formed by Huguenot (that is, Calvinist) families that had fled religious persecution in France and taken up residence abroad (primarily in Switzerland) in the sixteenth or seventeenth centuries and then had begun to return to France in the eighteenth century. The first members of this *haute banque protestante* to return to France were the Mallets. Originally from Rouen, the Mallets had followed John Calvin to Geneva in 1557, where they flourished in trade and banking. In 1709, twenty-five-year-old Isaac Mallet came to Paris as the agent of Geneva bankers anxious to exploit the financial opportunities expected to follow the end of the War of the Spanish Succession. Isaac soon decided to settle permanently in Paris and oversaw the fortunes of his family firm (with his son and grandsons) for the next seventy years, until his death in 1779. Despite the imprisonment of the grandsons during the Reign of Terror, the Mallet bank was one of the few pre-1789 houses to remain open and operating throughout the Revolution. In 1799, Isaac's chief heir, Guillaume Mallet, joined other Swiss bankers in backing Napoleon's coup d'état and in founding the Banque de France. As the first Baron Mallet, Guillaume occupied the third seat on the Banque's board of regents until his death in 1826. His son, grandson, and great-grandson subsequently occupied the "Mallet chair" until the nationalization of the Banque in 1936, making the Mallets the only family continuously represented on the board of the Banque de France from beginning to end.[27]

Second only to the Mallets among the charter members of the *haute banque protestante* from Switzerland were the Hottinguers, who had been prominent citizens of Zurich since the time of Ulrich Zwingli and who included a number of Protestant ministers in the seventeenth century. In the early eighteenth century, Johannes Hottinguer moved the family into the cloth trade. His grandson Jean-Conrad came to Paris in 1784, worked first for the powerful Paris financier Le Couteulx de Canteleu, and then set himself up as a cloth merchant and banker, acting as agent for Zurich bankers seeking to invest in the French royal debt. Hottinguer was closely associated with the early leaders of the Revolution, especially Talleyrand, and during the Reign of Terror he followed Talleyrand into exile in the United States, where he married Martha Redwood, daughter of a Newport shipowner and slave trader. In 1798 he returned to Paris and reopened his bank. In the early 1800s, Napoleon made Hottinguer a baron, and he joined the board of the Banque de France. His sons, grandsons, and great-grandsons kept the Hottinguer name in the forefront of French business and finance well into the twentieth century.[28]

Other Protestant merchants and bankers arrived in Paris from Switzerland or elsewhere in Europe from the 1790s to the 1840s and eventually took places in the *haute banque parisienne*. These included the Andrés, Mirabauds, Vernes, Odiers, and Bérards, Geneva families originally from the south of France, plus the Delesserts and Cottiers from Lausanne and the Bartholonys from Florence. All these families participated in *grand négoce*, merchant banking, and government finance in the capital; most were involved in running the Banque de France; and some played important roles in launching new industrial ventures in the 1820s and 1830s and the railroads in the 1830s and 1840s.[29]

A second distinct wing of the *haute banque* was constituted by the Jewish merchants and bankers who arrived in Paris from the provinces or from outside France starting in the 1780s and who quickly rose in wealth and influence after acquiring full civil rights during the Revolution. Among these was the Worms family of Sarrelouis in Lorraine. In 1787 Louis XVI granted limited citizenship to Hayem and Cerf Worms for their service to the crown in procuring arms. Soon after, Hayem's son, Olrey-Hayem, set up as a banker in Paris, where he prospered. In 1808, he acquired the château of Romilly-sur-Aube and became Worms de Romilly. However, the family continued in banking and commerce in the persons of Worms de Romilly's nephews, Adolphe, a banker in Metz, and Hipolyte, who made the Banque Worms a major force in the international coal trade (see Chapter 3).[30]

Equally successful was the Fould family. Beer-Léon Fould, son of a small-time wine dealer in the Moselle Valley, went to Paris in 1784 as the agent of Cerf Berr de Médelsheim, a leading Strasbourg arms dealer and banker. Once in Paris, Beer-Léon developed a brisk business in collecting interest on government bonds and other sums owed to his roster of clients back in Lorraine. From there he expanded into other areas, including after 1790 speculation in the new national currency *(assignats)* and in *biens nationaux* (confiscated church property). Despite going bankrupt in the late 1790s and again in 1810, Fould continued to widen his network of correspondents, especially among the Jewish merchants and bankers of Germany who needed a representative in the Imperial capital. The Foulds attained even greater prominence under the Second Empire, when Beer-Léon's son Achille joined the Pereire brothers in founding a new generation of joint-stock investment banks and then served Napoleon III as finance minister.[31]

Whatever the success of families like the Worms and Foulds, they ultimately were overshadowed within the ranks of the *haute banque* by the wealthiest and most famous Jewish bankers in France (and the world), the Rothschilds. The story of the meteoric rise of the Rothschilds has been told many times, most recently and most definitively (albeit from the perspective of the English branch of the family) in a two-volume work by Niall Ferguson.[32] The saga of the Rothschilds in France began in 1812 when twenty-year-old James (Jacob) Rothschild arrived in Paris to provide a key strand in the web of international financial dealings woven by his father, Mayer-Amschel, and his four older brothers. In the early 1800s, Mayer-Amschel had turned his modest merchant house in Frankfurt into a kind of multinational bank that reaped huge profits facilitating various war-related flows of money and goods, including the smuggling of contraband British manufactures to the Continent, the transfer of funds from London to Wellington's army in Spain, and the payment of subsidies to England's allies in the final war against Napoleon in 1812–1814. In Paris, James Rothschild played a key role in financing the defeat of Napoleon and the restoration of the Bourbons in France in 1814, and his influence continued to grow as the Rothschilds masterminded various loan packages for European governments during and after the Congress of Vienna. Whereas the share of the Paris branch of the Rothschild enterprise was modest in 1815 (one-sixth of the combined capital of 36 million British pounds), that share increased to 1,490 million pounds—one-third of the total—by 1825.[33] At the death of his older brother Nathan in 1836,

James de Rothschild became the unofficial head of the family firm.[34] Just as important from our perspective, James had emerged by then as the richest and most powerful capitalist in France (Anka Muhlstein, a descendant, estimates that by the 1830s James de Rothschild's personal wealth amounted to 40 million francs, ten times the wealth of Baron Hottinguer and twenty times that of Baron Mallet; only Jacques Laffitte and the Duke of Orléans, the future King Louis-Philippe, had comparable fortunes).[35] After James' death in 1868, the position of the French Rothschilds in world banking and finance would be maintained by his three sons, led by Alphonse, the first member of the family to serve as a regent of the Banque de France.

In the wake of the successful implantation of the Rothschilds in France, a number of other German Jewish banking families sent representatives to Paris. These included the Sterns, Kanns, and Ellissens of Frankfurt; the Bambergers and Hirsches of Mainz; and the Heines of Hamburg. Perhaps the most successful of these—and certainly the quickest to assimilate into the *haute banque*—were the Seligmanns of Munich, led by Aron-Elias Seligmann, who was created Baron d'Eichthal in 1814 for his financial services to the Allies in their war against Napoleon. Like Mayer-Amschel Rothschild, Seligmann sent his sons to various commercial and financial nerve centers, with his third son, Louis-Adolphe, going to Paris. Louis-Adolphe's son, Adolphe d'Eichthal, became the first regent of the Banque de France of Jewish descent (although by the time of his election he had converted to Protestantism to facilitate his marriage into one of the leading banking families of Geneva); Adolphe's son William would likewise sit on the board of regents of the Banque de France.[36]

The final cohort in the *haute banque* was made up of a number of Catholic families. Lacking the incentive of religious persecution, these families were less cohesive and formed a less distinct network than did the Protestant and Jewish banking families, yet their provincial origins led them to share the Protestants' and Jews' sense of being outsiders. The most influential Catholic banker in early nineteenth-century France, Jacques Laffitte, came from modest circumstances in Bayonne and rose to the top of the Paris banking world through his association with the Protestant banker, Jean-François Perregaux. Perregaux et Cie was renamed Perregaux, Laffitte et Cie in 1807; when Perregaux died in 1808, Laffitte succeeded to his seat on the board of regents of the Banque de France. Laffitte subsequently served as governor of the bank from 1814 to 1820 and became the dominant merchant capitalist in

Paris in the 1820s and 1830s.[37] Although Laffitte was assisted by several brothers—and although his nephew, Charles Laffitte, later had success as a railroad promoter and administrator—their family never constituted a true banking dynasty. However, three other Catholic banking families—the Davilliers of Montpellier, the Seillières of Lorraine, and the Periers of Dauphiné—played important roles in the *haute banque parisienne* over several generations.

In the 1770s, the brothers Jean-Antoine-Joseph Davillier ("Davillier the Elder") and Jean-Charles Davillier (later Baron Davillier) came to Paris from Montpellier to work with the Genevan merchant banker Jacques Bidermann in the international cloth trade. In 1805 Davillier the Elder joined with François Gros and Jacques Roman to set up the largest cotton mill in France at Wesserling (see Chapter 4). Meanwhile, J-C Davillier founded a banking house in Paris and became a charter member of the Banque de France's board of regents. Through the efforts of his son-in-law, his son, and his grandson (all of whom served as regents of the Banque de France), the Davillier bank remained a force in the Paris financial world into the twentieth century.[38]

The Seillière family rose to prominence in Lorraine in the eighteenth century as wool traders and arms dealers. In the early 1800s Florentin Seillière founded a bank in Nancy and played a key role in financing the Wendel iron enterprise. Meanwhile, his sons, Nicolas and François-Alexandre, came to Paris and pursued the family's dual business of banking and industrial finance in association with Charles Demachy. The Seillières supplied much of the munitions for the Algiers expedition in 1830 but were particularly noted for bankrolling the relaunching of the Le Creusot ironworks by the Schneider brothers in 1836 and for their continuing role as bankers to the Wendel family, with whom they intermarried.[39]

Of the great Catholic merchant banking families of France, however, it was the Periers who rose the highest and assembled the widest range of interests in the nineteenth century. Their rise began with Jacques Perier, who set up a successful trade in cotton cloth at Grenoble in the 1730s. One of his sons entered the colonial trade and became director of the Compagnie des Indes in the 1780s, only to fall victim to the guillotine in 1793. The oldest son, Claude, fared considerably better. In the 1790s he established a banking house in Paris and joined in the takeover of the Anzin Coal Company, which came to be the Periers' most valuable property in the next century (see Chapter 5). Shortly before his death, he also participated in the founding of the Banque de France. Claude's son Casimir took over the management of the Perier bank and played a leading role in the financial and political affairs of the capital under the Restoration, helped engineer the accession of Louis-Philippe to the throne in 1830, and served as prime minister until his premature death during the cholera epidemic of 1832. His younger brother Joseph carried on the family businesses, served as regent of the Banque de France, and at his death held a wide array of administrative positions in mining, metallurgy, insurance, and banking. Grandsons and great-grandsons of Claude Perier bore the name and influence of the family into the next century.[40]

As the foregoing sketches reveal, responding to the challenges and opportunities afforded by France's changing political circumstances— from the crisis of the Bourbon monarchy in the 1780s to the fall of the Napoleonic Empire—was central to the fortunes of the families that came to make up the *haute banque parisienne* in the early nineteenth century. At the same time, we should note that it was the traditional activities of merchant capitalism that mostly occupied these "banking houses" on a daily or weekly basis. Indeed, as Bertrand Gille has pointed out, the term *"haute banque"* is misleading in that these firms were not banks as we now understand them; rather they were "merchant houses and financial establishments involved in international trade and the placement of securities [*valeurs mobilières*]."[41] The Mallets, for example, continued to trade in woolens, lace, crystal, coffee, soap, and other luxury commodities in the early nineteenth century just as they had in the eighteenth century, and their firm continued to maintain a *bureau des marchandises* in Paris until 1857, by which time the advent of the railroad was rendering the traditional forms of jobbing and brokerage obsolete. Thanks to their long-standing ties to Rouen and Le Havre and to the cotton manufacturer Oberkampf, the Mallets also moved into the importation of raw cotton, the most expansive and potentially profitable commodity trade in early nineteenth-century France. In this, they were following the lead of the Andrés, who from the 1790s imported cotton from the Levant as part of a diverse trade in the Mediterranean that included silk, woolens, diamonds, pepper, indigo, and cognac.[42] The Mirabauds also became major importers of Levantine cotton into France thanks to their connections in Trieste and Milan. But the heart of the cotton trade was the importation of American cotton through Le Havre, and the leading figures in this trade were the Hottinguers, who according to Max Gérard "were among the biggest importers of this fiber" into Europe from 1815 to 1840.[43]

Then there were the Rothschilds, who continued a wide range of purely commercial activities even as they were underwriting bond issues for the major states of continental Europe and developing such arcane financial specialties as exchange-rate arbitrage. Although the evidence is sketchy, it appears that the Rothschilds, after financing cotton imports from America in the 1830s, became cotton importers themselves in the 1840s. They also imported tallow, lard, and sugar and, in the aftermath of the crop failures of 1846, became major importers of Russian grain. Mostly, however, they liked to deal in high-priced commodities with limited sources of supply that offered the possibility of monopoly profits, particularly nonferrous metals. The Rothschilds were the exclusive importers of the copper produced by the Demidoff family in Russia that went to the cannon foundries and shipyards of western Europe, and they cornered the supply of mercury used in refining precious metals by becoming the exclusive sales agents for Europe's only mercury mines, Almadén in Spain and Idria in Austrian-controlled Dalmatia.[44]

While playing the role of *grands négociants*, the members of the *haute banque* also carried on the traditional business of merchant banking, discounting bills of exchange and other commercial paper and earning commissions by receiving funds and making payments for clients outside of Paris. Although commission and discount rates were modest, there was an enormous volume of commercial paper to be processed in the first half of the nineteenth century since all movement of funds from one city to another in France, as well as the movement of funds between Paris and foreign cities, required the drawing of bills of exchange.[45] In addition, commerce at all levels depended on both the short-term credit inherent in the use of bills of exchange and the ability of merchants to meet their own obligations by discounting (that is, selling) the bills of exchange they received in payment for goods. Ultimately it was the growing awareness among merchant bankers of the inadequacy of the traditional mechanisms of payment and credit in an era of expanding trade, along with the ever-present threat of bankruptcy during momentary liquidity crises, that led the leaders of the *haute banque* to pool their resources to form new collective credit institutions. This was part of a larger effort to use joint-stock companies to provide the new financial and business services needed to maintain France at the forefront of European and world economic development in the nineteenth century.

Prelude to the Revolution in Finance and Transportation

When leading merchant bankers from Paris and beyond started to form joint-stock companies to provide services that none of them could provide individually, they were embracing a rising theme in the public discourse of France in the early 1800s that emphasized the need for economic modernization through cooperation and association among people of wealth and expertise. The great apostle of economic-development-through-association in France was Henri Saint-Simon, the eccentric aristocrat who, at various points in his life, played the roles of soldier of fortune, venture capitalist, and *philosophe,* and who late in life authored a series of treatises that earned him the titles of "utopian socialist" and "father of technocracy" in the history books.[46]

By the time of his death in 1825, Saint-Simon had attracted a brilliant band of disciples from the rising generation of would-be financiers and entrepreneurs in Paris. These included Prosper Enfantin, son of a failed banker who became the intellectual leader of the Saint-Simonian movement and "father" of the short-lived Saint-Simonian "church"; Michel Chevalier, a brilliant young engineer in the Corps des Mines; and François Arlès-Dufour, a rising figure in the Lyon silk trade who had first met Enfantin in Frankfurt in 1817 when both were traveling salesmen. However, the men who would eventually do the most to translate Saint-Simonian ideas into practice were the Pereire brothers, Emile and Isaac, and Paulin Talabot.

The Pereires came from the Sephardic Jewish community in Bordeaux. Their grandfather had gained international renown as a teacher of the deaf, but their father had gone bankrupt in trade before dying at the age of thirty-five in 1806, leaving his wife and children penniless. Emile and Isaac were forced to end their formal education early and to enter trade. In 1822 Emile came to Paris to work for his uncle, Isaac Rodrigues, an accounting teacher and tutor of the children of the banker, Beer-Léon Fould. Isaac followed a year later and became a bookkeeper for Vital Roux, a regent of the Banque de France. Emile, however, turned to journalism, writing for various Saint-Simonian journals and the liberal newspaper *Le National,* and soon emerged as an indefatigable promoter of railroads.[47] Paulin Talabot was one of five sons of a successful Limoges magistrate. His older brother Léon, a graduate of the Ecole Polytechnique, entered the iron industry in the south of France in the employ of Marshal Soult in the 1820s. Paulin graduated from the Ecole Polytechnique in 1819 and served for ten years as a state engineer, and also became involved in Soult's industrial pursuits in the South, before meeting the Saint-Simonians in Paris in the early 1830s through his younger brother Edmond, an ardent Saint-Simonian activist who died in the cholera epidemic of 1832.[48]

Between 1825 and 1832 these "Saint-Simonians" refined and publicized Saint-Simon's ideas for social and moral regeneration through economic development in a series of short-lived journals such as *Le Producteur, L'Organisateur,* and *Le Globe.* Central to the Saint-Simonian vision was the idea that poverty and other social ills can be eliminated by using the power of science and technology to increase the total wealth of society. The best way to do this, in their estimation, was with joint-stock industrial development banks, which could siphon existing wealth from the non-productive upper class and put it in the hands of the productive class—*les industriels*—who would then use it systematically to increase the productive capacity of the economy, first and foremost by building a national and international transportation system with canals and railroads.[49] Saint-Simonism as an organized movement ended in 1832 when the authorities put the Saint-Simonians on trial on various charges and dissolved their "commune" outside Paris. It would be twenty years before some of these men would make good on their youthful ideals by helping to revolutionize banking and transportation in France (see the next chapter). What is often overlooked, however, is that before then an older group of Saint-Simon's friends and backers—the people who kept Saint-Simon going and subsidized his publications in the last ten years of his life—undertook to promote economic development through capitalist association in the early 1800s. These "proto-Saint-Simonians" included some of the leading figures in the *haute banque parisienne,* most importantly Jacques Laffitte.[50]

Laffitte and his allies seemed to have no master plan for renovating the French economy, but they addressed bottlenecks and deficiencies in existing business institutions and practices on a number of levels. One of their principal concerns was to expand and modernize the provision of short-term commercial credit by pooling their resources to offer discounting services beyond what individual merchant banks could offer. A first step in that direction had been taken as early as 1776 with the founding of the Caisse d'Escompte, which gave Paris bankers additional capacity to discount commercial paper until 1793, when the Committee of Public Safety dissolved the Caisse along with all other joint-stock companies.[51] After the fall of the Jacobins, a second such discount bank, the Caisse de Comptes Courantes, was launched in 1796. As its name implies, it allowed clients to set up and borrow against current accounts, but its main business was in fact discounting high-quality commercial paper (bearing three signatures and payable at Paris within thirty days) at reasonable rates (6 percent, at a time when private discounters charged three to six times as much). In 1797, yet another joint-stock discount bank, the Caisse d'Escompte du Commerce, was launched to serve merchants whose paper did not meet the stringent standards of the Caisse de Comptes Courantes. Both these banks were successful to a degree but had limited impact since they mainly discounted the paper of their shareholders. In any event, they were both soon outflanked and absorbed by the Banque de France, founded in 1800 in the aftermath of Napoleon Bonaparte's accession to power.[52]

The Banque de France eventually came to play the role of modern central bank for France, notably by establishing and maintaining a national paper currency based on its exclusive right to issue banknotes. In the beginning, however, it was just another vehicle of the leading Paris bankers to expand short-term credit. According to its 1808 by-laws, the Banque was set up to do three things for its clients: accept deposits of securities and bullion and make advances against those deposits; recover and discount commercial paper; and establish and administer current accounts. Of these, discounting was the most important (the advent of the Banque significantly lowered the cost of discounting high-quality, three-signature bills of exchange). Beyond its lower discount rates, what made the Banque de France an improvement over its predecessors was its right to issue banknotes which, by greatly increasing the money supply, at least for merchants in Paris, decreased the incidence of illiquidity crises. The Banque also came to play an important role in government finance when it assumed functions, such as making short-term advances to the Treasury, that Paris bankers had previously offered through a syndicate called the Négociants Réunis.[53]

With its shareholders normally receiving annual dividends equal to 5–10 percent of their invested capital, the Banque de France was unquestionably successful as a business venture. But as a vehicle for expanding commercial credit in France, it was less successful. Although the Banque endeavored to expand its operation beyond Paris in 1807–1810 by setting up *comptoirs* in Rouen, Lille, and Lyon (over the objections of local bankers in each city), those *comptoirs* were closed when Napoleon fell from power. For the next thirty years, the Banque's operations were restricted to Paris, and even there its impact was limited. Only merchants and bankers "admitted" by the Banque's discount committee could discount paper at the Banque (and it had to be three-signature paper), so most Paris merchants still had to go to high-cost "street discounters," who were little better than pawnbrokers. Yet even for those qualified to use it, the Banque did not really serve as discounter of last resort, since it limited its discount business according to the amount of specie on deposit (it would not issue banknotes uncovered by deposits). Moreover, while the Banque gradually extended the range of securities on which it would make loans (adding government bonds to the list in 1834 and warehouse warrants in 1848), it continued to offer only short-term loans on negotiable securities, eschewing long-term loans for industrial ventures. For all these reasons, Laffitte and other bankers began to look beyond the Banque de France for ways to expand commercial and industrial credit.

The 1820s brought the creation of various *comptoirs spéciaux* to aid specific businesses, such as the Caisse d'Escompte de la Boucherie Parisienne. In 1825, at the height of his interest in Saint-Simon, Laffitte tried unsuccessfully to set up the kind of joint-stock industrial investment bank that the Pereires eventually succeeded in launching in the 1850s. In 1837, however, Laffitte managed to launch the Caisse Générale du Commerce et de l'Industrie, which attempted to democratize commercial credit in Paris by discounting two-signature paper at 5 (and later 4) percent and by issuing its own *billets à crédit* as substitutes for the banknotes of the Banque de France. Although Laffitte was not able to raise enough capital to make the Caisse the dominant financial institution in Paris, it was still a moderate success, greatly increasing the amount of commercial paper discounted or rediscounted in Paris in the early 1840s and posing enough of a threat to the Banque de France that the Banque's discount committee expanded its weekly days of operation from three to five. Laffitte's Caisse also inspired other Paris bankers to launch joint-stock discount banks of their own. As a result of all these initiatives, the quality and capacity of banking services in the capital were gradually improving by the 1840s.[54]

Setting up joint-stock companies to offer commercial credit was only one way in which the leading bankers sought to expand and improve business services in Paris in the early decades of the nineteenth century. They also created—or re-created—the French insurance industry. To be sure, merchants in France's ports had long pooled their resources to insure individual shipping ventures, much as was done at Lloyd's Coffeehouse in London, and in the waning years of the Ancien Régime the French government began chartering joint-stock companies to write fire and life insurance policies as well as marine insurance. But the companies founded in the 1780s—notably the Compagnie Royale set up by the Geneva financier, Etienne Clavière—were swept away in the Revolution. The Napoleonic Code allowed new insurance companies to be formed with the approval of the Conseil d'Etat, but since the Emperor shared the popular view of insurance as a form of gambling, no new insurance companies came into being before 1815.[55]

In return for financing the restoration of the Bourbons in 1814–1815, the leading bankers of Paris received official support in relaunching the insurance industry. From 1816 to the 1840s, a steady stream of new joint-stock insurance companies made their appearance in Paris, with four companies dominating the market. Foremost among these was the Compagnie Royale d'Assurances, founded in 1816 by a prestigious group of financiers that included five regents of the Banque de France (Laffitte, Davillier, Perier, Hottinguer, and Delessert) plus James de Rothschild. After a ruling by the Conseil d'Etat in 1818 that any given company could write only one kind of insurance (that is, fire, life, and marine policies had to be written by different companies), the Compagnie Royale reorganized itself as three related companies (Royale-Incendie, Royale-Vie, and Royale-Marine)—a practice that became standard thereafter. In 1819, a second major group of insurance companies—the Assurances Générales group—was founded by the Mallets, who continued to dominate the administration of the company down to the twentieth century. The same year also saw the founding of the Phénix group with backing from Laffitte, the Hottinguers, the Mallets, and the Andrés. Ten years later the fourth main insurance group—the Union group—was launched by Benedict Fould-Oppenheim with backing from (again) Laffitte and other members of the *haute banque*. Paris bankers also took the lead in reviving marine insurance in the port cities, particularly Le Havre, in the 1820s and 1830s. All these companies struggled in their early years, especially in the areas of marine and fire insurance, as they groped their way toward sound pricing of fixed-premium insurance policies. An agreement in 1834 to end price warfare allowed the surviving companies to gradually build up reserves and establish a sound financial footing, and by the 1840s big joint-stock insurance companies were an integral part of the Paris business scene.[56] By then, the leaders of the *haute banque parisienne* were increasingly preoccupied with a third area of business renovation: transportation and communication.

In the 1820s and 1830s, France's political and business elite came to realize that, if their country was to industrialize and remain among the world's leading nations, it had to have a modern, multilevel system of transportation consisting of national and regional roads, canals and canalized rivers, and railroads. French bankers and financiers played only a limited role in the expansion of roads and canals for which the French government—especially the Corps des Ponts et Chaussées (Department of Bridges and Roads)—took primary responsibility. However, as it became apparent that the government would not take similar responsibility for building railroads, the *haute banque* joined with the young civil engineers and promoters associated with Henri Saint-Simon to found the private companies that, after many false starts, eventually succeeded in giving France a world-class system of rail transportation.

On the eve of the French Revolution, France had possessed perhaps the best system of roads in the world, at the heart of which were the *routes royales* that radiated from Paris and connected the capital to the leading administrative and commercial centers of the provinces. Lack of maintenance during the Revolution and Empire caused these roads to deteriorate badly, so it became a high priority of the Restoration government after 1815 to repair and expand them. This effort continued after 1830 under the July Monarchy, which also worked on expanding regional and local roads. As a result, by 1848 France had some 35,000 kilometers of national routes, 43,000 kilometers of departmental roads, and 60,000 kilometers of *routes vicinaux* in reasonably serviceable condition. Almost all of this work was paid for by the government and carried out by personnel of the Ponts et Chaussées. Private enterprise played at best a supporting role, mainly in bridge building, as seen in the work of Marc Seguin, who designed and built sixty-three suspension bridges for the road system over a period of fifteen years (starting with the world's first suspension bridge, at Tournon on the Rhône River, in 1824).[57] The one area of road transportation in which French capitalists took the lead was in providing express freight and passenger services. In 1828 Jacques Laffitte merged three small stagecoach companies into the Messageries Générales to challenge the Messageries Royales, which had enjoyed a virtual monopoly in passenger service on France's major highways since the days of the Empire. Soon these two firms agreed to divide the national market, and their duopoly continued into the 1840s, while myriad small companies provided passenger service on feeder roads.[58]

If French officials expected the road system to handle most passenger traffic, they counted on waterways to carry a growing share of the interregional movement of freight. To that end, in 1820 François Becquey, the director of Ponts et Chaussées, put forward an ambitious plan for 126 river and canal improvements that encompassed 25,000 kilometers of waterways, but the French parliament cut that back to ten projects totaling 2,252 kilometers. Becquey initially hoped that these projects could be conceded to private companies for construction and operation, but French capitalists were reluctant to invest in large-scale enterprises for which costs and revenues could be only roughly estimated. Ultimately the government fell back on a public-private partnership in which the government built and operated the canals, but private companies raised the capital in return for a guaranteed return on their bonds and a share of any eventual profits. One such company, which financed the Canal de Monsieur connecting the Rhône and Rhine, was organized and controlled by Strasbourg financiers. However, most of the other canal companies, including the two largest that financed the building of the Burgundy, Berry, Nivernais, Brittany, and Loire canals, were controlled by various members of the *haute banque parisienne*.[59]

Eventually some 3,000 kilometers of new canals and waterways were opened between 1820 and 1850, quadrupling the size of the French canal system. Some of these canals had a major economic impact: The opening of the Mons-Saint-Quentin Canal cut the cost of transporting Belgian coal to Paris by 75 percent; the opening of the Rhône-Rhine canal lowered the cost of Burgundian coal in Mulhouse from 62 francs per ton to 39.[60] But the economic impact of the canal system as a whole was less than expected because of the lack of standardization (the Canal de Bourgogne, for example, was too narrow to accommodate barges coming from the Rhône-Rhine Canal) and because navigability was intermittent due to floods and droughts. So while the Paris bankers continued to reap good returns on the bonds and shares issued by their canal companies, they ultimately had to look elsewhere—to the railroad—for the basis of a national transportation system.

It was simply not possible to start building railroads in earnest to serve as general regional and interregional carriers in France until the government worked out ground rules for when, where, and how railroads were to be built. Preoccupied as they were in the 1820s with roads and canals, the authorities turned to the railroad question only in the 1830s in response to growing disillusionment with canals and especially in response to a concerted effort by young engineers and Saint-Simonian journalists to promote the construction of a national rail system. In 1832 the director-general of the Corps des Ponts et Chaussées, Victor Legrand, floated a plan for a system of national rail trunk lines, five of which would radiate from Paris in a star pattern. Over the next decade, the French parliament repeatedly debated the legal framework for the rail system and the role of the state in railroad construction. Parliament eventually determined that the government would not build and operate the railroads directly, but it reserved to itself the right to approve the granting of concessions to private companies for each route. It also delegated to the Ponts et Chaussées broad powers over all aspects of railroad construction and administration, including the terms of concessions, technical specifications, and the schedules of charges. However, the Ponts et Chaussées badly underestimated the costs of railroad construction, so when companies that were granted early concessions to build railways started running out of money, the government stepped in with subsidies and then had to revisit the financing issue more systematically. The result was the Railroad Law of 1842, which confirmed the Legrand Plan as the blueprint for the national rail system and determined that future railroads were to be built through a public-private partnership: The state would buy up and prepare the right-of-way; then a private company would be granted a concession to lay track, build stations, and operate the railroad for a specified period. Although the government ended up supplying 35 percent of the total funds expended on railroad construction between 1842 and 1847 and continued to exercise broad authority over the planning, building, and operation of railroads, the initiative for construction continued to come from private joint-stock companies, which brought together the engineers and promoters with the vision and expertise to build railroads and the bankers and financiers who had the capital.[61]

France's first railways were built in the Southeast in the 1820s to facilitate the marketing of the coal produced around Saint-Etienne. The real beginning of the railway age in France, however, is usually dated from the building of the Paris–Saint-Germain railroad, conceived by Emile Pereire as a way to demonstrate the feasibility and potential of railroads to the movers and shakers of the capital. Pereire received a concession for the line in 1832, but construction began only in 1835 after James de Rothschild agreed to invest 6 million francs in the project, the first major commitment from the Paris *haute banque* to railroads. The Paris–Saint-Germain line opened on August 24, 1837, amid much fanfare and was an immediate success, prompting other Paris financiers to jump on the railroad bandwagon.

Over the next four years, two lines were built from Paris to Versailles, one by Pereire and the Rothschilds, and one by a group headed by Benôit Fould. A group led by François Bartholony began construction of the Paris-Orléans line, the first stage in the planned southwestern trunk line from Paris to Tours to Bordeaux. A group tied to the prime minister, François Guizot, and supported by English capitalists began construction of the Paris-Rouen line (the first stage in the western trunk line to Le Havre). Paulin Talabot, with Rothschild backing, built a railroad from Alais to Beaucaire in the Gard, which put him in position to take the lead in developing the crucial rail links between Lyon and the Mediterranean Sea. A group of Alsatian industrialists built lines from Mulhouse to Thann and, more importantly, from Strasbourg to Basel. Numerous companies began to compete for concessions on the eastern and southeastern trunk lines (Paris-Strasbourg and Paris-Lyon) and especially for the biggest prize of all, the northern trunk line connecting Paris to Belgium via Lille and Valenciennes. After years of maneuvering and negotiation, the Ponts et Chaussées conceded the northern line to a company dominated by the Rothschilds. With much of the groundwork for the line already completed by the government, Rothschild's right-hand man for railroads, Emile Pereire, succeeded in laying 800 kilometers of track and in building 43 train stations in nine months, which allowed France's first complete trunk line, the Chemin de Fer du Nord, to begin service in June 1846.[62]

The years from 1842 to 1848 saw a boom in the formation of railroad companies, in the granting of concessions, and especially in speculation in railroad shares. But, except for the Paris-Orléans, the Paris-Rouen, and the Northern, little progress was made in actually building railroads. As of January 1848, France had only 1,860 kilometers of railroads in operation, compared to 5,900 in Great Britain and 5,200 in Germany.[63] Part of the problem was insufficient supplies of iron rails and other building materials, which railroad managers blamed on France's prohibitively high duties on imported industrial products. An even larger part of the problem was the railroad companies' inability to raise sufficient capital: François Caron estimates that only 12 percent of the railroad shares being offered were actually subscribed and, on subscribed shares, only a third of the nominal capital had been paid in by January 1849.[64] Investors were scared off by the severe terms of concessions, which were so short in duration and called for such low fares (based on unrealistically low estimates of construction costs) that it was unlikely that the concessionaires could ever recoup their original investments or turn a profit before the expiration of the concession.

As the inadequacies of the government's plan for railroad building were becoming clear to all, crop failures in 1846 and a general recession in 1847 pricked the speculative bubble in railroad shares; 488 million francs in nominal share value disappeared practically overnight. Then, in February 1848, an uprising in Paris brought down the July Monarchy and cast the future of the railroads into even greater doubt. Through the spring and summer of 1848, the provisional government of the Second Republic debated the wholesale nationalization of the French rail system. Although it ultimately rejected nationalization, the government took control of certain key lines like the Paris-Lyon, and concessions for other lines reverted to the government when the concessionaires failed. By the end of 1848, railroad construction in France had slowed to a trickle. Resumption of construction—seen by many as critical to the nation's economic future—would await a fundamental rethinking of the legal and financial framework for public works in France by the incoming president, Louis-Napoleon Bonaparte, and his advisers.

Viewed from the perspective of what had preceded it, the half century 1800–1850 was undeniably a period of innovation and progress in the world of French merchant capitalism. Banking facilities were expanded and business services such as insurance improved. Palpable progress was made in transportation and communication. Yet France still lacked an efficient, truly national banking system and, with the railroads incomplete, a national transportation system. It would only be in the next quarter century—1850 to 1875—that the French would finally overcome these deficiencies and effect a dual revolution in banking and transportation that made possible the full maturation of merchant and finance capitalism—and the full flowering of industrial capitalism—at the end of the nineteenth century.

CHAPTER TWO

The Revolution in Banking and Transportation, 1850s–1870s

In France, as in most Western countries, the expansion and what we can justifiably call the "modernization" of financial and transportation facilities in the nineteenth century turned out to be as much a political as an economic process. This was especially true in France because efforts to address deficiencies in banking and to launch the construction of a national rail system had made only limited progress in the 1830s and 1840s before being engulfed by the mid-century political crisis. The fall of the July Monarchy and the advent of the Second Republic in early 1848 provided an opportunity for the Saint-Simonians and other advocates of reform to emerge from the shadow of their conservative elders, as reflected in the growing influence of the Pereire brothers and the apparent eclipse of James de Rothschild. But the ability of the Pereires and their allies to recast and relaunch the economy was severely constrained by incessant wrangling within the Constituent Assembly between Radicals and Conservatives in 1848 and later by a fundamental dispute between the popularly elected National Assembly and the popularly elected president, Louis-Napoleon Bonaparte, over who had ultimate authority.

The political stalemate was finally broken by the coup d'état of December 2, 1851, which dissolved the National Assembly and gave virtually dictatorial powers to Louis-Napoleon Bonaparte as Prince-President. Within a year, Bonaparte had assumed the title of Emperor Napoleon III, and the Second Empire had replaced the Second Republic. Although unquestionably a setback for the rule of law and the development of democracy in France, the advent of the Second Empire ended the gridlock among competing economic and bureaucratic interests that had made it impossible to deal effectively with critical issues of economic policy for three years. Indeed, in the year following the coup d'état, Napoleon III and his advisers mobilized the powers of the national government to stimulate the economy more effectively than did any other French government in the nineteenth century. Central to these efforts was their commitment to fostering the innovations in banking and transportation that many viewed as the sine qua non for France's future development.

The revolutions in banking and transportation that unfolded under the Second Empire were in many ways two parts of a single phenomenon. They were functionally interrelated in that the new joint-stock banks were founded in part to finance the building of the railroads, and both revolutions were the work of the same group of men, mainly the Saint-Simonian promoters and Paris financiers who had already risen to prominence in French business and government in the 1830s and 1840s. Still, for clarity's sake, it makes sense to look at each revolution separately in this chapter.

The Banking Revolution

The transformation of banking in France was not a matter of inventing new kinds of banks or new forms of credit but rather a matter of transferring to France techniques and structures previously developed elsewhere, particularly in Britain and Belgium. In the words of Jean Bouvier, "it was a revolution in the organization of banking, in the scale of firms, in the volume of the banks' own resources (capital and reserves), and especially in the amount of resources banks drew from the public."[1] It is too much to say that credit and banking were "democratized" in the 1850s and 1860s, since the services of banks remained unavailable to the great majority of the French people, but certain segments of the French population—middle-class people with savings to invest, merchants in need of short-term credit, entrepreneurs in need of long-term financing—became regular customers of banks for the first time. Moreover, as the Banque de France and later the new deposit banks set up branches in the provinces, a truly national credit system emerged that allowed capital to move easily from one part of the country to another (and to foreign countries) following the dictates of supply and demand. By twentieth-century standards, the French system of credit and banking remained incomplete as of 1870, but it had unquestionably crossed a critical threshold on the path to modernity.

One of the first manifestations of the banking revolution was a significant expansion of the scope and volume of the operations of the Banque de France. Amid the political and financial turmoil of March 1848, the Banque assumed control of nine departmental banks of issue that had recently failed and turned them into miniature versions of itself. Though this was not the beginning of the Banque's branch system—it had created some thirteen branches between 1831 and 1848 to counter the competition of local banks in the discount business— the expansion in 1848 for the first time extended the Banque's monopoly in issuing banknotes beyond Paris and gave it a much greater presence in the major commercial centers of provincial France. The crisis of 1848 led to the liberalization of the Banque's conservative discount policy, as it began discounting warehouse warrants as well as government securities and three-signature commercial paper. The Banque was also authorized to begin issuing banknotes in 100-franc denominations, which increased the popularity of Banque de France banknotes nationwide. Together these reforms significantly strengthened the position of the Banque de France and provided a firmer foundation for the expansion of other sectors of French banking in the years that followed.[2]

Just as important as the expansion of the Banque de France was the founding of a new cohort of banks and credit institutions—some private, some public; most in Paris, but some in the provinces. Of these, the first to appear was the Comptoir d'Escompte Nationale de Paris (CNEP)—the National Discount Bank of Paris—which was founded by the provisional government of the Second Republic on March 8, 1848, scarcely a week after the overthrow of the July Monarchy, to head off massive bankruptcies by providing emergency liquidity to Paris merchants. Within a week of its founding, the CNEP had raised 1.6 million francs (of its total authorized capital of 20 million francs) and had made these funds available to Paris businessmen through various *sous-comptoirs*. Some of these *sous-comptoirs* lasted only as long as the crisis in 1848, but some continued into the next decade and were eventually taken over by the new joint-stock banks. As for the CNEP itself, its charter was renewed for six years in 1850, but in 1854 it abandoned its semipublic status at the urging of the government, was converted into a conventional joint-stock company *(société anonyme)*, and soon shifted from financing Paris commerce to financing foreign trade (see below).[3]

The same law that authorized the creation of the CNEP in March 1848 led to the founding of seventy-six *comptoirs d'escompte* outside of Paris to provide short-term assistance to provincial merchants by discounting their bills of exchange and other commercial paper. The size of these *comptoirs* varied according to local resources and needs. The largest, at Bordeaux, was capitalized at 3 million francs; the smallest, at Rethel in the Ardennes, at only 60,000 francs. As a response to emergency conditions, the *comptoirs* were authorized only to 1853, but most were turned into private banks and continued to serve their communities after that year. One of these—the Comptoir National d'Escompte de Lille—was renamed the Crédit du Nord in 1871 and eventually became France's most important regional bank (and today is a bank of national importance).[4]

The conversion of the *comptoirs d'escompte* into departmental banks was part of a larger expansion of local banking for which the creation of a national network of branches by the Banque de France served as a catalyst.[5] Drawing on reports of the Banque de France inspectors, Alain Plessis has estimated that the number of local banks in France amounted to 2,500 under the Second Empire (if all those discounting paper at branches of the Banque de France are counted as banks). Drawing on a report of tax officials, Louis Bergeron has estimated that there were 1,258 banks in France outside of Paris by 1892, which is perhaps a more realistic estimate. Whichever estimate is used, provincial France had undoubtedly acquired a much denser banking network and achieved a level of banking services much closer to that of the British by 1870 than was once thought.[6]

The chief function of these new local banks was the discounting of the commercial paper of local merchants and manufacturers. This was, of course, indispensable for the workings of local trade. By effecting a threefold increase in the discount volume, from 7 billion francs to 22 billion, the proliferation of local banks under the Second Empire clearly contributed to the strong growth of the French economy between the 1840s and 1870s.[7] Still, these local private banks did not offer new services (like checking accounts) to their established customers, nor did they bring many new customers into the system. Most importantly, they did little to mobilize the latent wealth of the provinces in the cause of industrial and infrastructure development, the highest priority of the economic reformers around Napoleon III. Thus, the expansion of local banking, however noteworthy, was ultimately not as important for the banking revolution under the Second Empire as was the creation of the great joint-stock banks of Paris.

The Saint-Simonians and others concerned with France's long-term economic development—and particularly with building canals, railroads, and large-scale industrial enterprises—had concluded as early as the 1820s that the most efficient way to mobilize the large amounts of capital needed for these enterprises was to set up limited-liability joint-stock companies that could issue shares or interest-bearing bonds in denominations small enough to attract the savings of the middle class. Such institutions were operating in Belgium with great success by the 1830s. Some reformers also looked to a British innovation, deposit banking, as an additional way to gain access to large pools of previously inaccessible capital. However they did it, once these joint-stock institutions had mobilized sufficient capital, they could then direct it into the areas where it could do the most good, first and foremost to build the railroads.

Broadening the use of the limited-liability joint-stock company in French banking and finance in the early 1800s, however, was no easy matter. Under the Commercial Code in effect since 1808, setting up full-fledged limited-liability joint-stock companies *(sociétés anonymes)* was subject to strict government oversight and, in particular, required the approval of the Conseil d'Etat. But the Conseil d'Etat, which perfectly embodied the ingrained official suspicion of limited liability that could be traced back to the failure of John Law's financial schemes in the 1720s, was reluctant to grant such approval. In his study of joint-stock enterprise in France, Charles Freedeman discovered that the Conseil d'Etat authorized only 400 *sociétés anonymes* between 1809 and 1848—an average of ten a year—and only seven of these were banks.[8] Traditional merchant bankers also remained reluctant to form or participate in limited-liability companies, fearful of losing their financial power in a world of very large joint-stock banks. Thus Jacques Laffitte had only limited success in creating large joint-stock credit institutions on the model of the Belgian joint-stock investment banks in the 1830s and 1840s. With the collapse of Laffitte's Caisse Générale du Commerce et de l'Industrie in the crisis of 1847–1848, the movement to modernize the French financial sector by creating big joint-stock banks seemed to be back to where it had started.[9]

The real breakthrough for joint-stock banking came with the coup d'état of December 1851. Starting in early 1852, Louis-Napoleon Bonaparte did what his uncle and the constitutional monarchs of 1815–1848 had never done: He threw the full authority of his government behind the creation of joint-stock banks in defiance of the entrenched resistance in the Conseil d'Etat and the conservative financial establishment. This was first manifested in February 1852 in a decree authorizing the formation of a national mortgage bank, the Crédit Foncier de France. The Crédit Foncier was yet another brainchild of Emile Pereire, who viewed it as the first of a phalanx of government-backed joint-stock banks that would operate on an unprecedented scale and undertake the systematic transformation of all sectors of the French economy. The initial expectation was that the Crédit Foncier would rescue French farmers from dependence on usurious local notaries and, more broadly, that it would organize and coordinate mortgage credit on a national scale. Although the Crédit Foncier did succeed in mobilizing huge resources (it was capitalized at 60 million francs and was authorized to issue bonds up to twenty times the amount of its paid-in capital), it ended up serving urban real estate developers more than farmers. By 1866 its chief client was the City of Paris, to which it loaned some 350 million francs in support of Baron Haussmann's urban renewal projects.[10]

The decisive step in the government's program to expand and transform the banking system came in the fall of 1852 with the founding of the Crédit Mobilier, which was conceived by Emile and Isaac Pereire as the principal means of promoting and orchestrating the industrial development not only of France but of the whole continent of Europe. It would do this first by mobilizing unprecedented amounts of capital—perhaps 1.2 billion francs—by selling shares in the company in small denominations (500 francs) and by issuing large numbers of interest-bearing bonds in even smaller denominations (100 francs) directly to the public. It would then use that capital as seed money to launch an array of subsidiaries in France, including railroads, steamship lines, and engineering and construction companies, and also replicas of itself—other crédits mobiliers—outside of France to build railroads and to promote industrialization in other countries. If the Crédit Mobilier proved to be successful, it would, among other things, allow the Pereires and their allies to supplant the Rothschilds as the dominant force in European finance, and James de Rothschild was quick to recognize this. In a letter to the Prince-President, Rothschild opposed the authorization of the Crédit Mobilier, warning that, if approved, the new bank would take control of the great part of the public fortune and would eventually become "more powerful than the government itself."[11]

In a high-stakes battle fought at the top levels of the French government in the fall of 1852, Louis-Napoleon Bonaparte came down on the side of the Pereires against Rothschild, and the Crédit Mobilier was authorized without the normal review by the Conseil d'Etat. At the same time, perhaps heeding Rothschild's warning, the Prince-President established strict government oversight of the new bank. In addition to giving the government the right to approve the company's directors and its issuance of foreign bonds, the decree of authorization put clear limits on the indebtedness of the new bank.

As a result, the initial resources of the Crédit Mobilier amounted to little more than its paid-in capital of 60 million francs plus 120 million francs in the current accounts of its principal clients, rather than the 1.2 billion francs envisioned by the Pereires. Yet, according to Rondo Cameron, these resources allowed the Credit Mobilier to "perform prodigious feats of industrial promotion and financial manipulation" in its first three years of operation.[12] These included the organization and financing of three of France's six trunk-line railroads (the Eastern, Western, and Southern); the founding of the Paris Gas Company, the Paris omnibus company, two insurance companies, and a steamship company; and the underwriting of sixteen major industrial firms. And that was just within France. Beyond France, the Crédit Mobilier helped to found the Darmstadter Bank in Germany and, through its "sister" *crédits mobiliers*, soon engaged the Rothschilds and their allies in a titanic struggle for control of the railroads in Austria, Switzerland, Italy, Spain, and Russia.

Eventually, and perhaps inevitably, the Pereires overplayed their hand and acquired powerful enemies whose influence could not be permanently offset by the Pereires' relationship with the Emperor. The most important of these enemies was the Banque de France, whose monopoly of note issue the Pereires dared to challenge in the 1860s. In the financial downturn of 1866–1867, the Crédit Mobilier could not meet its current obligations because much of its assets were tied up in long-term loans for construction in Paris. With the bank's stock price plummeting, the Pereires were forced to seek a loan from the Banque de France. The Banque agreed to save the Crédit Mobilier from immediate failure, but it used the opportunity to force out the Pereires and to initiate a gradual transformation of their company into a much smaller bank, the Société Française du Crédit Mobilier.

It was not the downfall of the Crédit Mobilier, however, but its astounding initial successes that were of greatest significance for the course of French banking history. The founding and early triumphs of the investment bank finally persuaded the Paris financial community that joint-stock banks represented the wave of the future, and this in turn generated a barrage of proposals for additional such banks. As Charles Freedeman has shown, most of these proposals were rejected by the Conseil d'Etat, which remained resolute in its distrust of limited-liability enterprises.[13] But in time a number of new banks succeeded in winning official approval, including the five banks that would come to dominate and define the French banking scene for the rest of the nineteenth century and much of the twentieth.

The first of these to appear was the Comptoir d'Escompte de Paris, born (or reborn) in 1854 when the official discount bank set up to alleviate the credit crunch in 1848 was reorganized as a *société anonyme* capitalized at 20 million francs. At the time, with the Crédit Mobilier focusing its attention and resources on railroads and other long-term capital investments, there remained an unmet need for short-term commercial credit. James de Rothschild and his allies wanted to set up a joint-stock bank to meet this need, but in the charged atmosphere left by the battle over the Crédit Mobilier, the Conseil d'Etat refused to approve it. Instead, the Conseil allowed the Comptoir d'Escompte to double its capital in order to serve more customers.[14]

The signing of the Anglo-French Trade Treaty in 1860, ushering in an era of freer trade and raising expectations for a big increase in France's foreign trade, prompted the directors of the Comptoir d'Escompte to take the firm in a new direction. Instead of financing domestic trade, the Comptoir henceforth concentrated on financing France's foreign trade, and it began to set up offices overseas to carry out this new mission. It started with an office in New York to finance the importation of cotton from the United States and later added offices in Calcutta, Bombay, and Alexandria to finance trade in Indian and Egyptian cotton. It also set up offices in Buenos Aires, Sydney, and Melbourne to finance the importation of wool by Roubaix manufacturers and an office in Saigon to serve the new protectorate of Cochinchina.[15]

Even before the Comptoir d'Escompte decided to specialize in overseas trade, financiers from Paris and abroad were jockeying to set up an additional joint-stock bank to offer short-term commercial credit to the growing business community of the capital. In January 1859, three

years of complex negotiation and maneuvering on this question culminated in the founding of the Crédit Industriel et Commercial (CIC)
by two groups of French financiers, one associated with Napoleon III's
half-brother, the ubiquitous promoter Comte Charles de Morny, and
another associated with the Saint-Simonian entrepreneurs, François
Arlès-Dufour and Paulin Talabot. Although the CIC was the first Paris
bank to offer British-style deposit banking and to introduce checking
accounts when those were legalized in 1865, its raison d'être was financing the daily movement of goods into, out of, and through France
by the discounting of bills of exchange and warehouse warrants.[16]

To pursue this line of business, the directors of the CIC realized that
the bank would need a network of correspondents or branches beyond
the capital. This was initially provided by the Sous-Comptoir de
l'Industrie et du Commerce, which set up offices in various provincial
trade centers—including Marseille, Bordeaux, Nantes, Reims, Le
Havre, and Dunkirk—through which it offered commercial credit,
mainly by discounting warehouse warrants that by prior agreement the
CIC re-discounted at rates comparable to those offered by the Banque
de France. This re-discount business burgeoned from 67 million francs
to 167 million francs in just three years and became the principal focus
of the CIC's operations by the mid-1860s. However, widespread fraud
in warehouse warrants—specifically the issuing of warrants on non-
existent merchandise—soon undercut this business and led to the liquidation of the Sous-Comptoir in 1868. By then, however, the CIC
was putting in place an alternative network of correspondents by
launching smaller versions of itself in Marseille, Lyon, and Lille. Although initially quite dependent on the CIC, all three of these subsidiaries soon moved out of the CIC's orbit and became important independent regional banks, the Société Marseillaise de CIC in particular.[17]
The CIC and its associates also moved into financing overseas trade,
especially in Asia and the Pacific, which led to the founding in 1875
of the Banque de l'Indochine as a joint-venture with the Comptoir
d'Escompte.[18]

The third new commercial bank founded under the Second Empire,
and the only one originating outside of Paris, was the Crédit Lyonnais.
Its backers included some of the same Saint-Simonian entrepreneurs
involved in the CIC (notably Arlès-Dufour and Talabot) as well as Lyon
silk merchants, local iron manufacturers, and financiers from Paris and
Geneva. However, the largest shareholder and the man who would
direct and indeed personify the Crédit Lyonnais from its founding until

the early 1900s was Henri Germain. Son of a well-to-do silk merchant, Germain had studied and practiced law in Paris in the 1840s before returning to Lyon in 1848, where he married the daughter of another silk merchant, dabbled in local politics, and worked with Hugues Darcy, head of the Châtillon-Commentry iron and steel combine, who put Germain on his company's board of directors.

The initial purpose of the Crédit Lyonnais was to support regional trade and industry. In particular, Arlès-Dufour and other *marchands de soie* needed funds to turn Lyon into a center for the international silk trade, and leaders of the regional iron and steel industry needed financial support for the adoption of the Bessemer process and other technological innovations (see Chapter 6). Both groups had at first expected the CIC to supply this support through a branch in Lyon, but when negotiations with the CIC stalled, they were able to bypass Paris and create their own bank under the Incorporation Law of May 1863. This law legalized a new kind of joint-stock company, the *société à responsabilité limitée* (SARL), which was not subject to the restrictions and government oversight that still applied to the *société anonyme*. Thus the Crédit Lyonnais, capitalized at 20 million francs (the maximum for SARLs), opened its doors in late 1863.

More than the CIC or the later Société Générale, the Crédit Lyonnais utilized the techniques of British deposit banking, offering its customers a variety of interest-bearing accounts. The bank eventually multiplied its resources a hundredfold or more by setting up branch banks throughout France to "drain" middle-class savings into its coffers. But at first it limited its branches to one in Marseille, which promptly failed in the financial crisis of 1866, and one in Paris. The latter soon overshadowed the home office in Lyon, especially after 1869 when Henri Germain, widowed in 1867, married the daughter of the governor of the Banque de France and was absorbed into Parisian financial circles. This transfer of power from Lyon to Paris was reinforced in 1878 when the Crédit Lyonnais opened the Italianate "palace" on the Boulevard des Italiens that has remained the architectural symbol of the bank ever since (formal transfer of the bank's corporate headquarters from Lyon to Paris followed four years later).

This geographical reorientation mirrored a shift in the bank's lending and investment activities. In the 1860s it concentrated on supporting Lyonnais enterprises, including the ill-fated La Fuchsine Dye Company, France's first major effort to develop synthetic dyestuffs. However, after turning a handsome profit in 1871–1872 by helping to underwrite the loan to pay the indemnity to Germany, the Crédit Lyonnais quickly moved to vying with the Rothschilds and other Paris financiers for a share of the government loan business, for which it soon opened branches in Constantinople, Madrid, Amsterdam, and Saint Petersburg. It was largely to raise funds for foreign lending that Germain set up the bank's network of domestic branches in the 1870s. By 1880, the capital of the Crédit Lyonnais had risen to 200 million francs—ten times its original amount—and its 382 million francs in assets made it the largest commercial bank in France.[19]

The second great French deposit bank, which became the Crédit Lyonnais' principal rival, was founded in 1864 as the Société Générale pour Favoriser le Développement du Commerce et de l'Industrie en France, or Société Générale for short. As its full name indicates, the creators of the Société Générale considered it primarily an investment and development bank—another Crédit Mobilier—not a deposit bank. Its origins can be traced back to efforts in the 1850s by James de Rothschild and his allies to create a rival to the Crédit Mobilier. By 1864, however, Rothschild was preoccupied with government finance and with his duel with the Pereires elsewhere in Europe, so promotion of the new bank fell to others, notably Edouard Blount, the British banker who headed the Chemin de Fer de l'Ouest; Eugène Schneider of the Le Creusot Iron Company; Guillaume Denière, a Paris bronze maker who served as a regent of the Banque de France and later as chairman of the Marine Steel Company; and Paulin Talabot of the Paris-Lyon-Mediterranean Railroad (P-L-M).

Once launched, the Société Générale quickly moved beyond pure investment banking to embrace deposit banking, which led it to create a network of branch banks in Paris and the provinces. By 1870, when the CIC and Crédit Lyonnais still had only rudimentary branch systems, the Société Générale already had twenty offices in Paris and thirty-three outside Paris. Largely because of its success in attracting deposits through its branches, the assets of the bank rose rapidly, from 150 million francs in 1864 to 307 million in 1873, which enabled it to offer critical financial support to various enterprises—particularly those of Paulin Talabot (the P-L-M Railroad, the Mokta-el-Hadid Mining Company, and Talabot's new steamship company, the Société Générale des Transports Maritimes à Vapeur). The Société Générale also moved aggressively into financing the national debts of developing countries such as Mexico, Brazil, Peru, Rumania, and the Ottoman Empire, which left it open to criticism at home for betraying its original purpose but which greatly contributed to the 11 to 16 percent annual returns on paid-in capital that the bank posted in its first five years of operations.[20]

The last of the new banks created in this era that would play a major role in French and international finance in the succeeding century was the Banque de Paris et des Pays-Bas, or "Paribas." This was very different from the joint-stock banks in that it did not aspire to mobilize the previously untapped resources of the general public but only to bring the private capital of a number of investment bankers together under a single corporate umbrella. In essence it represented the transition of merchant banking from the family capitalism of the Rothschilds, Mallets, and Hottinguers to the corporate age. It was the first of the modern *banques d'affaires*.

Paribas was founded in 1872 through the merger of the Banque du Crédit et des Dépôts des Pays-Bas with the Banque de Paris. The first had been created in 1863 by German bankers living in Paris—Louis and J-R Bischoffsheim and their nephew Henri Bamberger—with support from the Geneva banker Edouard Hentsch to manage various interests in Brussels, Antwerp, and Amsterdam. The Banque de Paris had been set up in 1869 under Adrien Delahante (previously the director of the Société Générale) to challenge the Rothschilds in the lucrative government loan business in the aftermath of James de Rothschild's death in 1868. The merger of the two banks was a response to the Rothschilds' success in nearly monopolizing the first installment of the French bond issue to pay the indemnity to Germany after the Franco-Prussian War. Paribas' first success was in securing 35 percent of the second installment in cooperation with the Crédit Lyonnais.

In the beginning Paribas was managed collectively by its principal partners from multiple locations to allow them to establish and maintain personal contacts with capitalists and politicians across Europe. However, financial reversals for the Bischoffsheims in Belgium and America weakened the Pays-Bas wing of the bank and tipped the balance of power toward the Paris wing, which succeeded in installing Ernest Dutilleul as the first chairman of the board with authority over the whole company in 1877. Still, the bank remained at heart a confederation of private bankers who depended on personal contacts to generate two types of business: syndication of government bond issues and the underwriting of corporate stock and bond offerings. The latter inevitably gave Paribas a financial stake in a wide array of companies, particularly the new companies in electricity, urban transit, gas, and chemicals—the industries of the Second Industrial Revolution—that were launched in the 1880s and 1890s.[21]

The emergence of the new *banques d'affaires*—not only Paribas but also the Banque de l'Indochine, the Banque Impériale Ottomane, and eventually others—and the survival and continued importance of the private merchant banks amply demonstrate the continuities at certain levels of French banking from the first half of the nineteenth century to the second. At the same time, the new joint-stock banks did effect a revolution in banking in two ways. First, they introduced new financial services that made banks and banking an increasingly important part of daily life, at least for businessmen and the affluent, most of whom had previously avoided banks as too risky, too expensive, or simply unhelpful. The Société Générale, for example, offered this clientele four new kinds of accounts: running or current accounts, which replaced the cashbox in daily business operations; checking accounts; interest-bearing savings accounts; and certificates of deposit, which paid higher rates of interest on funds deposited for periods of up to five years. In addition, the deposit banks also played the role of stock-brokers, giving middle-class people a convenient and secure way of acquiring and holding the stocks and bonds that, because they were being issued in smaller denominations than previously, were becoming more and more a part of their investment portfolios.

Drawing middle-class savings out of the strongbox and into bank accounts or investment portfolios in turn played a major role in the mobilization of capital that was the second and most significant aspect of the banking revolution. Maurice Lévy-Leboyer has assembled various quantitative indicators of the dimensions of this mobilization that together suggest that the stock of capital in the French economy increased threefold between the 1840s and the late 1860s.[22] How was this increased stock of capital distributed?

The long-standing criticism of French banks is that they committed "lèse croissance industrielle nationale,"[23] depriving the national economy of much-needed investment capital, by funneling so much of their available funds into unproductive loans to potentates in the Near East, South America, and Eastern Europe. To be sure, government finance was a big part of the business of French banks throughout the nineteenth century. However, banking historians now tend to see this not so much as depriving the French economy of needed capital but rather as a response to declining domestic demand for capital in the downturn of the late 1860s and 1870s. In any case, the new joint-stock banks did play a big role in mobilizing capital for French commerce and industry. The CIC did this for domestic commerce, the Comptoir d'Escompte for import and export merchants, and the Crédit Lyonnais and the Société Générale for industry. Moreover the latter two followed in the footsteps of the Crédit Mobilier in financing or assisting railroads, steamship companies, and other infrastructure enterprises. Thus was the revolution in banking integrally linked to the other economic "revolution" of the mid-nineteenth century, the creation of a modern transportation system.

The Transportation Revolution

The expansion of the French transportation system in the mid-nineteenth century was a complex event that involved a broad range of technological and organizational innovations. It was intimately bound up with the development of French industry, especially the production of coal, iron, steel, and machinery (a connection that will be explored more fully in Part II). Here the emphasis is on the development of the institutions and enterprises that served to bring together the different parts of France into a single national market and to connect that national market to the outside world. In particular, we focus on the creation of the national rail system and the development of oceangoing steam navigation.

Building the Railroads

As we saw in Chapter 1, the French government had established a plan for a national rail system by 1842, and France experienced a boom in railroad promotion, as well as some actual railroad building, in the mid-1840s. In 1846, the first of five projected trunk lines radiating from Paris—the Chemin de Fer du Nord—was completed, and train service between Paris and the Belgian border began. But the expected rapid completion of the entire primary rail system did not follow. The heart of the problem was railroad finance, and this could be traced to the overly stringent terms placed on concession holders by the government. For one thing, the technical specifications formulated and enforced by the Bureau of Bridges and Roads (Ponts et Chaussées) made railroad construction in France an expensive proposition, significantly more expensive than in Belgium, Germany, or the United States. By 1847 it was apparent that raising the money needed for the trunk lines was going to strain the capacity of the Paris money market even under the best of circumstances.[24] Financing the railroads was further complicated by the short duration of the concessions (thirty-eight years, in the case of the Chemin de Fer du Nord), which made it unlikely that railroad companies would be able to recover their initial investment before the concession expired and so made people reluctant to buy railroad shares and bonds in the first place. Added to these man-made problems were natural ones. Crop failures in 1846 led to a general economic downturn that deflated financial markets. As their stock prices plummeted, railroad companies suspended (or never began) construction. By the end of 1847 several companies were in bankruptcy, and a number of concessions had been abandoned.

The future of the French railroads was thrown further into doubt by the Revolution of February 1848 that brought to power a republican government overtly hostile to the "féodalités financières" that controlled the railroad companies. The finance minister of the new government, Louis-Antoine Garnier-Pagès, called for nationalization of the entire rail system, and as a down payment he sequestered two completed lines, the Paris-Orléans and the Avignon-Marseille. In June the newly elected Constituent Assembly took time out from repressing a worker uprising in Paris to debate and reject nationalization as a general policy, but the Assembly proceeded to revoke the concession for the Paris-Lyon line in August, so the legal status of the railroads and the relationship between the railroad companies and the state remained uncertain as the revolutionary year came to an end.

For the next three years, the government of the Second Republic continued to concede new railroad lines to private companies one-by-one through a time-consuming, highly politicized process that harked back to the situation before the law of 1842. Construction continued, but at a halting pace. The government itself undertook the building of the Paris-Lyon railroad, and all but the Chalons-Lyon section was completed by 1851. The Northern Railroad opened branches to Calais and Dunkirk in September 1848, and by 1850 it had opened the first segment of a projected second trunk line from Paris to the Belgian border via Saint-Quentin.[25] The first section of the Paris-Strasbourg line opened in September 1849. Indeed, the total length of the French railroads more than doubled, from 1,860 kilometers to 3,900, between 1848 and 1851, but they still amounted to little more than a collection of unconnected local and regional lines. The railroads would have the desired economic impact only when the entire projected system was finished, and that could happen only when basic policy issues were resolved concerning the terms under which the companies were to build and operate the various segments of the national system.[26]

As with banking policy, indecision on railroad policy ended with the coup d'état of December 1851. In assuming dictatorial powers, Louis-Napoleon Bonaparte threw his support behind a program that Emile Pereire and other railroad executives had been advocating unsuccessfully throughout the Second Republic. This program had three essential points:

1. *Fusion.* This involved the creation of a single company to build and operate each of the six planned trunk lines—the Northern, Eastern, Western, Southwestern (Paris-Orléans-Bordeaux), Southeastern (Paris-Lyon-Marseille), and Southern (Bordeaux-Cette)—and the merger of the secondary lines in each region with the trunk line to form six coherent regional systems. As François Caron has put it, "in place of bidding, competition, and isolated concessions, there was to be concentration and systems organized around major axes considered as natural monopolies."[27]

2. *Extension of all concessions to ninety-nine years.* This gave companies time to recoup their initial investment, and, more importantly, it increased the period over which the capital of each company could be amortized and its debts retired. This would have the effect of greatly reducing annual finance charges and freeing up more of annual revenues to cover operating expenses and to pay dividends, greatly increasing the attractiveness of railroad shares and bonds to investors.

3. *State interest guarantees.* The terms that had first been negotiated to support the building of the Paris-Orléans line—state guarantee of interest to be paid on bonds issued by railroads—were to be extended to all trunk-line companies and their regional lines. In other words, the government was to become the ultimate guarantor of all investments in the railroads. This meant that, in the eyes of the investing public, railroad bonds would become indistinguishable from government *rentes,* and this alone insured that the reorganized railroad companies would be able to raise all the capital they needed.

By supporting this plan for reorganizing and relaunching the railroads, Napoleon III accepted that the French railroad system would be owned and operated by large, monopolistic, government-supported companies. But he also made sure that the power of these companies was balanced and constrained by the power of the French state acting through the Ministry of Public Works, the Bureau of Bridges and Roads, and other agencies that exercised broad authority over how the railroads were built and how they operated. Even more than the large joint-stock banks, the French railroad companies had to accept close government oversight as the price for government support.

With the new government policies in place, four years of stalemate and uncertainty swiftly gave way to five years of frenzied railroad construction. Between 1852 and 1857, the length of railroad concessions tripled, from under 5,000 kilometers to over 15,000, and the length of lines actually in operation doubled to 7,300 kilometers.[28] As expected, construction was accompanied by reorganization, with various smaller companies merging to form the six regional companies that would dominate the French railroad industry until their nationalization and fusion into the Société Nationale des Chemins de Fer (SNCF) in 1937. The ultimate shape of the "Big Six" was not preordained by the government but was worked out through intense maneuvering by a handful of railroad executives and promoters, each of whom aspired to control as much of the national rail system as possible. Supporting parts in this drama were played by various members of the *haute banque,* each of whom sought to win a piece of the most lucrative companies on the best terms. Above all, the battle for the railroads mirrored the battle of the banks, with the Pereire brothers and their allies in the Crédit Mobilier competing with James de Rothschild and his allies, especially François Bartholony of the Paris-Orléans (P-O) and Paulin Talabot, who eventually parlayed his control of the Avignon-Marseille into control of France's largest railroad, the Paris-Lyon-Méditerranée (P-L-M). There was also a wild card, the Emperor's half-brother, the comte de Morny, who worked diligently in the mid-1850s to put together a seventh regional system—the Grand Central—in the south-central part of the country. The Grand Central, however, proved not to be economically viable, and Morny's lines were soon divided up between the P-O and the P-L-M. When the dust settled in 1857, the Pereires controlled three of the six companies (the Western, Eastern, and Southern), and their rivals controlled the other three (the Northern, Paris-Orléans, and Paris-Lyon-Méditerranée).

The key events in the creation of the French rail network in the 1850s concerned the completion of the trunk line from Paris to Marseille, the consolidation of most of the railroads in the southeastern quadrant of France around that trunk line in the P-L-M Company, and the determination of who would control this vital network. The Paris-Lyon had long been viewed as a pivotal line in the national rail system, and the 1840s witnessed a protracted battle for this concession that attracted all the major players, including Rothschild, Bartholony, and the Saint-Simonians (Enfantin, Arlès-Dufour, the Pereires). In 1845 the concession was awarded to a company put together by Isaac Pereire with the participation of the Rothschilds, but it failed in the financial crisis of 1847, and in 1848 the government cancelled the concession and began to build the railroad itself.[29] By 1851 much of the construction on the Paris-Lyon was completed, and the section from Paris to Dijon was open to traffic. But privatization was the order of the day following the coup d'état, and in March 1852 the Paris-Lyon line was taken over by a new company, control of which was finely balanced between the Rothschild and Pereire forces (by then at odds over the Crédit Mobilier). On important matters of company policy the decisive vote was cast by the chairman of the board, the Genevan financier Auguste Dassier.

Meanwhile, Paulin Talabot had been establishing himself as the master of the section of the Paris-Marseille trunk line south of Lyon. Talabot had won the concession for the Avignon-Marseille line in 1843. Despite facing formidable topographical challenges that necessitated building twelve viaducts and digging a 4.6 kilometer tunnel through the Nerthe Mountains north of Marseille, he and his partners completed the line and opened it for traffic by January 1848.[30] Talabot also took control of the concession for the Lyon-Avignon line, and in late 1852 he won government approval for the merger of the Lyon-Avignon, the Avignon-Marseille, and three regional railroads (including Talabot's original Alais-Beaucaire line) into the Compagnie des Chemins de Fer de Lyon à la Méditerranée. The line from Lyon to Avignon was completed in 1855, at last making possible through train service from Paris to Marseille. Finally, in 1857, the Paris-Lyon joined with the Lyon-Mediterranean, the Lyon-Geneva, the Bourbonnais line of the defunct Grand Central, and various regional lines to form the Paris-Lyon-Méditerranée (P-L-M). Capitalized at 400 million francs and operating 4,010 kilometers of rail lines throughout the Southeast, the P-L-M was not only the largest railroad company but also the largest corporation of any kind in France. At first the two halves of the railroad (north and south of Lyon) were administered separately, but in 1862 they were united under a single managerial hierarchy headed by Paulin Talabot. From an administrative point of view, the P-L-M remained very much Talabot's railroad until his death in 1885.[31]

Although the Pereires were ultimately excluded from control of the P-L-M, they used the financial power of the Crédit Mobilier to orchestrate the creation of three other trunk systems: the Eastern, Western, and Southern. The Eastern Railroad was created in 1853 through the merger of the Paris-Strasbourg with various regional lines, including the Strasbourg-Basel, the Nancy-Gray, and the Ardennes. The Western Railroad was created in 1855 through complex negotiations among the Pereires (who controlled the Paris–Saint-Germain and Paris-Versailles), Edouard Blount and Charles Laffitte of the Paris–Le Havre, and François Bartholony of the Paris-Orléans, who agreed to split the lines in Brittany, giving the lines in northern Brittany to the Western. The Southern Railroad, by contrast, was a purely Pereire creation, assembled out of unclaimed or previously abandoned concessions in the Southwest. In 1852, with backing from the city fathers of Bordeaux and Toulouse, the Pereires acquired the trunk line from Bordeaux to Cette on the Mediterranean coast west of the Rhône, the only trunk line in the 1842 plan that did not emanate from Paris. This line finally opened in 1857 when Emile Pereire, traveling east from Bordeaux, met his brother, traveling west from the Mediterranean, at ceremonies in Toulouse that foreshadowed those that accompanied the completion of the first American transcontinental railroad twelve years later. Prevented by prior concessions to the P-O from expanding north of their trunk line, the Pereires endeavored to extend that trunk from Cette to Marseille in the early 1860s, but Talabot blocked them. As a result, the Southern remained the smallest, poorest, and least traveled of the Big Six.

While the P-L-M, Eastern, Western, and Southern railroads were products of the new regime put in place in 1851, the Paris-Orléans and Northern systems were extensions of successful lines that predated the Second Empire. More than any other railroad in France, the P-O was the work of one man, the Geneva-born financier François Bartholony. Bartholony had won the concession for the key route south from Paris in 1838, and fifteen years later he leveraged that 160-kilometer railroad into the system serving the Center and Southwest of France by merging it with three other railroads: the Centre (Orléans-Chateauroux), the Orléans-Bordeaux, and the Tours-Nantes. Subsequently, in negotiations with the Pereires, he added southern Brittany (the Nantes-Lorient-Quimper line), and in 1857 he divided the Grand Central with Talabot's P-L-M, taking the lines south and west of Clermont-Ferrand.

Meanwhile, the Rothschilds' Chemin de Fer du Nord—potentially the most profitable of all French trunk lines because of its strategic position in the most populous, most industrialized part of the country—had been marking time from 1848 to 1851, constrained by its heavy obligations to repay state construction expenses and to amortize shareholder capital by the end of its thirty-eight year concession. These constraints largely disappeared, however, as a result of what Louis Girard called "the miracle of December 2nd." When the government extended the Northern's concession to ninety-nine years and reduced the interest on its debt to the state from 5 percent to 3 percent, the company's fixed expenses fell dramatically, and its profits tripled in one year even though operating revenues hardly increased at all. Instead of watching every centime of expense, the railroad was suddenly in a position to expand its services. It soon completed a second trunk line from Paris to the Belgian border that, coupled with strategic acquisitions of southern Belgian railroads, gave it a virtual monopoly on shipments of Belgian coal into northern France and also assured its control of passenger service from Paris into northern Germany. All of this, plus sound financial management, allowed the Northern to post the strongest financial performance of any French railroad in the period from the Second Empire to the First World War.[32]

The six trunk-line rail companies that emerged in the 1850s were the largest private enterprises (in terms of assets and number of employees) yet created in France, and they maintained that distinction into the twentieth century. As such, they were the first French companies to face the managerial problems associated with modern big business and, like their counterparts in the United States, they pioneered many of the solutions to those problems between the 1860s and World War I (see Chapter 16). However, the large French railroads never exercised the independent power over their domestic economy that the American railroads did, largely because obligations arising out of their initial dependence on the French government created financial problems that led to further dependence on—and subordination to—the government. In particular, as the price for approving the mergers of the late 1850s, the government of Napoleon III required the Big Six to undertake 2,500 kilometers of new construction to complete the so-called second network of feeder and connector lines.

Because so many of these additional lines were expected to be unprofitable, this new requirement threatened the long-term financial viability of the railroads and made it that much harder for them to raise needed capital. Of course, the Second Empire could not countenance the failure of the railroad companies with which it was by then so closely identified, so it entered into a new round of negotiations with the companies to revise the terms of their concessions yet again. These negotiations culminated in 1859 in conventions (agreements) that extended to bonds issued on the second network interest guarantees that the government had given to earlier railroad bonds in 1852. That is to say, if in a given year the revenues of a railroad were not sufficient to pay the mandatory 4 percent interest on its new bonds, the state would make the interest payment for it, and the railroad would reimburse the state out of future revenues. Since the need for such payments was considered all but inevitable, the conventions required the companies to put aside all profits in excess of statutory dividends to fund repayments to the government starting in 1872. The Conventions of 1859 thus drew the railroad companies into an even tighter web of government regulation and supervision. But in the short run they allowed the companies to finance continued construction by floating government-backed obligations, and by 1865 the French rail system reached 11,500 kilometers, triple its size in 1852.[33] By 1883, when another set of conventions with the Big Six settled a long-running battle over the building of the third network of local rail lines and defined the legal framework for railroad operations for the next half century (see Chapter 11), the French rail system had grown to more than 25,000 kilometers and was second in length in Europe only to the German system. By then, no point in France was farther than 15 kilometers from a rail line, and the railroads, supplemented by an ever-expanding road network, effectively tied all parts of France together into a single market.

This new rail-centered transportation system proved to be far more reliable, more capacious, and faster than the existing canal- and road-based system. It was also much cheaper. According to Alfred de Foville, the cost of moving one passenger one kilometer fell by 60 percent between 1840 and 1870, while the cost of moving a unit of merchandise one kilometer fell 75 percent. This alone insured that the volume of passenger and freight traffic would increase continually from the 1840s onward.[34] The completion of the rail system therefore had a profound impact on all facets of the French economy and the French business system. We will explore some of the effects on commercial enterprise in the next chapter and the effects on the development of industrial enterprise in Part II. For now, however, we must note that the building of the railroads served not only to tie the different regions of France together more tightly but also to integrate the whole of France more fully into the international economy.

The Saint-Simonians thought in global terms, and from the beginning they set out to build a European rail network, not just a French one. Indeed, all the leading French railroad promoters aspired to control the flow of people and goods across national borders as well as within them. The Pereires laid out the Southern Railroad with an eye to facilitating the rail traffic between France and the Iberian Peninsula. The Northern Railroad extended its lines into southern Belgium to control the traffic between France and northern Germany. The P-L-M invested in lines in Switzerland and northern Italy to give it control of as much of the transalpine commerce of Europe as possible. Such coordination between the building of French railroads and those of its neighbors helped to bring about a threefold increase in France's overland foreign trade between 1850 and 1870. Yet, in the final analysis, the growth of France's foreign trade depended even more on the progress in oceanic communication and transportation made possible by the development of oceanic steamer service, the modernization of France's ports, and the building of the Suez Canal.[35] These were indispensable ingredients in France's transportation revolution and are thus the appropriate subject for the concluding section of this chapter.

Connecting France to the Wider World

In the early decades of the nineteenth century, steamships were so expensive to operate and had such limited carrying capacity, compared to the best sailing vessels, that they were employed on the open seas only for those cargoes for which high speed and adherence to a regular schedule were paramount—mainly passengers and mail. But as the technology of shipbuilding improved, as iron construction greatly increased the size of steamships, and as the operating costs fell, steamships gradually drove sailcraft from the world's principal shipping lanes. From 1850 onward, the iron-hulled, screw-propelled steamship became as much a symbol of the transportation revolution as the steam locomotive, and the extent to which a nation participated in that revolution came increasingly to depend on its ability and willingness to support a steamer fleet and to accommodate its ports to the steamships of other nations.

As we saw in Chapter 1, the French had taken some early, tentative steps toward developing oceanic steam navigation in the 1830s and 1840s, mainly on the short, heavily traveled routes between the Continent and the British Isles and in the Mediterranean. Most of the early French steamship companies were organized in the traditional way, as partnerships or family firms. Although increases in the size and sophistication of steamships were rapidly raising capital requirements beyond the means of these companies, a certain number of family firms survived and even prospered. These included Maurel et Prom of Bordeaux, which employed steamers in its trade with West Africa; Delmas-Vieljeux of La Rochelle, which carried coal and iron ore between Bilbao, Cardiff, and France's channel ports; and Nicolas Paquet et Cie of Marseille, which established regular steamer service between Morocco and France in the 1860s. The largest of these family-run steamship lines, though, was Fraissinet et Cie, founded by Marc-Constantin Fraissinet in 1843. Starting with the coasting trade that tied together France's Mediterranean ports, Fraissinet added service between Marseille and the Mediterranean ports of Spain and Italy in the 1840s and 1850s. In the late 1860s Fraissinet expanded into the eastern Mediterranean and profited greatly from carrying construction materials for the Suez Canal project to Egypt in 1867–1869. In 1870, its steamer *Asie* was the first ship to traverse the whole canal north to south (part of an effort to expand service to India that eventually failed). Thereafter Fraissinet concentrated on Mediterranean shipping.[36]

As late as 1881, the Marseille merchant Cyprien Fabre launched a new steam navigation company that by 1900 had surpassed Fraissinet's to become France's largest family-owned steamship enterprise. But overall, French family firms did poorly in oceanic transport in the steam era, compared to the British and later the Germans, especially after the abolition of the *surtaxe de pavillon* in 1866 put foreign shipping on an equal footing with the French in French ports.[37] That the French enjoyed even limited success in steam navigation in the second half of the nineteenth century was due to the efforts of the Paris financiers and the Saint-Simonian entrepreneurs who saw steam navigation as the necessary extension of the railroads and who had the resources and expertise to found joint-stock companies that could raise the huge sums required for a competitive operation. They also had the connections to mobilize government support for steam navigation, first in the form of postal contracts and later in the form of direct subsidies. Two companies in particular epitomized the role of the Paris financial elite and the contribution of public-private cooperation in the development of France's oceangoing steamer service: the Messageries Maritimes and the Compagnie Générale Transatlantique.

In 1851 the French government, looking to divest itself of the money-losing steamer service it had operated in the Mediterranean since the 1830s, signed a contract with the Messageries Nationales, the country's oldest and largest coach company, to carry French mail from Marseille to various ports in the Mediterranean in return for an annual payment of 3 million francs. On the basis of this subsidy, the Messageries Nationales launched the Service Maritime des Messageries Nationales, which was renamed the Messageries Impériales in 1853 and the Messageries Maritimes in 1870. The new company took over fourteen steamships previously operated by the government plus three more from the Marseille *armateur* Albert Rostand, who became the company's Marseille director. The headquarters of the company, however, remained in Paris. The chairman of the Messageries Nationales, Edouard Besson, also served as the first chairman of the Messageries Maritimes. He was joined on the board by various Paris financiers, including Armand Béhic, who succeeded Besson as chairman in 1861 and held that position (except when he was the minister of commerce and public works in 1863–1867) until his death in 1891. Second only to Béhic in the company's top management was Henry Dupuy de Lôme, France's leading naval engineer, who founded and ran the company's shipyards at La Ciotat and designed many of its ships.[38]

Messageries Maritimes began by offering scheduled steamer service from Marseille to Alexandria, Constantinople, and Syria, and by 1860 it regularly sent steamers to some forty ports in the Mediterranean. It also expanded into the South Atlantic, the Indian Ocean, and the Pacific by contracting to provide postal service from Marseille to Brazil, Argentina, and Indochina. By 1869 the Messageries Maritimes had sixty-five ships in service, representing an investment of over 100 million francs, which made it not only France's largest steamer company but also one of the world's largest.[39] It was also France's most heavily subsidized company, receiving some 12 million francs a year from the government by 1886 to support its services.

In contrast to the Messageries Maritimes, which started out as (and largely remained) a veritable agency of the French government, the Compagnie Générale Transatlantique (CGT, or "Transat") had more speculative origins. In 1855, the Pereire brothers, convinced of the bright future of the shipping industry, joined with representatives of leading Paris merchant banks (Mallet, Eichthal, Perier, Delessert) to found the Compagnie Générale Maritime, which acquired the assets of a Norman shipping company and set out to pursue an array of ventures including steamer service from Le Havre to the New World. However, in its early years, most of its profits came from a less savory enterprise, a kind of neo-slave trade that involved transporting 18,000 Indian and Chinese coolies to Martinique and Guadeloupe to work the sugar plantations. Despite those profits, heavy losses in commodities speculation reduced the company's initial capital by one-third, and large loans were needed to stave off bankruptcy in 1859.[40]

The salvation of the company came in October 1860 when it took over the lucrative government contract for postal service between Le Havre and New York, Mexico, and the Antilles that had originally been granted to a Rothschild company, the Union Maritime. The contract required that the company be reorganized and recapitalized. In the process Isaac Pereire replaced Adolphe d'Eichthal as chairman, and the company got a new name, the Compagnie Générale Transatlantique. With new steamships built in Scotland and at the company's shipyard at Penhoët near Saint-Nazaire, the CGT inaugurated its service to Vera Cruz in 1862 in time to profit from the French military intervention in Mexico. In 1864 the steamer *Washington* began the company's Le Havre–New York service, and in 1867 the CGT expanded into the Pacific with service from Panama to Valparaiso.

The rapid growth of the CGT in the 1860s was cut short in 1868 by a cluster of setbacks, including the overthrow of the French-backed regime in Mexico and the fall of the Crédit Mobilier, its chief source of financial backing. The Pereires were forced off the board of the CGT, and over the next seven years the company staggered from one setback to another. By 1875, with new German companies moving aggressively into the carrying trade in the Atlantic, it seemed only a matter of time until the CGT failed. In that year, however, an aging Isaac Pereire, along with his son Eugène and nephew Emile II, regained control of the company by buying up two-thirds of the outstanding shares. The Pereires then proceeded to engineer a stunning turnaround. Over the next five years, they cut costs, poured 25 million francs into renovating and expanding the CGT's steamer fleet, and expanded service in the Atlantic. Passenger volume doubled, and profits rose 77 percent by 1880. The CGT also moved into the Mediterranean by taking over the contract for postal service to Algiers and by adding service to Tunis just in time to profit from the French military intervention there in 1882. By then thirty-nine of the company's sixty-five steamers were based in Marseille, and Marseille personnel and capital poured into the company. Among the new investors was Jules Charles-Roux, the future president of the Suez Canal Company, who eventually succeeded Eugène Pereire as chairman of the CGT. With strong positions in both the Atlantic and the Mediterranean, the CGT was solidly established as France's second largest steam navigation company by the 1880s.

In addition to the Messageries Maritimes and the CGT, three other joint-stock steamship companies established themselves between 1850 and 1880. The Compagnie de Navigation Mixte was founded in 1850 by three Lyon bankers to operate *navires mixtes* (ships that combined sail and steam power) in the Mediterranean and South Atlantic. After running up huge costs trying to extend its operations into the eastern Pacific with *clippers mixtes,* the company was reorganized as a *société anonyme,* ceded its South American routes to the Messageries Maritimes, and thereafter concentrated on offering regular steamer service from Marseille to various Mediterranean ports.[41] The Société Générale de Transports Maritimes à Vapeur (SGTMV) was founded in 1865 with backing from the Société Générale to carry iron ore from the Mokta-el-Hadid mine in Algeria to the smelters of southern France via Marseille. From the beginning, the company was dominated by the ubiquitous Paulin Talabot, and its nine ships were known as "talabots." In the late 1860s the SGTMV moved beyond ore transport by acquiring four new steamers to carry emigrants from Genoa and Naples to South America. By the end of the 1870s, it operated fourteen ships with a combined tonnage of 16,500 tons, making it the third largest French steamer company based in the Mediterranean.[42] Meanwhile, Paris bankers and exporters, led by Jean Vignal and Henri Fould, founded the Chargeurs Réunis in 1872 to provide the first regular service between Le Havre and the ports of Brazil and Argentina (the first such direct service between a northern European port and South America). Taking advantage of the 1881 law that offered substantial subsidies to French ship builders and operators, the Chargeurs Réunis expanded its fleet to twenty-six steamers and inaugurated service to sub-Saharan Africa and East Asia in the 1880s. By the end of the century it had firmly established itself as France's third largest steam navigation company, after the Messageries Maritimes and the CGT.[43]

As a group, France's steam navigation companies held their own in the highly competitive marine transport business in the second half of the nineteenth century by adopting an approach similar to that of many French manufacturers: emphasizing quality over quantity and focusing on niche markets. The French companies ceded much of the bulk carrying trade, both in passengers and freight, to others and especially to Britain's huge fleet of non-scheduled tramp steamers. But they did relatively well in the area of high-end scheduled passenger service with their well-designed liners, particularly on the routes between continental Europe and South America, Africa, and East Asia. And they also held their own in the transport of non-human cargoes between France and the expanding French Empire, for which they received postal sub-ventions and other subsidies, and between France and the ports of certain overseas trading partners (Italy, the Ottoman Empire, Brazil, Argentina). As a result, even though France fell further and further behind the British and was even surpassed by the Germans in total steam tonnage in the closing decades of the nineteenth century, France's three largest steam navigation companies—Messageries Maritimes, the CGT, and Chargeurs Réunis—ranked among the largest in the world at the outset of the twentieth century.[44]

The development of steam navigation and the expansion of France's maritime trade necessitated the expansion and modernization of its ports, or at least those ports that received the oceangoing steamers. As home port for the South American service of the Messageries Maritimes and as a port of call for the CGT, Bordeaux made limited improvements in its channel and wharves in the 1860s and 1870s.[45] Le Havre made more extensive renovations in the 1840s and 1850s that quintupled the area of its port and, indeed, briefly made it the largest port on the Atlantic coast of continental Europe. However, the Havrais did not continue this expansion when oceanic steam navigation took off in the 1860s, and by the 1870s the CGT actually had to limit the size of its new ocean liners to continue to use Le Havre as its home port. By the early 1900s it was widely agreed that Le Havre was fifty years behind the times.[46] So the principal example of successful port modernization in France was found in Marseille.

The growing traffic in the Old Port, Marseille's ancient natural harbor, and especially the influx of steamships after 1830 led in 1844 to the formulation of a plan to build an artificial harbor, the Bassin de Joliette, on the coast north of the city. Using new techniques for constructing artificial breakwaters that had been first developed for the port of Algiers, state engineers completed the Joliette Basin in 1853. By then, however, the founding of the Messageries Maritimes, the burgeoning of steamer traffic, and the arrival of the railroad had prompted outside interests led by Paulin Talabot to formulate more ambitious plans for the expansion of Marseille. In its mature form, the Talabot plan called for a new port north of the Joliette Basin that was modeled on the London docks and equipped with hydraulic cranes to move cargoes from steamships to fireproof warehouses or directly into the freight cars of the P-L-M. When Talabot's plan was finally approved over strong local resistance in 1859, a new company, the Docks et Entrepôts de Marseille, was formed to undertake the construction and to manage the new port. Completion of two new basins and the associated Docks Talabot in 1863, followed by the completion of the Bassin Impérial in 1870, added 102 hectares of harbor area and 3,940 meters of new quais to the port of Marseille and provided the most rationalized and mechanized handling and storage facilities in any continental European port. Additional basins with even more sophisticated handling facilities were completed under the direction of the Marseille Chamber of Commerce in the 1880s. These and other improvements allowed Marseille to avoid the bottlenecks experienced in Le Havre and preserved its status as one of the leading ports of continental Europe into the twentieth century.[47]

The modernization of the port of Marseille was closely linked to another key event in France's mid-nineteenth-century transportation revolution, the building of the Suez Canal. Connecting the world's oceans with interoceanic canals had long been a dream of the Saint-Simonians. In the 1830s, Prosper Enfantin and a group of his followers went to Egypt to study the feasibility of a canal across the Isthmus of Suez connecting the Mediterranean and Red Seas, and Paulin Talabot drew up plans for such a canal in the 1840s. But it was a retired diplomat, Ferdinand de Lesseps, who in 1854 won the right to build the canal, thanks to his long friendship with the incoming viceroy, Muhammed Saïd Pacha. In 1859 de Lesseps founded the Compagnie Universelle du Canal Maritime de Suez and, eschewing the normal underwriting services of the Paris bankers, proceeded to raise the 200 million francs needed for construction from his Egyptian patrons and by selling stock in the company directly to the public. With timely help from Napoleon III (whose consort, the Empress Eugénie, was de Lesseps' cousin), the Suez Company overcame enormous technical and logistical challenges and completed the canal in 1869. Its opening in 1870 immediately cut 4,000 kilometers off the voyage from Marseille to Saigon (reducing the travel time by 40 percent), and it offered even greater potential savings to the large number of British steamers operating between the British Isles and India and Australia. The canal thereby provided a new impetus to the growth of trade between Europe and Asia and played a key role in the development of the British and French Empires in the late nineteenth century. After its shaky start, the Compagnie Universelle became France's largest publicly held company and one of the most profitable private enterprises in the world. Transformed into a financial holding company after the nationalization of the Suez Canal in 1956, it remains a power in international business to this day.[48]

The revolutions in banking and transportation that unfolded in France between 1850 and 1880 changed forever the underlying structure of the French economy—and to a large extent the structure of the European and world economies—and transformed the French business system in fundamental ways. Specifically, this dual revolution gave rise to a collection of large enterprises—the big joint-stock banks, the railroad and steam navigation companies, public-service companies like the Docks de Marseille—that continued to play central roles in the economic and political life of the country well into the twentieth century. It also provided the impetus for an array of changes in the structures and practices of French commerce and finance that became fully apparent only in the final decades of the century. We examine these changes in the next chapter.

CHAPTER THREE

The New World of Financial and Commercial Capitalism, 1870s–1900s

In spite of the economic slump that engulfed France and much of the developed world from the mid-1870s to the mid-1890s, the institutional and organizational modernization of French financial and commercial capitalism that began in the early nineteenth century and accelerated with the revolution in banking and transportation in the 1850s and 1860s continued and broadened in the last quarter of the nineteenth century. The maturity and sophistication attained by French banking and commerce by 1900 in turn set the stage for the surge of industrial growth and the emergence of big business in the early years of the twentieth century. This chapter explores the three developments in the waning years of the nineteenth century that contributed the most to forming this new world of financial and commercial capitalism:

- continued growth and specialization in the banking sector, resulting in an ever-wider array of services being offered to an ever-expanding clientele by an increasingly dense network of financial institutions

- the transformation of wholesale trade, marked by the rise of specialized commodity traders for staple goods and industrial raw materials, the rise of a new class of middlemen *(négociants-commissionnaires)* in the trade in certain manufactured goods, and, in the case of others, the elimination of middlemen entirely as manufacturers' representatives increasingly dealt directly with large-scale retailers

- the revolution in retailing, in which the highly fragmented world of shopkeepers and peddlers was challenged and to some degree replaced by a new class of mass marketers, first and foremost department stores and chain stores.

The Maturation of Banking and Finance

French banks experienced recurring crises in the last quarter of the nineteenth century, notably in 1882 and 1889, yet, according to Alain Plessis, their total resources tripled from 1873 to 1895 and grew even faster from 1895 to 1914.[1] Concurrently, the banking system as a whole acquired greater complexity and density as the Banque de France and the big Paris deposit banks expanded their branch networks, as the established local banks assumed greater importance as partners and rivals of the Paris banks, and as a new generation of *banques d'affaires* carved out a place in investment banking alongside Paribas. In an era of capital export and resurgent imperialism, French banks also refined and extended their international operations, enabling French capitalists to continue to play a prominent role in mobilizing (or exploiting) the resources of the developing world. How these trends unfolded can best be seen by looking at the histories of the three main types of banks that emerged out of a century-long process of specialization: the Paris-based joint-stock deposit and investment banks; the private merchant banks that comprised the *haute banque parisienne;* and the local and regional banks.

The Joint-Stock Banks

However one gauges the size of banks—assets, deposits, total lending volume, profits, or whatever—the four largest French joint-stock banks (the Crédit Lyonnais, the Société Générale, the Comptoir d'Escompte, and the Crédit Industriel et Commercial) occupied an increasingly important place in French banking in the closing decades of the nineteenth century.[2] Of these four banks, the Crédit Lyonnais was already the largest in 1880 and had increased its lead over the other three by 1900.[3] Indeed, according to figures assembled by Youssef Cassis, it was the largest bank in Europe in 1910.[4] As such it tended to set the pattern and priorities for the entire deposit banking sector.

Over the course of the 1870s, the Crédit Lyonnais moved away from direct investment in domestic industry (its original raison d'être) and increasingly channeled the funds collected through its growing system of branch banks into loans to governments, especially those of developing countries. In 1878, the Crédit Lyonnais established an office in Saint Petersburg to participate in the underwriting of the first Russian bonds marketed directly to Western investors. By the 1890s it was the principal distributor of Russian bonds in France, and by the turn of the century the marketing of Russian bonds accounted for 30 percent of the profits earned by the bank on the sale of stocks and bonds.[5] Of comparable importance was the business conducted by the Crédit Lyonnais in Egypt through branch offices in Alexandria, Cairo, and Port-Saïd, each of which did more business than any other office of the bank except Paris. By 1900 the Alexandria branch alone was yielding profits of 33 million francs per year—three-fifths of the total profits of the Crédit Lyonnais' overseas offices.[6]

To sustain its foreign operations, the Crédit Lyonnais modified and expanded its domestic banking business in the 1880s and 1890s. In 1882, the risk inherent in using current account deposits and other short-term assets to make long-term loans to governments was revealed when the collapse of the Union Générale, a high-flying new investment bank headquartered in Lyon, precipitated a run on banks throughout the Southeast that briefly threatened the solvency of the Crédit Lyonnais. Vowing never to be put in such a vulnerable position again, Henri Germain, the founder and chairman of the bank, ordered an immediate restructuring of the bank's business that emphasized the discounting of commercial paper in order to insure liquidity. As a result, the share of the bank's total assets devoted to commercial banking rose from 31 percent to 43 percent by the early 1890s.[7] At the same time, the Crédit Lyonnais accelerated the opening of new branches (bringing the total to 257 by 1904) not only to collect more deposits to fund its discount business but also to provide an outlet for its growing portfolio of foreign securities. Indeed, the *service des titres* organized across the branch network after 1888 became the indispensable complement to its foreign lending business and an increasingly important "profit center" for the bank by the early 1900s.[8]

Though quite successful, the strategy of the Crédit Lyonnais—eschewing direct investment in domestic industry and emphasizing foreign lending coupled with the marketing of foreign stocks and bonds to the bank's middle-class clientele through an expanded network of branch banks—was not immediately emulated by the other joint-stock deposit banks. The Crédit Industriel et Commercial saw its subsidiaries break away and become independent banks in the 1870s, and it did not seek to replace them until after 1900. In the meanwhile, it de-emphasized discounting and, playing the role of an investment bank, increased its direct participation in other banks and in industrial firms. This shift was even more pronounced in the case of the Comptoir d'Escompte, which became the principal backer of the Société des Métaux, founded in 1881 to make copper wire and other capital goods for the nascent electrical industry. In 1887 the head of the Comptoir, Edouard Hentsch, followed the president of the Société des Métaux, Eugène Secretan, into an elaborate scheme to corner the world copper market. When copper prices collapsed in 1889, both men were arrested and both companies were forced into receivership. The Comptoir was then relaunched as the Comptoir Nationale d'Escompte de Paris (CNEP) under new, conservative managers who soon adopted the policies of the Crédit Lyonnais, reverting to the discount business and building a system of domestic branches that numbered 110 by 1900. By 1913, the CNEP had solidified its position as the third largest French deposit bank by developing a particular strength in the Paris metropolitan area, where it had fifty-two offices.[9]

While avoiding the excesses of the Comptoir d'Escompte, France's second largest deposit bank, the Société Générale, also continued to put money into domestic industry in the 1870s and 1880s, notably coal, steel, cement, sugar refining, and the enterprises of Paulin Talabot, who remained very influential in the bank until his death in 1885. At the same time, the Société Générale invested even more heavily in foreign enterprises. In Spain, it backed lead, zinc, and manganese mines. In Egypt, it took a major stake in the Crédit Foncier Egyptien, the country's principal mortgage bank, and it bankrolled the Egyptian operations of the Say Sugar Company. In South America, the Société Générale financed Brazilian railroads and joined with Dreyfus Frères to take control of the Peruvian guano industry. Most importantly, it moved into Russia in the 1870s and 1880s, before investing in Russia was fashionable, helping to found the Rutchenko Coal Company, the Krivoi-Rog Iron Company (another Talabot project), and the Makeevka Steel Company. It was only after 1893, when Louis Dorizon became director-general, that the focus of the Société Générale's foreign operations shifted from direct investment to underwriting the issue of stocks and bonds, which the bank then sold to middle-class customers through a branch network, as did the Crédit Lyonnais.[10]

To the extent that much of their business centered on international finance, the largest French deposit banks were indistinguishable from the country's leading investment bank, the Banque de Paris et des Pays-Bas. Since its founding in 1872, Paribas had remained a uniquely multinational affair whose cosmopolitan board of directors operated out of offices in Brussels, Amsterdam, and Geneva as well as in Paris, and maintained close ties to various foreign investment banks, including Kuhn Loeb in New York. From 1880 to 1914, the bank continued to rely mainly on shareholder equity to pursue two areas of business, direct investment in industrial enterprises and the underwriting of public and private securities. Paribas made direct investments in a new French steel company, Nord-Est, and in the Parisian electrical power industry, but most of its investments were outside France: in Russian steel, Belgian coal, and Rumanian oil; in railroads in Spain, Argentina, and Russia; and in the Norwegian power company, Norsk Hydro. Paribas participated in the syndicate that underwrote the Russian bond issue of 1888, but it also underwrote bond issues for Spain, Norway, Bulgaria, the Ottoman Empire, the Sultan of Morocco, Argentina, Uruguay, Venezuela, Mexico, China, and Japan. To market these securities, Paribas worked through the branch networks of the French deposit banks, especially the Société Générale, which became a close ally after Paribas helped the deposit bank raise much-needed capital in 1905.[11]

These five big Paris joint-stock banks also participated in the renascence of France's formal and informal colonial empire by investing in and virtually controlling various colonial banks, including the Banque Impériale Ottomane, the Banque de Sénégal, the Banque de Maroc, and especially the Banque de l'Indochine. As mentioned earlier, the Banque de l'Indochine (BI) was founded in 1875 as a joint venture of the Crédit Industriel et Commercial and the Comptoir d'Escompte to serve as a bank of emission for the emerging colony of French Indochina. It also provided commercial banking services to the oil seed exporters of Pondicherry and the rice merchants of Saigon. In the course of the 1880s and 1890s, the Société Générale, the Crédit Lyonnais, and Paribas gained financial stakes in the bank and places on its board, which, for all intents and purposes, made it the official representative of the "Big Five"—and indeed of the whole French banking establishment—in East Asia. The founding of branches in Hong Kong, Shanghai, Canton, and Hankow in the 1890s allowed the BI and its associated banks to gain a foothold in China, especially in the silk trade, while new branches in Bangkok, Singapore, and Djibouti enabled them to expand their activities in Southeast Asia and the Indian Ocean in the 1900s.[12]

Thus, from 1875 to 1914, the big French deposit banks greatly expanded the volume of their domestic business by using their branch networks to capture the lion's share of discounting and other forms of short-term commercial credit and to develop a large customer base among the French middle classes. At the same time, along with Paribas and other *banques d'affaires,* they played an important and sometimes dominant role in many theaters of international finance and staked out a strong position in the financing of the new colonial empire through quasi-subsidiaries like the Banque de l'Indochine. Yet the big joint-stock deposit and investment banks were neither omnipresent nor omnicompetent. They left openings in both the domestic and foreign money markets that were ultimately filled by other French banks.

The Private Merchant Banks

One of the biggest stories in French banking and finance from the 1870s to 1914 was the survival and resurgence of the "old" private merchant banks of Paris—the *haute banque parisienne*—that had played a dominant role in French (and world) finance in the first half of the nineteenth century and then had seemingly been muscled aside by the new joint-stock banks in the 1850s and 1860s. In truth, the leaders of the *haute banque* had not been averse to the creation of these new banks. The Foulds, Hottinguers, Mallets, and Seillières had all been associated in some way with the Crédit Mobilier. James de Rothschild and his allies had proposed the creation of a joint-stock bank in the mid-1850s to rival the Crédit Mobilier, and only when those proposals were rejected did Rothschild turn against the idea of corporate banking. But many of his allies persisted, and several of them participated in the founding of the Société Générale in 1864. Later, the Hottinguers played a prominent role in the reorganization of the Comptoir d'Escompte in 1889, and a Delessert sat on the board of the Banque de l'Indochine. Still, on the whole, the old-line merchant bankers of Paris did not play a particularly prominent role either as shareholders or as directors in the joint-stock deposit banks, and this reduced their influence over domestic commercial banking in the final quarter of the century. They still possessed substantial resources, however, particularly the French Rothschilds, whose share of the capital of the Rothschild family partnership fluctuated between 450 million and 625 million francs between 1870 and 1900.[13] With such resources, it is not surprising that the *haute banque* maintained a high profile in French and world business after 1870, especially in three capacities: as owners and directors of the Banque de France, as directors of important industrial and infrastructure companies, and as major players in international government finance.

The Banque de France remained a unique institution and a force to be reckoned with in the last quarter of the nineteenth century—first and foremost as France's sole bank of issue (the only bank that could print money) and as the principal supplier of banking services to the French treasury, but also as a provider of commercial credit, the largest discount bank in France. Indeed, by expanding its branch network in France and by relaxing its previously stringent rules on the discounting of commercial paper in the 1890s, the Banque de France came to play a larger part in the life of the average French businessman than ever before. Jean Bouvier has pointed out that the resources of the Banque de France—mainly banknotes and current accounts—were not growing as fast as the resources of the three largest deposit banks at the end of the nineteenth century, but what is most striking about the figures he presents is that the Banque's resources remained twice as great as the combined resources of those deposit banks in 1900.[14] Of course, the Banque de France continued to be a private joint-stock company run by a self-perpetuating board of fifteen regents, who were drawn principally from the families that founded the Banque in 1800 (especially the Mallets, Hottinguers, and Davilliers) and from families that later ascended to the *haute banque* (including Alphonse de Rothschild, who sat on the board of regents for fifty years, 1855 to 1905).

If the Paris merchant bankers continued to participate in the domestic economy of France indirectly through the Banque de France, they participated more directly as owners and directors of a number of major corporations, notably the six trunk-line railroad companies. The Chemin de Fer du Nord had started out as the Rothschilds' railroad and it remained so into the twentieth century, with five or six members of the family sitting on the board of directors at any given time, and with Alphonse de Rothschild succeeding his father, James, as chairman in 1868 and being succeeded in turn by his son Edouard in 1905. Meanwhile Adolphe d'Eichthal continued to preside over the Southern Railroad until 1892, and Charles Mallet served as chairman of the Paris-Lyon-Méditerranée (P-L-M) from 1878 to 1891. Other Mallets continued to serve on the boards of the Southern, Western, and Paris-Orléans, while Hottinguers occupied seats on the boards of the Northern, Eastern, and Western. Another continuing interest of the *haute banque* families was insurance. Mallets, Hottinguers, and Andrés had participated in the founding of the major insurance companies in the 1820s and 1830s, and they remained prominent in the management of those companies at the end of the century. Some of the Paris merchant banks also continued to have interests in domestic industry (such as the Mallets and Rothschilds in the electrical industry, Alfred André in the Evian mineral water company, and the Hottinguers in the Compagnie Générale des Eaux).

More than ever after 1870, however, the chief métier of the *haute banque* was international finance, especially the underwriting of the bond issues of foreign governments and the organization of companies to exploit the natural resources of foreign countries. Here again the Rothschilds remained preeminent. Alphonse de Rothschild began his tenure as head of the Paris branch of the Rothschild bank by taking the lead in underwriting the indemnity loan floated by the French government after the Franco-Prussian War. Next he assumed his father's role as the czar's principal agent in the Paris money market. The French Rothschilds did distance themselves from the Russians when Alexander III unleashed a virulent anti-Semitic campaign in the 1880s, which allowed the Crédit Lyonnais and other French banks to take charge of the Russian loan of 1888. But, as the pogroms subsided and as official relations between Paris and Saint Petersburg warmed, the Rothschilds returned to underwrite two large issues of Russian bonds in 1889 and additional smaller issues in 1894, 1896, and 1901.[15]

In addition to underwriting government loans, the Rothschilds continued to administer the railroads in Spain, Italy, and Austria that James de Rothschild had "won" in his long-running battle with the Pereires. But the family also sought out new foreign direct investments, particularly in extractive industries. While the London Rothschilds staked out strong positions in gold and diamond mining in South Africa, the Paris Rothschilds invested heavily in the mining and refining of nonferrous metals, using their existing stake in Spanish mercury to capture a dominant position in lead and silver mining in Spain through the Peñarroya company in the 1880s. At the same time, they started mining nickel in New Caledonia, and, following the collapse of the French copper syndicate in 1889, they joined the Mirabaud bank in taking over the Boléo copper mine in Baja California (the London Rothschilds invested at the same time in the leading Spanish copper mine, Rio Tinto). Another "mining" interest of the French Rothschilds was petroleum. In 1886, they moved into oil production and refining in the Russian Caucasus by buying the Batum Oil Company and building a refinery at Novorossiisk. Two other Rothschild companies marketed the refined oil within Russia and in the Mediterranean, while sales east of Suez were handled by Marcus Samuel's Shell Oil Company (see Chapter 14).[16]

No other Paris merchant bank assembled as large or as important a collection of foreign business interests as the Rothschilds did in the last quarter of the nineteenth century, but many were doing similar things, underwriting the bonds of foreign governments and participating in the founding and management of various commercial and industrial enterprises in the developing world. A case in point is the Hottinguer bank. Baron Rodolphe Hottinguer helped to found the Banque Impériale Ottomane in 1863 and long served on the bank's board of directors. In 1869, the Hottinguers began a long association with the Russian government by organizing a successful loan flotation in Paris. One of Rodolphe's sons oversaw the Hottinguers' participation in a series of Imperial loans from 1895 to 1907, while two other sons supervised the building of the Trans-Siberian and Trans-Manchurian railroads. After 1904, the Hottinguers also developed extensive interests in Latin America and the Balkans through their position as major shareholders and officers of the new Banque de l'Union Parisienne.[17]

All in all, even a cursory examination of the interests and activities of the Paris merchant banks reveals a surprising degree of similarity to the interests and activities of the large joint-stock banks. This fundamental unity of outlook and purpose meant that the Paris banks tended to share the same strengths and weaknesses. As a group, they did a good job of providing commercial banking services—especially the discounting of commercial paper—to a growing clientele both in the capital and nationwide (the Paris merchant bankers did this indirectly through the Banque de France). As a by-product of their zeal for financing foreign governments, they also provided banking services to French businessmen abroad, but only in certain regions. The French banks were strongest in Eastern Europe (especially Russia), the Mediterranean and North Africa, and East Asia. They were also strong in South America but were surprisingly weak in the largest, most expansive market in the world, the United States—perhaps because high American import duties were decreasing French exports to the United States and because stiff competition from American and British banks simply made the American market less lucrative than other markets. Then there was the matter of financing domestic industry. After taking the lead in developing French industry and infrastructure from the

1820s to the 1860s, the Paris banks seemed to lose interest in that area after 1870. This was actually truer for the Crédit Lyonnais than for the other big banks and mainly applies to the period 1870–1890, since the Paris banks took a growing interest in the new industries emerging after 1890. Ultimately, even this limited failure of the Paris banks to support domestic industry after 1870 was less serious than once thought because it was largely offset by the growing activities of a new generation of investment banks that included the Banque Parisienne (which became the Banque de l'Union Parisienne in 1904), the Banque Suisse et Française (which later became the Credit Commercial de France), and the Banque Internationale de Paris and the Banque Française de l'Afrique du Sud (which came together to form the Banque Française pour le Commerce et l'Industrie [BFCI] in 1901).[18] It was also offset by the activities of local and regional banks, which historians only recently have begun to appreciate fully.

The Local and Regional Banks

In the late eighteenth and early nineteenth centuries, small specialized merchant banks were established in all parts of France to serve the needs of local businessmen, especially in discounting commercial notes. Among the banks founded before 1850 that continued to operate in the second half of the nineteenth century were the Banque Durand in Montpellier, the Banque Courtois in Toulouse, the Banque Adam in Boulogne, the Banque Dupont in Lille, and the Banque Samazeuilh in Bordeaux. As we saw in Chapter 2, the expansion of the branch system of the Banque de France in the 1850s served to strengthen and increase the population of local banks in France by giving them a way to re-discount the bills they took from their local clients. Indeed, a symbiotic relationship developed between the Banque de France branches and the local banks inasmuch as the latter provided the third signature that allowed the Banque de France to discount otherwise ineligible paper (since the Banque still adhered to a three-signature standard). Thus the local banks provided the vital link between the world of small local lenders and bill brokers and the emerging national system of banking and credit.

As the Société Générale and the Crédit Lyonnais built their branch systems from the 1860s onward, they began to challenge the position of the local banks in the discount business, but not always successfully. In some areas, the local banks already had their own branch networks and were able to resist the interlopers from Paris. This was true in the department of the Nord, where three well-established commercial banks—the Crédit du Nord, Devilder, and Verley-Decroix—maintained their dominant position in spite of the creation of nineteen branch offices by the Crédit Lyonnais and the Société Générale (the three local banks had 22 offices among them).[19] In other cases, the local banks survived by working around and complementing the services offered by the Paris banks. For example, when the Société Générale set up an office in Bayonne in 1874 and started discounting the bills of the biggest merchants, the local banker Jules Gommès shifted to serving smaller clients, mainly in the food industry. And when the arrival of the Crédit Lyonnais in 1894 forced the Société Générale to move into this industry as well, Gommès turned to financing the cod fisheries, the Landes timber industry, and the importation of Spanish wine. This kind of flexibility, coupled with long-standing relationships with local families and an unmatched feel for local business opportunities, allowed the Banque Gommès—the "Rothschilds of Bayonne"—to survive and prosper well into the twentieth century.[20]

More serious for the survival of local banks than the expansion of the Paris deposit banks was the decision by the Banque de France in the 1890s to accept two-signature paper for discount, which for the first time put it in direct competition with both the local banks and the branches of the Paris deposit banks for the local discounting business. In these new circumstances, some local banks followed the Gommès strategy and looked for new commercial customers, some sold out to competitors, and some merged to form regional banks that had sufficient resources to meet the head-to-head competition of the Paris banks. But what was most significant for the overall evolution of the French banking system was the decision by some local banks to turn themselves into small investment banks that would provide the critical aid to industrial start-ups, usually in the form of direct loans and underwriting services, that the big banks were reluctant to offer. Indeed, with the deposit banks increasingly following the Paris merchant banks and investment banks into international finance after 1880, these local investment banks came to play a crucial role in launching the new enterprises of the Second Industrial Revolution.

In Lorraine, the Société Nancienne de Crédit Industriel emerged as the region's leading backer of the new steel companies, but a number of smaller industrial banks also played important roles. Among these was the Banque Thomas in Longwy, which financed the adoption of the new Thomas-Gilchrist basic steel process by local ironmasters in the 1880s and 1890s. By 1900, the Banque Thomas had become, in J-M Moine's words, "une véritable petite banque industrielle" that underwrote the stock issues that enabled the local steel companies to expand rapidly and attain world-class status in the years leading up to World War I.[21] Meanwhile, the Charpenay bank was playing a similar role in southeastern France. Starting out as a commercial banker in Grenoble, Georges Charpenay underwrote a crucial stock offering in the 1880s to relaunch Allevard, one of the oldest ironworks in France, and eventually invested in some fifty industrial enterprises in the region, especially those connected with hydroelectric power.[22] In Marseille, the leading local joint-stock bank, the Société Marseillaise de Crédit (SMC), reflecting the interests of the Marseille merchant elite, participated in developing the trade and finance of Egypt and France's new colonies in North Africa. It also supported various local enterprises, including a land development company (the Société Immobilière Marseillaise), a steam navigation company (Cyprien Fabre), a sugar refiner (Raffineries de Saint-Louis), and a soap manufacturer (Huileries et Savonneries Méridionales). Later it helped launch many of the companies that would rejuvenate the regional economy in the twentieth century, including the Grands Travaux de Marseille in public works and the Energie Electrique du Littoral Méditerranéen in power and light.[23]

Thanks to the various activities of the big joint-stock deposit and investment banks, the private merchant banks of Paris, and the local and regional banks, the French business community had access to a wider array of financial services than ever before by 1900. Capital was moving more smoothly and was being mobilized and utilized more efficiently than ever before. What the French banks had not achieved, however, was the full democratization of credit and the mobilization of the resources of the small saver. To the extent that these goals were being met, it was the work of the *caisses d'epargnes* (savings banks) being created by municipal governments and non-profit organizations. By 1913, the funds accumulated by French savings banks were substantial, amounting to 6.2 billion francs (equal to about two-thirds of the deposits and current accounts in the private joint-stock banks). Most of these funds were deposited with a government agency, the Caisse des Dépôts et Consignations, which in turn invested them in government bonds.[24] Business historians can view this outcome negatively, as a failure by the banks to mobilize a major pool of capital for the private sector, or positively, as freeing the banking system of the responsibility of financing the French government and thereby relieving the banks of the heavy hand of government tutelage that had marked the first two-thirds of the nineteenth century. Either way, the rise of this large state-run system of savings banks truncated or segmented the French money market in a way that probably reduced its efficiency in the early twentieth century.

Transforming and Transcending the Wholesale Trade

The emergence of banking and transportation as distinct industries in the mid-nineteenth century tended to reduce wholesale trade—the traditional core of merchant capitalism—to the pure buying and selling of goods, separate from the movement and storage of goods and from the financing of trade. Even so, because of the enormous increase in the volume of trade in the first two-thirds of the nineteenth century, the wholesale sector expanded, and with expansion came greater division of labor and specialization. Then, after 1850, the unification of markets and the speeding up of market transactions made possible by the advent of railroads, steamships, and the electric telegraph brought a measure of consolidation, integration, and simplification to commercial operations that tended to marginalize the traditional wholesale merchant. More and more the buying and selling of industrial raw materials, semi-finished producer goods, and finished consumer goods fell under the purview of various brokers and commission agents who facilitated the movement of goods and the functioning of markets without exercising the control or reaping the large profits previously associated with *grand négoce*. But there were exceptions to this overarching trend. The world of wholesale trade remained sufficiently varied to defy easy generalization. Drawing an accurate picture of what happened to the wholesale merchant in late nineteenth-century France requires taking a closer look at specific sectors. Leaving aside the huge and still little-studied trade in agricultural produce, we will limit ourselves here to the port-centered trade in imported industrial raw materials (the commodities trade) and the Paris-centered trade in domestic manufactures.

The Commodities Trade

At the end of the eighteenth century, the most prominent and lucrative form of merchant capitalism had centered on the importation of commodities grown on tropical plantations—especially cane sugar from the Antilles—and the subsidiary trade in African slaves. As we saw in

Chapter 1, this trade was first disrupted by the French Revolution and then permanently undermined by the ending of the slave trade in 1818 and the replacement of imported cane sugar with home-grown beet sugar in the 1840s. By then, however, the demands of an industrializing economy for certain raw materials were drawing the port merchants of France into the importation of new commodities. In terms of the value of goods imported, the biggest trades were in cotton, wool, silk, and coal. We will look at how each of these was organized and how each evolved, emphasizing the changing role of the importing merchants and in some cases their decline and disappearance.[25]

As we will see in the next chapter, the manufacture of cotton cloth emerged as a major industry in France during the nineteenth century. Virtually all of the raw cotton used in the production of cotton cloth was imported from overseas, primarily from the United States and secondarily from India and Egypt. At the outset of the nineteenth century, cotton entered France not only through various French seaports but also overland from European ports such as Genoa, Trieste, and Antwerp. In 1816, however, the French parliament prohibited the overland importation of cotton, which gave the French seaports control of the trade. Marseille established and maintained a trade in Egyptian jumel, employed mainly by the cotton manufacturers of eastern France, but the great majority of imported cotton came from America and entered through Le Havre, which was well situated to supply the cotton industries of Normandy and northern France. By 1845, Le Havre handled 72 percent of French cotton imports, and by 1861, 89 percent. Le Havre's ability to access new supplies of cotton from India during the American Civil War, when the importation of American cotton fell 93 percent, preserved its dominant position in the trade through the 1860s and after. In 1875 Le Havre received over 676,000 bales of cotton (surpassing the previous high of 1861), and by the early 1900s it was receiving over 800,000 bales annually, which allowed it not only to maintain its position as the nearly exclusive supplier of the French cotton industry but also to compete with Antwerp and Rotterdam in supplying other European countries.[26]

In the first half of the nineteenth century, prior to the laying of the transatlantic cables, information about the American cotton harvest arrived at the same time as the commodity itself, so it was perhaps inevitable that the buying and selling of cotton in Europe (at least new cotton) came to be centered at the ports of entry. Initially, the cotton trade at Le Havre was seasonal. For a few months every fall, following the American harvest, representatives of the cotton manufacturers flocked to Le Havre from all over France to deal directly with the *négociants-armateurs* arriving with the raw cotton. Because the manufacturers generally had to buy and pay for their entire yearly supply of cotton at this time, Le Havre quickly attracted moneymen from Paris, the Hottinguers and Mallets among them, who offered the necessary financing. By the 1840s, however, the trade had given rise to a new class of specialized merchants, drawn from the ranks of local merchants and manufacturers' representatives, who traded year round from permanent stocks of cotton, reducing somewhat the power and profits of the financiers. By the 1870s, four distinct types of traders could be found operating in and around the Le Havre cotton exchange: representatives of the American exporters based in New Orleans and Memphis; import merchants, who bought from those representatives and sold to French cotton spinners (often through traveling salesmen armed with cotton samples); local commission merchants, who also served as middlemen between importers and manufacturers; and local brokers who acted as intermediaries between merchants.[27]

Just as Le Havre was solidifying its position as the center of the raw cotton trade in France, the laying of the transatlantic cables in the 1860s and 1870s threatened to subordinate Le Havre and other national markets to an international market centered in New York and a few other cities in the United States, plus Liverpool/Manchester in England. In theory, the advent of international telegraphic communications, coupled with the rise of public warehouses, the commerce in warehouse receipts, and an internationally accepted system of grading, should have eliminated the need for commodity traders to meet face-to-face or to operate where a commodity was physically located. In other words, the new conditions should have fostered decentralization in the trading of cotton and other commodities. What encouraged continued centralization was the rise of futures markets, which enabled consumers of commodities to reduce risk by locking in the cost of future purchases and enabled commodities traders to reduce their risk by hedging (balancing purchases in the spot market with simultaneous sales in the futures market or vice versa). The first full-fledged futures market was established at the New York Cotton Exchange in 1870. As more and more of the trading activity in American cotton became centered in this exchange, all the leading cotton merchants had to set up offices nearby or send representatives to New York. Thereafter, only those trading centers with a futures market maintained a position in the forefront of the world cotton trade, and it was to the credit of the Le Havre merchants that their city was one of those (there were only six cotton futures markets in the world by the twentieth century).

The Le Havre cotton futures market opened at the new Bourse de Commerce building in 1880 and soon gave rise to yet another group of market specialists, futures brokers. These brokers collected bids and offers at the offices of the other cotton merchants each morning, assembled at the Bourse at 10 A.M. to set opening prices on futures contracts based on the opening spot price in Liverpool, and returned in the afternoon to trade on the basis of the opening prices in New York. The smooth functioning—indeed the survival—of this futures market depended in turn on the creation in 1882 of a clearinghouse (the Caisse de Liquidation des Affaires à Terme), which took in deposits from member brokers to guarantee payment on all futures contracts. Once established for cotton, the facilities of the futures market and clearinghouse were extended to the trade in coffee and other tropical commodities, thus reinforcing Le Havre's position as one of the three or four leading commodities markets in continental Europe.[28]

The growing transparency, efficiency, and interconnectedness of the world cotton market benefited those at either end of the commodity pipeline—the cotton growers and manufacturers—who now enjoyed the same access to information about market conditions and prices as the middlemen. Competition among these middlemen continually reduced margins and commissions to the point that only massive transactions, which were beyond the resources of most merchants, could yield large profits. Of course, the cotton market, like all commodities markets, continued to attract speculators hoping to parlay inside information or special circumstances (bad weather, the outbreak of war) into quick profits, but the sheer size of the cotton trade and the multiple sources of cotton production made it virtually immune to corners and other speculative maneuvers. Eventually only the most efficient brokers and traders, operating on a global scale through trading companies, managed to make big money in commodities (the American firm of Anderson-Clayton accomplished this in the mid-twentieth century). In the short run, cotton trading in France and elsewhere became routinized in the hands of various specialized dealers content with modest but regular, low-risk returns. Merchant families that had made fortunes in the early phases of the cotton trade rarely stayed in it in this new era simply because other sectors of the economy offered better prospects for success.[29]

The organizational evolution seen in the French cotton trade was replicated to some degree in the wool trade. In the early nineteenth century, French woolens manufacturers still got most of their raw materials from domestic sheep. France's limited imports of wool came mainly from London, the world's largest wool market, and were delivered to all of France's major ports, where local merchants dealt with the representatives of the various inland wool manufacturers in the traditional manner. This began to change after 1850 in response to two separate but mutually reinforcing developments: the rise of sheep herding in Argentina, Uruguay, Australia, and South Africa, which brought about a doubling of world wool output between 1860 and 1913; and the emergence of a dynamic new woolens industry at Roubaix and Tourcoing in northern France, which was based on mechanical woolcombing and the mechanized production of high-quality worsted cloth (see Chapter 4). The raw material for worsted was merino wool, the domestic supplies of which were relatively inelastic and largely controlled by the older manufacturing center of Reims. The rising worsted manufacturers of Roubaix-Tourcoing therefore had to import, but to minimize their costs they sought to circumvent the high prices and high commissions charged by the established middlemen in London, Antwerp, and Le Havre. They did this by sending agents directly to the emerging export markets for merino wool in Buenos Aires, Montevideo, Melbourne, and Sydney. These agents purchased a year's supply of wool between October and December, following the spring sheepshearing in the Southern Hemisphere. They then arranged to ship it to Roubaix and Tourcoing initially through Le Havre and later through Dunkirk, which expanded and modernized its port facilities to accept transatlantic steamers in the 1880s and 1890s and soon became the dominant port of entry for wool in France.

As the worsted and woolcombing industries of Roubaix and Tourcoing expanded in the last quarter of the nineteenth century, the twin cities became centers not just for manufacturing but also for buying, selling, and distributing South American and Australian wool. This was due in part to the efficiency of the "pipeline" established to move wool from the export ports to Roubaix-Tourcoing via Dunkirk and in part to the superiority of Roubaix and Tourcoing's facilities for washing, degreasing, and combing wool (wool spinners from elsewhere soon realized that they could avoid these expensive and difficult preparatory procedures by simply buying combed wool from Roubaix-Tourcoing). Yet another crucial factor was the creation in 1888 of a futures market for wool in Roubaix and Tourcoing, which attracted wool merchants from around France and Europe, just as the cotton futures markets attracted cotton dealers to New York and Le Havre. By 1899, Roubaix-Tourcoing was handling 87 percent of the more than 400 million francs' worth of wool imported into France annually, half of which was being re-exported to other parts of Europe. This made Roubaix-Tourcoing one of the leading wool markets in Europe, rivaling London, Antwerp, and Bremen. As had happened with the cotton trade of Le Havre, the rise of the spot and futures markets for wool in Roubaix-Tourcoing called forth a corps of specialized commission agents and brokers, but the real powers behind the trade were not independent wholesale merchants—these in fact had scarcely ever existed in Roubaix-Tourcoing—but rather the purchasing departments of the leading woolcombing and spinning companies. In a sense, the wool market of Roubaix-Tourcoing was a new type of market, a manufacturers' market, a market without merchants in the traditional sense.[30]

The cotton and wool trades were the largest and most complex staples trades in the late nineteenth century and went the furthest down the path of modernization, the furthest toward eliminating the traditional wholesale merchant. In other commodities the wholesale merchants managed to hang on longer, as happened in silk. In the mid-nineteenth century the city of Lyon remained Europe's leading center for the manufacture of silk cloth, and the Lyon silk industry continued to be dominated by *marchands de soie,* a class of merchant-manufacturers who organized and financed all phases of the silk business, from the domestic production or importation of raw silk to the export of the finished cloth. When the pebrine blight permanently undercut the production of raw silk in southeastern France in the 1850s, the Lyon silk merchants set out to establish direct importation of Asian silk. Indeed, as noted in the last chapter, one of the motives for the founding of the Crédit Lyonnais in 1863 was to finance this new trade. The first direct shipment of silk from China arrived in Lyon in 1857, and by 1860 a Lyon silk trader named Buissonnet had taken up residence in Shanghai. A second Lyon silk trader, Ulysse Pila, set up an export house in Shanghai in the 1870s. But in the end only a few Lyonnais were willing to go to China and Japan to establish the new trade in raw silk, so the *marchands de soie* came to rely on foreign traders to execute their orders. Arlès-Dufour, for example, became a client of the British house, Jardine Matheson. By 1877, 33,000 bales of China silk went from Shanghai to Lyon, exceeding the amount sent to London, but only 12,000 of those bales were handled by French merchants resident in Shanghai. Likewise it was not French banks but rather British banks such as the Shanghai and Hong Kong Bank that financed the China-Lyon silk trade although, as we have seen, the Banque de l'Indochine belatedly moved into this area in the 1890s.

Even if the Lyon silk merchants ended up playing only a minor role in the supply end of the China-Lyon silk trade, they continued to dominate the receiving end as well as the importation of raw silk from the Near East and Italy. Much of the raw silk utilized in silk manufacturing elsewhere in Europe continued to move through Lyon (or at least through Lyon-controlled facilities in Marseille) because European manufacturers wanted silk that had been "conditioned" in Lyon (conditioning involved cleaning and drying the raw silk to verify its weight and quality), and the Lyonnais merchants continued to dominate this re-export trade. Lyon remained the largest silk market in the Western world until the mid-1890s and was still third (behind Milan and New York) as late as 1910. Whereas traditional merchant capitalists were disappearing from the trade in other textile raw materials, there were still 75 *marchands de soie* operating in Lyon in 1890 (down from 127 in 1870) and 60 in 1920.[31]

While cotton, wool, and silk were imported from long distances— sometimes from halfway around the world—France's third most valuable import, coal, came from closer to home, mainly from Great Britain, Belgium, and at the end of the nineteenth century from Germany. Most of the coal imported from Belgium and Germany was sold directly by mining companies to industrial consumers (gas companies, railroads, iron and steel makers) on long-term contracts. However, coal from Britain, constituting the largest portion of France's coal imports in most years, was traditionally handled by specialized merchants operating out of the chief coal exporting ports, Cardiff and Newcastle. The great majority of these merchants were British, but not all. At least one French firm played a major role in this trade in the second half of the nineteenth century, Worms et Cie.[32]

Hypolite Worms was a member of the Jewish merchant family of Sarrelouis that produced the merchant banker Worms de Romilly in the early nineteenth century and was allied to another family of Paris bankers, the Goudchauxs (Hypolite Worms temporarily managed the Goudchaux bank in 1848 while his brother-in-law, Michel Goudchaux, served as minister of finance). In the 1840s, Hypolite Worms' main business was supplying plaster as an export cargo to English ships delivering coal to Rouen. In 1848 he began importing coal from Cardiff and Newcastle to Rouen and Dieppe, and by 1851 he was reputedly the largest French purchaser of English coal. Among his chief customers were the steamship companies operating out of Le Havre and Marseille, and during the Crimean War he supplied coal to the French navy. In 1855 he bought his first ships and contracted to supply the coaling stations of the Messageries Impériales in the South Atlantic and Indian Oceans. In the 1860s, Worms supplied coal to the Suez Canal Company and set up coaling stations at Port Saïd and Suez that later gave him a virtual monopoly on the sale of coal to steamers traversing the canal. By 1871, Worms et Cie was handling 7 percent of all British coal exports and furnishing coal to all the navies of continental Europe.

After the death of Hypolite Worms in 1877, Worms et Cie continued to be run by various Goudchauxs and Worms, who kept the company at the forefront of the international coal trade. Through the Goudchauxs' backing of Marcus Samuel of Shell Oil, Worms et Cie also gained a foothold in the international petroleum trade. Under the direction of the founder's grandson, Hypolite Worms II, the company continued in the wholesale coal trade and the shipping business after World War I, but it also entered banking and shipbuilding, thereby reconstituting the cluster of interests long associated with merchant capitalism that had tended to become separate specialties during the nineteenth century.[33] Indeed, by the 1920s Worms et Cie, no longer just a wholesale import company, had joined the ranks of a small group of multiline trading companies that would play prominent roles in the economic life of France and its empire down to the 1950s.[34]

The Wholesale Trade in Domestic Manufactures

While the wholesale trade in imported raw materials still harbored a few old-style merchant capitalists like the Worms family at the end of the nineteenth century, the wholesale trade in domestic manufactures was undergoing profound changes that in some cases turned the traditional *négociant* into a more specialized middleman and in other cases eliminated the wholesaler altogether. A lot depended on the nature of the product and its market. Many of the new products of the Industrial Revolution were made to order for a specific industrial customer and never entered the general market, and thus were never handled by wholesale merchants. These included locomotives and other railroad equipment, steam engines used to power factories, and feedstocks employed in the production of chemicals. In the marketing of consumer goods, however, the role of the wholesaler had long been crucial, and in certain areas of the export trade (for example, the export of French luxury goods to North and South America) it remained so to the end of the nineteenth century. In the domestic trade in consumer manufactures, however, there was a clear trend toward circumscribing and even eliminating the role of the general wholesale merchant. How this happened can be seen in the marketing of textiles, paper, and hardware, three products for which we have good information.

In the early nineteenth century, the wholesale trade in consumer manufactures was still controlled by the merchants who organized and financed their production. This trade was seasonal, reflecting the annual cycle of a predominantly agrarian society, and to a large degree still involved face-to-face encounters between buyers and sellers at fairs and public markets. According to Pierre Léon, there were some 26,000 fairs held annually in France as late as 1836. Most were of purely local interest, but some played vital roles in national and international trade. Most important was the Beaucaire fair, which attracted dealers in a wide range of goods—textiles, leather, hardware—from all over southern, central, and eastern France to the banks of the Rhône River each July. There was also the fair at Guibray in Normandy, which continued to be an important market for certain kinds of woolen and cotton cloth into the 1840s. Also integral to the textile trade were numerous fixed exchanges *(bourses)* and market halls. The Rouen cloth hall, for example, dating back to medieval times, still attracted hundreds of cloth merchants in the 1830s and recorded its all-time peak sales—250,000 pieces—in 1835. The Mulhouse cotton exchange, founded in 1828, continued to serve as a market for finished cotton goods even after it had lost its role as a market for raw cotton in the 1850s.[35]

The railroad and the telegraph eventually killed off these long-established public markets in the 1860s and 1870s, but well before then the appearance of alternative forms of wholesale trade had already assured their decline. Thus, although the Beaucaire fair survived until 1876, the amount of business transacted there had fallen steadily from 30 million francs in 1819 to 1.4 million in 1842 and to only 25,000 in 1853. Likewise, the Rouen cloth hall continued to serve small local producers until the 1860s, but its role in the national and regional cloth trade had all but disappeared by 1842.[36]

What rendered the fairs and bourses obsolete—even before the full development of modern transportation and communication—was the appearance of networks of specialized wholesale merchants called *négociants-commissionnaires*. In the textile trade, the most important group of these was found in Paris in the Sentier district east of the stock exchange, where they supplied a diverse assortment of goods to export merchants and retailers. At the same time, they used the extensive knowledge of market conditions and consumer tastes gleaned from their customers to formulate production orders that were then communicated to textile manufacturers in the provinces, skilled artisans and factory masters alike. The *négociants-commissionnaires* maintained particularly close contact with their largest suppliers, buying cloth on their own account or, more commonly, accepting consignments of cloth to be sold on commission through their warehouses. Similar specialized middlemen emerged in other trades that involved supplying a variety of products to a numerous or dispersed clientele. In the paper industry, *marchands-papetiers* collected orders from printers and stationers for various kinds of papers and then distributed these orders among the large number of small paper mills that made up the industry in the early nineteenth century. Viewed from the other end of the pipeline, the function of these merchants was to assume the responsibility for selling the output of a given papermaker, thereby relieving the latter of the expense in time and money required to develop and maintain relations with a large number of paper dealers.

Specialized wholesale merchants remained key players in industries and trades that involved small production runs of a wide variety of goods by domestic handworkers or small factories. For example, as Louis Bergeron has emphasized, the *négociants-commissionnaires* of the Sentier district retained their control over much of the French garment and accessories trades well into the twentieth century.[37] But in those industries where large-scale production of standardized goods was taking shape, there was a growing trend after 1850 toward commercial integration and simplification. This involved either manufacturers circumventing the wholesaler and dealing directly with retailers or wholesalers integrating backward into production (often as a defensive maneuver to prevent being squeezed out by the manufacturers). In the latter scenario, the *négociant-commissionnaire* in essence became a *négociant-fabricant*. This happened in the paper industry as early as the 1820s, when the advent of machine production undercut the position of *marchands-papetiers* first in the marketing of newsprint and wrapping paper, which manufacturers increasingly sold directly to the end users, and later in the marketing of printing and writing paper. In self-defense, the leading paper merchant in Paris in the 1850s, Louis-Stanislaus Prioux, acquired his own paper mill to assure supplies for his wholesale trade.[38] Gustave Roy and his sons employed a similar strategy in the cotton textile industry. In the 1850s and 1860s, Roy was one of the leading cloth wholesalers in France, acting as a middleman between the cloth manufacturers of eastern France and the Paris market. As the cotton manufacturers increasingly circumvented Roy and other wholesalers in the 1870s and 1880s, Roy's sons purchased a factory in Rouen and moved into the production of shoddy cloth for the emerging (and protected) colonial market.[39]

The survival of Prioux and Roy notwithstanding, wholesalers of mass-produced consumer goods increasingly fell by the wayside in the second half of the nineteenth century as more and more manufacturers integrated forward into marketing. This was usually a two-step process. First, the manufacturers would set up depositories for their goods in Paris or other centers of distribution to eliminate the commissions paid on consignments entrusted to wholesalers. These depositories were staffed by the manufacturers' own employees, with salesmen dispatched to deal directly with retailers. Then, as transportation and communications improved, the manufacturers realized that they could eliminate the expense of maintaining large inventories in the distribution centers by using factory representatives (or simply telegraphed orders) to create a direct pipeline from factory to retail outlet.[40]

In the cotton industry, this two-stage process is seen in the history of the Mequillet-Noblot enterprise of Héricourt. Up to the 1840s, this firm still arranged sales to cloth merchants at the Beaucaire fair or placed its goods with *négociants-commissionnaires* on consignment. By the 1850s, it was sending these goods to its own depôts in Besançon, Lyon, and Paris, where they were sold by company salesmen. By the 1860s, however, the firm was employing traveling salesmen to take orders, shipping directly from the factory to its customers (mainly the new department stores). Accordingly it gradually closed its depôts, starting with the one in Besançon in 1863.[41] A similar evolution occurred with Japy Frères of Montbéliard, makers of watch movements and hardware. While the Japys always sold their watch movements directly to Swiss watchmakers, they sold their hardware through wholesale merchants in Paris until 1828. In that year, however, the Japys established a warehouse and sales office in Paris that soon became the primary channel for marketing their hardware production. Direct sales from factory to retailer followed in the 1860s and 1870s, and what was not sold directly was increasingly marketed through the Comptoir de Quincailleries Réunis de l'Est, a common sales agency set up by the hardware manufacturers of the region.[42]

Ultimately, whether the independent wholesalers survived or were eliminated by manufacturers integrating forward depended on the degree of concentration at the retail level. No matter how efficient a sales and distribution system a manufacturer set up, it rarely paid for him market directly to large numbers of small retailers. Just as wholesalers survived in industries where production remained divided among many small producers, so too did they survive in trades where retail sales remained fragmented among many small shopkeepers. So the decline and elimination of wholesale merchants were closely tied not only to the rise of mass production but also to the advent of mass retailing, the final development in the new world of French merchant capitalism that we will examine.

The Beginnings of Mass Retailing

In France, as elsewhere in Europe, retail commerce began with periodic local markets, where small producers of consumer goods dealt face-to-face with individual customers. For some goods, such markets persist today. Indeed, for Americans, one of the joys of European travel is experiencing market day in a small town. By the early modern era, however, France had specialized retail merchants—itinerant peddlers in the countryside, sedentary shopkeepers in the towns and cities—who maintained permanent inventories and offered continuous access to goods supplied by wholesale merchants. Shopkeeper retailing, of course, is still very much around. But the upsurge in industrial production of consumer goods in the nineteenth century and the concomitant improvements in transportation and communication brought two challenges to the shopkeeper economy. One came from working-class consumers seeking to free themselves from the petty tyranny and outright fraud associated with shopkeepers and was embodied in the cooperative and mutual aid movements, which in the short run were mainly important in the context of working-class politics.[43] The other and more economically significant challenge came from a new class of merchant-entrepreneurs, who created France's first department stores and chain stores. These stores and the techniques of mass retailing they pioneered continue to define the world of French retail commerce today.

To modern eyes, perhaps the most striking characteristic of retail commerce in France at the beginning of the nineteenth century was its high degree of fragmentation. This fragmentation was first of all spatial: The lack of mobility within as well as between towns meant that most consumers depended on small shops serving their immediate neighborhood. Because their clientele was small and captive, the owners of these shops had little incentive to offer a wide selection of goods or to worry too much about their quality. Retail commerce was also fragmented by product. Partially as a legacy of the guild system, which had prohibited those practicing one trade from moving into neighboring trades, and partially as a function of low capital and small potential markets, most shops dealt in a single product or product line. Such fragmentation in turn locked shopkeepers into a low-volume, high-price strategy. Entering a shop carried an obligation to buy, so browsing was difficult. There were no fixed prices—indeed there were no prices marked on goods at all—so making a purchase always involved haggling and was thus time consuming. In short, "shopping" as it has come to be known simply did not yet exist.

While these conditions persisted throughout the nineteenth century and into the twentieth in small towns and the less-trafficked quarters of cities, things began to change in the larger French cities even before the increase in urban mobility in the mid-nineteenth century. Paris in particular became a laboratory for innovative retailing from the mid-eighteenth century onward. By the 1780s, the *merciers* (notions dealers)—the only merchants allowed to sell a diversity of goods under the Ancien Régime—were already opening the first *magasins de nouveautés,* which offered a variety of dry goods and fashion accessories and even the first ready-made clothing at fixed prices. The pace of innovation in Paris accelerated in the nineteenth century, especially after 1828 when the inception of omnibus service afforded middle-class consumers greater access to stores beyond their own neighborhoods. This stimulated the development of specialized shopping districts, most notably in the first and second arrondissements and later in the ninth arrondissement around the new Gare Saint-Lazare, where trains arrived bringing affluent day-trippers into Paris from Versailles and Saint-Germain.

One innovation in the 1820s was the grouping of fashionable shops in interior courtyards or along covered pedestrian streets—such as the Passage Choiseul, the Galeries Vivienne, and the Passage Colbert near the Bibliothèque Nationale (all recently restored)—which were precursors of the shopping malls of the late twentieth century. Another innovation was the "bazaar," where dozens and even hundreds of dealers in housewares and clothing occupied adjoining stalls in a single building. The years from 1815 to 1848 also witnessed the building of ever-larger *magasins de nouveautés* in Paris. On the Left Bank, these included the Petit Saint-Thomas on the Rue du Bac; the Deux Magots, which offered the newly fashionable oriental goods in the Faubourg Saint-Germain; and the Belle Jardinière, founded on the Ile de la Cité near Notre Dame in 1824, which became the foremost menswear store in Paris (also a major manufacturer of mens clothing—see Chapter 10). On the Right Bank, Charles Gallois opened Aux Trois Quartiers on the Boulevard Madeleine in 1829, Joseph and Lecoq were running Au Coin de Rue east of the Palais Royal by the 1830s, and in 1843 Deschamps opened the biggest *magasin de nouveautés* yet, A la Ville de Paris, on the Rue Montmartre.[44]

Some of these *magasins de nouveautés* survived into the twentieth century as speciality stores or high-end clothing stores (for example, Belle Jardinière and Aux Trois Quartiers). A few continued to expand and made the transition to what by the 1860s were being called department stores in the United States and in France simply "big stores" *(grands magasins)*. This happened to Au Coin de Rue. In 1843, a former employee of the store, Romain Renouard, took control of Au Coin de Rue and initiated aggressive expansion that included organizing distinct departments around a glass-covered courtyard and adding a second building that made it, in Bernard Marrey's estimation, "the first *grand magasin* conceived and constructed as a whole." By 1860, Au Coin de Rue had 33 *galeries* (departments) on six floors, 250 salesmen, and sales of 14 million francs a year.[45] However, a handful of new stores founded between 1852 and 1872 came to epitomize the idea of the *grand magasin* and dominated the retail sector of Paris and the nation by the end of the nineteenth century. The first of these new stores to appear and the one that served as the industry pacesetter for half a century was the Bon Marché.

The Bon Marché was opened in 1852 in an affluent residential section of the Left Bank at the corner of the Rue du Bac and the Rue de Sèvres by Aristide Boucicault and Paul Videau. Boucicault had worked as a peddler and as a salesman in various Paris stores before becoming a department head *(chef de rayon)* at the Petit Saint-Thomas. Videau had previously operated a store at the Rue de Sèvres location with his brother, and the Videaus furnished most of the 441,000 francs needed to launch the Bon Marché in 1852. In its first year, the store had four departments, employed twelve people, and had sales worth 450,000 francs, which made it just another *magasin de nouveautés*. The next sixteen years in the store's history are largely unknown except for two things: In 1863 Boucicault bought out the Videau brothers and became the sole proprietor; and the Bon Marché managed to raise its annual sales from less than half a million francs in 1853 to 22 million francs by 1869–1870. This growth in turn prepared the way for what set the Bon Marché apart from all other Paris stores: the construction of an enormous new building designed by Gustave Eiffel on the model of the exhibition halls of the world's fairs of the era. Construction of the new building commenced in September 1869, and the first stage opened in April 1872. When eventually completed in 1887, the new store had over 52,000 square meters of floor space and covered the entire block bounded by the Rue de Sevrès, the Rue du Bac, and the Rue de Babylone, making it the largest commercial building in the world. By 1877, the Bon Marché employed 1,788 people and had sales of 77 million francs. After Boucicault's death that same year, his widow converted the store into a joint-stock company with the shares closely held by ninety-five long-term employees. After her death in 1888, the direction of the store passed to her lawyer and to two department heads. Under this system of collective ownership and management by the employees, the Bon Marché continued to expand and prosper. By 1906, it employed 4,500 people, and its sales had risen to 227 million francs, which, according to Michael Miller, was a third higher than the sales of its nearest Paris competitor and which probably made the Bon Marché the largest retail business in the world.[46]

For all its success, the Bon Marché by no means had the Paris retail market to itself at the outset of the twentieth century. Its rise had been shadowed at every step by the development of a number of other *grands magasins*, all of which were founded, like the Bon Marché, by men and women of modest origins who had worked as small-scale retailers or as employees of other dry-goods stores or *grands magasins*. These included the Grand Magasin du Louvre, founded like the Bon Marché by two former department heads at other *magasins de nouveautés*; Au Printemps, launched in the new shopping district near the Gare Saint-Lazare in 1864 by Jules Jaluzot, head of the silk department of the Bon Marché; La Samaritaine, founded near the Pont Neuf in 1871 or 1872 by a former street hawker, Ernest Cognacq, and his wife, Louise Jay, head of the womenswear department at the Bon Marché; and the Bazar de l'Hôtel de Ville (BHV), launched by another former street hawker, Xavier Ruel, as a store for toys and knick-knacks *(bim-beloterie)* on the Rue de Rivoli in the early 1860s. In addition to the Bon Marché and its imitators, a second generation of *grands magasins* began to appear in the 1890s, led by the Grand Magasin Dufayel, which briefly rivaled the Bon Marché in sales but lasted only until 1916, and by the Galeries Lafayette, founded by two Alsatian merchants in 1895, which exhibited much greater staying power and eventually became the leading store in Paris after World War II.[47]

The emergence of the *grands magasins* of Paris in the 1850s and 1860s, their subsequent growth, and their increasing dominance of the French retail scene resulted from a number of related innovations in marketing and financial management. Although the increased mobility associated with new transportation facilities (railroads, omnibuses, tramways) made it feasible for a single store to attract a citywide and even national clientele, turning that possibility into a reality required doing a number of things right, starting with finding the right location. Renouard's Au Coin de Rue was initially as successful as the other *grands magasins*, but it found itself increasingly marginalized as the rebuilding of Paris directed traffic westward, away from its location east of the Palais Royal; following Renouard's death in 1878, the store was liquidated. Beyond securing the best location, stores had to offer in a single location the widest possible selection of goods in as many different lines *(rayons)* or departments as possible (the Louvre went from thirteen departments in 1855 to fifty-five by 1882; the Bon Marché tended to stick with dry goods but still had thirty-six departments by the early 1880s and forty-seven by 1900). Moreover, the stores had to make purchasing these goods a pleasant experience for the customer by providing attractive surroundings, an artful display of goods, and fixed, marked prices that eliminated haggling and encouraged browsing and comparison shopping. Many stores also offered home delivery of purchases so that women could spend extended periods in the store and make multiple purchases without being weighed down with packages (the goal was to maximize not just the number of visits but also the number of purchases per visit). Some stores extended their customer base by offering mail orders from catalogues that again put a premium on the artful presentation of the merchandise (mail orders accounted for one-sixth of total sales for the Bon Marché by 1902).

The *grands magasins* could offer a wide array of goods and services at or below the prices charged by smaller competitors thanks to policies and practices that continually lowered costs per unit of sales. First and foremost, the founders of the *grands magasins* understood that concentrating more and more goods under a single roof lowered overhead per unit of goods sold (according to Philip Nord, annual rent expenses for the *grands magasins* ran around 1 percent of sales, versus 2.5 percent for smaller stores).[48] They also knew how to leverage economies of scale with economies of speed. By turning over stock four times a year instead of once a year, as was usual, Boucicault quadrupled the sales that could be generated annually by a given amount of working capital or by a given area of floor space, which further lowered costs per unit of sales. Additional savings came from operating as much as possible on a cash basis, which spared stores the expense of carrying and collecting accounts receivable and gave them the ability to pay cash to suppliers, which in turn enabled them to demand from those suppliers lower prices and such concessions as staggered deliveries, which greatly reduced inventory costs.[49] Costs were lowered further by eliminating middlemen. Instead of buying through wholesalers, the *grands magasins* increasingly sent buyers directly to the manufacturers, and in some cases the stores became their own manufacturers (by 1900 the Bon Marché employed hundreds of garment workers turning out ready-made clothing in workshops attached to its main store). Yet another source of savings—and a cornerstone of the operating independence of the store owners—was the avoidance of borrowing. Most of the founders were able to scrape enough money together from partners and family to get started (Jaluzot launched Au Printemps shortly after marrying a former Comédie Française actress who had a substantial fortune), which they then expanded by reinvesting retained earnings. The exception to this rule was the Grand Magasin du Louvre, which began as a joint-stock enterprise backed by leading Paris financiers, including Emile Pereire, and continued to depend on outside sources of capital. Not coincidentally it was the only one of the five biggest stores to pass into the hands of outsiders before 1900. (After the surviving founder, Alfred Chauchard, retired in 1885, Emile Pereire II became chairman of the board, and the Pereire family continued to control the store down to the 1930s.)

Beyond specific financial and operational policies, the success of the *grands magasins* depended on the development of organizations and management structures that allowed them to monitor, coordinate, and refine the complicated daily flow of messages and merchandise. Indeed, the large department stores were among the leaders in the development of the managerial capitalism that in France, as in the United States and Germany, became a hallmark of big business in the twentieth century (a topic we will return to in Part III). For now, we must note that the birth of the Paris department stores was not the only manifestation of the rise of mass retailing in late-nineteenth-century France.

Although the Bon Marché and other *grands magasins* cultivated a clientele beyond Paris by distributing catalogues and by encouraging provincials and suburbanites to come to the capital to shop, there was plenty of room for entrepreneurs to launch imitations of the Paris stores in provincial France. The history of these stores is yet to be written, but we know that each major provincial city from Lille to Marseille had some sort of department store by the 1890s. These included the Grand Bazar in Lyon, Les Nouvelles Galeries in Le Havre, the Magasin Decré in Nantes, and the Grand Magasin des Nouvelles Galeries in Bordeaux. Perhaps most important was the Bazar Saint Nicolas, founded by Antoine Corbin in Nancy in the early 1870s. In the 1880s, Corbin replicated this store in Lunéville, Toul, Troyes, and other cities of eastern France under the name Magasins Réunis, and in 1894 he began setting up branches in Paris. In this way the rise of the department store merged with the development of the other major vehicle for mass retailing, the chain store.[50]

Chain stores exploited the same economies of scale and scope that department stores did. Like department stores, they sold at low prices standardized goods that they bought directly from the manufacturer or that they manufactured themselves. While department stores provided a wide range of goods in a single location to a mostly urban clientele, the chain stores offered more specialized lines of goods to suburban and small-town customers. As in England, where "multiple shop retailing" was highly developed, one of the principal products sold in chain stores in France was shoes—mass-produced, machine-made shoes. By the end of the nineteenth century, there were three major chains of shoe stores in France: Chassures Incroyables with 140 stores, and Chassures Raoul and Chassures André, with 50 stores each.[51]

Another sector of French retailing where chain stores developed was groceries. The pioneer in this area was Félix Potin, who owned and operated six grocery stores in Paris in the 1860s. The big expansion of this chain was engineered after Potin's death in 1871 by his widow, sons, and sons-in-law. It was based not on operating company-owned grocery stores but on manufacturing a wide array of branded, packaged foods (coffee, sugar, jams and jellies, canned goods, condiments, and the like), which were then distributed by the company's fleet of delivery wagons to independent grocery stores operating under the Félix Potin name. It was, in fact, an early example of franchising. The first true chains of grocery stores in France arose in Reims as a response by food wholesalers to the growth of a cooperative movement among the city's large population of textile workers. Docks Rémois was founded in 1887 and operated some 500 stores in various parts of France by 1910, as did a second Reims-based grocery chain, Comptoirs Français. A third Reims chain, Goulet-Turpin, had 300 stores, while Casino, founded in Saint-Etienne in 1898, had 200 stores (primarily in the Southeast) by 1914.[52]

Over the course of the nineteenth century, in France as in Great Britain and America, the largely undifferentiated world of merchant capitalism gave rise to the modern sectors of banking and finance, transportation, and wholesale commerce. In the process a number of firms arose that would continue to dominate these three sectors into the twentieth century, including the big joint-stock deposit and investment banks, the great railroad and steamship companies, and several major companies in trade and distribution. At the same time, the retail sector, which hardly qualified as "capitalism" at all at the outset of the nineteenth century, brought forth the first mass-retailing enterprises—the Paris department stores and provincial chain stores—that would also play vital roles in defining the framework of French business in the twentieth century.

Of course, all these achievements in the commercial and financial spheres constituted only half the story of French business in the nineteenth century. Indeed, it has been impossible to sketch the evolution of French banking, railroads, and commerce in the preceding pages without constant reference to the development of mining and manufacturing and the world being created by the Industrial Revolution in the 1800s. Therefore, before turning to the rise of modern big business in France in the early twentieth century, it is necessary to look more closely at the other side of French business in the nineteenth century, the world of industrial capitalism.

PART TWO

THE FLOWERING OF
INDUSTRIAL CAPITALISM

The rise of modern manufacturing in France began in the seventeenth and eighteenth centuries when traditional city-based, guild-controlled craft production began to be supplanted by a system of craft production centered in the countryside and in small towns and organized and controlled by so-called merchant-manufacturers. In some cases, these new merchant-manufacturers brought the artisans in their employ together under one roof; in other cases they "put out" work to artisans working at home. In either case, once established, this system of merchant-manufacturing continued to develop in city and countryside alike through the nineteenth century, and in some industries it persisted into the twentieth. However, as early as the late eighteenth century, merchant-manufacturing and craft production in general started to give way to mechanized production centered in water- and steam-powered factories controlled by true industrial capitalists. At first this occurred only in certain product areas and only in some stages of production (such as the spinning of cotton yarn and the printing of cotton cloth, but not the weaving). In much of French manufacturing, craft production and factory production continued to coexist and to depend on each other. But this symbiosis gradually eroded as mechanized factory production, which had originally supplemented and supported craft production, increasingly came to dominate and replace craft production as the nineteenth century wore on. As Whitney Walton has shown, some economists and industry observers in the mid-1800s lamented this trend and stressed the need to preserve and strengthen the craft system in order to maintain France's competitive advantage in the luxury trades.[1] However, even more observers, including most of the Saint-Simonians we met in Chapter 1, argued that France's long-term well-being—indeed its very survival as a great power—depended on its following Britain into mechanized factory production, and by and large this was the path that France took. Thus the central theme in French industrial development in the nineteenth century was not the persistence of small-scale, craft-based enterprise but the advent of large-scale, machine-based enterprise.

The origins of the new industrial enterprises were diverse: Some arose from government initiatives; some through the efforts of engineers, inventors, or skilled craftsmen with knowledge of new technologies; and some as off-shoots of foreign companies. But most were founded by merchant capitalists—either merchant-manufacturers already involved in an industry as organizers of cottage production or merchant bankers seeking new investment opportunities (including many of the same merchant bankers who were backing new enterprise in banking, railroads, and commerce).[2] Whatever their origins, the new industrial enterprises that survived the intense competition of the early and mid-nineteenth century came to form the basis for France's industrial economy down to the mid-twentieth century.

Because of the varied nature of industrial enterprise, Part II describes the rise of industrial capitalism in nineteenth-century France industry by industry, starting with those industries that developed earliest and gave rise to the largest firms (textiles, coal, iron and steel). It then moves on to industries where factory production often coexisted with artisanal production but which nonetheless gave rise to large industrial enterprises in the course of the nineteenth century (hardware and machinery, chemicals, glass, paper and print, sugar refining and flour milling, oil and soap, and clothing and household furnishings). Chapter 11 then completes this section by describing the new circumstances and new challenges faced by virtually all of the new industrial capitalists in nineteenth-century France, whatever their field.

As we explore the creation of the new industries in nineteenth-century France, we will encounter certain recurring patterns and themes that will help to unify an otherwise highly fragmented story. It is perhaps useful to enumerate these in advance:

1. *The primacy of technological innovation.* Among the factors that promoted the rise of large-scale mechanized manufacturing in the nineteenth century, none was more important or more universal than tech-

nological innovation. If there was ever a time when Say's Law (production creates its own demand) was valid, it was the early years of the Industrial Revolution, when new technologies dramatically lowered the cost of producing traditional items and, just as important, made possible the introduction of new products for which no demand previously existed. From textiles to iron, paper, glass, sugar, and all sorts of hardware and machinery, technological innovation and the transfer of technology from elsewhere played decisive roles in the advent of the new industrial enterprises in France.

2. *The tendency to consolidate and concentrate production.* As new technology revolutionized production in one industry after another and as markets were expanded and unified, economies of scale took on increasing importance in France. Consequently, the production of common goods that was scattered among dozens or hundreds of small firms in the early stages of industrialization became more and more concentrated in a small number of larger, more technically advanced firms by the late nineteenth century.

3. *Specialization.* The same technological advances and market growth that made possible the concentration of production of the most common standardized products also promoted the development of new products and provided a rationale for a countervailing movement toward specialization. Alongside the large firms mass-producing standardized goods arose new firms serving various market niches, which gave French industry an increasingly dualistic structure. This dualism also arose when, for whatever reasons, large manufacturers chose not to move into the production of necessary raw materials, feedstocks, or sub-assemblies and instead came to depend on other specialized firms to supply these goods.

4. *The emergence of the four classic growth strategies.* Early in the process of industrialization, companies in France began to employ—or contemplated employing—what would later be viewed as the classic growth strategies for modern big businesses: horizontal integration, vertical integration, product diversification, and geographic diversification. In many industries—including glass, paper, woolens, and steel-making—the last of these involved expansion into foreign countries and the precocious emergence of multinational enterprises.[3]

5. *The role of the state as customer and overseer.* Even in an age dominated by the ideology of free enterprise, the French state remained heavily involved in all facets of the French economy in the nineteenth century, as we have already seen in Part I. In the realm of mechanized

manufacturing, there were many instances where demand from the French state provided the key incentive for the creation of new industrial enterprises and even more instances where the state played a key role as overseer and regulator of industrial practices. Nor was the relationship between government and industry entirely one-sided. In Chapter 11, we see how French industrialists attempted to mobilize the power of the state on their own behalf on a number of issues over the course of the nineteenth century.

CHAPTER FOUR

Textile Capitalism

In the late eighteenth century, textile manufacturing was a ubiquitous and mature industry in France. On one level, it remained a craft industry, highly structured and closely regulated by the state and by what remained of the guild system, in which the various procedures—preparing the fibers, spinning fibers into yarn, weaving yarn into cloth, and finishing cloth through fulling, bleaching, dyeing, and printing— were carried out in small workshops by skilled workers with the help of journeymen and apprentices (often members of their own families). At the same time, as the demand for textiles waxed and the authority of the guilds waned, putting-out merchants were creating an alternative system of production in the countryside based on the labor of non-guild workers. The development of this domestic system has been called "proto-industrialization," implying that it was somehow a transitional phase between traditional craft production and modern industrial production. In truth, both craft production (minus the guild structure) and merchant-led domestic production continued in many sectors of the French textile industry contemporaneously and sometimes symbiotically with factory production to the end of the nineteenth century and even into the twentieth.[1] Although of unquestionable social and political significance, the persistence of these earlier forms of manufacturing serves only as background to what will be related here, the story of how large-scale enterprise emerged in textiles through mechanization and concentration in factory settings.

The mechanization of French textile production supposedly began in

1753 when John Kay introduced his flying shuttle in France after being chased out of England by angry weavers.[2] Of course, the flying shuttle and the spinning jenny (the latter brought to France by another Englishman, John Holker, in 1773) depended on human muscle, so they were easily absorbed into the existing structure of craft production. It was the introduction of machines that could be powered by waterwheels or steam engines—first in carding, spinning, and finishing, and later in weaving—that launched the real industrialization of French textiles and brought into existence large industrial concerns based on factory production. As in England, this happened first in cotton—the most workable and forgiving of fibers, and thus the easiest to mechanize—and subsequently in woolens, linen, jute and hemp, and eventually (but only partially) in silk. The survey that follows respects this chronology and thus begins with cotton.

Cotton

As Serge Chassagne has shown,[3] the driving force behind the rise of mechanized cotton manufacture in France, as in England, in the late eighteenth and early nineteenth centuries was the growing demand for printed cotton cloth, called variously *toiles peintes* (painted cloth) or *indiennes* (after its chief place of origin). First introduced and popularized among the upper classes in France in the early seventeenth century, *indiennes* came to be viewed as such a threat to the traditional textile industries (woolens and linen) that their importation and manufacture were banned in 1686. However, in the 1700s the crown allowed numerous exceptions to this ban, notably by allowing the production of *indiennes* in the south of France for export through Marseille. By the 1750s, the ban was being openly flaunted, with a Paris banker, Joseph-Daniel Cottin, establishing an *indiennage* at the Arsenal in 1754, right under the noses of the royal authorities. So in 1759 the pro-development general director of manufactures, Daniel-Charles Trudaine, won the lifting of the ban. There followed a rush to set up printing works in France by Swiss, German, and Alsatian printers, including descendants of the Huguenots who had left the country after the ban of 1686 and had settled near France's eastern border in towns like Mulhouse, Basel, and Geneva. Within two years, forty of these printing works were in operation in France, and by the eve of the French Revolution that number exceeded 120.[4] The foremost of these belonged to Christophe Oberkampf, who set up operations at Jouy, south of Paris, in 1760 to serve the court at Versailles and the larger market of the capital. Oberkampf's enterprise was soon designated a royal manufacture, and by the 1780s it was not only the largest *indiennes* producer in France but also one of the largest enterprises of any kind in France. In 1793 Oberkampf constructed a new four-story plant at Jouy that was reputedly the largest factory building in the world at the time. By 1800, *indiennes* printing, a classic artisanal industry, was rapidly moving toward mechanization and mass production in the modern sense, at the Oberkampf works and elsewhere, with the introduction of the cylindrical press, which could print 5,600 yards of cloth per day (versus 224 for a manual block printer or 336 for the flat copper press).[5]

The rapid growth of cotton printing naturally stimulated demand for unfinished white cotton cloth and soon led to the creation of mechanized spinning mills to supply yarn to the burgeoning population of handloom weavers (Oberkampf himself opened a spinning mill at Chantemerle near Jouy in 1804). As Louis Bergeron has shown, Paris itself was briefly a major center for cotton spinning and weaving under the Empire,[6] and it would continue to be the hub for commerce in cottons and all other French textiles (except silk) throughout the nineteenth century. But the manufacture of cotton in Paris depended on a particular set of circumstances: the ban on the importation of English cottons under Napoleon's Continental System and the momentary availability of cheap real estate following the nationalization of church property. Once these conditions passed, the progress of mechanization, coupled with the high cost of labor in the capital and its lack of water power or cheap coal, dictated that cotton manufacture would be increasingly dispersed in the provinces.

Parisian capitalists played a leading role in this dispersion, as reflected in the careers of the Davillier brothers. In 1805 Jean-Antoine Davillier, with his partners François Gros and Jacques Roman, took over Wesserling, Alsace's foremost *indiennes* manufacturer, and by adding mechanized spinning turned it into one of the leading integrated cotton enterprises in France. At the same time, Davillier's younger brother Jean-Charles began manufacturing cotton cloth near Paris to supply Oberkampf. In 1816, he took over and expanded the cotton spinning mill founded by the Englishman Frank Morris at Gisors in upper Normandy. Although J-C Davillier devoted more and more of his time to banking and finance in Paris, cotton manufacturing remained a major part of his family's business, and his sons continued to manage the Gisors factory into the middle of the nineteenth century.[7]

With or without the intervention and support of Paris bankers and merchants, numerous centers of cotton production appeared in provincial France in the late eighteenth and early nineteenth centuries, usually in towns long associated with the traditional textile industry—like Saint-Quentin in Picardy, Thizy and Roanne in the Beaujolais, and Troyes in Champagne. However, three regions in particular came to dominate the industry and produced France's largest and longest-lived cotton enterprises: Normandy in the West, Alsace and the Vosges in the East, and the department of the Nord along the Belgian border.

Normandy

The province of Normandy—and especially upper Normandy, the lands drained by the lower Seine and its tributaries and centered on the old seaport of Rouen and the newer deep-water port of Le Havre—was the first area of implantation of the English-style mechanized cotton industry in France, and it remained the largest center of cotton production in France to the end of the nineteenth century. Normandy had three attributes that account for its leading role in the cotton industry:

1. *Excellent water resources*, including myriad small rivers that could be harnessed with water wheels to power spinning and weaving.

2. *Excellent location*. Normandy was close to the Paris market; it had good connections with England, which allowed easy importation of coal when steam engines began to supplant water power in textile production; and it had good access to raw cotton through Le Havre (raw cotton was much cheaper in Normandy than anywhere else in France before the railroads were built).

3. *Skilled workforce*. It had a large population with long experience in domestic industry, including thousands of skilled weavers who could be integrated into the new industry.

German and Swiss *indienneurs* came to Normandy at the same time they arrived in Paris and Alsace, after the prohibition on *indiennes* was lifted in 1759, and they had made Rouen and Bolbec important centers for cloth printing by the 1780s. The growth of cloth printing in turn provided a growing market for cotton cloth, which encouraged the introduction of English spinning machines to furnish cheap yarn to rural weavers. The chief agent for this transfer of English technology was John Holker, a Jacobite soldier of fortune and mechanic, who came to Normandy in 1752 and created a *manufacture textile à l'anglaise* at Saint-Sever with the support of the French government. Later, as French inspector-general of manufactures, Holker recruited other English cotton spinners and machine builders, including John Milne, Henry Sykes, and Frank Morris. Just as important, native French entrepreneurs, drawn from local merchant families and from the ranks of skilled artisans, also entered the industry.[8] Then, in the early nineteenth century, when the domestic market was shielded from English competition by highly protective tariffs and even the outright prohibition of cotton cloth imports, spinning and weaving mills proliferated along the tributaries of the Seine in upper Normandy and spread to towns in lower Normandy such as Flers, Falaise, Condé-sur-Noireau, and Ferté-Macé. As one observer put it, "cotton mills [were] popping up like mushrooms in springtime."[9]

This "first growth" of water-powered mills gave way by the 1840s and 1850s to a second growth of larger, more technologically advanced mills equipped with self-acting mules and mechanical looms powered by steam engines. With the turn toward freer trade in 1860 and the "cotton famine" that accompanied the outbreak of the American Civil War came a process of culling. Increasingly, Norman cotton found its niche in the production of heavy yarns and cloth for the rural domestic market and the colonial market (especially with the return to protection under the Méline Tariff of 1892), and more and more this production was concentrated in large mills in and around Rouen and other towns with good transportation (Le Havre, Bolbec, Oissel).[10]

As would be true of the entire French textile industry, the growth and transformation of Norman cotton unfolded through the medium of family firms. Atypically, however, few of these family firms lasted longer than the life span of the founder or at most two generations. Instead, entrepreneurs would typically enter the textile business, make their fortune (and achieve social status), and then exit into government service, landed property, and a life of leisure, leaving the field to others. There were exceptions, to be sure. As elsewhere, Protestant cotton printers in Normandy *did* form dynasties. The Keittinger printing firm, founded in 1788, continued in the family until the line of male heirs died out in 1910 (at which point the firm became a *société anonyme*). Similarly, the Fauquets of Bolbec constituted a multilineal dynasty in both printing and cloth manufacture that remained prominent in the industry into the twentieth century.[11] And the Waddington family, which in 1812 inherited the cotton complex at St. Rémy-sur-Avre founded by Henry Sykes, sustained its enterprise over six generations until 1961.[12] More representative, however, is the story of Augustin-Thomas Pouyer-Quertier, the largest cotton spinner in Normandy after 1860 and the most prominent industrialist to come out of Normandy in the nineteenth century.

Son of a successful putting-out merchant (Augustin-Florentin Pouyer) who had married into a prosperous merchant family (the Quertiers), Augustin-Thomas Pouyer-Quertier was sent to England to study the latest cotton machinery in the 1830s, after which he set up a water-driven mill at Fleury-sur-Andelle in the 1840s. In 1859, Pouyer-Quertier abandoned Fleury to create "La Foudre," a giant steam-driven spinning mill at Petit-Quevilly near Rouen, which he gradually expanded to a maximum size of 106,000 spindles in 1868 (in the face of supposedly murderous competition from the British!) and then shifted more into mechanical weaving by adding 283 power looms. Meanwhile he entered the Corps Législatif in 1867, served as finance minister in 1871 (and helped to negotiate the Treaty of Frankfurt, which ended the Franco-Prussian War), and became a leader in the National Assembly of the Third Republic. While pursuing a political career, he also pursued new investments (launching a transatlantic cable company later known as the PQ)[13] and social prominence (by marrying his two daughters into old aristocratic families). Thus distracted—and lacking a son to take over the business—he neglected to keep his cotton enterprise competitive in the increasingly difficult economic climate of the so-called Great Depression of the 1880s. In 1883, Etablissements Pouyer-Quertier was turned into a joint-stock company under a salaried director, but the influx of new capital and managerial talent was not enough. Pouyer-Quertier died in debt in 1891, and his company limped on, producing shoddy goods for the colonial market at low profits until it finally closed its doors in 1932, a victim of the other Great Depression.[14]

The Great Depression of the late nineteenth century that fatally wounded Pouyer-Quertier's enterprise did not destroy the Norman cotton industry, but it did mark a transition in its control and organization. Always an "industry of implantation" dependent on outsiders for its impetus, Norman cotton increasingly fell under the sway of other wings of the French textile industry after 1870, notably the Alsatian cotton masters who, following Germany's annexation of their homeland in 1870, were seeking new footholds on French soil. The result was noted by the geographer Levainville in his 1913 study of Rouen: "The current progress of Rouen's manufacturing is of foreign origin. Elbeuf and Rouen would probably have lost their importance as centers of weaving and printing by now if several large Alsatian firms had not migrated into their suburbs after 1870. . . . Thanks to their forceful action, the industry of Rouen maintains its reputation while the local bourgeoisie, once so active, seems to sleep."[15]

Alsace and the Vosges

Alsace—the half-French, half-German province on the right bank of the Rhine that was added to France piece by piece between 1648 and 1790—and more precisely upper Alsace—the southern part of the province around the city of Mulhouse that became the department of the Haut-Rhin—did indeed play host to the most expansive and entrepreneurial cotton industry in continental Europe in the nineteenth century. Like so much of the Rhineland, Alsace was greatly influenced by the Protestant Reformation, and the commercial and industrial elite of the province was drawn mainly from the Protestant community, making it a prime illustration of Max Weber's thesis about the role of the Protestant ethic in the rise of modern capitalism.

As elsewhere in France, the cotton industry in Alsace began with cloth printing. The first Alsatian cloth printing enterprise was founded in 1746 at Mulhouse, then a city-state independent of the French crown (and thus not subject to the French prohibition on *indiennes*) that was well situated to serve the French taste for contraband *toiles peintes*. When the French ban was lifted in 1759, the industry quickly moved into the French part of the province, starting with the printworks at Wesserling (which later formed the basis of the Gros-Davillier-Roman enterprise). The full incorporation of Mulhouse into France in the 1790s propelled the industry forward, and the first decade of the 1800s, when Napoleon's commercial policies gave French manufacturers favored status in the continental economy, brought even greater growth. However, unlike other segments of French textiles that wilted after the hothouse atmosphere of the Napoleonic Empire disappeared in 1814, the cotton industry of Alsace had acquired sufficient technological expertise by 1815 that it continued its upward path after Waterloo, combining production for the domestic market with exports of high-quality printed calicoes to the rest of continental Europe and to America. As a result, the output of *indiennes* in and around Mulhouse continued to expand (quintupling between 1815 and 1834) until the

American financial panic of 1837 disrupted the transatlantic cloth trade and the more general "climacteric" in the printed cloth industry of the 1840s ushered in an era of consolidation.[16]

Cloth printing, of course, was only a beginning for the Alsatians. The growing appetite of the presses for unfinished cloth led the printers to integrate backward into spinning and weaving, especially after 1800 when they began to set up steam-powered mule jennies to spin yarn that was woven at first by the handloom weavers of the region and later by power looms added to the spinning mills. By the 1820s, Alsace's production of white goods—unfinished calicot and muslin—exceeded the needs of the local *indienneurs*, so manufacturers began to "export" their *toiles d'Alsace* to other parts of France, notably to Normandy. In turn, the raw cotton coming into Le Havre was being sent on to Alsace to be turned into cloth that was then returned to Normandy for printing—eloquent testimony to Alsace's position as the low-cost producer!

Along with their move from printing to cloth manufacture, the cotton masters of Alsace diversified into related industries, including the printing of wallpaper, the building of textile machines and steam engines, and the production of acids, alkalis, and dyestuffs. Eventually, the spirit of diversification took the Alsatian cloth printers beyond cotton into the manufacture of silk ribbon and especially the spinning and weaving of combed wool. Indeed, according to Michel Hau, the manufacture of woolens rather than cottons accounted for most of the growth in Alsatian textiles from 1840 to 1870.[17]

From the beginning, the creation, expansion, and diversification of the Alsatian cotton industry was the work of a remarkable collection of intermarried Protestant families. Indeed, so great was the incidence of intermarriage, as even a casual perusal of the various published genealogies of this community reveals, that it would be more accurate to say that the Alsatian success story was the work of a single extended family from which sprang the hundreds of partnerships and family firms that controlled and directed all aspects of the industrial development of the province.[18] Even so, three family names stand out as particularly important for the textile capitalism of Alsace: Dollfus, Koechlin, and Schlumberger.

The Dollfus family came to Mulhouse from Strasbourg in 1540 and was one of the leading families of the city by 1746, when Jean-Henri Dollfus, a painter, joined Samuel Koechlin and J-J Schmaltzer to found Mulhouse's first cloth printing firm. Breaking with Koechlin and

Schmaltzer in 1765, Dollfus continued in cloth printing with his sons (who later started Mulhouse's wallpaper industry). Meanwhile, Jean-Henri's younger brother Jean (Johannes) also got into cloth printing, founding the most successful of many parallel lines of the family. Jean's son Daniel, who took the name Dollfus-Mieg after marrying into yet another important textile dynasty, became a leader in technological innovation, installing Mulhouse's first steam engine in 1812 and its first power looms in 1817. Under the direction of Dollfus-Mieg's son-in-law André Koechlin, and later his four sons, the Dollfus-Mieg enterprise became the most important of all the integrated spinning, weaving, and printing companies in Mulhouse. In the 1820s, it led the industry out of common prints and into the production of more profitable luxury prints, and in 1837—amid a severe contraction in the world *indiennes* market—it began to manufacture the cotton sewing thread that increasingly became its specialty and assured the national and international reputation of the DMC (Dollfus-Mieg et Cie) trademark. After the German annexation of Alsace in 1871, DMC continued to operate in Mulhouse and on French soil through a subsidiary in Belfort. Eventually, in the contraction and consolidation of the European cotton industry after World War II, Dollfus-Mieg, alone of all the great Alsatian cotton houses, survived as a company and trademark (not, however, under the control of the Dollfus family, but rather under the Thiriez family of Lille).[19]

The second great Mulhouse textile dynasty was founded by J-H Dollfus' original partner, Samuel Koechlin. Like the Dollfuses, Samuel Koechlin and his sons developed integrated spinning, weaving, and printing enterprises in the late eighteenth century that continued to grow and prosper into the nineteenth. However, the Koechlins, more than the Dollfuses, diversified into related industries, as reflected in the careers of two of Samuel Koechlin's grandsons, Nicolas and André. While continuing in cotton manufacturing, Nicolas Koechlin took the lead in promoting railroads in Alsace, starting with the Mulhouse-Thann and Strasbourg-Basel lines in the 1830s. André Koechlin, after running the *indiennes* plant of his father-in-law, Daniel Dollfus-Mieg, turned to the manufacture of textile machinery in association with Sharp and Roberts of Manchester. In the 1830s, he added steam engines and turbines to his line, and when the cotton industry contracted in 1837, he turned to wool spinning and began building locomotives and other railroad equipment (filling orders from Nicolas Koechlin's companies). In 1872, A. Koechlin et Cie merged with Graffenstaden, the other major Alsatian maker of railroad equipment, to form the Société Alsacienne de Constructions Mécaniques (SACM) which, through its Belfort branch, continued to serve the French market after the German annexation of Alsace in 1871 (see Chapter 7). Meanwhile, other Koechlins played important roles not only in textiles and machine making but also in automobiles, chemicals, electric power, and investment banking.[20]

The third big name to come out of Alsatian cotton was Schlumberger. Long involved in the commerce and industry of Mulhouse and its environs, the Schlumberger family entered the cotton industry when Pierre Schlumberger "du Loewenfels" joined his friends and relatives among the Dollfuses, Koechlins, and Rislers in spinning, weaving, and printing enterprises in the 1780s. Two of Pierre's sons continued the family cotton business, while another son, Nicolas, moved into machine building at Guebwiller. The mechanical aptitude of the Schlumberger family would bear its greatest fruit in the twentieth century, when Conrad and Marcel Schlumberger (great-grandsons of Nicolas) invented electronic oil exploration technology that would underpin one of the most successful high-tech firms of the post–World War II era, Schlumberger Ltd. Other members of the extended family would gain prominence in publishing (Jean Schlumberger of Le Figaro), banking (Marcel Schlumberger of Banque de Neuflize, Schlumberger), petroleum (Etienne Schlumberger of Shell Française), and plastics (Paul Schlumberger of Compagnie Française des Matières Plastiques).[21]

The Alsatian cotton industry thus not only served as the motor of growth that turned what was a relatively backward and rural province in the eighteenth century into the industrial cockpit of France by the mid-nineteenth century; it also served as a launching pad for industrial innovation on a broad scale by the leading capitalist dynasties of the region. However, the Alsatian cotton industry itself was lost to France in 1871, when the Treaty of Frankfurt ceded the departments of the Bas-Rhin and Haut-Rhin (except for Belfort and its environs) to the new German Empire. Although Alsace was returned to France in 1919, by then its place in the French textile industry had been largely taken over by its offshoot to the west in the Vosges Mountains.

The cotton industry of the Vosges was launched in the 1760s when a weaving plant was set up at Remiremont to supply cloth to the *indienneurs* of Mulhouse. In 1806 the expatriate English mechanic John Heywood built the first mechanical spinning mill in the Vosges at Senones (a mill that later passed through Heywood's son-in-law to the noted Lorraine merchant banking family, the Seillières). However, the real takeoff of the Vosges cotton industry came in the 1840s and 1850s, when the perfection of water turbines led to the founding of numerous turbine-powered spinning and weaving mills on the upper reaches of the Moselle and Meurthe rivers and their tributaries by members of the Mulhouse cotton patriciate as well as by "new men" such as Jean-Thiébaut Géhin, Georges Perrin, and Nicholas Géliot. By 1860, these and other cotton masters operated mills with some 368,000 spindles and over 13,000 power looms and employed some 15,000 workers (by comparison, the parent industry in the Haut-Rhin had 1.2 million spindles, perhaps 18,000 power looms, and employed twice as many workers).[22]

The Vosges cotton industry entered a second, more expansive phase after 1870 in response to two developments, one political and one economic. First, the Franco-Prussian War cut off Alsace from the rest of France, necessitated the creation of a new finishing industry in the Vosges (because Vosges cloth could no longer be sent to Mulhouse for bleaching and dyeing), and occasioned a considerable movement of Alsatians to the west, mainly to Belfort and the Vosges, to preserve their French citizenship. Second, the completion of the Nancy-Epinal railroad and the opening of the Canal de l'Est connecting the Moselle and the Saône integrated the Vosges much more into the national economy than ever before and, more particularly, brought cheap coal into the Vosges, making possible the creation of a steam-powered textile industry in and around Epinal. The result was an influx of Alsatian money, machinery, and manpower into the Vosges in the 1870s, reflected in the transfer of the firms of Charles Laederich and David, Trouillier, & Adhémar from Mulhouse to Epinal; the building of new cotton mills at Rambervilliers, Ramonchamp, and Hericourt by Fritz Koechlin, younger brother of André; and the founding of the Blanchisseries et Teintureries de Thaon (BTT) to provide the bleaching and dyeing services previously available in eastern France only at Thann in upper Alsace.[23]

What began as an effort to re-create the Alsatian cotton industry on French soil in the 1870s and 1880s received new impetus in the 1890s, when the passage of the Méline Tariff of 1892 significantly raised duties on cotton cloth imported into either metropolitan France or its colonies, in essence reserving both the domestic and colonial markets to French cotton masters.[24] By 1900, the spindlage of the Vosges had risen from 412,475 in 1873 to 1.7 million and had surpassed that of the annexed Haut-Rhin. By 1913, the Vosges had surpassed both Normandy and the Nord in the number of spindles and looms to become the largest center of cotton production in France. In the process, some of France's most profitable textile enterprises appeared in the Vosges, including Charles Vélin et Cie (successor of Géhin); Vincent, Ponnier et Cie (successors of the Seillières); Les Heritiers de Georges Perrin S.A.; and the Société Cotonnière des Vosges, a joint venture of the Laederich family, Jules Favre of BTT, and Henri Géliot.[25]

The triumph of Vosges cotton was also reflected in the continued growth of BTT. While expanding its bleaching and dyeing capacity to meet the demands of the colonial trade, BTT also pursued vertical and horizontal integration. In the early 1900s, it moved into cloth printing and starch production, and it began to buy up bleaching and dye works in the rest of the country, in cooperation with the Motte family of Roubaix and the Gillet family of Lyon. By 1914, the company possessed "a quasi-monopoly of bleaching and dyeing" in France.[26]

In the interwar years, a trend toward concentration and consolidation already evident before 1914 picked up pace and eventually led to the creation of the three groups that dominated Vosges textiles after World War II: Texunion (controlled by Lyonnais and Nord interests, especially the Gillet and Motte families), the Laederich group (put together by Charles Laederich's son René and grandson Georges), and the Comptoir de l'Industrie Cotonnière (founded by Marcel Boussac, a protégé of René Laederich and the leading textile entrepreneur of twentieth-century France).[27]

The Nord

The third major focus of the French cotton industry in the nineteenth century was French Flanders, especially the department of the Nord and the cities of Lille, Roubaix, and Tourcoing. This region had long been associated with the traditional linen and woolens industries of the Low Countries, whose roots went back to the golden age of Ghent and Bruges in the late Middle Ages. These industries had become stagnant by the late eighteenth century, so it took little to entice the French merchants and merchant-manufacturers of the region to turn to mechanized cotton production at the outset of the nineteenth century, especially since the Nord, unlike Normandy and Alsace, had good access to coal. Mule jennies powered by steam engines were set up in Lille as early as 1792 and at Roubaix by 1804, and by 1808 there were twenty-six mechanized spinning mills operating in Lille, nineteen at Roubaix, and ten at Tourcoing.[28] The industry continued to expand steadily over the course of the nineteenth century so that by 1900 the Nord possessed some 2.2 million cotton spindles and 15,000 looms (compared with 1.75 million spindles and 27,000 looms in Normandy and 2.3 million spindles and 56,000 looms in the Vosges).[29] With this growth came the emergence, as in Alsace, of a large community of intermarried textile dynasties—or rather two communities, one in Lille and one in Roubaix-Tourcoing, that, for reasons specific to this region, continued to remain distinct (although Lille, Roubaix, and Tourcoing are so close as to form one metropolitan area).[30] Of all these dynasties, perhaps the two that best exemplify the dynamic and expansive nature of the Nord cotton industry in the nineteenth century are the Thiriez of Lille and the Mottes of Roubaix.

The Thiriez were relative latecomers to the cotton *patronat* of the Nord. Julian Thiriez founded a spinning mill in Lille in 1833 after working several years as a foreman in the cotton mills of Roubaix. But the Thiriez joined the ranks of the leading Nord cotton families only in the mid-1800s, thanks to the innovations and efforts of Julian's son Alfred. In the 1860s, Alfred Thiriez perfected a glazing process that gave his twisted cotton thread a silken appearance that not only gave it an advantage as sewing thread but also made it highly desirable for tulle and ribbon making. From 17,000 spindles in 1857, Thiriez et Cie expanded to 140,000 in 1889, which made it the largest cotton spinning firm in France. Under Alfred Thiriez's sons and grandsons, the firm continued to prosper into the twentieth century. By merging with Dollfus-Mieg (DMC) in 1961, Thiriez et Cie preserved its position as one of the few remaining world-class cotton enterprises in France in the late twentieth century.[31]

The saga of the Mottes in Roubaix can be traced to the 1820s, when Jean-Baptiste Motte-Brédart, son of a Tourcoing wool merchant (Motte-Clarisse), entered the cotton spinning business. However, the family's dominant role in the local industry dated from 1843 when Motte-Brédart's son, Louis Motte-Bossut, taking advantage of the legalization of British textile machine exports in 1842, founded his "filature monstre," a Manchester-style, five-story spinning mill equipped with 44,000 English-made self-acting spindles (the first in France) powered by two steam engines. After fires in 1853 and 1865, Motte-Bossut rebuilt the mill on an even larger scale as a mock-Gothic fortress in brick and iron that still stands (added to France's list of historic monuments in 1978, it now houses the business history section of the

French National Archives).[32] While Motte-Bossut's sons continued in the cotton business, Motte-Bossut himself and other members of the family diversified, especially into woolens manufacture, and in this they typified the behavior of most of the leading textile firms of the Nord. Indeed, we cannot really understand the history of the Motte clan or the larger development of textile capitalism in the Nord without turning from cottons to the industrialization of linen and woolens production in nineteenth-century France. Before doing that, however, we should briefly note the overall evolution and impact of the French cotton industry in the nineteenth century.

Between the 1780s and the 1850s, the consumption of raw cotton in France increased twentyfold and the value added by French cotton spinners, weavers, and finishers increased sixfold,[33] making cotton manufacturing one of the fastest growing industries in France in the first half of the nineteenth century. But the growth rates of the early 1800s could not be sustained in the late 1800s—in part because the domestic demand for cottons leveled off as population growth slackened, and in part because French cotton exports fell in the face of continued expansion by the low-cost producers (the British) and the emergence of cotton industries in other countries. From its position as the world's second largest manufacturer of cotton goods in the 1840s, France fell to sixth place by 1900 behind the United States, Germany, Russia, and India as well as Great Britain. Even so, the spinning and weaving of cotton remained one of the largest sectors of French industry in the years before World War I, accounting for 5.5 percent of the value added in the manufacturing sector (exceeding in those years even woolens, traditionally the largest French textile industry).[34] More importantly, by 1900 the cotton industry had already served as the principal conduit for the transfer of manufacturing technology into France and as the indispensable catalyst for the mechanization of the French textile industry and for the broader development of industrial capitalism in France, especially in the years from 1800 to 1860. And, as we have seen, many of the family firms and entrepreneurial dynasties that arose in cotton in the early nineteenth century would continue to play important roles in French business well into the twentieth.

Linen

The manufacture of linen cloth was much older and still much larger than the manufacture of cotton at the beginning of the nineteenth century.[35] It was a two-tiered industry, with small-scale production of common cloth for local consumption dispersed across much of the country, and larger-scale (but still pre-industrial) production of certain specialties for regional or even national and international consumption located in certain towns (for example, lace in Cholet and sailcloth in Angers). Because of the industry's ingrained traditions and perhaps because of complacency born of its sheer size, production in the linen industry remained artisanal and essentially unmechanized for a generation (or more) after the mechanization of cotton production had begun. So, while cotton took off and became the motor of growth in French textiles between 1800 and 1840, linen languished. But this began to change in the 1830s.

Philippe de Girard invented machines to comb and spin flax (the raw material for linen) in the first decade of the nineteenth century, but these were initially ignored by the leaders of the French linen industry.[36] In the 1820s, however, Marshall of Leeds successfully put the machines into production in England. In the following decade, Antoine Scrive-Labbe and Julien Le Blan, scions of the leading linen houses of Lille, smuggled copies of these machines out of England (for which they were hailed as national heroes by King Louis-Philippe) and introduced mechanical flax spinning to Lille and the nearby town of Armentières. Mechanized weaving of linen came to France in the 1860s and turned Armentières into a boom town (the "cotton famine" occasioned by the blockade of the southern ports during the American Civil War gave both linen and woolens a chance to expand at the expense of cotton in what Claude Fohlen calls "the competitors' revenge"). From the late 1860s onward, when resurgent cotton production began to erode the overall demand for linens, the mechanized linen industry of Lille-Armentières—the low-cost producer in the industry—began to drive the artisanal linen producers elsewhere in France out of what remained of the market. By the 1890s, Lille-Armentières had a virtual national monopoly.[37] Thanks to this, many of the family firms of the Nord that pioneered mechanization of the linen industry in the middle of the century remained viable and prosperous at the end of the century. Most important of these was Droulers-Agache.

Droulers-Agache began in 1828 when Donat Agache and Florentin Droulers formed a partnership to spin cotton in Lille. In 1848, when Julien Le Blan, one of the founders of mechanized linen spinning, went out of business, Droulers-Agache purchased Le Blan's mill at Perenchies and shifted to spinning linen. Under the management of Edouard

Agache, the Perenchies mill expanded to 1,500 employees during the cotton famine. Breaking with the Droulers family, Agache converted the firm to the S.A. des Etablissements de Perenchies in 1888. Under the direction of Edouard's son, Donat Agache II, the Perenchies enterprise grew to 55,000 spindles and 3,500 employees, and provided fully 10 percent of the linen yarn sold in France on the eve of World War I. Destroyed during the war, Perenchies was rebuilt with government aid and the latest technology, and the firm integrated forward into weaving and finishing in the course of the 1920s. As "the crown jewel of the traditional French textile industry," the Agache enterprise later formed the basis of the Agache-Willot conglomerate that dominated French textiles in the 1960s and 1970s.[38]

Woolens

Throughout the nineteenth century, the French woolens and worsteds industry was not only the largest sector of the French textile industry but also probably the largest woolens industry in the world.[39] Unlike the cotton industry, where the necessity of importing all of the raw materials from abroad tended to concentrate production in peripheral areas near ports of entry, the woolens and worsted industry, using locally grown as well as imported wool, developed in virtually every part of France. Indeed, as late as 1875, the *Annuaire statistique* listed woolens manufacturers in seventy-seven of France's eighty-seven departments.[40] Even so, the industry came to be identified with those towns that, in the industry's long evolution since the Middle Ages, had emerged as specialists in one form of woolens manufacture or another. These included Louviers, Lisieux, and Elbeuf in Normandy; Sedan in the Ardennes; Reims in Champagne; and Castres, Lodève, Bédarieux, and Carcassonne in Languedoc.

At all these locations, woolens manufacture remained a craft industry at the end of the eighteenth century, with various skilled artisans working at home or in small workshops for merchant capitalists who supplied the raw materials and took responsibility for the finishing and marketing of the final product. Within this framework, however, a few large-scale enterprises emerged, often as royal manufactories, which brought together large numbers of workers in "proto-factories." Unlike cotton, where the concentration of production was associated with the adoption of powered machinery for spinning and weaving, the creation of these proto-factories in wool derived from the need for quality control in the preparation of the raw wool and in the finishing of wool cloth. Thus proto-factories served mainly the beginning and end of the chain of production. Even so, they were impressive facilities. For example, Dijonval in Sedan, founded in 1644 but greatly expanded in the late eighteenth century, brought together 1,100 workers in a richly ornamented, four-story structure that Maurice Daumas has described as being "in a class apart" among industrial buildings of the eighteenth century. Almost as impressive was the three-story manufactory built in 1779 in Louviers by J-B Decretôt, which Arthur Young judged to be "the foremost *fabrique de draps* in the world" at the time of his visit in 1788.[41]

These proto-factories were a manifestation more of the old order of merchant capitalism than of the coming order of industrial capitalism, and the transition from the one to the other was slower and less clear-cut in woolens than in cotton. It began with the introduction of water- and steam-powered spinning, fulling, and shearing machines in response to increased demand for cheap cloth for military uniforms during the wars of the Revolution and First Empire (according to Christopher Johnson, the army absorbed one-half of all *draps* produced in France in 1800–1810).[42] This first wave of mechanization was especially identified with the rise of the remarkable multiplant, multinational enterprise of Guillaume Ternaux,[43] but its impact in France is perhaps best illustrated by what happened at Reims.

On the eve of the Revolution, Reims had a well-founded reputation for its light woolens, which were made in the standard artisanal fashion. The city itself played host to 300–400 master drapers, eight dyers, twelve fulling mills, and nearly 5,000 hand-loom weavers, but another 35,000 spinners and weavers "worked for Reims" in some twenty villages in the surrounding country. During the Revolution, Reims suffered the loss of much of its traditional market for ecclesiastical garb but soon picked up a larger market for military cloth. It was partially on the strength of army contracts but also to serve the expanding Europe-wide market for consumer goods created by Napoleon's Continental System that certain Reims entrepreneurs began setting up true factories that combined mechanized spinning, fulling, and shearing with manual combing and weaving. Among these was Pierre Jobert-Lucas, brother-in-law of Guillaume Ternaux, who opened three factories: a spinning mill at Bazancourt; a second plant that employed 900 workers making "toilinettes" and swansdown; and a third plant in a former convent employing 1,000 workers to make shawls and "merinos" for men's and women's clothing.[44]

With the fall of the Empire, the French woolens manufacturers lost their privileged position in continental markets and saw military demand contract as well. As a result, the impetus for mechanization and concentration waned. Indeed, in the volatile and highly competitive conditions after 1815, those needing to produce long runs of standardized goods to amortize their heavy investments in machinery were at a disadvantage, and some of the most ambitious enterprises failed in the 1820s, including Ternaux's.[45] Through the 1830s, the advantage lay with what Philip Scranton has called "endless novelty": new patterns and new fabrics for the constantly changing men's and women's apparel market, including various mixtures of wool, cotton, and silk that could be most efficiently made in small runs by skilled artisans, including weavers equipped with the new Jacquard loom.[46]

Where it still paid to have concentrated mechanized manufacturing was in production for the military. Indeed, the French army encouraged consolidation in woolens production by imposing the 50,000 meter rule in 1824 (to qualify for an army contract, a company had to be able to produce at least 50,000 meters of cloth per year).[47] The military market was particularly important for the woolens towns of the southern Massif Central, which were increasingly unable to compete with the northern woolens centers in the French domestic market and which found that the wars of the Revolution and Empire had permanently disrupted their once-secure markets in the Mediterranean basin. Lodève, in the department of the Hérault, had been producing cloth for the army since 1729, when the king's chief adviser, Cardinal Fleury (son of a Lodève cloth merchant), gave it its first contract. Its military production boomed during the Napoleonic Wars, fell off after Waterloo, but then rebounded sharply on the basis of new orders from the National Guard during the July Monarchy. Consequently, the number of mechanized spinning mills in Lodève rose from one in 1815 to fifteen in the 1830s, with most of these tied to a handful of relatively large firms created by merger to meet the 50,000 meter qualification.[48] Lodève's neighbor, Bédarieux, also expanded in this period, mainly by subcontracting work on Lodève's military orders. By the 1840s, Bédarieux's largest firms rivaled those of Lodève in size and, like Lodève's, combined mechanized spinning with hand-loom weaving.[49]

Mazamet, in the neighboring department of the Tarn, followed a similar line of development when Marshal Soult, Louis-Philippe's minister of war (who was born ten kilometers from Mazamet), channeled a contract for 18,000 meters of military cloth to the town's leading firms in 1831. As of 1849, the foremost Mazamet wool manufacturer, Houlès-Cormouls, employed 738 workers and ranked sixth among woolens manufacturers in France.[50]

As of the 1840s, the French woolens industry was prosperous and even expansive but was only partially mechanized. There were a few instances of true factory production—mainly for the military—but many of the leading firms remained essentially merchant operations that contracted with skilled artisans to turn out small quantities of a wide range of cloths in response to the rapidly changing tastes of middle- and upper-class consumers in Paris and other cities. Full-fledged industrial capitalism arose only after 1850, when the influx of cheap wool from Argentina and Australia and major advances in production technology—improved spinning machines, power looms, and mechanical woolcombing—finally made possible mass production of woolens and worsteds for a mass market. Mechanical woolcombing was especially crucial. It led directly to the mechanization and expansion of the manufacture of the highly prized light worsteds and merinos of northern France and made Reims, and even more Roubaix-Tourcoing, the leading centers of woolens manufacture in continental Europe.

A machine to comb wool—the critical step in preparing fibers to be spun into yarn—had been introduced in England as early as 1789. But truly effective machine combs appeared only in the 1840s—principally the Heilmann comb in France (manufactured by Nicholas Schlumberger at Guebwiller) and the square motion comb (developed by Isaac Holden and Samuel Cunliffe Lister in England). By systematic purchase of patents, Holden and Lister took control of the new woolcombing technology both in Britain and on the Continent, and in 1849 Holden came to France to commercialize the Lister-Holden machine, setting up specialized woolcombing plants at Saint Denis, Reims, and Croix near Roubaix. By the 1870s, the surviving Holden plants at Reims and Croix were producing almost 12 million kilograms of combed wool a year (twenty times as much as twenty years earlier) and accounted for 27 percent of all the wool consumed by French industry. By then, however, the Holden-Lister patents were beginning to expire, and other woolcombing enterprises were emerging, notably Desmoulin et Droulers at Fourmies and Amedée Prouvost at Roubaix. At the same time, more and more worsted manufacturers were integrating woolcombing into their operations using the smaller Heilmann machine comb, which was well suited for this application. In Reims, the number of machine combs rose from 63 in 1853 to 709 in 1878; the number in Fourmies rose from 42 to 520 in the same period.[51]

The breakthrough in mechanical woolcombing dramatically lowered the cost of wool for the worsted manufacturers of northern France and made possible the development of a mass market for light woolen cloth. This opportunity was enhanced by the cotton famine during the American Civil War, which further increased demand for light woolens in the 1860s. It now made sense for worsted manufacturers to invest heavily in mechanical spinning and weaving. Accordingly, mules, self-actings, and power looms first developed for the cotton industry were soon adapted to woolens production. In the 1860s, woolens manufacture experienced a takeoff unmatched by any other segment of the French textile industry. At Reims, where Jobert-Lucas had pioneered the mechanical spinning of combed wool in 1812, there were some sixty-three spinning mills with 270,000 spindles by 1848, but most weaving remained unmechanized and under the control of putting-out merchants. This began to change in the 1850s, and by 1860 six firms had installed a total of 577 power looms, with the largest operating 177. Then, in the following decade, a new generation of industrial capitalists started constructing integrated spinning and weaving mills in and around the city. By 1870 there were 4,000 mechanical looms in Reims, and that number climbed to 7,000 in 1875 and 8,000 in 1887.[52]

Even more spectacular was the development of Roubaix and Tourcoing. These neighboring towns had arisen in the seventeenth and eighteenth centuries as second-echelon wool centers operating in the shadow of the older, better-established wool industry in Lille. As we saw earlier, the Roubaisians joined the first rush into mechanized cotton production in the early 1800s, but, when that boom ended in the crisis of 1827, they had moved back into wool and pioneered the cotton-wool blends that became a Roubaix specialty. It was only after 1850 that a combination of events tipped the balance definitively toward wool at Roubaix and Tourcoing. First, the Heilmann woolcombing machine revolutionized the wool preparation that had long been Tourcoing's forte. Then the emergence of the world transportation system based on steamships and railroads made possible the massive importation of raw wool into Europe from Australia and South America and simultaneously facilitated the combing of that wool in one place just as the cotton famine of the early 1860s increased demand for other fabrics. Displaying the opportunistic, competitive entrepreneurship inculcated in them by their years of laboring in Lille's shadow (see Landes), the Roubaisians and Tourquenois took advantage of these circumstances better than anyone else in Europe. While Tourcoing specialized in woolcombing and spinning, Roubaix became a center for combing and weaving, and, as we saw in Chapter 3, it also eclipsed London as the center of the European raw wool trade.[53]

Among the leading firms in Roubaix were four major woolcombing enterprises, the most important of which belonged to Amedée Prouvost.[54] Scion of an old Roubaix-Tourcoing textile family, Prouvost set up a plant with twenty-one Heilmann combs in 1851. Thanks to the woolens boom of the 1850s and 1860s, Prouvost et Cie grew to 150 machine combs and 1,500 workers by 1875. Following the founder's death, the firm continued under his sons and nephews as a *société anonyme*, integrating forward into spinning in 1910 with the creation of Lainières de Roubaix. After temporarily transferring its operations to Elbeuf during World War I, Prouvost et Cie rebuilt its plant in Roubaix after 1919. In the 1920s, Prouvost had the largest woolcombing capacity in France and was second in wool spinning only to Masurel (with which it eventually merged). It also moved into retail sales with its Pingouin chain of knitting goods stores. By the 1970s, Prouvost-Masurel was one of the three largest textile groups in France, along with DMC-Thiriez and Agache-Willot.[55]

While Prouvost built an empire on the first stage of wool manufacture, other Roubaix-Tourcoing woolens manufacturers specialized in downstream processes. Foremost among these were the Mottes of Roubaix. The firm of Louis Motte-Bossut, the family's leading enterprise in the mid-1800s, continued to produce both cottons and woolens until 1982, when it finally closed its doors. Long before then, however, the center of the Motte enterprise had shifted to the company founded by Motte-Bossut's younger brother Alfred in 1870. Beginning as a dyeworks that complemented the other Motte operations, Etablissements Alfred Motte grew by 1914 into a diversified and integrated textile giant employing 7,000 in woolcombing, wool spinning, cotton spinning, and dyeing under the direction of Eugène Motte, who succeeded his father in 1887. It also became a multinational company with plants in Belgium, Poland, and Russia. After losing its Russian investments and being forced to rebuild its Nord facilities after World War I, the firm moved aggressively into the United States and Canada to maintain its position as a world leader in textiles.[56]

As the woolcombers and worsted manufacturers of the Nord came increasingly to dominate the French woolens industry in the late nineteenth century, the long-established centers of carded wool production declined. Yet even in decline, they sometimes harbored examples of entrepreneurial success. Elbeuf is a case in point. Along with the rest of the French woolens industry, it had enjoyed strong growth in the boom of 1850–1870, yet growth did not bring industrialization. As a specialist in *nouveautés* for men, in which variety and novelty were paramount, Elbeuf had remained a commercial center dependent on an extreme version of the putting-out system. Of the 234 *fabricants du drap* doing business in Elbeuf in 1870, only thirty-six operated water- or steam-powered spinning or weaving plants. Most were simply finishing cloth produced by traditional artisanal methods in the surrounding countryside. However, as styles moved away from carded woolens to lighter worsteds and as prices on their specialties fell (privileging more mechanized and efficient producers of those specialties elsewhere), these firms faced a seemingly irreversible decline. Yet one Elbeuvian firm bucked this trend and enjoyed considerable success in the closing years of the century.

The Alsatian firm of Blin et Blin had pioneered the mechanized production of *drap noir* at its plant in Bischwiller (Bas-Rhin) in the 1850s and 1860s. When Germany annexed Alsace in 1871, the Blins decided to move their operation—lock, stock, and barrel—to Elbeuf and to expand it greatly. In 1872 they opened a four-story mill with 7,300 square meters of floor space and the latest equipment. As demand for *drap noir* fell off, they moved into other products, including *drap de troupe* and *tissus peignés* (using combed wool from Reims and Roubaix), and their annual sales rose steadily, from 1.2 million francs in 1872 to 8.8 million in 1891. As of 1900, Blin et Blin had one of the largest woolen mills in France, with 22,000 square meters of floor space and over 1,600 workers.[57]

Meanwhile, in the south of France, most of the old woolens towns of Languedoc—Lodève, Bédarieux, Villeneuvette, Clermont, Castres, Carcassonne—sank into a long twilight, generally maintaining the level of production achieved in the 1850s and 1860s but accounting for a smaller and smaller share of France's overall woolens output as the northern woolens centers expanded. The region's one success story in the late nineteenth century was Mazamet. In 1851, Mazamet's foremost woolens manufacturer, Pierre-Elie Houlès, imported two bales of sheepskins from Argentina and stripped them for the wool, thus introducing a new specialty, *delainage*. The great expansion of dressed meat exports from Argentina to Europe after 1870 also brought a concurrent influx of sheepskins, and Mazamet became the world center for stripping them. With woolens manufacturing surviving but not expanding in Mazamet, more and more of the city's manufacturers, including the grandsons of Houlès, abandoned textile production to specialize in *delainage*. A strike by woolens workers in 1887 accelerated this shift, and by 1899 Mazamet was importing annually some 100,000 bales of sheepskins that yielded wool worth 50–60 million francs, most of which went to other woolens centers for further processing. *Delainage* did not support particularly large-scale enterprises. The fifty-four firms that specialized in wool stripping in Mazamet in the early 1900s typically employed 100 or fewer workers (in contrast to the largest surviving woolens manufacturer, which employed 400). But it proved to be a highly profitable niche industry that kept Mazamet from suffering the decline and depopulation that was the fate of many other woolens towns in the south of France.[58]

However detailed it may appear, this discussion of the cotton, linen, and woolens industries hardly does justice to the varied nature of the textile capitalism that arose in nineteenth-century France. Several other towns and regions developed specialties of national and international repute and played host to important family firms: the jute industry of the Somme led by the firms of Bocquet, Carmichael et Dewailly, and Saint Frères; the hosiery industry of Troyes; the tulle and lace of Calais; the cotton industries of Amiens, Roanne, and Saint-Quentin. However, for the sake of brevity, we shall forego a detailed discussion of these and turn to France's fourth largest textile industry and the last to mechanize, the silk industry of southeastern France.

Silk

From its beginnings in the sixteenth century, the manufacture of silk fabric in France centered on the city of Lyon and was bound up with that city's far-flung international trade. Unlike other fabrics, which ranged in quality from shoddy to deluxe (with mechanization of production usually starting with the former and progressing to the latter), silk was an "aristocratic" fiber that, because of its delicacy and costliness, resisted processing with powered machinery, required skilled handling, and was used almost exclusively in high-quality, high-priced fabrics. Accordingly, at the end of the eighteenth century, the trade in and manufacture of silks remained a classic example of merchant capitalism, with a small group of silk merchants *(marchands de soie)* controlling the movement of silk thread from the sites of production in the Rhône Valley and Italy into Lyon and its distribution to the city's hand-loom weavers *(les canuts)* as well as the finishing and eventual sale of the cloth—both plain silk *(soie unie)* and figured silk *(soie façonnée)*—produced by the weavers. The manufacture of silk cloth remained an artisanal enterprise that was strictly regulated by a guild, *La Grande Fabrique,* made up of master weavers and merchants and governed by overseers appointed by the municipal government. It was thus a "pre-industrial industry," an industry without factories or true industrial capitalists.[59]

The abolition of guilds at the end of the Ancien Régime and the proclamation of freedom of enterprise at the beginning of the Revolution ended the strict regulation of production by the *Grande Fabrique* and opened the way for *marchands de soie* to expand production to meet the growing demand for French silks in Europe and America. They did this not by mechanizing but by improving and expanding the traditional system of artisanal production. The introduction of the Jacquard loom led to an increase in the production of figured cloth, mainly in the hilly suburb on the north side of Lyon called the Croix Rousse, while weaving of plain cloth continued in the older parts of the city.[60] At the same time, the merchants, freed from guild restrictions, proceeded to cut wages in the 1820s in order to maintain Lyon's position as a low-cost producer. The result was class warfare, the "revolt of the *canuts*" in 1831 and 1834. Armed force took care of these challenges in the short term, but the merchants found it increasingly prudent to put out their silk to rural weavers who were willing to work for lower wages (and who lacked the organization and class consciousness of the *canuts*). They did this especially for the production of *soie unie,* which involved less expensive looms and required less supervision than the production of *soie façonnée.* According to Yves Lequin, the number of looms serving the Lyon silk industry rose from 37,000 in 1830 to 60,000 by 1850, with two-thirds of these located in the suburbs of Lyon or in the surrounding countryside in the departments of the Rhône, Loire, Ain, and Isère.[61]

Meanwhile, steps toward mechanization and factory production—and thus true industrial capitalism—were being taken, not in the weaving of pure silk cloth but in the preparation of silk thread and in the production of blends and specialty fabrics. The preparation of silk thread for weaving involved two steps, *devidage* and *moulinage,* usually translated in English respectively as "reeling" and "throwing." *Devidage* consisted of immersing the cocoons in hot water to loosen the silk and then drawing out the single strand that made the cocoon and winding it on to a bobbin or reel. Because these single strands lacked the bulk or strength needed for weaving (especially on the new Jacquard looms), they were then combined and twisted to form threads on a throwing mill *(moulin)*. From the beginning, both processes employed fairly sophisticated machines. But since these machines were hand-powered and since the work was seasonal (following the harvesting of cocoons in late spring), both reeling and throwing were usually carried out by the silk growers and their families in or near the houses where the silkworms were raised.

Change came in the late 1700s, when improvements in this machinery required outlays of more capital than the silk growers could muster and thus occasioned a first, albeit modest, move toward the separation and concentration of reeling and throwing in workshops and mills financed and controlled by the *marchands de soie*. In the case of *devidage*, this involved the use of steam engines to heat the basins in which the cocoons were soaked and to power the reeling machines. Maurice Daumas has described the transfer of this work in the Cévennes from family-run sheds to factory settings between 1800 and the 1840s, epitomized by the building of a two-story plant at Laroque (Hérault) in 1838 that was equipped with 117 basins. As of 1869 there were some 600 such plants operating 30,000 basins, located mainly in the departments of the Gard, Ardèche, and Drôme.[62] Meanwhile, silk throwing came to be concentrated in specialized mills mainly in the Ardèche, which was halfway between Lyon and the silk-growing regions to the south. In the 1770s, the royal silk inspector and great patron of the industry, Jacques Vaucanson, had developed an improved machine for throwing silk *(moulin à organsiner)*, which was first utilized in the royal manufactory at Pont d'Aubenas. The first steam-powered version of this mill was set up by Louis Blanchon near Privas in 1825, and similar plants—either water- or steam-powered—were built in the next decade by Arlès-Dufour at Clérieux (Drôme), Armandy et Cie at Taulignan and Grignan (Drôme), and C-J Bonnet at Jujurieux (Ain). By mid-century there were some 109,000 throwing spindles in operation in 277 mills scattered through the southeast of France. Although Bonnet's *usine pensionnat* (boarding school mill) at Jujurieux employed upwards of 220 women and children, most of these mills employed 15–60 workers—hardly factories in the modern sense.[63]

As time passed, *devidage* and *moulinage* came to be combined more and more in the same plant, as Louis Blanchon did in his two-story mill at Chomérac on the Ardèche River in the 1840s. Moreover, both processes were increasingly integrated with weaving, first hand-loom weaving and later mechanical weaving. This occurred to a limited degree in the production of pure silk cloth but even more in the production of blends and specialties made with silk waste *(bourre de soie)*, which behaved more like cotton than silk and could be spun and woven on machines used for cotton. The first such operation, with 200 looms and 600 workers, was set up in 1817 at Sauvagère de Saint-Rambert near Lyon by a Frankfurt *négociant* to make shawls with *bourre de soie,* but it apparently failed by 1845.[64] Of longer-lasting significance was the enterprise of Victor and Frédéric Chartron, founded at Saint-Vallier in 1834, which combined *tirage, moulinage,* and weaving (mostly of crêpes). By 1858 it employed 1,200 workers at three locations and was described by the prefect of the Drôme as "one of the most colossal industrial enterprises in the South."[65] Still, with all these developments, the industrialized sector of the silk industry remained small at mid-century, with hand-woven pure silk cloth still accounting for some 65 percent of the total value of the industry's output in 1847.[66]

As in the other textile industries, the pace of industrialization in silk quickened after 1850, with the most striking changes occurring in the production of pure silk cloth. The emergence of low-cost silk manufacturing in Germany and Switzerland and changes in fashions at home (with figured weaves giving way to plain silk cloth brightly colored with synthetic dyes) induced France's *fabricants de soie* to increasingly abandon the traditional hand-loom weaving of Lyon and its environs for mechanized production in rural factories. Also contributing to mechanization was the influx of raw silk from Asia discussed in Chapter 3 (Asian silk was stronger than home-grown silk and thus more amenable to being woven on power looms). The shift to mechanized weaving was especially pronounced in the Bas-Dauphiné. There the number of power looms went from 295 in 1850 to 1,500 by 1860 and 4,667 by 1879. In the industry as a whole, the number of power looms tripled in the decade of the 1870s, rising from 3,400 to 10,400.[67]

Pierre Cayez has identified sixty-five Lyonnais silk firms that either set up their own factory operations in the second half of the nineteenth century or employed the services of factory owners who worked on contract (called *façonniers*). These firms included producers of specialties, many of whom had taken the lead in mechanization before 1850. Among them: Baboin et Cie, employing 1,300 at Saint-Vallier (Drôme) in tulle manufacture; Montessuy et Chomer, with 1,250 workers at Renage and Vienne (Isère) making crêpes; Durand Frères, whose 1,500 workers at Vizille and Condrieu (Rhône) made crêpes and foulards; and J-B Martin, employing 3,500 at Tarare for velours and plush.[68] However, forty-eight of these sixty-five firms manufactured pure and blended silk cloth through various combinations of mechanized factory production and traditional domestic production. Their approach to this task is well illustrated by the story of Léon Permezel.

Starting out with modest capital in 1870, Permezel had great success in designing and marketing the newly fashionable mixtures of silk and other fibers. By the early 1880s he was producing and selling more cloth than any other *fabricant* in Lyon. He did this, however, without ever building, buying, or even renting a factory of his own. Instead, he worked through *façonniers* who, under contract to Permezel, operated 3,200 looms and employed 7,200 workers at various locations in eight different departments. All the while, Permezel himself concentrated on building the most efficient marketing operation in the business, which Pierre Cayez identifies as the key to his success:

> Thirteen industrial departments linked by telephone occupied two office buildings in Lyon. The commercial organization was the largest of any Lyonnais firm with ten branches (Paris, New York, Bombay, Como, London, Calcutta, Yokohama, Zürich, Barcelona, and Melbourne). The firm's success depended heavily on the talent of Permezel . . . Possessing detailed knowledge of markets and fashions, he knew how to fully exploit the demand for blended fabrics. The American consul described him in 1883 as "one of the biggest exporters to the United States and one who has the rare talent of creating new and original types of merchandise."[69]

Permezel's success notwithstanding, the silk industry of Lyon was in almost continuous crisis and underwent profound structural changes from the 1870s to the turn of the century. Silk growing in France never recovered from the pebrine blight of the 1850s, and this spelled decline for the steam-reeling industry (the number of reeling plants fell from 723 in 1872–1875 to 173 by 1914, with the number of basins dropping by half, from 22,500 to 11,600).[70] Moreover, as the Lyonnais became more and more dependent on the importation of raw silk from the Orient (mainly from China), silk throwing was transferred from France to Italy.[71] Consequently, in the late nineteenth century there was a move away from what had appeared to be the wave of the future in the mid-

1800s—namely, the integration of reeling, throwing, and weaving in large mills—and a move toward what Sabel and Zeitlin call "flexible specialization," wherein *fabricants* produce short runs of a wide array of fabrics in response to ever-changing prices and fashions (essentially the strategy pioneered by Permezel in the 1870s).[72] At the heart of this system was a weaving plant that by the 1900s was entirely mechanized, with some looms powered by steam engines in factories but most powered by electric motors in the homes of the weavers (a prime example of how electrification headed off industrial concentration and, in essence, preserved artisanal production by modernizing it). But none of this could mask the fact that Lyon's day as world leader in silk manufacturing was over. Although the amount of silk processed by the Lyonnais remained stable, their share of world silk consumption fell precipitously, from 83 percent in 1882 to 19 percent in 1911–1913 (largely reflecting the rapid growth of the American silk industry). While the total value of Lyon's production remained in the early 1900s what it had been in the 1870s, the value of its exports contracted, from 443 million francs in 1869 to 250–300 million francs per year in 1900–1905.[73] The strongest of Lyon's half-commercial, half-industrial silk enterprises survived, but none were expanding at the outset of the twentieth century. The future of the Lyon textile industry lay with artificial silk, first synthesized by Chardonnet in 1890, and with other artificial fibers that would be developed and commercialized, not by the established silk manufacturers, but by the chemical manufacturers that had grown up around Lyon silk.[74] We will examine the rise of those enterprises in Chapter 15.

Despite the varying fortunes of its constituent parts, the French textile industry as a whole experienced steady growth over the course of the nineteenth century and, according to Markovitch, became the largest sector of French industry, exceeding even construction and food processing by the beginning of the twentieth century.[75] Interestingly, however, as the French textile industry grew, it did not fall under the control of a few giant firms (as happened in many other industries) but rather continued to support dozens—even hundreds—of small and medium-sized firms. This reflected the fact that the central trend in the development of the textile industry in France, as in most countries, was not concentration but specialization—specialization by fiber, by region, and by process:

Specialization by fiber. Although some textile firms combined production of different fibers (cotton and wool in Alsace and Roubaix, cotton and silk in the Lyonnais), the trend over the course of the century was to specialize in one fiber not only because of the differences in the skills and technology associated with each fiber but also because of the separate sourcing of raw material for each one. By the end of the nineteenth century, all four principal fibers were imported—cotton from America, Egypt, and India; flax from Russia; wool from South America and Australia; silk from Italy and East Asia—and each involved different channels of supply. This kind of specialization naturally led to another:

Specialization by region. As certain cities emerged as ports of entry and entrepôts for certain fibers (Le Havre for cotton, Dunkirk for flax, Roubaix for wool, Lyon for silk), it made sense for the spinning, weaving, and finishing industries for those fibers to cluster nearby (although the rise and persistence of the Alsatian/Vosges cotton industry argues against absolute geographic determination of location).

Specialization by process. Early on, there was a trend within textile enterprises, especially in Alsace, toward vertical integration (the combination of all processes within one firm and even within a single plant). But, according to Maurice Lévy-Leboyer, vertical integration brought overcapitalization and often bankruptcy in the periodic financial panics of the early nineteenth century, whereas leaner, more specialized firms could ride out hard times.[76] The French eventually did move toward deintegration and specialization by process in textiles, but perhaps not to the extent that occurred in the larger British textile industry. This was, of course, a concomitant of regional specialization in that the close proximity of many firms working the same fiber let some specialize in spinning, some in weaving, and some in dyeing without the need to put all processes under one roof or one management.[77]

Going hand-in-hand with specialization in the textile industry was the predominance of firms owned and managed by single proprietors, two or three partners, or a family. Although the limited-liability joint-stock model of organization was readily available to French businessmen by the 1860s, few textile firms adopted it. Those that did were usually family firms that had reached the third generation and needed to find a way to cope with ownership divided among dozens of the founder's grandchildren. In any event, in France as elsewhere, the textile industry remained a bastion of the family firm well into the twentieth century. Indeed, as Louis Bergeron has argued, families rather than firms remained the most meaningful basis of industrial organization in French textiles, with the family providing the integrative force that compensated for the seeming overspecialization at the level of the firm.[78]

Of course, when there was sufficient longevity of family firms dynasties arose, and, as we have already seen, there were many such dynasties in French textiles. However, whereas in Britain and America textile dynasties tended to stay in textiles, somewhat encapsulated and isolated from the mainstream of capitalism, many French textile dynasties developed interests and influence far beyond textiles. Perhaps this was because many of these dynasties came out of merchant capitalism in the first place and never gave up the merchant's eye for the larger picture. In any case, one can quickly gauge the place of the textile dynasties in the world of modern French capitalism by scanning the pages of *Who's Who in France*, where since 1954 one finds a Thiriez at the head of the Aciéries du Nord et de l'Est, a Prouvost as publisher of *Le Figaro* and *Paris-Match*, a Masurel in Morgan Guaranty Trust and Paribas, a Mathon heading Dun & Bradstreet France, a Wibaux in frozen foods, and various Seydoux at Schlumberger, Chargeurs, and Gaumont.

But even if the great French textile families continue to be important, the leading textile companies have tended to wane in their influence as time goes on. As mechanized textile production spread throughout Europe and the world in the late nineteenth century, French textiles took on the air of a mature industry with few opportunities for dramatic growth. Indeed, as early as the mid-1800s, the technological cutting edge and its associated prospects for high profits were passing to other fields such as metallurgy, engineering, and chemicals—in short, to "heavy industry." It is to these that we now turn, starting with the most basic of heavy industries, coal.

CHAPTER FIVE

The Capitalism of Coal

In France, as in Great Britain, industrialization and the rise of industrial capitalism progressed not only through the mechanization of textile manufacture but also through the development of heavy industry, which typically includes the extraction and refining of mineral raw materials with the aid of mineral fuel (coal), the production of intermediary goods (metals, bulk chemicals), and the manufacture of various capital goods such as engines, machinery, and transportation equipment. The mining of metallic and chemical ores was so thoroughly bound up with the production of specific metals and chemicals that, by the late nineteenth century, it was rarely undertaken through independent ventures. By contrast, coal mining—although sometimes combined with other industries in large integrated enterprises, especially in the making of iron, steel, glass, and chemicals—did give rise to independent firms.

France's coal deposits were small, geographically remote, and hard to work compared to those of Great Britain, Germany, and the United States (this is often cited as a cause of France's supposed economic retardation), yet coal mining developed steadily in France over the course of the nineteenth century. By 1870, France had surpassed Belgium to become the third largest coal-producing nation in Europe (and fourth in the world), and it remained in that position into the twentieth century. Although its output was only a fraction of that of the British, German, or American industries,[1] the French coal industry gave rise to some of the largest industrial enterprises in France, and indeed in the world, in the years before World War I.[2] For this reason, and because of its position as the most fundamental of heavy industries, coal mining is the next logical subject in our survey.

The Birth and Maturation of an Industry, 1700s–1860

From the beginning, the development of the French coal industry was molded by three factors: rising demand for fuel; the size, quality, and location of coal deposits; and governmental initiatives, particularly as expressed in French mining laws. In France as in England, the progressive exhaustion of woodlands—reflected in the 100 percent rise in wood prices from 1816 to 1843—coupled with the growth of heat-based production (brewing, metalworking, sugar refining) dictated a rising demand for coal as an alternative to wood fuel even before the advent of coal's major applications as fuel for steam engines, iron smelting and steelmaking, and gas lighting in the nineteenth century. How much of this demand could be satisfied by domestic production was determined in turn by geography and geology. Although it would not be definitively known until the twentieth century, France's exploitable coal resources were modest compared to those of Great Britain and Germany. Moreover, they proved to be more expensive to work, and, except for France's sector of the "Austrasian" coalfield straddling the border with Belgium, they were remote from existing population centers and posed transportation problems. Consequently, most French colliers found it difficult to compete with cheaper coal coming from England and Belgium in the major urban markets (especially Paris) and had to find local outlets for their production. Although French consumption of coal rose steadily, from 2.4 million tons per year around 1830 to 65 million tons per year on the eve of World War I, domestic producers never supplied more than 70 percent of that amount.[3] To these economic constraints were added legal and political ones. The French monarchy, claiming ownership of all subsoil rights, determined who could set up mining operations, and, in both the court-centered political system of the late eighteenth century and the ostensibly parliamentary system of the early nineteenth, connections and influence tended to determine how the royal government granted mining concessions.[4]

Since the Middle Ages, outcrops of coal had been worked by peasant-miners in much of France and particularly in the wood-scarce Massif Central, which reached from the Bourbonnais in the center of the country to Languedoc in the South. In the eighteenth century, growing demand for fuel prompted the aristocratic landlords whose estates included significant coal deposits to begin commercial mining, and this in turn prompted the French crown to reassert its ownership of the subsoil by edict in 1744 and to require a formal royal concession for anyone to undertake mining operations. From the 1760s to the 1780s, the crown issued some fifty major coal-mining concessions, invariably to great nobles (thus, in its early stages coal mining was an "aristocratic" industry, in contrast to the distinctly "bourgeois" nature of textile capitalism). In Burgundy, the duc Delachaise won the concession to mine coal at Blanzy; in the upper Loire near Saint-Etienne, the duc du Charost founded the Roche-la-Molière mine (later exploited by the duc d'Osmond); in Languedoc near Alais, the marquis de Castries took control of the Grand'combe mine; to the west, the marquis de Solages began mining coal at Carmaux; and in lower Normandy the marquis de Balleroy founded the Littry mine.[5] However, the most important concessions were awarded in French Flanders in the North.

The cession of Hainaut to the Austrian Habsburgs in the Treaty of Utrecht in 1713 restricted the flow of coal from Mons and Charleroi into France and stimulated the search for coal deposits on the French side of the new border. Vicomte Jacques Desandrouin, already involved in coal mining near his hometown of Charleroi, began prospecting around Valenciennes in 1717. After several false starts and minor discoveries, he and his partner, Pierre Taffin, found the mother lode of bituminous coal—the western extension of the Mons coalfield—at the village of Anzin in 1734. They began mining there the next year, but their claim to the concession was challenged by the *grands seigneurs* of the region, the marquis de Cernay and the duc du Croy. Twenty years of haggling and litigation postponed serious exploitation of the concession until the three parties came together (with royal encouragement) to form the Compagnie d'Anzin in 1757. The Anzin Coal Company quickly developed into the largest mining enterprise in France. On the eve of the French Revolution, Anzin employed some 4,000 workers in thirty-seven pits (some over 300 meters deep), utilized a dozen Newcomen steam engines for drainage, produced almost 300,000 tons of coal a year, and earned profits of 50 percent on sales of 3.75 million livres. There was only one other coal mine in what would soon be the department of the Nord, Aniche, conceded to the marquis de Trainel in 1773, but it was not at that time a significant producer.[6]

Anzin operated normally to 1792, but the invasion of northern France by the Prussian and Austrian armies in 1792–1794 forced the closing of its pits, and the onset of the Reign of Terror precipitated the emigration of several of its noble owners and the confiscation of their property (the Desandrouin family did not emigrate, however, and kept their share of the company). Then, the French counterattack in 1794 and the subsequent annexation of the Austrian Netherlands again gave Belgian coal free access to the French market, discouraging further expansion of coal mining at Anzin and elsewhere in the North for twenty years.[7]

Only after 1815 did circumstances again favor the development of the French coal industry. In particular, the new mining law of 1810 ended years of ambiguity about ownership and control of the coal beds. While validating many previous royal concessions, the law reasserted state ownership of the subsoil and set up a procedure by which the new Conseil Général des Mines and the Conseil d'Etat awarded new mining concessions. In addition, the tariff laws of 1816 and 1822 gave French producers a measure of protection against Belgian and English coal imports, and the advance of industrialization—or rather the expectation of rapid advance in the use of coal to power steam engines (especially steam locomotives), to smelt and refine iron, and to provide gaslight in cities (all of which came to pass only at mid-century)—spurred the organization and expansion of coal enterprise after 1815.

The development of the French coal industry during the Bourbon Restoration and July Monarchy was not so much the work of the great noble families (although at some mines the noble heirs of the founders remained in charge) but rather the work of Paris financiers and their political allies, who were in a position to win concessions from the Paris government and to raise the often staggering sums of money needed to get mining operations started. This was seen at Anzin, where rebuilding after 1795 required the infusion of new capital from Paris bankers who replaced the emigré nobles as the leading shareholders. While the Parisian takeover was muted at first by the continued presence of the Desandrouins, it came into full view in 1817, when Casimir Périer acceded to the presidency. In the following fifteen years, Périer oversaw major technological improvements at Anzin and the territorial expansion of the concession, especially the acquisition of Denain in 1831. Under Périer's successor, the Orleanist politician Louis-Adolphe Thiers, Anzin acquired the Hasnon concession and grew to its maximum size, remaining by far France's largest producer of coal in the 1840s.[8]

The success and continued profitability of Anzin encouraged further exploration of the Valenciennes coal basin, peaking in what Marcel Gillet calls "la fièvre des houillères"—a fever of speculation in new concessions in 1834–1839—and the relaunching of the Aniche mine in 1840 after fifty years of stagnation and mismanagement. Moreover, it led to systematic efforts to find the westward extension of the northern coalfield beyond Aniche, which culminated in the discovery and definition of the Pas-de-Calais coal basin in the 1840s and 1850s.[9]

Meanwhile, other well-connected financiers and politicians were active in reorganizing and expanding the coal industry of the Center and the Massif Central, often as part of an effort to develop coal-based metallurgy or to create freestanding enterprises to meet the growing demand for fuel. In the Saône-et-Loire, Jean-Conrad Hottinguer, of the Paris merchant bank that dominated the Le Havre cotton trade, took over the Epinac mine in the 1820s (it would remain in the Hottinguer family into the twentieth century), and the Paris paper merchant Jean-François Chagot and his sons took control of the mining, glass-, and ironmaking complex in and around Le Creusot. The Chagots sold the Le Creusot ironworks to Manby and Wilson of Paris in 1826 and the glassworks to Baccarat in the early 1830s, and concentrated their attention on Blanzy, a coal mine fifteen kilometers from Le Creusot. In 1834, Chagot's youngest son, Jules, took over management of the mine, and within ten years Blanzy was producing nearly 100,000 tons of coal a year, making it one of France's largest (although still dwarfed by Anzin, which produced up to 700,000 tons a year in the 1840s). Meanwhile, at Le Creusot, the Schneider brothers of Lorraine, backed by the Seillière bank, took charge in 1836, after the failure of Manby and Wilson, and expanded coal production as part of their relaunching of the metallurgical enterprise (see the next chapter). Although most of its output was used internally in the smelting and refining of iron, Le Creusot produced nearly as much coal as Blanzy in the 1840s.[10]

In the neighboring department of the Allier, the Commentry coal mine, first conceded in 1788 but not well exploited, fell into the hands of the ironmaster Nicolas Rambourg in 1815. In 1840, Rambourg's three sons hired Stephane Mony, the engineer who directed the building of the Paris–Saint-Germain railroad for the Pereires, to manage the mine. Mony devoted the rest of his life to developing and assuring markets for Commentry coal, which soon took him and the Rambourgs into metallurgy (the Hauts-Fourneaux et Forges de Commentry) and railroad building (the Commentry-Montluçon line). In 1853, Mony merged the Houillères de Commentry with the Fourchambault ironworks and the Société des Hauts-Fourneaux de Montluçon to form Commentry-Fourchambault-Montluçon, and Commentry—like Le Creusot—disappeared into an integrated metallurgical enterprise.[11]

Meanwhile, to the south, Paris financiers and their allies spearheaded the development of major coal-mining companies at four locations along the southern edge of the Massif Central: Alais in the department of the Gard, Aubin in the Aveyron, Carmaux in the Tarn, and Grais-sessac in the Hérault. At Grand'combe, Rochebelle, and other sites in the Gardou Valley near Alais, the Norman entrepreneur Pierre-François Tubeuf set out to introduce large-scale pit mining under a broad grant from the royal government in the 1770s, only to be frustrated by entrenched local interests led by the marquis de Castries. In an effort to relaunch capitalistic coal mining in this region after the Revolution, the Napoleonic authorities set up eight new concessions in 1809, with the sons of Tubeuf receiving the Rochebelle concession and the new duc de Castries receiving the Grand'combe concession. But given low local demand, high costs of exploitation, and the lack of good transportation links to outside markets, the new concessionnaires did little to develop these mines over the next twenty years.[12]

Coal mining did not really take off in the Gard until the late 1820s, when the Napoleonic marshal, Nicholas Jean de Dieu Soult, duc de Dalmatia, in association with various Paris financiers, purchased Rochebelle and other mines as part of a larger plan to set up English-style, coal-fired iron production at Alais. At the same time, two local businessmen purchased Grand'combe from the Castries family with financial support from Odilon Barrot, a prominent Paris politician who hailed from the nearby Lozère, and merged it into a united Grand'combe Mining Company. However, the ultimate success of both Grand'combe and Soult's iron enterprise depended on building a railroad linking the region to Beaucaire on the Rhône River. To build that railroad, Soult brought in the young engineer Paulin Talabot. In a complex series of maneuvers between 1833 and 1837, Talabot merged his railway company with Grand'combe, secured a 6 million franc loan from the central government to finance railroad building, and attracted additional backing from the Rothschilds, who ended up with the controlling interest in Grand'combe. Talabot then expanded coal production at Grand'combe to supply fuel to the Alais forge (which in turn was supplying rails to the new Alais-Beaucaire Railroad), and, once the railroad was operating, Grand'combe began sending coal to Marseille and other urban markets. Coal production in the Alais basin increased from a mere 30,000 tons in 1830 to 100,000 tons in 1840 and 300,000 in 1846. At mid-century, Grand'combe was France's fifth largest coal company.[13]

Elsewhere in the southern Massif, Louis XVIII's former prime minister, the duc Decazes, launched an ambitious venture to develop the coal and iron deposits of the Aubin basin in the department of the Aveyron. By the 1840s, the Houillères et Fonderies de l'Aveyron—known simply as Decazeville, after the company town—had emerged as a major producer of coal as part of its primary business, supplying rails to the Paris-Orléans Railroad.[14] Meanwhile, in the department of the Tarn, the Solages family, which was mining coal at Carmaux in the early 1800s mainly to provide fuel for the family's glassworks, began expanding and modernizing the mine in 1835 in anticipation of an industrial takeoff in southwest France. Production at Carmaux rose to 40,000 tons a year by the 1840s, but it soon became clear that, as elsewhere, further growth would depend on better transportation. Thus, in 1853, Achille de Solages reorganized the Mines de Carmaux, until then a closely held family firm, as a joint-stock company in order to undertake the building of a railroad from Carmaux to Albi, only to see the new company swept up in the speculative fever that accompanied the construction of the national rail system in the 1850s. Another decade would pass and the Carmaux Company would undergo further reorganization before it finally came into its own as a coal enterprise of national stature (see below).[15]

The fourth major coal mining basin of the southern Massif was found along the Orb River around the town of Graissessac in the department of the Hérault. As elsewhere in the region, the Graissessac basin had been exploited by artisan-miners and small-time entrepreneurs until the central government stepped in and divided it into a half dozen major concessions in 1808. Because of their isolation from industrial and urban markets and the lack of good transportation, these concessions remained little developed through the 1820s (total output of the basin was only 12,000 tons in 1830). Change came in the person of Philippe Usquin, a former Napoleonic officer with ties to moneymen in Paris and Montpellier, who succeeded in merging the various concessions in the 1840s in the hope of turning Graissessac into a major supplier of coal to southern railroads and Mediterranean steamships. To realize this ambition, however, Usquin needed a railroad to move his coal forty kilometers over rugged terrain to Béziers. When that railroad was finally completed in 1858, coal production at Graissessac took off, and by 1869 Graissessac was the fifteenth largest coal company in France, with an annual output of 188,000 tons.[16]

The most important coal basin in France in the first half of the nineteenth century, eclipsing those of the southern Massif and even the Nord, lay in the department of the Loire around the city of Saint-Etienne, fifty kilometers southeast of Lyon. Because numerous outcrops made it so easy to mine coal in the Loire basin, early efforts to define and assign specific concessions failed. Instead, as happened throughout the Massif Central, myriad small-scale, freelance mining operations proliferated in the closing years of the eighteenth and the first decade of the nineteenth centuries. As one mining engineer complained in 1808, "nature has spread mineral coal abundantly around Saint-Etienne; it is revealed on the slopes of the hills in every direction, and this very abundance, combined with the unrestricted freedom to exploit it, has engendered a mass of abuses."[17] By 1810, haphazard mining had left hundred of pits abandoned, flooded, and plagued by chronic underground fires.

Under the mining law of 1810, the French government sought to organize and relaunch coal mining in the two basins of the Loire, Saint-Etienne and Rive-de-Gier. The government recognized eight pre-existing concessions, including Roche-la-Molière, the "fief houiller par excellence" of the basin, which in 1820 passed from the Osmond family to the new Compagnie des Mines de Roche-la-Molière et Firminy, headed by Jean-Jacques Baude, a former Napoleonic prefect and a future leader of the Revolution of 1830. Beyond that, the basin was divided into twenty-four "perimeters" which were further divided into some sixty-four new concessions in 1824–1826. Amid interminable haggling and maneuvering over the next decade, these concessions fell into the hands of various local notables, mostly from the ribbon and metals trades, as well as outside entrepreneurs, mainly bankers and merchants from Paris, Lyon, and Geneva. Despite the lack of order in the exploitation of the coal basin, production shot up as the metallurgy of the region expanded after 1815. As early as 1826, the output of the Loire surpassed that of the Nord basin (560,000 tons versus 360,000), and it continued to grow in the 1830s, when the completion of France's first two railroads—from Saint-Etienne to the Loire River at André-zieux and from Saint-Etienne to Lyon—gave the Loire colliers access to the two largest markets in France, Paris and Lyon.[18]

As other coal basins opened in the 1830s and as Anzin increasingly gained access to Paris via the Saint-Quentin Canal, Loire coal tended to be forced back on the local market, and hyper-competition ensued among the many Loire producers. To bring order to the industry and alleviate cutthroat competition, the leading investors in Loire coal undertook to merge concessions, starting in 1838. Within five years, two combines had emerged, the Mines Réunis de Saint-Etienne in the western half of the basin and the Compagnie Générale des Mines de la Loire in the eastern half. It was then easy for Paris financiers, led by François Bartholony of the Paris-Orléans Railroad and Gustave Delahante, to complete the merger. In 1845, Bartholony and Delahante brought the two Loire companies into a single company, which nearly monopolized coal production in the basin (accounting for 1.2 million of 1.7 million tons produced in 1847) and immediately displaced Anzin as the largest coal company in France.[19]

An array of local industrialists in the Loire—all important consumers of coal—feared the market power of the new Compagnie de la Loire and sought from the beginning to have it broken up as an illegal monopoly. Eventually they gained the support of the authorities in Paris. In October 1852, after overthrowing the Second Republic and assuming dictatorial powers, Louis-Napoleon Bonaparte intervened to block a proposed merger between the Loire Company and Grand'combe, directing that henceforth no mining concession could be acquired by the owner of another concession and thus outlawing mergers like the one that had created the Loire company. Two years later, under threat of prosecution for restraint of trade, the Compagnie de la Loire dissolved itself and was replaced by four *sociétés anonymes*: Mines de la Loire, Houillères de Saint-Etienne, Mines de la Rive-de-Gier, and Montrambert-La Beraudière. Henceforth, the coal industry of the Loire was controlled by an oligopoly of large companies instead of a giant monopoly. Without formally renouncing the movement toward concentration favored by Paris financiers, the French government had put constraints on that movement.[20]

Beyond the Loire itself, the government's decisions on the organization of the Loire coal industry had their greatest impact on the new Pas-de-Calais coalfield. To avoid both the extreme fragmentation that characterized the Loire in the 1830s and the excessive concentration in 1845–1852, the Conseil Général des Mines and the Conseil d'Etat decided to create a limited number of medium-sized concessions in the Pas-de-Calais, with each exploited by a single, independent mining company. Fourteen such concessions had been surveyed and approved by 1862. Because the 1852 decree effectively precluded empire builders

from the industry, the new companies formed to exploit these concessions were not, as elsewhere, the creations of Paris financiers, railroad
companies, or metallurgical interests, but largely the domain of local
interests. Even among the local interests, the new mines as a rule were
not controlled by the established coal companies. Courrières, for example, was founded by Louis Bigo-Danel, a Lille linen spinner who
had bankrolled much of the early exploration of the Pas-de-Calais, and
his nephew Léonard Danel, head of the Nord's largest printing house.
Bigo-Danel and Danel later left Courrières and presided in turn over
the Mines de Lens, which had been founded by local sugar and textile
families, including the Mottes. Béthune was headed by bankers from
Cambrai, the Boittelles, and a Bailleul lawyer and politician, Charles-
Ignace Plichon.[21]

The Coal Companies in Their Prime, 1860–1914

The years from 1860 to the outbreak of World War I proved to be the
golden age of French coal mining, even though coal prices fell continuously in the closing decades of the nineteenth century, the result of
the permanent reduction of import duties on coal after 1860 and the
general economic stagnation of 1875–1895. With the completion of
the French rail network providing a double stimulus (lower transport
costs plus greater demand for coal from the railroads) and with the
continued expansion of coal-based metallurgy, gas lighting, and coal-
powered industry of all types, the consumption of coal in France rose
steadily from an average of 16 million tons a year in 1860–1864 to 42
million tons a year in 1895–1899. The percentage supplied by imports
actually declined, from over 40 percent in 1860 to 25 percent in 1900,
as French coal production tripled in the forty years from 1860 to 1900
(from 10 million tons a year to 30 million).[22]

This dramatic growth in production was accomplished not by adding
new coal basins or concessions but through the efficient exploitation
of existing ones. Indeed, by the end of the Second Empire in 1870, the
French coal industry had more or less attained the geographical and
organizational configuration that it would possess until the nationalization of the industry after World War II. By 1870, there were 611
active coal-mining concessions in France; this figure rose only slightly,
to 636, by the end of the century. Although coal-mining activity continued in all parts of France in the late nineteenth century, the lion's
share of French coal in 1900 came from the seven departments—the

Nord, Pas-de-Calais, Loire, Saône-et-Loire, Allier, Aveyron, and Gard—
and the fifty or so largest concessions in those departments that already
dominated the industry in 1860. Indeed, as Table 1 shows, the list of
the top twenty coal companies in France was remarkably stable from
the 1860s to the 1890s; only the rankings changed, mainly because the
new Pas-de-Calais mines supplanted the older mines of the Nord, Loire,
and Massif Central at the top of the list. This means that the French
coal industry, despite the antitrust action of mid-century, continued to
be dominated by an oligopoly of large firms (the decree of 1852 and
the division of the Pas-de-Calais field simply assured that the oligopoly
consisted of twenty to twenty-five firms instead of five to ten). Even
more paradoxically, it means that the French coal industry—small in
comparison to its British, German, and American counterparts in the
late nineteenth century—played host to some of the largest industrial
enterprises in France (and in Europe) at the end of the nineteenth century.

In the North, given the newness of the Pas-de-Calais coalfield, it is
hardly surprising that the companies with the largest holdings in the
Pas-de-Calais—Lens, Courrières, Vicoigne-Noeux, Béthune, Bruay—
rose to the top of the industry by the end of the century. More surprising, however, was the continued importance of Anzin. Although
declining in relative terms (it would never again dominate the French
coal industry as it had before 1840), Anzin nonetheless expanded its
output from 900,000 tons in 1860 to almost 3 million per year in the
mid-1890s and thereby remained the largest mining company in
France. Indeed, visiting Anzin in the early 1880s, the journalist Julien
Turgan pronounced it still "in a class by itself." With eight concessions
covering 28,000 hectares (a quarter of the entire area of the Nord–Pas-
de-Calais field) and with 10,000 miners working twenty-one of the
sixty-seven active pits in the region, Anzin clearly justified Turgan's
awe.[23] According to Bertrand Gille, Anzin was the sixth largest business
enterprise in France in 1881 (only the five largest trunk railroads were
larger).[24]

Beyond its sheer size, the interesting thing about Anzin in the late
nineteenth century is how this already well-worked mine managed to
increase output and lower production costs at the same time (as mines
age, the natural tendency is for costs to rise as pits are deepened and
galleries extended). Keeping Anzin competitive and profitable was the
achievement of Commines de Marsilly, the managing director from the
1860s to the 1880s. To meet the twin challenges of increased British

imports and the growth of the Pas-de-Calais field (from which Anzin was excluded), de Marsilly undertook systematic modernization. He concentrated financial resources on the most efficient pits, adopted new mining technology (such as the use of inclined planes to improve underground haulage), and expanded the sales organization. Most importantly, de Marsilly aggressively attacked labor costs by switching

Table 1. The twenty largest French coal companies, 1860s–1890s

	1865–1869		1890–1894	
Rank	Company/Department[a]	Output (in thousands of tons)	Company/Department[a]	Output (in thousands of tons)
1	Anzin (N)	1,390	Anzin (N)	2,855
2	Saint-Etienne (L)	629	Lens (PdC)	1,959
3	Firminy Roche-la-Molière (L)	503	Courrières (PdC)	1,338
4	Blanzy (S-L)	483	Blanzy (S-L)	1,261
5	Grand'combe (G)	480	Vicoigne-Noeux (PdC)	1,103
6	Aniche (N)	450	Béthune (PdC)	1,072
7	Mines de Loire (L)	394	Grand'combe (G)	929
8	Montrambert-La Béraudière (L)	383	Bruay (PdC)	895
9	Lens (PdC)	350	Aniche (N)	821
10	Vicoigne-Noeux (PdC)	308	Firminy Roche-la-Molière (L)	735
11	Rive-de-Gier (L)	300	Marles (PdC)	712
12	Courrières (PdC)	252	Liévin (PdC)	677
13	Le Creusot (S-L)	220	Montrambert-La Béraudière (L)	636
14	Béthune (PdC)	183	Dourges (PdC)	566
15	Graissessac (H)	180	Saint-Etienne (L)	521
16	Douchy (N)	171	Escarpelle (PdC)	466
17	Carmaux (T)	122	Mines de Loire (L)	453
18	Escarpelle (PdC)	122	Carmaux (T)	418
19	Dourges (PdC)	107	Douchy (N)	340
20	Marles (PdC)	100	Meurchin (PdC)	285

Sources: Marcel Gillet, *Les Charbonnages du nord de la France au XIXe siècle* (Paris, 1973); Jean Bouvier et al., *Le Mouvement du profit en France au XIXe siècle* (Paris, 1965); (for Graissessac) Christopher Johnson, *The Life and Death of Industrial Languedoc* (Oxford, 1995); and (for Rive-de-Gier), L-J Gras, *Histoire économique générale des mines de la Loire* (Saint-Etienne, 1922).

a. Abbreviations for departments are as follows: G = Gard, H = Hérault, L = Loire, PdC = Pas-de-Calais, N = Nord, S-L = Saône-et-Loire, T = Tarn.

from day wages to piece rates, which allowed management to extract as much work from miners in five days as it previously got in six; he also laid off maintenance workers and reassigned timbering to the miners. As a result, between 1883 and 1885, the number of miners at Anzin increased from 4,600 to 5,400 even as the total workforce was reduced from 10,000 to 8,000, and output per worker rose from 200 tons a year in 1869–1882 to 300 tons a year in 1882–1895. Labor costs per ton fell from 6 francs to 4.25 francs, and total costs per ton fell from 11.6 francs in 1875 to 7.14 in 1892.[25] Of course, such economic policies had their social repercussions: In 1884 Anzin was the scene of the largest coal miners' strike in an era of strikes (serving as the model for Emile Zola's *Germinal* and cementing Anzin's reputation as a labor exploiter). But the failure of the strike postponed unionization at Anzin for twenty years and secured labor peace, albeit grudging, into the twentieth century. The company continued to pay handsome dividends to the small circle of grand bourgeois and noble families that controlled the mine throughout the nineteenth century. Among these were the Périers, led by Jean Casimir-Périer, who took time out from his tenure as president of Anzin to serve briefly as president of France in 1894–1895.

To the south, changing economic conditions brought the relative decline—and in some instances the absolute decline—of the mining companies of the Center and Massif Central that had been so prominent at mid-century. This was particularly true in the Loire, where the collapse of iron- and steelmaking in the 1880s deflated local demand for coking coal, and where some concessions were starting to be played out. The latter was the case at the Société des Houillères de Rive-de-Gier. Hailed in 1855 as the "most favored" of the four companies that emerged from the break up of the Compagnie de la Loire, Rive-de-Gier's production declined from 489,000 tons in 1855 to 300,000 tons in 1866 and to only 69,000 tons by 1887. Rive-de-Gier shares that sold for 260 francs in 1862 were worth only 8 francs by 1889. In 1911 the company was liquidated. The second of the four successors of the Mines de la Loire—the eponymous Société des Mines de la Loire— avoided the fate of Rive-de-Gier but declined relative to the other large coal companies largely because the conservative managers, strapped with high fixed financial and production costs, put off needed improvements in mining technology.[26] Meanwhile, the other big coal companies of the Loire did better. Under the innovative management of Félix de Vilaine, Montrambert-La Béraudière increased its output from 146,000 tons in 1855 to 376,000 in 1888 and to 754,000 by 1897. Through similar good management and new technology, including mechanical washing, electric lighting, and conveyor belt sorting, Firminy Roche-la-Molière maintained its position as the largest producer in the Loire basin, with output rising to 905,000 tons by 1899.[27] But not even Firminy Roche-la-Molière could match the growth of the big mines in the Nord–Pas-de-Calais field. Consequently, as Table 1 shows, it fell from third position among French coal companies in the 1860s to tenth in the 1890s.

To the south of the Loire in the department of the Hérault, the Graissessac mine sank into a long decline that Christopher Johnson attributes to the poor regional infrastructure: The Graissessac-Béziers railroad was so poorly constructed that it could handle coal trains of only twenty cars, versus the fifty to sixty cars that were standard on other lines. This raised Graissessac's freight costs to the point that it could no longer compete in the lucrative market for steamer coal in Marseille. Production fell from its all-time high of 269,000 tons in 1875 to 248,000 tons in 1891, and the company maintained its profitability only through draconian cuts in wages and benefits that precipitated a bitter strike in 1894.[28]

Elsewhere in the South, the story was more positive. In the Aveyron, Decazeville all but abandoned iron production in the 1860s and limped through the Great Depression of the 1870s and 1880s by selling coal to the railroads. It was reborn as a center for steelmaking in the 1890s after being acquired by Commentry-Fourchambault in 1892 (see Chapter 12).[29] In the Tarn, the Carmaux Mining Company, after almost being destroyed in the speculation associated with the Grand Central Railroad in the 1850s, was relaunched as a *société anonyme* in 1862 and received an infusion of new capital and new management in the person of Baron Réné Reille, who joined the board as a representative of the Paris-Orléans Railroad and served as chairman from 1884 to 1898. In the 1860s, the company sold off its glassworks and started "exporting" its coal and coke to other industrial areas via the recently completed Toulouse-Lexos railroad. In the 1870s and 1880s it upgraded its equipment and added a plant to make the coal briquettes used more and more by steamships and locomotives. As a result, Carmaux's output quadrupled to over 475,000 tons a year, which placed it among France's twenty largest coal companies in the last quarter of the nineteenth century.[30] At Grand'combe in the Gard, the story was similar. Under the long-term leadership of Edouard Graffin,

Grand'combe modernized its underground and surface operations and, most importantly, compensated for the decline of metallurgy at Alais by turning, as did Carmaux, to the manufacture of briquettes to fuel the steamships operating out of Marseille. As a consequence, Grand'combe doubled its production between the 1860s and 1890s and remained one of France's ten largest coal companies at the turn of the century.

Even more impressive was the performance of Blanzy in the Saône-et-Loire. Under the continued leadership of various members of the Chagot family, Blanzy increased its production steadily, from 581,000 tons in 1873 to 1.5 million tons in 1895, thereby keeping it in fourth place among all French mining companies. Instrumental to this success was a series of technical improvements that kept costs under control as output rose. Devised mainly by Léonce Chagot, Blanzy's chief mining engineer from 1846 to 1876 and managing director from 1877 to 1893, these improvements included the pioneering use of compressed air to power drilling and cutting; long wall mining (rather than "room and pillar mining"), which maximized the amount of each seam mined; mechanical ventilation to remove dangerous gases from the pits; and large-scale, mechanized washing and sorting at a central location at Montceau-les-Mines, the company town. Just as important for Blanzy's success was its skill in marketing. Blanzy was well situated to distribute its coal throughout much of France via the P-L-M Railroad and the Canal du Centre, which ran along the entire length of the concession and which the company fully utilized with its fleet of 200 canal barges. To this was added the largest sales organization of any French mining company, including twelve coal depots scattered around the country.[31] Sales in the open market, however, gradually gave way to long-term contracts to supply coal to the P-L-M Railroad and Châtillon-Commentry, and ultimately Blanzy fell under the control of the latter, reflected in the fact that in 1900, when the last Chagot departed and Blanzy was turned into a *société anonyme*, Henry Darcy of Châtillon-Commentry became president. As we shall see below, this sort of vertical integration of big coal with big steel became increasingly common in France after 1900.

In concluding this brief survey of the rise of the French coal industry, we should note that coal mining presents an especially good example of a paradox that, to a greater or lesser extent, is present in all areas of industrial capitalism in nineteenth-century France. On the one hand, we see the French state playing a central, dominant role in the affairs of the leading French coal companies, first via the concession system that allowed officials in Paris to determine who entered the industry and on what terms, and second through the close regulation of day-to-day operations in the pits by the inspectors and engineers of the Corps des Mines (an important facet of the industry that space limitations kept us from examining). On the other hand, in spite of all this government oversight and "interference," coal mining in nineteenth-century France proved to be a remarkably dynamic and entrepreneurial industry. We can see this in the efforts of the people—mainly financiers and politicians from Paris and Lyon or engineers in their employ—who founded or assumed control of the big coal companies in the early 1800s at a time when the viability and profitability of these ventures were by no means assured. It can also be seen in the efforts of the professional managers—usually trained engineers like Commines de Marsilly or Léonce Chagot—who later addressed the myriad challenges of working France's thin, convoluted coal beds. By introducing new technologies and by squeezing more labor from their miners, they succeeded in extracting ever-larger quantities of coal at steady or even declining unit costs (the opposite of what normally occurs in mining), and this in turn allowed the French companies to maintain their share of the domestic market—and their profit margins—in an age of strong foreign competition and declining prices.

For all its dynamism and success, however, coal mining, even more than textiles, was a mature industry in France by the end of the nineteenth century. No amount of technological progress or labor exploitation could overcome the finite limits to France's coal resources or postpone forever the increase in production costs that would end the industry's competitiveness (or force it to seek unacceptable levels of tariff protection). Consequently, even as French mines continued to expand their output, French capitalists were looking outside France for new sources of coal. By the early 1900s they had launched a number of firms to find and exploit the coal deposits of Russia, Belgium, Germany, and the colonies. Beyond that, they were eyeing the next generation of fuels—petroleum and hydroelectricity—and moving toward commercializing the most promising applications of coal chemistry. Coal would remain important in the twentieth century but mainly as the source of coke, an indispensable ingredient in the making of iron and steel, and as the raw material for organic chemicals. Thus it was increasingly bound up with those sectors of heavy industry.

CHAPTER SIX

The Capitalism of Iron and Steel

In France, as in Great Britain, the rise of industrial capitalism in the nineteenth century was bound up with the advent of large-scale production of various metals, of which iron and steel (a special form of iron) were by far the most important.[1] Although the French iron and steel industry never matched the British industry in total output and was eventually outstripped by the German and American industries in the course of the nineteenth century, it nonetheless grew tenfold between the 1820s and the 1880s. As late as 1869, France produced more iron and steel than any other country in continental Europe.[2] As the French iron and steel industry developed, it joined coal in giving rise to some of the country's largest industrial enterprises.

As in the case of textiles, the rise of the iron and steel industry depended on utilizing and adapting technology first developed in Great Britain. The transfer of this technology and the emergence of the principal French iron and steel companies unfolded in three more or less chronological stages. Stage 1 (1815–1860) saw the "old metallurgy"— the smelting of iron ore and the refining of wrought iron from pig iron with charcoal—challenged and gradually replaced by the new "English" metallurgy of coke-fired smelting and coal-fired refining. The new metallurgy brought with it larger, more concentrated ironmaking enterprises, usually organized as joint-stock companies. It also brought the founding of firms to produce steel in small quantities using the new crucible and cementation processes. Stage 2 (1860–1880) witnessed the advent of mass-produced steel through the introduction of the Bessemer converter and the Siemens-Martin open-hearth process. This in turn forced a retooling of the big iron companies, brought the expansion of the small-scale steel producers, and marginalized traditional iron producers that could not modernize. Stage 3 (1880–1914) was the era of the Thomas-Gilchrist "basic steel" process (versus the "acid steel" processes in Stage 2). This was especially significant for France because it allowed the full exploitation of the iron of Lorraine—previously worthless for steelmaking because of its high phosphorous content—and brought about the rapid shift of the French steel industry from central France to the northern and eastern border. It was in this stage that French iron and steel firms attained the size that, even by British, German, or American standards, qualified as "big business." This stage will be discussed in Part III; here we will concentrate on the rise of France's leading iron and steel enterprises during the first two stages from 1815 to 1880.

From the Old to the New Metallurgy, 1815–1860

Throughout France in the eighteenth century, as in prior centuries, numerous small, water-powered forges, using local iron deposits and charcoal from nearby forests, produced small quantities of iron (and less frequently steel) to meet the mostly agrarian population's need for farm implements, knives and files, pots and pans, and other traditional kinds of hardware. These forges were operated as a sideline by landlords as a way of deriving cash income from their wooded property, or as a full-time business by professional forgemasters *(maîtres de forge)* who leased the woodlands and water mills from their aristocratic owners. In either case, most iron production remained small-scale, seasonal, and geographically dispersed.[3]

The needs of an expanding merchant marine for anchors and other naval fittings and the growing demand of the French state for cannon and other military hardware created opportunities to organize iron production on a larger scale in the course of the eighteenth century. Moreover, the government seemed ready to promote the adoption of English-style, coal-based iron production by the 1780s when it sponsored Ignace de Wendel's effort to set up the first coke-fired blast furnace in France at Le Creusot.[4] The outbreak of war in 1792 and the almost continuous warfare from then until 1815 might have served as a catalyst for the rapid expansion of French iron production on the basis of the new technology. But, as Denis Woronoff has shown, this did not happen for a variety of reasons: the difficulty in solving technical problems with the coal-based technology when access to English know-how was restricted; the availability of additional iron supplies on advantageous terms after the conquest of the Low Countries and the Rhineland; and the elasticity of charcoal-based production within France, which allowed it to be expanded to meet new demand.[5] The upshot was that the French put the implementation of the new coal- and coke-based metallurgy on hold, so the French iron industry remained in 1815 what it had been in 1789—rural, dispersed, and charcoal based. More specifically, as a detailed foldout map in Woronoff's book shows, the industry in 1811 consisted of hundreds of small water-driven forges situated on the upland tributaries of major rivers in those areas with good woodlands and good iron deposits, notably the Nivernais, Berry, and Burgundy in the Center, the Franche-Comté in the East, the Pyrenees in the South, and the Dauphiné in the Southeast.

But this situation soon began to change. Even as the traditional metallurgy survived and expanded after 1815, forgemasters seeking to emulate the success of their English counterparts and, even more, financiers seeking attractive investments for their wartime profits began forming partnerships, *sociétés en commandite,* and even full-fledged *sociétés anonymes* to undertake the mass production of iron with English technology in the decade after Waterloo. By 1822 they had won the imposition of an ultra-protectionist tariff on imported iron goods, which Bertrand Gille has called "the indispensable pre-condition for innovation" in metallurgy.[6] Still, even with tariff protection, development of the industry was held back by continuing problems in applying the new technology to the kind of iron and coal found in France and by the lack of demand for large quantities of middling-to-poor-quality iron (which is what "English" forges could produce).

It was only in the 1830s and 1840s, when railroad construction began, that the new metallurgy took off. As the biggest public works project in French history to that time, the building of the railroads accomplished what the wars of 1792–1815 had not: the creation of a real market for mass-produced iron (Serge Benoit estimates that between 1850 and 1880 the railroads absorbed 25 percent of French iron production and 80 percent of French steel production). Also important was growing demand for structural iron—T-beams, I-beams, ornamental ironwork—especially during the massive rebuilding of Paris in the 1850s and 1860s.[7] With the advent of the mass market for iron and steel there arose a cluster of large-scale enterprises that proved to be precocious in their degree of vertical integration (that is, each firm combined several discrete stages of production, from iron and coal mining to smelting, refining, and fabrication) and equally precocious in their degree of concentration (by 1869, the ten largest iron companies accounted for more than 50 percent of output).[8] Some of these firms would continue to dominate the industry in France until the mid-twentieth century.

In looking at the early history of the major French iron and steel companies, we confront the question of origins. Bertrand Gille has characterized the new metallurgy in France as the work of men coming from outside the circle of established forgemasters. More specifically, he sees it as the work of the same merchant capitalists and financiers—mainly from Paris and Lyon—who were spearheading the building of the railroads and for whom development of coal and iron production was simply a way to ensure the availability of critical raw materials for their railroads through a kind of backward integration.[9] While there is much truth in this, we must also recognize that the financiers and railroad promoters could not revolutionize the iron industry by themselves. They also needed engineers with the expertise to set up and operate the new smelters, forges, and foundries. Some of these engineers came from merchant capitalist families, some from the old service nobility, and some from modest origins. Moreover, a few of the established ironmaking families proved to be dynamic and resourceful enough to play a role in the new metallurgy independent of the big financiers and railroad promoters, thereby providing a measure of continuity between the old and new metallurgy. This is best seen in the case of the Wendels.

The Wendel iron enterprise was founded in 1704 when Martin Wendel, son of an officer in the service of the Duke of Lorraine, acquired the Hayange forge on the Fensch River between Metz and Thionville. Exploiting local supplies of iron and wood, Wendel and his son Charles built Hayange into the largest iron enterprise in Lorraine in the eighteenth century. Charles' son Ignace experimented with a coke-charcoal mixture in the blast furnaces of Hayange before moving on to Le Creusot in the 1780s (see below). Following the death of Charles de Wendel in 1784, his widow, known as "Madame d'Hayange," kept the enterprise going into the years of the Revolution. However, other family members emigrated, and in 1795 the Revolutionary government confiscated Hayange and imprisoned Madame Wendel. The same year Ignace de Wendel died of an opium overdose in Vienna. By 1800 it seemed that, in the words of the firm's historian René Sedillot, "a century of effort [by the Wendels had been] annihilated."[10]

In 1803, however, Napoleon offered an amnesty to emigrés, and François de Wendel, the son of Ignace, returned from exile. With financial help from relatives and local bankers, he repurchased Hayange from the French government and in 1811 acquired a second forge at Moyeuvre on the Orne River. After studying the new metallurgy in England in 1817, he set up coke-fired blast furnaces and coal-fired puddling furnaces, along with rolling mills and the other elements of an up-to-date *forge à l'anglaise* at Hayange and Moyeuvre. When François de Wendel died in 1825, his ironworks were producing 6,000 tons of pig iron and 5,000 tons of "English iron" a year, making Wendel et Cie the third largest iron enterprise in France.[11]

To capitalize on the burgeoning demand for rails for the railroads and iron plate for naval construction, François de Wendel's successors—his son Charles and son-in-law Theodore de Gargan—greatly expanded operations at Hayange and Moyeuvre in the 1840s and 1850s. Moreover, both plants were connected by rail to the company's coal mines and coke furnaces at Stiring, near Saarbrücken, and at Seraing in Belgium, thereby alleviating what had long been Wendel's biggest problem, a chronic shortage of coal and coke. By the time Charles de Wendel died in 1870, Wendel et Cie was the largest iron company in France, employing some 7,000 workers and producing 134,500 tons of pig iron and 112,500 tons of iron a year—roughly a fortyfold increase since 1825.[12]

While the Wendel family enterprise spearheaded the development of modern ironmaking in Lorraine, to the south, in the ironfields of Berry and Burgundy and in the coal fields ringing the Massif Central, the new metallurgy was introduced by new joint-stock companies. Chief among these was Le Creusot, founded by Ignace de Wendel and later brought to maturity by two other Lorrainers, Adolphe and Eugène Schneider.

Located in the uplands between the Loire and Saône valleys in southern Burgundy, Le Creusot was one of the few places in France where good quality coking coal was known to lie in proximity to substantial deposits of iron ore in the late eighteenth century. It is thus not surprising that in 1781 Ignace de Wendel chose it as the site for the first major effort to bring the English system of ironmaking to France. With capital raised from a wide variety of investors, including King Louis XVI, and with the technical assistance of the English forgemaster

William Wilkinson, Wendel built France's most technologically advanced forge. In 1785, Le Creusot turned out 5,000 tons of iron (compared to 900 tons at Hayange), but in the 1790s, amid the turmoil of the Revolution, Wendel fled the country and production at Le Creusot fell dramatically. Over the next forty years, Le Creusot passed through various hands, never ceasing production but never living up to its potential. The Chagots of Blanzy took control in 1818 but soon passed it on to Aaron Manby and Daniel Wilson, the English steam engine makers at Charenton. Although Le Creusot was the second or third largest producer of iron in the country in the early 1830s, low demand and low prices rendered its production largely profitless. By 1833 Manby and Wilson were bankrupt.

In 1836, Le Creusot was purchased by four outside investors—Louis Boigues, a Paris iron merchant (and proprietor of the Fourchambault ironworks), the banker F-A Seillière, and Seillière's longtime associates, Adolphe and Eugène Schneider. The new owners proceeded to relaunch Le Creusot as a *société en commandite*, with the Schneider brothers as managing directors. Aided by a professional engineer, Francis Bourdon, and helped even more by the onset of railroad building, the Schneiders quickly brought production at Le Creusot up to capacity. In 1838, they expanded that capacity by installing their first hot-air blast furnace and a rolling mill for rails. They also began to integrate forward into the production of steam engines and locomotives and even began to build steamboats in their shipyard at Chalon-sur-Saône.[13]

Like all the major ironmakers, the Schneiders concentrated on furnishing matériel to the railroads in the decade of the forties. Between 1841 and 1847, Le Creusot quadrupled its rail production, mostly to fill a 34,000-ton order from the Paris-Lyon line. It also expanded its production of locomotives and steam engines. Indeed, on the eve of the 1848 revolution, Le Creusot was rapidly moving beyond the manufacture of iron to become France's first fully integrated machinery manufacturer, and much of its subsequent history must be considered as part of that industry (see the next chapter). Suffice it to say here that Le Creusot remained a leader in coal and iron production through the middle decades of the nineteenth century. We should also note that, having started out as a joint-stock company, Le Creusot soon became a family enterprise à la the Wendels. Although the Seillières continued to play an important role in the financial affairs of Le Creusot, a majority of the shares came to be concentrated in the hands of the Schneiders, and, after the death of Adolphe in a riding accident in 1845, Le Creusot was for all intents and purposes the property of Eugène Schneider.[14]

By contrast, most of the other major iron and steel companies moved toward ever more fragmented ownership and toward professional management, with day-to-day control vested in a salaried *directeur-général* responsible to a board of directors. This was the case with the six iron companies that, next to the Wendel and Schneider firms, were the largest in France in the mid-nineteenth century: Decazeville, Alais, Fourchambault, Châtillon-Commentry, Terrenoire, and Marine. As we saw in the last chapter, Decazeville and Alais were the brainchildren of two Paris politicians (the duc Decazes and Marshal Soult), who in the 1820s set out to create from scratch new coal-based iron smelting and refining centers that were supplied by their own coal and iron mines in the south of France. Both nearly failed for lack of customers in the early 1830s but were ultimately saved by big orders for rails in the late 1830s and early 1840s (from the Paris-Orleans Railroad in the case of Decazeville, and from Paulin Talabot's Alais-Beaucaire line in the case of Alais).[15] Terrenoire and Marine Steel arose out of efforts to establish large-scale iron and steel production in the department of the Loire by combining the coal resources of the Saint-Etienne–Rive-de-Gier region with the iron resources of the lower Rhône Valley. Fourchambault and Châtillon-Commentry were created by complex mergers of coal and iron mines, traditional forges and blast furnaces, and new English-style iron mills in Berry and Burgundy; they represented a transitional approach to the new metallurgy, in which wrought iron was refined with coal from pig iron that was produced with charcoal.

Fourchambault was the product of a collaboration between one of France's leading metallurgical engineers, Georges Dufaud, and the Paris iron merchant and army contractor Louis Boigues. After studying the new metallurgy in Wales, Dufaud had set up what has been often cited as the first *forge à l'anglaise* in France at Trézy in the Nivernais in 1818. Two years later, Louis Boigues bought Dufaud's forge and moved it (and Dufaud) to Fourchambault, on the Loire River downstream from Nevers, as part of a larger plan to get in on the ground floor in the mass production of iron by combining the new coal-based refining with the established charcoal-based smelting of Berry. Over the next fifteen years, Boigues, Dufaud, and their associates built Fourchambault into one of the largest metallurgical complexes in France by buying up ten blast furnaces in the surrounding region along with various existing ironworks, including a sheet metal plant at Imphy and a nail factory at Cosne, and by commissioning Dufaud's son-in-law, Emile Martin, to create a foundry near Dufaud's forge at Fourchambault.[16]

The death of Louis Boigues in 1838 led to the reorganization of Fourchambault as a *société en commandite* with authority shared by Dufaud and Boigues' heirs. At the same time, the advent of railroad building gave Fourchambault a chance to greatly expand its customer base. The Boigues, Dufaud, Martin, and other partners in Fourchambault had been deeply involved in promoting the railroads since the 1820s, and that gave Fourchambault the inside track in bidding on rail contracts. Even so, its bids had to be competitive, which meant it had to lower its raw materials costs by switching to *fonte au coke* and by obtaining coal at the lowest possible price. This in turn brought Fourchambault into contact with pig iron producers in Montluçon and the coal mine of Commentry, both of which were accessible to it via the Berry Canal. Eventually, the Fourchambault partners joined with Denys Benoist d'Azy of Montluçon and the Rambourgs and Stephane Mony of the Commentry coal mine to create Commentry-Fourchambault-Montluçon, which was the second largest metallurgical company in France in terms of balance-sheet assets at the time of its founding in 1854.[17]

The birth and evolution of Châtillon-Commentry followed a course similar to Fourchambault's in that it began with the grouping of traditional charcoal-fired blast furnaces around a new *forge à l'anglaise,* followed by a shift to coke-fired smelting and coal-fired refining in the Montluçon-Commentry area. In this case the old iron industry was in northern Burgundy and southern Champagne—the departments of the Haute-Saône, Haute-Marne, and Côte d'Or—the foremost iron-producing region in France at the outset of the nineteenth century. In 1824, Auguste-Louis Viesse de Marmont, Napoleonic marshal and Duke of Ragusa, set out to convert his family's charcoal-fired forge near Châtillon to the English system, using equipment built by Manby and Wilson and coal brought in by barge on the Canal de Bourgogne. This precipitated the consolidation of many of the independently owned forges and blast furnaces in the Châtillonais into a single loose-knit company that, in the words of Bertrand Gille, "took the form of a constellation, with a great refining center [Châtillon] surrounded by an array of small blast furnaces."[18] Marshal Marmont soon dropped out of the enterprise because of financial difficulties, but the process of consolidation continued into the 1830s and 1840s under the leadership of Edouard Bouguéret, J-B Martenot, and Jacques Palotte. By 1845, according to Gille, "there no longer remained in the south of the Haute-Marne or the north of the Côte d'Or a forge that was not dependent, directly or indirectly, on this firm."[19]

Meanwhile, to the southwest in the department of the Allier, Nicolas Rambourg and his sons were creating an ironmaking complex (unrelated to what was developing in the Châtillonais) that included the Tronçais ironworks and the Commentry coal mine. As we saw earlier, when Nicolas Rambourg died in 1835, his three sons brought in Stephane Mony to manage the mine. In 1843, Mony and the Rambourgs founded the Société des Hauts-Fourneaux et Forges de Commentry, which used coal from their Commentry mine to refine wrought iron from pig iron brought in from Berry on the newly opened Montluçon–Saint-Amand section of the Berry Canal. Among the partners in this venture were Jacques Palotte and J-B Martenot of the Châtillon group. Seeking to combine the best of the old and new technology to take advantage of the burgeoning demand for iron by the railroads, Palotte and Martenot proceeded to engineer an informal merger of the Châtillon and Commentry ironmaking enterprises in 1845. For the next ten years, this new entity, known as "Châtillon-Commentry," remained a loose combine that grouped the forges of the Châtillonais and the charcoal-fired forges and furnaces of the Tronçais with various mines, blast furnaces, puddling ovens, and forces in the Montluçon area.[20]

The disparate operations of Châtillon-Commentry were finally brought under unified management in 1856 through the efforts of Hugues Darcy, a well-connected Paris lawyer who had joined Bourguéret, Martenot et Cie (the Châtillon half of the combine) after Louis-Napoleon's coup d'état had ended his political career. In 1862 Châtillon-Commentry was turned into a *société anonyme*, with Darcy as chairman and CEO and Henry Germain (the future founder and president of the Crédit Lyonnais) as vice president. Darcy and Germain then proceeded to streamline the operations of the company by concentrating iron production at four principal sites, each of which had its own specialty. For example, the Saint-Colombe forge near Châtillon—the original *forge Marmont*—specialized in making wire and nails, while Ancy-le-Franc, the forge of the Martenot brothers, specialized in rolling I-beams for Haussmann's new construction projects in the capital. As of 1867, Châtillon-Commentry employed 9,000 workers (second only to Le Creusot) and produced 75,000 tons of various forms of iron, which made it the largest purely metallurgical enterprise in France at that time.[21]

Still other joint-stock iron companies appeared on the scene between 1815 and 1850. Among these was Saut-du-Tarn, a steelmaking enterprise near Albi in the department of the Tarn. Launched by Toulouse capitalists in the 1820s, it was later run by Paulin Talabot's brother Léon. Léon Talabot was also instrumental in the creation and management of Denain-Anzin, the foremost metallurgical enterprise in the department of the Nord, which was formed in 1849 by the merger of Talabot's Forges et Laminoirs d'Anzin (founded in 1836 to supply rails to the projected Northern Railroad) and the nearby ironworks of Serret, Lelièvre, Dumont et Cie of Denain. Meanwhile, in the department of the Oise, the Forges et Fonderies de Montataire was set up to produce sheet iron and tinplate using pig iron smelted from English coal and Spanish ore at Outreau on the Atlantic coast.[22] Of greater significance, however—at least in the mid-nineteenth century—were the iron and steel companies that arose in the department of the Loire and the neighboring departments along the lower Rhône River.

The sources of the Loire's rise to prominence are not hard to find. By 1800, Saint-Etienne and its environs were well established, not in the making of iron and steel, but in the working of iron and steel produced elsewhere. The region's twin specialties were *quincaillerie* (nails, chains, wire, saws, and other hand tools) and *armurerie* (swords, rifles, and other hand weapons). In addition, as we have already seen, the Loire emerged as the leading coal-producing department in France by 1840. This combination of heavy local demand for iron and steel and the local abundance of coal made it almost inevitable that the Loire would become a leader in the new coal-based metallurgy. The development of the iron and steel industry in the Loire involved the rise and fall of numerous enterprises, but the story is best and most simply told by focusing on the two firms that came to dominate the metallurgy of the region by the 1850s, Terrenoire and Marine Steel.

From the beginning, Terrenoire was a regional enterprise that combined the coal of the Loire, the iron of the Ardèche, and the commercial and financial resources of Lyon within the framework of the river, canal, and railroad systems of the lower Rhône Valley. Its origins went back to 1818, when Georges and Louis Frèrejean, Lyon metals dealers and arms makers, set up a coke-fired blast furnace at Pont-l'Evêque near Vienne to smelt the iron ore of La Voulte (Ardèche) using coal from Rive-de-Gier (Loire).[23] In 1821 this became the Société Anonyme des Fonderies et Forges de la Loire et de l'Isère (the first *société anonyme* organized in Lyon). This company soon added an English forge at Terrenoire near Saint-Etienne (the second in the Loire) and acquired nearby mines to supply coal to it. In 1829–1830, Louis Frèrejean moved most of the company's *fonte* production from Pont-l'Evêque to the iron mine pitheads at La Voulte because, thanks to the Givors Canal and the opening of the Saint-Etienne–Lyon railway, it was cheaper to ship Loire coal downstream to La Voulte than to ship iron ore upstream to Pont-l'Evêque. By 1837, in spite of a decade-long depression in the iron market that undermined weaker rivals, "Loire-Isère" was producing 40,000 tons of ore, 15,800 tons of pig iron, and 7,300 tons of wrought iron a year, the largest overall output of any metallurgical company in France.[24]

The railroad boom made the 1840s an age of "beaux bénéfices" for Terrenoire. Indeed, the profits accumulated in 1841–1847 kept the company afloat through the bust of 1848–1851 and allowed it to move aggressively during the subsequent upturn to consolidate its position as the dominant iron producer in the Saint-Etienne–Lyon–lower Rhône region. During the 1850s the company took over the Privas iron mines in the Ardèche, the Saint-Julien and Lorette forges in the Loire, and the Forges et Fonderies de Bessèges in the Gard, and in 1858 it assumed the name Compagnie des Fonderies et Forges de Terrenoire, La Voulte, et Bessèges (Terrenoire, for short). On the eve of the Bessemer revolution, Terrenoire was probably the largest metallurgical company in France, with four coal mines, five iron mines, seven smelting plants, and six ironworks spread over the departments of the Loire, Ardèche, Isère, Gard, and Jura.[25]

Meanwhile another giant was emerging in the Loire out of the world of steelmaking. In contrast to English ironmaking, which put the emphasis on producing large quantities of a relatively low-quality, low-priced commodity, steelmaking remained in the first half of the nineteenth century a quasi-artisanal industry in which skilled workers produced small quantities of a high-quality product at correspondingly high prices. Although the arms makers of Saint-Etienne had long utilized steel in their work, steel was made locally only after 1816, when James Jackson of Birmingham set up France's first crucible steel plant at La Trablaine with a subsidy from the government of Louis XVIII. In 1830 the Jackson steelworks were moved to Assailly, where Jackson's four sons continued to have a virtual monopoly in the production of crucible steel *(acier fondu)* into the 1840s (in 1844, they accounted for 900,000 of the 1.4 million kilograms of *acier fondu* produced in France).[26] At the same time, the Loire also became a center for steel made by the cementation process *(la méthode allemande)* after the state mining engineer Beaunier and the financier Milleret teamed up to bring in German technicians to found a second steelworks at La Bérardière.

From the 1820s to the 1850s, there was a steady increase in the number of steelmaking enterprises in the Loire as, one after another, the artisans first employed by the Jacksons or Beaunier and Milleret struck out on their own, often to exploit patents on new products and processes. Thus in 1825 Jean and Jacob Holtzer, Alsatian steelmakers brought to the Loire by Beaunier, founded their own works at Unieux to make crucible steel from high quality *fonte au bois* imported from Sweden and the Pyrenees. Splitting with his brother in 1842, Jacob Holtzer, assisted by his wife and collaborator Caroline Toussaint, became a leader in technical innovation, producing puddled steel with the Wolf-Lanmüller process and taking the lead in making large steel castings for the armaments industry.[27] In 1853, the five sons of another Loire *forgeron*, François Marrel, began making large steel forgings for the railroads and later became leaders in making armor plate. At the same time, Félix and Xavier Verdié, sons of a local metal worker, formed the Aciéries et Forges de Firminy to exploit a patent for the making of *aciers mixtes* (rails and other products that combined a steel surface with an iron core). Even more important was the enterprise founded by two former employees of Frèrejean, Hippolyte Petin and Jean-Marie Gaudet.

Petin and Gaudet set up their steelworks at Rive-de-Gier in 1839, and in 1841 they installed the first steam hammer in the Loire. Seven years later, they took over a Saint-Chamond firm that had a patent for making seamless steel tires for railroad wheels. By the early 1850s they were major suppliers to both the railroads and the armaments industry. Faced with a possible takeover of the Loire steel industry by the Pereire brothers in 1854, Petin and Gaudet engineered a preemptive strike—a grand merger within Loire steel that put their firm together with Jackson Frères of Assailly, Neyrand and Thiollière's steelworks at Lorette, and the blast furnaces and forges of Parent and Shaken at Vierzon (Cher) and Clavières (Loire). Thus emerged the awkwardly but appropriately named Compagnie des Hauts-Fourneaux, Forges, et Aciéries de la Marine et des Chemins de Fer, known as Marine Steel or Petin and Gaudet (especially after the last of the Jackson brothers sold out in 1858).

Described by Turgan as "one of the industrial glories of our country,"[28] Marine Steel made a variety of products at its various plants in the Loire—rails and other forms of rolled iron at Saint Chamond, steel castings at Assailly (including the prows of the new battleships *Solferino* and *Magenta,* weighing sixteen tons each), springs and other railroad equipment at Lorette, and armor plate and components for giant marine steam engines at Rive-de-Gier, including the 2,300 kilogram crankshaft for the battleship *Eylau,* which was described as "the most colossal and complicated forging ever undertaken within France or abroad." As the largest steel company in France, it employed 8,000 workers, did 30 million francs in business, and paid out 2.7 million in dividends (50 francs per share) in 1860.[29] Of course, Marine was in no position to rest on its laurels. As things turned out, 1860 marked the end of an era in French metallurgy and ushered in a period of accelerating technological and organizational change that would transform Marine and all the other major iron and steel companies of France in the next two decades.

The Age of Steel Begins, 1860–1880

The year 1860 was a double turning point for the French iron and steel industry. First, the signing of the Anglo-French Treaty of Commerce in January overturned the policy of ultraprotection for French metallurgy in place since 1822 (although, in fact, import duties on iron had already been progressively reduced in the course of the 1850s to allow the railroad companies to bring in rails and rolling stock more easily). Henceforth, at least until 1892, the French iron and steel companies found themselves operating in a more or less open market in which increased competition at home was balanced by new opportunities for sales abroad, especially in southern and eastern Europe. Along with the "free trade revolution," 1860 also brought a technological revolution embodied in the Bessemer converter, which made it possible to mass produce the cruder forms of steel, mainly cast steel, for the first time. This was soon followed by the introduction of the open-hearth steelmaking process patented by Pierre-Emile Martin, son of Emile Martin of Fourchambault.[30] By making possible the large-scale production of more sophisticated forms of steel, the Siemens-Martin process (so named because Martin employed a reverbatory gas furnace invented by Siemens of Germany) was in the long run more important than the Bessemer process. In any case, the two innovations together enabled companies already making steel to greatly expand production and to take customers away from the ironmakers, and this meant that the established iron companies had to contemplate shifting to steel-making to keep those customers. The upshot was that, even as the output of iron continued to increase in response to the ever-growing demands of an industrializing economy, the focus of investment and technology decisively shifted from iron to steel. Those companies that successfully made this transition ended up larger and stronger by 1880, while decline awaited those that did not, including not only most of the charcoal-based ironmakers (now two revolutions behind) but also some of the coal-based ironmakers who, only a few years before, had been at the forefront of the French metallurgical industry.

Not surprisingly, those already familiar with making steel led the way in applying the Bessemer and Siemens-Martin technologies. The first Bessemer converter in France was set up in 1858 at Saint-Seurin-sur-l'Isle in the Dordogne by William Jackson, grandson of the founder of France's crucible steel industry, who was seeking to relaunch the independent family enterprise after Jackson Frères was absorbed into the Marine Steel Company in 1854.[31] A more systematic and economically significant application of Bessemer technology was undertaken by the steelmakers of the Loire, who sought to meet the burgeoning demand from the French army and navy for steel guns, steel projectiles, and steel armor and who also saw the opportunity to substitute steel for iron in rails and other railroad equipment.[32] Marine Steel set up the first Bessemer converter in the Loire at Assailly in 1861 and added six more before the end of the decade. Terrenoire had four converters in operation by 1862 and soon led the nation in Bessemer output (in 1868 it produced two-fifths of all steel rails made in France). Verdié et Cie (Firminy) undertook the first large-scale application of the Siemens-Martin process at a new plant near Rive-de-Gier in 1865, and Marine, Terrenoire, and several smaller specialty steel companies (Marrel Frères, Holtzer) quickly followed suit. By the early 1870s, many of the biggest iron companies outside the Loire—notably Wendel, Le Creusot, Châtillon-Commentry, and Denain-Anzin—had moved into Bessemer and/or Siemens-Martin production as well.[33]

Because of the interdependence and linkages among the various stages of metallurgical production, the adoption of the new steel-making technology necessitated huge investments, not just in Bessemer converters and Siemens-Martin furnaces but also in new forges, rolling mills, and sheet metal mills. Above all, it required the renovation and expansion of blast furnaces to produce the larger amounts of pig iron needed by the new steelworks. Bertrand Gille estimates that the conversion from iron to steel cost 120 million francs, with the big companies undertaking "investments that [they] had never before known."[34]

At the same time, the iron companies had to find new sources of iron ore. The early "acidic" Bessemer converters and Siemens-Martin furnaces produced usable steel only from pig iron made with high-grade ore (the phosphorus found in most of the iron ore of continental Europe made it unsuitable for steelmaking). The most famous instance of the problem was the *minette* ore of Lorraine, which was plentiful but so high in phosphorus that the rising *fonte* producers of Lorraine who depended on it had to forego the mass production of steel until the Thomas-Gilchrist basic steel process was invented in 1878 (see Chapter 12). Meanwhile, the iron companies of central France that did move into steelmaking were forced to look for sources of high-quality hematite ore outside of France. Some found it in northern Spain, others went to the Mediterranean. Marine Steel was already mining and smelting ore on Corsica in 1860 and soon opened mines on Sardinia. Le Creusot found high-grade ore on the island of Elba. But the largest and most promising deposits were discovered in the new French colony of Algeria.

Algeria had a special place in the hearts of the Saint-Simonian engineers who envisioned a "grande système de la Méditerranée" and who were so instrumental in the industrial development of France in the mid-nineteenth century. One of these, Henri Fournel, formerly of Le Creusot, found iron and lead in the Edouah Mountains near Bône (Annaba) in the early 1840s. Another Saint-Simonian, Jules Talabot (brother of Paulin Talabot), was given the first concession to mine this iron in 1845. The concession was revoked for non-exploitation in 1848 but reinstated in 1852, at which time Jules ceded it to Paulin. In contrast to other would-be developers of Algerian resources, who tried unsuccessfully to smelt Algerian ore in Algeria with imported coke, Paulin Talabot looked toward exporting the ore to the existing smelters of southern France. This plan took on new urgency when a lode of very pure hematite was discovered at Mokta-el-Hadid in 1857 and when the unsuitability of most French ore for Bessemer steel became evident a few years later. In 1861 Talabot built a railroad from Mokta-el-Hadid to Bône, where new facilities for handling ore exports were being constructed. Then, as we saw in Chapter 2, he founded the Société Générale des Transports Maritimes à Vapeur (SGTMV) to transport the ore from Bône to Marseille, whence he could distribute it to steelworks throughout the southeastern quadrant of France via his Paris-Lyon-Mediterranean Railroad. By 1866 the first shipments of Algerian ore had arrived at Le Creusot, but other companies found it more advantageous to process the ore closer to the port of entry. Thus Hugues Darcy and Henri Germain of Châtillon-Commentry joined in the creation of the Compagnie des Hauts-Fourneaux de Marseille in 1862–1863, and Châtillon-Commentry later moved its smelting operations from Montluçon to Beaucaire on the lower Rhône. This trend toward what Bertrand Gille calls "métallurgie littorale" was also manifested in the creation of steelworks at Boulogne, Dunkirk, and Boucau (near Bayonne) by Montataire, Denain-Anzin, and Marine Steel, respectively—all to utilize ore from Bilbao.[35]

As a consequence of all these developments, the production of Bessemer and Siemens-Martin steel—only 9,647 tons in 1865—reached over 280,000 tons by 1878. To be sure, total steel output that year (313,000 tons) was still below iron output (843,000 tons), which would not achieve its all-time peak until 1882 (1,073,000 tons).[36] But the trend was clearly toward steel. Moreover, because Bessemer and Siemens-Martin production was so capital intensive and was undertaken by only a dozen or so firms, the trend toward steel reinforced the tendency toward concentration that the iron and steel industry had long exhibited. Gille has estimated that by 1869 the ten largest firms controlled more than 50 percent of production, versus only 14 percent in 1845.[37]

Continued technological change (of which the introduction of the mass production of steel was only one manifestation), coupled with intensifying international competition under free trade, promoted a winnowing out process in the 1860s and 1870s that did not just favor large companies at the expense of the small but also favored the technologically advanced and economically efficient, large or small, over the obsolescent and inefficient, large or small. Thus, among the highly capitalized iron companies that had been created to serve the mass market for cheap, middling-to-low-grade iron, those that did not or could not move into production of cheap steel were destined to decline. This happened to Alais, which decided to forego investment in the new steel technology in the 1860s because of the softening of demand for rails and its chronic problems in finding suitable supplies of coal and iron. In 1875 it turned its ironworks over to Terrenoire and for the next decade concentrated on supplying coal to the railroads.[38] A similar path was taken by Decazeville. The quality of the iron ore and coal it mined in the Aubin basin did not allow it to adopt Bessemer technology, and Decazeville was too far from the coast to use Algerian ore. Stuck in an increasingly non-competitive position, the company declared bankruptcy in 1865. Three years later it was relaunched as a coal company—La Nouvelle Société des Houillères et Fonderies de l'Aveyron—under the direction of Alfred Deseilligny of Le Creusot.[39]

If relatively large, modern firms like Decazeville and Alais declined in the heightened competition of the 1860s and 1870s, what became of the smaller firms still practicing the "old" metallurgy? With the construction of the national rail system, many firms that had survived to the 1850s by serving isolated local markets lost their geographical protection and succumbed, especially those whose costs were rising as local iron mines and forests were depleted. However, those firms that adapted themselves to the new metallurgy and, even more, those that found a market niche for high-quality specialty goods often proved surprisingly resilient. Both situations were well represented in the metallurgical industry of Burgundy and the Franche-Comté in eastern France.

Although the formation of Châtillon-Commentry in 1845 had brought together dozens of the smaller forges and foundries of Burgundy in a single company, many others continued to operate independently into the 1850s and 1860s. However, those that made no concessions to technological and economic change rarely survived to 1870. In the Côte d'Or, for example, the Magnin family continued to refine iron with charcoal at Brazey in the 1850s and even expanded during the railroad boom of 1855–1856. The downturn of 1857–1858, however, all but killed the enterprise. By 1860 Joseph Magnin employed only eighteen workers, and in 1865 he decided to close the forge entirely and to convert the buildings into a sugar mill. Shortly thereafter he left for Paris to pursue a political career, quite successfully as it happened (he eventually served as minister of finance and Governor of the Banque de France before ending his career as a leader of the French Senate). Another Côte d'Or forgemaster, Paul Thoureau, took a different tack. In 1855 he attempted (à la Châtillon-Commentry) to merge the remaining obsolete forges in the department into a joint-stock company, the Société des Hauts-Fourneaux et Forges de la Côte d'Or, but he did not subsequently invest in modern technology as Châtillon-Commentry had done. With the arrival of the railroad (and thus outside competition) in the Côte d'Or in 1858, the company failed.[40]

Although most of the old metallurgy of Burgundy had been killed off by 1860, there were exceptions. Perhaps the most notable was Gueugnon in the Saône-et-Loire. Founded in the 1720s by Latour-Maubourg, Louis XIV's inspector-general of the infantry, Gueugnon continued to refine pig iron into wrought iron with charcoal into the 1840s, even though English-style puddling furnaces and rolling mills had been installed there as early as 1825. However, when Pierre-Joseph Campionnot acquired the forge in 1845, he set out to turn it into a modern coal-fueled ironworks to produce *fer blanc* (tin- and lead-plated sheet iron) with financial and technical aid from his friend, Eugène Schneider. The transformation was a success. Gueugnon's workforce grew from 80 in 1845 to 600 at the time of Campionnat's death in 1888. Under the direction of Campionnat's son and grandson, Gueugnon continued to lead France's small iron companies in technological innovation (it was Gueugnon that introduced the British hot-rolled steel process into eastern France in the 1940s).[41]

In the Franche-Comté—the departments of the Jura, Doubs, and Haute-Saône—the small forgemasters proved even more adept at adjusting to the new environment and at finding ways to survive in the increasingly competitive environment after 1850. Some perpetuated independent family firms through partial modernization and specialization. At Aillevillers (Haute-Saône), Rodolphe de Buyer sold off his charcoal-fired blast furnaces, bought a share of Ronchamp, the largest coal mine in the region, and proceeded to use an English forge dating back to the 1820s to produce *fers blancs* and *tôles lustrées*. In the Jura, Edmond Monnier rebuilt and modernized the family forge at Baudin, making him "one of the rare metallurgists of the Jura to preserve his enterprise from the decadence of the *forge comtoise*," while his brother-in-law, Alphonse Jobez, saved his forge at Syram from sure demise by specializing in nailmaking with the help of a young *polytechnicien*, Honoré Reverchon, future director of Audincourt.[42]

Other *comtois* forges survived by imitating Châtillon-Commentry and banding together in joint-stock companies. One of these centered on Audincourt, one of the oldest forges in France (dating back to 1616). Converted into a *société anonyme* in 1824 by the Strasbourg financiers Georges Humann and Florent Saglio, Audincourt combined the smelting of high-quality *fonte au bois* with English-style wrought iron production in the 1830s and 1840s (like Fourchambault) and ranked as one of France's ten largest ironworks in 1845. Because of its reputation for high quality, Audincourt became a pole of attraction for less efficient neighbors seeking to sell out in the 1850s. Under Frédéric Strohl, a former railroad director from Alsace, Audincourt merged with four of these firms and also integrated backward by acquiring the Exencourt iron mine. Under Honoré Reverchon, who took over after Strohl died in 1868, Audincourt continued to find an outlet for its charcoal iron in various high-quality applications such as telegraph and telephone wire.[43]

Still other *comtois* forgemasters found refuge in an entirely new joint-stock company, the Société des Forges de Franche-Comté, created in 1854. One of these, Jules Vautherin of Lods, poured 800,000 francs of his own money into the new company, obtained a 1 million franc loan from the government to modernize, and oversaw Franche-Comté's acquisition of an up-to-date coal-fired forge in the late 1850s. However, the depression in the rail market in 1857–1858 and the general increase in competition after 1860 kept the company from turning a profit. Facing bankruptcy in 1868, it was reorganized, and new capital was brought in, but it remained too vertically integrated for its own good (one critic wrote in 1878 that the company "will not cease to decline as long as it keeps its blast furnaces going"). Eventually it dropped smelting and limited its operations to making structural iron, still the building material of choice for many civil engineers even in the age of steel. In 1887, it furnished 2,200 tons of puddled iron for the Eiffel Tower and later won contracts to provide structural iron for bridges in Lyon, Cairo, and Haiphong, as well as the Alexandre III Bridge in Paris.[44]

Specialization and niche strategies also allowed many of the smaller steel companies to survive and to prosper in the shadow of giants like Terrenoire, Marine, and Le Creusot. Indeed, the crucible steelmakers of the Loire like Marrel Frères and the Holtzers were not initially threatened by Bessemer and Siemens-Martin steel, which was of low quality (suitable mainly for rails), and they continued to expand in the 1860s to meet the growing demand of the army and navy for high-grade steel for weapons and armor plate. Moreover, by the 1870s, Marrel and Holtzer were themselves adopting the Siemens-Martin furnace to produce their specialties. Meanwhile, the widening applications of steel spawned yet more specialized manufacturers. In 1865, for example, Charles Barrouin, chief engineer at Marine Steel, founded the Aciéries de Saint-Etienne to produce puddled steel railroad tires and armor plate in competition with Marine, and in 1875 former employees of the Rive-de-Gier forges founded the Aciéries et Forges de la Lorette.

Nor was the trend toward specialization in steelmaking limited to the department of the Loire. It is also seen in the case of Allevard in the Isère.

Allevard was one of the oldest continuously operating forges in France. Iron smelting had begun there in the reign of Louis XI in the fifteenth century, and the forge long prospered by supplying high-quality charcoal-fired *fonte* to the steelmakers of Rives. In the early nineteenth century, however, the development of cheaper coke-fired pig iron and the introduction of crucible steel by Jackson threatened Allevard and Rives with extinction. Allevard passed through several hands until, virtually bankrupt, it was acquired in 1842 by Emile Charrière. Charrière decided that the future of Allevard lay in forward integration from iron smelting to steelmaking and the fabrication of steel parts for the railroads. In 1856 Allevard became the first (and for a while the only) maker of steel tires for locomotive wheels, a product that soon absorbed its entire output of pig iron (1,600 to 1,900 tons a year). From 300 employees in 1842, Allevard grew to 900 by 1860. By the 1870s, however, the big joint-stock steel companies were selling steel tires at prices below Allevard's costs, and Allevard was forced to abandon what had once been its virtual monopoly. Yet the company survived by selling high-quality "spathic" iron ore to Le Creusot and by manufacturing steel railway car springs, mainly for the P-L-M, using a Siemens-Martin furnace installed in 1867.[45]

By the 1870s, fifty years of extraordinary technological innovation and economic growth in the French iron and steel industry had brought into existence a hierarchy of important capitalist enterprises. At the top of this hierarchy were the great joint-stock companies, the most sophisticated of which integrated iron and coal mining with smelting, refining, and the fabrication of a variety of finished products. In terms of social capital, these were the largest manufacturing firms in France, exceeded in size only by the trunk railroads, the big steamship companies, the largest gas and water companies, and the largest coal companies.[46] Below and around these were the smaller specialty firms—such as Holtzer and Allevard—which were often the most technologically innovative. Although most of these would survive into the twentieth century, the next wave of technological change, stemming from introduction of the Thomas-Gilchrist process, would profoundly alter the pecking order. Even more, it would bring forth new firms to challenge and supplant many of the older ones. All of this will be treated in Chapter 12. For now, our survey of the new industrial capitalism of the nineteenth century must turn to the enterprises in engineering and metallurgical manufacturing that arose downstream from, and often in close conjunction with, the iron and steel enterprises.

CHAPTER SEVEN

Hardware, Machinery, and Construction

Ferrous metallurgy did not end with the production of bars, beams, wire, sheet, and other basic forms of iron and steel. These were merely the raw materials for the increasingly wide variety of products that came to be made from metal in the course in the nineteenth century. These products ranged in complexity from simple farm implements to sophisticated motors and precision instruments and in size from tiny watch movements to the grandiose undertakings of French civil engineering, epitomized by Gustave Eiffel's 1,000-foot-high tower for the 1889 Paris World's Fair. Some of these products were made by the companies that smelted and refined iron and steel (we have already noted Le Creusot's interest in building machines and Marine Steel's involvement in manufacturing armaments). By and large, however, metallurgical manufacturing and construction involved separate sets of firms, some of which came to rival the big iron and steel companies in size and influence and eventually joined the ranks of France's biggest business enterprises in the twentieth century.

Just as we contrasted the old charcoal-based metallurgy and the new coal-based metallurgy in the last chapter, we can make a useful distinction here between the old metallurgical manufacturing—the making of the various forms of hardware that had been around for centuries—and the new metallurgical manufacturing—the making of entirely new products such as steam engines, machine tools, textile machines, and locomotives (or the use of iron and steel in the making of old products like bridges and buildings). Of course, these two forms of metallurgical manufacturing were never entirely discrete. Some firms that started out making traditional products shifted to the new products, and makers of both old and new products could and did make the transition from shop production to factory production, thereby moving toward the greater size, greater capital intensity, and greater organizational complexity associated with modern industrial capitalism. Even so, it is useful in presenting a survey of this highly diverse set of enterprises to distinguish between these two categories.

The Hardware Industry Transformed

At the outset of the nineteenth century, metallurgical manufacturing in France consisted mostly of skilled craftsmen—"village smiths"—fabricating one at a time the various tools and utensils needed by their local communities or cottage workers making hardware or parts of hardware for the iron merchants who served larger markets. For certain kinds of products and for certain areas—especially those that, for lack of good transportation facilities, remained outside the larger market economy—this kind of production continued throughout the century. At the same time, however, true industrial capitalists using machine tools clustered in factories began to mass-produce certain kinds of hardware for sale in regional, national, and even international markets. One line in which this occurred was farm implements.

In the course of the nineteenth century, all sorts of new farm machines were introduced in Europe and America, including seed drills, harrows, cultivators, and threshing machines, while traditional tools like plows and scythes were improved and adapted to specific crops and soils. In the United States, the settling of the Midwest and Great Plains created a vast market for standardized, mass-produced versions of these new implements and machines, which made possible the success of giant farm equipment manufacturers like Cyrus McCormick and John Deere. In France, the smaller size of land holdings and the smaller scale of cultivation—as well as the greater regional variations in crops and growing conditions—precluded the development of a unified national market for expensive, labor-saving machinery produced by a few giant manufacturers turning out a few standardized models. Therefore, no French McCormick or Deere appeared on the scene. Instead, the industrialization of farm implement production in France proceeded along two tracks that gave rise to two kinds of firms: (1) "proto-factories," which specialized in a single product and often clustered in a particular region but nevertheless sold their output regionally or even nationally, and (2) larger, less-specialized firms making an array of products for a specific region.

Good examples of the first kind of firms are found in the edged-tool industry of the Franche-Comté. On the upper Doubs River and its tributaries, dozens of water-powered *taillanderies* appeared in the eighteenth and early nineteenth centuries, each employing a handful of skilled workers in the production of edged tools, especially scythes (the Comtois scythe was renowned throughout eastern France). Despite the small size of these enterprises, they were collectively significant, accounting for 40 percent of the 100,000 to 200,000 scythes produced in France annually by the mid-1800s. A few of these micro-enterprises went on to become national leaders in the farm implement industry in the second half of the nineteenth century. Among these was the *taillanderie* of Nans-sous-Sainte-Anne, acquired by the Philibert family in 1865. Using a variety of water-powered machine tools, the Philiberts engaged in an early version of flexible mass production, turning out 180 models of scythes and 540 other kinds of edged tools in surprisingly large numbers with a workforce that never exceeded twenty-two (between 1895 and 1914, the company produced 15,000–22,000 scythes and 6,000–13,000 edged tools each year). These implements were sold under the Philibert Frères brand through local blacksmiths and hardware dealers in the Franche-Comté and throughout central and southeastern France.[1]

Meanwhile, in western, central, and northern France, dozens of larger, less-specialized firms appeared, each employing 100 to 200 workers to manufacture a variety of tools and light machinery tailored to the needs of their home region. As described by Julien Turgan in his report on the farm equipment displayed at the 1878 Paris Exposition, these firms included Delahaye et Bazar of Liancourt ("great propagators of the double Brabant plow"); Souchu-Pinet of Langleais ("one of the youngest stars in the constellation of Indre-et-Loire manufacturers"); and Joseph Pinet of Abilly (Indre-et-Loire), who displayed a well-regarded harvester called the Abilienne and who, in Turgan's estimation, was largely responsible for the "popularization of mechanical processes in the center and west of France."[2] Perhaps foremost of these farm manufacturers, however, was Charles Meixmoron de Dombasle of Nancy.

In 1822, Alexandre Mathieu de Dombasle, one of France's leading agronomists, founded an experimental farm at Roville (Meurthe-et-

Moselle) to which he added workshops to make plows, cultivators, harrows, seeders, and other farm machines. In 1842, his son-in-law Charles Meixmoron (who later added "de Dombasle" to his name) moved the manufacturing operation to Nancy. Meixmoron's son took over in 1860 and proceeded to expand production of the famous Dombasle plow and other implements by adding steam-powered machinery. In 1882, Turgan described the plant: "Completely rebuilt, it consists today of many fine workshops arranged around a large courtyard, including a forge, assembly shop, and wheelwright's shop. Opposite the forge is a magnificent showroom where buyers can select what they want at their convenience. Farther on stand vast storerooms containing thousands of implements ready for delivery."[3] Twenty years later, Dombasle remained the most important farm equipment maker in eastern France, and one writer noted that "Dombasle tools and implements are distributed worldwide and have been the object of the highest awards at all the regional competitions and at the Paris world's fairs."[4]

Farm implements, of course, constituted only one of the many kinds of hardware that had long been fabricated by skilled artisans who either worked alone and sold to local customers or worked for merchants who sold to wider markets. In either case, over the years hardware makers in particular areas or towns came to specialize in particular products, as happened also in textiles. Many of these centers of specialized artisanal production continued unchanged to the end of the nineteenth century, thereby providing the "alternatives to mass production" much lionized in recent years by critics of big business.[5] For example, in the Vimeu region of Picardy, located between Abbeville and Le Tréport in the department of the Somme, lock making continued to occupy some 8,000 craftsmen in such villages as Fressonneville and Frivelle-Escarbotin in the early 1900s. Meanwhile, in the Auvergne, 18,000 knife makers employed in some 500 separate enterprises in and around the town of Thiers continued to account for 80 percent of the cutlery produced in France.[6]

In some areas, however, hardware manufacture moved beyond cottage industry and small workshops to the large-scale factory production found in the iron and steel industry. This happened in and around Saint-Etienne, long a center for the production of swords, firearms, and general hardware *(quincaillerie)*. To be sure, severe restrictions on the private manufacture and possession of firearms in France limited the growth and development of the Saint-Etienne arms industry in the first half of the nineteenth century. In contrast to what happened in Liège and Birmingham, which were under no such restrictions and which thus became world leaders in small arms manufacturing by the 1850s, the arms industry of Saint-Etienne remained largely artisanal as late as the 1860s. However, to facilitate production of the new Chassepot rifle after 1866, the state arms manufacture at Saint-Etienne was concentrated at a single new mechanized plant at Treuil in 1869. Then after 1885, when restrictions on arms manufacturing by private companies were relaxed, the commercial side of the industry was similarly transformed: the large metallurgical firms of the Loire began massproducing rifle barrels and other components; these were then assembled and finished by the new Manufacture Française d'Armes et Cycles and by various Saint-Etienne machine shops, some of which were also turning out parts and assemblies for bicycles and automobiles.[7]

Meanwhile, production in at least some sectors of the traditional hardware industry of Saint-Etienne and its environs was also being mechanized and concentrated by the late nineteenth century. At Saint-Etienne, Chambon, and Montsirol, the firms of Mermier and Martouret built factories to make various kinds of locks with steampowered machine tools. At Chambon, Neyrand Frères et Thiollière—having sold their steelworks to Marine and Terrenoire in the 1850s—pioneered the factory production of tacks (pointes), while Barbier et Cie adopted Norwegian methods and employed 100 workers to mass produce 800,000 kilograms of horseshoe nails per year by the end of the century. Also at Chambon, Pallet Frères (who introduced boltmaking to the Saint-Etienne region in the 1830s) and seven other firms employed modern thread-cutting machinery and a total of 1,000 workers to produce 7–8 million kilograms of bolts per year by 1900.[8]

More striking than what happened in the Saint-Etienne arms and hardware industry, however, were developments in the Pays de Montbéliard, in eastern France near the Swiss border, which became the undisputed leader in the factory production of watch movements, clocks, and certain kinds of hardware in the course of the nineteenth century. As in the adjacent province of Alsace, the rise of industry around Montbéliard was the work of a community of interrelated, intermarried Protestant families. Two of these families, the Veillards and Migeons, created a long-lived family firm that produced screws and bolts at plants at Morvillars and Grandvillars.[9] But the foremost enterprises in the Montbéliard region were associated with the Japy and Peugeot families.

The Japy family had been active in the artisanal industry of the

Montbéliard region since at least the sixteenth century, but the modern history of the Japy enterprise began in the 1770s when Frédéric Japy, after studying watchmaking in Neuchâtel (which was then supplanting Geneva as the center of the Swiss watch industry), returned to his hometown of Beaucourt, east of Montbéliard, and set up a factory to make watch movements using newly invented machine tools.[10] This enterprise brought under one roof and at least partially mechanized what had been a highly segmented system of domestic manufacture in which a single watch movement might pass through the hands of 150 different cottage workers. As a result, Japy cut the cost of making a watch movement by two-thirds and soon became the principal supplier of *ébauches* (rough movements) to the Neuchâtelois. French territorial expansion after 1794 brought first Montbéliard and then Switzerland and much of the rest of western Europe under French control, opened a wider market to Swiss watchmakers, and thereby promoted the continued growth of the Japy enterprise. By the early 1800s, Japy employed 500 workers to turn out over 12,000 dozen watch movements a year.[11]

In 1806, Frédéric Japy retired and turned his business over to his three eldest sons—Fritz, Louis, and Pierre—who not only continued what their father had begun but also greatly expanded and altered it over the next half century. While the manufacture of watch movements at Beaucourt remained the core business of Japy Frères, the construction of new water- and steam-powered plants enabled them to move into clockmaking and, more significantly, into general hardware manufacturing. The Japys had begun making screws as early as 1806, when Napoleon's Continental Blockade cut off imports from England, but they decided to move into this business on a large scale in the 1820s when Louis Japy developed new screw-cutting machinery. Turning out 18,000–20,000 gross of screws per month by 1830, the Japys quickly dominated the French market and began exporting screws to Belgium, Germany, and even the United States. This success prompted them to diversify, and soon they were manufacturing bolts, nails, pins, hooks, corkscrews, buckles, chains, and many other hardware products. They also added wrought iron household utensils, for which they built yet another new plant in 1834.

With 3,000 employees working in six different locations in the 1830s, the three Japy brothers found it increasingly difficult to manage their growing enterprise by themselves, so in 1837 they reorganized their partnership, bringing in four of their sons and two sons-in-law to form a nine-man partnership. Subsequently, in the 1850s, Japy Frères was converted into a *société en commandite par actions*, with all shares closely held by the family and power vested in a self-perpetuating board of directors selected from the male successors of the three original partners. Meanwhile, the business continued to expand in the 1840s and 1850s as Swiss watches made with Japy movements came to dominate the growing American market, and as the Japys continued to add more and more products to their hardware and utensil lines (by 1855 screws, hardware, and utensils accounted for 3.8 million of the company's 5.6 million francs in annual revenues). At this time, the firm integrated forward into marketing their products—thus foreshadowing what would be a common strategy for modern big businesses—by cutting out the traditional middlemen and selling their watch movements directly to Swiss watchmakers and by setting up sales offices and warehouses for their other products in Paris and elsewhere, as we saw in Chapter 3.

The advent of factory production of cheap watches in the United States in the 1860s and 1870s drove the Swiss out of the American market and permanently undercut that segment of the Japys' business, but the continued growth of their hardware and utensils business seemed to more than compensate for that loss. Annual revenues rose steadily from 5.8 million francs in 1856 to 12.4 million by 1874–1875, and by the 1870s the Japys had over 5,500 workers on their payroll, making them one of the largest employers in France. Behind the favorable figures, however, lurked serious problems. Starting in the 1860s, the firm eschewed investing in new production technology that would have allowed it to continue to compete on the basis of price in Europe and America. According to the company's historian, Pierre Lamard, such investment would have required the Japys to bring in outside money, and that would have threatened family control of the firm. Instead, Japy Frères continued to produce the same goods in the same way and increasingly depended on tariff protection and cartelization to maintain sales at home and in the French colonies.

By the 1890s, Japy Frères was also pursuing a policy of hyper-diversification, seeking a small piece of the burgeoning market for various new products—electric motors and dynamos, phonographs, cameras, bicycles, and many more—without making the investment in research or production required to make the company a leader in any one of these markets. As Lamard points out, this strategy was ultimately counterproductive, for "in seeking to fight on all industrial fronts at once, the management incontestably weakened its position in manufacturing."[12] Japy Frères continued to turn a profit as long as the protected home and colonial markets absorbed the traditional goods produced in its increasingly obsolete plants. But long before the firm was finally dismantled and sold off piece by piece in the 1950s and 1960s—a classic example of what happens to once-successful family firms unwilling or unable to change with the times—leadership in metallurgical manufacturing in the Pays de Montbéliard had passed to the Peugeot family, which had risen in the shadow of the Japys in the course of the nineteenth century.

The Peugeots were long established as craftsmen, millers, and petty merchants at Herimoncourt and other villages south of Montbéliard by the mid-eighteenth century. Jean-Pierre Peugeot and two of his sons helped to launch cotton production in the region in the 1780s—just as the Koechlins and Dollfuses were doing around Mulhouse—but the true founding of the family enterprise was the work of Jean-Pierre's two other sons, Jean-Pierre II and Jean-Frédéric. In 1810, these two Peugeot brothers converted a mill at Sous-Cratet on the Gland River into a forge and began refining local *fonte* into steel, which was then made into saw blades and springs. Overextended and facing bank-ruptcy during the economic crisis of 1814, the Peugeot brothers decided to stop making steel and to concentrate on transforming steel purchased from others. In 1819, they invented a new way to make saw blades by cold rolling and tempering (instead of hammering), which enabled them to match the quality of imported English saw blades at a fraction of the cost. By the 1830s, Peugeot Frères employed seventy workers at Sous-Cratet making saw blades, steel corset stays, and watch springs (for the Japys). Business was good enough to warrant building a second plant at Terre-Blanche in 1839.[13]

The firm split in 1842, with the three sons of Jean-Frédéric joining some of the Jackson brothers of Assailly (their brothers-in-law) in a partnership to make saw blades, watch springs, and umbrella frames at Sous-Cratet, while the three sons of Jean-Pierre II continued to run the plant at Terre-Blanche plus a new plant at Valentigny that they purchased with the help of the Japys. It was the latter firm—known simply as Peugeot Frères—that emerged as the most innovative and dynamic of the Peugeot family enterprises in the second half of the nineteenth century. In 1850, Peugeot Frères started manufacturing steel cages to support women's skirts just as the fashion for crinolines was taking hold; soon their workforce of over 500 was using 8 tons of steel a month to produce 25,000 cages. When the crinoline craze died out in the 1860s, they shifted to making coffee mills, scissors, tableware, and the like.

Under Jules Peugeot, the last surviving son of Jean-Pierre II, and then under Jules' son Eugène and his nephew Armand, Peugeot Frères continued to pursue this kind of business in the final decades of the nineteenth century. But, most importantly for its long-term success, the firm had also become by then a leader in one of the growth industries of the *belle époque,* bicycles, thanks to the efforts of Armand Peugeot.

Bicycles first caught the attention of Armand Peugeot in the 1870s when he was studying metallurgy at Leeds, and he quickly recognized the potential of the "safety bicycle" when it appeared in the 1880s. In 1887 he converted the family's plant at Beaulieu into a bicycle factory. By 1900, the 650 workers in the Beaulieu plant were turning out 20,000 bicycles a year with components produced at Valentigny. By then, however, Armand had turned his attention to a potentially even more lucrative gadget, the automobile. In 1897 he left Peugeot Frères to found the Société Anonyme des Automobiles Peugeot. That company eventually emerged as one of the "Big Three" of the French automobile industry, giving the industrial economy of the Pays de Montbéliard a new lease on life and making the Peugeots one of the wealthiest and most influential industrial families in twentieth century France (we will return to the Peugeots and the automobile industry in Chapter 14).

The New Metallurgical Manufacturing

Even as the manufacture of traditional metal products was being transformed in the course of the nineteenth century and was giving rise to new industrial enterprises, the manufacture of entirely new kinds of products (particularly machines, such as the steam engine, that are closely identified with the Industrial Revolution) was forming the basis of a new sector of the industrial economy of France. Such a progression was not inevitable. By 1815, the British had a substantial head start over the French (and everyone else) in the design and manufacture of the new machinery, and they could have easily met the French demand for the new machines through exports. But two things prevented this. First, the French government enacted a high tariff to promote the development of domestic machine manufacturing (a good example of the use of import duties to protect an infant industry). Second, the British themselves encouraged France and other countries to develop their own machine industries by treating the new machines as state secrets (the nineteenth-century version of nuclear or rocket technology). In the early 1800s, the British government banned not only the export of the new machines but also the licensing of foreign manufacturers and even the emigration of those with knowledge of the machinery (none of which, of course, kept the new technology from spreading but only kept British firms from fully profiting from the spread). As a result of these policies, a French machine industry appeared and developed rapidly in the early nineteenth century, often with the direct participation of British engineers and mechanics.

One important sector of the new industry was textile machinery. As French entrepreneurs endeavored to set up factories to spin and weave cotton, wool, and flax on the British model, they did whatever was necessary to gain access to British machinery, including smuggling machines out of England part by part (often with the complicity of the British manufacturers), recruiting British mechanics to build the machines in France, and traveling to England to study the new machinery (often returning with blueprints in their bags or, as in the case of Nicolas Schlumberger, in the lining of their coats!). By the 1820s, the largest, most technically advanced textile manufacturers all had machine shops attached to their textile mills. Soon those most proficient in making the new machines were turning these shops into separate enterprises or were giving up textile manufacturing to specialize in machine building. Nowhere was this better seen than in Alsace.

In Alsace, Nicolas Schlumberger began building a range of spinning and weaving machines at his cotton mill at Guebwiller in 1818. In 1836 he built one of France's first self-acting mule jennies, and four years later he introduced the Heilman woolcomb, which, as we saw in Chapter 4, was destined to transform the French worsted industry. At the Paris Exposition of 1839, the judges lauded Schlumberger's "vast construction shops" that produced machines "as well made *(soignés)* and as perfect as the best English products."[14] Meanwhile at Cernay, Mathieu and Jérémie Risler, who had begun building machinery before 1820, were joined by the English mechanic, Job Dixon, who helped make Risler et Dixon the leading machine makers in Alsace for a decade, until the firm failed in the financial crisis of 1829–1830. Thereafter, Jérémie Risler contributed his expertise to the machine-building enterprise of another Mulhousian, André Koechlin. As we saw earlier, Koechlin began making textile machinery in 1826 after an eight-year stint as manager of the Dollfus-Mieg cotton enterprise. He soon entered a virtual partnership with Sharp and Roberts, the leading machine makers in Manchester, who agreed to supply Koechlin with plans, machine tools, and skilled workers in return for 30 percent of Koechlin's profits. Richard Roberts himself came to Mulhouse to oversee the installation of the new equipment (after it had been smuggled out of England). The Koechlin enterprise prospered in the 1830s and soon became independent of Sharp and Roberts. By 1839, Koechlin employed 1,800 workers to build *métiers complets* for spinning cotton, wool, and flax plus looms, printing machines, and steam engines. At the 1839 Paris Exposition, where Koechlin was awarded a gold medal, the judges were especially impressed with his version of the Sharp self-acting jenny ("we call this remarkable machine to the attention of manufacturers in the hopes that, by trying it, they will put it in the ranks of those inventions that have most advanced industry").[15]

Paralleling the rise of the textile machinery industry—and ultimately outstripping it in economic impact—was the manufacture of steam engines and other power sources (water wheels and turbines). James Watt's version of the steam engine, which transformed a pumping machine into an all-purpose power source, first appeared in 1776. Within three years, Jacques Constantin and Auguste Périer, who had the concession to build a waterworks for Paris, had acquired the right to manufacture (or rather to assemble) Watt engines at their machine shop at Chaillot near Paris. According to Jacques Payen, the Chaillot enterprise prospered in the 1780s by building steam engines for Anzin, Le Creusot, and various waterworks. But demand for steam engines remained limited in France and became more so during the Revolution, and the Chaillot firm went into decline after 1790.[16] Growth of the cotton industry after 1800 did present a new and potentially large market for steam engines, and machine builders like Etienne Calla, Charles Albert, and the Englishman John Collier joined the Périers in making steam engines for the cotton industry under the Empire, but there were still only 200 steam engines in France by 1810, a fraction of the number in Great Britain.[17]

The real takeoff in both the use and production of steam engines in France came after 1815, when the English mechanic Humphrey Edwards introduced the Woolf double expansion compound engine, which was much more fuel-efficient than the Watt engine and thus became the standard in coal-poor France. Edwards was appointed director of the Chaillot works when Scipion and Casimir Périer of Anzin took it over following the death of Constantin Périer (no relation) in 1818, and Edwards proceeded to build thirty steam engines for Anzin and a total of 200 engines by 1835. Rising demand for steam engines soon brought others—both immigrant Englishmen and native Frenchmen—into the industry. Thirty-nine firms were assembling steam engines in France by 1825 and fifty by 1840. Those in and around Paris included Joseph Farcot, a former employee of Chaillot, who introduced the horizontal steam engine in the 1820s; the English forge-master Aaron Manby, who set up a machine works at Charenton with Daniel Wilson in 1822 and, as we have seen, briefly controlled Le Creusot before going broke in 1833; and Christophe-François Calla, who took over his father's foundry and machine works in 1835. Beyond Paris, Verpilleux and Revollier introduced the building of steam engines in the Loire, Alphonse Duvergier built steam engines at Lyon, and in Alsace Stehelin and Huber of Bischwiller, André Koechlin of Mulhouse, and other textile machine makers entered the field by the 1830s. By 1840, there were some 2,900 steam engines in operation in France, and hundreds more were being installed every year as the proprietors of sugar refineries, foundries, flour mills, and sawmills came to appreciate the new power source previously found only in coal mines and textile mills.[18]

Throughout the nineteenth century, the harnessing of water power was as important as the development of steam power for French industrialization. Accordingly, several important enterprises emerged in the design, construction, and installation of water wheels and water turbines. The early leaders were Benoit Fourneyron and his brother-in-law, Jean-Claude Crozet-Fourneyron, who introduced the first practical low-pressure turbine in the 1830s and had installed it in some 129 factories across France by 1843.[19] In the late 1840s, the Fourneyron turbine was supplanted by the Jonval turbine manufactured by André Koechlin of Mulhouse, and it in turn was superseded by the axial turbine developed by Pierre Fontaine of Chartres for the flour mills of the Beauce. Between 1850 and 1873, Fontaine and his partner Alexandre Brault installed more than a thousand of these turbines in textile, paper, and flour mills in France.[20] After 1870, however, leadership in the turbine industry passed from specialists in harnessing low and medium waterfalls, such as Fontaine and Brault, to the makers of high-pressure turbines for the new paper mills and hydroelectric plants of the Vosges and the French Alps. These included Singrün Frères of Epinal and Casimir Brenier of Grenoble.[21]

Another sector of the new machinery industry centered on making boilers and distilling equipment, especially for sugar refiners. Dozens of firms entered this field in the first half of the nineteenth century, but one stood out: Derosne et Cail. Charles Derosne, a noted chemist who had invented a system for the continuous distillation of sugar in response to the Napoleonic effort to develop French sugar beet production during the Continental Blockade, founded a works in 1818 to make distillation equipment at Chaillot, near the Périers' steam engine works. In 1824, Jean-François Cail, a twenty-two-year-old boilermaker from the Deux-Sevres, joined the firm and soon invented a double-effect evaporator that reduced coal consumption in sugar refining by two-thirds. Promoted to plant director, Cail became Derosne's partner by 1834, and after 1836 the firm was known as Derosne et Cail. As the refining of both cane and beet sugar increased in western Europe in the 1840s, Derosne et Cail expanded its manufacturing capacity, not only in Paris but also in the department of the Nord (the heart of French beet-sugar country) and in Brussels and Amsterdam (to supply equipment to the refiners of Belgian beet sugar and East Indian cane sugar). From only fifty workers in 1834, Derosne et Cail expanded to 2,500 (1,500 in Paris, 1,000 at the subsidiaries) by 1848.[22]

Charles Derosne died in 1846, and J-F Cail became sole proprietor of the firm, which he continued to manage until his death in 1871. Throughout this period, the Cail company remained France's foremost manufacturer of refining equipment, specializing in complete refineries—turnkey plants—that it installed for sugar companies all over the world. At the same time, it began to diversify into steam engines (of which it was the largest French producer by 1860) and, more importantly, into locomotives, bridges, and other railroad equipment (see below).[23] It also produced more and more machine tools—lathes, shearing machines, and machines for boring, punching, and stamping—which enabled it not only to further mechanize its own production but also to add a profitable new line to its product mix.[24]

Whether they got their start in building textile machines, steam engines, boilers, refining equipment, or whatever, all machine makers tended to move into neighboring product lines and into machine tool construction. This was certainly true of Schlumberger and Koechlin in Alsace, and it was true of most of the Paris machine makers. For example, François Cavé, who apprenticed with John Collier and then opened his own textile machine shop in Paris in 1822, soon moved into steam engine production, specializing in marine engines for the French navy, and also into steam-powered machine tools, including his version of the steam hammer. Indeed, according to James Edmonson's study of the French engineering industry, "direct application of steam power to a broad range of machine tools constituted Cavé's chief practical contribution to machine building."[25] Similarly, Pierre-André Decoster, who pioneered the manufacture of English-style flax-spinning machines in France in the 1830s, added the manufacture of machine tools and by 1844 had outfitted some seventy French factories.[26]

While diversification was the watchword in the French machinery industry in the mid-nineteenth century, the continuing evolution of engineering technology seemed to reward specialization and niche strategies later in the century. As a result, by 1900 there were in France—mainly in Paris—dozens of small-to-medium engineering firms that typically employed 50 to 200 machinists to turn out high-quality engines and machines for particular markets and applications.[27] In addition, the refitting of France's arsenals for the production of the Chassepot and Lebel rifles in the 1860s and 1870s supported some ten specialized toolmakers, the most important of which were Bouhey and Bariquand et Moore.[28] These and similar firms provided the engineering infrastructure that allowed Paris to take the lead in the world automobile and airplane industries at the outset of the twentieth century. In the mid-nineteenth century, however, it was the manufacture of railroad equipment that drove metallurgical construction and machinery production in France and everywhere else, and it was this industry that produced the handful of very large firms that dominated metallurgical manufacturing in France throughout the second half of the nineteenth century.

According to François Caron, the French railroad companies spent an average of 151 million francs a year on rails and equipment between 1845 and 1852 and 400 million francs a year between 1853 and 1867.[29] Of course, the biggest single expenditure was for rails, which sustained the growth of the big joint-stock iron and steel companies. But the railroads also needed hundreds of locomotives and tenders, thousands of passenger and freight cars, plus turntables, loading and signaling equipment, and metal bridges and tunnels. While the big iron and steel companies manufactured axles, wheels, springs, and other parts for rolling stock as well as the girders and plate used in iron construction, except for Le Creusot they were reluctant to take responsibility for the final assemblage. This left open an equipment market so large and potentially profitable that it naturally attracted most of the existing engineering firms and called many more into existence. We can see this happening most clearly in steam locomotives, the sector of the industry we know the most about, thanks to the work of François Crouzet and Jacques Payen.[30]

The builder of France's first railroads, Marc Séguin, also assembled its first locomotives at his plant at Perraches (Lyon) in the early 1830s. Séguin, however, left the railroad and locomotive business by 1835 to concentrate on bridge building. A few years later the building of the first passenger lines around Paris—the Paris–Saint-Germain and two lines to Versailles—prompted François Cavé, Stehelin et Huber, and the Schneiders to start building locomotives, while the construction of the Strasbourg-Basel line prompted André Koechlin et Cie to do the same. In Lyon, Alphonse Clément-Desormes, son of the noted chemist Nicolas Clément-Desormes, built locomotives at Séguin's old plant at Perrache before founding the Ateliers et Forges d'Ouillins in the early 1840s. Various other steam engine and machine makers soon tried their hand with locomotives, including J-J Meyer of Mulhouse (successor of Risler et Dixon), Pauwels of Paris, and even the Anzin Mining Company. However, the slow initial pace of railroad building in France, coupled with an influx of British imports after the railroad companies got import duties on locomotives cut in half in 1837, discouraged heavy investment in plant and equipment by any French firm before 1845. As of 1842, the two largest French locomotive makers—Schneider and Koechlin—had delivered only 18 and 22 locomotives, respectively. The largest locomotive maker in France at that point was the firm of Allcard and Buddicom, set up at Rouen by two English engine makers at the behest of the English engineers directing the construction of the Chemin de Fer de l'Ouest.[31]

This situation changed dramatically in 1844 when the French government raised import duties on locomotives back up to 30 percent ad valorem—effectively closing the French market to imports—just as the implementation of the 1842 Railroad Act was generating an upsurge in railroad construction. Except for the depression of 1848, demand for locomotives remained strong from 1845 to the early 1860s, and in response Schneider and Koechlin made major commitments of money and manpower to locomotive production. Le Creusot's output rose to a peak of 147 locomotives in 1857, and Koechlin turned out 91 the same year. Just as important, new firms entered the field.

In 1844, Cail et Derosne, which had never before even made a steam engine, won a contract to supply the Crampton high-speed locomotive to the Northern Railroad, and it succeeded in delivering 64 of them by 1847. Surviving bankruptcy and reorganization in 1848–1851, Cail produced 136 locomotives in 1853—more than all other French companies combined. By 1863, the company was capable of assembling twenty-five locomotives at once at its Paris works while turning out additional machines for the Belgian market at Brussels and for the Russian market at Saint Petersburg. Overall, Cail produced more than 1,000 locomotives between 1845 and 1870.[32] Meanwhile, in Alsace another established metallurgical manufacturer, the Société de Graffenstaden, also made the transition to locomotive production. Founded in 1824 as a steel and hardware company, Graffenstaden was transformed in 1838 into the Etablissements de Construction Mécanique de Strasbourg to manufacture scales and machine tools, but like so many others the enterprise failed during the financial and political crises of 1847–1848. Taken over by the Strasbourg financier Alfred Renouard de Bussière in 1848, Graffenstaden shifted to steam engines and in 1855 started making locomotives. By the early 1860s, it was turning out 45–62 locomotives a year and had become France's fourth largest locomotive maker behind Schneider, Koechlin, and Cail.[33]

Two other new firms emerged as leaders in locomotive production in these years. In 1846 the young railroad engineer Ernest Gouïn launched the Société des Constructions de Batignolles with backing from James de Rothschild and other railroad promoters and financiers. Gouïn's goal was to turn out a locomotive a week, mainly for Rothschild's Northern Railroad. Despite a sputtering start, Batignolles met and surpassed that goal by 1854.[34] In the same year, what would soon become France's sixth large railroad equipment maker, Fives-Lille, was founded by Basile Parent and Pierre Schaken, who, after selling their steelworks at Vierzon and Clavières to Marine Steel in 1854, turned to providing rolling stock to the Lyon–Saint-Etienne Railroad. Parent and Schaken initially leased the Ouillins railroad works in Lyon that had been founded by Clément-Desormes, but in 1861, when the P-L-M Railroad acquired Ouillins as a repair and maintenance center, they transferred their operation to Fives-Lille in the Nord. Drawing capital from thirteen partners and then going public as the Compagnie de Fives-Lille in 1868, Parent and Schaken created France's largest railroad works outside of Le Creusot. With 1,700 workers and 500 machine tools, Fives-Lille produced 40–50 locomotives a year through the

1860s along with steam engines, cranes, hydraulic lifts, pumps, and refining equipment. At a separate plant at Givors near Lyon, the company turned out wheels and axles, boilers, and other locomotive components.[35]

Six firms thus came to dominate locomotive production in France at the height of railroad-building activity in the 1850s and 1860s: Schneider (Le Creusot), Koechlin, Cail, Gouïn (Batignolles), Graffenstaden, and Fives-Lille. These six became five after the Franco-Prussian War and the German annexation of Alsace-Lorraine in 1871, when Koechlin and Graffenstaden merged to form the Société Alsacienne de Constructions Mécaniques (SACM). Although a "German" company, SACM maintained its share of the French locomotive market—first through exports and then through a French subsidiary at Belfort. Not only did these five firms continue to supply most of the locomotives purchased by French railroads, but they also supplied locomotives to the new railroad systems in Italy, Spain, Portugal, and Russia in the 1860s and later exported locomotives to South America, China, and the French colonies.[36]

Locomotives constituted only one segment of the railroad equipment industry. Another was railroad cars. In Lyon in 1847, one of the promoters of the Lyon-Marseille railroad launched the Chantiers de la Buire, which specialized in freight car construction (700 per year in 1857–1867). It later merged with the Compagnie de Fonderies et Forges de l'Horme, and the resulting firm eventually moved into production of equipment for electric tramways.[37] More important for the railroad car industry were the Dietrich family enterprises in Alsace, which dated back to 1685 when the Strasbourg banker Jean Dietrich acquired the mines and forges of Jaegerthal. In the eighteenth century, the Dietrichs built blast furnaces, forges, and rolling mills at Rauschendwasser, Reichshoffen, Zinswiller, and Niederbronn. As the charcoal-based metallurgy of the Dietrichs came to be challenged by the new coal-based metallurgy in the nineteenth century, they transferred their smelting and refining operations to Mouterhouse in Lorraine, where they installed the first Bessemer converters and Siemens-Martin hearths in eastern France in the 1860s. At the same time, they converted their Alsatian plants to the manufacture of steam engines, turbines, and machine tools, and in 1848 they began building passenger and freight cars for the railroads at their Reichshoffen plant. After the annexation of Alsace-Lorraine in 1871, the Dietrichs became major suppliers of equipment to the German State Railway, but they also continued to supply the French railroads through a new subsidiary at Lunéville created in 1876 and eventually spun off as an independent company, the Société Lorraine des Anciens Etablissements de Dietrich.[38] Dietrich did not, of course, have the French market to itself. François Caron lists seven railroad car makers that supplied the Chemin de Fer du Nord (and probably the other French railroads) at the end of the nineteenth century. In addition to Dietrich, these included the Ateliers de Construction du Nord de la France at Douai, the Société Franco-Belge (Raismes), the Compagnie Française de Matériel de Chemin de Fer (Ivry), and Desouches et David of Pantin.[39]

Beyond locomotives and rolling stock, the building of the French railways offered many other opportunities for metallurgical manufacturing and engineering companies. Particularly important from the 1850s onward, when lines were being extended across the rugged topography of central and southern France, was the fabrication of iron bridges, viaducts, and tunnels, which required less mechanical proficiency than the manufacture of locomotives and other machinery but which the railroad companies were happy to delegate to outside contractors nonetheless. The equipment manufacturers found this work especially welcome in times of slack demand for their other products. The Société des Batignolles, for example, contracted to build its first railroad bridge in 1851 when orders for locomotives were few and far between. Building bridges proved to be so successful and profitable that it eventually supplanted locomotive building as the company's main line of business. Indeed, on the basis of this new expertise, Batignolles became a general contractor for railroad construction outside of France (initially in Italy and Russia and later in the Ottoman Empire, Greece, and South America), and it also built and operated a number of the railroads in the emerging French Empire, including the Bône-Guelma in Algeria and the Dakar–Saint-Louis in Senegal. Batignolles also diversified into the manufacture of heavy construction equipment (dredges and the like) and even attempted to build steamships at a shipyard in Nantes between 1855 and 1872.[40]

Cail and Fives-Lille followed a similar path. Taking advantage of their position as neighbors in the Nord, these two companies cooperated in building locomotives in the 1860s and also undertook a number of construction projects as joint ventures, including buildings for the 1867 Paris World's Fair and some 800 railroad bridges and viaducts in France and elsewhere. After the joint manufacturing agreement between the two expired in 1871, Fives-Lille proceeded to compete with

Cail in building sugar refineries (and ended up owning and operating several large refineries in northern France in the 1880s). It likewise competed with Batignolles in the manufacture of construction equipment and participated in a variety of public works projects including the Peking-Hankow Railway in China and the Gare d'Orsay (now the Musée d'Orsay) and the Alexander III Bridge in Paris.[41]

Schneider et Cie also moved into metallurgical construction, mainly at the plant at Chalon-sur-Saône, where it had been making steam engines, steamboats, and locomotives since 1839. Starting with the Lyon-Vaisse railroad bridge in 1853, the company supplied iron bridge flooring, caissons, and other components to bridge builders such as Hildevert Hersent. In the 1860s, the company began to fabricate iron building frames for public buildings such as the Entrepôt de Bercy and the Austerlitz railroad station in Paris, as well as lock doors for canals. However, it was not until the 1890s, when Schneider established a separate public works division, that it became a prime contractor for major construction projects (see Chapter 12).[42]

Metallurgical construction was undertaken not just by the large, diversified joint-stock companies but also by much smaller, specialized engineering companies. As described in the older work of Rondo Cameron and in the recent work of Dominique Barjot, the French were international leaders in the diverse and expanding field of public works construction, which included not only railroads, bridges, and tunnels, but also harbors and ports, waterworks and sewer systems, and canals. This activity brought forth and sustained a number of civil engineering firms. Among these were Fougerolles, which became a world leader in tunnel excavation after participating in the digging of the Saint-Gothard railroad tunnel in the 1860s; Vitali, Picard, et Cie, later renamed the Régie Générale des Chemins de Fer, which built railroads in the Mediterranean basin, China, and South America; and the firm of Hildevert Hersent, which became the leader in port construction in France and the French Empire in the late nineteenth century. Several firms specialized in the use of iron and steel in the construction of railroad bridges and tunnels, for which the French had no rivals in the second half of the nineteenth century. The largest firm of this ilk was that of Henri Daydé, but the best known was Gustave Eiffel et Cie.[43]

Gustave Eiffel was raised in a comfortable family of Dijon coal merchants (his *mother* started a coal trading business after Gustave's birth in 1832 to earn some extra money and ended up as the regional distributor for the Epinac Mining Company). After studying chemistry at the Ecole Centrale in Paris, Gustave began his career working for his brother-in-law in the iron industry at Châtillon-sur-Seine. In 1856, he became secretary to Charles Nepveu, a consulting engineer in Paris, and he followed Nepveu when the latter's firm was absorbed by the Compagnie Belge de Matériel de Chemins de Fer (Pauwels et Cie) in 1857. On behalf of Pauwels and Nepveu, Eiffel directed the construction in 1858–1860 of the iron bridge across the Garonne at Bordeaux that joined the Paris-Orléans and Midi railroads, after which he became the head of the firm's bridge division. In 1867, Eiffel left Pauwels to found his own company at Levallois-Perret, an industrial suburb on the northwest side of Paris. His first commission was for two viaducts on the Commentry-Gannet line in central France, undertaken in co-operation with Cail and Fives-Lille. Completion of these viaducts firmly established Eiffel's reputation for finding innovative solutions to engineering problems and, more importantly, for bringing projects in on time and at low cost.

Over the next fifteen years, Eiffel emerged as one of the leading contractors for iron construction in the world, building dozens of bridges and viaducts in France, Europe, and Asia; developing the portable, prefabricated iron bridges widely used by French colonial officials in Africa and Indochina; and advancing the use of structural iron in buildings as diverse as the Bon Marché department store, the Paris pavilion for the 1878 World's Fair, the Budapest train station, and the Church of San Marcos in Arica, Chile (prefabricated at Levallois-Perret and shipped to Chile section by section). In 1884, Eiffel constructed the iron framework that supported Bartholdi's Statue of Liberty, and two years later he won the right to design and build the monumental tower that became the centerpiece of the 1889 Paris Exposition (and eventually the most famous man-made structure in the world). In 1889, Eiffel agreed to construct the locks that the Panama Company belatedly commissioned to salvage its canal, but funds ran out before these were completed. Sucked into the scandal that followed the failure of the Panama Company in 1893, Eiffel resigned as managing director of the Etablissements Eiffel. However, the company went on as the Société de Construction de Levallois-Perret under Eiffel's protégé, Maurice Koechlin. Reverting to the Eiffel name in the 1920s, the firm survived until 1975.[44]

Examples could be multiplied, but it should be clear at this point that the steadily rising demand for an ever more diverse and sophisticated array of metal products over the course of the nineteenth century gave rise to a host of new capitalist enterprises in France.[45] These ranged in size from the giant Schneider Company at Le Creusot with its 8,000 employees to the large, diversified machinery and construction companies (Cail, Fives-Lille) that competed with Le Creusot in supplying the railroads, to the many small-to-medium firms (and the few quite large firms like Japy and Peugeot) that turned out the enormous variety of engines, tools, and hardware that were available in France by the end of the nineteenth century. In 1900, this industry was anything but static, as the demand for equipment for the new electrical industry burgeoned along with demand for a variety of new consumer durables such as bicycles and automobiles. Many of the firms introduced in this section will reappear in subsequent chapters when we consider these emerging industries. For now, we shall continue our survey of the flowering of industrial capitalism with a look at yet another essentially new industry of the nineteenth century, chemicals.

CHAPTER EIGHT

The Capitalism of Chemicals

At the heart of industrial capitalism in the nineteenth century was the processing of various vegetable and mineral raw materials to make semi-finished producer goods, which in turn served as the raw materials for finished consumer goods. The textile and metallurgical industries discussed earlier were simply special cases of this wider materials industry, which also included the production of vegetable oils, soap, glass, paper, cement, sugar, alcohol, and various pure chemicals. Though chemicals by no means constituted the largest materials industry in the nineteenth century, over the long run it proved to be one of the most important because of its linkages to other industries. In particular, the advent of large-scale production of inorganic acids (especially sulfuric acid) and alkalis (soda and potash), while most closely tied to the expansion of textiles production, made possible the greatly increased production of glass, soap, paper, and many other products. Similarly, the development of organic chemistry—above all the chemistry of coal-tar derivatives—gave rise to artificial dyes, new pharmaceuticals, synthetic fibers, and a host of other "miracle" products by the beginning of the twentieth century. This chapter deals with both sides of the new chemical industry in the nineteenth century, starting with the production of acids and alkalis and then turning to the development of organic chemicals, especially dyes, and hybrid products such as photographic plates and high explosives. The production of closely related materials like glass, paper, vegetable oils, and petroleum will be taken up in later chapters.

Heavy Chemicals: Acids and Alkalis

At the outset of the nineteenth century, dozens of chemicals and chemical compounds were produced in western Europe for industrial applications, but the emergence of a capitalistic, factory-based chemicals industry centered on the production of four things: "oil of vitriol" (sulfuric acid); the alkalis soda and potash (sodium carbonate and potassium carbonate); and various forms of chlorine, especially hydrochloric acid and chlorine bleach.[1] Alkalis were essential for making glass and soap, glazing pottery, and bleaching and finishing cloth, and potash could also be used to make artificial saltpeter, a key ingredient in gunpowder. Sulfuric acid was at first used mainly as a substitute for buttermilk in the souring of cloth (part of the bleaching process in the pre-chlorine era). Eventually, though, it was applied to many other processes—including curing and tanning leather, felting hats, purifying vegetable oil, and fixing blue and green dyes in wool. It also became a crucial ingredient in the production of other chemicals, notably hydrochloric acid and soda.

Sulfuric acid had been manufactured commercially in England since the mid-eighteenth century. It was made by burning sulfur over water, first in glass chambers and later in much larger lead chambers. The rise of the cloth printing industry in France created a need for sulfuric acid to fix blue dye in cotton, and demand for it burgeoned. John Holker *fils* brought the lead chamber process to France in the early 1770s, and by the end of the 1780s a number of acid works had been set up in France. Meanwhile, chlorine gas was first produced in 1773, and the French chemist Berthollet discovered its bleaching properties in 1785. Soon thereafter, the manufacture of chlorine bleach began as an offshoot of sulfuric acid production (hydrochloric acid—the starting point for most chlorine products—was produced by treating common salt with sulfuric acid). By 1789, various kinds of chlorine bleach were on the market in France, notably "eau de Javel" (potassium hypochlorite), produced under Berthollet's supervision at the Javel Chemical Works in Paris by combining hydrochloric acid and potash.[2]

While sulfuric acid and chlorine were essentially new products made possible by scientific and technological breakthroughs, alkalis were traditional products that continued to be extracted from natural sources using age-old methods. Potash was produced by burning wood, and soda by burning marine vegetation, mainly saltwort on the Spanish coast and kelp on the Scottish coast. By the 1780s, the French depended on foreign sources for both of these alkalis, so there was growing interest in finding ways to produce them at home artificially and cheaply. It was already understood that soda could be made through the combustion of salt; the trick was to find an economically feasible way of doing this. To that end, the Académie des Sciences offered a prize in 1775, but it was not until 1789 that Nicolas Leblanc, the household physician to the duc d'Orléans, came up with a workable solution. The Leblanc soda process consisted of two stages: Salt was first treated with sulfuric acid to produce sodium sulfate ("saltcake," Na_2SO_4), with hydrochloric acid as a by-product; the saltcake was then burned in combination with limestone (calcium carbonate) to yield sodium carbonate and various by-products. It was the second stage that was Leblanc's true innovation, and not until he developed a reverbatory furnace to handle the combustion of the saltcake and limestone did his process become commercially feasible.

In September 1791, the French government awarded Leblanc a fifteen-year patent on his soda production process, and he then proceeded to construct a plant at Saint-Denis near Paris with the financial backing of the duc d'Orléans. In trial runs in 1793, the plant produced over 30,000 pounds of soda, but the onset of the Reign of Terror prevented it from becoming fully operational. Although he embraced the Revolution, changed his name to Philippe Egalité, and even voted in favor of the execution of his cousin Louis XVI, the duc d'Orléans was arrested and guillotined in November 1793. The Revolutionary government thereupon seized the Saint-Denis sodaworks as a part of the Orléans property. During the next six years the plant went out of production as Leblanc haggled with officials over control. Finally, in 1800 Leblanc regained control of the plant, but he lacked the capital necessary to put it back into full operation. Despondent over this and other business failures, Leblanc committed suicide in 1806. The Saint-Denis plant ended up in the hands of J-P Darcet.[3]

Meanwhile, in 1794 the Committee of Public Safety had revoked Leblanc's patent and had placed the Leblanc process in the public domain in the hope of increasing soda production so that potash could be used exclusively in making saltpeter, which was in critically short supply. However, the real takeoff in Leblanc soda production came only in 1809, when the government of Napoleon Bonaparte granted sodamakers an exemption from the salt tax, which had remained high in spite of the reforms of the Revolution and had thereby discouraged full utilization of the new technology. In 1810, a total of 24,000 tons of Leblanc soda was produced at some twenty-seven plants located mainly in five departments—the Seine (Paris), the Seine-Inférieure (Rouen), the Aisne (including Saint-Gobain), the Hérault (Montpellier), and the Bouches-du-Rhône (Marseille)—where the necessary raw materials were readily available and there were important industrial customers (mainly, makers of textiles, glass, or soap). Because firms set up to manufacture Leblanc soda inevitably became the largest producers of sulfuric acid (more of which was employed in soda production than all other uses combined) and hydrochloric acid (which was the chief by-product of the first stage of the process), these firms ended up dominating France's heavy chemicals industry through most of the nineteenth century.

Among the largest integrated producers of soda, acids, and sulfates in France in the early 1800s were the Dieuze chemical works in Lorraine; the Malétra family enterprise at Petit-Quevilly near Rouen, which came to virtually monopolize the supply of chemicals to the Norman cotton industry by the 1860s; and the firm of Charles Kestner at Thann, which similarly became the leading supplier of chemicals to the Mulhouse textile industry. In the Paris region, the most important chemical enterprise was the firm of J-P-C Darcet and his partners, which at its height in the early 1820s operated three plants, including the original Leblanc sodaworks at Saint-Denis. In the department of the Bouches-du-Rhône, which had the largest concentration of chemicals works and accounted for three-fourths of all the soda produced in France in the 1820s (two-thirds of which went to the soap industry), the largest firm was the Compagnie des Salines et Produits Chimiques de Plan d'Aren. With 460 workers and an annual output of 5,000 tons of crude soda, it was arguably the largest chemical company in France in 1830.[4]

In the mid-1820s, the British entered the Leblanc soda industry on a large scale, and over the next quarter century they supplanted the French as the world's largest soda and acid producers (in 1853, British alkali production exceeded 151,000 tons, more than three times the French production of 45,000 tons). The British gained their supremacy because, as the low-cost producer, they were able to push the French out of third-country markets. Moreover, after 1860, when the Anglo-French Treaty of Commerce cut French import duties on soda from a virtually prohibitive 100 percent to 10 percent, the British made significant inroads into the French market (between 1860 and 1868 imports of soda into France rose from zero to 9,850 tons).

Under these circumstances, only the largest-scale, lowest-cost French manufacturers could survive and prosper. By and large these did not include the first generation of French Leblanc sodamakers, who were operating aging, relatively small-scale plants. To be sure, firms such as Malétra, Dieuze, and Saint-Denis continued to produce acid and soda for local and regional markets, and Kestner in Alsace survived and expanded by making a wide range of specialized chemicals for the textile industry. But the Marseille sodaworks disappeared in the face of the growing competition. In their place, leadership of the French chemical industry passed to a second generation of Leblanc soda enterprises, founded after 1820, which developed more efficient and larger-scale production, made better use of chemical by-products, and were simply better managed. By the 1860s, four of these second generation firms dominated the French chemical industry: Saint-Gobain, Perret-Olivier, Kuhlmann, and Alais et Camargue.

As we saw earlier, Saint-Gobain had been one of France's great industrial success stories of the eighteenth century. At the outset of the nineteenth century, it was still the world's leading producer of plate glass for mirrors and display windows, and, as we shall see in the next chapter, it continued to lead the French glass industry throughout the century. At the same time, it also became France's largest producer of sulfuric acid and Leblanc soda. Faced with a shortage of natural soda (a key ingredient in making glass) during the trade embargo of 1806–1807, Saint-Gobain began buying artificial soda from various suppliers, and in 1819 it acquired its own Leblanc plant at Charlefontaine. In 1822 this production was transferred to a larger, more sophisticated plant at Chauny near Saint-Gobain. However, the key date for Saint-Gobain's entry into the chemical industry was 1829, when, as part of a larger reorganization to meet growing competition in the glass industry, the directors brought in the eminent chemist Nicolas Clément-Desormes as general agent and head of a new separate chemical division. In his six years at Saint-Gobain, Clément-Desormes rebuilt the Chauny sodaworks, doubling the size of its furnaces and increasing its overall capacity fivefold. He further enhanced production and profits by improving the recovery of by-products, especially hydrochloric acid, which was used to make bleaching powder.

The development of Saint-Gobain's chemical division continued under an even more eminent scientist, Joseph Gay-Lussac, who joined the management in 1832 and served as president from 1843 to his death in 1850. Gay-Lussac introduced "Gay-Lussac towers" to recover nitric acid used in the lead-chamber process, thereby cutting the cost of making sulfuric acid 20 percent, and he generally promoted technical improvements in the production of both acid and soda. At his death, revenues from chemical production had surpassed those from glass production (3.36 million francs versus 2.6 million). In the 1850s and 1860s, Saint-Gobain further expanded acid production and maintained its position as France's largest producer of acid and soda (from the 1830s to the 1870s, it consistently provided 15 percent of annual French soda production and up to 37 percent of the annual output of sulfuric acid). Instead of technical innovation, however, the company increasingly followed a strategy of horizontal integration, seeking to protect existing production and profits by eliminating competition through mergers with other French acid and soda makers. In particular, Saint-Gobain successfully negotiated a merger with the second largest soda company, Perret-Olivier of Lyon, in 1872, which gave Saint-Gobain control of 40 percent of French soda output.[5]

At the time of its merger with Saint-Gobain, Perret-Olivier was the dominant chemical company in Lyon. In 1819 Claude-Marie Perret had established a Leblanc sodaworks in the Lyon suburb of Les Brotteaux, using locally produced vitriol to treat sea salt brought up the Rhône on riverboats from the Camargue. In 1822 he moved his plant to Perraches at the confluence of the Saône and Rhône and began making his own sulfuric acid. The key to his success, however, lay in research undertaken in the 1830s by his sons, Michel and Jean-Baptiste, and his son-in-law, Jules Olivier, to perfect the making of sulfuric acid by roasting cupriferous pyrite ores. In 1836, the Perrets and Olivier patented their method, which cut the cost of making sulfuric acid in half. Armed with this new technology and with pyrite mines purchased in the early 1840s, Perret-Olivier (as the firm was by then known) proceeded to take control of acid and soda production in southern France. In the 1850s, the firm moved production out of Lyon proper to the suburb of Saint-Fons, built additional plants along the Saône-Rhône corridor north and south of Lyon, and integrated backward by purchasing its own coal mine and assembling its own fleet of riverboats to bring raw materials to its factories and to distribute its finished products to markets throughout southeastern France. By the 1860s, Perret-Olivier not only monopolized acid and soda production in the South but also furnished pyrites to acid makers elsewhere in France, including Saint-Gobain. So, in its drive to consolidate French acid and soda production in the face of British competition, it is not surprising that Saint-Gobain looked to Perret-Olivier.[6]

A third possible partner in the 1872 merger was Etablissements Kuhlmann, the principal acid and soda producer in the department of the Nord. This firm was founded and for fifty years managed by Frédéric Kuhlmann. A native of Colmar in Alsace, Kuhlmann studied with the chemist Vauquelin in Paris and then went to Lille, where he taught public courses in chemistry and began manufacturing chemicals. In 1825 he set up a plant near Lille at Loos to make sulfuric acid and soda and then added two more plants in 1847 and 1852. By the 1850s, Kuhlmann was the principal producer of a wide variety of chemicals used by the textile industry of the Nord. In the early 1860s, the firm became a *société en commandite*, which Kuhlmann continued to run with the help of his son and two sons-in-law, Auguste Lamy (professor of industrial chemistry at the Ecole Centrale) and Edouard Agache (the leading linen manufacturer of Lille). Seeking to broaden its markets and assure its supply of raw materials, Etablissements Kuhlmann considered merging with Saint-Gobain and Perret-Olivier in the late 1860s, but the negotiations failed. Choosing to remain independent, the S.A. des Manufactures des Produits Chimiques du Nord (as it became in 1870) accounted for some 15 percent of French inorganic chemical production in the 1870s, and it was the second largest chemical company in France at the time of Kuhlmann's death in 1881.[7]

The third largest Leblanc soda manufacturer—and thus the third largest chemical company in France—in the 1870s was the newest, the Compagnie des Produits Chimiques d'Alais et de la Camargue, founded in 1855 by Henri Merle and a group of Lyon and Marseille industrialists, including J-B Guimet of Lyon, one of France's leading dyemakers. After studying chemistry with J-B Dumas at the Ecole Centrale in Paris in the 1840s, Merle had worked in soda production in Belgium, England, and Germany. At the urging of Guimet and his associates, Merle went to the south of France in 1855 to find a location for a state-of-the-art Leblanc soda factory where raw materials could be brought together most economically. Merle selected Salindres, near Alais on the Alais-Bessèges railroad in the department of the Gard, where coal from Bessèges and local pyrites and calcite could be combined with salt that Merle and Guimet produced at the Salins de Giraud in the Camargue. By 1857 what was probably the single largest Leblanc sodaworks in France went on line at Salindres, first producing sulfuric acid, then soda and other products made with sulfuric acid. One of these was the then little-known light metal, aluminum.

In the early 1850s, Henri Sainte-Claire Deville had invented the first commercially viable method for refining aluminum from bauxite, which was particularly prevalent in the south of France (the name of the ore comes from the town of Les Baux near Arles). Looking for ways to utilize his sulfuric acid output profitably, Henri Merle purchased the rights to the Sainte-Claire Deville process, which required large amounts of sulfuric acid, in 1859. From then until the invention of the more efficient electrolytic process for refining aluminum in the 1880s, Alais et Camargue was virtually the only producer of aluminum in Europe. But at the time this was of little consequence. Output of aluminum remained miniscule, the price high, and industrial applications limited (it was mainly a curiosity, used in a set of tableware for Napoleon III in the 1860s and later in an alloy for medals and medallions).[8] Meanwhile the success of Alais et Carmague continued to depend on the production of other chemicals: soda, chlorine and chloride of lime (bleaching powder), copper sulfate and other copper compounds derived from the pyrites of Salindres, and caustic soda for the soapmakers of Marseille. In 1877 Henri Merle died prematurely and was replaced as *gérant* by Alfred Rangod Pechiney, whose name would henceforth be synonymous with the firm. However, ultimate power remained in the hands of the Guimets and the other founding families, and the basic strategy of the firm continued as before.[9]

Even as Alais et Camargue (Pechiney) was bringing Leblanc soda production to a new level of technical efficiency, Ernest Solvay in Belgium was introducing a new method of making soda that, for all practical purposes, rendered the Leblanc process obsolete. Almost from the beginning, soda manufacturers had recognized that there were certain inefficiencies inherent in the Leblanc process, notably the need for large amounts of fuel and the inability to retrieve and reuse such valuable ingredients as sulfur and calcium, all of which kept soda prices up. As early as 1811, Auguste Fresnel had proposed that soda could be synthesized more cheaply by converting ammonia to ammonium bicarbonate and then combining the latter with salt, but the key to making this economically feasible was the recovery and reuse of the ammonia. It was this recovery that Solvay worked out in the 1860s. The opening of his first ammonia process sodaworks near Charleroi in 1864 dramatically reduced costs and prices and dealt a mortal blow to Belgium's Leblanc soda production.[10]

In 1872, Solvay entered the French market with a soda plant at Varangéville near the Dombasle saltworks in the Meurthe-et-Moselle. Although Saint-Gobain, Kuhlmann, and Pechiney made numerous small improvements in their Leblanc production to cut costs, the inherent superiority of the ammonia process allowed Solvay to quickly take control of soda production in France. By 1890, Solvay et Cie accounted for fully one-half of world soda production, and its revenues in France were three times those of Saint-Gobain's chemicals division. Leblanc soda output in France fell from 57,000 tons in 1873 to 20,000 by 1900, as Solvay's output rose from 44,000 tons to 207,500.[11] The last Leblanc soda plant in France closed in 1910. By then Solvay's patents had expired, and Saint-Gobain had begun producing soda with the ammonia process at a plant near Varangéville. Pechiney, however, chose to get out of soda production entirely and signed a long-term contract to supply salt from its Salins de Giraud plant to a new Solvay soda plant set up there in 1896. By 1914, the production of artificial soda in France, once scattered in dozens of plants throughout the country, was concentrated in four giant works: the Solvay plant at Salins de Giraud and three plants in Lorraine operated by Solvay, Saint-Gobain, and Marchéville, Daguin et Cie, France's largest makers of table salt.[12]

The demise of Leblanc soda production and the virtual takeover of the French soda market by Solvay did not mean the end of the heavy chemical industry in France or the decline of the big firms that had dominated the industry in the mid-nineteenth century. While maintaining Leblanc soda production as long as possible (and, in the case of Saint-Gobain, eventually adopting the Solvay process), France's three largest chemical companies responded creatively to the challenge posed by Solvay, mainly by finding new uses for their sulfuric acid production, which in contrast to their soda production faced no threat. For Saint-Gobain this move involved substituting sodium sulfate—still made by treating salt with sulfuric acid (the first stage of the Leblanc process)—for sodium carbonate in the making of glass. In other words, the advent of the Solvay soda process posed less of a threat to Saint-Gobain because glassmaking no longer required soda; it could and did phase out the second stage of Leblanc production without great sacrifice. At the same time, Saint-Gobain found a new outlet for its excess sulfuric acid in the production of superphosphates, artificial fertilizer made by treating phosphate ores with acid. France represented a potentially large market for all varieties of artificial fertilizer in the late nineteenth century, and as early as 1872 one-fourth of Saint-Gobain's sulfuric acid output went into making superphosphates. However, it was only in the 1890s that Saint-Gobain made a major commitment to superphosphate production. In 1892 it opened a huge new fertilizer plant at Balaruc

(Hérault) and proceeded to build more than a dozen additional plants in various parts of France over the next fifteen years. At the same time, it invested heavily in phosphate mining in France, Morocco, Algeria, and Tunisia. By 1913 superphosphate production was absorbing 60 percent of Saint-Gobain's sulfuric acid output, and chemicals again became the company's most profitable division.[13]

Meanwhile in the Nord, the Kuhlmann Company, under Frédéric Kuhlmann's successors (notably Edouard Agache), continued and even expanded its traditional production technology, adding four new plants in the 1870s and 1880s. However, like Saint-Gobain, it shifted its emphasis to sulfuric acid and to the first stage of the Leblanc process, producing sodium sulfate and hydrochloric acid for the textile industry. It also followed Saint-Gobain into superphosphate production in the 1890s with a new plant at Dunkirk to treat imported phosphate ore. Although Kuhlmann did little more than hold its own among French chemical companies at a time when the French were being outdistanced by rapidly growing German, Belgian, Swiss, and American chemical companies, it nonetheless raised its total output of chemicals from 90,000 tons in 1889 to 200,000 tons in 1900.[14]

In the South, Pechiney also exploited the existing technology as long as possible, producing caustic soda (which could not be made with the ammonia process until the 1890s) for the soapmakers of Marseille along with bleaching powder and copper sulfate for the wine industry. Meanwhile, it faced the loss of its monopoly in aluminum production after 1890, when new firms began producing aluminum much more cheaply with the Héroult and Hall electrolytic processes. In the late 1890s Pechiney relaunched its aluminum production by taking over a plant that made aluminum with the Hall process. As we shall see in Chapter 15, the firm increasingly concentrated on aluminum after 1900, using the sulfuric acid produced at Salindres to extract alumina—the raw material of the electrolytic process—from bauxite.[15]

As a result of these modifications, Saint-Gobain, Kuhlmann, and Pechiney managed to maintain their positions as the three largest chemical companies in France at the end of the nineteenth century. At the same time, other firms found new niches in the French heavy chemicals industry. For example, the Compagnie Française des Produits Oxygénés pioneered the production of hydrogen peroxide (eau oxygéné) for bleaching wool and also became France's leading maker of barium salts. At Clermont-Ferrand, Jacques-Louis Kessler emerged as the leading French manufacturer of fluorine products, particularly hydrofluoric acid for etching glass. In Rouen, the Malétra Company, while continuing to produce acid and soda, diversified into other inorganic salts and became the leader in cobalt compounds, thanks to the opening of a cobalt mine on New Caledonia in the South Pacific in 1891. In Paris, Poulenc Frères produced fine inorganic salts for medical uses (iodides, bromides), pure chemicals for scientific research (lithium, chromium, molybdenum), and photographic supplies (potassium bromide). In the Nord, the Société Anonyme des Usines de Produits Chimiques d'Hautmont used Belgian pyrites to make an array of products similar to Kuhlmann's. In Lyon, Coignet et Cie, founded in 1818 to manufacture gelatin and glue by treating bone with hydrochloric acid, became the leading French manufacturer of pure phosphorus and a major manufacturer of matches until the latter became a government monopoly in 1872; thereafter Coignet concentrated on making superphosphates from bonemeal as well as copper phosphate, phosphoric acid, and phosphate of soda. The match monopoly itself was leased to the Compagnie Générale des Allumettes de France, which consolidated match production in some ten plants that it operated until the government took over direct administration—and further consolidated production—in 1889.[16]

The New Chemicals: Artificial Dyes and High Explosives

In addition to the inorganic (mineral-based) chemical industry, there was, of course, a new organic chemical industry emerging in the late nineteenth century. Histories of this industry usually focus on the development of artificial dyes and pharmaceuticals and emphasize how the French failed to capitalize on early opportunities and were soon relegated to the periphery of the industry by innovative German and Swiss firms. There is certainly much evidence to support this view, but one should not overestimate the degree of French failure.

In the first half of the nineteenth century, France was the world's leading producer of colors and dyes, and a number of French dyemakers developed new dyes or perfected old ones using traditional animal or vegetable raw materials. One of these was Charles Meissonnier of Saint-Denis, who introduced a superior grade of garancene—the red dye extracted from madder root—in 1829 and remained its leading manufacturer for the next fifty years.[17] Another was J-B Guimet of Lyon, who in 1834 introduced the dye that made him rich and famous, an inexpensive ultramarine blue made from kaolin, sodium carbonate, and other inorganic chemicals (previously this color could only be made at great expense by pulverizing lapus lazuli). Guimet later added other dyes to his product line, and his son Emile continued the family dye business into the second half of the nineteenth century while also serving as a director of Alais et Camargue (which, as we saw earlier, was founded by his father).[18] Another Lyon dyemaker, François Gillet, made his mark by manufacturing *noir de Lyon*, a black dye extracted from chestnut wood that was in great demand among the makers of silk cloth. Gillet's sons and grandsons continued to produce natural dyestuffs into the twentieth century while also putting together France's leading bleaching and dyeing company, Gillet-Thaon, and helping to launch the artificial silk industry (see Chapter 15).[19] Meanwhile still other Lyon chemists and dyemakers played critical roles in the development of synthetic dyes.

In 1845 the Lyon firm of Guinon Marnas et Bonnet synthesized picric acid, the first artificial dye made from coal-tar derivatives, and within ten years this became the principal yellow dye used in the French silk industry. In the mid-1850s, however, demand in the women's fashion industry was shifting to purples. To capitalize on this demand, the British chemist William Perkin created an artificial purple dye based on the coal-tar derivative aniline and introduced it in France as "mauve" in 1857. Because Perkin failed to secure a French patent on his new dye, various French dyemakers soon introduced competing versions of aniline purple. But because Perkin remained the low-cost producer and because French import duties on foreign dyestuffs were reduced under the terms of the Anglo-French Trade Treaty of 1860, Perkin continued to send large quantities of aniline purple to France until the "mauve mania" subsided.[20]

In the early 1860s, fashion on both sides of the English Channel turned from purple to red, prompting the French chemist François-Emmanuel Verguin to create the first aniline red dye. The Lyon dyers François and Joseph Renard quickly acquired the rights to Verguin's aniline red, patented it in their name, and brought it to market in France as "fuchsine" (from fuchsia). They simultaneously licensed it to English dyemakers, who introduced it in Britain as "magenta red," in honor of Napoleon III's recent victory over the Austrians in Italy. Aniline red proved to be highly lucrative (according to Jean Bouvier, Renard Frères earned 2.5 million francs just from their licensing agreement with the British in 1860–1863), and the Renards soon faced challenges to their ownership of the new dye from many quarters. The ensuing commercial and legal battles over fuchsine to a great degree determined the fate of the synthetic dye industry in France.

When another Lyon dyemaker, Emile-Hippolyte Franc, introduced a substitute for fuchsine made from toluidine instead of aniline, Renard Frères headed off a ruinous price war by merging with Franc's company. Similarly, when other Lyon chemists discovered a more efficient way to synthesize aniline red, Renard Frères et Franc absorbed them and their patents. But as still other potential threats to their control of aniline red emerged, the Renards changed tactics and brought suit to enforce their patent rights (under French law they could claim exclusive rights to all aniline red, regardless of how it was made). By 1863, the French courts had ruled definitively in favor of Renard Frères et Franc. To get maximum benefit from this victory, the Renards and their associates enlisted the aid of the newly created Crédit Lyonnais to launch a joint-stock company to take over and exploit the French patent on aniline red. Thus was the Société La Fuchsine born in December 1863.

At the insistence of Henri Germain, the president of the Crédit Lyonnais and the leading director of the new company, La Fuchsine immediately spent millions of francs to stockpile aniline feedstock, to acquire two aniline plants in England, and to expand the Renard dyeworks in Lyon, all in order to meet the expected demand for fuchsine. As things turned out, however, Germain had overestimated this demand, leaving the company with large unsold inventories and heavy operating losses in its first two years. The firm's situation worsened when a number of deaths in the Lyon area were traced to pollution from La Fuchsine's plants, which prompted the government to close those plants in 1866 and 1867 just as German chemical companies started to flood the French market with aniline red in defiance of La Fuchsine's patent. Germain and his allies on the company's board decided to cut their losses by selling the fuchsine patent to the Paris dyemaker Alcide Poirrier. In April 1870 Société La Fuchsine was liquidated.[21]

The decline of the French dye industry that seemed to begin with the demise of La Fuchsine was to a large degree due to the successful enforcement of the fuchsine patent in France. Many of the French chemists on the losing side in the battle over the aniline red patent in 1863 moved across the border to Basel, Switzerland, where they set up aniline dye production for Geigy, Bindschedler and Busch (the future CIBA) and Durand and Huguenin. Concurrently, four German firms —BASF, Casella, Bayer, and Meister, Lucius, Bruning (the future

Hoechst)—not only moved into aniline dye production but also took the lead in developing a second generation of coal-tar derivative dyes that soon superseded the aniline dyes. In 1868, German chemists discovered how to make an artificial form of alizarin (the chief component in garancene, the red dye extracted from madder), which cost one-third as much as garancene and was easier to use. When Meister, Lucius, Bruning and BASF in Germany and William Perkin and Sons in Britain began to produce the artificial alizarin in volume, garancene was quickly driven off the market, and madder cultivation in Holland and France collapsed. The principal French maker of garancene, Les Héritiers de Charles Meissonnier, survived, however, by shifting to the production of wood-based dyes such as *brésilene* from brazilwood.[22]

By the 1890s the five largest German chemical companies—Bayer, BASF, Hoechst, Casella, and AGFA—dominated world dye production, and most of the dye made in France was produced by the French subsidiaries of these companies. According to Claude Ferry, fully 87 percent of the dyestuffs employed in French industry came from German companies or their subsidiaries on the eve of World War I.[23] However, the dramatic rise of the German dye industry did not mean that the French industry "withered away" at the end of the nineteenth century, as L. F. Haber asserted in his history of the European chemical industry.[24] Two French makers of synthetic dyes and pharmaceuticals managed to survive the German-Swiss onslaught and later played key roles in the renascence of the French chemicals industry after World War I.

One of these was the Société Anonyme des Matières Colorantes et Produits Chimiques de Saint-Denis (Poirrier et Dalsace), founded in Paris by Charles Mottet in 1824 to extract natural colors from dyer's moss, indigo, and the like. When Mottet retired in 1857, one of his employees, Alcide Poirrier, took over the firm and soon moved into the production of aniline dye, starting with an aniline violet *(rosalene)* in 1861 and scoring a greater success with *violet de Paris* in 1867. The next year, Poirrier acquired the patents of La Fuchsine, but these lost much of their value when synthetic alizarin was introduced. Because the Germans held the French patents on alizarin, Poirrier was blocked from producing it until the patents expired in 1885, by which time BASF had achieved such market dominance that Poirrier could not catch up. However, he compensated for this defeat by moving into the production of the new azo (nitrobenzene-based) dyes and coal-tar-based pharmaceuticals in the 1870s. In 1881, Poirrier merged with another firm, Dalsace, and the new company was soon reconfigured as the Société Anonyme des Matières Colorantes et Produits Chimiques de Saint-Denis. As of 1900, the company employed 500 workers at four plants that produced various organic and inorganic feedstocks and a wide range of dyes and pharmaceuticals, many of which had been developed in the company's research laboratory. It also maintained sales offices in the principal textile centers of France, Great Britain, continental Europe, the United States, and Japan.[25]

A second major French dye company was founded by a Lyon chemist, Prosper Monnet, who, like Alcide Poirrier, played a prominent role in the early aniline dye industry in France. When Monnet's efforts to compete with Renard Frères in red dye production were foiled by the 1863 patent ruling, Monnet became the director of production at La Fuchsine. When La Fuchsine sold out to Poirrier in 1868, Monnet moved to Geneva, where he set up a new firm with Marc Gilliard and Jean-Marie Cartier to manufacture aniline dyes. In 1881 the fuchsine patents held by Poirrier expired, and the French government put new duties on artificial dyes imported into France, so Gilliard, Monnet, et Cartier moved back to Lyon. Building a new plant at Saint-Fons, the firm increased the number of dyes it manufactured and added artificial flavors and fragrances as well as pharmaceuticals (antipyrines and salicylates) to its line. In 1895 the firm was reorganized as a *société anonyme*, the Société Chimique des Usines du Rhône. As we will see in Chapter 15, Usines du Rhône later metamorphosed into the leading French chemical company of the twentieth century, Rhône-Poulenc.[26]

Although the French (and, it might be noted, the British) had only limited success in competing with the Germans and Swiss in coal-tar dyes and pharmaceuticals in the late nineteenth century, they fared better in other new industries that straddled the border between organic and inorganic chemicals. One of these was photographic supplies. In Lyon, Antoine Lumière and his sons Auguste and Louis founded a plant to manufacture gelatin-silver bromide photographic plates in 1881 (before then, photographic paper and plates were so unstable that each photographer prepared his own as needed). In 1894, the Lumières introduced the first color photographic plates, further cementing their position as the foremost makers of photographic plates in the world. Even as the Lumière brothers entered the nascent motion picture industry in 1896—the basis of their historic reputations today—they continued to expand their photographic plate production. By 1906, they employed 800 workers and technicians, turned out 2.5 million plates and 2,200 kilometers of photographic paper, and had sales worth 9 million francs.[27]

Another new hybrid chemical industry that the French did well in at the end of the nineteenth century was high explosives. Until the Franco-Prussian War, the production of explosives in France had centered on gunpowder and remained a government monopoly under the Administration des Poudres et Salpêtres. Two new "high" explosives discovered in the 1840s, nitrocellulose (guncotton) and nitroglycerine, were destined to supplant gunpowder in blasting and demolition and in the warheads of artillery shells, but both were initially so dangerous to manufacture and handle that France and other countries banned their production. In 1864, however, the Swedish chemist Alfred Nobel introduced a more stable form of nitroglycerine that he called dynamite. Nobel soon began manufacturing dynamite at plants in Sweden, Germany, and Austria with financial backing from a French embroidery maker turned forgemaster, Jean-Baptiste Barbe-Schmitz, and his son, Paul Barbe, a *polytechnicien* and military engineer. As demand for dynamite took off in the late 1860s, Barbe became Nobel's right-hand man in managing production and sales on the Continent, even though the French ban on nitroglycerine precluded the production of dynamite in France.[28]

In 1870, the invading Prussian armies used dynamite with great success to blow up bridges and fortifications, and in the autumn of 1870 Léon Gambetta, the minister of national defense in the new government of the Third Republic, gave Barbe permission to set up a dynamite factory at Paulilles near the Spanish border. At the end of the war, the French government closed the Paulilles plant, but Barbe was allowed to continue to make dynamite for export at his father's forge at Liverdun in the Meurthe-et-Moselle. In 1875, the ban on dynamite production in France was finally lifted, and Barbe and Nobel founded the Société Générale pour la Fabrication de Dynamite to produce dynamite and other Nobel-patented products in France. In 1884, that company merged with its only significant domestic rival, thereby establishing a virtual monopoly in the manufacture of high explosives in France.[29]

Meanwhile, Nobel and Barbe proceeded to found similar firms in Spain, Portugal, Switzerland, and Italy. To eliminate competition among the various Nobel companies in western and southern Europe, these were brought together with the French Nobel Company in 1887 under a holding company, the Société Centrale des Dynamites, headed by Barbe and headquartered in Paris, where Nobel by then was living.

The Société Centrale came to be known as the Latin Trust and worked closely with a second Nobel holding company, the Anglo-German Trust, to fix prices and divide up markets for high explosives throughout Europe. As of 1896, the French Nobel company produced a mere 1,500 tons of explosives annually, but the 26 factories controlled by the Société Centrale produced 8,500 tons yearly (compared to 36,000 tons produced by the Anglo-German Trust and a total of 66,500 tons produced by all Nobel companies worldwide).[30]

In 1886, the French Nobel company began supplying explosives to Ferdinand de Lesseps' Panama Company. The following year, Paul Barbe, by then a member of the National Assembly and minister of agriculture, along with other deputies tied to the Dynamite Trust, accepted bribes to support the Panama Company's campaign for parliamentary approval of a lottery loan to stave off bankruptcy. But the Panama Company failed in 1889 anyway, and a parliamentary inquiry and revelations of illegal payoffs soon followed. Paul Barbe's sudden death in 1890 spared him prosecution, but other directors of the Société Générale and the Société Centrale were caught up in the scandal (and one went to prison).[31] As a result, there were wholesale resignations within the top management of both companies, and a Paris banker, Emile Mercet, was brought in as chairman to restore credibility. Yet the long-term effects of the Panama Scandal were minimal. Under the direction of Paul Clemenceau, the younger brother of Georges Clemenceau, the Société Centrale remained part of the bicephalous trust that continued to control the production and sale of dynamite and other Nobel products in Europe and in much of the rest of the world into the twentieth century. At the same time, the French Nobel company moved into new product areas, including cellulose, artificial silk, and chlorate-based explosives such as cheddite. Both the Société Générale—renamed the Société Nobel Française after its merger with the Société du Celluloïd in 1927—and the Société Centrale continued to play major roles in the French chemicals industry into the post–World War II era.[32]

Finally, we should note that dyestuffs, pharmaceuticals, photographic supplies, and explosives represented just the high end of the organic chemicals industry. The nineteenth century also witnessed the advent of bulk organic chemical production, which included the processing of coal for gas, coke, and coal by-products. In the coal-processing industry, the clear leader in France was the Compagnie Parisienne d'Eclairage et de Chauffage par le Gaz—the Paris Gas

Company—founded in 1855 by the merger of the original six gas companies in the capital. As discussed by Lenard Berlanstein in his social history of the company,[33] the Paris Gas Company did more than produce gas for lighting and coke for home-heating and industrial uses. Through its by-products division, it also became a principal supplier of coal tar and coal-tar derivatives like anthracene to the dye industry, as well as a major producer of ammonium fertilizers. Beyond the coal processors, the bulk organic chemical industry included the various companies that refined sugar cane and sugar beets into sugar, syrup, and alcohol, as well as the oil-seed refiners and other manufacturers whose products straddled the line between industrial raw materials and consumer goods. For the sake of coherence, however, those firms will be discussed in Chapter 10, which discusses the capitalism of consumer goods.

To conclude our discussion of the capitalism of chemicals, suffice it to say that chemicals production remained a dynamic and expansive area of enterprise in France throughout the nineteenth century in spite of deficiencies and failures that relegated the once-dominant French to the role of supporting players in the European and world chemicals industry. No less than textiles, metallurgy, and machine building, the chemicals industry in nineteenth-century France gave rise to a complex assortment of small, medium, and large firms, some of which continued to play—or came to play—important roles in the French and world economies in the twentieth century.

CHAPTER NINE

The Capitalism of Glass, Paper, and Print

Closely allied to the chemical industry—indeed, treated as a subset of that industry in some industrial classifications—were the industries of glass and paper. More than the bulk chemicals discussed in Chapter 8, glass and paper (and the printing industry tied to the latter) straddled the line between producer and consumer industries. Discussing these industries thus provides us with a transition from the producer industries that have so far monopolized our attention to the consumer-oriented industries with which we will complete our survey of industrial capitalism in the next chapter.

Glass

The consumer revolution of the nineteenth century depended less on the introduction of new products than on the expanded production and wider dissemination of old products. Among these was glass. At the end of the eighteenth century, virtually any form of glass was expensive and was possessed mainly by the rich and powerful. But as production expanded and costs and prices fell in the nineteenth century, the consumption of glass was democratized. Window glass, once found only in public buildings and the houses of the wealthy, spread everywhere, even to the domiciles of the poor. Plate glass mirrors—a royal preserve when Louis XIV built his palace at Versailles with its Hall of Mirrors in the late seventeenth century—became common elements of interior decoration for the growing middle class in the nineteenth century. Plate glass display windows—virtually unknown because of their prohibitive cost at the outset of the nineteenth century—had become defining fixtures of urban retailing by the close of the century. Where once only those at the summit of French society took their drink from crystal or glass vessels, everyone was using "glasses" by the late 1800s. Moreover, the wine, beer, and mineral water that everyone drank by then was packaged and sold in glass bottles, the result of a revolution in container technology that allowed all sorts of food and drink, plus perfumes, medicine, and many other consumer products, to be stored and consumed in cheap glass jars and bottles. In short, glass was an integral part of the emerging consumer society in France, and production of the various forms of glass became a major industry in the course of the nineteenth century.[1]

At the beginning of the nineteenth century, there was already one giant manufacturing enterprise in the French glass industry, Saint-Gobain, but this was hardly typical. Most glass produced in France in 1800 came from one of some sixty much smaller glassworks, each of which operated a single wood-fired furnace and employed at most forty skilled glassmakers and their apprentices. Leaving plate glass to Saint-Gobain, these firms tended to specialize in one or two other forms of glass: window glass *(verre à vitre),* hollowware (bottles, jars, *gobeletterie*), beads and trinkets *(verroterie),* or crystal (a luxury good like plate glass).

Starting from this base, the French glass industry followed a course of evolution similar to that of many other industries in the nineteenth century. In the more open, competitive environment that resulted from the reforms of the French Revolution, there was a proliferation of glassmaking enterprises (even in the field of plate glass that Saint-Gobain had previously monopolized), with the number of firms peaking at 182 in 1870. Then in 1870–1900, with the growth of demand slowing during the Great Depression and the introduction of the tank furnace making true mass production possible, a process of concentration and consolidation took hold, reducing the number of firms and increasing the scale of operations within each specialty, although not to the degree seen in steel or chemicals. Meanwhile, the shift from wood fuel to coal was bringing about the same geographical concentration that occurred in other heat-based industries. In particular, the departments of the Nord and the Loire, adjacent to France's largest coalfields, emerged as the two largest centers of glassmaking by the 1860s and remained in that position in 1900.[2] Thus, by the end of the nineteenth century the twin processes of geographic and technological concentration had created within each branch of the industry an oligopoly of leading firms that continued to dominate the industry into the twentieth century. First among these firms, of course, was Saint-Gobain.

In the late eighteenth century, the Saint-Gobain Company, operating under privileges first granted to it by Louis XIV in 1665, was the world's leading producer of *glace,* the distortion-free plate glass used principally in the manufacture of mirrors. Stripped of its monopoly in France in 1790, Saint-Gobain nonetheless continued to dominate plate glass manufacturing thanks to the quality of its product and the efficiency of its production. That production consisted of two phases: first, the formation of plates by pouring molten glass onto large tables, and second, the grinding and polishing of the resultant rough plates to produce the finished product, which was then sold to the mirror makers of Paris. In the late 1700s, the company expanded and reorganized the first phase of production in a factory setting at the former chateau of Saint-Gobain in the Aisne, a site valued for its supply of natural soda (a necessary ingredient in glassmaking) and for its access to Paris via the Oise River. The more labor-intensive grinding and polishing work remained at the company's original works at Reuilly, an industrial suburb of Paris adjacent to the famous Faubourg Saint-Antoine. In the early 1800s, however, the finishing work was also transferred to Saint-Gobain and to the nearby plant of Chauny, where grinding was mechanized with water power. Also, as we have seen already, to compensate for the dwindling supply of natural soda, Saint-Gobain moved into the production of Leblanc soda by purchasing the Charlefontaine works in 1819 and moving them to Saint-Gobain three years later.

Even though Saint-Gobain modernized and expanded its production facilities in the years following the loss of its monopoly, its sales stagnated as new competitors came on the scene. In the 1770s, using workers from Saint-Gobain, the Cast Plate Glass Company of Ravenshead introduced plate glass production to England and challenged Saint-Gobain's position in its principal export market. More importantly, the Verrerie de Saint-Quirin in eastern France, which had started out making window glass in the 1730s and had added the production of *glace soufflée* (blown plate glass) in the 1770s, began to compete directly with Saint-Gobain in 1804, when it hired former workers from Saint-Gobain to make *glace coulée* (poured plate glass). By 1814, Saint-Quirin's production amounted to one-half of Saint-Gobain's, and in the next ten years, thanks to a new plant at Cirey, the upstart drew abreast of its older rival. Soon other competitors appeared. Nicolas Rambourg set up plate glass production at Commentry in 1823; in 1836, the former director of Saint-Gobain, Clément-Desormes, founded the glassworks of Sainte-Marie d'Oignies in Belgium; another glassworks opened at Montluçon in 1845; and the Verrerie d'Aniche started making plate glass in 1850.

As related in the various works of Jean-Pierre Daviet, the story of the French plate glass industry, 1830–1900, is largely the story of how Saint-Gobain regained and maintained its industry leadership in France and Europe in the face of this competition.[3] Saint-Gobain's rebound began with what Daviet calls "a revolution from above, a revolution in the spirit of top management" in the 1830s.[4] Reorganized as a *société anonyme* in 1829, Saint-Gobain continued to be run by aristocrats, but increasingly these were aristocrats with engineering and managerial expertise, such as the *polytechnicien* Comte Armand de Kersaint. Also important were representatives of the Geneva bankers who had bankrolled the firm since the early eighteenth century and men with governmental experience like Baron Mounier, A-P Hély d'Oissel, and duc Albert de Broglie. The latter were, in Daviet's words, "men of state who had learned the sense of the general interest and collective action through bureaucratic procedures by which it was necessary to combine information, weigh arguments, compare hypotheses, and reason in writing, all at the price of a certain slowness in conception but with the benefit of rigor and sureness."[5] As students of the Napoleonic wars, these directors took a military approach to strategic planning, still a novelty in business circles in the early 1800s. They reformed the company's accounting practices, demanded that plant managers report regularly to the directors (who met twice weekly to make strategic decisions), and revamped the pay system to base the compensation of all workers on productivity. They brought in leading scientists like Clément-Desormes and Gay-Lussac not only to set up chemical production but also to oversee the modernization of glassmaking. The latter included the application of steam power to grinding and polishing and the shift from wood to coal fuel (a step facilitated by the adoption of new Siemens "gazogenes" that converted coal into gas for use in the glass furnaces). These measures greatly reduced Saint-Gobain's production costs between 1830 and 1860, which allowed the company in turn to lower its prices to discourage new competitors and to broaden consumption.

Even while improving its competitive position through technological and managerial innovation, Saint-Gobain also sought to reduce competition through cooperation, and eventually merger, with its rivals. In 1852 it set up a new plant at Stolberg in Germany as a joint venture with Saint-Quirin, and six years later it merged with Saint-Quirin completely, a move reflected in the inclusion of Saint-Quirin's Cirey plant in the company's new name (Saint-Gobain, Chauny, et Cirey). In 1868, Saint-Gobain took over Montluçon, which further consolidated its position in plate glass production in France, and, as we saw earlier, the merger with Perret-Olivier in 1872 similarly consolidated Saint-Gobain's position in soda production.

In the last quarter of the nineteenth century and the first decade of the twentieth, Saint-Gobain maintained its dominant position in plate glass in France and Europe, but not without effort. The return to protection throughout Europe in these years forced the company to move a growing proportion of its production abroad to get around tariff barriers, so that by 1913 eight of its twelve glassworks were outside France. Meanwhile, within France, Saint-Gobain faced new competition that could not be entirely contained through its traditional methods of cartelization and horizontal integration. This competition came in part from the largest British glassmaker, Pilkington Brothers, which set up a plant in Maubeuge in 1891 to secure a position in the French market on the eve of France's return to protection. More threatening, however, was new competition from the Belgians, who built four new glassworks in France between 1870 and 1890. In 1893, Jeumont and Recquignies, the French subsidiaries of the biggest Belgian glass companies, Oignies and Floreffe, merged to form the Compagnie des Glaces et Verres Spéciaux du Nord. In 1899, the Compagnie du Charleroi entered France by erecting a plant at Boussois, across the Sambre River from Recquignies, near Maubeuge. In 1908 this plant combined with Recquignies and Jeumont to form the Compagnie Réunis de Glace et Verres Spéciaux de la Nord de la France (known simply as Boussois). As of 1913, Boussois accounted for 33 percent of French sales of plate glass, which reduced Saint-Gobain's market share to 45 percent (versus 70 percent in 1870).[6]

In addition to challenging Saint-Gobain's dominance in plate glass, Boussois also forced it to move into the previously separate field of window glass. Traditionally, window glass had been produced by skilled glassblowers in small-scale artisanal works, in contrast to the large-scale industrial production of plate glass. By the early 1900s, however, new technologies appeared that made possible for the first

time the large-scale production of window glass, potentially at the expense of plate glass. When Boussois launched window glass production
using one of these new technologies (the Fourcault process), Saint-
Gobain had to respond. Merging with Aniche, one of its friendly competitors that already had window glass capabilities, Saint-Gobain purchased the European rights to another new window glass process from
American Window Glass Company, and it set up two new plants to
exploit this process in 1912–1913. It also began to produce window
glass at its Italian and Spanish subsidiaries. These initiatives preserved
Saint-Gobain's position as the leading glass manufacturer in continental
Europe in the years prior to World War I.[7]

While Saint-Gobain was establishing and defending its dominant position in the plate glass industry, another old aristocratic company came
to dominate the production of a second form of luxury glass. The
Cristallerie de Baccarat, located twelve miles east of Lunéville in the
department of the Meurthe, was founded in 1765 by Montmorency-
Laval, the bishop of Metz, to bring to France the production of lead
crystal, theretofore a Spanish specialty. Utilizing local sand, soda, and
lime, wood from nearby forests for fuel, and imported lead, Baccarat
produced a high-quality crystal that enjoyed great commercial success
in the 1770s and 1780s. As a royal manufactory, it was nationalized
during the Revolution and later sold to Pierre-Antoine Godard-
Desmarest, an expert in accounting who had also made a fortune in
military provisioning under the Empire. Under Godard-Desmarest's
management, production and sales of Baccarat crystal grew steadily
from the 1820s to 1850s. By 1863, when Turgan visited and wrote it
up, Baccarat employed 1,500 men, women, and children and accounted
for 4 million of the 9 million francs of crystal sold annually in France
(by comparison, Saint-Gobain's annual glass sales were around 14 million in the 1860s). Of the other leading crystal works in France—Lyon,
Sèvres, Bercy, Pantin, Saint-Louis—only the last named, with 2.4 million francs in sales, was in Baccarat's league in the mid-nineteenth century.[8] Enjoying a brand name recognition that few companies in any
field could match (then or now), Baccarat continued to lead the French
crystal industry into the twentieth century.[9]

While Saint-Gobain and Baccarat dominated France's production of
the most expensive forms of glass, production of the more common
forms of glass was left to a collection of much less well-known companies, few of which have attracted historians. The companies that we
know the most about came to specialize in bottle making, which in

1830 accounted for 50 percent of all glass sold in France. From 1800 to the 1870s, bottle production in France grew steadily in response to rising demand, first and foremost from the wine industry but also from a new industry, the bottling of mineral water. In the absence of economies of scale in what remained a labor-intensive industry dominated by skilled glassblowers, this growth was manifested more in the appearance of many new firms than in the expansion of existing firms. These firms were found in virtually all parts of France, but as in the case of other forms of glassmaking, they came to be concentrated in regions well endowed with coal (the Nord and the Loire) or near regions of high demand (such as the wine country of Burgundy and Champagne).

In the 1870s and 1880s, when the phylloxera blight undercut wine production and an economic downturn tempered demand for consumer goods in general, demand for bottles softened, and bottlemakers looked for ways to cut costs and gain a competitive edge. They found both in the tank furnace, which made possible the continuous melting of raw materials (and thus around-the-clock glassblowing) and mandated large-scale operations to capture the potential economies of scale. For example, when the Verrerie Sainte-Clothilde in Carmaux installed the new furnace in 1884, its workforce jumped from 350 to 800 and output rose from 21,000 to 33,000 bottles a day.[10] Along with the new furnaces, new kinds of bottle molds were introduced that allowed firms to cut costs by substituting semi-skilled workers for master glassblowers. This move precipitated a wave of unionization and strike actions by glassworkers in defense of their craft, but it ultimately gave owners and managers control of the shop floor, and thus the pace of production, at all the major bottleworks by the end of the 1890s.[11]

Just as important from our perspective, these changes in manufacturing technology promoted concentration and consolidation, as technologically advanced firms expanded at the expense of their less advanced competitors and as bottlemakers within a given market banded together to reduce competitive pressures. Naturally, this winnowing process took on a geographical dimension as the strongest firms in the best-endowed locations came to dominate what, in the age of railroads, was rapidly becoming a single national market. How all this unfolded can be better understood by looking at the evolution of the glass industry in the department of the Loire, for which we have good company histories.

As the forests of eastern France became ever more depleted in the course of the eighteenth century, glassmakers from the Franche-Comté migrated to the Gier Valley south of Lyon—and particularly to the coal-mining towns of Givors and Rive-de-Gier—where they began making bottles and window glass with coal-fired furnaces. In the early nineteenth century, the number of glassmaking firms in the Gier Valley rose steadily, mainly to produce bottles for the wine industry. In the 1840s, seventeen of these glassworks came together in a regional combine, the Société Générale des Verreries de la Loire et du Rhône, which mimicked the consolidation of the Loire coal industry carried out at the same time by the Mines de la Loire. With some thirty furnaces producing over 20 million bottles a year, the Société Générale may have been the largest glassmaking company in the world in the 1860s. But success bred complacency. Failing to invest in the new technology in the 1870s, the company ended up going out of business in the 1880s when demand for wine bottles collapsed. By then, however, leadership in the Loire bottle industry had already passed to two more technologically progressive family firms, Richarme Frères and the Nouvelles Verreries de Givors (Neuvesel, Momain, et Cie).[12]

Richarme Frères of Rive-de-Gier escaped the effects of collapsing wine production by contracting to supply bottles to one of the rising mineral water bottlers, the Société Saint Galmier (Source Badoit). More importantly, in 1877 Richarme became the first French bottlemaker to install the Siemens tank furnace and thereby to make the transition to true industrial production. By the 1890s, the company employed approximately 700 workers and operated four furnaces around the clock to turn out 65,000–70,000 bottles a day (25 million a year).[13] The chief rival of Richarme in the Loire, the Nouvelles Verreries de Givors, had been founded in 1864 when two partners in the Société Générale, J-B Neuvesel and J-B Momain, left the combine to make bottles and demijohns for the wine industry. Following the lead of Richarme, Neuvesel and Momain installed a Siemens furnace in 1878, and by the 1890s the Nouvelles Verreries was producing 21 million bottles a year, putting it in second place in the Loire. In the next decade, however, Richarme marked time, and the Nouvelles Verreries (by then known as Neuvesel et Cie) emerged as the more expansive of the two firms under the direction of Eugène Souchon, a graduate of the Ecole Centrale, who became plant manager in 1900, married J-B Neuvesel's daughter, and as Souchon-Neuvesel became head of the firm when Neuvesel's son died in 1907. In 1903, Souchon-Neuvesel was the first French bottlemaker to install the Boucher semi-automatic bottlemaking machine. He then signed an exclusive contract with Evian to furnish its entire yearly supply of bottles, and in 1911 Souchon-Neuvesel et Cie became the exclusive supplier of bottles to another major mineral water company, Vittel.[14]

Meanwhile, in the western part of the department of the Loire, another important bottle manufacturer was emerging under the aegis of the Badoit Mineral Water Company of Saint-Galmier. Until 1882, Badoit had purchased bottles from Richarme, but losses due to transport and difficulties in matching the supply of bottles to the need prompted the company to set up its own bottleworks. In 1883, the Société de la Verrerie de Saint-Galmier was launched. Under the direction of Irenée Laurent, it proceeded to build a state-of-the-art plant at nearby Veauche that included the largest Siemens furnace in the region. By 1889 Veauche was turning out 12 million bottles a year, which allowed it to supply not only Badoit but also various makers of lemonade, wine, and spirits, including the Grande Chartreuse distillery. By 1906, Veauche was making forty-six different kinds of bottles and twenty-two kinds of clear glass and, although still supplying Badoit with bottles, it was "entirely emancipated" from its control. What it had not yet done was to mechanize bottlemaking as Souchon-Neuvesel had done, mainly because Laurent could not choose between the Boucher machine, the Owens machine from America, and others coming on the market. Eventually, after World War I, Veauche installed the even better O'Neill automatic bottle-making machine along with automated loading equipment and new gas furnaces. By 1930, its production was 50 percent above the prewar level.[15]

The 1920s brought a decisive movement toward consolidation of the Loire bottle industry. Already in 1917, Souchon-Neuvesel had taken control of Richarme and guided its modernization. It also promoted the creation of a national consortium of bottlemakers to control production and allocate sales in the uncertain postwar environment, largely in response to Saint-Gobain's decision to start producing hollowware during and after World War I. By 1930, stock swaps had bound Souchon-Neuvesel, Richarme, and Veauche together in an arrangement that allowed close coordination of all bottle production in the Loire. However, a full merger of these firms did not occur until the 1960s, when Souchon-Neuvesel and its dependencies, Charbonneaux of Reims and Boussois of the Nord, came together to form a single national bottle manufacturer, BSN.[16]

Paper

Like the manufacture of glass, the manufacture of paper was well established in France at the beginning of the nineteenth century. According to Louis André, there were more than 700 paper mills in operation in France in 1812, with at least one mill in seventy of France's ninety departments, but the thirty-three largest mills were clustered in four regions—the Ile-de-France in the Center, the Lyonnais and Dauphiné in the Southeast, Alsace in the East, and the Charente in the West.[17] The most important French papermaking enterprises at that time belonged to the Didot family, which operated mills on the Essonnes River south of Paris, and the Montgolfier family, which operated two mills on the Deûme River near Annonay in the Ardèche. Whatever their position in the industry in 1800, however, all these firms were soon transformed by the introduction of mass-production technology and by the dramatic expansion of paper production in France in response to rising demand.[18]

To some degree, rising demand for paper was a function of rising literacy and the resulting demand for reading matter—which, as we will see below, fostered the emergence of printing and publishing as a major form of industrial capitalism by 1900. However, the production of books, newspapers, and other printed material absorbed only about one-third of France's annual output of paper in the nineteenth century. The growth in paper production also stemmed from the growing demand for writing paper (the other side of the advent of mass literacy) and from demand for new kinds of paper (such as cigarette paper). Even more important was the rise of industrial paper—wrapping paper, packaging, and cardboard—which directly derived from the overall increase in commercial activity that accompanied the advent of a consumer economy.[19]

An increase in the kinds and amount of paper consumed would not have been possible without a revolution in papermaking technology. For France, this revolution began in 1781, when Etienne de Montgolfier introduced Dutch methods of making rag paper at his family's mill near Annonay. The Dutch method still formed sheets of paper one at a time, by dipping a wire screen in a vat of pulp, but it replaced water-driven mallets with a rotating cylindrical vat to tear up rags to make the pulp. The use of this "hollander" speeded up the production of pulp (and thus lowered its cost), but hollanders were expensive and required an even more expensive upgrading of a paper mill's power train. Consequently, in the absence of machinery to increase the speed and volume of paper formation—the heart of the manufacturing process—only one-fifth of French paper mills had adopted the hollander and the related Dutch methods by 1812.[20]

The advent of true mass production of paper awaited another invention, a water- or steam-powered machine that could turn out paper continuously—paper by the roll, rather than by the sheet. Such a machine was built and patented in 1798 by Nicolas Robert, production manager at Essonnes, but a prolonged and rancorous dispute over legal rights to the machine between Robert and his boss, Léger Didot, delayed the adoption of the machine by French papermakers. Instead, the Didots took the machine to England, where it was improved and widely adopted for the production of newsprint. This improved version was introduced in France in 1816 at the Didots' mill at Sorel, and by 1830 thirty-one papermaking machines had been installed at twenty-two French paper mills, mainly to produce wrapping paper, wallpaper, and newsprint.[21]

The real takeoff in mechanized papermaking in France came in the 1830s, when the introduction of a second generation of paper machines made possible the large-scale production of writing paper and other high-quality forms of paper, in addition to newsprint and wrapping paper. There were 148 paper machines in operation in France by 1840 and probably more than 500 by 1860. All the while, the speed and capacity of paper machines were being steadily improved, and the introduction of various ancillary machines, like rotating bleaching vats and pulp presses, further enhanced the production process. The growing size and complexity of paper mills in turn required manufacturers to replace water wheels—the normal source of power for papermaking through the 1840s—with water turbines and steam engines. There were only 17 steam engines in use in French paper factories as of 1848, but by 1864 there were 240. As a result of these interrelated technical advances, the total output of paper in France rose from 25,000 tons in 1830 to 93,000 tons by 1860 (virtually the same as the output of the British paper industry). But the high cost of staying abreast of the new technology meant that more and more of this production became concentrated in the mills of the dozen or so firms with annual sales in excess of 2 million francs. These included the Didot mills at Mesnil-sur-l'Estrée in the Eure, the Papeteries de Marais et de Sainte-Marie in the Morin Valley east of Paris, Laroche-Joubert, Lacroix et Cie in Angoulême, and Blanchet Frères et Kléber in the Dauphiné, but the two leading firms in 1860 (as in 1800) remained the Papeteries d'Essonnes and the Montgolfier family enterprise.[22]

The development of Essonnes by no means followed a straight line. In 1809, Léger Didot, preoccupied with capitalizing on the English rights to the Robert paper machine, sold Essonnes, and the new proprietors promptly turned it into a cotton mill. It was only in the 1830s, amid the boom in mechanized papermaking, that a group of Paris paper merchants and financiers formed a joint-stock company that took control of Essonnes and relaunched it as a paper mill to mass-produce newsprint. In 1840, Amédee-Louis Gratiot, son of a prominent Paris printer, took the helm of the new Papeteries d'Essonnes, and over the next twenty years he and his team of technicians guided Essonnes back to a leading position in the French paper industry. By 1860, when Turgan featured Essonnes in the first volume of his *Grands usines*, the company employed 500 workers and operated nine papermaking machines powered by a combination of water turbines and steam engines that turned out 4,000 tons of rag paper a year, approximately 5 percent of total French production.[23]

Although Essonnes and a few other major paper enterprises—notably Marais et Sainte-Marie—were either created or later reorganized as limited-liability joint-stock companies, most of the largest French paper companies were family firms, or, as in the case of the Montgolfier enterprise, interlocking networks of family firms similar to the textile enterprises of Alsace and the Nord. The Montgolfier enterprise had been launched in the early 1700s when Raymond de Montgolfier founded two paper mills—Vidalon-le-Haut and Vidalon-le-Bas—on the Deûme River near Annonay. These mills and several others in the vicinity continued to be run at the end of the eighteenth century by various descendants of Raymond, including Etienne and Joseph de Montgolfier, who in their spare time invented the hot-air balloon (and thus aeronautics). Although Etienne's introduction of Dutch technology in the 1780s represented an important milestone for the Montgolfier enterprise, its modern history dates from 1799, when he was succeeded by his son-in-law, Barthelémy Barbou de Canson, as head of Vidalon-le Haut.

Canson expanded Vidalon-le-Haut by acquiring a nearby flour mill that controlled the largest waterfall in the Deûme Valley, and he took over Vidalon-le-Bas from other members of the family, thereby re-uniting the two halves of the original Montgolfier enterprise. In 1822 he installed one of the first French-made paper machines at Vidalon and added four more over the next twenty years. Because of the limited hydraulic resources of the Deûme Valley, these were smaller paper-making machines designed for short runs of high-quality papers rather than the large machines for newsprint installed at Essonnes. From the 1830s to the 1850s, Canson and his son Etienne, who served as the firm's technical director after studying at the Conservatoire des Arts et Métiers in Paris, continued to make technical improvements that re-inforced Vidalon's position as France's leading maker of high-quality paper and earned it a steady stream of prizes at the Paris expositions of the era.

While the Cansons expanded and modernized the original Montgol-fier mills at Vidalon, other members of the family founded or acquired a dozen additional paper mills in France between the 1790s and the 1850s. These included three mills upstream from Vidalon on the Deûme River at Saint-Marcel, Thelly, and Grosberty; a mill at Les Ar-dillats near Beaujeu to serve the Lyon market; and another at Leysse near Chambéry to serve Savoy. They also included Fontenay, a re-nowned Cistercian abbey in Burgundy, where in 1832 Elie de Mont-golfier founded a Fourierist "phalanstery" that combined papermaking and printing with an agricultural school and industrial museum under the grandiose title of Société Nationale pour l'Emancipation Intellec-tuelle (the utopian socialist agenda did not last, but Fontenay remained an important part of the Montgolfier enterprise into the second half of the nineteenth century).[24] Taken together, the various Montgolfier mills constituted the largest papermaking enterprise in France (and one of the largest in the world) in 1860. But as things happened, 1860 proved to be the high water mark for the Montgolfiers and for the entire French rag paper industry in the nineteenth century, as the growing scarcity and rising cost of raw materials (rags) were already bringing about a fundamental transformation of the industry.[25]

As early as the 1830s, French papermakers had begun experimenting with alternative raw materials, including straw, palm leaves, esparto grass, and even dried horse dung. Straw and esparto eventually became the standard raw materials for certain kinds of paper, but they did not provide the sheer quantity needed for the kinds of paper in greatest demand, namely newsprint, wrapping and packing paper, and card-board. For these, the solution was wood pulp. The Germans developed a mechanical wood-pulping process in the 1840s, and the British and Americans followed with chemical processes to break wood into pulp using caustic alkali. By the 1860s, timber was being harvested on a large scale as a source of wood pulp throughout Europe—especially in Scandinavia and Russia—and in the United States. Coupled with the continued improvement of papermaking technology (the speed of papermaking machines rose from 20 feet per minute in the early 1880s to over 400 feet per minute in 1900), this elevated the mass production of paper to a new level in the last quarter of the nineteenth century.[26]

Because the French played a distinctly secondary role in the development and commercialization of wood pulp technology—in contrast to their leadership in rag paper technology in the late eighteenth and early nineteenth centuries—the conventional wisdom is that France was left behind by the British and Americans, and especially by the Germans, in the mass production of paper in the late nineteenth century. To be sure, in terms of overall output, German paper production grew much faster than French production after 1870, and by 1908 the Germans were turning out twice as much paper as the French (1,350,000 tons versus 600,000 tons). However, France continued to lead the world in the production of the most coveted and expensive forms of rag paper, including fiduciary paper for banknotes, stock certificates, and legal documents. France was also the world's leading producer and exporter of cigarette paper. And France did move into the production of newsprint, industrial paper, and cardboard using wood pulp imported from abroad or harvested from its forests in the Southwest (Landes) and Southeast (Dauphiné and Savoy). This allowed it to increase its paper production fourfold between 1875 and 1908 and kept it among the world's top five paper producers at the turn of the twentieth century.[27]

The rise of a wood pulp-based paper industry in France involved both the conversion of existing enterprises and the founding of new ones. The first development is best illustrated in the history of the Papeteries d'Essonnes. Essonnes had been especially hard hit by the rising cost of rag pulp in the 1860s, when its rapid expansion had overextended its financial resources, and the company declared bankruptcy in 1867. The following year the mills were taken over by one of the principal shareholders in the bankrupt company, the flour magnate Aimé-Stanislaus Darblay, in association with his son Paul and his son-in-law Matherin Béranger. The new firm of Darblay et Béranger quickly moved Essonnes into wood pulp paper production using wood pulped in Rouen from Scandinavian logs brought up the Seine. According to Alain Plessis,[28] Essonnes was the largest paper mill in the world by

1885, employing 2,500 workers to turn out 120 tons of paper products a day, or approximately 36,000 tons a year (more than 10 percent of French production), including much of the newsprint used by the daily newspapers of Paris.[29] In 1905, the Papeteries d'Essonnes was reorganized as a *société anonyme*, but the Darblay family continued to run it with Aimé-Henri Darblay succeeding his father Paul as director-general and being succeeded in turn by his son Robert Darblay.[30]

Although the continuing success of Essonnes meant that the Paris basin remained a leading producer of wood pulp paper into the twentieth century, the center of gravity of the French paper industry shifted in the last quarter of the nineteenth century to areas of timber production (the Alps and the Southwest) and to points of entry for imported wood pulp (the lower Seine). This trend is especially well illustrated by developments in the Dauphiné, where water power from the high falls of the Alps combined with large stands of fir and aspen to provide the basis for the dynamic new paper industry that emerged after 1860.

In the mid-nineteenth century, the Dauphiné already possessed a substantial rag paper industry, located on the lower Romanche River at Vizille and along the Fure and Morge Rivers that emptied into the Isère downstream from Grenoble. Its principal enterprises included Blanchet Frères et Kléber at Rives and Montgolfier at Charavines (both on the Fure) and Lafuma et Cie on the Morge. The introduction of *cylindres hollandaises* and Robert papermaking machines allowed all these firms to expand in the 1830s and 1840s, and they continued to prosper in the 1850s and 1860s by applying *pâte chimique* (pulp produced by treating wood with caustic soda or bisulfites) to the manufacture of fine papers. But the big expansion in Dauphiné paper after 1860 came in the Grésivaudan Valley—the stretch of the Isère upstream from Grenoble between Pontcharra and Domène—where harnessing high falls on the tributaries of the Isère offered the large quantities of cheap power needed for the large-scale application of the new mechanical wood pulping technology that made the Isère France's foremost paper-producing department by 1873.[31]

The key figure in the launching of this new industry was Amable Matussière, who came to the region in 1856 to found a sawmill at Domène to supply parquet flooring to the building trades in Lyon. Matussière soon saw the potential for papermaking in the Grésivaudan. In 1860, after studying the new mechanical wood pulp technology in Germany and lining up financial backing from local bankers, he set up a mill to furnish wood pulp to the existing paper manufacturers of the region. At the same time, he recruited a cohort of young engineers from established paper companies to help him found new paper mills and to harness the high falls of the Grésivaudan to power them. This cohort included Alfred Fredet, who collaborated with Matussière in founding the Pontet *pâte chimique* plant at Pontcharra in 1864, and Gaspard-Zephyrin Orioli, a former chemist at Marais, who worked with Matussière and Fredet at Pontet before founding the Moulin-Vieux paper mill in 1869.[32] But the most important of the engineer-entrepreneurs attracted to the Grésivaudan by Matussière was Aristide Bergès.

Son of a paper manufacturer at Lorp (Ariège), Aristide Bergès studied engineering at the Ecole Centrale and then went to Spain to develop mountain-going locomotives for the Andalusian Railroad. In 1863 he returned to the family *papeterie,* where he designed and patented improved wood pulping machinery. Brought to the Isère in 1865 to install his machines at Matussière's pulp mill at Domène, he stayed on to found his own combined pulp and paper mill at Lancey. In the process, he became an expert in harnessing the high falls of the area for water power. In particular, Bergès solved the problem of radical seasonal variations in water flow on the Alpine streams (too much in the spring melt off, too little the rest of the year) by damming the existing lakes to form reservoirs, which provided a controlled water flow year round. Realizing that the most efficient way to utilize this power was through the generation of electricity, he became one of the principal architects of the hydroelectric industry of Grenoble and coined the term "white coal" to characterize this resource. At the same time, he continued to expand his papermaking enterprise at Lancey. As of 1900, Bergès employed some 1,800 workers to operate five *defibreuses* for *pâte mécanique,* three *lessiveurs* for *pâte chimique,* five paper machines, and two cardboard machines. By 1920 Lancey was turning out 10,600 tons of cardboard and 21,000 tons of paper each year, and six years later it remained, in Raoul Blanchard's estimation, "the most striking and most complete expression of the paper industry of the Alps."[33]

While the wood pulp paper industry grew apace in the Dauphiné and elsewhere in France in the last decades of the nineteenth century, several of the long-established rag papermakers resisted the shift to wood pulp paper and continued to produce small quantities of high-quality rag paper that commanded high prices and generated high profit margins. The most successful practitioners of this high-quality/limited-production strategy were the Montgolfiers. As we saw earlier, as of 1860 the Montgolfiers owned and operated a dozen paper mills in the Southeast, the foremost of which were the family's original mills at Vidalon, controlled by the Cansons. When Barthelémy and Etienne de Canson died within a year of one another in 1859–1860, Louis de Canson sold Vidalon to Marc Seguin, the great civil engineer and "father of French railroads," who was himself a member of the Montgolfier clan. Seguin proceeded to partially reintegrate the scattered Montgolfier holdings with the aid of the three sons of Elie de Montgolfier who, in the inbred world of the Montgolfiers, were both his sons-in-law and brothers-in-law. In this arrangement, Laurent de Montgolfier took over the direction of Vidalon, upgraded its power plant with a powerful new steam engine, and created a depot in Paris to handle the sales of all Montgolfier paper and much of the rest of the rag paper produced in the Southeast. On the eve of his retirement in 1881, he converted the firm into a limited-liability joint-stock company, the Société Anonyme des Papeteries de Vidalon. At the end of the nineteenth century, Vidalon remained a medium-sized manufacturer of rag-based writing, typing, and tracing papers with an impeccable reputation for quality and technological leadership that was reflected in the grand prize awarded it at the 1900 Paris World's Fair and in the encomium of the jury: "We could write the history of paper by recounting the successive phases in the growing prosperity of the Vidalon paper mill."[34]

Vidalon continued to manufacture and market what Raoul Blanchard called "aristocratic paper" throughout the twentieth century, mainly under the Canson brand. In 1976, it merged with several other major French paper companies, including Papeteries du Marais and Blanchet Frères et Kléber, to form a division of the pan-European paper conglomerate Arjomari (which became Arjo-Wiggins in 1991). However, at least thirty other French paper companies dating back to before 1860 continued to operate independently at the end of the twentieth century.[35]

When viewed as a whole, the development of the French paper industry in the nineteenth century reveals many similarities to the French glass industry. As in glass, technological innovation did much to determine the overall structure of the paper industry as well as the success or failure of individual firms. Specifically, the invention, perfection, and diffusion of the Robert continuous papermaking machine made possible economies of scale that virtually mandated larger units of production and the concentration of production in a smaller group of much larger firms. But, as in the glass industry, the process of concentration went only so far. Along with the rising demand for standard-ized, mass-produced forms of paper (especially newsprint and pack-aging), there was continuing and growing demand for specialized papers, for which economies of scale in production were limited and which continued to support a number of small firms that employed smaller-scale machinery or, in some cases, traditional manual methods of production. Thus, as happened in other French industries, the French paper industry remained dualistic at the end of the nineteenth century, with a dozen or so relatively large-scale producers co-existing with hun-dreds of small-scale producers.[36]

A more distinctive characteristic of the French paper industry was its close association with its chief customer, the printing and publishing industry. Many of the leading paper mills were founded or acquired by leading printers (such as the Didots' mills at Mesnil-sur-l'Estrée and Essonnes), and many ostensibily independent paper companies were closely linked to publishing. Indeed, up to a point, these were two halves of a single industry, so in completing our examination of the paper industry it is logical to turn next to printing and publishing.

Print

The nineteenth century brought a dramatic rise in the production and consumption of printed matter in France, as in other Western countries. Frédéric Barbier has estimated that the output of books increased twenty-five–fold in France between 1840 and 1914 (from 12.4 million per year to 310 million), while according to others the total circulation of Paris daily newspapers increased a hundredfold (from 50,000 a day in the 1820s to 5 million in 1912).[37] And this was just the tip of the iceberg. There were similar increases in the output of many other kinds of publications, including government documents, commercial cata-logues, and all sorts of magazines and periodicals. Indeed, by 1900 France was awash in printed matter that ran the gamut from "perish-ables" (like daily newspapers, train schedules, election posters, and handbills) to "consumer durables" like the Bibles and "great books" printed on fine paper and bound in leather that were handed down from generation to generation in middle- and upper-class families.

The increased production and consumption of printed goods were the result of the interaction of many factors, including the spread of literacy, the opening of the printing trades after 1789, the gradual lifting of government censorship and regulation of book and newspaper publishing, and improvements in the distribution of all consumer goods after the advent of the railroads. However, most important were the innovations in manufacturing technology that made mass production possible. These included the mechanization not only of papermaking but also of printing and related processes.

In 1800, printing was still done on manually powered wooden presses that differed little from Gutenberg's. In 1811, Koenig installed the first mechanical (steam-powered) press in the printing plant of the *Times* of London, and similar English presses were set up in Paris in the 1820s to print the *Journal des Débats,* the *Bulletin des Lois,* and *Le Globe.* The first French-built mechanical press was installed at *Le National* in 1831, and by the 1840s more than a dozen firms were building mechanical presses in Paris. Foremost of these was the firm of Auguste-Hippolyte Marinoni, who installed a reciprocating press for Emile de Girardin's *La Presse* in 1845 and subsequently emerged as one of the world's three leading makers of high-speed rotative presses. Along with mechanical presses came other innovations in printing—stereotyping, lithography for printing illustrations, color printing, linotype and monotype machines for composing text—as well as machines to handle subsidiary processes like folding newspapers and binding books.[38] All these innovations inevitably transformed the nature of business enterprise in printing and publishing and indeed the very structure of the industry.

At the beginning of the nineteenth century, the production and distribution of books was a collaborative process that involved the contributions of writers, editors, printers, bookbinders, and booksellers, all operating as independent entities. Similarly, newspapers consisted of little more than editorial offices that remained distinct from the printers who made the physical product and the newsdealers who distributed it. This functional fragmentation was still prevalent in many areas of French publishing at the end of the nineteenth century. There were still thousands of small artisanal printing shops with manual presses in France turning out everything from exquisite limited editions of Greek and Latin classics to posters and handbills for local merchants—indeed, most of the 4,000 printers in France at the turn of the twentieth century fell into this category. In journalism, there were still hundreds of small-town newspapers and weekly, monthly, or quarterly journals serving highly limited audiences. And there were still thousands of small booksellers serving the general market in small towns or, in the case of Paris, serving myriad specialized clienteles and niche markets (to this day,

Paris remains one of the most fragmented and variegated publishing scenes in the world).

At the same time, at certain points in the production and distribution of books, newspapers, and other printed goods, true industrial enterprises began to appear in France—not only in the production of paper but also in printing. The adoption of steam-powered presses involved unprecedented capital investments, amounting to several hundred thousand francs in the early nineteenth century and over a million francs by the end of the century. Installing the equipment often required a further investment in a new plant, typically located on the outskirts of the city, where the machines and the expanded workforce to tend them could be efficiently deployed. Many of these emerging industrial printing houses remained single-function enterprises, printing books and other materials on contract with private publishers or public authorities. However, the temptation to integrate forward into publishing and backward into papermaking was great, so in a number of cases industrial printing became the basis for multifunctional publishing enterprises.

One of these new industrial printing and publishing companies was founded in Lille by Léonard Danel, whose family had been in the printing trade there since the 1690s. Louis Danel rose to the status of royal printer before retiring in 1846. His business then passed to his nephew Léonard, who capitalized on the expansion of government printing contracts under the Second Empire and became the official printer for the Chemin de Fer du Nord. Between 1850 and 1863, Danel increased his plant from four mechanical presses to thirty-four and his workforce from 112 to 420. By the 1890s, Imprimerie Danel employed 500 workers operating fifty-two mechanical presses and did 2–3 million francs of business annually, which made it the largest of the some 250 printing enterprises in the Nord at the turn of the twentieth century. Danel, meanwhile, had branched out into other businesses, helping to found and administer the coal mines of Lens and Courrières and becoming the publisher of a daily newspaper, the *Journal de Lille*. Danel was succeeded by his son-in-law, Emile Bigo, and Bigo's sons and grandsons continued to run the firm as the S.A. des Petits Fils de Léonard Danel until the 1970s.[39]

The other major printer-publishers of provincial France were Berger-Levrault and Mame. Founded in Strasbourg in 1676, Berger-Levrault mechanized in the 1850s and 1860s; following the Franco-Prussian War, it relocated to Nancy, where it continued to specialize in government publications such as the *Statistique générale de la France* and the *Almanach national*.[40] Mame et Cie was founded as a printworks in Angers by Charles-Pierre Mame in the 1760s. In 1796 Armand Mame moved it to Tours, where it grew in the next century into one of France's largest integrated printing and bookbinding enterprises, becoming a major publisher of missals, prayer books, Bibles, and Catholic religious literature. By the 1860s, Mame operated twenty steam-powered presses and employed 1,200 workers in printing and bookbinding. In 1868, it integrated backward into papermaking by taking over the La Haye–Descartes paper mill near Tours. By 1900, the Mame empire had expanded to Paris where, through intermarriage with the Dalloz family, the Mames became major shareholders in the country's largest publisher of law books and also acquired extensive interests in the newspaper and periodical press through the S.A. des Publications Périodiques.[41]

As the evolution of the Mame enterprise underscores, Paris remained the center of printing and publishing in France in the nineteenth century, and it was there that the largest number of industrial printers were to be found. In the eighteenth century, the printing industry in Paris had been controlled by the thirty-six members of the Paris Book Guild. The abolition of guilds and the declaration of freedom of the press by the Revolutionary assemblies after 1789 destroyed this closed oligopoly, and the ranks of Paris printers swelled to 187 by 1810, when Napoleon cut the number down to eighty as part of a broader plan to control the press. By then, however, there had been considerable turnover at the top of the trade, because many of the established, "breveted" printers (who were heavily invested in crown publications that no one wanted anymore) went bankrupt after 1789 and were replaced by the up-and-coming printers of new journals and pamphlets that were in high demand.[42] Yet one family—the Didots—made a graceful transition from the closed, privileged world of Old Régime printing to the more open, market-driven printing scene of post-Revolutionary France and remained in the vanguard of French printing and publishing in the nineteenth century.

François Didot, son of a master butcher, had made a place for himself in the Paris book trade in the mid-eighteenth century by publishing and selling translations of Greek classics and the novels of the Abbé Prévost, author of *Manon Lescaut*. Late in life, Didot acquired patents as one of the thirty-six privileged printers of Paris, and his two sons, François-Ambroise and Pierre-François, were appointed official printers to the royal family in the 1780s. As discussed earlier, Pierre-François Didot also took over the Essonnes paper mill, which soon drew his son and heir, Léger, into the battle over the Robert papermaking machine. Meanwhile the two sons of François-Ambroise Didot remained in printing and publishing, weathered the Revolution (despite their close association with the Bourbons), and re-emerged as official printers during the Restoration. Pierre Didot continued to produce high-quality editions of classics, while his younger brother Firmin Didot moved into the new world of mechanized, industrial printing by reinventing stereotyping, which enabled printers to produce larger runs of first editions and to reprint editions cheaply. Firmin also set up an integrated papermaking and printing complex at Mesnil-sur-l'Estrée that included a paper mill, inkworks, type-casting foundry, and mechanized print shop. In the hands of Firmin's two sons, who adopted the hyphenated surname Firmin-Didot, this enterprise prospered by combining the production of deluxe limited editions of fine literature with mass-market publications like the *Annuaire générale de commerce,* which later merged with the better known directory of Bottin to become the *Didot-Bottin,* the foremost business guides and references in modern France. In the second half of the nineteenth century, the Société Firmin-Didot expanded the Mesnil complex, added a new paper mill in the Eure-et-Loir, and remained one of the four largest printing companies in France at the outset of the twentieth century.[43]

In the mid-nineteenth century, the two best customers for French printers were the French government and the new railroad companies, which enjoyed quasi-governmental status. Not surprisingly, the new industrial printers were attracted to and dependent on both of these. We have already seen this in the rise of Léonard Danel of Lille, and it was even more evident in the rise of two of the most successful industrial printers in Paris, Paul Dupont and Napoléon Chaix.

Paul Dupont served an apprenticeship with Firmin-Didot and then opened his own print shop in Paris in 1818. Using his wife's dowry, Dupont soon invested in mechanical presses and began turning out school books and cheap editions of literary classics. By developing a lithographic printing process that anticipated offset printing, he was also able to underbid competitors for government printing contracts. The increase in government printing that followed the July Revolution and the new demand for school materials (as primary education expanded under the Guizot Law of 1833) helped Dupont's business take off after 1830. By 1834, Dupont was printing a newspaper and several important periodicals, including the *Journal Générale de l'Instruction Publique*. More importantly, he had achieved a "virtual monopoly in the decisive sector of administrative printing."[44] After the fall of the July Monarchy in 1848, Dupont shifted his allegiance to Louis-Napoleon Bonaparte in time to capitalize on the advent of the Second Empire. In the 1850s and 1860s, Dupont displaced Hachette as the leading French printer of schoolbooks while maintaining its position as the leading administrative printer. By 1865, the company had added a second printing plant in Clichy that Turgan characterized as "the largest French factory in its field," a huge facility of 20,000 square meters with 650 workers operating two steam engines, twenty mechanical printing presses, six mechanical lithographic presses, and forty-five manual presses.[45]

By 1870, Dupont's main rival among Paris printers was a firm founded by a former employee, Napoleon Chaix. After apprenticing with his father, the departmental printer of the Indre, Chaix went to Paris in 1832 where he worked for Dupont. In 1845, Chaix formed a *société en commandite*—the Imprimerie Centrale des Chemins de Fer—to print train schedules and other materials for the new railroads using steam-powered presses set up in the Paris suburb of Saint-Ouen. In 1848, he expanded into political pamphlets and newspapers *(La Liberté)* and then into government printing and general literature (the *Bibliothèque Universelle des Familles*). After the death of Napoleon Chaix, the firm continued under his son, Edmond-Albion. In 1881 new capital from Paribas allowed the firm to double its plant at Saint-Ouen and to continue to dominate railroad printing in the closing decades of the nineteenth century.[46]

Meanwhile, the Imprimerie Paul Dupont lost its privileged position in administrative printing after the fall of Napoleon III. In 1871 it reorganized as a *société anonyme* with Paul Dupont II as president, which allowed it to raise new capital but did nothing to alleviate its loss of political favor. Henceforth, Dupont et Cie had to bid for contracts like everyone else, and increasingly it found itself at a disadvantage vis-à-vis provincial presses that enjoyed lower production costs. Between 1889 and 1899, the value of Dupont shares fell by more than a third, and when Paul Dupont II died in 1906, he left the company in "deplorable financial condition." However, the firm survived by specializing in the new field of color printing and was still around in 1968 when the French government relaunched it as the Société Nouvelle des Imprimeries Paul Dupont (SNIPD).[47]

While the growing demand for books and other printed matter allowed a certain number of large-scale printing enterprises to emerge in the course of the nineteenth century, it also led to the appearance of the dozens of modern publishing houses whose names are intertwined with the literary and intellectual history of modern France, including Calmann-Levy, Dalloz, Masson, Charpentier, Plon, Flammarion, Fayard, and Gallimard. Publishing is a complex creative and commercial process that centers on commissioning or buying literary works, preparing them for publication (but not necessarily printing and binding the books themselves), and then marketing the final product to booksellers (but not necessarily handling retail sale of the books). In nineteenth-century France, some publishers (Firmin-Didot, Dupont, Chaix, Mame, Berger-Levrault, L. Danel) were in fact printers who had integrated forward and who continued to combine printing and publishing. By the same token, some book publishers and sellers integrated backward into printing and took on the nature of industrial enterprises in the process. Most publishers, however, continued to contract out printing and binding and remained simple, one-function enterprises with anywhere from a few dozen to a few hundred editorial and clerical employees. One publishing firm, however, not only integrated backward into printing and bookbinding but also forward into distribution and even into retail sales, emerging before the end of the nineteenth century as a multifunction publishing giant unique in France and perhaps in the world. This was Hachette.

Hachette was founded in 1826 by Louis Hachette, a brilliant student at the Ecole Normale Supèrieure, whose bright prospects for an academic career had been dashed in 1822 when the Bourbon government closed the Ecole Normale and prevented its mostly liberal students, including Hachette, from standing for the *agrégation.* Hachette then became a tutor to the sons of a wealthy Paris notary, Fourcault de Pavant, who subsequently loaned Hachette the money to purchase a bookseller's license. Setting up his business in the heart of the Latin Quarter, Hachette drew on his academic connections to issue a Greek-French dictionary and to start publishing textbooks and teaching aids. In 1835, thanks to his backers' connections to Guizot (the minister of education), Hachette won an order for 500,000 alphabets, 100,000 reading primers, 40,000 arithmetic books, and 40,000 copies of Madame de Saint-Ouen's *Petite Histoire de France.* At the same time, Guizot promoted Hachette's monthly review for teachers, the *Revue d'Instruction Publique,* virtually making it the official bulletin of the new primary education system. Because of this kind of patronage,

Hachette enjoyed a dominant position in educational publishing in France by the 1840s.[48]

In the 1850s, Hachette lost ground to Dupont in the schoolbook trade (the Bonapartist authorities considered Hachette and his people too liberal), but this loss was more than offset when the railroad companies awarded Hachette an exclusive contract to set up bookstalls in train stations throughout France. To stock these *bibliothèques de gare,* which numbered 900 by 1890, Hachette moved into the publishing of guidebooks, itineraries, general-interest periodicals *(Journal pour Tous),* children's literature *(Tour du Monde),* and cheap editions of popular novels *(Bibliothèque des Chemins de Fer).* He also began publishing new works of fiction by popular authors such as Victor Hugo, George Sand, and Charles Dickens. By the time of Louis Hachette's death in 1864, his company was putting out 200 new titles a year and employed 3,000 at its editorial and sales offices, its printworks, and its bookbindery. In the years that followed, his heirs and successors continued to increase the company's output of books and periodicals and also moved into the area of news distribution. In 1898 Hachette et Cie purchased two existing newspaper distribution companies and merged them into a new subsidiary, the Agence Générale de Librairie et de Publicité, which gave Hachette a dominant position in news distribution in Paris and the provinces. With annual revenues of 45 million francs, Hachette was not only France's largest publishing company but also one of the largest business firms of any kind in turn-of-the-century France.

In the world of publishing, the only enterprises that rivaled Hachette in late nineteenth-century France were the mass-circulation daily newspapers of Paris. Despite continued government censorship and regulation of the press in France until passage of the Press Law of 1881, the nineteenth century saw an enormous profileration of daily and weekly newspapers, both in Paris and the provinces. In addition, all sorts of biweekly, monthly, and quarterly reviews and magazines came into existence. Most of these hardly qualified as industrial enterprises for, whatever their intellectual and political influence (and it was often great), they usually employed only a handful of writers, artists, editors, and secretaries. Not until the advent of what the British called the "penny press"—daily newspapers printed in runs of tens of thousands and later hundreds of thousands—did true industrial enterprises emerge in the world of French journalism. Not surprisingly, such enterprises were found mainly in the capital.

The coming of the mass-circulation daily in France is usually dated from 1836, when Emile de Girardin launched *La Presse* and Armand Dutacq launched *Le Siècle*. Unlike existing Paris dailies, which were sold on a subscription basis at high prices (typically 80 francs a year) and were thus aimed at an upper-class clientele, *La Presse* and *Le Siècle* catered to the middle class with features like serialized novels *(romans-feuilletons)* and were sold at lower subscription rates of forty francs a year (still not a penny press and still out of the financial reach of the working class). Both papers struggled initially, but by 1845 the daily circulation of *Le Siècle* reached 34,000 and that of *La Presse* 22,000. This was apparently sufficient to justify Girardin setting up his own printing plant with the first mechanical press designed specifically for the needs of newspaper publishing.[49] However, the full realization of the mass-circulation newspaper in France came only with the founding of four true penny-press dailies in Paris between 1863 and 1892: *Le Petit Journal, Le Petit Parisien, Le Matin,* and *Le Journal.*

The first and most important of these was *Le Petit Journal,* launched in February 1863 by Moïse Millaud. The paper was distinguished from earlier popular dailies by its smaller size (a *demi-format* instead of the usual *grand format*) and by its lower price (five centimes, half the price of previous low-priced dailies). Most important, *Le Petit Journal* was *depolitisé* (nonpolitical), which exempted it from the government stamp tax on regular, "political" newspapers. Not only was this a cost savings in itself, but it also meant that the paper could eventually be printed on high-speed rotative presses using roll paper, instead of individual stamped sheets, which gave it an even greater price advantage over its competitors. Almost as important as price for attracting the common man was the paper's content, an amalgam of hard news, court reports, theater schedules, stock quotations, and serialized novels. Millaud's formula worked: The paper's circulation reached 250,000 before the end of 1863, and by 1869 it was up to 400,000.

Moïse Millaud died in 1871, and *Le Petit Journal* was taken over by a syndicate that included Hippolyte Marinoni and Emile de Girardin. Under this new ownership, the paper's circulation rose to 700,000 by 1882, making it by far the largest newspaper in Paris. Indeed, it accounted for one out of every four papers sold daily in the capital. After Girardin died in 1881, *Le Petit Journal* was dominated by the aging Marinoni, who installed Ernest Prevet as editor-in-chief. Under the Third Republic the earlier distinction between political and nonpolitical newspapers had disappeared, so Prevet was free to take an aggressively nationalistic line that became *anti-dreyfusard* at the time of the Dreyfus Affair in the late 1890s. This apparently alienated some readers, for the paper's circulation fell from its peak of 1 million a day in the mid-nineties to between 725,000 and 850,000 a day in the early 1900s, which relegated it to third place among Paris dailies behind *Le Petit Parisien* and *Le Matin*. Still, on the eve of World War I it remained the most popular Paris newspaper in the French provinces.

Le Petit Parisien was launched in 1876 by two Radical politicians, Louis Andrieux and Jules Roche, but it was Jean Dupuy, a successful Paris lawyer who later served in several governments, who turned the paper into a going concern. Assuming control in 1888, Dupuy used the usual mix of sensational news, crime reports, and serialized novels—plus heavy coverage of the Boulanger Affair—to increase circulation from 100,000 to 300,000 in 1889 and to 600,000 by 1896. In the early 1900s Dupuy was succeeded by his sons, Pierre and Paul, and his son-in-law, François Arago, who brought the daily circulation to a peak of 1.5 million, making *Le Petit Parisien* the largest newspaper in Paris and in France—and by their claims the largest in the world—on the eve of the First World War. More than that, they turned *Le Petit Parisien* into something of a publishing empire, with an illustrated supplement and an array of collateral publications, including an American-style photomagazine. The newspaper operated its own printing plant at the headquarters building at 16–18 Rue d'Enghien and its own paper mill in the Eure-et-Loir (to avoid dependence on the Papeteries d'Essonnes); to circumvent Hachette, it had developed its own national distribution apparatus.[50]

The other two big Paris dailies at the turn of the twentieth century were *Le Matin* and *Le Journal*. *Le Matin* was started in 1884 by two Englishmen and an American as an American-style tabloid featuring short, punchy news stories under large headlines. After doing poorly in its initial years, *Le Matin* finally hit its stride in 1898, when it was reorganized as a *société anonyme* by Maurice Bunau-Varilla, brother of Philippe Bunau-Varilla, the civil engineer who promoted the Panama Canal and played a key role in the American acquisition of the Panama Canal Zone. Generating headlines with a string of well-publicized feuds, Bunau-Varilla boosted *Le Matin*'s circulation to 600,000 in his first decade at the helm, and he continued to run the paper for the next forty years, until it was closed down in 1944 for collaboration with the Nazis. Meanwhile, *Le Journal* was launched in 1892 in a blaze of publicity by Fernand Xau, a journalist and impresario who also brought Buffalo Bill and his Wild West Show to Paris. With backing from the Darblays, Xau recruited a stable of famous writers to provide *romans-feuilletons,* and he installed a state-of-the-art printing plant that included France's first linotype machines. The paper was almost an instant success: The circulation hit 300,000 in 1894, 600,000 by 1904, and surpassed 1 million by 1913, putting it in second place behind *Le Petit Parisien.*

Although each of these four mass-circulation dailies had its distinct characteristics, they were very similar as business enterprises. Reflecting the enormous costs involved in newspaper publishing, each was organized as a limited-liability joint-stock company and resorted to frequent stock offerings to raise needed capital. Each had its own printing plant housed in a large headquarters building that combined editorial, production, and marketing operations under one roof. Each employed about 1,000 people, although the composition of the personnel varied (*Le Matin* had more editorial employees in the home office than *Le Petit Parisien,* but the latter required 450 "correspondents" to run its distribution system in the provinces). All depended on advertising revenues to offset production and distribution costs, and all promoted themselves heavily to maintain circulation in a highly competitive environment (*Le Petit Journal,* for example, sponsored auto, air, and bicycle races). Finally, each was more than a one-product firm. They all turned out families of journalism "products," including illustrated supplements and special-interest magazines. All of this points up the extent to which in France—as in Britain and the United States—newspapers, magazines, and books had become consumer commodities to be mass-produced and marketed by the beginning of the twentieth century. As such, the business of printing and publishing was but one part of a much larger consumer goods capitalism that emerged in France in the course of the nineteenth century.

CHAPTER TEN

Industrial Capitalism and Consumer Goods

Like Great Britain and the United States, France experienced the beginnings of an unprecedented consumer revolution in the nineteenth century. American business historians tend to equate this revolution with the appearance of standardized, branded, packaged goods that were mass-produced in huge factories and "marketed" (not just "sold") through mass retailers with the help of new methods of advertising and promotion.[1] In truth, the advent of widely marketed branded goods represented the final stage in a multistage process by which the quantity and variety of consumer goods were expanded over the course of the nineteenth and twentieth centuries, and it is a stage that France (and most Western countries) reached only after World War II. In the nineteenth century, France experienced a different kind of consumer revolution (or an earlier stage of "the" consumer revolution, if one sees it as a single global phenomenon). This consumer revolution had two sides. On the one hand, it involved a transformation in the way items of general consumption (such as food and clothing) were produced and distributed. On the other hand, it involved making available to the middle class, and even to the urban working class, goods once viewed as luxuries meant only for kings and nobles. That is to say, it involved a transition from "aristocratic" consumption to "bourgeois" consumption.

On both levels, the expansion of consumption affected only certain goods. Yet when it occurred on either level, it often gave rise to mechanized manufacturing. One obvious example of this was the textile industry, which we have already considered because of its primacy in establishing the model of industrial capitalism in France. Other consumer goods that came to be produced in factories in the nineteenth century included glass and paper, which we have likewise already considered because they served as industrial raw materials as well as products of direct consumption. In this chapter we will look at additional consumer goods—both goods of general consumption and goods of luxury consumption—that came to be produced in factories and thus supported the rise of large-scale industrial enterprise. However, the coverage will necessarily be selective both because of limitations of space and because the consumer goods industry remains relatively unexplored by historians of French business.

Flour and Breadstuffs

The production of food and drink—*alimentation*—was one of the largest sectors of the French economy throughout the nineteenth century, and, within this large and varied sector, the production of breadstuffs dwarfed all other areas. Indeed, the manufacture of flour, bran, bread, biscuits, and pasta accounted for 83 percent of food production in the period 1815–1824, and eighty years later it still accounted for 65 percent.[2] The process of providing the French with their daily bread—from the growing of grains to milling flour and baking bread in its myriad forms—had been at the center of French life from time immemorial. By the beginning of the nineteenth century, that process was locked into well-established routines that, on the whole, changed very little over the course of the century, in part because two of the major participants in the process—farmers and bakers—persuaded the French government to intervene to block or slow down such changes. However, as France became more urban and was increasingly knitted by the railroads into a single market, two stages in the process—flour milling and the manufacture of packaged baked goods—became increasingly susceptible to large-scale, centralized, mechanized manufacturing methods, and it was there that true industrial enterprises appeared.

In the nineteenth century, milling went from being a small-scale, geographically dispersed, artisanal industry to a highly capitalistic industry dominated by a few dozen entrepreneurs who set up large water-powered (and later steam- and electricity-powered) mills to supply flour to the large cities and regional markets of France.[3] The outstanding figure in this evolution was Aimé-Stanislas Darblay. Between the 1820s and 1860s, Darblay joined with his brother and later with his son Paul to build and operate a series of large mills that supplied flour on long-term contracts to the bakers of Paris under the Six Marques label.

In the early years, the Darblay enterprise centered on the Saint-Maur mill, constructed in 1838 near the junction of the Seine and Marne rivers. It was powered by Fourneyron water turbines and incorporated the "American" system of milling—that is to say, it was a multistory, gravity-fed mill where grain went into the top and flour and bran came out at the bottom with a minimum of human handling.[4] In the 1860s, the center of the Darblays' operations shifted from Saint-Maur to Corbeil, southeast of Paris on the Essonne River. One of the oldest flour mills in France, Corbeil was probably the first one in the country to have the American system installed (in 1817) when it was owned by the Hospices Générales de Paris. The Darblays leased Corbeil in 1838 and became outright owners in 1863, whereupon they sold Saint-Maur to the City of Paris and transferred its equipment to Corbeil.[5]

As we saw in the last chapter, the Darblays moved into papermaking in 1868 by purchasing the Papeteries d'Essonnes. Because Paul Darblay focused increasingly on papermaking after his father died in 1878, the Corbeil mills were reorganized as a *société anonyme* in 1882. In 1888, the "Hungarian" milling system (in which cylinders replaced grindstones) was installed at Corbeil, and by 1900 the daily capacity of the mill had risen from 180 metric tons to 350 metric tons. That, plus the opening of an additional mill at Le Havre, kept the Grands Moulins de Corbeil in first place among French milling companies at the turn of the century.[6]

Following the lead of the Darblays at Corbeil, large-scale milling enterprises emerged in other parts of France. In Lorraine, the mayor of Metz, Emile Bouchotte, entered the milling business in 1837. After the annexation of Metz by the Germans in 1871, Bouchotte moved to Nancy and leased a water-powered mill from two other Lorraine millers, Léon Simon and Louis Vilgrain. After Bouchotte's death, his enterprise was merged with those of Simon and Vilgrain in a *société anonyme*. In 1885, this firm acquired the Grands Moulins de Nancy and assumed its name. Under the direction of Ernest Vilgrain, Grands Moulins de Nancy continued to expand by acquiring mills throughout eastern France, and at the turn of the twentieth century it was one of the largest milling companies in France. Meanwhile, in the department of the Nord, the Schotsmans brothers combined a traditional grain-trading business at Dunkirk with heavy investments in oil-seed and flour milling, particularly at new mills at Brebières near Douai and at Don near Lille. The latter, a "superb installation" with forty-eight pairs of grindstones (Corbeil then had fifty-eight), processed 100 metric tons of wheat per day, the largest output in the Nord. Although the Schotsmans were ruined in the grain speculations of the 1890s, two of their cousins, J. and P. Schotsmans, salvaged the mills at Don and Brebières and continued to operate them profitably in the early 1900s.[7]

The other sector of the breadstuffs industry that gave rise to industrial enterprises by the end of the nineteenth century was the manufacture of biscuits, pasta, and other flour-based packaged foods. Although the leading companies in this sector adopted many of the techniques of modern mass marketing, including brand names and heavy advertising, we know surprisingly little about the companies themselves. In 1900, there were some 225 firms manufacturing and marketing *pâtes alimentaires* (pasta) in France, but only twenty-one of these employed fifty or more workers. The most important were in Lyon and included Bertrand, Yberty et Cie, Société Générale des Pâtes Alimentaires, and, especially, Carret et Fils. The last of these was still a relatively small enterprise in the mid-1880s. In 1888, however, it built a new plant in Lyon, and it added plants at Marseille and Mulhouse in the 1890s. By 1900, Carret et Fils had raised its daily output to 50,000 kilograms—versus only 15,000 in 1892—and had become, according to the jury report for the 1900 World's Fair, "probably the largest producer [of pasta] in the world."[8]

Meanwhile, the manufacture of branded, packaged biscuits was being developed by Honoré-Jean Olibet, who first produced British-style sea biscuits at Bordeaux in 1862 and whose son later added plants near Paris and in Spain.[9] Just as important was the firm of Lefevre-Utile, founded in Nantes in 1846 when Jean-Roman Lefevre set up a plant to produce *biscuites de Reims* with the mechanized methods recently introduced by the English, particularly Huntley and Palmers of Reading.[10] By 1850, Lefevre had married Pauline-Isabelle Utile, and after 1860 the firm was known as Lefevre-Utile, or LU. In 1882 Louis Lefevre-Utile succeeded his father, moved the family's business to a new building on the banks of the Loire, and invested in the latest American manufacturing technology. In the 1890s, Lefevre-Utile introduced an automated production line, using conveyor belts, continuous ovens, and liquid dough shot into cookie molds by "pistols" to mass produce the "Paille d'Or" *gaufrette*. He also began to promote his various brands vigorously, employing leading artists like Alphonse Mucha to design packaging, posters, and advertisements.[11] As of 1913, LU was turning out twenty tons of branded baked goods each day with a workforce of 1,200, making it the largest food processing company in Nantes and one of the largest in France.[12]

Sugar and Confectionery

Cereals and breadstuffs continued to be the main ingredients in the diets of the French and other European peoples throughout the nineteenth century, but they did not really constitute a growth industry. Per capita consumption of bread and other flour-based foods was already high at the beginning of the nineteenth century and remained relatively inelastic (that is, consumption did not necessarily rise as prices fell and disposable income increased).[13] By contrast, the demand for sugar and confections proved to be highly elastic, and indeed a dramatic rise in the consumption of them was a key component in the consumer revolution of the nineteenth century.

In France and elsewhere, sugar had been an expensive luxury good at the end of the eighteenth century, but in the course of the nineteenth, production of sugar took off and prices fell—from 300 francs per 100 kilograms for refined sugar in Paris in 1815–1818 to 63–65 francs in the five years before the outbreak of World War I. Although the French never developed the sweet tooth of the British, per capita consumption in France rose from less than one kilogram a year in 1815 to over fifteen kilograms by 1900.[14] When combined with population growth, this meant that France's gross domestic consumption of sugar increased roughly twentyfold, from 30,000 tons in 1815 to nearly 600,000 tons by 1900. At the same time, France continued to export refined sugar to the rest of Europe, as well as to North Africa and the Near East. Indeed, French exports of refined sugar rose thirtyfold between 1825 and 1875; even though they declined somewhat after 1875, the average annual export of 137,500 tons in 1901–1905 was still twenty-five times the level of seventy-five years before. Overall, France's production of refined sugar increased by a factor of twenty-eight from 1816 to 1900, from around 25,000 tons to 700,000.[15]

The sugar that was sold to food processors, pastry bakers, confectioners, and the general public was produced in three stages, each of which supported a distinct industry: (1) the cultivation of sugar cane in France's tropical colonies (Guadeloupe and Martinique in the Caribbean and Réunion in the Indian Ocean) and of sugar beets in metropolitan France; (2) the processing of sugar cane and sugar beets in *sucreries* to yield raw sugar; and (3) the further purification and concentration of this sugar in *raffineries* to yield refined sugar. The high cost of transportation dictated that the second stage be located as near as possible to the point of cultivation, so each plantation or cluster of plantations on the sugar islands maintained its own *sucrerie*, while hundreds of *fabriques-sucreries,* scattered across the sugar beet country of northern France, crushed and extracted raw sugar from the sugar beets harvested in their vicinity.[16]

In theory, there was nothing to keep the refining phase of sugar production from also locating near the point of cultivation. Indeed, the Cail family became the leading French producers of cane sugar in the mid-1800s by setting up refineries on the islands of Guadeloupe and Réunion. However, it was a long-standing policy of the French government, dating back to the origins of the French sugar industry in the seventeenth century, that sugar destined for the domestic market be refined on French soil, and this policy was maintained into the nineteenth century by a prohibition on the importation of refined sugar. As a result, the refining of cane sugar continued to be located at the ports long associated with the sugar trade, especially Nantes, Marseilles, Bordeaux, and Le Havre. Later, with the rise of beet sugar production, a new refining center was established in Paris, the principal market for beet sugar, although nothing prohibited the refining of beet sugar elsewhere. Eventually, the dominance of the Paris refiners came to be challenged by entrepreneurs who appended refineries to their sugar beet mills in northern France at the end of the nineteenth century. Before then, however, that sort of vertical integration was rare, and refining for the most part remained a separate industry. But it was not a static industry. Sugar refining proved to be highly susceptible to increases in the scale and efficiency of production through technological innovation and the infusion of capital, and this eventually led to the concentration of production in a handful of large industrial enterprises.

At the outset of the nineteenth century, the technology of sugar refining was rudimentary. The first step was "clarification," which involved heating the raw sugar syrup with animal blood and lime water to bring impurities to the surface, where they were skimmed off. After this, the syrup was cooled in a succession of pots or vats, during which the sugar crystallized, was separated from molasses and other waste products, and formed into loaves (the waste was later further refined into lower-grade forms of sugar called "bastards"). Because the pots were heated by direct fire and needed to be supervised closely at all stages, this process tended to preclude large-scale operations. So sugar refining remained fragmented among dozens of small, artisanal enterprises—perhaps 167 in all in 1832—each employing ten to fifty skilled workers. This pattern changed, however, with the introduction of new technology.

As early as 1812, Charles Derosne demonstrated the use of animal black as a substitute for blood in the first stage of sugar refining, and by the 1830s it was being employed in large filters that simplified and improved the purification process. At the same time, steam replaced direct fire in heating the vats, and the concentration process was revolutionized by the vacuum pan, first developed by the English refiner Edward Howard and later improved by Derosne and Cail in their multiple-effect evaporation apparatus. Together, these innovations greatly increased the optimal size of sugar refineries and required refiners to make large capital investments to adopt "best practice" (the Derosne-Cail apparatus cost 50,000–60,000 francs, plus the use of animal black usually meant building a rendering plant at the refinery). But the payoffs were a higher quality refined sugar ("Derosne train white") and substantial savings in fuel costs.[17] By the 1840s, a process of concentration was under way. Refiners willing and able to invest in the new technology expanded output, and those who did not went out of business or at best survived at the margin (in the Paris region, for example, the number of refineries fell from eighteen in 1848 to only four in 1868).

The trend toward concentration continued throughout the second half of the nineteenth century as improvements in refining technology continued to appear. Among these were the Rousseau process, which substituted carbonic acid for animal black in clarification; paddle boilers, which eliminated manual stirring and increased the scale of operations; *turbinage*, which substituted physical separation for chemical reactions in purification; the Steffen process for the bleaching and formation of granulated sugar; and the Adant process, which allowed sugar to be formed in lumps as well as loaves. These innovations, when coupled with market forces and government policy (including the protection of domestic refining, the protection of colonial sugar cane production and later domestic sugar beet production by import duties on foreign raw sugar, and the promotion of refined sugar exports through direct and indirect subsidies) transformed the French sugar industry in the course of the nineteenth century and gave rise to modern industrial enterprises of European and worldwide importance. We can best understand these firms by looking at the development of the chief sugar refining centers.

The recovery of colonial sugar production and the implementation of policies to promote sugar exports after 1815 worked to the benefit of the established sugar ports of the Atlantic seaboard in the early 1800s. These included Bordeaux, which had been the leading sugar refiner among the Atlantic ports in the late eighteenth century but had suffered grievously from the loss of Saint-Domingue and the interruption of maritime trade during the Revolution and Napoleonic Empire. By 1839, Bordeaux was back up to thirty-nine refineries, but these were all traditional artisanal operations that failed to make investments in the new technology in the 1840s. Consequently, the Bordeaux industry was already in decline by 1848, when the abolition of slavery disrupted colonial sugar production and further undercut the Bordeaux industry. By 1860, sugar refining had virtually disappeared at Bordeaux. For a time Le Havre did better, supplanting its old rival Rouen as a sugar refining center between 1815 and 1848 and attracting true industrial enterprises. But in the face of competition from Paris, Le Havre sugar refining declined in the 1860s, and its last refinery closed in 1898. Thus, of the traditional sugar ports on France's Atlantic coast, it was Nantes that had the greatest success in the nineteenth century.

The development of a modern sugar refining industry in Nantes began in 1812 when Louis Say, the younger brother of the renowned political economist J-B Say, came to the city to manage a new sugar refinery set up by the Paris financier Benjamin Delessert. Delessert soon left the company, and Say took J-B Etienne as his new partner. As colonial sugar production boomed, their business prospered. Louis Say moved to Paris in 1832 and set up a new beet sugar refinery at Ivry (see below), leaving the Nantes refinery in the hands of Etienne and Say's two oldest sons. The Says and Etienne invested in the new technology in the 1830s and 1840s, and their output increased fourfold—from 5,800 tons a year in the 1820s to 25,000 tons in 1860.[18]

The reform of trade policy in the early 1860s ended the *pacte coloniale* that had long given colonial sugar a privileged position in the French market, and this hurt all port refiners in their continuing competition with domestic beet sugar, including Say and Etienne. In addition, the firm was hurt by the deaths of Achille Say in 1858 and J-B Etienne in 1866. Under Etienne's son Emile, the company invested in new equipment and attempted to expand into beet sugar refining, but this strategy did not pan out. In 1878, Etienne merged his refinery with another owned by Nicolas Cézard, but in the absence of functional integration of the two refineries, the new firm followed its predecessors into bankruptcy in 1883.

More successful in the long run was the Raffinerie du Chatenay, founded in 1866 by Nicolas Cézard's son Louis. In the 1880s, Chatenay became part of the Cail family sugar enterprise. J-F Cail had become France's largest refiner of colonial (cane) sugar—as well as its leading maker of refinery equipment—by the time of his death in 1871. Subsequently, under the direction of Cail's widow and his son-in-law, the Cail firm managed to turn Chatenay into a profitable operation in spite of severe competitive pressures. Taken over in turn by Albert Dehaynin, another important Paris entrepreneur, Chatenay was Nantes' largest sugar refinery (and the seventh largest in France) in the early twentieth century.

Of the port cities of France that refined sugar, Marseille emerged as the most important in the course of the nineteenth century on the strength of its production for export. Although Marseille's location put it in a poor position to supply the domestic sugar market, it was well situated to import raw sugar from the colonies and the Near East and to export refined sugar throughout the Mediterranean world. This business was aided by the French government's policy of drawbacks, whereby duties on imported raw sugar were refunded on exported refined sugar, which actually made it more profitable to sell sugar abroad than at home. In 1864, however, government policy turned against Marseille: A system of temporary admissions replaced drawbacks in such a way that indigenous beet sugar acquired the same advantages in the export trade as imported cane sugar. Paris refiners immediately started exporting sugar, especially to Great Britain. Driven from the British market by the Parisians, the Belgians and Dutch then moved into the Mediterranean at the expense of Marseille, whose exports declined from their nineteenth-century high of 71,315 tons in 1865 to less than 24,000 tons twenty years later. However, Marseille eventually reclaimed its position as France's leading sugar exporter in the early 1900s when new colonial markets opened up and changes in government transportation policy allowed the Marseillais to start using beet sugar from northern France, which they "imported" by sea from Dunkirk.

Within this century-long cycle of boom, crisis, and recovery, the sugar refining industry of Marseille experienced a pattern of business development similar to that of other refining centers: namely, the proliferation of firms as production expanded in the early 1800s, followed by a weeding out and concentration in the hard times of the late 1800s, with an overall trend toward ever-larger, more technically sophisticated and capital-intensive enterprises. This pattern is well illustrated in the history of the two joint-stock companies that came to dominate Marseille sugar by the end of the century, the Raffineries de la Méditerranée and the Raffineries de Saint-Louis.

The origins of the Raffineries de la Méditerranée went back to the enterprises founded by Joseph Grandval—"le Napoléon de la cuite"—in the early 1800s. Grandval set up a distillery in 1821 and in 1831 moved into sugar refining with a partner, Girard. By 1839, Grandval et Girard was the largest sugar refinery in Marseille and virtually monopolized Marseille's exports to Italy. In the 1840s, Grandval moved on to banking and leased his refinery to the marquis de Forbin-Janson, who modernized the equipment but went bankrupt in the crisis of 1847. Grandval thereupon reclaimed the refinery and relaunched it as the Raffinerie Marseillaise in 1848. Buoyed by the business recovery of the 1850s, Grandval's refinery grew and prospered. By 1863 it employed 1,500 workers, processed 36,000 tons of raw sugar annually (compared to 80,000 tons processed by all Paris refiners), and was reputedly the largest sugar refinery in Europe.[19]

The rapid expansion of French sugar exports in the early 1860s attracted outside money into the Marseille industry in what Jacques Fierain calls "a fever of investment in sugar refining."[20] Three new refineries were set up including that of Charles Rostand, scion of the old Marseille merchant family that also produced Edmond Rostand, author of *Cyrano de Bergerac*. Rostand got his start in the Cuban sugar trade in the 1840s and 1850s, made a killing in sugar speculation in 1861–1862, and then returned to Marseille in 1863 to invest his winnings in a huge new refinery that processed 60,000 tons of raw sugar in its first year. Fearing hyper-competition, Grandval sold out to Rostand in 1864. The next year, sugar prices collapsed in Marseille, and the Rostand enterprise, already overextended by its buyout of Grandval, collapsed. In 1867 the Rostand refineries merged with yet another Marseille refinery and were relaunched as the Raffineries de la Méditerranée. The new company—headed by Amédée Armand, a Marseille merchant with interests in shipping, shipbuilding, and banking—was backed by some of the leading families in Marseille, including the

Grandvals. Despite its size and the names on its prospectus, however, the Méditerranée proved to be surprisingly undynamic. Paying out most of its income in dividends to shareholders, the company invested in new technology reluctantly and late, and its output of sugar scarcely increased from the 1860s to the 1900s, fluctuating between 32,000 and 42,000 tons per year over these years. It soon took a backseat to the other large joint-stock sugar refinery created in the aftermath of the 1864–1865 crisis, the Raffineries de Saint-Louis.

Raffineries de Saint-Louis was the brainchild of Henri Bergasse, member of an important merchant family of Marseille, who participated in many of the major ventures of the 1860s, including Paulin Talabot's Société des Transports Maritimes à Vapeur and the Docks et Entrepôts de Marseille. Not incidentally, he was a principal backer of Charles Rostand in 1863. In 1867 Bergasse led a group of investors, drawn from many of the leading families of Marseille, in taking over another new refinery that had recently failed and relaunching it as the Raffineries de Saint-Louis. Under the leadership of Bergasse, who remained the dominant figure in the firm until his death in 1901, Raffineries de Saint-Louis embraced a strategy of continuous modernization and expansion that succeeded in simultaneously lowering its costs and raising the quality of its product. The company further lowered production costs by shifting from cane to beet sugar, much of which was brought from Dunkirk on Saint-Louis' own steamships. As the city's low-cost producer, Saint-Louis led the way into new markets for Marseille sugar in North Africa and Persia in the 1890s and 1900s. Reflecting these initiatives, the company's annual sales, after hovering in the 33–50 million franc range during its first two decades, rose steadily after 1886 to a prewar peak of 81.3 million francs in 1913. By then, Saint-Louis was well-established as the largest sugar refinery in Marseille and second largest in France, processing almost 115,000 tons of raw sugar annually (versus 36,000 for the Raffineries de la Méditerranée).

Despite the success of the Raffineries de Saint-Louis, the sugar industry of Marseille came to be overshadowed by the sugar industry of Paris in the course of the nineteenth century. Sugar refining in Paris was based on beet sugar, and its rise to preeminence paralleled the growth of sugar beet production.

Sugar beets had been planted experimentally in France in 1800–1802 and then more extensively during the Continental Blockade of 1806–1814, but the reopening of France to cane sugar in 1814 had virtually killed off this first, hothouse growth of sugar beet cultivation. However, the continued protection of colonial sugar kept domestic prices artificially high, which helped beet sugar production gradually recover, rising from a mere 50 tons in 1820 to 5,500 tons in 1830 and then to more than 50,000 tons in 1850, when it exceeded the production of colonial sugar for the first time. Thereafter, government policy increasingly favored domestic production over colonial production—perhaps a reflection of the progress of democratization in a country with a large farming population—and sugar beets became the preeminent source of raw sugar in France (in 1900, French sugar refiners processed over 600,000 tons of beet sugar but less than 100,000 tons of cane sugar).

The rise of beet sugar in turn gave rise to a new sugar refining industry separate from the established cane sugar refining industry of the ports. The first beet sugar refinery was set up in Arras by Crespel-Dellisse in 1810, but the most important beet sugar refineries appeared in Paris and its suburbs. In 1832, 24 of the 167 sugar refineries in France were in or near Paris, but this number fell to 18 in 1848 and to 6 by 1870. By 1900, there were only three refineries in Paris, but these three—Say, Lebaudy, and Sommier—were three of the four largest in France, and together they made Paris the country's premier center for sugar production.

As we have seen, Louis Say left his Nantes refinery in the hands of his eldest sons and moved to Paris in 1832. There, in association with Constant Dumeril, he purchased the Raffineries de Jamaïque in the industrial suburb of Ivry. Despite its name, this refinery processed beet sugar, and as the domestic production of sugar beets—still untaxed—grew at the expense of imported cane sugar in the course of the 1830s, the Say-Dumeril company prospered. With the death of Louis Say in 1840, his share of the Ivry refinery passed to his youngest sons, Constant and Louis-Octave. In 1858, after the death of Louis-Octave and the retirement of Dumeril, Constant Say became sole proprietor. In the 1860s, the Paris sugar industry entered its period of great expansion thanks to technical advances in the extraction of sugar from beets, the opening of the British market under the 1860 trade treaty, and the granting of indirect export subsidies to beet sugar under the temporary admissions regime set up in 1864.[21] Responding to these favorable circumstances, Constant Say rebuilt the Ivry refinery with the latest equipment and increased its output. At his death in 1871, the firm employed between 600 and 800 workers and produced 65,000 tons of refined sugar per year, making it France's largest.

The growth and prosperity of the Say enterprise continued in the 1870s and 1880s under the management of Ernest Cronier, a professional engineer who ran the company while Constant Say's children were still minors. In 1890, Constant's son Henri took control of the firm and again renovated the equipment. At the same time, he expanded into the Mediterranean market with the founding of the Raffineries et Sucreries d'Egypte.[22] After Henri Say's premature death in 1899, the company was reorganized as a *société anonyme*, with Cronier back in charge. In 1905, however, Cronier got caught up in a speculative bubble that burst with the crash of the Paris sugar market. Facing financial ruin and possible prosecution, he shot himself. The company went through yet another reorganization but managed to maintain its position as France's largest sugar refiner on the eve of World War I.[23]

The second largest refinery in Paris was founded by the Lebaudy brothers at La Villette in 1829. The Lebaudys, already established merchants and bankers at Le Havre and Paris, were prominent in the colonial sugar trade. Two of the brothers, Jean and Adolphe, continued to focus on these businesses while the third, Guillaume, specialized in sugar refining with help from Derosne et Cail (Adolphe was married to Derosne's daughter). After attempting unsuccessfully to take control of the colonial sugar trade through their Société des Antilles in the 1840s, the Lebaudys concentrated on beet sugar. Under the leadership of Guillaume's son Jean-Gustave and grandson Paul, the firm expanded steadily in the second half of the nineteenth century, mimicking the development of Say, except that Lebaudy remained under family control. Its production of 82,000 tons in 1912 put it in third place behind Say and Saint-Louis.[24]

The third great sugar refining enterprise of Paris was owned and operated by the Sommiers, a family of Paris *négociants* who rose as much by brilliant marriages as by entrepreneurial acumen (they were connected by marriage to the Périers, de Voguës, and Barantes). Following the lead of the Lebaudys, Pierre Sommier joined with his nephew Achille to set up a sugar refinery at La Villette in 1829. The firm was reorganized in 1869 under Pierre's son Alfred, who is also noted for his purchase and restoration of the chateau of Vaux-le-Vicomte near Paris. Alfred was in turn succeeded by his son Edme. At the turn of the twentieth century, the Sommier enterprise was turning out 50,000–65,000 tons of sugar a year.[25]

Beyond Paris, beet sugar refining developed in conjunction with the cultivation and processing of sugar beets in the rich farmlands north of Paris. Members of the merchant and industrial elite of the Nord, such as Henri Bernard and his son-in-law Charles Kolb-Bernard, had set up modest refineries in and around Lille, Valenciennes, Douai, and Cambrai by the 1840s. However, it was really in the second half of the nineteenth century that this industry came into its own, spreading south into the Aisne, Oise, and Seine-et-Oise and giving rise to a new class of farmer-industrialists who combined the growing of sugar beets with milling and even refining. The prototype for these *betteravier-sucriers* was Louis Crespel-Dellisse of Lille, who built France's first beet sugar refinery in 1810 and went on to assemble an empire consisting of eleven *domaines agricoles* and nine *fabriques* employing 2,500 workers before he lost it all in the financial panic of 1857. Another of these new farmer-industrialists was Armand Decauville, a big Seine-et-Oise farmer who began refining sugar in 1854 and whose son Paul took what his father had begun and built it into a major industrial enterprise by the end of the century. A third was Aimé Ternyck, who moved from textile production in Roubaix to sugar refining at Chauny and Nogent in the 1890s.[26] In the long run, however, the most important of the new sugar refining enterprises in northern France was that of the Beghin family.

In 1826 Ferdinand Beghin took over his father-in-law's *sucrerie* at Thumeries in the department of the Nord, and over the next twenty years he built it into a profitable small refining enterprise with fifty workers and annual sales of over 100,000 francs. However, the Beghins attained national stature only toward the end of the century when the efforts of the Syndicat des Raffineurs to maintain sugar prices by limiting production inadvertently gave the small refiners of the Nord their big opportunity. Led by the grandsons of Ferdinand Beghin, Joseph and Henri, the Beghin Company expanded its refinery at Thumeries and added new ones at Beauchamp (Somme) and Corbedem (Pas-de-Calais). By 1913, the Beghins employed 4,000 workers and processed 35,000–43,000 tons of raw sugar yearly, putting them in fifth place among all French refiners.[27]

Along with the family-run enterprises of the Nord, a number of joint-stock sugar refining enterprises appeared in the late 1800s, including the Raffineries et Sucreries de Pont d'Ardres and the Sucrerie Centrale de Cambrai. In the wake of the consolidation and concentration that dominated French sugar refining in the 1870s and 1880s, this represented something of a renewal and expansion of the industry, as sugar beet growers and processors integrated forward into refining. Even so, as of 1912 there were only twenty-six refineries in France, and (with the exception of the Beghin company) the ten largest continued to be found in the long-established centers of sugar refining: Paris, Marseille, and Nantes.

Much of the sugar refined in France was not sold directly to individual consumers but instead went to other food manufacturers, the most important of which were the makers of chocolate and sweets.[28] Many firms in this industry were small craft businesses turning out deluxe specialties for an upper-class clientele or less expensive sweets for a local or regional market. However, the growth of Paris and the knitting of the French provinces into a national market by the railroads provided the necessary conditions for the advent of mass production in this area, as in many others. Thus, the years after 1850 witnessed the emergence of relatively large-scale enterprises such as that of Eugène and Auguste Pelletier, who employed 300 in factories in Paris, Strasbourg, and London, turning out "bonbons of all shapes, colors, and flavors," and that of J. J. Jacquin, who erected "a veritable factory to mass-produce bonbons" at Dammarie-les-Lys near Melun in 1872.[29] However, the emergence of large-scale enterprise in *chocolaterie* and *confiserie* is best seen in the case of the Menier Company.

By the end of the nineteenth century, Menier et Cie was by far the largest manufacturer of chocolate in France and perhaps in the world. It was founded by Antoine-Brutus Menier, a Paris pharmacist who in the 1820s built a horse-powered mill to grind the ingredients for medicines that he sold in his Paris shop. In 1825, he shifted this production to a water-powered mill at Noisiel on the Marne. Four years later, he began grinding cacao beans at Noisiel and added chocolate to his line of products. After receiving a gold medal at the 1832 Paris Exposition, Menier introduced the yellow wrapper and gold medal trademark that would be associated with Menier chocolate down to the twentieth century. By 1847, Menier had shifted most of his pharmaceutical production to a new plant at Saint-Denis, and the Noisiel plant was increasingly devoted to chocolate. By the early 1850s, Menier was producing some 600 tons of chocolate a year, about one-fifth of France's total consumption.[30]

Succeeding his father as proprietor in 1853, Emile Menier initially expanded pharmaceutical production at both Noisiel and Saint-Denis, but in 1867 he sold that half of the business, and the Saint-Denis plant, to the Pharmacie Centrale. By then the development in Holland of the Van Houten process for the production of pure powdered cocoa—

"Dutch chocolate"—had created large supplies of cocoa butter as a by-product. Most of this was sent to Menier, who used it to make solid chocolate bars and chocolate-covered bonbons at Noisiel, which was renovated and expanded for that purpose. Menier also began growing his own cacao beans at a plantation in Nicaragua. While Noisiel turned out 2,500 tons of chocolate a year (one-fourth of French consumption), a new plant in London produced three times that amount for the British market by the 1870s.[31]

After Emile Menier's death in 1881, the firm continued under his three sons, led by Henri. By 1889, the company was producing one-half of all the chocolate made in France, it continued to be the leading chocolate manufacturer in Great Britain, and it was also producing chocolate in the United States. In the 1890s, Menier pioneered modern marketing techniques with aggressive advertising and the installation of vending machines in railroad stations. At Henri Menier's death in 1913, Noisiel was turning out 17,000 tons of chocolate a year with 2,400 workers—making it one of France's largest factories[32]—and Menier et Cie had come to dominate its field as much as any company in France.

Soap and Vegetable Oil

The production of soap in France more than quadrupled in the course of the nineteenth century, from an average annual output of 62,000 tons in 1803–1812 to 285,000 tons in the decade before World War I.[33] This reflected not only the growing demand for cleansing agents in industry but also the growing emphasis on cleanliness in general, especially within the expanding middle classes of Europe and America.

The expansion of soap production involved surprisingly few technological innovations. True industrialization occurred not so much in soapmaking as in the production of the raw materials for soap—that is, the manufacture of artificial soda, the refining of vegetable oils, and the recovery of by-products. Soapmaking itself remained an artisanal trade little changed from antiquity. Cooking animal fats or vegetable oils with alkalis produced a solution of soap and glycerol. Heating this solution in salt water rendered the soap insoluble so it could then be skimmed off, formed into cakes, and dried. The liquid residue—the "wash"—was then thrown away. Throughout the nineteenth century, the size of the heating vats and drying racks increased, and heating became more efficient through the substitution of steam generators for direct heat. By 1900, some firms had vats with capacities of 5,000 hectoliters that could make 80 tons of soap at a time, but most French soapmakers used vats half that size. Because the scale of production remained small, there was little to be gained from vertical integration. Thus soapmaking remained independent from alkali and oil production in France, whereas in England, starting in the 1870s, William Lever constructed integrated oil refining, soda, and soap works that made possible true mass production of soap. In France, the primary innovations were in product rather than in process. The advent of artificial soda and the introduction of new tropical oils led to a shift from traditional hard soaps made with olive or rapeseed oil to blue marbled soap made with sesame oil. Later came a second shift to lighter, softer *savon blanc* made with palm, coconut, or peanut oil.[34]

By mid-nineteenth century, soapworks could be found in virtually every region of France, but the majority were located in and around Paris, the principal market for soap, or near the seaports, where oilseeds arrived from the tropics. Among the Paris soapmakers, perhaps the leading firm in 1900 was Michaud et Cie. Founded in 1849 and still owned and managed by the Michaud family fifty years later, the company produced and sold over 6,500 tons of industrial and toilet soaps annually. Its Savon de Paris brand was apparently the first French soap marketed in individually packaged bars stamped with the brand name on all six faces, in the manner of British and American national brands and in contrast to traditional French practices (as late as 1900 most French soapmakers still produced soap only in ten pound "loaves," and indeed forty pound loaves were still the norm in the Midi; retailers would cut and wrap smaller pieces from these loaves for individual customers just as delicatessens slice ham and cheese today).[35]

Notwithstanding the success of Paris soapmakers like Michaud, the soapmakers of Marseille continued to dominate the French industry in the nineteenth century as they had since the Middle Ages, accounting for as much as 70 percent of French soap production. From the thirteenth to the end of the eighteenth century, the Marseillais made soap using olive oil produced locally or imported from Italy and natural soda imported from Spain. At the beginning of the nineteenth century, they made the transition to artificial soda (as we saw earlier, Marseille was an early leader in the application of the Leblanc process). As a port city with strong ties to the Levant and Africa, Marseille also pioneered the importation and utilization of tropical oilseeds. Even so, Marseille soapmaking remained a conservative industry with a guild-like solidarity among its members. While Marseille soapmakers used individual brand names and competed among themselves on the basis of fragrance, shape, and color, their central concern remained the defense of the industry's collective reputation for quality, symbolized by the words "Savon de Marseille," which by law had to be stamped on each cake produced in the city.[36] Reflecting this ingrained conservatism, no Marseille soapmaker adopted true mass production practices that could challenge Lever for dominance in the emerging mass market for toilet soap.

The total output of soap at Marseille rose from 25,000 tons on the eve of the French Revolution to 50,000 tons in 1842, 70,000 in 1863, and 90,000 in 1890. As we have seen in many other industries, this growth came about at first through the addition of new firms, the number of which peaked at around ninety in 1890. Thereafter a process of consolidation and concentration set in, and the subsequent growth of the industry (from an annual output of 90,000 tons in 1890 to 180,000 tons in 1913) resulted from the expansion of a small group of established firms. In 1913 there remained forty-one independent soap companies in Marseille, but the six largest of these accounted for fully one-half of the total output. These were Arnavon, Charles-Roux (Canaple), Emile Baron, Félix Eydoux, Charles Morel, and J-B Paul.[37]

The oldest of these, Honoré Arnavon et Cie, dated back to the end of the eighteenth century. With some one hundred technicians and workers operating fourteen vats heated by five steam generators, Arnavon turned out a variety of marbled and white soaps made from olive, palm, and peanut oils at the outset of the twentieth century. The second oldest of these firms was founded by Charles Roux in 1828. Roux's son, Jules Charles-Roux, initially entered the family business but soon moved into finance, shipping, and politics.[38] The family soap business passed into the hands of Charles-Roux's brother-in-law Charles Canaple, who in 1900 continued to make the *savon marbré* that had first established the firm's reputation, plus an array of *savons blancs* for household and industrial uses. The rest of the six largest firms were all founded in the 1860s to produce the new *savon blanc*, which they continued to manufacture under established brand names at the turn of the twentieth century.[39]

Although the French soap industry maintained its reputation for high quality in the early twentieth century, exporting a sixth of its total output in 1913, the impetus for growth and innovation in the industry was increasingly coming from outside—from foreign companies like Lever Brothers, which took over Félix Eydoux and Canaple in 1914 in order to get a foothold in the Marseille industry, and from the oilseed processing companies, which were originally set up to supply raw materials to the soapmakers but which were moving into soap production and the manufacture of edible oils and fats by the turn of the century.

Since most oilseeds came from abroad—cottonseed from the American South, sesame seeds from India, peanuts from West Africa and India, palmetto seeds and coconuts from Africa and the South Pacific— it was natural that port cities came to dominate oilseed processing in France. At Bordeaux, Maurel and Prom began pressing oil from West African peanuts at their Huilerie de Bacalan in 1857, and they opened the Grande Huilerie Bordelaise at La Bastide in 1896. At Nantes the firm of Talvende Frères et Douault produced some 10,000 tons of cottonseed and coconut oil yearly by 1900.[40] But, because of the close association between oilseed processing and soapmaking, it was Marseille that emerged as the largest center for the vegetable oil industry in the nineteenth century.

In the early 1800s, the soap works of Marseille depended on olive oil imported from Italy and Spain. In the 1820s, linseed processing plants appeared in Marseille. But the real takeoff of the city's oil industry came in the 1830s, when Greek merchants, driven from the Aegean by the Turkish massacres, settled in Marseille and began importing oilseeds from the Levant, especially the Indian sesame that became the basis for Marseille's blue marbled soap. By 1844, Marseille had forty *huileries* producing 50 percent of France's annual output of 72,000 tons of vegetable oil.[41] Despite the imposition of new duties on imported oilseeds in 1845 to protect domestic producers, the Marseille oil industry continued to expand into the 1850s, propelled by the introduction of new sources of vegetable oil. In 1851 the discovery of a way to decolorize cottonseed oil allowed it to be used in soapmaking for the first time, and imports of cottonseed from the United States and Egypt burgeoned. Soon after, peanuts started arriving from Africa and India, and palm seeds and copra (dried coconut meat) from Zanzibar and Mozambique. The expansion of the industry continued into the 1860s as the rising importation of oilseeds from the tropics more than made up for the decline in cottonseed imports during the American Civil War. By 1869 Marseille had 44 oil refineries with 930 presses employing 2,300 workers and processing 120,000 tons of oilseeds annually (compared to an annual production of domestic oilseeds in France of around 220,000 tons).[42]

The Marseille industry expanded further in the late 1870s when the establishment of direct steamer service between Marseille and the Coromandel coast of India via the new Suez Canal made large new supplies of high-quality sesame seeds available to the Marseille oil processors. The general economic slump in France and new competition from American and Italian oil processors stalled the growth of the industry in the 1880s and early 1890s, but it gained a new lease on life in 1897 when a new technology to purify and decolorize vegetable oils gave birth to a whole new industry, the production of edible oils. As of 1913, there were 48 *huileries* in and around Marseille employing 8,000–10,000 workers and producing some 600,000 tons of vegetable oil annually. Most of these were medium-sized plants processing sixty tons of oilseeds daily, but two firms—Verminck and Rocca-Tassy-de Roux—operated plants with the capacity to process 200 tons per day and were probably the largest vegetable oil enterprises in France.[43]

Etablissements Verminck was established in 1855 by Charles-Augustin Verminck, a Belgian *brasseur d'affaires* who had started trading with West Africa in the 1840s and later developed the direct trade with the Coromandel coast of India. In 1881, Verminck converted his West African business into a joint-stock company, the Compagnie du Sénégal et de la Côte Occidentale d'Afrique (CSCOA), only to lose control of it as a result of the trade slump of the mid-eighties. Seeking to retrench by unloading unprofitable properties, the CSCOA sold back to Verminck in 1884 the oilseed processing plants that Verminck had originally set up in Marseille. This was the beginning of a new, highly integrated Verminck enterprise that by 1900 included a soapworks, glassworks, the manufacture of sacks and containers, and five oil refineries.[44] After Verminck's death in 1911, the company was converted into a *société anonyme* that was capitalized at 6 million francs and had assets of over 17 million francs, which made it one of the 100 largest publicly held manufacturing companies in France on the eve of World War I.[45]

Rocca-Tassy-de Roux (R-T-R) was formed in 1890 by the merger of the oil refining businesses of Félix Tassy, Emilien Rocca, and François and Barthélemy de Roux. In 1897 this firm introduced the purification technology that made copra and other vegetable oils and fats fit for human consumption. This in turn led to the launching of Végétalene, a cocoa butter–based cooking grease that anticipated by fifteen years a similar product, Crisco, that was introduced in the United States by Procter and Gamble in 1912. To support and complement this venture, R-T-R operated plants that made packing materials, metal cans, and soap, as well as three oil pressing plants, including the largest in Marseille. Together these operations made R-T-R "one of the most important and most complete enterprises in Marseille" at the beginning of the twentieth century.[46]

Despite the success of the soap and oil processing businesses of Marseille, the largest single enterprise to emerge in the *corps gras* industries of the city—and of the whole country—was found neither in soapmaking nor oil refining but in candle making. More specifically, it was found in the production and commercialization of stearic acid, which was first undertaken in 1831 when Adolphe de Milly opened a plant in Paris to refine stearin from sheep suet and to use it in the manufacture of *bougies* (wax candles) as a lower-cost alternative to *cierges* (beeswax candles) and *chandelles* (tallow candles). In 1836, Louis and Frédéric Fournier joined with Milly to launch a second plant to manufacture *bougies stéariques,* this one situated in Marseille. The Fourniers' enterprise prospered and soon separated from de Milly's, which continued to operate in Paris. After 1864, the Fournier enterprise was in the hands of Félix Fournier, Frédéric's son, who gradually took control of all *bougie* production in Marseille. By the 1880s, Fournier's Le Chat brand was dominant in France and accounted for three-fourths of French candle exports.

As Fournier's production expanded, vegetable oils were added to, and eventually substituted for, animal fats in the making of stearin, which led Fournier not only into vegetable oil refining but also into soapmaking (to utilize oil not needed for candle making). In 1898, Fournier retired and transformed his company into a *société en commandite par actions*. At that time, the company accounted for 21 million of the 56 million packets of wax candles sold in France annually and virtually all of the 15 million packets exported from France. At Fournier's death in 1911, his company still employed 2,000 people in *stéarinerie* and *savonnerie,* was perhaps the largest industrial enterprise in Marseille, and, in the category of chemicals and allied products, was surpassed only by France's Big Three, Saint-Gobain, Kuhlmann, and Pechiney.[47]

Clothing and Home Furnishings

No realm of French manufacturing seemed more impervious to the development of industrial capitalism in the nineteenth century than personal and home furnishings (such as clothing, furniture, and dinnerware). These goods have long epitomized the devotion of the French to high-quality craft production and their commitment to style and artistry at the expense of affordability and accessibility. Indeed, several recent studies have sought to explain how the development of a middle-class market for high-quality furnishings, buttressed by a characteristic "bourgeois" sense of taste, sustained craft production of these products and prevented the rise in France of the mechanized mass production that was taking hold elsewhere in the mid-1800s.[48] However, notwithstanding the continuing importance of craft production in this area, industrial capitalism—meaning above all factory production—was in fact starting to appear in some segments of the French clothing and home furnishings industries by the end of the nineteenth century.

Clothing, Shoes, and Gloves

Although *haute couture,* the designing and sewing of one-of-a-kind gowns for wealthy women, is the most famous branch of the French clothing industry, it has always been a small part of that industry, economically speaking. Much more important has been the production of men's coats, pants, and suits (including uniforms); men's shirts, cuffs, and collars; and shoes, stockings, and gloves for both sexes. These were the focus of the "clothing revolution" of the nineteenth century—the advent of standardized, mass-produced, ready-to-wear clothing—in which France fully participated, led by merchant capitalists (including the founders of the great retail emporia of Paris) who created vast networks of artisan outworkers to make the garments that they sold. In some instances, however, these merchants crossed the invisible line between merchant and industrial capitalism by setting up factories with machine production and wage labor, in effect becoming industrialists. The best documented example of this process—thanks to the work of François Faraut—is provided by La Belle Jardinière.[49]

La Belle Jardinière was launched in Paris in 1824 by Pierre Parissot, whose family already operated several clothing stores in the capital. Parissot's first store was located on the Ile de la Cité and sold woolen cloth for men's clothing. Sometime in the late 1820s or early 1830s, Parissot moved into *confection,* the manufacture of ready-to-wear clothing, primarily for workers. Like other *confectionneurs,* Parissot organized his production around domestic handicraft workers. He bought wool cloth in bulk, had it cut in standard-sized pieces by skilled cutters working in-house at the Ile de la Cité store, distributed the pieces to outworkers who sewed the pieces into garments at home, and finally had in-house *pompiers* (touch-up sewers) finish the garments for sale.

When Pierre Parissot died in 1860, La Belle Jardinière passed into the hands of Parissot's son-in-law Charles Bessand and Bessand's son Paul, who transferred it from the Ile de la Cité to the right bank of the Seine near the Pont Neuf. At the same time the company was reoriented toward the manufacture and sale of higher quality menswear for the growing middle-class market, and operations began to be industrialized. To be sure, the assembly of men's suits, pants, and coats continued to be done by hand by domestic workers. But to produce the cuttings in standard sizes for those garments, the Bessands turned two floors of the new Pont Neuf store into what amounted to a factory, where hundreds of cutters worked in a controlled environment. Eventually, when the pool of part-time domestic garment workers dried up after 1900, the company put the assembling and finishing of garments in a factory equipped with steam-powered sewing and pressing machines.

Even more clearly industrial was the plant that the Bessands founded in Lille in 1866 to make shirts, work clothes, hunting clothes, and accessories. By 1900, this plant employed over 900 and was but one part of a much larger commercial and manufacturing enterprise that produced lines of ready-to-wear clothing for women and children as well as for men. These lines were distributed via the main Pont Neuf store, branch stores elsewhere in Paris and in Lille, Bordeaux, and Nancy, and mail order. La Belle Jardinière also made uniforms for the Eastern Railroad Company and ecclesiastical garb for the French Catholic Church.[50]

La Belle Jardinière may have been the largest and most successful French enterprise in *confection* at the end of the nineteenth century, but it was by no means unique. In 1859, Alexis Godillot, son of a Paris leather merchant, took over a plant in the Rue Rochechouart originally set up by the French government to assemble boots and uniforms for the French troops going to Italy. According to Turgan, the plant turned out over 1 million pairs of boots and shoes and 1.2 million uniforms in 1867; by the 1880s it was the headquarters of a multiline business—"une groupe encyclopédique de nombreuses spécialités"—that included the mechanized manufacture of uniforms and the largest boot and shoe factory in France.[51] Meanwhile, mass retailers were following the lead of La Belle Jardinière and integrating backward into garment making. In 1876, the Bon Marché, the largest of the Paris department stores, set up a clothing factory in Lille. In 1891, Maurice Schwob set up a mechanized factory in Chateauroux that employed 700 workers to make shirts for his growing chain of clothing stores, 100,000 Chemises, and in 1910 he added a second factory in Creil.[52] By then, there were clothing factories in a number of French cities, including eight in the Lille-Roubaix area that employed 2,300 workers.[53]

The advent of industrial capitalism was even more evident in the manufacture of boots and shoes. At the outset of the nineteenth century, shoemaking in France was a well-established craft industry with a worldwide reputation for quality. The growth in foreign demand for high-quality handmade French shoes sustained this craft production until the 1880s, when exports began to decline in the face of mounting protectionism abroad. Meanwhile, the manufacture of middling- and lower-grade boots and shoes in standard sizes, especially for the military, was transformed by the advent of machinery, first and foremost the sewing machine, but also piercing, punching, warping, and cutting machines. The first mechanized (or, more likely, partially mechanized) shoe factory in France opened in Blois in 1850, followed in 1859 by the Godillot factory in Paris.[54] However, it was the introduction in 1889 of the Goodyear sewing machine by the United Machinery Company, making possible the machine stitching of soles to uppers comparable in quality to hand sewing, that brought about the real triumph of mechanized production of shoes and boots in France.[55] In 1906, Alfred Aftalion wrote that "a profound transformation of the industry occurred in a relatively brief period of time [in the 1890s]. Today the factory incontestably dominates the industry."[56] By then, the two largest shoe manufacturers in France were the Monteux Company of Limoges, which employed 800, and Dressoir et Premartin of Paris, whose plant in the Butte-Chaumont section of northeast Paris employed 1,200 workers and a variety of machinery to turn out 2,500–3,000 pairs of shoes daily.[57]

Glovemaking was another old artisanal industry that underwent mechanization and consolidation in the closing years of the nineteenth century. The focal point for this transformation was the city of Grenoble, located at the edge of the French Alps southeast of Lyon. In the Middle Ages, Grenoble had emerged as a center for the dressing and tanning of skins from the sheep and goats raised in the surrounding mountains. As early as 1343 and increasingly after 1700, master glovemakers in Grenoble had organized the cutting and sewing of fine gloves from these skins. On the eve of the French Revolution, there were a hundred such masters employing 4,500 workers in and around

Grenoble, and the city had come to be dominated, in the words of a recent history, by a "virtual leather monoculture."[58]

Growing foreign demand for kid and lambskin gloves promoted the steady expansion of the industry in the first half of the nineteenth century, and the advent of free trade and the arrival of the railroad in 1860 continued this expansion into the second half of the century. Output rose from 400,000 dozen pairs of gloves in 1850 to 1 million dozen in 1870 and 1.5 million dozen by 1893. In the process, a number of large enterprises appeared, most important of which was Veuve Perrin et Fils. Founded in 1860, Perrin at first combined traditional artisanal production with innovative marketing. Under the leadership of Valerien Perrin after 1875, the firm bypassed established middlemen by creating its own sales subsidiaries in New York, London, and Latin America, and by hiring its own corps of traveling salesmen to serve the domestic market. By 1900 it even had its own retail outlets and had also integrated backward into skin preparation and dyeing. Finally, after 1900, the company scrapped the putting-out system of production, brought its corps of *coudeuses* together in a central factory, and equipped them with sewing machines (mainly because the worldwide shift to protectionism had undercut Perrin's exports of high-quality handmade gloves and forced it to compete with lower-quality gloves in the domestic market). By World War I, Perrin had become an integrated industrial enterprise employing some 4,000 workers.[59]

If Perrin and the other Grenoble glovemakers industrialized only belatedly and under duress, glovemakers elsewhere in France moved toward mechanized production more readily. The best example of this is Trefousse, Goguenheim et Cie, which in the 1890s employed 1,600 workers in steam- and electricity-powered plants in Chaumont (Haut-Marne) that combined leather curing, dyeing, and glovemaking, and another 1,500 outworkers in the nearby towns and villages. Trefousse, Goguenheim gloves were known for their "brilliance, suppleness, and solidity" and were sold through company-owned sales offices in Paris, London, New York, Frankfurt, Belgium, and Switzerland. The London and New York offices were especially important, accounting for 11 million of the 13.5 million francs in total sales. To augment its production for the American market, the company acquired a plant in the United States in 1896. Overall, Trefousse, Goguenheim was the leading firm in French glovemaking at the turn of the twentieth century. According to the jury report from the 1900 Paris World's Fair, "it occupie[d] an absolutely exceptional position in the leather industry."[60]

Home Furnishings

As in clothing, the French were the undisputed style leaders and trend-setters in home decoration at the beginning of the nineteenth century. Paris was home to a large population of artists and craftsmen who produced an astonishing array of furniture, wallpaper, tableware, objets d'art, and what for lack of a better term were simply called *articles de Paris* (all sorts of items of personal consumption from umbrellas to chess sets). Given the Parisian emphasis on making high-quality, one-of-a-kind goods for affluent consumers around the world, it is not surprising that much of this production remained artisanal until the twentieth century. Yet, as in the clothing industry, new technology allowed some entrepreneurs in certain product lines to move into larger-scale production without compromising quality. Indeed, by affording a new degree of precision in manufacturing, machine production enhanced the quality of some products even as it raised output and lowered unit costs. One place this happened was in the manufacture of silver-plated dinnerware.

In 1842, Charles Christofle, scion of a well-established family of goldsmiths and jewelers in Paris, purchased the patent for a new method of electroplating developed by the Elkington Brothers in Great Britain and by Baron Henri de Ruolz-Montchal in France. Three years later, Christofle set up the world's first factory to exploit this technology, and he was soon winning prizes at the Crystal Palace and other international exhibitions for his mass-produced and relatively inexpensive silver plate. By 1860, Christofle had two plants in Paris and one in Karlsruhe, Germany, that together employed a total of 1,380 workers and sold goods worth 6 million francs annually.[61]

Another luxury consumer good that underwent partial industrialization in the nineteenth century was wallpaper. The manufacture of wallpaper had grown rapidly in France in the second half of the eighteenth century through the application of techniques developed by Alsatian *indienneurs* for printing cotton cloth. Like textile printing, wallpaper printing became a concentrated factory industry even before the application of water and steam power. This was certainly true of J-B Reveillon of Paris, the "Oberkampf of wallpaper," who in the 1780s produced high-quality wallpaper in nine-foot rolls (versus the standard sheets) in a plant employing 300 workers in the Faubourg Saint-Antoine. This plant was sacked by a mob on April 27–28, 1789, in one of the first *journées* of the French Revolution, but Reveillon soon recovered and resumed production. In 1791 he sold out to Jacquemart

and Benard, who maintained the firm as the foremost wallpaper manufacturer in France throughout the turbulence of the Revolution, First
Empire, and Restoration. The firm finally ceased production in 1840
after the death of Jacquemart's sons.

Leadership of the industry then passed to Jean Zuber of Rixheim
(Haut-Rhin), who had gotten his start managing an *indiennes* plant for
the firm of Dollfus, Hartmann, and Risler. Zuber introduced the steam-
powered rotative press to wallpaper printing in 1827. When Zuber
combined wallpaper printing with continuous production of paper on
rolls in 1830 (using one of the first Robert paper machines to be installed in France), the industry moved into true mass production for
the first time. The mechanization of wallpaper printing continued with
Louis-Isidore Leroy, who began printing wallpaper in Paris in 1842
and operated one of the three steam-powered presses in the industry
as of 1860. At the end of the century, there were perhaps two dozen
major manufacturers of wallpaper in France who employed various
combinations of mechanized and hand presses to print the wide array
of wallpapers in various finishes and patterns that had come to be
essential elements of interior decoration in France and throughout the
civilized world.[62]

A third item of home furnishing that became an object of mechanized
production and industrial enterprise in the nineteenth century was fine
porcelain dinnerware (china). This is yet another example of how a
product manufactured at high cost in small quantities for the wealthy
in the eighteenth century became an item of mass consumption—or at
least an item of bourgeois consumption—in the nineteenth century.
Markovitch's estimates of porcelain output suggest what happened: Average annual output of porcelain in France rose from 30 tons in the
1780s to 145 tons in the decade before World War I, with the value
of annual production rising seventeenfold, to 175 million francs, over
the same period.[63] Industrial production of porcelain and its near competitor, *faïence fine,* developed in a number of places in France in the
nineteenth century—at Vierzon and Gien in Berry, at Lunéville and
Sarreguimines in Lorraine, at Bordeaux in the Southwest, and of course
at Sèvres near Paris—but it was especially associated with the city of
Limoges and the firm of Haviland et Cie.

Early efforts by Europeans to produce a good substitute for Chinese
porcelain had been handicapped by the lack of suitable raw materials
(or, more precisely, by ignorance of the right kind of clay to produce
china). In the 1730s, the Germans discovered that kaolin from Saxony

produced high-quality chinaware, and this led to the founding of the porcelain works at Meissen. At first, the French had to import Saxon kaolin to supply the royal porcelain works at Vincennes (later transferred to Sèvres), but in 1769 large deposits of kaolin were discovered at Saint-Yrieix near Limoges. Under the patronage of the *contrôleur-général des finances*, Turgot (a native of the Limousin), porcelain manufacture was set up in Limoges in the 1770s, but it was not until the early 1800s that the industry began to turn a profit.[64]

As it began to expand in the early nineteenth century, the Limoges industry became segmented. One set of entrepreneurs specialized in quarrying kaolin; a second set specialized in grinding the clay and making *pâtes;* a third set turned the *pâte* into porcelain dishes, vases, and figurines; and a fourth set took this whiteware, decorated it, and marketed the finished product. The first two sets remained small independent operators because the porcelain manufacturers preferred to buy *pâtes* from several different suppliers and wanted to avoid the expense of making their own (thus resisting the temptation to integrate backward). However, the third and fourth sets tended to merge to form large-scale enterprises that combined porcelain manufacture, decoration, and marketing.

From 1800 to 1830, the leading porcelain manufacturer in Limoges was Alluard Frères, but in the following decade the lead passed to a new firm founded by a New York porcelain merchant, David Haviland. Haviland came to Limoges in 1836 in search of new goods for the rapidly growing American market. Impressed by what he found, he stayed on and in 1842 set up a plant to decorate Limoges whiteware to his specifications. Under Haviland's guidance, the export of Limoges porcelain took off, accounting for most of the French porcelain exports to the United States, which rose from 231,000 kilograms in 1840 to 1,132,000 in 1850.[65] The success of this trade prompted Haviland to add porcelain manufacture to decoration and exporting. In the 1850s, he constructed the largest porcelain works in France. By the 1860s it included two giant kilns and twenty smaller ovens, plus workshops for molding, color preparation, decoration, dusting, and polishing, and a sixty-meter-long warehouse, and it employed over a thousand workers.[66]

Haviland's timing seemingly could not have been better. In 1860, France's exports of porcelain to the United States reached an all-time high of 2,167,000 kilograms just as the arrival of the railroad in Limoges made possible the substitution of coal for local wood as fuel, bringing down production costs and providing, in Camille Grellier's words, "the point of departure for a new era of prosperity."[67] In fact, the years from 1860 to 1900 were filled with crises for Limoges porcelain, starting with the disruption of the American trade by the Civil War, followed by the upheaval of the Franco-Prussian War in 1870–1871, labor unrest in 1882, and the depression of the 1880s—along with the rapid expansion of the German industry and the closing of foreign markets through protective tariffs. Yet the French industry survived and continued to prosper through artistic leadership and steady improvement of its production technology, led by Haviland et Cie, which passed into the hands of David Haviland's sons Charles and Theodore at David's death in 1879.

Shifting toward everyday dinnerware and restaurant services in the 1870s, the Havilands pioneered the mechanized mass production of porcelain plates using new steam-powered machinery and replacing hand decoration with chromolithographic presses. At the same time, however, they maintained the artistic reputation of their dinnerware by contracting with famous artists to provide the designs for their mass-produced lines. The technological improvements continued in 1892–1893, when Theodore Haviland built a new plant outside Limoges featuring continuous ovens and electrically powered molding machines. Although twice the size of the old plant, the new one required 20 percent fewer workers. Despite a violent strike by porcelain workers in 1905 and continued disputes with U.S. customs officials over porcelain exports, the Limoges industry continued to prosper into the twentieth century, and the Haviland enterprise (actually two firms, after a split between Charles and Theodore) continued to dominate the French industry, accounting for 3,500 of the 8,000 porcelain workers in France.[68]

In 1900, France remained a largely rural, peasant society and lacked the large, rapidly growing urban population that was making possible the mass production of standardized consumer goods in the United States and, to a lesser extent, in Great Britain. The full impact of the consumer revolution, with its characteristic proliferation of heavily advertised branded products, still lay in France's future. Yet France had witnessed the rise of large-scale production of certain consumer goods under the aegis of true industrial enterprises in the nineteenth century. In some industries like flour milling, this occurred when the building of the railroads and the emergence of a functional national market brought about the concentration of processing that had previously been dispersed and decentralized. In other industries, notably sugar refining, it occurred when the government decided to pursue an import substitution strategy and aggressively promoted the domestic production of goods that might have otherwise been imported. But it mostly happened when new technology allowed handmade luxury goods, many of which were already associated with the French, to be produced in larger quantities at lower prices without a significant diminution of quality, thereby making possible the democratization, or at least the *embourgeoisement,* of luxury consumption in France and abroad. This occurred across a wide range of products, including toilet soap, chocolate, ready-to-wear clothing, wallpaper, silver plate, porcelain, and others not discussed in this chapter (such as champagne and musical instruments), thanks to the efforts of dynamic entrepreneurs like Emile Menier, Charles Christofle, Jean Zuber, and David Haviland. Thus did France participate in the early stages of the consumer revolution, and thus did industrial enterprise arise in France in the realm of consumer as well as producer goods.

Having now established the range of industrial enterprise and the identity of the leading industrial firms in nineteenth-century France, we shall conclude this section by looking more closely at the practices and challenges that distinguished the new world of industrial capitalism in France.

CHAPTER ELEVEN

The New World of Industrial Capitalism

The new industrialists of the nineteenth century faced certain challenges that set them apart from merchant and finance capitalists. In contrast to the mobility associated with merchant capitalism, industrialists tended to be rooted in a particular place by their dependence on factories and other fixed production facilities. At the very least, investing in such facilities greatly reduced the liquidity and mobility of their assets and forced them to operate with a longer time horizon than that observed by merchants and merchant bankers. In addition, factory production involved hiring, retaining, and managing large numbers of wage workers, also a rarity for merchant capitalists. Moreover, the frozenness of their assets made industrialists more dependent on the goodwill of the state than those who could pick up and move easily. Indeed, industrialists often needed the active support of government to succeed. In short, while industrialists often came out of the world of commerce and banking, founding and managing industrial enterprises separated them from the merchant world in fundamental ways.

This chapter explores three issues that were particularly important in defining the new world of industrial capitalism in nineteenth century France: (1) how the new industrial enterprises were financed and kept profitable (or at least solvent), (2) how industrialists recruited and managed their labor force, and (3) how they managed their external environment, especially how they attempted to mobilize the power of the state in support of their efforts to control markets.

Financing Industrial Enterprise

The first challenge for the new industrialists of the nineteenth century—as for all entrepreneurs through the ages—was to raise enough money to get started. Of course, the truly colossal start-up costs in the nineteenth century were associated with the great infrastructure projects, especially the railroads. As we saw earlier, raising the money to build the railroads precipitated a revolution in banking and finance in France. Financing early industry involved no such revolution. When little or no water- or steam-powered machinery was involved, the costs of setting up industrial enterprises were no greater than those of traditional merchant enterprises.[1] Even when such machinery *was* involved, it was often still possible to start small and gradually increase the size and scale of operations from retained earnings, as merchants did. Yet, as a rule, industrial investment was "lumpy," and getting started in industry was more expensive and more complicated than it was in trade.

The founding of a true industrial enterprise in manufacturing involved assembling an array of machines that were usually (but not always) attached to an inanimate source of power (a waterwheel or steam engine) within a separate, dedicated factory building. While the factory buildings could be leased, the machinery usually had to be purchased. According to Serge Chassagne, by the early nineteenth century new waterwheels cost anywhere from 1,000 to 84,000 francs, with 20,000 being typical. A small steam engine cost 7,000 francs (not including installation), but a ten-horsepower steam engine, installed with two boilers, could run 30,000 francs. *Grands filatures* cost anywhere from 100,000 to 1,000,000 francs, with most costing around 200,000; mechanized cloth printing plants ran anywhere from 50,000 to over 800,000 francs.[2] In 1841, a well-equipped sugar refinery cost from 600,000 to 950,000 francs. A paper factory equipped with the new papermaking machines in the 1830s ran 96,000 to 134,000 francs. An integrated works to make iron by the English method—including iron and coal mines, blast furnaces, forges, and rolling mills—cost 500,000–700,000 francs in the 1820s and 1830s.[3]

In addition to plant and equipment, industrialists often had to provide housing and amenities for their workers, create or improve the millrace for their waterwheels, and build or improve the roads that connected their factories to the outside world. In addition to these up-front investments in fixed assets, industrialists had to have substantial working capital to begin operations—funds to buy raw materials and fuel and to pay wages during the sometimes lengthy period until the sale of finished goods started to bring in money. According to Maurice Lévy-Leboyer, as a rule of thumb, working capital represented one-half of the total capital needed to launch an enterprise.[4] Exact figures for the total start-up costs of large-scale mechanized enterprises in early nineteenth-century France are not easy to come by, but reasonable estimates are embodied in the available financial records of various family firms and especially in the initial social capital raised by new joint-stock companies. In the cotton industry, for example, we know that the enterprises of both Dollfus-Mieg at Mulhouse and Davillier et Cie at Gisors started out with capital of more than 2 million francs in 1816–1818, while the Société de la Filature et du Tissage Mécanique du Bas-Rhin was capitalized at 1.8 million francs in 1826. In the paper industry, the limited partnerships formed in 1830–1840 to build or acquire mechanized mills raised 200,000 to 1 million francs each, but a few paper firms raised substantially more, including Essonnes (1.6 million) and Marais et Sainte-Marie (1.8 million). In sugar refining, Louis Say got started in Nantes in 1820 for 150,000 francs, but the relaunching of his firm thirty-five years later required 4 million francs, and the founders of the Raffinerie de la Méditerannée in Marseille in 1865 raised 8.5 million. The capital needed to launch an integrated ironworks similarly escalated between 1820 and 1860. Audincourt was capitalized at 4.5 million in 1824, Alais at 6 million (4 million paid-in) in 1829, and Decazeville at 7 million by 1832. That the Schneiders needed only 4 million to relaunch Le Creusot in 1836 was something of a bargain. By contrast, the founding of the Marine steelworks in 1854 required 22.5 million.[5]

How was this start-up money raised? In a society in which 100,000 francs represented a substantial fortune,[6] the launching of an enterprise for mechanized manufacturing posed an enormous challenge to all but the wealthiest. In fact, a few established manufacturers—or more often the merchants who traded in the goods produced by traditional handicraft workers—were able to self-finance the setting up of mechanized production by doing it gradually. A classic example of such *autofinance-ment* is provided by the Alsatian cotton firm, Mequillot-Noblot, which started out with rudimentary, secondhand machinery in the 1820s and added more sophisticated equipment over the next twenty years as conditions (and profits) allowed. But this approach was the product of particular circumstances: In the pre-railroad age, the Mequillots and Noblots did not have to compete in their regional market with the largest, most technically advanced French and British producers. They could afford to grow slowly and to industrialize piecemeal.[7]

In cases where the nature of the technology or the pressures of competition mandated setting up machine production all at once and at a cost that exceeded available resources, even established industrialists could rarely go it alone. Typically, they would first look to the resources of their own extended family or follow what Patrick Verley calls the "matrimonial strategy," tapping their wives' dowries or the resources of their wives' families.[8] When those avenues were exhausted, industrialists would then have to bring in new partners, necessitating a reorganization and refounding of their enterprise. From a legal standpoint, this process was indistinguishable from the launching of a new enterprise. In either situation, industrialists could choose among several models of organization. Most partnerships and family firms were set up as *sociétés en nom collectif,* with full authority and unlimited liability for all participants. However, under the Code de Commerce of 1808, three other legal forms were available: (1) the *société en commandite simple,* with authority vested in one or more *gérants* with unlimited liability and backed by sleeping partners *(commanditaires)* with limited authority and liability; (2) the *société en commandite par actions,* a rudimentary form of limited-liability joint-stock company with a small number of shares in large denominations held by a few sleeping partners; and (3) the *société anonyme,* a full-fledged limited-liability joint-stock company with freely transferable shares that required government authorization (until the incorporation laws were liberalized in the 1860s). The latter two forms were particularly used in the early nineteenth century in those industries—mining, metallurgy, paper, glass, and sometimes textiles—in which large amounts of money had to be raised up front from a wide circle of investors in order to launch mechanized production.[9]

Raising start-up funds by forming associations with other businessmen—either as partners, sleeping partners, or anonymous investors in joint-stock companies—more often than not brought professional moneymen into the picture. In contrast to the long-held conventional wisdom that French bankers avoided industrial investment in the nineteenth century (supposedly out of fear of illiquidity), the research of the last four decades has demonstrated that bankers were deeply involved in the organization and financing of industrial enterprises in France in the early 1800s. The Strasbourg bankers Jean-Georges Humann, Florent Saglio, and Alfred Renouard de Bussière invested in Alsatian cotton and Le Havre sugar refining. Lyonnais bankers backed a wide range of manufacturing enterprises in the Southeast. In the Nord, Jules Decroix of the Caisse Commerciale du Nord bankrolled the wool-combing business of Amédée Prouvost. The Seillière bank underwrote François de Wendel's acquisition of Moyeuvre in 1811 and the Schneiders' relaunching of Le Creusot in 1836. Most importantly, leading Paris financiers participated in the founding of a variety of industrial enterprises, including ironworks in the Nord (Denain-Anzin), the Center (Fourchambault), and the South (Decazeville, Alais).[10]

Once an enterprise was launched, its owners or directors—even the bankers among them—sought to avoid further recourse to outside capital by financing day-to-day operations and subsequent expansion from earnings. Indeed, industrialists went to great lengths to retain maximum funds within the firm for these purposes. The statutes of many limited partnerships and joint-stock companies required a certain percentage of yearly earnings to be retained as a reserve. Many also required that partners deposit the minimum dividends mandated by law, usually 5 percent of paid-in capital, in a current account *(compte courante)* with the firm. In essence this amounted to a forced loan to the firm from its shareholders.[11] In addition, company administrators used various accounting tricks to minimize the amount of annual profits that would be subject to possible payout to shareholders. Chief among these was the expensing of the full cost of new machinery in the year of purchase.[12]

Using these policies and tactics, many companies managed to retain the lion's share of annual earnings—even in the face of shareholder pressure to distribute more earnings as dividends—and thereby to self-finance not only current operations but also much of their subsequent growth. For example, the paper manufacturing firm, Blanchet Frères et Kleber, made no payouts at all to partners in its first fifteen years; at the end of twenty years, the value of the company had quadrupled with partners' funds (essentially retained earnings) comprising 90 percent of the liabilities on the balance sheet. Similarly, 85 percent of the increase in Saint-Gobain's assets between 1830 and 1847 came from retained earnings. And at Le Creusot the sharp increase in annual revenues in the company's first decade, coupled with the retention of shareholders' profits in current accounts, allowed the company to finance all operations and new investments internally.[13]

Such triumphs of *autofinancement* notwithstanding, few firms succeeded in covering all financial needs from internally generated resources at all times. Even in the expansive middle years of the nineteenth century, there were serious business contractions or out-and-out crises about every ten years (1827–1829, 1837–1839, 1847–1850, 1857–1858, 1867–1869) that eroded or completely eliminated profits and forced companies to seek outside financial assistance. At the other extreme, pressure to expand output in good times, even when it did not entail additions to plant and equipment, could increase demands for working capital beyond the firm's capacity to generate it. In either case, industrial firms often needed short-term credit just as commercial firms did, and typically they got it in the same ways—via advances from customers, credit from suppliers, or the discounting of commercial paper by banks. For longer-term needs, they might take out a mortgage loan or use bankers as conduits for issuing various kinds of "obligations." The eclectic nature of industrial finance is illustrated by Le Creusot's situation in 1847–1848, when it cobbled together some 8 million francs in working capital from a variety of sources, including 1.5 million from its own social capital, 525,000 from a mortgage loan, another 1.9 million in loans from shareholders, 650,000 from the *compte courante* of M. Seillière, and a 1.25 million credit from the Banque de France.[14]

The combination of resources and strategies that kept industrial firms solvent and functioning in normal times often did not suffice when competitive pressures or the opportunities that arose from technological breakthroughs mandated massive renovations or expansion. A case in point is France's big iron companies. From their beginnings in the 1820s and 1830s, these firms faced almost continual pressure to expand and modernize. This was especially true in the 1860s, when the trade treaty with Great Britain opened France's domestic market to strong new competition and the advent of the Bessemer and Siemens-Martin processes for mass-producing steel presented forgemasters with a stark choice between expensive modernization and obsolescence. For most of the big iron companies, it was not just a matter of setting up Bessemer converters and Siemens hearths but also a matter of finding improved sources of iron and coal and upgrading their production of pig iron (both new processes required purer pig iron than the big companies were accustomed to producing). According to Bertrand Gille, French forgemasters invested some 120 million francs in iron and pig iron production between 1860 and 1865. Total new investment in the sixties and seventies amounted to 16.8 million francs for Terrenoire,

14.7 million for Marine, and 23.8 million for Châtillon-Commentry.[15] Although plowed-back profits furnished some of the required new capital, all the big iron- and steelmakers had to tap into outside funds for the rest. Terrenoire, Le Creusot, and Marine issued new stock; Denain-Anzin secured a 2 million franc loan from its chief customer, the Chemin de Fer du Nord; Marine borrowed heavily from various Lyon banks; Le Creusot issued 5.1 million in corporate bonds in 1867. Perhaps most importantly, executives of many of the biggest iron and steel companies participated in the founding of two new joint-stock deposit banks in 1863–1864, the Crédit Lyonnais and the Société Générale, to channel funds from the general public to the firms.[16]

Dealing with the complexities of financial management perhaps inevitably led French industrialists to develop new accounting practices in the nineteenth century. As early as the 1820s, the owners and managers of France's largest industrial enterprises realized that the profitability (and ultimately the survival) of their companies depended on developing accurate information on production costs as a basis for pricing decisions or, in cases where companies had little control over prices, as a basis for maintaining profitability by controlling and lowering expenses. Such information on costs could not be gained from the traditional single-entry bookkeeping ("charge and discharge" accounting) that mining companies inherited from land management, nor from the double-entry bookkeeping ("Italian" accounting) that originated in commerce but was increasingly being adopted by industry in the early nineteenth century. Mercantile accounting, after all, was aimed principally at keeping track of a firm's external relations—its purchases from suppliers and sales to customers—rather than its internal costs, which tended to be simple and straightforward for firms that simply bought finished goods in one place and sold them in another.

To meet these needs, managers at a number of French industrial companies worked out the rudiments of industrial or cost accounting between 1820 and 1870.[17] At Baccarat Crystal, Pierre Godard-Desmarest set up separate accounts for each input and intermediate product to trace costs through the production process as well as to accurately determine the magnitude and source of total costs. He also pioneered the analysis of fixed and variable costs as a basis for strategic management. Meanwhile, at Decazeville an elaborate *service comptable* was created in the late 1820s to produce monthly cost reports for the board of directors in Paris. At Saint-Gobain, the double-entry bookkeeping adopted in 1820 soon evolved into a system of cost accounting that in the 1830s allowed the directors to address such thorny accounting issues as the allocation of overhead and transfer pricing. The latter was a major issue for a company that produced most of the chemical raw materials for its glassmaking operations, because what the glass division was charged for these chemicals determined whether chemicals or glass was to be the chief source of profits. By the 1870s, Saint-Gobain's cost-accounting system had evolved into a management system in which each branch and each plant within what amounted to a multidivisional, multinational organization could be treated as a potential profit center.[18]

In seeking to understand and control internal costs as a corollary to successful financial management, French industrialists followed a path remarkably similar to that taken by British industrialists. As a recent comparative study of industrial accounting in Britain and France makes clear, the industrialists in both countries who addressed issues of cost analysis, cost allocation, and depreciation did so in very similar ways.[19] To be sure, industrialization had a twenty-to-fifty-year headstart in Britain, so British companies like Wedgwood were dealing with cost-accounting problems in the 1780s that French companies did not face until the 1820s and 1830s. But in dealing with these problems, industrialists in the two countries developed similar practices and solutions. This was not because British expertise in industrial accounting was transferred to France along with technological know-how (British industrialists did not even start writing texts on cost accounting until fifty years after the appearance of the first French texts). Rather it was a case of "simultaneous discovery"—similar problems being addressed in similar ways at corresponding stages of industrial development in spite of the very different institutional settings and business traditions in the two countries.

Much the same was true in the wider field of financial management. There was nothing particularly new or unique about the French approach to financing industrial enterprises. The French raised the initial capital for industrial investments in much the same ways and from the same sources as the British. Although the British banking system was quite different from the French, there was great similarity in the prominent role that banks played in industrial finance in both countries. Industry in both countries was organized mainly in family firms, but there was a similar trend toward joint-stock companies in both countries over the course of the nineteenth century. The major difference was that the British lacked the limited partnership *(société en com-mandite)* available to the French, so they began to liberalize regulations on the full limited-liability joint-stock company (the *société anonyme*) twenty years before the French.[20]

Given these similarities, those concerned with the "retardation" of French industrialization relative to the British are hard-pressed to attribute that retardation to deficiencies in industrial finance, or more particularly to institutional rigidities and the aversion of French bankers to invest in industry. The normality of the French industrial experience—that is, its similarity to the British experience—is no less apparent in the realm of labor relations, which we examine next.

Managing Labor

In France as in Britain, the rise of industrial capitalism is associated with the concentration of large numbers of wage workers in centralized work sites. Of course, not all mass employers were found in industry (if we mean by that mining and manufacturing). Some of the largest French employers were in transportation (the railroads) and commerce (department stores). Conversely, not all industrial enterprises employed large numbers of workers. The majority of French workers in food processing, garment making, and woodworking were employed in establishments with fewer than five employees, even at the end of the nineteenth century, and in hides and leather, printing, and quarrying, the majority of workers were employed in establishments with fewer than 100 employees. However in five industries—chemicals, glass, textiles, and especially mining and metallurgy—firms employing 500 and even 1,000 or more workers appeared early in the nineteenth century, and plants in these industries were employing on average well over 100 workers by the end of the century.[21] It was particularly in those industries that, in the course of the nineteenth century, French employers worked out solutions to the problems of recruiting, retaining, controlling, and "managing" large numbers of workers.

Recruiting and Retaining Workers

The difficulty of recruiting and retaining workers in industrial enterprises varied with the industry and with the level of skill and the kinds of skills needed. Coal mines needed men who could hew coal at the pitface, handle explosives, and timber galleries. The new joint-stock mining companies that took control of mining concessions in the early nineteenth century initially found plenty of men with these skills already in place in the existing mining communities (unless the companies were fighting with those communities over rights to the concessions). Once the mines were up and running, skills could be passed from older to younger miners in the course of day-to-day operations without formal schooling or long apprenticeships. The main concern of the mine managers was maintaining a sufficient flow of new workers into a line of work that was inherently dangerous and suffered from chronically high rates of turnover.[22] Most mining companies turned this task over to independent contractors *(marchands)*, who hired, paid, and supervised the mining crews. In densely populated departments like the Nord and the Loire, these contractors usually found the needed manpower locally. But mines in the less populous South sometimes had to go far afield to find enough miners (or sufficiently skilled miners). In the 1860s, the Carmaux Company brought in miners from as far away as Brittany, Belgium, and Alsace, while Grand'combe in the Gard imported a contingent of cotton workers recently laid off in Rouen and tried unsuccessfully to turn them into coal miners.[23]

In the manufacturing sector, the initial focus of labor recruitment was more on the quality of the workforce than on sheer numbers. The successful launching of mechanized factory production often depended on finding workers with particular skills, especially mechanics who could set up and operate the machinery. Although the transition from artisanal to machine production of textiles is usually portrayed as a process of de-skilling, operating mule jennies was itself a skilled trade. Only the introduction of self-acting spinning machines in the 1850s allowed cotton masters to replace skilled mule spinners with more easily recruited and cheaper machine tenders, usually women and children. Similarly, mechanized weaving depended on the skills of the *pareurs* who prepared and mounted the warp. Iron- and steelmaking likewise required an array of skilled forge- and foundrymen.

Setting up these new technologies in early nineteenth century France inevitably meant bringing in workers with the requisite skills from outside. The founders of the Loire steel industry recruited skilled steelworkers from Germany. The Alsatian cloth printers brought in engravers from Switzerland. The new coal-based iron smelting and refining and the mechanized cotton industry all depended heavily on English workers.[24] Given the high cost of these foreign workers and the difficulties of retaining them, French industrialists moved quickly to train French replacements, either by apprenticing them to the skilled foreigners or by setting up formal training programs. The Alsatians were particularly assiduous in the latter: By 1860, some 3,000 students were getting technical instruction at thirty-six public and private educational institutions scattered through the Haut- and Bas-Rhin.[25] Also, a number of industrialists provided primary and secondary schooling for their workers' children with the intention of preparing the next generation of skilled workers for their factories, the Schneiders of Le Creusot being a leading example.[26]

Of course, even in the early years of mechanized manufacturing, industrial enterprises employed more unskilled than skilled workers, and this tendency increased in the course of the nineteenth century as improvements in industrial technology allowed more and more skilled workers to be replaced by less skilled machine tenders.[27] So as time went on, labor recruitment became less of a problem, at least for firms located in towns or in densely populated rural areas where there were pools of unemployed or underemployed workers. Indeed, some enterprises—such as the cotton manufacturers of Normandy and the Nord—virtually created their own labor force by displacing local artisanal spinners and weavers and then recruiting them for factory work. However, when setting up factory production in remote, thinly populated locations in order to access water power or raw materials, industrial entrepreneurs often found it difficult to recruit and retain enough workers, whether skilled or unskilled. In these situations, finding and keeping workers was not just a matter of paying good wages but also of providing non-wage benefits such as housing, schools, churches, insurance, recreation, and shopping facilities often embodied in an entire worker village *(cité ouvrière)* or company town. Companies that were not geographically isolated also started providing such benefits when they found themselves competing for available workers in their region (this was the case for the Anzin Coal Company after the opening of the Pas-de-Calais coalfield).[28]

To attract and maintain a stable workforce at its rural soda and glass works at Chauny (Aisne), Saint-Gobain offered a comprehensive array of services and benefits that included sickness and accident insurance, pension eligibility for all workers after three years on the job, churches, schools, hospitals, and free housing and free heating fuel for about one-fourth of its workers.[29] The great metallurgical companies provided similar benefits. At Le Creusot, the Schneiders spent 1 franc on services for every 10 francs in wages. To some workers they provided detached garden homes in a *cité ouvrière* modeled on the Cité Rochechouart in

Paris, and they provided low-interest mortgage loans to workers not living in company housing. There was a 128-bed, state-of-the-art hospital that was free to all workers by the 1890s, plus day care, schools, savings plans, pensions, and other benefits that constituted a system of social protection that was consistently judged the best in France at the expositions of the late nineteenth century.[30] At Hayange, Moyeuvre, and Stiring, the Wendels followed suit, building worker housing, schools, and churches, and offering pension plans, medical services, and other social services. Most of the Loire metallurgy firms provided similar benefits.[31]

Among the major mining companies in southern France, Carmaux and Decazeville did little to provide housing, in part because the fiercely independent peasant-miners were loath to accept company largesse and thereby become dependent on their employers. But Grand'combe built a completely company-owned and operated town.[32] In the Nord and Pas-de-Calais, coal companies competing for miners provided housing for up to half of their employees, as well as a long menu of social services and recreational activities that included choral societies, shooting clubs, and, at Douchy, a philharmonic orchestra.[33] In the woolens centers of Roubaix and Tourcoing and in the Alsatian cotton industry, employers behaved much like the leading iron and steel manufacturers. Indeed, the Protestant cotton masters of Alsace were probably the most paternalistic employers in France: When Armand Lederlin transferred the Alsatian bleaching and dyeing industry from Thann to Thaon-les-Vosges in the 1870s, he also replicated the social works of the Alsatian cotton industry, providing housing, a hospital, a library, a co-op, day care, and recreational facilities for his workers.[34] In the paper industry—which tended to combine isolated rural locations with a need for highly skilled workers—the patrons were equally paternalistic. The Montgolfiers offered not only free housing but also guaranteed year-round employment, a seniority bonus after ten years, and a "panoply of institutions" that included dining halls, company stores, libraries, schools, nurseries, and musical societies.[35]

In all these cases, the provision of housing and other benefits did not spring just from Christian charity, although the religious roots of industrial paternalism should not be overlooked. Nor did it serve only to attract and retain needed workers. As recent work on industrial paternalism has stressed, it was also part and parcel of the industrialists' desire to mold their workers into loyal, efficient employees and to control those employees within the workplace.[36]

Controlling the Workplace

Whether mining coal or manufacturing textiles, glass, paper, iron, or chemicals, the new industrialists of the early nineteenth century needed workers who came to work healthy, sober, and, above all, on time; who stayed at work the required time and followed instructions; and who identified with the firm and respected the plant and equipment. In the highly mechanized industries (such as cotton and paper), where the role of the workers was to keep the machinery running smoothly, punctuality and the willingness to work long hours (typically twelve hours, six days a week) were the highest priorities. For people of the twenty-first century who are inculcated with time awareness practically from birth and who learn to function in regimented groups starting in pre-school, it is hard to comprehend how difficult it was to impose the new factory discipline on workers accustomed to coming and going at will, working at their own pace, and exercising considerable control over how a task was done. Suffice it to say that industrialists addressed this problem from several angles simultaneously:

1. *Control of access.* To limit entry and exit and to keep track of who was coming and going, factory buildings often had only one main door, and work sites were enclosed with fences with a single gate manned by a gatekeeper. Gates and doors were locked except at shift changes.[37]

2. *Legal authority.* The French legal system clearly favored the authority of the employer over the rights of workers through much of the nineteenth century. This authority was symbolized in the *livret,* a kind of passport, which a worker had to present to a new employer when changing jobs (with the *livret* signed by the previous employer), thereby providing yet another mechanism for controlling and disciplining the workforce (the *livret* system was not abolished until 1892).[38]

3. *Rules and regulations.* Under the Napoleonic Code, employers could include lengthy rules and regulations in their contracts with workers, and any fines or penalties assessed for violations of those rules were legally enforceable. Hundreds of examples of these rules from the nineteenth century remain extant.[39] The rules issued by early textile manufacturers and quoted *in extenso* by Serge Chassagne reveal not only the mindset and preoccupations of the industrialists but also the practical problems inherent in employing workers fresh from the farm or small workshop who were often very young (the majority of millworkers were in fact teenagers). One concern was getting workers to accept and adhere

to the daily work schedule; another was avoiding precipitous or unanticipated departures that would leave the mill shorthanded. At the wool-spinning plant of Henri Gagneau, for example, workers contracted to stay at least a year and lost what amounted to several weeks' pay if they quit early or did not give the required notice or if their departure violated the rule allowing only one worker to leave a given department in a given month. Workers could also be fined 2 francs (a day's pay) for refusing overtime beyond the normal thirteen-hour workday. Workers arriving ten minutes late for work were fined 25 centimes; those leaving without permission forfeited a day's pay. Workers could be fined for various forms of dereliction of duty (for example, stopping their spinning machines too early or too late), and fines were meted out for a wide variety of misbehaviors, starting with drunkenness, but also including playing, swearing, shouting, singing, fighting or quarreling, eating, sleeping, running, bathing, using the toilet at unauthorized times, or washing up with the company's soap. Theft or destruction of company property brought immediate dismissal.[40]

Seventy years after the Gagneau rules were issued, Eugène Schneider II published new work rules at Le Creusot in the aftermath of the great strike of 1899–1900. These demonstrated a certain progress in labor relations since Gagneau's time in that specific monetary fines for infractions were eliminated and procedures were in place to allow workers to express their grievances through elected spokesmen. But the tone of the rules was still punitive, with the emphasis on a long list of offenses for which a worker could be summarily fired. These included:

> unwarranted absences . . . insubordination, lack of respect for or disobedience toward supervisors, injurious or obscene inscriptions on the plant or equipment, refusal to do work as ordered, bad will or negligence in doing work, leaving one's post, insults or threats toward other workers, harmful or inappropriate comments to personnel, visitors, or management, drunkenness in the shop, bringing alcoholic beverages on the shop-floor, bringing merchandise to sell in the shop, stealing from other workers or from the plant, making objects for personal use in the plant, willful damage or sabotage, divulging a company secret, bringing outsiders into the plant, entering or leaving by climbing over fences, breaking the security rules.[41]

Suffice it to say that, in an era when the ideas of human rights and democratic government were taking hold in the public sphere, French industrialists continued to believe that the success and indeed the very survival of their private enterprises depended on maintaining their absolute authority and a kind of military discipline within their factories and mines. Of course, establishing and maintaining such discipline and obedience required more than posting written rules and regulations.

4. *The chain of command.* Alfred Chandler has argued that early industrial enterprises were comparatively simple organizations that did not require the elaborate managerial hierarchies that characterized the big businesses of the late nineteenth and twentieth centuries.[42] Even so, as the workforce of these enterprises grew from a few dozen to hundreds and even thousands, it became clear that more than the personal authority of the *patron* or plant director was needed to maintain discipline and to assure smooth operations. At first, workplace supervision was delegated to some of the workers themselves in the manner of the domestic system. In textile mills, for example, male spinners and weavers might be responsible for hiring, training, paying, and supervising their assistants, usually their wives and children. In mining, glassmaking, and ironworking, there was a variation on this theme, known as *marchandage,* in which a subcontractor hired and supervised an entire crew or team of workers. Such practices relieved the *patron* of the burden of personnel management but inevitably also limited his contact with and authority over his workers.

As the growing complexity of production processes made the direct exercise of authority over workers more necessary, industrialists turned to salaried overseers and works managers, sometimes as a substitute for subcontractors or crew bosses, but more often as a new layer of authority between the *patron* and the crew bosses. Initially this involved hiring doormen, or *concierges,* to verify the presence of the workers and to control their comings and goings. By the middle of the nineteenth century, however, simple surveillance was giving way to a more comprehensive supervision of workers and machinery by a new class of industrial foremen. Le Creusot, for example, employed only eight foremen to supervise a workforce of 1,800 in 1846, but this number rose to 38 in 1856 (for a workforce of 6,300) and further increased to 58 in 1881 (when the workforce exceeded 8,000).[43]

In summary, the French approach to labor relations—what historians now call "industrial paternalism"—had three main facets: (1) use of non-wage benefits such as housing and medical care to attract and retain workers and to inculcate in them a sense of obligation to the *patron* or the firm; (2) use of company educational programs to indoctrinate adult workers and to perpetuate a compliant, loyal workforce by training the children of workers to follow in their parents' footsteps; and (3) strict, top-down management of production processes and the work environment on the basis of the *patron*'s absolute authority. Although this approach to labor relations worked in some cases, it was not uniformly successful, in part because some industrialists used the "stick" but not the "carrot." Indeed, from the first appearance of large-scale capitalistic mining and factory-based manufacturing, workers bridled at the restrictive regulations, the "tyranny of the clock," the even more galling tyranny of overseers and foremen, and in general the sheer prisonlike atmosphere of many industrial work sites. More importantly, there were disputes over pay—not just the level of wages but also their manipulation (withholding wages to enforce work rules, paying different workers different wages for the same work, cutting wages without warning or recourse). Worker discontent was endemic in the industrial system in France from its beginnings. This discontent not only erupted in individual acts of defiance; it also increasingly led to collective action, especially work stoppages, in spite of the provisions in the commercial code that outlawed the formation of "coalitions" to block or impede the operations of mines and mills. In the second half of the nineteenth century, when the workers' right to organize and to strike was recognized, dealing with these challenges became a central theme in the management of the industrial labor force.

Dealing with Conflict

Work stoppages occurred in French textile mills from the early 1800s, and over the course of the nineteenth century the textile industry experienced more strikes than any other industry in France. The coal mining industry was a close second, with the largest and most violent strikes, notably at Anzin in 1833, 1847–1848, and 1884, and at Decazeville in 1867 and 1886. The issues in the textile and coal strikes were almost always wages and hours. In good times, workers sought to increase their pay and reduce hours; in bad times, especially the 1880s, they sought to block pay cuts or increases in work hours (or new work rules that squeezed more effort out of workers in the same hours and for the same pay). Meanwhile, metallurgy and metalworking were less vulnerable to strikes, at least before the great expansion of iron and steel at the end of the century. Le Creusot, for example, experienced collective actions by its workers in 1848 and 1871 that were tied to the political upheavals in those years, but it avoided a classic economically motivated strike until 1899. Strike activity was particularly a phenomenon of the last third of the century, no doubt because the government recognized the legality of strikes only in 1864 and legalized labor unions only in 1884.[44] In any event, it was the rare industrialist who did not confront a strike or the threat of a strike at some point in his career. How did industrialists respond to these challenges?

The response of industrialists to strikes and related challenges to their authority changed as legal circumstances changed. Before 1864, when strikes were illegal, industrialists could act in the secure knowledge that the law and the state were on their side. Indeed, many strikes in this era ended with the prosecution and imprisonment of the strike leaders (although this did not preclude offering concessions to the strikers to end their walkout, as the administration of the Anzin Coal Company did in 1833). Moreover, in the absence of labor unions in this period, workers in one plant rarely tried to coordinate strikes with workers in other plants—except in towns like Rouen and Lille, where mills were in close proximity to one another—so industrialists could act independently and individually and did not have to coordinate their reaction.

With the legalization of strikes in 1864, things began to change. In the strike wave of 1867–1870, industrialists for the first time confronted workers who had the sympathy if not the overt support of the national government. Not surprisingly, many made concessions: Michelle Perrot's figures show that a higher percentage of strikes ended in success in 1867–1870 than at any other time in the nineteenth century. Indeed, as David Gordon, Sanford Elwitt, and others have argued, the strike issue played a major role in swinging industrialists away from the Second Empire and toward Republicanism.[45] Accordingly, the advent of the Third Republic brought a shift in government policy in favor of the industrialists and against striking workers. Increasingly government troops were sent in to "protect" factories and mines during strikes, and this anti-strike position hardened after 1884 when the legalization of unions supposedly gave workers a more peaceful alternative to strikes in seeking redress of grievances.

By the last decade of the nineteenth century, the dominant issue for industrialists was how to deal with unions or the threat of unionization. In general, there were two strategies. The first, epitomized by the Schneiders at Le Creusot, combined staunch refusal to recognize any independent union as a bargaining agent with the formation of a company union (which Le Creusot succeeded in setting up in the aftermath of the 1899–1900 strike).[46] The second strategy was for industrialists to come together in patronal associations to finance resistance to strikes collectively. This approach was epitomized by the mining companies in the Nord/Pas-de-Calais coalfield, which came together in the Union des Compagnies Houillères du Nord et du Pas-de-Calais to create and administer an anti-strike fund.[47] As it happened, this shift to collective quasi-political action in the labor sphere was part of a larger trend toward collective action by French industrialists in managing the political and economic environment in which they operated. By the end of the nineteenth century, management of that environment had long occupied the leading industrialists.

Managing the Business Environment

In seeking to create and maintain as favorable an environment for their business activities as possible, French industrialists of the nineteenth century had to work within a political and legal system that manifested a dual personality in economic matters, at once both liberal and statist. On the one hand, the reforms of the French Revolution had established a competitive free market in France, at least in theory. On the other hand, the French state retained vast powers to define the terms of economic activity and to regulate commerce and industry.

By and large, industrialists accepted the ambiguities of this situation and exploited them to their own advantage, acting individually or collectively outside the purview of the state when the law allowed it and when it served their purposes, but also encouraging government intervention in economic matters when such intervention seemed beneficial. How industrialists went about using both private initiatives and state authority to create an optimal business environment, and the extent to which they succeeded in this, can be ascertained by looking at their efforts on three fronts:

1. the formulation of trade and tariff policy to secure control of the home market for French industry

2. the utilization of the government's regulatory authority to force the railroad companies to serve the needs of industry

3. the curbing of "excessive" competition through the creation of cartels in apparent violation of the anti-trust clauses of the French commercial code

Tariff Policy and the Control of the Home Market

The making of tariff policy illustrates the difficulties that industrialists encountered in getting the government to act on their behalf. Even more, it shows how, as industrialization proceeded, the interests of industrialists diverged, making it increasingly difficult for them to form a common front and making the formulation of economic policy an increasingly contentious, adversarial process.

At the outset of the nineteenth century, French industrialists seemed united on what kind of tariff policy they wanted, and they enjoyed great success in getting it. To begin with, the wars of the French Revolution had brought them a great windfall: a prohibition on British imports that eliminated their principal outside competitors in the domestic market. When later extended beyond France by Napoleon, this prohibition gave the industrialists privileged access to the whole continent, at least temporarily. In 1814, however, the fall of Napoleon and the collapse of the Continental System brought an influx of cheap British goods, and French industrialists immediately turned to the new government of Louis XVIII to enact high import duties to shelter the home market from foreign competition. Fortunately for the industrialists, the restored Bourbon monarchy provided ample channels through which they could influence economic policy making, including the new bicameral parliament. Consequently, starting with a December 1814 law that increased import duties on iron fivefold and prohibited the importation of a long list of goods (including most cotton and linen cloth), the French parliament passed a series of measures that by 1820 gave French manufacturers effective control of their home market.[48]

This control came at a price in that, for the benefit of other domestic interests, high import duties were also placed on coal, foodstuffs, and some industrial raw materials (such as wool). From the perspective of French manufacturers, all of those items would have been better left unprotected. While the price seemed worth paying for the textile and metallurgical manufacturers in the forefront of the drive for protection, it was not worth paying for certain other businessmen, including Bordeaux wine merchants and dealers in silk cloth and other high-quality French manufactures, who had no fear of British competition at home and who normally exported much of their output. For them, the adoption of high protection in France only served to inspire like measures abroad that restricted their access to foreign markets. Consequently, a countermovement for free trade—or at least trade liberalization— sprang up in the 1830s and began pushing for a general reduction of import duties through negotiation of a trade treaty with Belgium. In response, the protectionists organized at the sectoral level (in the Comité des Filateurs de Lille, the Comité des Intérêts Métallurgiques, and the Comité des Houillères Françaises, among others) and then nationally (in the Association pour la Défense du Travail National).[49]

The protectionists prevailed in this first battle over trade liberalization, and the *régime prohibitif* remained intact as of 1847. However, with the fall of Louis-Philippe in 1848 and the eventual rise to power of Louis-Napoleon Bonaparte, the balance of power shifted. The Saint-Simonians who advised Louis-Napoleon tended to favor free trade, so the new government of the Second Empire began chipping away at the protectionist system, particularly by cutting duties on the iron rails, locomotives, and other materials needed for railroad construction. Then, with the signing of the Anglo-French Treaty of Commerce in 1860, the Second Empire in one fell swoop replaced high protection, not with free trade, but with a more moderate regime in which low "conventional" tariffs written into trade treaties superseded the prohibitive "general" tariffs legislated earlier.[50]

While many industrialists were unalterably opposed to Napoleon III's liberalization of French tariff policies, a number of major industrialists, including the chocolate manufacturer Emile Menier, supported the trade treaties because they opened up new markets for French manufactures abroad. Others supported the treaties because they gave French industries access to cheaper sources of the semi-finished goods that served as their raw materials. For example, after 1860 the Mulhouse cloth printer Jean Dollfus could import unfinished English muslin as print stock and Eugène Gouïn of Batignolles could import the iron and copper he used in building locomotives and bridges. These industrialists joined forces with the commercial and transport interests that had long favored freer trade to head off the efforts of protectionists to scuttle the trade treaties after the fall of Napoleon III.[51]

Instead of bringing a quick return to protection, the advent of the Third Republic unleashed a twenty-year battle between the evenly matched forces of free trade and protection to determine the future shape of French trade policy. In 1881–1882, the free traders won a double victory when the French parliament replaced the prohibitive general tariff established under the Bourbon Restoration with a new, more moderate general tariff and then ratified a new series of trade treaties that extended the existing conventional duties on manufactures for ten more years. However, advocates of a return to protection for agriculture succeeded in exempting farm products from the new trade treaties and then succeeded in legislating substantial increases in import duties on grain, wine, and livestock as a remedy for the ongoing agricultural depression. This seemed to turn the tide against the free traders, and in 1890–1892 industrial and agricultural protectionists in parliament joined together to overthrow the system of trade treaties. They put in their place a legislated two-tier tariff consisting of minimum duties, which applied to imports from countries granting France its best trade terms, and a set of maximum duties to be applied to the products of countries that did not extend most-favored-nation status to France. This was the Méline Tariff, named for the Vosges deputy who for twenty years had led the fight for a return to protection for both industry and agriculture.[52]

While the Méline Tariff represented a return to high protection for French agriculture, it represented, in the realm of industrial tariffs, a carefully crafted compromise between protectionists and the so-called free traders who had favored the lower import duties on industrial products embodied in the trade treaties. Thus, by the terms of the Méline Tariff, duties on coal and basic forms of iron and steel remained at their existing moderate levels, partly to help French manufacturers who drew on foreign sources of coal, coke, and pig iron, and partly to prevent tariff retaliation abroad on exported French metallurgical products. At the same time, the Méline Tariff substantially raised import duties on higher-value metallurgical products, from locomotive wheels to steam engines, as well as on specialized forms of iron and steel like the tinplate used in canning. There was a similar balancing act for textiles. Domestically oriented cotton and linen manufacturers got higher import duties on most of their products (plus privileged access to the emerging colonial markets); export-oriented silk and woolens manufacturers got continued duty-free access to foreign sources of their raw materials and new trade treaties to maintain or open foreign markets for their finished goods.[53]

In the end, the prolonged battle over the tariff demonstrated that, by participating in the formulation of policy as deputies, senators, ministers, and advisers and by becoming proficient in the techniques of pressure-group politics, French industrialists could enlist the power of the French state in the cause of furthering their collective economic interests. But it also demonstrated that the economic interests and policy needs of the various sectors of French industry were complex and often in conflict with one another as well as with the interests and needs of French commerce and agriculture. Determining what policies most benefited industry and then getting those policies enacted involved compromise; industrialists had to accept that getting half a loaf was better than getting none at all. The battle over the tariff also demonstrated something else: Even the limited goal of protecting the home market from outside competitors required more than just a favorable tariff policy; it also required the assistance of the French railroads. Getting that assistance embroiled French industrialists in another long and difficult political fight in the 1870s and 1880s.

Railroads and the Promotion of National Industry

From the beginning of the railway age, French industrialists had understood that their future economic success depended on where the railroads were built, how they were built, and how they were operated. Industrialists participated in the public debate on the building of a national rail system in the 1830s and took the initiative in building many of the early local and regional lines. However, state engineers ultimately decided where the trunk lines and main feeder lines were placed, and they did this mainly with an eye to the military and administrative needs of the state, not the needs of French industry. Similarly, it was the bankers and financiers who controlled the six major trunk lines who ultimately decided how the railroads were run. Not surprisingly, their main goal was to make the railroads as profitable as possible, and this often meant promoting imports and international traffic at the expense of the industrialists' efforts to control the national market. Accordingly, railroad executives like Emile and Isaac Pereire and François Bartholony became leading advocates of freer trade in the 1850s and 1860s.[54]

In addition to quarreling with the railroad companies over operation of the existing lines, French industrialists challenged the railroad companies on when and how the system was to be expanded. In the late 1860s, provincial industrialists were particularly concerned with the building of a third network of local feeder lines to complete the first network of trunk lines laid in the 1840s and 1850s and the second network of regional feeder lines laid in the early 1860s. The Big Six trunk carriers were reluctant to build the third network because of its projected unprofitability and because the government did not guarantee dividends on investments in these lines. So, with the help of a 1865 law that allowed local interests to build local railroads, provincial industrialists set out to construct these lines themselves. By the mid-

1870s, however, all the resultant local rail companies were in financial trouble, and interest in launching new ones as independent enterprises waned.

In this situation, provincial leaders turned to Paris for help. With Republicans taking control of the national government in 1876 and calling into question all aspects of the ownership and operation of the railroads, their demands got a sympathetic hearing. The result was the Freycinet Plan of 1878, by which the government was to finance the building of the third network. The Republican leaders were reluctant to turn these lines over to the "financial oligarchs" who controlled the Big Six, but the crash of the Union Générale in 1882 and the ensuing financial crisis seemingly precluded continued state support and management of the third network. Therefore, in the railroad conventions of 1883, a deal was struck. In return for government subsidies and dividend guarantees on their new investment, the Big Six agreed to take over and complete the third network. In exchange for allowing the Big Six to consolidate further their control of the French rail system, the provincial interests got the expansion of the system they had long sought. They also got, it turned out, concessions in the area of rates and service.[55]

From the 1840s to the 1870s, the French railroads had developed multitiered freight rate schedules with the approval of the Ministry of Public Works. These included several categories of general fares that varied with the type of merchandise carried and the distance traversed plus special fares for certain goods on certain routes. French shippers—including French industrialists—raised four basic complaints about these fares: They were too high, they were needlessly complex, they were arbitrary and discriminatory, and they favored foreign goods over domestic goods in the national market, thereby undermining the protection provided by customs duties. In the realm of general fares, which applied to small shipments not eligible for special fares, complaints centered on the high overall level of fares and the lack of uniformity in fare schedules from line to line. When two parliamentary commissions looked into these complaints, they found them justified and recommended wide-ranging reforms in general fares, but virtually none of these had been enacted by 1880.

Meanwhile, special fares applied to the great majority of rail freight in France, and these attracted the most attention from reformers. Indeed, the files of the Ministry of Commerce and the proceedings of French chambers of commerce for the late 1870s and early 1880s fairly overflow with complaints about special fares. Some complaints asserted that existing or proposed special fares were discriminatory and aided certain businesses at the expense of others. Others alleged that the railroads were not offering enough aid to particular interests via special fares.[56] Beyond the complaints about specific special fares on specific lines, there was a general feeling that special fares were inherently unfair. This sentiment was expressed not only by the small provincial industries, which could not qualify for special fares or which competed in the national market with foreign producers who benefited from special import fares. It was also expressed by large cosmopolitan interests that often benefited from special long-haul rates. Thus in 1881, in a report to the Paris Chamber of Commerce, the dye manufacturer Alcide Poirrier denounced various station-to-station fares that caused goods of the same type moving the same distance on the same line to pay different fares, or goods moving between the same stations in different directions to pay different fares, or goods moving different distances on the same line to pay the same fare. Heeding Poirrier's assertion that "equality in the application of fares is the only guarantee of commerce," the Paris chamber thereupon went on record in favor of a reform of all freight rates to make them proportional to the distance traveled (on a decreasing base) and applicable to all sections of a given line.[57]

Addressing these concerns and reforming the rate-making practices of the Big Six was an important issue in the negotiation of the Railroad Conventions of 1883. However, from the point of view of industrialists and other shippers, the rate reforms that eventually emerged were at best an imperfect compromise among the interests involved. Because the government was headed by politicians sympathetic to the railroad companies—notably Léon Say, the finance minister, who was also a director of the Compagnie du Nord—it did not drive a hard bargain on rate reform. Moreover, as François Caron has suggested, there may have been a deal to leave fare structures alone in return for the companies' cooperation in completing the third network.[58] In any case, the conventions themselves contained no clauses on rates, nor did the government assume greater control of rate making after the conventions, as some politicians had demanded. However, in letters attached to the conventions, the companies did make concessions on freight rates. For one thing, they promised that transit fares previously applicable only to foreign goods bound for foreign destinations would be applied to domestic goods being exported on the same route. For another thing, five of the companies offered specific fare reductions. For example, the P-L-M promised to lower general fares 6–10 percent on cereals, coal, fertilizer, refined sugar, and certain metallurgical products; and the Eastern Railroad offered 4–11 percent reductions in fares on grain, coal, and fertilizer.[59] The Northern Railroad did not offer specific reductions in its 1883 letter but, according to Caron, provided "revolutionary" fare reductions in the ensuing three years that gave the Compagnie du Nord by far the lowest schedule of freight rates of all French railroads at the end of the nineteenth century.[60]

In the end, industrialists had gotten some but not all of what they demanded of the railroads. They had gotten the third network and thus better rail connections between industrial regions and their markets in France and Europe, and they had achieved a generally more equitable rate structure with significantly lower fares on some categories of freight on some lines. However, all railroads still gave preferential fares to international long-haul shippers and large-scale importers—so-called penetration fares—despite a promise in the 1883 conventions "to modify all combinations of fares having the effect of altering the economic conditions that result from our customs regime."[61] Protectionist politicians continued to wrangle with the railroads over penetration fares until the passage of the Méline Tariff seemed to settle the issue by providing sufficient protection to offset the pro-importation effects of those fares.

Ultimately, in the realm of railroad rates and service, as in the realm of tariff policy (and, for that matter, labor policy), industrialists found that they could enlist the power of the national government in promoting the welfare of industry, but only up to a point. However, at the same time, they discovered that any failures and frustrations in the public sphere could be offset with private agreements to manage the economic environment. Specifically, with the government relaxing legal strictures on industrial cooperation and collusion, industrialists began to divide up markets and to fix prices, either directly though *ententes* and cartels or indirectly through the creation of common selling agencies *(comptoirs)*.

Taking Control of Markets

The road to cartelization in France was neither straight nor smooth, in part because Article 419 of the Commercial Code of 1810 outlawed all "coalitions" having the purpose of raising the price of a product above what it would be under "natural and free competition." Although this article was originally aimed at grain speculators, the French government occasionally invoked it to break up would-be industrial cartels and monopolies, as it did in the cases of the Marseille soda manufacturers' cartel in 1838 and the Compagnie des Mines de la Loire in 1852. However, as the nineteenth century wore on, French governments and courts gradually became more tolerant of cooperation among industrial firms, particularly since the depression of 1876–1896 demonstrated the deleterious effects of "excessive" competition. By the early 1900s, after the defendants had been exonerated in a series of antitrust cases, the prosecution of industrialists for violation of article 419 virtually ended, and cartelization became open and commonplace.[62]

In the final analysis, however, changes in the legal environment had less influence on the timing and extent of cartelization than did changes in the structure and competitive environment of French industry. In order for French producers to be able to negotiate and enforce market-sharing and price-fixing agreements, there had to be sufficient protection of the domestic market to eliminate foreign competitors, or, alternatively, foreign competitors had to be included in the agreement (that is, the cartel had to be international). In either situation, successful cartelization required a certain level of concentration. Ideally, there needed to be twenty or fewer major producers of a product, inasmuch as it was very difficult to negotiate agreements—and even harder to enforce them—when there were too many producers. Thus the earliest successful agreements were found in the glass and chemicals industries, where the number of major producers in France was limited.

As described by J-B Daviet, Saint-Gobain was the key mover in the cartelization of both glass and chemicals. In 1829, Saint-Gobain made an informal arrangement with Saint-Quirin, the only other French manufacturer of plate glass, to set up a common marketing system. In 1862, after it had absorbed Saint-Quirin, Saint-Gobain made more formal market-sharing agreements with two other French firms and two Belgian firms that had entered the French plate glass market since 1830. This agreement was extended to Saint-Gobain's British competitors in 1863, and thereafter Saint-Gobain managed to maintain what amounted to an international plate glass cartel, which probably explains the French glassmakers' relative indifference to the issue of tariff protection. At the same time, Saint-Gobain also sought market-sharing agreements in its sector of the chemicals industry, starting with soda and sulfuric acid in the 1830s. Thanks largely to its efforts, the whole French chemicals industry was highly organized by the 1890s, with market-sharing agreements in place for alkalis, acids, chlorine, phosphates, and dyestuffs.[63]

French metallurgists first organized on a national scale in the Comité des Intérêts Métallurgiques in the 1840s to combat the efforts to lower import duties on iron and steel. In the early years of the Second Empire, the leading ironmasters continued to work behind the scenes to uphold high protection against the efforts of the railroads to open up the French market, but the influx of British iron and steel into France under the 1880 trade treaty, coupled with the relaxation of restrictions on industrial organization under the new law on coalitions, prompted them to create a formal association, the Comité des Forges, in 1864. The Comité's stated purpose was not price-fixing or overt control of the market but rather the exchange of technical information and common action on economic policy, especially tariffs and temporary admissions. But disagreements among the leading participants blocked meaningful action in even that limited sphere through the 1870s.[64] Only in 1880, in response to the deepening crisis in French metallurgy, did the Comité des Forges start meeting regularly. According to Robert Pinot, the Comité's long-time executive director, it voted in 1886 to undertake a five-step program to regulate production and markets that included allocating a portion of the domestic market to each member, formulating a uniform system of classification and pricing of iron and steel, penalizing members who exceeded their production quotas, and setting up a fund to encourage exportation.[65] Ultimately, however, successful cartelization of French iron and steel depended less on the efforts of the Comité des Forges than on the efforts of regional and product-specific associations of forgemasters. Particularly important was the example set by the pig iron producers of the Meurthe-et-Moselle.

Because the emerging pig iron industry of Lorraine was new and somewhat isolated from the rest of the French iron industry and even more because the high phosphorus content of its pig iron limited its applications, the ironmasters of the Meurthe-et-Moselle had cooperated from the beginning in marketing their output. This cooperation was formalized in December 1876, when the leading forgemasters in the northern part of the department founded the Comptoir de Longwy as a partnership to sell their excess pig iron. The Comptoir did not formally set production quotas, but it did assign a share of predicted domestic sales to each member company. This amounted to a quota, since no one wanted to produce beyond what the Comptoir was willing to sell. Under the management first of Alexandre Dreux and then Philippe Aubé, the Comptoir was so successful that it soon absorbed the neighboring *comptoir* founded in Nancy in 1879. By the end of the century its membership had risen to fourteen, and it was responsible for the sale of 30 percent of the pig iron produced in the Meurthe-et-Moselle. By 1900 the Comptoir de Longwy "had become virtually the only supplier of pig iron to independent metallurgical firms that did not smelt their own pig iron,"[66] which, for all intents and purposes, made it the cartel for French pig iron. Soon its structure and methods were imitated by other sectors of the iron and steel industry. From the early 1890s to the early 1900s, similar *comptoirs* were set up by the makers of basic (Thomas) steel as well as by the manufacturers of axles, steel beams, sheet and plate steel, steel tubes, coach springs, wire net, nails, horseshoes, hinges, and general hardware. Because no *comptoir* was attempting to corner the market in its respective product (what the French call *accaparement*), the government did not view them as illicit coalitions under Article 419, especially after the legality of the Comptoir de Longwy was upheld in two high-profile court cases in 1902.[67]

French colliers also formed national and regional associations from the 1840s onward, first to defend the protectionistic tariff system and later to lobby for transportation improvements and to meet the challenge of organized labor. In the Nord/Pas-de-Calais (the coalfield about which we know the most thanks to the work of Marcel Gillet), there were numerous short-lived agreements to set prices on various kinds of coal from the 1840s to the 1870s—mostly bilateral agreements between Anzin and its smaller neighbors. There was no attempt, however, to cartelize the whole industry before the end of the century, perhaps because the growing demand for coal, coupled with the moderate import duty on coal, gave French colliers a relatively secure market in the second half of the nineteenth century. In any event, it was only in 1901, in response to weakening domestic prices and the cartelization of the German coal industry, that the main producers of the Nord/Pas-de-Calais created an *entente* to set minimum prices and to allocate market shares. Unlike the *comptoirs* in metallurgy, the Nord/Pas-de-Calais *entente* did not act as a selling agent for coal. However, it did serve as a virtual *comptoir* for coke, with its president negotiating sales contracts with the leading Lorraine iron- and steelmakers on behalf of the entire industry as a way of countering intense competition from the well-organized Belgian and German coal syndicates.[68]

It was also in the early twentieth century that cartelization came to French textiles, or at least to cottons and linen. Throughout much of the second half of the nineteenth century, the large number of firms manufacturing cotton and linen, along with the access that foreign manufacturers had to the French market under the trade treaties, had precluded agreements to divide up the market and to set prices. Co-operation among cotton and linen manufacturers had been limited to participation in organizations dedicated to overthrowing the trade treaties and returning France to high protection (especially the Association de l'Industrie Française). In the 1890s, however, the passage of the Méline Tariff returned a measure of control of the domestic and the colonial markets to French cotton and linen manufacturers. At the same time, production was being concentrated in the hands of a relatively small group of companies clustered in specific regions. Virtually all French linen production was concentrated in Lille-Armentières, which put the flax spinners in a position to formalize an agreement to share raw materials, limit production, and set minimum prices on finished goods. Likewise, starting in 1899, the Comité Française de Filature de Coton, representing the leading cotton spinners of Normandy, the Vosges, and the Nord, set production quotas and collected penalties from those who exceeded their quotas (the penalties in turn subsidized exports and thereby further reduced price competition in the domestic market). The Nord cotton spinners went a step further and actually fixed prices. But unlike the coal and metals cartels, the cotton and linen cartels functioned at best sporadically. Adherence was a year-to-year matter, with many producers joining in hard years but dropping out when market conditions improved.[69]

In summary, the efforts of French industrialists to manage their markets through cartels and *ententes* faced formidable obstacles, not only in law but also in the structure of industry and in the divergent economic interests and individualistic mindsets of the industrialists themselves. Yet by the end of the nineteenth century these efforts had achieved considerable success, as had the industrialists' efforts to mold public policy to their economic needs. French industrialists by no means succeeded in every attempt at private organization or public policy-making, but the cumulative weight of their political activities, both public and private, greatly contributed to creating an overall business environment favorable to industrial enterprise. This industry-friendly political economy, in turn, became a necessary precondition for the rise of big business in France in the early years of the twentieth century.

Conclusion to Part II

Industrial capitalism was almost as old as merchant capitalism, but in France it remained clearly subordinate until the end of the eighteenth century. Only in the new economic circumstances of the 1800s—marked by the advent of the new manufacturing technology and the emergence of national and international markets based on modern systems of transportation and communication—did the industrialist come into his own and begin to play as large a role as the merchant and the banker. As demonstrated in the industry-by-industry survey we have just completed, France made enormous strides in industrial development over the course of the nineteenth century. This gave rise to some of the most important industrial enterprises in Europe and the world, including Saint-Gobain in glass and heavy chemicals, Anzin in coal, Wendel and Le Creusot in iron and steel, Thiriez and Dollfus-Mieg in cotton spinning, Prouvost in woolcombing, Moulins de Corbeil in flour milling, Essonnes in papermaking, Hachette in publishing, Say in sugar refining, Menier in chocolate, and Haviland in porcelain. By the end of the nineteenth century, the activities of these and other mining and manufacturing firms had become the focal point of economic life in France and to a substantial degree the focal point of political and social life as well. Most important from the perspective of this book, the rise of these firms provided the necessary technological and organizational resources so that France could participate in the next stage in the history of world capitalism: the Second Industrial Revolution and the advent of giant corporate enterprise—"big business." The nature of that participation is the subject of Part III.

PART THREE

THE SECOND INDUSTRIAL REVOLUTION AND THE BEGINNINGS OF MANAGERIAL CAPITALISM, 1880s–1930s

After suffering through twenty years of slow growth or even outright depression from the mid-1870s to the mid-1890s, France, Europe, and much of the rest of the world entered a long period of economic expansion that continued, except for the hiatus of World War I, to the onset of the Great Depression in the early 1930s.

Economic historians attribute this expansion mainly to the introduction of new technologies and the emergence of new industries—the industries of the so-called Second Industrial Revolution. For Alfred D. Chandler, however, something larger and more fundamental was happening, a kind of organizational revolution in business that made the period 1890–1930 even more of a watershed in modern economic history than is implied in the concept of the Second Industrial Revolution. As Chandler has argued, principally in *Scale and Scope,* it was in this period that the United States and other leading industrial nations witnessed the rise of firms of unprecedented size and complexity that first took control of their respective sectors of their domestic economies and then invaded and took control of markets abroad, thereby becoming enterprises of global reach and significance. Moreover, by developing "organizational capabilities" that enabled them to cope with changing environmental conditions, many of these firms managed to maintain their dominant positions throughout the twentieth century. Indeed, some remain as important today as they were seventy-five or one hundred years ago.

The traditional name for these new, very large, very complex firms is "big business," but Chandler prefers the terms "integrated industrial enterprise" or "managerial enterprise," which emphasize what he sees as their defining characteristics: the combining of a number of different functions and operations, especially by means of vertical integration, and the coordination of these operations (as well as the development of new corporate competencies) by a hierarchy of professional managers. In the United States, the prototype for this new kind of business firm was found in the national railroad companies that appeared between 1850 and 1900, but the new model found its widest application in the new manufacturing enterprises that developed mass production of both existing products (such as steel, machinery, and foodstuffs) and the new products of the Second Industrial Revolution (such as electrical appliances, automobiles, and organic chemicals).

By setting up large-scale manufacturing facilities to capture economies of scale and scope, by integrating backward to assure steady, low-cost supplies of raw materials, and in some cases by integrating forward into distribution of finished goods to maintain a high level of sales, these new integrated industrial firms emerged as the low-cost producers in their respective industries. This in turn allowed them to drive their higher-cost competitors out of business (or to take them over) and to join the small group of large, efficient firms controlling the home market in their respective industries (oligopoly being more common than monopoly). Many of these firms were also able to move into foreign markets on the strength of the same competitive advantages that had brought them success at home, which turned them into multinational enterprises. At that point, would-be challengers could dislodge these firms from their dominant positions only by replicating all at once the investments in production, organization, and distribution that they had built up gradually, so they in effect possessed "first mover advantages" that enabled them to maintain their dominance throughout the twentieth century despite environmental upheaval and technological change. Indeed, it is Chandler's contention that these large, integrated industrial enterprises—especially those that invested in in-house research laboratories—became important vehicles for innovation in product and process, which further insulated them from competition and allowed them to grow not only by geographical expansion in their original businesses but also by product diversification (taking advantage of economies of scope). Thus the great industrial enterprises that arose on the basis of the new technologies of the Second Industrial Revolution in the early twentieth century also became leaders in the science-based industries of the Third Industrial Revolution at the end of the twentieth century.[1]

In the decade following the publication of *Scale and Scope* in 1990, Chandler's interpretation of modern business history—the "Chandlerian paradigm"—was subjected to searching criticism from many quarters. Much of this criticism focused on his tendency to correlate national economic success (or failure) with the development (or lack thereof) of integrated managerial enterprises, and he was particularly criticized for his assertion that British economic decline in the twentieth century sprang from the persistence of family firms and from the failure to develop managerial enterprises in cutting-edge industries. Chandler has also been criticized for emphasizing big business as a source of growth and innovation to the exclusion of small entrepreneurial firms, and for emphasizing the mass production of standardized goods while ignoring the continuing importance of flexible batch production of a wide array of non-standard goods. Others have questioned the importance of first mover advantages and the superior survivability of the large industrial business.[2] None of these criticisms, however, has invalidated Chandler's central point about the importance of integrated industrial enterprises in the twentieth century or his explanation of how and why these enterprises came into existence. Thus, in examining the development of business in France in the period 1880–1930, it is important—especially because Chandler did not address the French case in *Scale and Scope*—to consider the extent to which France participated in the creation of big business and managerial capitalism and the extent to which a cohort of "Chandlerian" enterprises emerged in France as they did in the United States, Germany, and (to a lesser degree) Great Britain in these years. In short, how relevant is the Chandlerian paradigm to the development of French business in the twentieth century?

No one questions that France experienced a high rate of industrial growth between 1896 and 1929 or that its largest industrial enterprises were much larger in 1913, and especially in 1929, than they had been in 1880 or 1890. However, in part because no truly giant enterprise emerged in France in this period—no equivalent of U.S. Steel, Standard Oil, Ford Motors, or IG Farben—French business historians have been reluctant to apply the concept of "the rise of big business" or Chandler's analytical framework to the French case. For example, a recent collaborative history of French industry pointedly avoided any reference to Chandler and to big business in its discussion of the early twentieth century.[3] On the other hand, in his book *Big Business: The*

European Experience in the Twentieth Century (1997), Youssef Cassis did acknowledge that some French firms had become big businesses by 1929, although not as many as in Germany or Britain. Using a high threshold for what qualified as big business (10,000 employees or £2 million in paid-in capital in 1907, £3 million in 1929), Cassis identified thirty-four French big businesses in 1907 and 50 in 1929. Most of these, however, were non-manufacturing companies in "old" sectors of the economy such as banking, insurance, shipping, and coal mining. Only thirteen firms on his 1910 list and twenty firms on his 1929 list were in industries associated with the Second Industrial Revolution, and none of these possessed the sheer size or organizational complexity of the great American corporations. For this and other reasons, Cassis discounted the applicability of the Chandlerian paradigm to the study of big business in France and Europe.[4]

The argument here, however, is that French business was developing more along the lines of American (and German and British) business in the early twentieth centuries than is usually recognized and that—notwithstanding the criticisms of Cassis and others—the Chandlerian paradigm is relevant to describing and explaining that development. It is true that most of France's largest enterprises in the early twentieth century continued to be found in non-manufacturing sectors (such as banking, transportation, and mining). It is also true that, within the manufacturing sector, France lacked the giant firms found in the United States and Germany. Yet, as we will see below, France participated in most of the technological advances of the Second Industrial Revolution, and, in those sectors of the economy most closely associated with the Second Industrial Revolution, large French firms emerged in the early 1900s that were behaving like Chandlerian firms elsewhere—investing in new technology, moving from personal management to professional management, and in general developing the organizational capabilities that enabled them to capture and preserve dominant positions in their respective industries. Specifically, these firms clustered in two mature industries that underwent significant technological and structural change in the early twentieth century—steel and chemicals—and in five more or less new industries born of the Second Industrial Revolution: electricals, aluminum, automobiles, tire and rubber, and petroleum. Together these industries accounted for thirty-seven of France's fifty largest manufacturing firms by 1936 (see Table 2).[5]

The chapters that follow do not attempt to describe the development of all sectors of French industry in the early twentieth century, inas-

Table 2. France's fifty largest manufacturing firms, 1936

Rank	Product group	Assets[a]
	Food and Kindred Products	
43	Société des Raffineries et Sucrières Say	355
	Textile Mill Products	
21	Gillet-Thaon	552
37	Saint-Frères	402
41	Compagnie Générale des Industries Textiles	361
50	Dollfus-Mieg et Cie	319
	Chemicals and Allied Products	
4	Pechiney	1,151
11	Etablissements Kuhlmann	887
20	Ugine	566
25	Air Liquide	496
36	Rhône-Poulenc	407
	Petroleum and Coal Products	
3	Standard Française des Pétroles	1,317
8	Compagnie Française des Pétroles	1,023
17	Société Française Industrielle et Commerciale des Pétroles	632
23	Société Générale des Huiles et Pétroles	528
28	Raffinerie de Pétrole du Nord	450
35	Compagnie des Produits Chimiques et Raffineries de Berre	410
40	Compagnie Industrielle des Pétroles	375
	Rubber and Plastic Products	
7	Etablissements Michelin	1,037
39	Société de Pneumatiques Dunlop	376
	Stone, Clay, and Glass	
2	Saint-Gobain	1,432
49	Poliet et Chausson	321
	Primary Metal Products	
1	Wendel et Cie	1,492
6	Aciéries de Longwy	1,043
13	Schneider et Cie	710
14	Marine-Homécourt	707[b]
15	Forges et Aciéries du Nord et de l'Est	659
24	Denain et Anzin	522
27	Escaut et Meuse	484
29	Hauts-Fourneaux de la Chiers	442
30	Aciéries de Micheville	439
31	Société Lorraine des Aciéries de Rombas	438
32	Aciéries et Forges de Firminy	435
33	U.C.P.M.I.	417

Table 2. (continued)

Rank	Product group	Assets[a]
38	Société Métallurgique de Senelle-Maubeuge	399
42	Compagnie Générale Electro-Métallurgique	357
44	Hauts-Fourneaux et Fonderies de Pont à Mousson	350[b]
48	Louvroil-Montbard-Aulnoye	323
	Industrial Machinery and Equipment	
46	Société Alsacienne de Constructions Mécaniques	338
	Electrical Equipment	
12	Compagnie Générale d'Electricité	857[b]
16	Tréfileries et Laminoirs du Havre	644
18	Alsthom	576
34	Ateliers de Constructions Electriques de Jeumont	416
47	Thomson-Houston	326
	Transportation Equipment	
5	Penhoët	1,083
9	S.A. André Citroën	1,011
10	S.A. Usines de Renault	1,000?
19	Ateliers et Chantiers de la Loire	568
21	Forges et Chantiers de la Méditerranée	552
26	S.A. Peugeot	488
44	Compagnie Industrielle Maritime	350

Source: Adapted with corrections from Bruce Kogut, "Evolution of the Large Firm in France in Comparative Perspective," *Entreprises et Histoire* 19 (October 1998): 136–148.

a. Assets in millions of francs.

b. Assets in 1930.

much as many of these remained in 1930 what they had been in 1900 in terms of industry structure and in terms of the identity of the dominant firms. Rather, the chapters in Part III focus on the leading industries of the Second Industrial Revolution as enumerated above, which proved to be not only the most expansive French industries in 1900–1930 but also the key industries for France's subsequent industrial development. Each of the next four chapters traces the evolution of one or more of these industries, emphasizing the leading firms. A final chapter considers the degree to which the structures and practices of managerial capitalism were taking root in these industries and throughout French business in the early 1900s. At that point, it should be apparent that France was not the odd man out in the development of modern business but rather was moving, as were other advanced nations, toward an economy dominated by large industrial corporations run by professional managers. It should also be apparent that, despite all of its deficiencies and problems, France by the 1930s had already gone a long way toward assembling the roster of large dynamic firms that would serve as the vehicles for the country's economic resurgence—and its achievement of economic parity with Great Britain and Germany—in the second half of the twentieth century. Indeed, France's postwar boom—"les trentes glorieuses"—would not have happened without the prior emergence of large industrial firms possessing the technological competencies and organizational capabilities necessary for high-speed growth, a point we shall return to in the Conclusion.

CHAPTER TWELVE

Big Steel

Between 1880 and 1914, steel emerged as the material-of-choice for hundreds of products and applications, the result of myriad improvements in production technology that allowed an ever-increasing variety of steels to be produced in ever-larger quantities at progressively lower costs. Although the Americans and Germans led the way in the mass production of steel, the French also participated, despite losing the lion's share of one of the world's richest ironfields (in Lorraine) in 1871 just before it became possible to utilize its highly phosphoric ore in making steel. French steel output rose twelvefold between 1880 and 1913, from 389,000 tons to 4,687,000 tons, which kept France in fourth place among the world's steel producers, behind the United States, Germany, and Great Britain, and slightly ahead of Russia, whose steel production was advancing rapidly in the early 1900s thanks in no small part to the efforts of French entrepreneurs and engineers (many of Russia's largest steel companies were de facto subsidiaries of French companies).[1]

By the early twentieth century, the French steel industry consisted of scores of firms manufacturing a wide array of products. The two dozen largest steel firms (see Table 3) were among the one hundred largest industrial firms in France, and, like their counterparts in the United States and Germany, they were classic Chandlerian firms that mass-produced standardized products, were vertically integrated (especially backward into the production of their raw materials), and were organizationally complex, with multiple operating units overseen by a hierarchy of professional managers. The steel industry is thus a good place to begin our inquiry into the rise of big business in France.

This chapter traces the development of the largest French steel companies in the context of the broader evolution of ferrous metallurgy in France from the 1870s to 1920s. It first looks at the transformation between 1870 and 1914 of what had already been a mature industry by European standards in 1870. It then examines the impact of World War I and the rebuilding and reorganization of the industry in the 1920s, and it concludes by taking stock of the position of the French steel industry and the most important French steel companies on the eve of the Great Depression.

Table 3. The twenty-five largest French iron and steel firms in 1913

Rank	Firm	Assets (in millions of francs)
1	Marine-Homécourt	120.7
2	Schneider (Le Creusot)	110.0
3	Wendel et Cie	100.0?
4	Aciéries de Longwy	96.0
5	Aciéries de Micheville	89.5
6	Aciéries de France	82.5
7	Châtillon, Commentry, et Neuves Maisons	82.4
8	Denain-Anzin	64.1
9	Forges et Aciéries du Nord et de l'Est	61.2
10	Usines Métallurgiques de la Basse-Loire	57.7
11	Commentry, Fourchambault, et Decazeville	53.3
12	Aciéries et Forges de Firminy	46.5
13	Hauts-Fourneaux et Aciéries de Caen	45.5
14	Hauts-Fourneaux et Fonderies de Pont à Mousson	43.2
15	Société Métallurgique de Senelle-Maubeuge	37.6
16	Hauts-Fourneaux, Forges, et Aciéries de Pompey	31.6
17	Usines de l'Espérance à Louvroil	30.3
18	Hauts-Fourneaux de Saulnes, Marc Raty et Cie	29.9
19	Mines, Fonderies, et Forges d'Alais	25.6
20	J. J. Carnaud et Forges de Basse-Indre	23.2
21	Société Générale des Cirages Françaises	20.1
22	Société Métallurgique d'Aubrives et Villerupt	19.1
23	Société Jacob Holtzer	18.0?
24	Forges et Fonderies de Montataire	17.9
25	Escaut-Meuse	17.2

Source: Michael S. Smith, "Putting France in the Chandlerian Framework: France's 100 Largest Industrial Firms in 1913," *Business History Review* 72 (Spring 1998): 57.

The Remaking of French Iron and Steel, 1870s–1914

As we saw in Chapter 6, the production of iron and steel in France developed rapidly in the middle decades of the nineteenth century in response to the growing demand for rails and railroad equipment, steam engines and other machinery, structural iron and steel, and military and naval hardware. With growth came a certain degree of concentration, so that by the 1870s the industry was dominated by a dozen firms that were among the largest manufacturing firms in France and continental Europe.[2] These were the firms that had successfully implemented the English methods of smelting and refining iron with coal and coke in the 1830s and 1840s and then had moved on to the next new technology, the mass production of crude steel with Bessemer converters and Siemens-Martin furnaces, in the 1860s and 1870s.

The rapid evolution of metallurgical technology continued and even accelerated from the 1870s to the early twentieth century, as the size and nature of world demand for metals underwent profound changes. The completion of the basic rail systems of France and Europe in the 1870s ended the boom market for rails and railroad equipment, except for the brief revival in France in 1878–1882 occasioned by state-sponsored building of feeder lines under the Freycinet Plan. What followed was a twenty-year decline in iron and steel prices that put enormous pressure on firms to cut costs in order to survive and forced into bankruptcy those firms that could not do so. The depression also prompted firms to seek out products and markets less subject to price competition, such as the rising government market for steel armaments and munitions. In the 1890s, the slump finally ended as various developments conspired to raise the demand for steel and ushered in a new twenty-year boom for metallurgy. These included an accelerating Europe-wide arms race, the expansion of merchant fleets (by then made up mostly of steel-hulled steamships), the growing use of iron and steel in construction, the railroads' need to replace worn-out rails and equipment, and the rise of the automobile industry. At the same time, technological change was altering where and how steelmakers would meet this new demand.

The new iron and steel companies of the early nineteenth century had located mainly on or near the iron- and coalfields of the Massif Central or on the coalfields of the Nord. The introduction of the Bessemer process—which required very pure iron ore found in northern

Spain, the Mediterranean, and North Africa—precipitated a migration of steelworks to the coast in the 1860s. This migration was still in progress in the 1880s when the Thomas-Gilchrist process again revolutionized steelmaking technology.

In 1878, two British tinkerers, Sidney Thomas and his cousin Percy Gilchrist, patented improvements in the Bessemer converter that involved the use of a basic lining and basic flux, which for the first time allowed steel to be made from the highly phosphoric *minette* iron ore found in continental Europe, most notably in Lorraine. In 1879, Henri Schneider purchased an exclusive license to employ the Thomas process in France and set up production of basic steel on a limited scale at Le Creusot. He also entered into a joint venture with Henri de Wendel to set up Thomas production in French Lorraine, where it would have the greatest impact. The result was the new steelworks of Wendel et Cie at Joeuf (Meurthe-et-Moselle) that went on line in 1882. Schneider and Wendel also agreed to sublicense a second Thomas steelworks in the Meurthe-et-Moselle, the Aciéries de Longwy, and another Thomas works was set up at Trith near Valenciennes by the Aciéries du Nord et de l'Est, probably under license from the Belgian license holder.[3] Thomas production was thus initially limited to just four locations—Le Creusot, Joeuf, Longwy, and Trith—and had no wider application in France until the patent fell into the public domain in 1893. Then, however, came a veritable explosion of new investment in basic steel production in French Lorraine as local ironmakers integrated forward into steel production and as established steel companies from elsewhere in France tapped into the cheap and abundant *minette* ore of Lorraine. This boom continued into the 1900s with the opening of the even richer ironfield of the Briey basin and the proliferation of new plants to produce not only standard forms of basic steel but also specialty products such as iron pipes and steel tubes. By 1913 all this had brought about one of the most fateful developments in the history of French metallurgy, the concentration of the country's pig iron and steel production in the department of the Meurthe-et-Moselle.[4]

From the perspective of the rise of big business in France, the most significant result of the expansion and transformation of the steel industry was the emergence of a new oligopoly of large firms that, like the reigning oligopoly in iron and steel in 1870, were among the largest industrial enterprises in France (indeed, six of the ten largest publicly held manufacturing enterprises in France in 1913—and thirty of the largest one hundred—were in ferrous metallurgy).[5] As one would expect in an age of rapid economic growth, the largest members of the new oligopoly were substantially bigger than those of the 1870 oligopoly, perhaps by a factor of five.[6] They were also organizationally more complex and represented a wider range of specialties. To be more precise, the twenty-five or thirty largest iron and steel companies in France on the eve of World War I fell into three categories:

1. new joint-stock firms founded to commercialize new technology, especially the Thomas process, using new and cheaper sources of raw materials (iron ore, coal, and coke) with the goal of supplanting the older, less well-positioned iron and steel companies as the low-cost producers of standard forms of steel (rails, girders, bars, sheet, plate, and wire)

2. established firms—including those that were among the largest in France in the 1870s—that adopted new technology and relocated their plants to gain access to cheaper raw materials in order to preserve their dominant position in the production of generic forms of steel, or that alternatively specialized in higher-value forms of steel (such as alloy steel for armor plate) that were less subject to price competition from the new general producers

3. both old and new firms that pursued niche strategies—turning out specialties such as iron pipe, steel tubing, and tinplate on a scale sufficient to put them in the ranks of the largest metallurgical firms in France

The remainder of this section examines these three groups of large firms more closely.

The New Firms

Among the companies founded after 1870 that rose to the ranks of the largest metallurgical enterprises in France by 1913 were three that produced acidic Bessemer or Siemens-Martin steel at coastal locations using imported iron ore and/or coal. Foremost of these was the Société Anonyme des Aciéries de France, founded in 1881 during the brief boom in railroad construction engendered by the Freycinet Plan. This company rolled rails from Bessemer steel that it made at Isbergues (Pas-de-Calais) using local coal and Spanish and Swedish iron ore. Despite the collapse of demand for steel rails in the mid-1880s, the Aciéries de France stuck with rail production until the mid-1890s, when it started to diversify into other standard shapes and added a Siemens-Martin furnace to support high-quality steel castings. In 1905, the company decided to move into Thomas steel production, which necessitated geographical expansion and backward integration. Over the next eight years it acquired iron mines in the Orne and the Meurthe-et-Moselle and a coal mine in the Pas-de-Calais; it set up Siemens-Martin production at plants in Paris to make structural steel from scrap iron; and it acquired a huge new smelting plant near Calais through its takeover of the Aciéries de Sambre-et-Meuse. By 1913, Aciéries de France ranked as the sixth largest steel company in France in terms of assets.[7]

Two other coastal enterprises ranked among France's largest steel companies in 1913, at least on paper. The Usines Métallurgiques de la Basse-Loire traced its origins to the founding in 1879 of a steel mill at Trignac near the mouth of the Loire River to make steel rails using local iron ore and imported coal. Because the local ore proved to be unsuitable for Bessemer steel, Trignac struggled to stay in business using more expensive imported ore through the 1880s and 1890s. Eventually, it was taken over by a new company, the Société des Usines Métallurgiques de la Basse-Loire. By securing new supplies of ore in Spain and Normandy, by setting up efficient new coke furnaces and a new 250-ton-per-day iron smelter, and by adding a new Siemens-Martin steelworks and electrically powered rolling mills, Basse-Loire effected a striking turnaround in Trignac's fortunes. Whereas Trignac had produced only 70,000 tons of pig iron and 80,000 tons of steel in 1900, Basse-Loire turned out 135,000 tons of pig iron and the same amount of steel in 1913.[8]

That same year saw the beginning of construction of what promised to be France's largest, most productive coastal steelworks ever, to be built all at once on a site near Caen in lower Normandy. The project was the brainchild of the great German steel magnate, August Thyssen, who set out in 1910 to acquire iron mines in Normandy to feed his ever-hungry blast furnaces in the Ruhr. However, in order to obtain the French government's permission to build railroads from the iron mine to a new port at Colombelles (whence the ore would go by ship to Germany), Thyssen had to agree to convert 60 percent of the projected 1 million tons of iron ore to be mined annually into steel on French soil. The upshot was the founding of the Hauts-Fourneaux et

Aciéries de Caen as a joint venture of Thyssen and the Société Française des Constructions Mécaniques (Anciens Etablissements Cail). By 1913, the new company had raised 30 million francs in capital and assembled book assets worth 45 million francs, making it, on paper, the thirteenth largest steel company in France. However, production was not scheduled to begin until 1915, and the outbreak of war with Germany in 1914 put the entire project on hold. Future control of the property became embroiled in wartime politics and was only settled, in favor of the Schneiders, in the early 1920s. Not until the late 1920s did the Caen complex finally fulfill its early promise by emerging as one of France's most important centers of steel production.[9]

More typical of the new steel firms that appeared after 1870—and more important for the long-term development of French metallurgy— were the firms founded in French Lorraine by local ironmasters to undertake the mass production of steel using the Thomas process. These included the Wendels' new steelworks at Joeuf and the Aciéries de Longwy plus Micheville, Pompey, and Senelle-Maubeuge. All of these were created not only in response to the appearance of new steelmaking technology but also in response to the bifurcation of the Lorraine ironfield that resulted from the annexation of the department of the Moselle and part of the department of the Meurthe by the new German Empire in 1871.

The German chancellor Otto von Bismarck probably never sought to annex the entire Lorraine ironfield, even as it was imperfectly known in 1871. Certainly he did not countenance annexing the northern and southern extremities of the field—around Longwy and Nancy, respectively—that already supported significant iron production in 1870. It was only in response to the push by the French president, Thiers, to retain the fortress city of Belfort that Bismarck—late in the peace negotiations in Frankfurt in March 1871—demanded that the new border in the region between Thionville and Metz, in the center of the ironfield, be moved sufficiently westward to put on German soil the two largest ironworks in the province, the Hayange and Moyeuvre works of the Wendels.[10] Still, intended or accidental, Germany ended up in possession of most of the known iron deposits in Lorraine as well as most of the existing iron and pig iron production,[11] and the leading German ironmakers wasted little time in colonizing the ironfield, especially after the advent of the Thomas process made it clear that Lorraine ore would provide the basis of a world-class steel industry.

The only French firm to survive as a large independent producer in annexed Lorraine in the face of the invasion of the German iron companies after 1871 was Wendel et Cie. The transfer of the Wendel properties to Germany came only months after the death of Charles de Wendel had put his eighty-six-year-old mother, Madame François de Wendel, again in charge of the family firm (she had first run the firm after the death of her husband in 1825). In December 1871, to assure the survival of the firm in uncertain circumstances, Madame de Wendel converted what had previously been a simple proprietorship into a *société en commandite*, Les Petits-fils de François de Wendel et Cie, with her nine grandchildren as shareholders and with three of those, Henri and Robert de Wendel and Théodore de Gargan II, as *gérants*. Under the leadership of Henri de Wendel, who accepted German citizenship and served as on-site director, Hayange and Moyeuvre limped along through the 1870s, profitless, cut off from their former markets in France, struggling to adjust their operations to a new political and economic regime.

All this changed, however, in 1879 when Henri de Wendel, having decided to gamble the future of his company on basic steel, agreed to pay the German licensee 1 million reichsmarks over ten years for the right to use the Thomas process. Emptying the family coffers, he then proceeded to construct a state-of-the-art steelworks at Hayange and to redirect the entire enterprise toward the mass production of rails and other standard forms of steel. The gamble worked. Within two years of its opening in 1881, the Hayange steelworks had reaped sufficient profits to pay off the entire fee for the Thomas license.[12] By 1913, the output of the Wendel plants at Hayange and Moyeuvre had risen to 847,000 tons of pig iron and 661,000 ton of steel, making Wendel the largest iron and steel producer in German Lorraine and one of the largest in the whole German Empire.[13]

Meanwhile, in order to give the Wendels a continuing foothold in France and to preserve their entrée into the French market, the firm's three directors started laying plans soon after the annexation for a new iron mine and ironworks at Joeuf, upstream on the Orne River from Moyeuvre and just on the French side of the new border. However, before these plans could be executed, the Thomas process appeared, and the Wendel directors decided to totally recast Joeuf to produce Thomas steel instead of iron. To do this, a new French *commandite*, Wendel et Cie, was launched in 1880 as a joint venture of Les Petits-fils de François de Wendel and Schneider et Cie, the French license holder for the Thomas process. According to Claude Beaud, this firm was originally to be owned and controlled equally by the two partners, but Eugène Schneider was reluctant to invest heavily in an operation with such an exposed border location and ended up taking only a minority position, which gave effective control of the new firm to the Wendels. In any case, the first blast furnace was lit at Joeuf in 1882, and steel production began the following year. Thereafter, production increased steadily, first under the direction of Théodore de Gargan and after 1902 under the three sons of Henri de Wendel (François, Maurice, and Humbert). In 1913, Joeuf produced 393,000 tons of pig iron and 340,000 of steel, which made Wendel et Cie France's largest producer of pig iron and third largest producer of steel after Marine-Homécourt and the Aciéries de Longwy.[14]

The second largest of the new Lorraine iron and steel companies, and the only other firm licensed to make Thomas steel in the Meurthe-et-Moselle before the patent expired in 1893, was the Aciéries de Longwy, founded in 1881 by the leading ironmasters of the town of Longwy, located at the northern end of the Lorraine ironfield near the border with Belgium and Luxembourg. The two men who took the initiative in launching the company were Joseph Labbé and Baron Oscar d'Adelsward. They had previously collaborated in setting up the Comptoir de Longwy and viewed the new venture as simply another way to provide a profitable outlet for the pig iron they produced at Mont-Saint-Martin and Prieuré near Longwy.

The Aciéries de Longwy got off to a slow start because of technical problems and because of the downturn in demand for rails, the chief product of all the early Thomas steelworks, in the mid-eighties. To diversify its product line beyond rails, the company added wire and sheet metal production in 1887, but this did not immediately lead to profitability. To turn the company around, the directors brought in Alexandre Dreux as general manager in 1888. The orphaned son of a poor farmer in the Sarthe, Dreux had started as a clerk at a Le Mans foundry and then worked as an accountant for Armand Chappée, another Le Mans foundry owner who was setting up blast furnaces at Redon in Brittany. It was on Chappée's recommendation that Labbé and Adelsward hired Dreux in 1876 as the first executive director of the Comptoir de Longwy, a position he filled brilliantly.

In taking over as manager of the Aciéries de Longwy in 1888, Dreux immediately instituted cost-cutting measures and secured a large rail contract for the firm. As a result, the company moved quickly from the red to the black, earning a profit in 1888–1889 of 471,000 francs, which then increased sixfold to over 3 million francs by 1892.[15] In the period of the most rapid growth of the Lorraine steel industry, 1893–1913, Dreux steadily increased the physical plant of Longwy, setting up new blast furnaces to supply molten pig iron directly to six basic Bessemer converters at Mont-Saint-Martin and adding Siemens-Martin furnaces for special steels and mills to roll steel in a variety of forms and shapes. By 1913, Longwy employed some 7,000 workers to turn out 390,000 tons of pig iron and 345,000 tons of steel, which put it in third place among French pig iron producers and second place in steel. Dreux, it should be noted, continued at the helm of the Aciéries de Longwy until his retirement in 1919 and then returned for another ten years after the premature death of his son and successor, Edouard, in 1923. Over his forty-five years at Longwy, Dreux became one of the most powerful and respected figures in the French steel industry and came to personify the growing importance of professional managers in large-scale industry in France.[16]

Three other companies were set up to produce basic steel in the Meurthe-et-Moselle in the waning years of the nineteenth century, after the Thomas patents expired: the Aciéries de Micheville, Senelle-Maubeuge, and the Hauts-Fourneaux, Forges, et Aciéries de Pompey. The Aciéries de Micheville developed along lines similar to Longwy's but on a somewhat smaller scale because of its later start. Like Longwy, it was founded by local forgemasters to provide an outlet for their pig iron production, and like Longwy it was long directed by a professional manager brought in from the outside, Ernest Nahan. Senelle-Maubeuge had its origins in the Société Métallurgique de Senelle, a pig iron smelting firm owned by the Huart brothers, who were also founding partners in the Aciéries de Longwy. It became Senelle-Maubeuge in 1902 when it merged with the Hauts-Fourneaux de Maubeuge, and it moved into the production of Thomas steel in 1910.[17]

Whereas Longwy and Micheville were situated at the northern end of the Lorraine ironfield and Joeuf in the center, the fourth new Lorraine steel company was located to the south at Pompey, near the confluence of the Meurthe and Moselle rivers. The company had its beginnings in the ironworks founded at Ars-sur-Moselle near Metz in 1836 by Jewish timber and coal merchants, Auguste and Mayer Dupont and Adolphe Isaac Dreyfus. With the German annexation of the Moselle in 1871, Mayer Dupont and Dreyfus decided to move their entire operation south to Pompey, where they secured the concession for a new iron mine. Soon thereafter, control of the firm passed to

Alphonse Fould, scion of the renowned family of Jewish merchants and financiers, who had met and married Mayer Dupont's daughter while serving as an artillery officer at Metz. In the 1880s, Fould began moving the firm into new technologies and products, starting with a Siemens-Martin furnace in 1884. In 1895, he made the leap into Thomas steel production and converted Pompey into a joint-stock company in order to raise the capital needed to acquire iron mines in the Briey basin and to support the new scale of operations. By 1913, when Alphonse Fould died and was succeeded by his son René, Pompey was producing 175,000 tons of pig iron and 160,000 tons of steel annually.[18]

The last of the new companies that rose to national prominence producing Thomas steel had one foot in Lorraine and one foot in the Nord, a fact that was reflected in its name, the Forges et Aciéries du Nord et de l'Est (Nord-Est for short). The company's origins lay in the enterprises of the Leclerqs, a family of hardware manufacturers who had founded one of France's first *forges anglaises* at Trith-Saint-Léger near Valenciennes in the 1820s and who later acquired an iron mine and set up two blast furnaces at Jarville near Nancy. In 1881, the Leclerq company merged with a Jarville pig iron company and became the S.A. des Forges et Aciéries du Nord et de l'Est. The new firm was the handiwork not of the Leclerqs but of the Banque de Paris et des Pays-Bas (the first shareholders' meeting of Nord-Est took place at the Paribas offices in Paris, and its corporate headquarters remained at that address until 1903).[19] Under the tutelage of Paribas, Nord-Est entered basic steel production in 1882 by setting up a Thomas steel mill at Trith, the first in the Nord and only the fourth in France after Le Creusot, Joeuf, and Longwy. Although it continued to smelt pig iron at Jarville in the Meurthe-et-Moselle, Nord-Est increasingly centered its operations at Trith where, between 1906 and 1913, it constructed a new German-style integrated steelworks. In 1913, its "best year ever,"[20] the company produced around 250,000 tons of steel, well below the level of the great steel companies of Lorraine but second among the iron and steel companies of the Nord behind Denain-Anzin.[21]

The Survival of Established Firms

Alongside the newcomers on the list of the largest steel and iron companies in 1913 were a number of firms founded in the early and mid-1800s that managed to survive—and even thrive—in the new circumstances at the end of the nineteenth and beginning of the twentieth centuries. Among these were Denain-Anzin, Commentry-Fourchambault, Marine, Le Creusot, Châtillon-Commentry, and Firminy.

The survival of these firms was by no means preordained. The competitive pressures during the depression of 1876–1896, coupled with the advent of basic steel and the rise of Lorraine, led to the demise of several of the leading firms of the 1860s that could not, or would not, change with the times. By far the most important of these was Terrenoire, still the biggest producer of steel rails in France in 1870. Terrenoire's president, Alexandre Jullien, remained committed to rail production in the Loire and Ardèche into the 1880s, eschewed relocation and retooling, and put his hopes in political solutions to shrinking demand and falling prices in the form of the Freycinet Plan and a return to protection. But the collapse of the Freycinet Plan and the renewal of the trade treaties in 1882 doomed this strategy, and by then it was too late to catch up technologically. In January 1888, Terrenoire filed for bankruptcy, and Alexandre Jullien disappeared from the ranks of France's leading forgemasters.[22]

Other established firms by no means eschewed tariff protection and other forms of government aid, but they also undertook sufficient technological modernization and other changes in their way of doing business to survive and expand in the new circumstances at the end of the century. This was true, for example, of Denain-Anzin, the largest metallurgical enterprise in the department of the Nord. Under the leadership of the founding families, especially the Nervos (the descendants of Léon Talabot), Denain-Anzin moved into Bessemer and Siemens-Martin steel production in the early 1870s and assured its access to hematite ore by taking control of a Spanish iron mine in 1878; but it largely abstained from further investment during the depression years of the 1880s. However, in 1896 Robert de Nervo acceded to the chairmanship and set out to revitalize the firm. Nervo renovated the company's blast furnaces and secured increased supplies of lower-cost coal by acquiring the Azincourt Mining Company, which laid the foundation for the installation of one of the largest and most efficient Thomas steel mills in France in the early 1900s. By 1913, Denain-Anzin was turning out 335,000 tons of pig iron and a comparable amount of steel each year, which made it the fifth largest steel producer in France and the largest outside the Meurthe-et-Moselle.[23]

More surprising than the survival of Denain-Anzin was the comeback staged by another old-line iron company, Commentry-

Fourchambault, at the end of the nineteenth century. As we saw in Chapter 6, the company's longtime director-general, Stephane Mony, did not invest in the new steel technology in the 1860s and concentrated on selling coal. In 1879 the company belatedly installed three Siemens-Martin furnaces at Imphy and upgraded its blast furnaces at Fourchambault, but these efforts failed to stem the company's decline inasmuch as the aging Mony was still committed to mining coal at increasing costs at the by-then depleted Commentry mine (only the herculean efforts of the mine's young manager, Henri Fayol, kept it producing at all). Such was Commentry-Fourchambault's financial condition that, when Mony finally died in 1884, the board of directors voted to install Fayol as *directeur-général* only long enough to liquidate the enterprise in an orderly fashion with as little loss to the shareholders as possible. But, as described by Donald Reid, Fayol had other plans.[24]

Instead of simply liquidating Commentry-Fourchambault as instructed, Fayol set out to reinvent it by closing obsolete facilities, upgrading viable ones, and above all by committing the company to developing steel production at a new site in the South. In 1892, Fayol acquired the Decazeville Company in the Aveyron, which, like Commentry-Fourchambault, had principally been in the coal business since the introduction of Bessemer steel in the 1860s. In the course of the nineties, Decazeville was refurbished and relaunched as an integrated steelworks on the basis of new technology that enabled the company's blast furnaces to remove sulfur from local iron ore and to produce a high-quality pig iron, which was then refined in Siemens-Martin furnaces into a steel that, in the words of one expert, "left nothing to be desired from the standpoint of quality."[25] By 1913, Commentry-Fourchambault-Decazeville was producing almost 107,000 tons of iron and steel. Just as important, in partnership with the Lens Coal Company, it was in the process of launching the Société Métallurgique de Pont à Vendin to build and operate a much larger state-of-the-art steelworks in the Pas-de-Calais.[26]

While Commentry-Fourchambault-Decazeville survived by abandoning its original sites of production in the Center, four Loire steelmakers survived *in situ* by producing high-quality specialty steels for machinery and armaments. Marrel Frères operated five Siemens-Martin furnaces at Rive-de-Gier to produce steel for armor plate and for the cannon barrels, drive shafts, and other large pieces forged by the company's seven steam hammers. Similar equipment was used to turn out a similar array of products by the Fonderies, Forges, et Aciéries de Saint-Etienne. Holtzer et Cie of Unieux continued to specialize in the highest-quality crucible steel (as of 1913, Holtzer operated 330 crucibles, as many as all other French steel companies combined). Holtzer introduced the first steel alloy, chrome steel, in the 1870s, and it subsequently developed other alloys (nickel steel, tungsten steel) used in the manufacture of armor plate, armor-piercing projectiles, internal combustion engines, and other automobile components. The Aciéries et Forges de Firminy also moved into the manufacture of cannon, projectiles, and armor plate in the 1880s and became a leading maker of steel wire as well. At the turn of the century, Firminy operated the only blast furnace left in the Loire, plus five Siemens-Martin furnaces and 108 crucibles (second only to Holtzer), turning out 16,000–17,000 tons of various steel products annually. At the same time, it developed interests outside the Loire, participating in the founding and operation of the Huta-Bankowa steelworks in Poland in the 1880s and launching a steelworks at Dunes near Dunkirk in 1913 to produce steel and forge large pieces with the cheaper coal from the Pas-de-Calais.[27]

Of all the pre-1870 French iron and steel companies that still ranked among France's largest metallurgical enterprises in the early twentieth century, the largest and most organizationally complex were Marine-Homécourt, Le Creusot, and Châtillon-Commentry. All three moved beyond their original bases of operation in central France after 1870 and became geographically diversified, multiplant companies. Like the newer steel companies of Lorraine and the Nord, all three pursued vertical integration by mining iron ore and coal, smelting pig iron and refining it into crude steel (using both acidic and basic Bessemer converters), and then rolling the steel into standard shapes. Moreover, like the specialized steel companies of the Loire, they also produced the higher grades of steel and forged machine parts, armor plate, projectiles, and weapons components. Indeed, all three eventually went beyond making weapons components to manufacturing complete weapons systems for armies in Europe, Asia, and Latin America. And, as we have already seen in Chapter 7, Le Creusot took diversification even further, producing locomotives, steamboats (and later warships), bridge components, and all manner of heavy machinery, making it the only French iron and steel company that was also a major player in the engineering and construction industry.[28]

As we saw in Chapter 6, the Compagnie des Hauts-Fourneaux, Forges, et Aciéries de la Marine et des Chemins de Fer had become France's biggest metallurgical firm by 1860, only six years after its founding. Fifty years later, as Marine-Homécourt, it was again ranked number one. But its path from the first summit to the second was a circuitous one, and along the way the Marine Steel Company came perilously close to succumbing to the same forces and circumstances that destroyed Terrenoire and other leading firms of the 1860s. Only by reinventing itself twice—first in the 1870s and again in the early 1900s—did it survive to enjoy the growth and prosperity of the pre–World War I decade.

In the 1860s, the co-directors of Marine Steel, Petin and Gaudet, committed the company not only to the production of Bessemer steel but also to complete vertical integration, from iron and coal mining to the fabrication of various finished products. But nothing they tried quite worked out. Their fundamental mistake was to locate their Bessemer converters in the Loire at too great a distance from their old pig iron smelters at Toga (Corsica) and from their new pig iron smelters at Givors. In a desperate attempt to salvage their strategy, Petin and Gaudet moved their Bessemer production from Assailly to Givors in 1869, but it was too little too late. By 1871, their investment and expansion program "had almost completely failed for lack of proper [preliminary] studies." In that year, the stockholders ousted Petin and Gaudet and reorganized the company as a *société anonyme* under Guillaume Denière (president of the Société Générale). To carry out a thorough reorganization of the company's steel production, Denière brought in Adrien de Montgolfier as *directeur-général* in 1874.[29]

A member of the great paper-making family of the Ardèche, Adrien de Montgolfier had no previous experience in the steel industry, having served since 1856 as the state engineer for the department of the Loire and since 1871 as one of the department's representatives in the National Assembly. He nonetheless set out to rationalize Marine's specialty steel production and to reconceive and relaunch its failed initiative in Bessemer production. To handle the latter, Montgolfier hired Claudius Magnin, one of France's leading metallurgical engineers, who had launched the Bessemer steel production of the Terrenoire Company. Realizing that transportation costs made it impossible to produce Bessemer steel efficiently at Givors, Magnin decided to transfer this production to a new site, at Boucau near Bayonne on the Atlantic coast, where English coal and Spanish hematite ore could be brought together to produce high-quality steel at low cost. The Boucau plant opened in 1881 and was operating at full capacity by 1887; Givors was sold off in 1886.

Boucau gave Marine the means to remain competitive in the production of rails and other standard forms of steel and also provided a stable supply of high-grade pig iron for the company's crucible and Siemens-Martin steelworks in the Loire. The latter in turn supported the production of springs, wheels, and other parts for locomotives and railroad cars, the forging of drive shafts and other components for marine steam engines, and most importantly the manufacture of war matériel. Marine had pioneered the production of armor plate for France's first ironclad warships in the 1850s, and in the ensuing decades it had continued to make steel turrets for warships and shore batteries, and steel barrels and other components for the naval guns and field artillery assembled in state arsenals. In 1885, when French law was amended to allow private companies to manufacture complete weapons systems for export, Marine committed even more of its resources to military and naval production. In competition with Le Creusot, Châtillon-Commentry, and the crucible steelmakers of the Loire, it developed new steel alloys for armor and armor-piercing shells, and in the early 1890s it became the French licensee of the Harvey process for hardening steel armor. Overall, the combination of specialty steel production and sophisticated forge work in the Loire, much of it for the arms trade, and the mass production of pig iron and ordinary steel at Boucau kept Marine Steel reasonably profitable in spite of slack demand and declining prices in the 1880s and early 1890s.

By the mid-nineties, however, rapidly increasing competition at the low end of the steel market threatened to undermine the company's position. The expiration of the Thomas patent in 1893 set off a rush into Thomas steel production in Lorraine, and Montgolfier and Magnin decided that Marine, too, needed to be producing Thomas steel there. Their chance came in 1902 when Vezin-Aulnoye, a Belgian firm long established in Lorraine, virtually bankrupted itself building a huge new Thomas steel mill at Homécourt in the Orne Valley next to the Wendel's Joeuf complex. To acquire the Homécourt plant and its associated iron mine, Marine bought Vezin-Aulnoye lock, stock, and barrel in 1903 for 19.7 million francs in cash and 10,000 shares of Marine valued at 5 million francs.

Renamed Marine-Homécourt, the company proceeded to reorganize its operations in four regional branches. The Loire branch consisted of three plants—Saint Chamond, Assailly, and Rive-de-Gier—that made specialty steels and turned them into armor plate, projectiles, and artillery pieces, plus various components for locomotives, steamships, and automobiles. The Adour (Bayonne) branch was the Boucau plant, where 1,500 workers continued to turn out pig iron and Bessemer steel that was rolled into rails and other standard shapes. The Nord branch consisted of a rolling mill inherited from Vezin-Aulnoye that produced wire and other small-scale forms of steel. Finally, there was the Lorraine branch—Homécourt—on which the company's future ultimately rested. While the Crédit Lyonnais report of 1908 dismissed Boucau as "mediocre" and judged the war matériel produced in the Loire to be inferior to that of Marine's competitors, it lauded Homécourt as a steel mill "of the first order," with the second lowest costs per ton of steel produced in the Meurthe-et-Moselle (Joeuf had the lowest costs).[30] In 1913, Homécourt turned out 436,000 tons of steel, more than any other steel mill in France, and its balance-sheet assets of 120 million francs made it the largest publicly held metallurgical firm—and the third largest publicly held manufacturing firm (after Thomson-Houston and Saint-Gobain)—in France.[31]

Châtillon-Commentry's evolution closely paralleled Marine-Homécourt's in that it retained the most efficient of its original plants in the Center while jettisoning the obsolete plants; shifted increasingly into arms production as the rail market collapsed (or became too competitive); and moved its steel production out of the Center first to a coastal site and then to Lorraine in the 1890s to utilize the Thomas process. The overall results, however, were less successful than Marine-Homécourt's. Reputed to be France's largest metallurgical firm at the end of the 1860s, Châtillon-Commentry was at best number seven by World War I. Its main achievement in an era of rapid technological change was survival.[32]

Schneider et Cie (Le Creusot) did much more than survive, but its achievements in the period from 1871 to 1913 lay less in iron and steel production than in metallurgical manufacturing and engineering and construction. Under Henri Schneider, Le Creusot moved into the production of steel with Siemens-Martins hearths and Bessemer converters in the early 1870s and poured the first basic steel in France in 1879. Schneider then joined with the Wendels to set up the first Thomas steelworks in Lorraine in 1881, but, as mentioned earlier, he maintained only a minority interest in that project and hesitated to make additional investments in steel production there.[33] Eventually, after Henri's death in 1898, his son and successor, Eugene II, acquired an iron mine in the Briey basin and a coal mine in Belgium as the first steps toward setting up a Homécourt-style steel mill in Lorraine, but that plan had yet to be realized when war broke out in 1914. So for the time being the company's steel production remained at Le Creusot. But, with the coal and iron deposits at Le Creusot played out, more and more of the raw materials for making steel had to be brought in from elsewhere at relatively high cost (the coal came from a variety of sources, including the Brassac mine in the Puy de Dôme, while the iron ore came from company-owned mines in the Dauphiné, Spain, and Morocco), and the quantity of Le Creusot's iron and steel output scarcely increased between 1878 and 1900. Although its steel output surged from 125,000 tons a year to over 200,000 tons a year in the decade before World War I, this did not prevent Le Creusot from being eclipsed by the big Lorraine steel companies, which were turning out over 300,000 tons of steel annually by 1913.

Yet one should not be misled by the picture of stagnation and relative decline conjured up by these figures. The assets of Le Creusot increased steadily from the 1870s to the 1900s, and in 1913 the company was second only to Marine-Homécourt on this score among French metallurgical companies. Indeed, it remained one of the largest, most profitable, and most powerful industrial enterprises in France and Europe on the eve of World War I, not so much because of the size of its iron and steel output but because of the quality of its products and the diversified nature of its activities.[34]

As we saw earlier, the Schneiders started building steam engines and locomotives shortly after taking control of Le Creusot in 1836, and they added structural iron and building components to their product line in the 1850s and 1860s. After 1870, the company increased its involvement in *travaux publics* with contracts to build piers for the ports of Lisbon and Bordeaux and bridges for the Gap-Briançon railroad in the French Alps. But this branch of the business really took off after 1895 when a separate public works division was created under Maurice Michel-Schmidt, an engineer who had previously directed port construction for Hersent. Under Michel-Schmidt's guidance, this division constructed bridges for the Chilean State Railway, the Alexander III Bridge in Paris, and various exposition halls for the 1900 Paris World's Fair. The company also landed an even larger contract for the expansion and modernization of the Port of Le Havre and the commission to build the new Port of Rosario in Argentina, for which Schneider and Hersent jointly created the Société du Port de Rosario. In the early 1900s, Schneider moved into electrical construction (Grenoble tramways, the Paris Metro), for which it opened a factory to make electrical equipment at Champagne-sur-Seine under license from Westinghouse.[35]

Although complete production and revenue figures for the various divisions of Schneider et Cie are not available, it is likely that revenues from iron and steel production and public works were eventually surpassed by revenues from yet another line of business, war matériel and armaments. As early as the 1850s, Schneider had joined Marine Steel in making iron plate and steam engines for France's first ironclad warships, and in 1871 it forged France's first steel cannon at the behest of President Thiers. Schneider scientists subsequently developed a superior all-steel, hammer-forged armor plate, which became the world standard (Bethlehem Steel later produced this plate for the U.S. Navy under license from Schneider). Schneider maintained its leadership in this intensely competitive market by introducing nickel steel plate in 1888 and then by forming a consortium with Marine and Châtillon-Commentry in 1893 to license the Harvey steel-hardening process after field tests demonstrated that this process produced an armor plate superior even to Le Creusot's nickel steel plate.[36]

Meanwhile, Schneider acquired the Chantiers et Ateliers de la Gironde in 1881 and began building battleships for foreign navies in Bordeaux while continuing to build torpedo boats, destroyers, and tugboats at its Chalon shipyard. With the passage of the 1885 law allowing French companies to produce artillery and other land armaments for export, Schneider began producing complete artillery pieces, not just components, at Le Creusot. In the 1890s, it introduced its 75-millimeter rapid-fire field artillery, designed by General Canet, which it manufactured in a Le Havre armaments plant recently acquired from the Forges et Chantiers de la Méditerranée. Adoption of the Schneider-Canet cannon by the Transvaal and its successful deployment in the Boer War led to a flurry of orders from governments around the world. By 1910, the company was engaged in replicating its domestic arms production in Russia through a number of subsidiaries and partnerships.[37] Overall, Schneider et Cie emerged as a leader in a wide range of cutting-edge industries, from transportation equipment to heavy construction and armaments and even electrical manufacturing between 1871 and 1914. In the process, Schneider founded an array of foreign subsidiaries that made it one of France's leading multinational corporations by World War I and put it in a position unique among the firms that constituted Big Steel in France.

The Niche Firms

By the early 1900s, nine of the ten largest metallurgical firms—and perhaps seventeen of the thirty largest—were making standard forms of steel, most of them using the Thomas basic steel process. Yet a dozen other firms attained a place in the top thirty by producing specialized forms of iron and steel for specialized markets. These included the makers of high-quality crucible and Siemens-Martin steel that we have already considered. They also included two manufacturers of iron pipe (Pont à Mousson and Aubrives-Villerupt), two makers of steel tubes (Escaut-Meuse and Montbard-Aulnoye), and two makers of tinplate and tin cans (J. J. Carnaud/Basse-Indre and Société Générale des Cirages Françaises), which will be discussed in this section. It should also be noted that the introduction of electrolysis for the refining of copper and aluminum led to the rise of a number of firms in nonferrous metallurgy that were comparable in size to the large iron and steel companies. These included the Compagnie Française des Métaux and the Société d'Electro-Métallurgie de Dives, manufacturers of copper and bronze, and three large aluminum companies, which, because of their close association with electrochemicals, will be discussed in Chapter 15. A related industry—electrical wire and cable, of which the Tréfileries et Laminoirs du Havre was the leading manufacturer—is discussed in the next chapter on the electrical industry.

The development of urban water, gas, and sewage systems plus steam heating and the large-scale refining of petroleum and chemicals created a large and growing market for cast iron pipe, plumbing fixtures, valves, pumps, and the like in the second half of the nineteenth century. This market came to be served by a number of medium-sized firms scattered across France that specialized in foundry work—*moulage de fonte en seconde fusion*—using pig iron made by others. One of these was Armand Chappée et Fils of Le Mans, where Alexandre Dreux of Longwy got his start. Chappée employed 600 workers in two plants to make a wide variety of iron pipes, plus radiators, pumps, pots and pans, motor blocks, and decorative ironwork.[38] Another group of specialists in *moulage de fonte* integrated backward into pig iron production by attaching blast furnaces to their foundries. The largest of these was the Société Métallurgique d'Aubrives et Villerupt, which produced iron pipes up to two meters in diameter that were used in water and sewer systems and in construction (160 Villerupt pipes in six-meter lengths served as columns to support the floor of the Gare des Invalides in Paris).[39] A third group of iron pipe makers consisted of large-scale smelters of pig iron that integrated forward into pipe casting. Commentry-Fourchambault, for example, had pioneered the vertical casting of iron pipe in the mid-nineteenth century and still turned out 15,000 tons of pipe of various sizes at its Montluçon plant in 1900. In the Meurthe-et-Moselle, Joseph Labbé's Société Métallurique de Gorcy cast mine-shaft casings, cylinders for rolling mills, and valves for gas, heating, and air systems, among other things. But the undisputed leader in the manufacture of iron pipe was the S.A. des Hauts-Fourneaux et Fonderies de Pont à Mousson, acclaimed by the jury at the 1900 Paris World's Fair as "the most important company in France and even in Europe in this area of *moulage de fonte.*"[40]

Pont à Mousson was founded in 1857 to produce pig iron from a recently discovered seam of high-grade iron ore near the town of Pont à Mousson in the Moselle Valley between Metz and Nancy. Under the leadership of Xavier Rogé, Pont à Mousson prospered in the late 1860s and early 1870s selling its pig iron to iron refiners like Châtillon-Commentry, but softening demand and declining prices in the mid-seventies prompted Rogé to integrate forward into the production of iron pipe using the English system of vertical pipe casting. In 1883, the company got its big break with a contract to supply water mains to the City of Paris, which sustained the company through the depression of the 1880s and early 1890s (Pont à Mousson eventually supplied 82 percent of the water pipe installed in Paris from 1883 to 1897).[41]

Rogé and his designated successor, Camille Cavallier, worked relentlessly to dominate the domestic market for iron water pipe through the 1880s, and by 1890 Pont à Mousson had achieved a remarkable 90 percent market share.[42] In the following decade, the company moved into foreign markets—first Tunisia, then Europe and Latin America. To support the production needed to serve these markets, the company integrated backward into coal and iron mining, acquiring an iron mine at Auboué in the Briey ironfield and joining with Marine and Micheville (the beginnings of the postwar MarMichPont consortium) to acquire and exploit coal mines in Belgium and Germany. With its supply of raw materials assured, Pont à Mousson rapidly increased its output of pig iron (and thus of pipe) from 88,000 tons in 1900 to 305,000 tons in 1913, which made it the fifth largest pig iron producer in France after Joeuf, Marine-Homécourt, Longwy, and Micheville.[43]

Pont à Mousson was unique among the specialized metallurgical enterprises in turn-of-the-century France in its size and its ability to dominate its market niche. Yet several other specialized iron and steel manufacturers made it into the ranks of the top thirty metallurgical firms in France by exploiting emergent technologies and by supplying new kinds of products. One of these products was steel tubing, which was in growing demand for a variety of industrial uses, such as oil refining and refrigeration, as well as for the manufacture of new consumer products like bicycles and automobiles. Steel tubing also had important military applications, including the production of artillery shells. One of the first French companies to move into the manufacture of steel tubing was the Société Française des Métaux, the country's leading maker of copper, brass, and bronze. Another was Henri Rouart et Cie of Montluçon, one of France's leading manufacturers of ice-making and refrigeration equipment.[44] But the industry leaders were three new firms expressly created to manufacture steel tubes: Escaut-Meuse, Louvroil, and Montbard-Aulnoye.

The Société Métallurgique d'Escaut et Meuse was founded in 1882 by the Chaudoir brothers, Liège metallurgists, and Émile Laveissière (of the same family of copper refiners that founded the Société des Métaux) to produce welded steel tubing at plants at Anzin (on the Escaut) and Liège (on the Meuse). In 1888, the company reorganized as a *société anonyme* to raise the money needed to license the revolutionary Mannesmann process for making seamless tubes. With that license secured and with a battery of Siemens-Martin furnaces at Anzin supplying its raw materials, Escaut-Meuse became France's leading maker of steel tubing, with an annual output of some 33,000 tons in 1913.[45] Meanwhile, the Société Française pour la Fabrication des Tubes de Louvroil was founded in 1890 by a group of Belgian entrepreneurs to make the same kind of welded tubes that Rouart was making, except in larger diameters. By 1900, its 600 workers were turning out 10,000 tons of steel tubing, five times the amount produced by Rouart. In 1902 it added its own steel mill at Anzin and continued to expand its tube production, which reached 27,000 tons in 1913, second only to Escaut-Meuse.[46] The third member of the steel tube troika was Montbard-Aulnoye, founded in 1899 by Arthur Desmoulin of Châtillon-Commentry and Edmond Dupuis of Marine Steel to bring to France yet another new technology for the manufacture of seamless tubes, the Ehrhardt process. The company initially produced some 6,000 tons of tubing a year at its plant at Montbard (Côte d'Or), but it soon added a second plant at Aulnoye (Nord), where it also built its own steel mill. As of 1913, the company enjoyed expanding sales and rising profits as a producer of armor-piercing artillery shells and various forms of tubing for the automotive and aeronautical industries.[47]

The last specialty that supported large metallurgical companies at the beginning of the twentieth century was the manufacture of tinplate and metal containers. The making of tinned and untinned sheet iron (*fer blanc* and *fer noir*) had been pioneered in France by the Forges et Fonderies de Montataire. Although Montataire was increasingly drawn into the production of standard forms of steel through its ownership of a Thomas steelworks at Frouard in the Meurthe-et-Moselle, it continued to turn out some 13,000 tons of tinplate at its plant at Montataire (Oise) in 1900.[48] By then, however, Montataire was being eclipsed by two manufacturers of metal containers that had integrated backward into steel and tinplate production. One of these was the Société Générale des Cirages Françaises, which had been founded in 1881 to make waxes, ink, and other consumer chemicals, and which soon began manufacturing the containers for these products. By 1900 Cirages Françaises had acquired the Forges et Aciéries d'Hennebont, an established supplier of tinplate to Breton canneries. Using coal and pig iron imported from Britain, Hennebont produced almost 30,000 tons of Siemens-Martin steel in 1913, 20,000 of which was rolled into tinplate to supply the mother company's container factories.[49]

The chief rival of Cirages Françaises in can manufacture was J. J. Carnaud. As of 1900, J. J. Carnaud et Cie was just one of many firms in the Paris area that made tin cans for the fish canneries along the Atlantic coast and the vegetable canners of southern France; it was mainly known for the "irreproachable quality" of its printing on metal.[50] In 1902, however, the company merged with the Forges et Aciéries de Basse-Indre and formed a new joint-stock company, the Etablissements J. J. Carnaud et Forges de Basse-Indre. Basse-Indre had been founded near Nantes in 1825 as one of the first *forges anglaises* in France. In the 1880s, it began making Siemens-Martin steel and was rolling tinplate by 1893. As of 1913, Carnaud/Basse-Indre was producing 21,400 tons of steel and 6,000 tons of tinplate and was one of France's twenty-five largest metallurgical firms. By continually improving its technology, Carnaud/Basse-Indre eventually established itself as France's leading maker of metal containers.[51] By the 1980s, after merging with Metal Box, the leading British can maker, Carnaud had become one of the largest container manufacturers in the world.

The Sources of Success

Tracing the transformation of French metallurgy from 1880 to 1914 reveals that France's biggest steel companies were pursuing the same strategies and exhibiting the same corporate behaviors in this period as the biggest steel firms elsewhere even though they never attained the sheer size of their counterparts in America, Germany, or even Britain. These strategies and behaviors—such as investment in mass-production technology, vertical and horizontal integration, geographical expansion, and product diversification—were the ones identified by Alfred Chandler as critical for the rise of big business in all manufacturing industries at the end of the nineteenth and the beginning of the twentieth centuries. To conclude this section, let us briefly review what the French steel companies were doing in each area.

1. *Investment in technology.* The first key to success in the steel industry in France and elsewhere in the late nineteenth century was timely investment in new technology. In some cases, adoption of new technology allowed French firms to escape ruinous competition in the production of ordinary grades of iron and steel by moving into higher value-added specialties. But mostly it was a matter of achieving minimum efficient scale and minimizing costs in the production of generic iron and steel, which above all meant adopting the Thomas process for steel production. To be sure, for a variety of reasons—including the small size of France's domestic market and the relatively high cost of coal and coke in France—the French companies that produced Thomas steel never attained the total output of the largest American and German steel companies. Yet, as Eric Bussière has argued, at the plant level the French companies were installing equipment of similar size and sophistication to what was found in German steel plants by the early 1900s. For example, in 1906 Denain-Anzin erected two new blast furnaces that each had a daily capacity of 200–220 tons, and it added two more with daily capacities of 275–300 tons in 1913. The plans for the Pont à Vendin steelworks called for 250-ton blast furnaces, while the Hauts-Fourneaux de Caen were to have 300-ton blast furnaces.[52]

2. *Vertical integration.* Increased output depended not only on building larger units of production but also on increasing the rate of throughput and minimizing the cost of inputs through backward integration into the production of raw materials. The integration of iron- and steelmaking with the mining of iron ore had been standard procedure in France since at least the beginning of the nineteenth century

and remained so in the early twentieth century. As we have seen, the new iron smelters and steelworks in Lorraine were constructed adjacent to their own iron mines; the coastal steelworks and the big steel companies of the Nord bought into the iron mines of northern Spain; and the older steel companies of the Massif Central compensated for the depletion of their original iron mines by buying into mines elsewhere in France and abroad. On a different level, the new companies that fabricated seamless tubes and metal containers integrated backward into the production of sheet steel and tinplate at the outset of the twentieth century.

Backward integration into coal mining and coke making was more problematic. The iron companies founded in the Center and South in the early nineteenth century—Le Creusot, Decazeville, Alais, Châtillon-Commentry, Commentry-Fourchambault, Terrenoire—had operated their own coal mines, but as those mines were depleted these firms often had to resort to buying coal and coke on the open market. This was even more the case for the iron and steel companies founded later in Lorraine, where good domestic sources of coal and coke were lacking (the exception being the Wendels, whose Petite Roselle coal mine met their needs for coal and coke until the end of the century). Only after 1900, when coal and coke prices rose sharply, did the Lorraine companies make a concerted effort to acquire their own sources of coal and coke. For example, Pont à Mousson and Marine-Homécourt founded the Charbonnages de Beeringen and the Charbonnages de Limbourg-Meuse to assure them supplies of coal and coke from Belgium, and other French firms joined together to build a cooperative coking plant at Sluiskil in Holland to process coal from England.[53] The Schneiders likewise bought a Belgian coal mine on the eve of World War I, while Denain-Anzin and the Aciéries de France took over coal mines in the Pas-de-Calais.

Forward integration to secure outlets for their production was pursued less often by the big French iron and steel companies. To be sure, the creation of the entire Lorraine steel industry can be interpreted as an exercise in forward integration by pig iron producers anxious to secure their markets. Similar impulses propelled Pont à Mousson's move into pipe making and Le Creusot's move into weapons manufacture. In general, though, companies that made steel—whether generic forms or specialty steels—did not seek to take over the companies that employed steel in the next level of manufacturing, although there were instances of this (such as when Denain-Anzin acquired Tubes de Valenciennes in 1914). What was more common was the formation of *comptoirs* to promote and regulate the sale of iron and steel products in the open market, which was arguably more a matter of horizontal combination than vertical integration.

3. *Horizontal combination and cooperation.* Buying out or merging with one's competitors is a classic defensive strategy and was a significant contributor to corporate size at the end of the nineteenth century. This was particularly true in the United States, where antitrust legislation prohibited collusive market-sharing and price-fixing agreements. In Europe, however, such agreements were not illegal (or were often tolerated even if technically illegal). Thus, the big German steel companies formed a cartel in the early 1900s rather than emulate the American merger movement that resulted in U.S. Steel. In France there were a certain number of acquisitions and mergers in the steel industry as companies scrambled to keep up with technological change and the new geography of steelmaking (for example, Commentry-Fourchambault took over Decazeville, and Marine Steel acquired Vezin-Aulnoye in order to get Homécourt). But when it came to combining horizontally to control competition, the method of choice, as we saw in Chapter 11, was the creation of selling agencies that served the function of cartels by setting prices and dividing markets. These arrangements were reinforced by interlocking directorates, which seem to have been particularly important in Lorraine, and by the steel industry's penchant for cooperation on matters of economic policy through the Comité des Forges and other associations. In short, French steel's success in attenuating competition through organization probably prevented the more thorough consolidation—and the concomitant corporate giantism—that occurred in the United States.[54]

4. *Product and geographical diversification.* As Alfred Chandler has shown in *Scale and Scope,* product diversification and expansion into new geographical markets were important growth strategies in many industries in the early twentieth century, although not typically in steel. Indeed, as of 1914, most of the large French iron and steel companies remained in a single product or line and served mainly the French domestic market with domestic production facilities. But, as we have seen, there were important exceptions. After exhausting the domestic market for water mains in the 1880s, Pont à Mousson increasingly produced for export after 1890. Marine-Homécourt and Châtillon-Commentry moved into arms production for foreign markets. Schneider did this and much more, becoming by the end of the nine-

teenth century a highly diversified machinery manufacturer and engineering contractor and also one of France's most multinational enterprises. In sum, the big French iron and steel companies exhibited a high degree of dynamism and employed the full range of offensive and defensive strategies to make their way in the competitive business environment at the outset of the twentieth century.

World War I and Its Aftermath: Destruction, Reconstruction, Expansion, and Reorganization

The outbreak of World War I turned out to be both a blessing and a curse for French steel. The German invasion in 1914 and the subsequent four-year German occupation of northeastern France deprived France of its premier iron- and coal-producing region. Few of the steel and iron plants in that region escaped depredation or outright destruction. In the Nord, the Germans dismantled the new steelworks of Denain-Anzin, SFCM-Cail, and Nord-Est and reassembled them on German soil; the rest of the equipment of those three companies was cut up for scrap. In the occupied part of the Meurthe-et-Moselle, the Germans preserved a number of French-owned blast furnaces to supply pig iron to German steelmakers, but they destroyed the steelworks of Longwy, Micheville, and Homécourt plus most of the production facilities of Pont à Mousson. The Wendels, who had fled to Paris at the outbreak of hostilities, had their German properties, Hayange and Moyeuvre, sequestered and eventually put up for sale by the German authorities (although no sale had been finalized when the war ended in 1918). Meanwhile, the Wendels' French property, Joeuf, was stripped of machinery and closed. Overall, the war deprived France of one-third of its capacity for open-hearth steel and three-fourths of its capacity for Thomas steel. As a consequence, French pig iron production fell from 5.2 million tons in 1913 to only 585,776 tons in 1915 (it rebounded by 1917, but only to 1.7 million tons). Likewise, French steel production fell 75 percent from 1913 to 1915, from 4.6 million tons to 1.1 million, and recovered only to about 2 million tons in 1917.[55]

While the German occupation of the Northeast severely reduced France's capacity to produce iron and steel, the prosecution of the war greatly increased the army's demand for arms and munitions. By mid-1915, the Ministry of Armaments was calling for a daily production of 100,000 artillery shells, and by 1917 it wanted 250,000 shells a day.

To meet these goals, the government turned to the private sector. The promise of high prices, a guaranteed market, and generous advances to set up new factories enticed entrepreneurs like the automakers Louis Renault and André Citroën and the construction engineer Louis Loucheur, as well as the leading French electrical manufacturers, to get into munitions production, but it was the established iron and steel companies that benefited the most from the situation. In theory, the Ministry of Armaments exercised strict control over both the granting of munitions contracts and the supply of critical raw materials, but in practice the ministry delegated much of its authority to the Comité des Forges, which divided up orders for munitions and equipment among its members and oversaw the purchase and distribution of British, and later American, iron and steel.[56]

The loss of their production facilities in the Nord and the Meurthe-et-Moselle did not necessarily keep the big steel firms based there from sharing in the wartime bonanza inasmuch as their corporate headquarters remained in Paris and they remained members in good standing of the Comité des Forges. For example, Pont à Mousson set up a shell factory near its existing plant at Foug in the unoccupied part of the Meurthe-et-Moselle (until the German advance in 1918 forced its evacuation), and it also built a new pipe plant near Rouen and new forges at Sens and Toulouse, all with financial aid from the government. The Aciéries de Longwy set up plants at Aubervilliers and Saint-Denis to make large caliber projectiles, and the steel tube manufacturers Louvroil and Escaut-Meuse also built replacements for their lost plants in the Nord in the greater Paris region.

Steel companies with plants already in place in the unoccupied part of France did even better. The steel tube manufacturer Montbard-Aulnoye lost the use of its Aulnoye plant but still earned enough on the production at its main plant at Montbard to raise its yearly profits to 60 percent of paid-in capital by 1917. Châtillon-Commentry shut down its Neuves-Maisons plant outside Nancy at the beginning of the war, but it relit its blast furnaces in 1915 and maintained full-scale production for the remainder of the war even though the front lines were only a few kilometers away. Likewise, Firminy's steelworks at Dunes near Dunkirk and the Aciéries de France plant at Isbergues continued production within earshot of the fighting. Despite the loss of Homécourt, Marine-Homécourt prospered during the war by increasing Bessemer production at Boucau and crucible and Siemens-Martin production in the Loire and by expanding armaments and munitions production at its Saint-Chamond plant.[57] And then there was Schneider et Cie. Its new steel mill at Breuil near Le Creusot, in the works before 1914, went into production in 1916, doubling the company's output of open-hearth steel. Schneider was also awarded a contract and government loan to take over Thyssen's Hauts-Fourneaux de Caen and to bring its pig iron smelters into production (however, this plant became operational only at the end of the war). Most importantly, Schneider expanded the output of its existing munitions plants at Le Havre, Chalon, and Le Creusot. And because iron, steel, and munitions were sold to the government throughout the war at fixed prices that factored in start-up costs and generous profit margins to spur production in a life-or-death situation, Schneider and the others reaped monopoly profits on this wartime production, although we still do not have a clear picture of the amount of those profits, given loose accounting practices and official secrecy.[58] Suffice it to say that France's largest steel companies, even those that suffered significant damage, were in a stronger financial position at the end of the war than at the beginning.

The end of World War I ushered in a new era for steel. The unexpected Allied victory in the fall of 1918 ended the German occupation of the steel-producing centers of the Nord and Lorraine as well as the artificial hot-house conditions of forced wartime production in France. Just as important, it undid the German victory of 1871, with France recovering Alsace-Lorraine and also occupying the Saarland and part of the Rhineland. As a result, French steel underwent three simultaneous and interrelated processes of change in the postwar decade: (1) the rebuilding and modernization of the steelworks in the North and Northeast that had been destroyed or dismantled during the war; (2) the expansion of the French steel industry as a whole by transfer of German assets in Lorraine, Luxembourg, and the Saar to French ownership; and (3) reorganization, concentration, and integration in the reconstructed and expanded steel industry through the formation of enterprise groups and cartels.

Reconstruction and Rationalization at the Plant Level

Thanks to their wartime profits and government credits for reconstruction, the steel companies were able to move quickly to rebuild damaged or destroyed plants in the war zone after 1918 in order to capitalize on strong postwar demand. Because many of these plants had been refurbished with state-of-the-art equipment just prior to the war, much of the reconstruction involved simply putting plants back in their prewar condition, often by recovering and reinstalling machinery carried off by the Germans. But for some steel companies, postwar reconstruction provided an opportunity to redesign, reorganize, and upgrade their steel plants. Denain-Anzin, for example, had developed since the 1830s through the unplanned accretion of facilities in and around Denain (Nord) and, according to Odette Hardy-Hémery, was suffering from "une véritable strangulation logistique" by 1913. This problem was serious enough that there was talk in 1918 of Denain-Anzin abandoning its plants in the Nord altogether and taking over the confiscated German steelworks at Knutange in Lorraine as compensation, but Louis Loucheur, the minister of reconstruction, apparently blocked the deal.[59] Instead, Denain-Anzin used its indemnities to rebuild its blast furnaces at a new location in the Nord at Escaudin, which freed up space for larger steelworks and rolling mills at Denain. In the process, the company redirected its production away from rails and girders to sheet metal in anticipation of growing demand from the automobile industry. When it finally reopened in 1927, Denain-Anzin had the most advanced rolling mill in France (although not as advanced as the new Armco plant in the United States, the world's first continuous sheet metal plant).[60]

Other companies that used postwar reconstruction as an occasion to rationalize and upgrade their production included Marine-Homécourt and Aciéries de Micheville, which coordinated the rebuilding of their destroyed steelworks in the Meurthe-et-Moselle in order to capture additional economies of scale through specialization (Micheville henceforth concentrated on rails and sections, Homécourt on plates and semi-finished products).[61] Similarly, the Wendel family took the opportunity to unite what had been a bifurcated, binational enterprise since 1871. In regaining control of Hayange, Moyeuvre, and Joeuf in January 1919 and in rebuilding Joeuf, Francois de Wendel and his brothers created an integrated steel complex that by 1929 produced some 1,666 million tons of pig iron and 1,628 million tons of steel annually—thirty-three times the combined output of these three plants in 1913 and two or three times the output of the company's nearest French competitors.[62]

A fourth example of how postwar reconstruction led to plant expansion and rationalization is provided by the Aciéries de Longwy. At Longwy, reconstruction unfolded in three stages over a ten-year period. It began with the reopening of iron mines in 1919 and the recovery and reinstallation of about one-third of the equipment taken by the Germans during the war, which allowed two blast furnaces, a Thomas converter, and a rolling mill to resume production in 1920. In stage two, Longwy replaced what could not be recovered with new equipment and regained its prewar capacity by 1924. Stage three, from 1925 to 1929, involved upgrading and expanding the existing facilities, including the installation of 300-ton-per-day blast furnaces, which raised the yearly capacity of Longwy to some 760,000 tons of pig iron and steel, 70 percent above its prewar capacity.[63]

Expansion

While rebuilding, modernizing, and even expanding their prewar plants, many of the big steel companies of the Nord and Meurthe-et-Moselle used the double windfall of war profits and indemnities to expand via mergers and acquisitions. Nord-Est was particularly "imperialistic," taking over the Esperance Company of Louvroil, Basse-Loire (Trignac), Montataire, Sambre-et-Meuse, and most significantly the new Pont à Vendin steelworks that was launched before the war as a joint venture of Commentry-Fourchambault and the Mines de Lens (in the process, Lens received enough shares of Nord-Est to wrest control of the firm from Paribas, a rare example of a French coal company taking over a steel company).[64] Other major acquisitions in steel included Marine-Homécourt's takeover of Allevard and Châtillon-Commentry-Neuves Maisons' takeover of Aciéries de France. Although it remained an ostensibly independent firm, Senelle-Maubeuge was all but annexed by the Wendels, with Maurice de Wendel assuming the chairmanship. In steel tubing, Louvroil merged with the Forges de Recquignies, the first in a series of mergers that eventually culminated in the creation of Vallourec in 1938.[65] Meanwhile, Schneider continued the multinational expansion it began in the prewar era by acquiring the famed Skoda arms works in Czechoslovakia and other properties in central Europe through its new financial subsidiary, the Union Européenne Industrielle et Financière (UEIF).[66]

The principal theater for expansion of French steel companies after World War I was in the reannexed part of Lorraine, the newly occupied parts of Germany (especially the Saarland), and in Luxembourg. This expansion was made possible by the French government's sequestration of German properties in *Lorraine désannexée* in January 1919 and by its subsequent decision to sell them to French steel companies at far below their market value. Having lost their Lorraine iron mines and steel mills, the German companies thereupon decided to sell to the French those facilities in Luxembourg and the Saar that were dependent on Lorraine pig iron and iron ore, although they were not required to do so by the Treaty of Versailles. The French government delegated to the Comité des Forges the task of coordinating the transfer of all these properties. To avoid destabilizing the existing balance of power among the French steel companies, the Comité discouraged the takeover of any of the major German properties by a single French firm (such as Denain-Anzin wanted to do with Knutange). Instead, the French steel companies plus some of their principal customers shared control of the former German properties through seven new companies formed expressly for that purpose. These included:

- the Société Lorraine des Aciéries de Rombas—created by Marine-Homécourt, Micheville, and Pont à Mousson (the MarMichPont group) plus Alais and Aciéries de France—which purchased the Rombacher Hüttenwerke and the Usines et Mines d'Ottange, both formerly owned by Deutsche-Luxemburgische AG, for some 137 million francs. Through Rombas, the same group also controlled the Mines et Usines de Redange-Dilling and HADIR (S.A. des Hauts-Fourneaux et Aciéries de Differdange, St. Ingelbert, et Rumelange), which took over the properties of Hugo Stinnes in Lorraine, Luxembourg, and the Saar.

- the Société Métallurgique de Knutange—created by Schneider, Wendel, Châtillon-Commentry-Neuves Maisons, Senelle-Maubeuge, Denain-Anzin, and the Aciéries de Saint-Etienne—which took over the iron mines, blast furnaces, and steel mills operated by Aumetz-Friede at Knutange plus mining concessions belonging to Krupp, Phoenix, and other German steel companies.

- the Société Métallurgique de Terre Rouge, set up by Schneider, Wendel, and the Belgian company, ARBED, which acquired the Luxembourg properties of the Gelsenkirchener Hüttenwerke.

- the Forges et Aciéries du Nord et Lorraine, created by Nord-Est and Paribas to take over the holdings of the Stumm Brothers at Uckange in the Moselle and Neunkirchen in the Saar.

- the Union des Consommateurs de Produits Métallurgiques et Industrielles (UCPMI), founded by some of the leading French automakers (Renault, Peugeot, Panhard) to allow them to integrate backward into steelmaking by acquiring and operating Thyssen's Hagondange works, the largest in prewar Lorraine.

- the Sociéte Lorraine Minière et Métallurgique, founded by the Aciéries de Longwy and its partners to take control of the Roechling steelworks at Thionville and 40 percent of the Roechlingische Eisen- und Stahlwerke of the Saar.
- the Société des Aciéries et Usines à Tubes de la Sarre (SAUTS), through which the leading French steel tube makers took control of the Mannesmann tube works of the Saar.[67]

The absorption of all these German properties by the French steel industry was not without a downside in that it gave the French companies control of pig iron and steelmaking capacity far in excess of domestic needs and put them in a position of having to find export markets in order to operate profitably. The natural market for this production, of course, was Germany, but the German steelmakers succeeded in largely denying the French access to the German market in the early 1920s and, just as importantly, access to the Ruhr coal on which iron smelting in Lorraine had always depended. They accomplished this first by taking the money received from the German government for the properties given up in Lorraine and using it to build new iron smelting and steelmaking facilities in the Ruhr and Rhineland that were even larger and more cost-effective than those lost in Lorraine (according to Eric Bussière, while the biggest French blast furnaces were capable of producing 250,000 to 400,000 tons of pig iron a year, the new German smelters produced 800,000 tons a year).[68] Coupled with the rapid depreciation of the German mark, this gave the German iron and steel producers a distinct price advantage over the French. At the same time, the quick expansion of German iron and steel production absorbed much of the existing output of Ruhr coal and coke, which the French needed and had hoped to acquire in exchange for Lorraine iron ore. Moreover, by developing new sources of raw iron at home and in Sweden, the Germans simultaneously avoided dependency on Lorraine iron ore that might have given the French leverage in negotiating access to both Ruhr coal and the German market for finished iron and steel.

All of this represented a skillful use of German iron and coal assets to force a revision of the Versailles settlement. And, as has often happened in modern times, the Germans were too successful for their own good. The hardships experienced by French iron and steel companies in the early 1920s provided an important pretext for Poincaré's decision to occupy the Ruhr in January 1923.[69] Ultimately, as part of the post-occupation settlement, the French got sufficient access to Ruhr coke, sufficient protection of their home market, and sufficient reduction in price competition through the workings of a new international steel cartel to be able finally to operate their newly acquired iron and steel mills at full capacity and at a profit in the late 1920s.[70] Despite the Germans' efforts to foreclose the expansion of French iron and steel made possible by the transfer of Lorraine in 1919, French iron and steel production rose faster than German production after 1925 and by 1930 had attained virtual parity with German production.

Reorganization, Concentration, and Integration

Although the French steel industry was reconstructed and greatly enlarged in the 1920s, it failed to achieve the kind of gains in efficiency and rationalization achieved by the German industry, as Matthias Kipping and others have pointed out.[71] In 1926, much of Germany's basic iron and steel production was brought under the control of a single firm, the Vereinigte Stahlwerke (VSt), which immediately effected an industry-wide rationalization of production by closing obsolete plants and concentrating production at the most efficient locations and, above all, by setting up a unified management structure for much of the industry.[72] By contrast, the French industry ostensibly remained in the hands of one world-class firm (Wendel) and a dozen or more smaller firms, which jealously guarded their independence and resolutely opposed efforts at industry-wide rationalization.[73] Yet even if the French steel companies did not do as much as the Germans to attain integration and rationalization in the postwar decade, what needs to be emphasized is that, by French standards, they took major strides toward greater concentration and coordination (presumably the path to long-term viability and competitiveness in heavy industry) through the constitution of *comptoirs* and other common marketing agencies, through mergers and acquisitions, and through the formation of informal groups via interlocking directorates and cross-ownership. By the end of the 1920s, there was as yet no French equivalent of U.S. Steel or VSt, but an industry that had been dominated by twenty to twenty-five major firms before World War I was by then effectively under the control of three supergroups dominated, respectively, by Wendel, Marine-Homécourt, and Longwy.

By the end of the 1920s, the Wendel family enterprise was more than ever in a class by itself. By rebuilding, expanding, and integrating their three great steelworks at Joeuf, Hayange, and Moyeuvre, the Wendel family created a concentration of assets in steelmaking second only to the Vereinigte Stahlwerke in continental Europe. Moreover, the Wendels' influence extended far beyond the boundaries of their own firm through their participation in Terre-Rouge, Knutange, Senelle-Maubeuge, and other firms. All told, Claude Prêcheur has estimated that the Wendel-Schneider-ARBED group, of which Wendel was the dominant partner, accounted for 45 percent of the pig iron production of Lorraine and Luxembourg in 1929 (and presumably a comparable share of the steel production).[74]

With Eugène Schneider turning increasingly toward international finance and building Schneider et Cie into a multinational conglomerate, perhaps the only figure in the domestic French steel industry who could rival the power and influence of the Wendels was the *président-directeur-général* of Marine-Homécourt, Théodore Laurent. A graduate of the Ecole Polytechnique and the Ecole des Mines, Laurent began his career in the late 1880s as a state engineer and later served as chief engineer for the Chemin de Fer du Midi and the Paris-Orléans Railroad before joining Marine-Homécourt in 1908 as second in command to Claudius Magnin. Laurent quickly brought Marine together with Micheville and Pont à Mousson in the MarMichPont group to address their common chronic shortage of coal and coke by acquiring coal mines and coking ovens in Belgium and Germany. In 1911, Laurent succeeded Magnin as *directeur-général* and continued in that position under Emile Heurteau, his former boss at the Paris-Orléans, who served as chairman of Marine-Homécourt from 1915 to 1927; in 1927, Laurent succeeded Heurteau as chairman and held that post until a few months before his death in 1953. During World War I, Laurent resided at Saint-Chamond, where he directed the firm's munitions production. After the war, he turned to the rebuilding of the Homécourt plant and to extending the national and international reach of the company.[75]

Marine-Homécourt developed on three levels in the postwar decade. First of all, it continued to produce steel and armaments at its established plants in the Loire, the Meurthe-et-Moselle (especially Homécourt), the Nord, and the Southwest (Boucau). New wrinkles on this level included the acquisition of Allevard in 1917; the rebuilding of Homécourt and Micheville in tandem in 1919, and their subsequent sharing of a common administration; and the acquisition of the Etablissements Métallurgiques de la Gironde to provide a captive market for Homécourt's semi-finished goods. On the second level, Marine-Homécourt remained the dominant partner in the MarMichPont group, which continued to operate coal mines in Belgium and Germany for the benefit of its three members. MarMichPont also organized and managed three new iron and steel companies: Rombas, HADIR, and Redange-Dilling (as of 1930, Laurent served as chairman of all three). To market the production of the MarMichPont companies and their dependencies, which amounted to 25 percent of the pig iron and steel produced in Lorraine and Luxembourg in 1929, Laurent founded DAVUM (Compagnie des Dépôts et Agences de Ventes d'Usines Métallurgiques) and Davum Exportation as new versions of the prewar *comptoirs*. The MarMichPont group also participated in the creation of the international steel cartel in 1926. Indeed, Laurent served as president of the cartel's French section and played a key role in negotiating the underlying tariff agreement that protected French steelmakers from German competition in their domestic market and at the same time gave the new French iron and steel companies in *Lorraine désannexée* a guaranteed share of the German market.[76] Meanwhile, on yet another level, Marine-Homécourt was emerging as an incipient conglomerate by taking shares in a wide range of enterprises beyond the iron and steel industry, including Enérgie Electrique de la Basse-Isère (a power company based on Allevard), the Compagnie Française de Matériel de Chemins de Fer (a major customer for Homécourt steel), Sulzer (a maker of pumps, diesel engines, and the like), Gennevilliers (airplane engines), and the Compagnie des Constructions et d'Entretien de Matériel de Chemins de Fer which operated railroad repair yards.[77] By 1930, Laurent sat on no fewer that forty-one corporate boards. Humbert de Wendel called him "le monstre," presumably a term of respect if not endearment that recognized the power of Laurent—and thus of Marine-Homécourt—in the French and European industrial spheres.[78]

The third dominant firm in French steel by the end of the twenties was the Aciéries de Longwy. With the completion in 1929 of its postwar rebuilding program, Longwy was again one of the largest producers of steel in France, with an annual output exceeded only by that of four other Lorraine steelworks (Hayange, Rombas, Hagondange, and Knutange). But, as in the case of Marine-Homécourt, Longwy's economic interests far exceeded the production of its original plant. Along with other steel companies in the Longwy area, it had founded the Société Lorraine Minière et Métallurgique (SLMM) in 1919 to acquire and operate the mines and blast furnaces of Thionville (by 1930, the SLMM was the thirteenth largest metallurgical firm in France). Like Marine-Homécourt, Longwy created a common export agency for the members of its group, Longovica, which supplemented a domestic marketing system that was recognized as a model of commercial organization. Also like Marine-Homécourt, Longwy had significant investments in metallurgical manufacturing.[79]

Perhaps the most important thing that Longwy did in the 1920s—the thing that set it apart from Wendel and Marine-Homécourt—was to integrate forward into the production of steel pipes and tubing, which was becoming one of the fastest-growing sectors of the industry thanks to the takeoff in petroleum refining in France and Europe in the late 1920s. According to Catherine Omnès, in 1919 Longwy supplied the majority of the funds for the expansion of the Forges de Recquignies, one of France's two leading steel tube makers, and the next year Alexandre Dreux masterminded the merger of Louvroil and Recquignies (the other major French tube maker). Dreux subsequently sat on the board of the new firm, Louvroil-Recquignies (France's seventeenth-largest metals company in 1930); through Louvroil-Recquignies, Longwy held a stake in SAUTS, the twenty-second largest French metals company.[80]

A comparison of the list of the largest iron and steel firms in France in 1930 (Table 4) with the 1913 list (Table 3) makes it clear that World War I and its aftermath served to accelerate and intensify two trends that originated in the prewar era. One of these was the shift of the French iron and steel industry to the North and Northeast. By 1930, twenty-two of the largest twenty-five metallurgical firms in France had all or part of their operations in the Nord or Lorraine. With the single exception of the Société Métallurgique de Normandie, coastal metallurgy was in decline. The specialty steelmaking of the Center—notably the crucible steelmakers of the Loire—lived on and even prospered, but whereas these firms had been leaders in the industry in the mid-nineteenth century and were still among the largest twenty-five metals companies in 1913, they were little more than "boutique" operations by the standards of 1930. Of the leading niche firms of 1913, J. J. Carnaud remained in the top twenty-five in 1930, but it was particularly companies in the North and Northeast such as Pont à Mousson and Louvroil-Recquignies that qualified as Big Steel.

A second trend was consolidation of control. Even if French metallurgy remained fragmented in 1930 in comparison to the hyperconcentration found in Germany and the United States, the mergers of the 1920s, the formation of interest groups, and the interlocking of

Table 4. The twenty-five largest French iron and steel firms in 1930

Rank	Firm	Assets (in millions of francs)
1	Wendel et Cie	1,492.0[a]
2	Aciéries de Longwy	932.3
3	Schneider et Cie	715.6
4	Marine-Homécourt	707.6
5	Aciéries et Forges de Firminy	596.6
6	Denain-Anzin	592.5
7	Société Métallurgique de Senelle-Maubeuge	590.1
8	Forges et Aciéries du Nord et de l'Est	541.9
9	Aciéries de Micheville	496.4
10	Escaut-Meuse	484.0[a]
11	Société Lorraine des Aciéries de Rombas	438.0[a]
12	UCPMI (Hagondange)	417.0[a]
13	Hauts-Fourneaux de la Chiers	359.5
14	Société Lorraine Minière et Métallurgique	357.5
15	Hauts-Fourneaux et Fonderies de Pont à Mousson	349.9
16	Société Métallurgique de Normandie	297.8
17	Forges et Aciéries du Nord et Lorraine	261.0[a]
18	Louvroil et Recquignies	251.3
19	Hauts-Fourneaux, Forges, et Aciéries de Pompey	242.8
20	Châtillon, Commentry, et Neuves Maisons	227.8
21	Hauts-Fourneaux de Saulnes, Marc Raty et Cie	217.7
22	J. J. Carnaud et Forges de Basse-Indre	212.1
23	Aciéries et Usines à Tubes de la Sarre	168.2
24	Aciéries du Nord	141.2
25	Mines, Fonderies, et Forges d'Alais	111.6

Source: Annual Reports in *Les Assemblées Générales,* 1930. For the 1936 figures, see Bruce Kogut, "Evolution of the Large Firm in France in Comparative Perspective," *Entreprises et Histoire* 19 (October 1998): 143ff.

a. 1936 figures.

directorates all served to concentrate control of the French industry in a few firms and a handful of executives. In effect, Big Steel was no longer twenty-five or thirty independent firms but rather ten or twelve firms and their affiliates—and the case can be made that as few as a half-dozen firms really controlled the industry.

A third trend—growth and convergence—is reflected in the French and German production figures (see Table 5).[81] These show that France was catching up with Germany in steel production by 1930 and had actually surpassed Germany in pig iron production. Indeed, if French-

Table 5. French and German steel production (thousands of tons)

Product	Country	1913	1920	1925	1930
Pig iron	France	5,207	3,434	8,494	10,035
	Germany	16,761	7,044	10,177	9,695
Steel	France	4,637	2,706	7,464	9,444
	Germany	17,609	9,278	12,195	12,536

controlled production in Luxembourg and the Saar is factored in, the French were well ahead of the Germans by 1930—an enormous change of fortunes since 1913.[82]

At the level of the firm, the convergence was less evident. The mean assets of the ten largest German steel firms, which were 3.2 times those of the ten largest French steel firms in 1913, were 3.4 or 2.8 times the mean assets of the ten largest French steel firms in 1930 (depending on whether the Vereinigte Stahlwerke is treated as a combination of six prewar firms or as a single firm). Even so, the largest French steel firms were not only more complex structurally and organizationally in 1930 than they had been in 1913 but also much bigger, probably by 60 percent.[83]

More important than the convergence—or lack of convergence—of the big French and German steel companies in terms of the size of their assets was a convergence in outlook and behavior. As the case of Longwy demonstrates, the leading French steel companies came to understand in the 1920s that the survival and viability of their industry required more than greater concentration and rationalization in traditional areas of production. They also needed greater vertical integration between basic smelting and refining and specialty production and greater diversification into new product lines (like steel tubes) that could give them the ability to operate in an increasingly competitive international market. In pursuing these strategies, the major French steel producers were behaving more and more like the largest German, British, and American steel companies in the post–World War I period. In spite of renewed setbacks in the 1930s and 1940s, the technological and organizational capabilities that these firms had acquired by 1930 would allow them to survive massive restructuring after World War II and to continue to play a significant role in the economy of France and Europe down to the crisis and contraction of the 1970s and 1980s.

CHAPTER THIRTEEN

The Electrical Industry

The first commercial applications of electricity—electroplating and the electric telegraph—appeared in the 1840s, but these required relatively small quantities of low voltage electricity supplied by small generators and crude batteries. It was the introduction in the 1880s of a number of new electrical technologies requiring the production and transmission of large quantities of electricity—electric lighting, electric traction, and electrolytic processes for the production of metals and chemicals— that gave rise to what came to be regarded as the quintessential industry of the Second Industrial Revolution.

Modern electrical industries did not arise in all parts of the industrialized world simultaneously. Although many countries, including France, contributed to the development of the science and technology of electricity in the nineteenth century, the critical inventions and innovations that allowed large-scale commercial application occurred mainly in the United States and secondarily in Germany in the 1870s and 1880s. It was American and German inventor-entrepreneurs such as Thomas Edison, George Westinghouse, Elihu Thomson, Henry Sprague, and Werner von Siemens who took the lead in launching the first electrical enterprises. To some degree, the precocity of the Americans and Germans was simply a reflection of the larger social and economic forces at work at the time: The United States and Germany experienced faster urban growth than any other countries in the world in the last quarter of the nineteenth century, and both were highly receptive to using electricity as the basis for the new urban lighting and transportation systems needed to make their cities livable (gas lighting being less established there than in the older industrial nations, Britain, France, and Belgium). A handful of American and German firms—especially Edison, Thomson-Houston, and Westinghouse in the United States and Siemens and Halske, Siemens-Schuckert, and the Allgemeine Elektricitäts Gesellschaft (AEG) in Germany—took control of the critical technology in the 1880s and 1890s and soon were in a position to use the "first mover advantages" acquired at home to dominate the development of electric power and light elsewhere around the world.

The rapid rise of the leading American and German electrical firms and their drive into foreign markets did not preclude the development of a home-grown electrical industry in France. In the 1870s, French scientists and engineers had been in the forefront of innovation in electricity, and by 1881, when Paris hosted a major international exposition on electrical technology, France seemed poised to play a leading role in the new industry. Yet for a variety of reasons, including the entrenched position of the gas lighting industry, the economic depression of the 1880s, and a curious indifference to new technology among France's fashion setters (seen particularly in the case of the telephone), France lagged behind the United States, Germany, and even Great Britain in the installation of electric lighting and electric traction.[1] The one bright spot for the French before 1900 was the emergence of electrometallurgy and electrochemical production in the Southeast on the basis of the hydroelectric power being developed in the French Alps (see Chapter 15).

France's failure to take the lead in electrification in the 1880s and 1890s recalls France's slow start in building railroads in the 1830s and 1840s. Of course, with government aid, French entrepreneurs overcame the lag in building railroads in the 1850s, and by the 1860s and 1870s French companies were playing a leading role in building and operating railroads in other parts of the world. Such a transition from laggard to leader never occurred in electricity, at least not before World War II. However, after 1900 the French did stage a remarkable rally that put in place a modern system of electrical production and distribution and closed the gap in electricity consumption between France and its European neighbors by the 1930s.[2] This turnaround was not solely the work of foreign companies, as an observer in 1900 might have expected, but rather involved the efforts of French engineers and entrepreneurs and resulted in the emergence of a number of important French companies in electrical production and manufacturing. As products of a middle-sized market, these firms never attained the critical mass needed to challenge the American and German first movers in international markets, but they were Chandlerian enterprises of sufficient size and complexity to serve as the organizational vehicles for France's considerable success in the electrical and electronics field after 1945. Indeed, three of these firms—Thomson, CGE (later Alcatel-Alsthom), and Schneider-Jeumont—would play major roles in nuclear power and telecommunications in the closing quarter of the twentieth century. In this chapter we look at the rise of these modern, dynamic firms within the context of the overall development of the French electrical industry between 1900 and 1930.[3]

The Early Years, 1890s–1914

The founding of the French electrical industry unfolded in three roughly chronological stages from the late 1890s to the outbreak of World War I. The first stage centered on the electrification of tramways and the beginning of the Paris Metro (1895–1902); the second stage (1902–1908) saw attention turn to creating power and light companies; the focus of the third stage (1908–1914) was the development of electrical equipment manufacturing.

Traction

From the early 1880s, there were efforts in France to set up small power plants to support electric lighting in select neighborhoods of the larger cities or to supply power and light in specific buildings (usually department stores or factories). But the production and application of electric power on something approaching a national scale began only in the mid-1890s with the electrification of the horse-drawn tramways in the major cities and with the launching of the Paris subway system. These projects were mostly the work of foreign companies or French companies with access to foreign technology, in particular the French Thomson-Houston Company.

The Compagnie Française pour l'Exploitation des Procédés Thomson-Houston (CFTH, or later Thomson-Houston) was founded at the end of 1892 as a joint venture of the Compagnie des Compteurs (the French licensee for Thomson-Houston electric motors) and the American General Electric Company (recently created through the merger of Thomson-Houston and Edison Electric) to serve as a conduit for the marketing of General Electric equipment in France and in the rest of continental Europe. The Compagnie des Compteurs supplied the initial capital and some of the managers for the company; General Electric (GE) agreed to supply present and future technology in return for 40 percent of the company's first stock issue. Moreover, a GE executive, Ernest Thurnauer, supervised day-to-day operations as *administrateur-délégué* of CFTH from 1894 to 1915. However, as CFTH issued new shares to raise additional capital, it increasingly fell under the sway of the bankers who took up these shares, especially Emile Mercet of the Perier, Mercet bank, who assumed the chairmanship in 1898. Thus CFTH gradually went beyond being the joint subsidiary of General Electric and the Compagnie des Compteurs to become an independent French firm with a unique asset: privileged access to the patents of America's leading electrical manufacturer.

One of General Electric's chief proprietary technologies was the system developed by Henry Sprague to transfer electricity from central power stations to trams via underground or overhead lines (in the latter case, a "trolley" maintained contact between power lines and what came to be known as trolley cars). Soon after its formation, CFTH set out to apply the Sprague system to France's myriad horse-drawn trams, but it soon realized that doing this would require either buying the tramway companies outright or accepting stock in these chronically undercapitalized companies as payment for equipment. Therefore, the large amounts of capital raised by CFTH between 1894 and 1898— estimated by John McKay at 85 million francs—did not go into setting up manufacturing facilities but into taking over tramway companies— first in Rouen, then in Bordeaux, Marseille, Paris, and other cities. By 1902, CFTH had become primarily a holding company for some fifty tramways. This enabled CFTH to make money in two ways: by selling equipment to a captive clientele or by reselling the shares it held in refurbished tramway companies.

CFTH's initial ventures in tramway electrification were sufficiently lucrative that the price of its stock soared after being listed on the Paris Bourse, and this success soon attracted a number of other companies into the electric tramway business. Foremost among these were the Compagnie Générale de Traction (CGT), founded in 1897 by a group of Belgian entrepreneurs with backing from British and French investment banks, and the Empain group, founded in the 1880s by another Belgian entrepreneur, Edouard Empain, which began taking over and electrifying tramways in northern France in 1894. Buoyed by a rising stock market that enabled them to sell off the shares of tramways at inflated prices, CFTH and its rivals competed fiercely to take over and electrify as many tramways as possible between 1899 and 1902. As a result, the length of electric tramways in France quadrupled from less than 500 kilometers to 2,000 kilometers in three years. Those years also brought the launching of France's first and foremost subway company, the Compagnie de Chemin de Fer Métropolitain de Paris, under the auspices of a syndicate of traction companies dominated by Empain. The first line of the Paris Metro opened in July 1900 in time to serve visitors to the Paris World's Fair, and it expanded steadily thereafter. By 1913, the Metro was operating eight lines and carrying some 250 million passengers per year.

In contrast to the steady expansion of the Paris Metro, the outfitting of electric tramways was radically curtailed in 1901 when the bubble in tramway stocks burst. The stock market crash proved fatal for CGT, which had increasingly become a vehicle for speculation in overvalued tramway stocks and had no manufacturing capacity to fall back on. By contrast, CFTH was forced to write off a number of bad investments and write down its capital, but it still held a number of viable tramway and power companies and, thanks to its relationship with General Electric, was in a position to reinvent itself as an electrical manufacturer. Meanwhile, the electric tramway system put in place in France by 1901 continued to grow slowly over the next ten years, reaching a length of 2,300 kilometers by 1913. But it never attained the size or importance of the tramways of Germany, the United Kingdom, or the United States in large part because of the limited development of tramways in the capital (due to opposition on aesthetic grounds to putting overhead power lines in the heart of the city and also due to the growth and popularity of the Metro). Thus while electric traction played an important role in launching the French electrical industry in the late 1890s, it was superseded after 1900 by efforts to set up and operate general-purpose power and light companies.[4]

Power and Light

The holding companies that pioneered electric traction in France also set up companies to supply electric power to their tramways and subways. The Empain group, for example, founded the Société d'Electricité de Paris in 1903 to serve the Paris Metro, and Thomson-Houston helped to found the Compagnie Générale de Distribution d'Energie Electrique (CGDEE), which built and operated plants near Paris to supply power to the tramways of the Compagnie Générale des Omnibus. Meanwhile, the early electrometallurgy and electrochemical companies built hydroelectric plants in the French Alps to supply the enormous amounts of electricity they consumed. However, most of the plants set up before 1914 to generate electricity were not dedicated plants serving a single industrial customer, be it a tramway company or an aluminum manufacturer, but were general-purpose plants intended to provide electricity to a mixture of residential and business customers in France's major cities and industrial centers.[5]

In France as in other countries, the economics of power production and distribution dictated that, over the long run, the generation of electricity be concentrated in ever-larger plants connected to a system of power lines that would allow demand for the entire nation to be met efficiently. Such a national grid was gradually put in place in France between the end of World War I and the end of World War II. In the beginning, however, a number of factors—including a legal system that gave authority over power plant concessions to towns and communes; pessimism, or just lack of foresight about the potential demand for electricity; and the absence of technology to transmit power long distances—conspired to foster *cloissonnement* (partitioning or fragmentation) in the French power and light industry. Instead of a single company taking control of electricity production and distribution in each city and region, these markets were divided among a number of relatively small companies. Consolidating these into more coherent and efficient citywide and regional power systems would be addressed only after World War I.

The classic example of *cloissonnement* in early twentieth century France was found in Paris. In 1888, the Paris City Council ended the era of desultory, free-enterprise provision of electric power and light by dividing the city into six sectors and awarding eighteen-year, nonexclusive concessions for electrical service in these sectors to six different companies.[6] Showing little concern for the long-term consequences of its actions, the Council allowed each concession-holder to determine the type and voltage of current in its sector. This created incompatibilities that would haunt the Paris electrical system for seventy-five years (as late as 1968, some parts of Paris had 220-volt current, and some had 110!). Also, the short duration of the concessions encouraged the concession-holders to install small, coal-fired power plants that were inherently inefficient and that were quickly rendered obsolete by rising demand. Indeed, by 1900, all six companies were focusing on developing their distribution systems, running power lines to as many customers as possible, and increasingly buying electricity from a second generation of companies that were setting up larger production plants in the suburbs.

These newer production-oriented companies included the Empain group's Société d'Electricité de Paris (SEP), founded in 1903 to supply the Paris Metro. When SEP's state-of-the art plant at Saint-Denis went on line in 1905, it produced enough power (50,000 kilowatts) to furnish substantial amounts of electricity to the six Paris power and light companies while also meeting the needs of the Metro. Similarly, Thomson-Houston's CGDEE built plants at Vitry and Billancourt that supplied power not only to the Paris tramways but also to two suburban distribution companies, Sud-Lumière and Nord-Est Parisien, that lacked their own generating capacity. Another new production company, the Société Le Triphasé, built a power plant at Asnières that initially supplied power to part of Paris and to the Paris Metro prior to the opening of SEP's Saint-Denis plant. Starting in 1901, however, Le Triphasé's electricity went increasingly to Nord-Lumière and Electrique de Montmorency, two suburban distribution companies it founded with backing from a major holding company, the Société Lyonnaise des Eaux et de l'Eclairage (SLEE). After SLEE took control of Le Triphasé, SLEE's managing director Albert Petsche merged it with Nord-Lumière and Montmorency to create an integrated production-distribution giant. Another company that used this tactic in the greater Paris area was Ouest-Lumière, founded and controlled by the Swiss technology and finance company Franco-Suisse. Ouest-Lumière built and operated one of the largest power plants in the Paris basin at Puteaux and distributed electricity to the towns west of Paris. Like SEP and Le Triphasé, it also sold power to the six Paris power companies.[7]

The operational fragmentation bordering on anarchy that characterized the electrical system of greater Paris in the early 1900s, coupled with the approaching expiration of the original six concessions and the end of the concession of the Paris Gas Company and its monopoly over public lighting, induced the Paris City Council in 1905 to consider ways of consolidating and standardizing electrical production and distribution in the capital. As a result, in 1907 the council granted a single concession for power distribution within the city of Paris to a new company, the Compagnie Parisienne de Distribution d'Electricité (CPDE), which was formed and largely controlled by the original six concessionaires. Under the terms of the new concession, the property of the original six companies (which reverted to the city at the expiration of their original concessions) was leased to the CPDE, which in return agreed to build two new power plants and to lower rates to encourage consumption. However, the CPDE never became self-sufficient for its power supply and continued to buy power from SEP, Le Triphasé, and CGDEE until power production and distribution in greater Paris were completely reworked after 1919.

The pattern of *cloissonnement* that characterized power production and distribution in Paris was if anything more pronounced in other parts of France. By 1908 there were some 1,400 power plants operating in France, up from 421 plants in 1894. Of these, 1,000 were hydro-electric plants producing small quantities of electricity, often for a single industrial customer. As one would expect, most of these were found in the Alps, the Pyrenees, and the Massif Central. The 400 coal-fired thermal plants were on average much larger, especially those built or refurbished after 1905, when steam turbines began replacing piston steam engines as the power source for dynamos. In addition to the Paris region, these plants were concentrated wherever coal was plentiful, especially along the coasts and in the coal-producing regions of the North and Northeast. Some of these provincial power plants were owned and operated by local power and light companies that managed to remain independent of the big Paris holding companies in the pre–World War I period. Among these were the Société Havraise d'Energie Electrique, which came to control power distribution in much of the lower Seine region, and the Société Lyonnaise des Forces Motrices du Rhône, which harnessed the Rhône River above Lyon with the Janage Dam in the 1890s and supplied electric power to Lyon and its environs in the early 1900s.[8] However, in most of provincial France, the work of installing and operating power and light facilities fell to holding companies of national stature for the same reasons that holding companies dominated electric traction: They needed captive clients for the equipment they were selling, and they possessed the technological know-how and the ability to raise capital that local entrepreneurs lacked. Thus, four holding company–centered groups came to dominate the development of the power and light industry of provincial France between 1900 and 1914. Two were tied to equipment manufacturers (Thomson-Houston and the Compagnie Générale d'Electricité), one was centered on a construction company (Giros-Loucheur), and one was the vehicle of a Swiss finance company (Franco-Suisse).[9]

The origins of the Compagnie Générale d'Electricité (CGE) can be traced to the founding of the Société Normande d'Electricité (SNE) in 1888. The SNE was headed by Nemours and Charles Herbault of the Banque Française pour l'Afrique du Sud (a precursor of the Banque Nationale de Paris), but the person most responsible for the company's success was Pierre Azaria. Born Bedros Azarian, son of an Armenian merchant in Cairo, Azaria studied engineering at the Ecole Centrale in Paris and then joined Electricité de Rouen, the predecessor of SNE, in 1887. Under Azaria's leadership, SNE expanded rapidly in the early 1890s and became the foremost power and light company in France in terms of output of electricity per inhabitant. It was also extraordinarily profitable: The Crédit Lyonnais estimated that its *coefficient d'exploitation* was 50 percent (that is, one-half of its annual revenues were pure profit).[10] This financial success encouraged Azaria and the Herbaults to raise their sights from the local to the national arena. In early 1898, they merged SNE into a new company, the Compagnie Générale d'Electricité, with backing from French and Swiss banks. The CGE immediately acquired a number of electrical manufacturing companies, including makers of lightbulbs, storage batteries, and brass and copper wire.[11]

Despite these early acquisitions, CGE initially focused less on developing its manufacturing capacity than on acquiring a portfolio of power and light companies that would produce immediate profits and in the longer term serve as a captive market for its manufacturing subsidiaries. In essence, CGE was applying to power and light the strategy that Thomson-Houston had successfully applied to electric traction. It made its first acquisitions in Nancy, Amiens, and Nantes in 1899–1900, and in the decade that followed it founded or took control of additional power and light companies, including those in Bordeaux, Marseille, and Barcelona. Although it sold off a number of these companies after 1910 as part of a larger redeployment of assets (including its original property, SNE), CGE remained a major force in power and light production in the French provinces on the eve of World War I.[12]

The rise of CGE as a holding company in power and light was soon rivaled by Thomson-Houston. In the late 1890s, CFTH had founded or taken control of a number of power companies that supplied electricity to its tramways, and when the tramway boom collapsed in the early 1900s, it looked to take over additional power and light companies that could replace the tramways as a market for equipment sales. As noted earlier, CFTH backed the CGDEE, which built and operated two major power plants in greater Paris. In the south of France, CFTH also helped to launch Energie Electrique du Littoral Méditerranéen (EELM), which built four hydro plants and five thermal plants to supply power to tramways and to the power and light companies that came to constitute the EELM group. By the end of World War I, EELM had installed production capacity of 265,000 horsepower, making it the largest electricity producer in France. Another Thomson-Houston power and light company in provincial France was Energie Electrique du Sud-Ouest (EESO), founded in 1906 to construct a hydro plant on the lower Dordogne River. By 1917, EESO had built two additional hydro plants and was distributing electricity to some 149 communes in the Southwest as well as to the Paris-Orléans Railroad and the state munitions factories around Angoulême. Yet another CFTH subsidiary was the Compagnie Centrale d'Energie Electrique, which took over the Rouen power company from CGE in 1909.[13]

A third major group of provincial power companies was put together in the early 1900s by Alexander Giros and Louis Loucheur, the leading public works contractors in France. In the Nord, Giros and Loucheur acquired the concession for power production in Madeleine, the hometown of the Kuhlmann Chemical Company, and combined it with other local power companies to create Energie Electrique du Nord de la France (EENF) in 1907. EENF later built a huge new power plant at Wasquehal—hailed as "one of the most beautiful in France" when it opened in 1912—to supply power to distribution companies in Lille, Roubaix, and Tourcoing. In the South, Giros and Loucheur founded the Compagnie Hydroélectrique de la Loire et du Centre by merging the company that generated hydroelectric power for Montluçon with the one that produced thermal and hydroelectric power for Saint-Etienne and its environs. The new firm, Loire et Centre, took the lead in the long-distance transmission of the electrical power produced in the Alps by constructing a 117-kilometer high-tension line from Grenoble to Saint-Chamond, which took on additional importance during World War I when Saint-Etienne boomed as a center for the munitions industry.[14]

The fourth major group of provincial power companies was put together by the Société Franco-Suisse pour l'Industrie Electrique (Franco-Suisse), founded in 1898 by various Geneva banks plus Paribas and the Schneiders to develop power plants in France and Italy on behalf of the Swiss electrical equipment makers.[15] Under the leadership of

Auguste Boissonnas, a Geneva-born engineer, Franco-Suisse established a foothold in the Paris electrical industry through Ouest-Lumière, but its chief focus was on developing the hydroelectric resources of the French Alps, mainly through the Société Générale de Force et Lumière (SGFL). In the early 1900s, SGFL built or acquired six hydro plants plus a major thermal plant at Oullins near Lyon, which soon made it the principal supplier of electric power to Grenoble, Annonay, Lyon, and a number of other towns and cities of the region. By 1918, SGFL was producing 200 million kilowatt-hours of electricity per year and distributing it over 1,200 kilometers of high-tension lines to six departments in the Southeast, which constituted the largest service area in France outside of Paris.[16]

The Takeoff in Electrical Manufacturing

The growth of the general-purpose power and light industry brought about a fivefold increase in the production of electricity in France between 1900 and 1913 (from 530 million kilowatt-hours to 1,800 million); that in turn stimulated a surge in the production of electrical equipment. To be sure, in the years leading up to World War I, the French electrical equipment industry was small compared to the American and German industries, but four French electrical manufacturers had amassed sufficient assets to rank among the twenty-five largest manufacturing firms in France in 1913. Foremost among these were Thomson-Houston and CGE.

As early as 1895, Thomson-Houston had acquired a manufacturing subsidiary, Etablissements Postel-Vinay, to make motors and other equipment for electric tramways, but, as we have seen, CFTH at first functioned mainly as a holding company and as a marketing agent for GE products. As late as 1908, 90 percent of the capital of CFTH was tied up in the stock of tramway and power companies. However, under the leadership of Florent Guillain, who replaced Emile Mercet as chairman in 1902, CFTH gradually shifted its emphasis to manufacturing, even as it hung onto its tramways and power companies as sources of equipment orders.[17] As part of this reorientation, CFTH reached an agreement in 1905 with Germany's AEG, by which CFTH ceded the Spanish market and one-half of the Italian market to AEG in return for AEG's promise to stay out of France. In other words, CFTH curtailed its international ambitions to guarantee its primacy in the domestic market. It then set out to increase its manufacturing capabilities by acquiring various small-equipment makers and by expanding internally on the foundation provided by Postel-Vinay, which became the Ateliers Thomson-Houston in 1904. By 1913, CFTH operated five factories—four in the Paris area and one at Lesquin near Lille—where it produced a full line of equipment, from steam turbines and dynamos to cables, switchboards, telephones, electric motors, batteries, and lightbulbs.[18]

More than Thomson-Houston, CGE had been a major manufacturer of electrical equipment since its founding in 1898. Although the company focused on increasing its holdings in power and light production in the early 1900s, Azaria decided in 1909, inasmuch as manufacturing continued to provide 70–80 percent of the firm's gross revenues, to rededicate the company to the production of electrical equipment and matériel for the power and light industry and to the design and installation of power plants. To this end, CGE got out of the production of tramway equipment completely and sold off selected power and light holdings to raise cash so it could expand its existing manufacturing plants and acquire new ones. The latter included the Tudor Battery Company in Lille and the French properties of the Swiss electric equipment makers Sprecher et Schuh, which became a new subsidiary, the Ateliers de Constructions Electriques de Delle. Most importantly, in 1912 CGE took control of Câbles Electriques Berthoud-Borel of Lyon, which had pioneered the continuous manufacture of power transmission cable and which was already closely associated with CGE as a major consumer of CGE's wire and as a supplier of cable to CGE's power companies. By 1913, CGE employed some 4,000 workers in twenty manufacturing branches and subsidiaries (about the same number as employed by Thomson-Houston in manufacturing). In just three years, 1910–1913, CGE's total revenues increased from 36 million francs to 81 million francs, and electrical manufacturing and construction emerged as the firm's foremost activities, accounting for 36 percent of revenues (versus 30 percent from metallurgy and 11 percent from power production).[19]

Although Thomson-Houston and CGE were the largest electrical manufacturers in France on the eve of World War I, they hardly constituted a duopoly. Dozens of small and medium-sized firms found niches in the emerging market for electrical equipment in France. More significantly, that market attracted the attention of established French metallurgical and engineering companies and foreign electrical manufacturers. In the 1890s, two French makers of steam engines and locomotives, SACM-Belfort and Schneider, had begun building steam turbines and dynamos, and in 1901 Schneider created a separate electrical division that made triphase transformers for the CPDE, super-turbines for Ouest-Lumière, and switching equipment for the Paris Metro at a new plant at Champagne-sur-Seine. Meanwhile, the American Westinghouse Company, having had limited success marketing its processes and products through French licensees in the 1890s, founded a French subsidiary, S.A. Westinghouse, which manufactured an array of electrical machinery at a plant in Le Havre by 1914. In southeastern France, the growth of the hydroelectric industry supported a number of specialized manufacturers, including Neyret et Beylier of Grenoble, the leading French makers of turbines, and the Etablissements Grammont of Pont-de-Cheruy (Isère), which began by making gold and silver thread for the silk cloth industry in the 1840s, moved into the manufacture of electrical wire in the 1880s, and by the 1900s employed 1,700 in highly diversified electrical manufacturing.[20] However, three other firms founded before 1914—TLH, CEM, and ACENE—would have the greatest success in electrical manufacturing in France in the first half of the twentieth century, along with CGE and CFTH.

The Tréfileries et Laminoirs du Havre (TLH) was founded in 1898 by a group of venture capitalists to take over and expand the Le Havre factory where the inventor-entrepreneur Lazare Weiller had been producing a patented copper alloy for electric wire since the 1880s. Weiller stayed on as the general manager of the new joint-stock company, but when it faltered in the stock-market debacle of 1901–1902, he was replaced by two engineer-managers, Raymond Jarry and René Robard, who first restored the profitability of TLH's wire production and then moved the company into cable production through the acquisition of Canalisation Electrique. (Weiller moved on to other ventures, including the Yellow Cab Company in New York City.) By 1914, TLH was the third largest electrical manufacturer in France in terms of assets and had established a solid foundation for future growth.[21]

The Compagnie Electro-Mécanique (CEM) was founded in 1885 by three established French manufacturers—Delaunay-Belleville in steam boilers, Weyher et Richemond in steam engines, and the Société Industrielle des Téléphones—to assemble and install electrical power stations using the equipment they manufactured along with dynamos supplied by the American Edison Company. In 1892, CEM began manufacturing improved dynamos designed by a new Swiss company, Brown-Boveri, and in 1899 Brown-Boveri took control of CEM and installed Paul Desombre as the managing director. Under Desombre's leadership,

CEM built a factory at Le Bourget and moved into the production of large steam turbines and dynamos for the Paris power and light industry. CEM also became a major producer of power plants for French ocean liners and warships. In 1911, when Brown-Boveri acquired the Swiss electrical manufacturer Alioth, CEM inherited Alioth's Lyon factory, where it set up assembly-line production of motors and transformers.[22]

The most successful French subsidiary of a foreign electrical company, however, was the Ateliers de Constructions Electriques du Nord et de l'Est (ACENE). This firm originated in the decision of the Empain group in 1901 to acquire a factory at Jeumont on the Franco-Belgian border (one wall of the plant lay *on* the border) to produce electric motors for the Paris Metro and alternators for Empain's Paris power company, SEP. Jeumont soon expanded to build motors for other French traction companies, along with electric railroad locomotives and electric cranes. In 1906, Empain decided to spin off Jeumont as an ostensibly independent company, ACENE, in which Empain retained a controlling interest. Under the management of various Empain lieutenants, ACENE added a second plant at Saint-Ouen, but it concentrated primarily on modernizing and expanding Jeumont, adding a steelworks, foundry, and wire and cable mill in the process. By 1913, Jeumont was the single largest electrical manufacturing plant in France (with 40,000 square meters of floor space and 2,300 employees). Thanks to its integrated structure and state-of-the-art machinery, it boasted the highest output per worker of any electrical plant in France.[23]

By 1914, despite false starts and stumbles along the way, the production of electric power and the manufacture of electrical matériel and equipment were established as major industries in France, and the roster of companies that would direct the development of these industries in the future was largely in place. In electric power and light, holding companies provided a measure of financial coordination among the various operating companies, but on a functional level the industry remained highly fragmented and technically immature. The voltage and frequency of electric current had yet to be standardized even within single cities; there was as yet little integration between thermal and hydraulic power production; and there had been only minimal efforts to tie local producers and distributors together in regional grids. The availability of electricity remained restricted to urban areas, and per capita consumption of electricity remained low compared to other European countries. Important industrial applications—notably the electrification of the railroads—had scarcely begun. These deficiencies in the generation and distribution of electricity in turn limited the size of the electrical equipment industry, especially since it was clear by 1914 that, for the foreseeable future, French manufacturers would be confined to the domestic market, along with part of the Spanish and Italian markets, due to the size and strength of the leading American, German, and Swiss firms. The French were also constrained by their continuing dependence on these foreign firms for much of their technology. Overcoming these many deficiencies and constraints had become the foremost priority for the French electrical industry by 1914, but fully addressing this challenge was postponed by the outbreak of World War I.

Growth, Maturation, and the Rise of Big Business, 1914–1930

As happened in virtually all French industries, the mobilization of August 1914 brought the operations of France's electrical manufacturers to a standstill, and the German invasion and occupation of the northern departments led to major losses. Among the plants that were occupied and eventually destroyed were Thomson-Houston's turbine factory at Lesquin, CGE's battery plant at Lille, and ACENE's Jeumont plant, France's largest and most modern. The war forced the cancellation of orders for new equipment in both the occupied and unoccupied zones and put on hold plans for railroad electrification and the installation of long transmission lines. The war eventually produced windfall profits for the leading electrical manufacturers, but only because they diverted their assets and energies to munitions production between 1915 and 1917. Of course, when munitions orders began to dry up in 1917 and 1918, all these companies faced the challenges of converting their new or expanded facilities to electrical production and making up lost ground in product development and manufacturing proficiency.

Meanwhile, the wartime shortage of coal resulting from the loss of major coal-producing departments (especially the department of the Nord) and the inevitable rise in the price of coal[24] prompted the government to finally commit itself to the systematic development of hydroelectric power and to the building of the transmission lines needed to move that power from the remote locations of production to centers of consumption. The government also took up the cause of electrifying the railroads (by then electric engines had been shown to be much more efficient than steam engines for locomotives). But because of the long lead time needed to carry out these projects, the impact of these government initiatives was felt only after the war ended.

In the short run, coal-based thermal electricity producers actually benefited from the wartime coal shortage because they were given privileged access to available coal supplies (and were able to purchase coal at the government's official price), while private industries buying coal in the open market faced uncertain supplies and high prices. Not surprisingly, these industries soon started shifting from steam to electrical power, to the ultimate benefit of the thermal producers. In Normandy, for example, the Société Havraise d'Energie Electrique increased its output 250 percent to meet the new demand, and in Paris the CPDE expanded its coal-fired plants at Saint-Ouen and Issy and doubled its output. Meanwhile, increases in the production and consumption of hydroelectricity in France resulted mainly from the rapid expansion of the electrochemical industry in the South. Increasing the output of the chlorates, carbides, and cyanamid used in high explosives and other munitions (i.e., poison gas) necessitated expanding the dedicated hydroelectric plants operated by the chemical manufacturers. By 1918, these companies were among the largest operators of hydroelectric plants in France, and their need to find markets for their excess power after wartime munitions production ended would provide a major incentive for the building of long-distance transmission lines after 1918.

The unbalanced, halting growth of the French electrical industry during World War I gave way to a decade of sustained and balanced growth during which France's production of electrical power increased fourfold, from under 4,000 million kilowatt-hours in 1919 to almost 17,000 million kilowatt-hours in 1930.[25] This expansion was the result, first of all, of the new commitment by the French government in the wake of the national trauma of 1914–1918 to putting in place a national electric power system as a cornerstone of France's future economic development. Between 1919 and 1923, laws were passed to clear away long-standing legal impediments to the development of electric power and to make the state an active partner of private enterprise in the industry's future growth. The law of October 1919, for example, strengthened the government's ability to take control of nonnavigable waterways away from private owners and to put it in the hands of companies developing hydroelectric power. A law of July 1922 enabled the government to compel power companies to form collective organizations to build long-distance transmission lines, and a decree the following year put these long lines under a concessionary system similar to that of the railroads. A law passed in August 1923 finally committed the government to sponsoring rural electrification. Along with all this enabling legislation, the government created various offices and bureaus, mainly under the Ministry of Public Works, to plan each phase of the creation of the national electrical system, from the development of water resources for hydroelectric power to the electrification of the railroads.

Just as important as this new government activism in the 1920s was the appearance of a positive feedback loop, in which improvements in production brought down the unit cost of electricity in France, thereby prompting ever more industrial power consumers to switch from steam to electricity and ever more municipal and household consumers to seek access to electric power. This growing demand in turn stimulated further expansion of capacity that further lowered costs (Henri Morsel has estimated that the inflation-adjusted price of electric power in France fell 60 percent between 1918 and 1940, with most of that decrease coming in the years of peak expansion in the late 1920s). In thermal production, the major contribution to the increase in capacity and decrease in costs was the introduction of ever-larger steam turbines, which in turn led to a dramatic increase in the size of power plants and a corresponding decrease in the cost of generating power (the largest power plants in Paris before 1914 were rated at 50,000 kilowatts, whereas the "supercenters" built in the 1920s were rated at 350,000–500,000 kilowatts).

Although the increasing size and efficiency of thermal power plants were major sources of the growth of electrical production in France in the 1920s, most experts believed that, given the scarcity and high price of coal in France, the key to meeting the country's long-term electric power needs lay in the full exploitation of its water resources. In the early 1920s, however, the hoped-for increase in France's hydroelectric capacity was blocked by two obstacles: The difficulty in raising the money to dam rivers and build hydroelectric plants at a time when postwar reconstruction and the declining value of the franc made investment capital scarce; and the continuing lack of long lines to transmit power from the sites of hydroelectric generation to centers of consumption, especially Paris. The financing problem was overcome after 1925 by the appearance of new holding and finance companies, especially the American-European Utilities Company, which mobilized the resources of both American and European companies to support such projects as the damming of the Truyère River and the construction of Brommat, France's biggest interwar hydroelectric project. At the same time, the logjam in connecting hydroelectric plants to urban markets was broken by the adoption of high-capacity transmission lines first used in California and by the formation of new companies to construct transmission networks. The model for these companies was UPEPO (Union des Producteurs d'Electricité des Pyrenées Orientales), founded in 1922 to support the electrification of the Southern Railroad. By the early 1930s, there were some fourteen companies like UPEPO that were busy connecting the hydro plants of the Alps, Pyrenees, and Massif Central to Paris, Lyon, and other major cities, mostly in the southern half of the country. Through the remainder of the interwar period, the development of hydroelectric power increasingly drove the growth of the whole industry.[26]

As much as government planning and government subsidies contributed to the expansion of French electrical production after World War I, private companies remained at the heart of the industry. New domestic companies appeared in the 1920s, especially in the nascent radio industry, and there was a new invasion of foreign companies, particularly in the manufacture of telephone equipment (ITT and Ericsson).[27] But the core areas of the industry—production and distribution of electricity and the manufacture of equipment for production and distribution—continued to be dominated in the 1920s by the firms, whether of domestic or foreign origin, that had been established before 1914. Indeed, it was in the 1920s and 1930s that these companies solidified their place in the ranks of France's largest and most influential corporations and helped to usher in the era of big business and managerial capitalism in France. To illuminate how they did this, the remainder of this chapter focuses on the history of the twenty-two French electrical companies, listed in Table 6, that had at least 250 million francs ($10 million) in balance-sheet assets in 1930.

One of the first things one notices about the firms in Table 6 is the virtual absence of traction companies, which reflects the rapid decline after 1914 of the sector that had launched the electrical industry in France in the 1890s. The one great continuing success story in electrified urban transport in France after World War I was the Compagnie de Chemin de Fer Métropolitain de Paris (CMP), the Empain subsidiary that operated the Paris subway system. Between 1914 and 1930, the

Table 6. France's largest electrical enterprises in 1929–1930

Rank	Group	Assets (in millions of FF)
	I. Traction	
3	Métropolitain de Paris	1,008.9
20	Compagnie Générale Française des Tramways	260.7
	II. Power Production and Distribution	
1	Compagnie Parisienne de Distribution d'Electricité	2,105.5
4	Energie Electrique du Littoral Méditerranéen	915.6
5	Union d'Electricité	887.6
6	Société Lyonnaise des Eaux et de l'Eclairage	872.5
9	Energie Industrielle	714.8
12	Nord-Lumière (Le Triphasé)	468.1
15	Force et Lumière	363.7
16	Electricité de Paris	355.3
17	Energie Electrique du Nord de la France	333.3
18	Compagnie Electrique de la Loire et du Centre	313.9
19	Electricité et Gaz du Nord	282.1
21	Force Motrices de la Vienne	255.6
	III. Manufacturing and Construction	
2	Tréfileries et Laminoirs du Havre	1,156.6
7	Compagnie Générale d'Electricité	857.1
8	Alsthom	790.6
10	Thomson-Houston	641.6
11	Electro-Câble	507.2
13	Grammont	446.9
14	ACENE-Jeumont	367.2
22	Compagnie Electro-Mécanique	254.0

Source: *Les Assemblées Générales,* 1929–1930.

length of the Metro increased from 63 to 117 kilometers, and the number of passengers carried rose from 250 million a year to an interwar high of 685 million. The growing popularity of the Metro did not necessarily translate into rising profits (or *any* profits) for the CMP, which in fact suffered chronic operating deficits throughout the 1920s because of rising labor costs. Yet the Empain group still made money by selling to the CMP the power and equipment produced by its subsidiaries. So, viewed in the context of Empain's total operations, the Metro remained a viable business in the 1920s. But the same cannot be said for the Paris tramways. By 1921, the surviving tramway companies in the Paris region were virtually bankrupt, so the Department of the Seine repurchased them and turned the concession for their operation over to a new company, the Société des Transports en Commun de la Région Parisienne (STCRP). But this was at best a stopgap. After further declines in tramway traffic, the City of Paris decided in 1929 to replace the tramways with publicly operated buses, and between 1929 and 1931 some 800 kilometers of tramway lines in the Paris region were torn up. Meanwhile, tramways held on longer in the provinces. Indeed, the only traction company in Table 6 besides the CMP is the Compagnie Générale Française des Tramways (CGFT), which continued to operate trolley lines in Orléans, Nancy, Le Havre, Toulon, Saint-Quentin, and especially in Marseille, one of the few French cities where tramway service actually expanded during the 1920s. In 1930, the CGFT remained profitable in part because it was able to change with the times, winning concessions to operate motorbuses in towns like Nancy and Le Havre where electric trams were being phased out.[28]

If the 1920s marked the beginning of the end for private enterprise in electric traction in France, they marked the true coming of age for the electric power industry, and it is perhaps not surprising that five of the ten largest electrical companies in France in 1930 were in electric power production and distribution. In Paris, three giant firms came to dominate this sector of the industry in the 1920s. The largest of these (at least on paper) was the Compagnie Parisienne de Distribution d'Electricité (CPDE), which took over the operations of the original six Paris power companies after 1907, as we saw earlier. In the 1920s, the CPDE continued to operate power plants at Saint-Ouen and Issy-les-Moulineaux, but it increasingly concentrated on power distribution rather than generation and thus focused more and more on maintaining and expanding its extensive network of low-voltage transmission lines in the greater Paris region. By contrast, Empain's Electricité de Paris (SEP) remained a power generation company. In the 1920s, SEP upgraded its plant at Saint-Denis and built a new one at Ivry to meet the growing power needs of the Metro and other clients. But the most important power company in Paris by 1930 was a new one, the Union d'Electricité, founded in 1919 by the Messine Group (so-called because its headquarters were on the Rue Messine in the eighth arrondissement), which also controlled two other of France's top ten electrical companies, the Société Lyonnaise des Eaux et de l'Eclairage (SLEE) and Nord-Lumière (Le Triphasé).

SLEE had been founded in 1880 by the Crédit Lyonnais, the Banque Mirabaud, and various Swiss bankers to provide water and gas in a number of French cities (though not in Lyon!). In 1896, Albert Petsche, a young state engineer tied to the Koechlins and the Société Alsacienne de Constructions Mécaniques (SACM), joined the SLEE board and began moving the company into the electrical power industry, particularly in Paris, where SLEE took over Le Triphasé and its distribution arm, Nord-Lumière, in the early 1900s. After Petsche became the managing director of SLEE in 1909, he brought in another rising young engineer, Ernest Mercier, to be chief engineer at Nord-Lumière/Le Triphasé and to prepare a bold plan to standardize the electric power consumed in the Paris market and to unify its production under a single company. However, Petsche and Mercier were able to act on this plan only after World War I.

In 1919, on behalf of the Messine Group, Mercier founded a *société d'études,* the Union Française d'Electricité (UFE), to undertake the consolidation of power production in Paris by building a new state-of-the-art power plant to replace the smaller, outdated plants in the Paris area. Within months, Mercier had merged the UFE with one of the principal power companies in the Paris region, the CGDEE, to form the Union d'Electricité (UDE). The UDE proceeded to upgrade the CGDEE's existing power plants at Vitry and Billancourt to meet short-term power needs in Paris, while it started construction of the largest power plant in the world at Gennevilliers on the Seine. Gennevilliers was designed to produce power so cheaply that the other Paris producers would be hard-pressed to compete. Consequently, in 1920 and 1921, the distribution companies in the region that still operated power plants, like Ouest-Lumière and Nord-Lumière, sold those plants to the UDE, which continued to operate them until Gennevilliers went on line in 1922 and then shut them down. By 1923, the Gennevilliers plant was supplying one-half of all the electricity consumed in Paris. Within five years, the UDE had become the leading thermal power producer in France and was coordinating all power generation in Paris as the leading partner in a consortium formed with the CPDE and SEP. With SLEE controlling some fifteen power companies in France and North Africa (including the UDE) through a holding company, Albert Petsche and Ernest Mercier, chairman and president of the Messine Group, respectively, had emerged as the most powerful figures in the French electrical industry by the end of the 1920s.[29]

In provincial France, five regional companies founded before World War I continued to dominate power generation and distribution in the 1920s (along with the companies of the Messine Group), and these remained among the largest electrical companies in France in 1930.

They included Loire et Centre and Energie Electrique du Nord de la France, still part of the Giros-Loucheur group, and Franco-Suisse's Force et Lumière. The largest remained Energie Electrique du Littoral Méditerranéen (EELM), founded and still largely controlled by Thomson-Houston to provide electric power to tramways, local power and light companies, and various industrial customers in the south of France. Although EELM built two new thermal plants and one hydro plant in the 1920s, it ceased growing at its prewar rate and was surpassed in revenues and profits at the end of the decade by a more dynamic company, Energie Industrielle (EI), which had been founded in 1906 by Pierre-Marie Durand, a Lyon lawyer who had taken control of the tramways of Saint-Etienne in 1901. After World War I, EI methodically acquired local distribution companies in a wide area of southern France, connected them with each other and with the hydroelectric plants of the Alps and the Massif, and eventually became the largest provider of electric power in France, serving an area with a population of ten million by World War II. At first, EI bought power from the electrochemical and electrometals manufacturers in the Alps and from the established hydroelectric producers like Force Motrices du Rhône and Force et Lumière. In the 1930s, however, it integrated backward into production by taking control of some 130 hydroelectric plants that had a combined annual output of 1,625 million kilowatt-hours. This made EI and its subsidiaries—the Groupe Durand—the largest production group in France at the end of the 1930s.[30]

Despite the apparent health and dynamism of France's leading private electric power companies in the 1920s and even the depression decade of the 1930s, various factors were making it increasingly likely that the state would sooner or later take over the industry. These factors included the chronically shaky finances of most power and light companies, a problem traceable to their high debt loads and inconsistent revenue streams; the progressive knitting together of the power companies into a national power grid that cried out for centralized management and planning; and the resurgence of the socialist Left with its commitment to state ownership of the means of production. Ultimately, nationalization of the electric power industry came after the Second World War, amid the triumph of the Left-leaning parties of the Resistance, and the various private companies in production, transmission, and distribution of electricity disappeared into a new state corporation, Electricité de France. As a consequence, the firms that would dominate what remained of the private electrical industry in

France after 1946—and that would participate in the remarkable growth of the European electrical and electronics industry in the 1960s and 1970s—were the large electrical equipment companies founded before 1914 that had occupied prominent places on the list of France's largest firms in 1930.

Thomson-Houston remained France's largest electrical manufacturer in the early 1920s. Even before World War I had ended, CFTH had begun to recast its manufacturing resources to meet the needs of the anticipated postwar expansion in power and light production, telephone and wireless service, and railroad electrification. In 1918 it took over Eclairage Electrique, one of the oldest electrotechnology companies in France. This added five factories to CFTH's roster, effectively doubling its manufacturing capacity. At the same time, with a $10 million advance from General Electric, CFTH acquired a racetrack at Saint-Ouen where it built a 10,000-square-meter factory for electric locomotives and power generation equipment. By 1922, CFTH possessed 500,000 square meters of factory space and 4,000 machine tools; it employed 10,000 workers in its reorganized and upgraded manufacturing division; and it was about to launch new manufacturing subsidiaries in Italy, Spain, Belgium, and Rumania in cooperation with GE. General Electric also reaffirmed CFTH's status as the exclusive French licensee of GE technology and allowed CFTH to station engineers permanently at its laboratories in Schenectady, New York, to assure immediate access to new products and processes.

Delays in the anticipated postwar surge in key sectors of the electrical industry, particularly hydroelectricity, communications, and railroad electrification, forced CFTH's new general director, Auguste Detoeuf, to reconsider the company's commitment to diversified manufacturing in the mid-twenties. Already in 1922, at the urging of General Electric, CFTH had spun off its lightbulb manufacturing division into a new firm, the Compagnie des Lampes, controlled jointly with GE and CGE, in order to compete more effectively with Osram, the subsidiary of the German electrical companies.[31] In 1926, CFTH decided to pull out of the telephone business and sold its production facilities to International Telephone and Telegraph (ITT), which had taken over the international division of Western Electric and was fast becoming the principal telephone manufacturer in France. In the same year, Detoeuf entered into talks with Albert Petsche, in the latter's capacity as chairman of SACM, about merging their companies' manufacturing resources in heavy electrical equipment in a jointly owned company that could stand up to foreign competitors. Two years later, these negotiations culminated in the founding of Alsthom (the name combines Thomson and Alsacienne). The new firm took over SACM's Belfort plant (effectively taking SACM out of electrical manufacturing) and leased CFTH's big new plant at Saint-Ouen and its older plants at Lesquin (Nord) and Neuilly. Alsthom's resources were further increased in 1930 when it took over Constructions Electriques de France, an electrical construction company created after the war by Paribas and British electrical manufacturers that had not panned out. By 1930, Alsthom employed 12,000 workers, sold equipment worth 650 million francs (primarily to domestic power companies), and had surpassed its two parent companies in terms of assets. Meanwhile, CFTH retained its electrical manufacturing plants in Paris, where it concentrated on the production of batteries, cables, and railroad signaling equipment. It also retained its rights to GE technology, especially in the future growth area of telecommunications, and it remained a major holding company with participations in an array of power and light companies and manufacturing subsidiaries.[32]

Like Thomson-Houston, the Compagnie Générale d'Electricité, France's other diversified electrical manufacturer before 1914, had moved into munitions production during the war and faced the challenge of retooling for the postwar economy in 1918. At that point, CGE was still essentially two companies: an electrical manufacturer with a strong presence in metallurgy and a holding company for provincial power plants, especially in Lorraine and Marseille. Under the continued leadership of Pierre Azaria and his team, CGE maintained and expanded its holdings in power generation in the 1920s. Indeed, as of 1928, CGE's subsidiaries produced more electric power—245 million kilowatt-hours—than any other group in provincial France. They also provided an assured market for some of the electrical equipment and matériel that CGE continued to manufacture. In the immediate postwar period, CGE sold off much of the new capacity in metal production that it had developed during the war as well as its lightbulb division (in return for a one-quarter share of the new Compagnie des Lampes), and it proceeded to concentrate its resources in certain areas of manufacturing. One of these was electric batteries—thought to be a growth area in the age of the automobile and airplane—which it produced at the restored Lille plant of its Tudor battery division. Another area of concentration was electric transmission. In the course of the 1920s, CGE's Delle division became a major manufacturer of high-tension equipment, a new ceramics division (Electro-Céramique) produced power-line insulators, and Câbles de Lyon expanded to supply much of the transmission line being installed across France. On the negative side, CGE made a bid to enter telephone production by acquiring the French branch of Ericsson in 1928 but had to bail out two years later. On the whole, however, the story of CGE in the 1920s was one of successful restructuring and continued growth. As late as 1920, the majority of CGE's revenues came from metals production. By 1930, metals accounted for only 27 percent of revenues, and electrical equipment had become its leading division, accounting for 43 percent of revenues. This shift played a major role in boosting the company's total sales from 283 million francs in 1918 to 1,303 million in 1930. With assets of over 850 million francs in 1930, CGE had surpassed CFTH to become France's second largest electrical manufacturing company.[33]

The largest French electrical manufacturer in terms of assets in 1930, and perhaps the industry's greatest success story in the 1920s, was the Tréfileries et Laminoirs du Havre (TLH). Still led by the professional managers put in place before World War I, TLH continued to specialize in wire and cable after 1918 and increasingly served as the principal link between the electrical and metallurgical industries. To support its wire and cable production, TLH integrated backward into aluminum production during and after World War I and expanded its resources in steel and steel alloys through participation in several new steel companies, including Lorraine Minière et Métallurgique and Hauts-Fourneaux de Chiers. Meanwhile, it expanded its wire and cable production by refurbishing its Le Havre plant and by acquiring a number of others, including the Pont-de-Cheruy plant of Grammont. By 1929, TLH produced 40 percent of the steel wire and electric cable made in France. To assure the sale of these products, the company integrated forward, helping to found Lignes Téléphoniques et Télégraphiques, which became a leading supplier of telephone line to France's state-run telephone system. TLH's permanent capital rose sixfold in the 1920s, and by 1930 TLH was no longer just a manufacturing company but (like CFTH and CGE) the center of a group.[34]

In contrast to the consistent success of the Big Four of French electrical manufacturing—CFTH, CGE, Alsthom, and TLH—the performance of the other large home-grown electrical manufacturers was mixed in the 1920s. On the one hand, there was Schneider's electrical division, which in 1929 became the French licensee for Westinghouse and was relaunched as Matériel SW. There was also the Compagnie des Compteurs, which continued to specialize in electric and gas meters, remained close to GE and CFTH (which, of course, had started out as a joint venture of GE and Compteurs), and grew mainly by expanding into Holland, Austria, Spain, Great Britain, Germany, and Czechoslovakia after 1918. On the other hand, there was Etablissements Grammont, which had once rivaled TLH in wire and cable but which tried to diversify too rapidly and too widely in the 1920s, failed to establish a customer base, and by 1929 was on the brink of collapse (in spite of balance-sheet assets of 446 million francs that on paper made it the sixth largest electrical manufacturer in France).

In the final analysis, the strongest performance after World War I among the second tier of electrical manufacturers in France was registered by the subsidiaries of foreign conglomerates, ACENE-Jeumont and CEM. ACENE had suffered the loss of its modern and highly efficient plant at Jeumont during World War I, but thanks to continued financial backing from the Empain group and government reconstruction subsidies, Jeumont was quickly rebuilt and outfitted with the latest American machine tools after 1918. ACENE also converted its munitions plant at Saint-Denis to peacetime production and took over plants at Levallois and Saint-Ouen that had been formerly operated by another Empain company, Ateliers de Longueville. With these expanded and modernized production facilities and with Empain companies like SEP and the Paris Metro providing an assured customer base, ACENE soon reclaimed its position as a leading maker of heavy electrical equipment and enjoyed a steady rise in sales revenues from 110 million francs in 1921 to 265 million in 1930. Meanwhile, the Compagnie Electro-Mécanique (CEM), still closely tied to Brown-Boveri and its new British partner, Vickers, and still managed by Paul Desombre and his team, remained the leading producer in France of steam turbines for electricity generation and naval applications. In 1920, CEM acquired the French assets of the S.A. Westinghouse, including a plant at Le Havre that was one of the largest in France, as part of the deal by which Vickers took over British Westinghouse. In 1927, when Brown-Boveri and Vickers parted company, CEM lost its privileged access to Westinghouse patents (those soon went to Schneider), but it maintained its position in turbine construction by joining a cartel organized by Alsthom, which guaranteed it 30 percent of the domestic market for turbines. At the end of the 1920s, CEM remained a highly profitable enterprise.[35]

By 1930, France was well on its way to acquiring a national electric power system comparable to those of other industrial nations—a system owned and operated by private power and light companies that ranked among the largest industrial enterprises in France. What is perhaps more surprising, given the financial and technical domination of the international electrical industry by the American and German giants in the early twentieth century, is that France in 1930 also possessed a large and growing electrical equipment industry that supported some of France's largest manufacturing companies.

Although France's four largest electrical manufacturers—TLH, CGE, Alsthom, CFTH—were still dwarfed by the biggest American companies (GE, Western Electric, Westinghouse, RCA) in 1930, they matched up well in terms of assets and workforce with all but the three largest German electrical companies (see Table 7). These French electrical firms must be seen as part of the new world of big business, not only because of their size but also because they were following the same strategic imperatives and were exhibiting the same organizational and structural complexities as the large electrical firms elsewhere. To be sure, companies like CGE and Thomson-Houston that had integrated vertically to assure their supplies of raw materials and that were diversifying their product lines and extending (or at least maintaining) markets abroad in the 1920s did not necessarily concentrate their operations under a single corporate umbrella. In the electrical industry as in others, the French approach to concentration involved the creation not of giant corporations but of groups of small, ostensibly independent

Table 7. Assets and workforces of the four largest American, German, and French electrical manufacturing companies in 1929–1930

United States		Germany		France	
Assets (in millions of dollars)					
General Electric	493.9	AEG	137.9	TLH	45.3
Western Electric	379.0	Siemens-Schukert	100.2	CGE	33.6
Westinghouse	246.0	Siemens-Halske	96.7	Alsthom	30.9
RCA	168.5	Bergmann	23.0	CFTH	25.1
Workforces in 1930					
GE	78,380	Siemens-Halske	116,000	CGE	20,000
Westinghouse	36,900	AEG	65,000	Alsthom	12,000
		Bergmann	12,000	CFTH	10,000

Sources: Maurice Lévy-Leboyer and Henri Morsel, eds., *Histoire générale de l'électricité en France*, vol. 2 (Paris, 1994), 1033–1045, 1062–1066; Alfred D. Chandler, Jr., *Scale and Scope* (Cambridge, Mass., 1990), 649, 712 and passim; Youssef Cassis, *Big Business: The European Experience in the Twentieth Century* (Oxford, 1997), 253.

firms attached to a somewhat larger mother company by means of interlocking directorates or through the intermediation of a holding company. Yet these groups functioned much like the multidivisional corporations arising in the United States and Germany—notably General Electric and Siemens—in which semi-autonomous operating divisions were given great latitude to develop specific products for specific markets, while top management exercised overall strategic and financial control. This was particularly true at CGE, where a long-established team of top managers (still Pierre Azaria and his protégés in the late 1920s) set overall corporate policies and goals while leaving tactical decision making to the heads of the various branches and subsidiaries. In the words of the company's official historians, "CGE was becoming a structure for economic and financial control while the essential operational activities passed to subsidiaries where increasing technical autonomy required management that was ever more developed [étoffé] and close-to-the-ground."[36]

Whatever their individual corporate structures, France's leading electrical companies by 1930 had acquired much of the technical expertise and the resources in production, marketing, and management—in short, the organizational capabilities—that would allow them to survive the depression of the 1930s and the upheaval of war and occupation in the early 1940s and to reemerge as key players in the resurgent and expanding industrial economies of France and Western Europe in the second half of the twentieth century.

CHAPTER FOURTEEN

The Automobile and Its Allies

No products of the Second Industrial Revolution had greater impact on the fabric of life and on the economic development of the Western world in the twentieth century than the automobile and related forms of motorized road transportation. While the French played minor roles in the creation of other new technologies at the end of the nineteenth century, they were the world leaders in automotive technology in the 1890s and early 1900s, and they remained the leading producers of automobiles in Europe until the 1930s, when they were surpassed by the British and, more permanently, by the Germans. But by then there were several world-class automotive companies in France that would continue to play major roles in the European automobile industry through the rest of the century. Moreover, by the 1930s the French automobile industry had fostered allied industries that also gave rise to major industrial firms. These included tire and rubber, aviation, and petroleum. This chapter examines how this cluster of new industries developed in France from the 1890s to the 1930s and how each industry came to be dominated by a few very large enterprises that, along with the big firms in steel, electricity, and chemicals, served as vectors for the advent of modern managerial capitalism in France.

The Automobile Industry

Beginnings, 1889–1914

The automobile was born in Germany in the 1880s when Karl Benz and Gottfried Daimler mounted gasoline-powered internal combustion engines on wheeled vehicles, but it was the French who took the early lead in automobile manufacturing in Europe in the 1890s.[1] In 1888 the Paris engineering firm Panhard et Levassor acquired the license to make the Daimler engine in France, and it persuaded the bicycle manufacturer Armand Peugeot to put that engine on a quadricycle in 1891. Within a year, Peugeot had built and sold twenty-nine of these automobiles, and by 1894 his annual sales had risen to forty. This modest commercial success, reinforced by victories in early automobile races, convinced Peugeot to devote his full efforts to automobile manufacturing. In 1896, he left the family hardware and bicycle company near Montbéliard to found the Société Anonyme des Automobiles Peugeot. By 1899, this company was producing 300 vehicles a year at factories in Audincourt and Lille.[2]

Panhard et Levassor (P&L) also began to build automobile chassis, as well as engines, in the mid-nineties, and by 1902 P&L was turning out 1,000 cars a year. Another important car company was launched by Comte Albert De Dion, the wealthy Parisian sportsman who organized the Automobile Club de France and many of the early automobile races. In 1893, De Dion joined forces with the mechanic Georges Bouton to introduce a new automobile engine that was twice as powerful as the Daimler. Soon, De Dion and Bouton were supplying this engine to French automakers and mounting it on their own brand of tricycles. By 1899, the firm of De Dion-Bouton employed 950 workers at a plant in Puteaux to produce 5,000 tricycles and four-wheel *voiturettes* plus 5,000 engines a year for other carmakers.[3]

The early success of Peugeot, Panhard et Levassor, and De Dion-Bouton depended on growing demand for automobiles not just in France but throughout the world. Indeed, by the early 1900s the leading French automobile manufacturers were selling more cars abroad than at home.[4] Such an expansive market inevitably drew dozens of would-be manufacturers. Like Armand Peugeot, many of these came out of the bicycle industry, including Darracq, Clement, Richard, Rochet-Schneider, and Chenard et Walcker. Others had backgrounds in the machinery and engineering industries, including De Dietrich (railroad equipment), Delaunay-Belleville (steam engines and boilers), Mors (electrical wiring), and Hotchkiss (machine guns). Some were young engineers and mechanics with little or no prior industrial experience, such as Louis Renault.

As the teenage son of a well-to-do textile merchant, Louis Renault began tinkering with engines and road vehicles in the mid-1890s in a workshop on the family estate in Billancourt on the southwest edge of

Paris. In late 1898, Renault built and demonstrated an automobile of his own design, and the next year he began manufacturing it in partnership with his older brothers. Victories in road races in 1899 and 1900 established the reputation of Renault's cars for performance, durability, and technological innovation. In 1903, Renault started making his own engines, instead of buying them from De Dion-Bouton, and building the bodies for some of his cars (at that time most car manufacturers assembled only the chassis; the body was crafted separately by coach makers and added later). Renault's big break came in 1905 when the new Société des Automobiles de Place awarded him the contract to build the first fleet of metered taxicabs. Similar orders followed from taxi companies in London and New York. As of 1907, Renault had built two-thirds of the taxicabs operating in Paris and half the taxicabs in London. By 1908, Renault Frères was turning out 3,575 units a year at its Billancourt plant, making it France's largest automobile company.[5]

After the death of one brother in the Paris-Madrid auto race of 1903 (which ended the company's participation in racing) and the death of his other brother in 1909, Louis Renault controlled virtually all shares of the Renault Automobile Company and became, in the words of his foremost biographer, a "patron absolu."[6] Renault maintained absolute control of his firm for the next thirty-five years by self-financing all subsequent growth and by studiously avoiding any recourse to outside sources of capital. In this respect, he resembled the leading American automaker, Henry Ford, but in other ways Renault and Ford differed. Although Renault visited Ford's Highland Park plant and took away pointers in production efficiency, he did not follow Ford into the mass production of a single utilitarian model after 1908. Believing that there was not yet a market in France or Europe for a mass-produced small car, Renault instead tooled up to produce eleven different models, ranging from eight-horsepower runabouts to forty-five–horsepower touring cars. He also moved into the production of trucks, buses, and aircraft engines.

Along with product diversification, Renault pursued geographic expansion, as did Ford, by setting up assembly plants in Spain, Hungary, and Russia (Renault's Saint Petersburg plant was actually larger than his Billancourt plant in 1914). Renault also integrated vertically by setting up in-house production of components previously purchased from outside suppliers. This required doubling the size of the Billancourt plant and increasing its stock of machine tools fourfold between

1905 and 1913. At the same time, Renault departed from his early reliance on independent, non-exclusive auto dealers by creating an extensive network of company-owned sales agencies. Thanks to the new emphasis on higher-priced cars and trucks, Renault enjoyed strong growth in sales revenues and gross profits after 1908, but the company's modest increase in total production, from about 3,600 vehicles in 1908 to around 5,000 per year in 1910–1912, gave competitors a chance to claim a larger share of an expanding French auto market.[7]

Among Renault's principal domestic rivals in 1908–1914 was the Lyon company founded and managed by Marius Berliet. Berliet developed a two-cylinder water-cooled engine for the Audibert-Lavarotte Automobile Company in the 1890s and then started assembling cars under his own name in 1899. His first success was a four-cylinder roadster that won several regional road races in the early 1900s. With 500,000 francs earned from licensing the production of this roadster in the United States, Berliet was able to buy the Audibert-Lavarotte plant, install American and German machine tools, and begin producing heavy touring cars and light trucks that used a common chassis. By 1913, the Berliet Company was turning out 3,000 vehicles a year, putting it in fourth place among French auto and truck manufacturers.[8] Third place, meanwhile, was occupied by the Darracq Company. Founded in the late 1890s by the successful bicycle manufacturer Alexandre Darracq, this firm had been taken over by British investors in 1903 to build cars for the British market (and also the Italian market— Darracq's Milan assembly plant later provided the basis for the Alfa-Romeo company). After a series of bad decisions, including heavy investment in a steam-powered bus, the board of directors replaced Darracq as general manager with an Englishman, Owen Clegg, who concentrated on the production of two models of automobile and restored the company's profitability with sales of 3,500 vehicles in 1913.[9] By then, however, an even greater comeback had been staged by Peugeot, which emerged as France's second largest carmaker and Renault's principal domestic rival on the eve of World War I.

After its initial success in the 1890s, Automobiles Peugeot had suffered declining sales in the early 1900s as new companies began offering technically superior cars. To turn things around, Armand Peugeot set up a new bureau to funnel the latest technological innovations in Paris to Peugeot's factories at Audincourt and Lille. As the quality of Peugeot's cars improved, its sales rose, from 876 cars in 1903 to

1,500 in 1909.[10] Meanwhile, at the Peugeot hardware and bicycle company, Armand Peugeot's cousin Eugène had begun making motorbikes, motorcycles, and a best-selling small car, prompting the aging Armand, who lacked an heir, to begin negotiating the merger of the automobile and bicycle businesses of the two Peugeot companies. These negotiations culminated in the founding of the Société Anonyme des Automobiles et Cycles Peugeot (SAACP) in 1908. In 1912, Eugène Peugeot's son Robert succeeded Armand as managing director of the SAACP, but the key figure at the new company was Ernest Mattern, a young engineer who had learned American cost accounting at Westinghouse's Le Havre plant and was also familiar with Frederick W. Taylor's theories of scientific management. First as production manager at Peugeot's Lille plant and then as director of its Audincourt plant, Mattern reorganized Peugeot's production system between 1908 and 1912, raising output, productivity, and profitability in the process. In 1913, Peugeot turned out 5,000 automobiles and trucks (versus only 1,500 in 1909), generated sales revenues of 51.8 million francs (second only to Renault's 57.8 million), and earned profits of 4 million francs (four times its profits of 1909).[11]

In 1913, France produced 45,000 automobiles, less than one-tenth the number built by the fast-rising American auto industry but still more than were produced in any other country outside the United States. However, that production was spread over a large number of firms. According to James M. Laux, hundreds of firms manufactured automobiles in France at one time or another before 1914, but in 1913 only twelve made as many as 1,000 cars a year. The largest of these—Renault, Peugeot, De Dion-Bouton, Panhard et Levassor, and the British-owned Darracq and Delahaye—already ranked among the 100 largest manufacturing firms in France in 1913, but in terms of assets and workforce even Renault and Peugeot were less than half the size of France's largest steel, electrical, and chemical manufacturers.[12] More importantly, they were dwarfed by the largest American firm, Ford, which produced 200,000 cars in the United States alone in 1913, an astounding fact given that as recently as 1908 Ford and Renault were virtually equal in plant size and workforce. Renault and Peugeot were also substantially smaller than the next ten largest American carmakers, which were each producing between 10,000 and 37,500 cars a year in 1913.[13]

Ford's dramatic growth from 1908 to 1913 was a direct result of its decision to concentrate on building a low-priced "people's car," the

Model T, to be made from standardized parts using moving lines for the assembly of both major components (engines, transmissions, bodies) and the whole car. In setting up this production system, Henry Ford drew on a century of American experience in mass-producing complex machinery with interchangeable parts (the so-called American System of Manufacture).[14] By contrast, French carmakers had little experience in this area, and it took at least until the 1920s for them to achieve true standardization and interchangeability. Similarly, while some French carmakers were experimenting with assembly lines before 1914—notably Lorraine-Dietrich at Argenteuil and Berliet at Lyon-Montplaisir—most French cars and trucks in those years were still being assembled in batches by skilled workers laboriously fitting together non-standardized parts. In short, the French automobile industry remained a craft industry, albeit a very large one, before World War I. It was the war itself, or more specifically the automakers' participation in wartime munitions production, that finally put the French automobile industry on the road to mass production.[15]

Mass Production and Concentration, 1914–1935

With the outbreak of war and the subsequent occupation of northern France in August 1914, Peugeot lost its assembly plant in Lille and Panhard et Levassor lost a parts plant in Reims, but most automobile production in France escaped direct damage because it was concentrated in and around Paris and Lyon, far from the front lines. As the war dragged on, domestic demand for automobiles dried up and French automakers lost their export markets, but these losses were more than offset by orders from the French military for trucks and armored vehicles, aircraft engines, and especially munitions. Indeed, even more than the steel and electrical manufacturers, French auto companies—particularly Renault—benefited from the massive demand for war matériel between 1914 and 1918. Renault produced only 3,500 cars over the entire four years of the war (versus 5,000 a year before the war), but it turned out 9,320 trucks, 1,760 tanks, 12,500 aircraft engines, 1,160 aircraft, 5 million rockets, and 8.5 million artillery shells, which allowed it to triple the size of its Billancourt factory, double its stock of machine tools, and increase its sales revenues sixfold from 57.8 million francs in 1913 to 326–378 million per year during the war.[16]

Berliet also enjoyed dramatic growth during World War I, on the basis of contracts for artillery shells and 2,500 four-ton trucks that became famous for supplying Verdun over the *Voie Sacrée* in 1916. In 1917, Berliet opened a new plant at Venissieux (Lyon) that was one-third larger than Ford's Detroit plant, making it the world's largest automobile factory until the opening of Ford's River Rouge plant in 1919. Venissieux employed 10,000 workers, featured the first moving assembly line in the European auto industry, and included its own in-house steel mill to get around wartime metals shortages. Meanwhile, Peugeot benefited much less from the war—not so much because of the loss of its Lille plant but because the location of its other plants near the front in eastern France made the government reluctant to grant it major arms contracts. Peugeot eventually built 6,000 trucks at its Sochaux plant, as well as 6,500 aircraft engines, 1,400 tank engines, and 1.7 million artillery shells at two plants near Paris, but its total wartime sales were only 60 percent of Renault's, and its wartime profits of 37 million francs were only a fifth of Renault's.[17]

The French automobile maker that enjoyed the greatest success during World War I was surely André Citroën. The son of a Dutch diamond merchant who came to Paris in the 1870s, Citroën graduated from the Ecole Polytechnique in 1898, patented a new gearing system for railroad locomotives, and in 1905 founded his own company to manufacture those gears. Soon thereafter he joined the board of directors of the troubled Mors Automobile Company, which he took over in 1908 with the backing of friends in the diamond trade. Under Citroën's direction, Mors still made only 600–800 cars a year and continued to suffer operating losses through 1913. It was only after the outbreak of war that Citroën finally emerged as an important industrialist by applying Ford's techniques of mass production to making munitions. In 1915, Citroën convinced the French Ministry of Armaments to underwrite the construction of a huge plant on the Quai Javel in southwestern Paris, where he planned to produce artillery shells on a moving assembly line. The Quai Javel plant opened in mid-1915 and after a slow start became increasingly productive, turning out 10,000, then 15,000, and eventually 20,000 shells a day with 12,000 largely unskilled (mostly female) workers. By the end of the war, Citroën's factory had produced 26 million shells (three times the output of Renault's Billancourt factory) and had generated enormous profits (later estimated at 125 million francs). Most importantly, Javel had made Citroën a national hero.[18]

Thanks to wartime contracts, the plant, equipment, and personnel of the French automobile industry increased fourfold between 1914 and 1918.[19] The firms that had profited the most from this increase—Renault, Citroën, Berliet, and Peugeot—came out of the war with sufficient resources to contemplate moving from the craft production of automobiles to American-style large-scale production. But the question remained, how to do this within the constraints of the French and continental European markets, inasmuch as the huge growth of the American auto industry—and the accelerating growth of British auto production—had largely deprived the French of foreign markets. The experience of Berliet soon demonstrated that wartime expansion in itself did not assure success in the postwar decade. Marius Berliet possessed the largest, most modern automobile factory in Europe in 1918, but he squandered this advantage by staking the company's future on the mass production of a single truck model and a single automobile based on the American Dodge. Because the steel available to Berliet was not suitable for a large, American-style automobile, the Berliet Dodge soon acquired a reputation for poor quality, and it failed in the marketplace. Because of the glut of surplus army trucks, Berliet's truck sales also lagged. Three years of operating losses brought Berliet's company to the brink of bankruptcy and put it under the control of bankers. By the time Berliet regained control of his company in 1929, he had lost his competitive advantage in auto production and thereafter concentrated on making heavy trucks.[20] Clearly, it was the quality of strategic decision-making, and not just the money and capacity gained during the war, that was going to determine which companies survived and prospered in the competitive postwar environment.

For Citroën, Renault, and Peugeot, the strategic choices in 1918–1919 were not unlike those revealed in the titanic battle between the world's two largest automakers, Ford and General Motors. In the 1920s, Ford continued to pursue a production-oriented strategy by which it manufactured a single model (first the Model T, later the Model A) in the largest possible quantity at the lowest possible cost and marketed this car on the basis of price and value. General Motors, however, pursued a marketing-oriented strategy by which it produced an array of models using a system of flexible mass production and then marketed these cars less on price than on such "soft" characteristics as style and comfort. As Richard Tedlow has argued, Ford's strategy was tailored to first-time buyers looking for inexpensive, reliable transportation, whereas General Motors' strategy was tailored to those looking to replace their first car with something better. As long as first-time buyers were the chief customers, Ford dominated the American automobile market. But by 1925, when the demand for basic transportation had been met in the United States, the advantage shifted rapidly to General Motors, and within two years it had displaced Ford as the largest automobile company in the world.[21]

Although General Motors had the right strategy for the American market in the mid-twenties, it should be emphasized that the situation in the United States—precocious saturation of the market for first-time sales—was unique. Sales leveled off in the United States after 1925 (albeit at a high level), but sales in France continued to grow as more and more first-time buyers entered what, by American standards, was not yet a fully developed mass market. In such circumstances, it is not surprising that French carmakers looked to Henry Ford for inspiration after 1920, as they had before 1914, but they did so only up to a point. Whether because of lack of financial resources or because of skepticism about creating a true mass market for cars in Europe, Renault, Citroën, Peugeot, and the others leavened the Fordist emphasis on all-out mass production with elements of the General Motors approach. So the leading French firms ended up pursuing a hybrid strategy that had six main elements:

1. investment in the technology and organization required for mass production (but more the flexible mass production of General Motors than the Ford version)

2. backward integration into the production of components and even the raw materials for components (a Ford strategy)

3. forward integration into automobile marketing

4. geographic expansion of the market

5. diversification of automobile products and diversification beyond auto production (a General Motors strategy)

6. development of broader organizational capabilities, especially in research, testing, and product development (also associated mainly with General Motors)

The automaker who was most successful in implementing this hybrid strategy in the 1920s was André Citroën. Citroën set out after World War I to produce, à la Henry Ford, a reliable, low-cost car in unprecedented quantities (his goal was to turn out 500 cars a day—150,000 a year—which was three times the annual production of the entire French auto industry in 1913). To this end, he merged Mors and several other French auto companies into the Société André Citroën, turned his munitions plant on the Quai Javel into an automobile assembly plant, and introduced the Citroën Model A in 1919. However, production problems kept initial output below optimal levels, which in turn made it impossible to sell the Model A at as low a price as promised, so to boost sales Citroën temporarily set aside his single-model strategy by introducing the smaller, five-horsepower Citron (lemon!—so-named as a play on "Citroën" and because of its color, not presumably as a comment on its quality). Additional models soon followed, yet Citroën never abandoned his goal of setting up American-style mass production of a single model.

In the early 1920s, the Javel plant was completely rebuilt to give Citroën the most sophisticated moving assembly line in Europe. At the same time, Citroën brought in Ernest Mattern from Peugeot to apply Taylorist principles to job and factory design throughout the company. Mattern also set up new production facilities to support the Javel assembly plant, including Europe's only continuous casting plant at Clichy and a state-of-the-art stamping plant at Saint-Ouen ("one of the glories of the company," according to Sylvie Schweitzer). However, Citroën never managed to carry production rationalization to its logical conclusion by concentrating all operations at a single location. Lacking sufficient space at Quai Javel but not wanting to abandon that site, Citroën ended up producing parts at several plants scattered across the Paris metropolitan region and then trucking them to Javel for assembly, which added significantly to the construction costs of each auto. Citroën did eventually return to the production of a single model (the ten-horsepower B14) in 1924. Though output took off, rising from 55,387 units in 1924 to 102,891 in 1929—almost twice that of Citroën's nearest competitor, Renault—costs and prices remained too high for the B14 to become a true people's car like the Ford Model T.[22]

If André Citroën played the part of Henry Ford by emphasizing the mass production of a single car, in other respects his approach to making and marketing automobiles was closer to that of General Motors. The appeal of his cars rested less on price and value than on their reputation for advanced engineering (the all-steel body in 1924, front-wheel drive in 1933), and in the final analysis Citroën's genius lay in marketing, not in production. In the 1920s he created a network of elegantly appointed sales agencies and invested heavily in innovative advertising and production, putting his name in lights on the Eiffel

Tower and staging well-publicized expeditions of his half-track vehicles across the Sahara and central Asia. Ultimately, it was this marketing flair that propelled the company to its great success in the late 1920s. By 1929, Citroën was not only the largest automobile company in France; in terms of assets and workforce, it was also the country's largest publicly held manufacturing enterprise of any kind.

Like Citroën, Louis Renault came out of World War I with lots of money and plant capacity, and like Citroën he invested heavily in modernizing his production facilities. But Renault refused to limit production to a single low-priced model and instead offered a range of medium- and high-priced cars. The chief Fordist element in Renault's business policy continued to be his insistence on maintaining absolute control over operations, even after 1922 when the company became a *société anonyme* governed in theory by a board of directors (Renault preserved his authority by retaining ownership of 80 percent of the shares in the new stock company). Another Fordist element in Renault's strategy was his pursuit of self-sufficiency through vertical integration. While Citroën sought to reduce production costs by achieving greater efficiency in the assembly process, Renault sought to cut costs by controlling as many production inputs as possible (Renault and Citroën each adopted only half of the total Ford production strategy, so neither achieved the overall cost reductions that Ford achieved). In the 1920s, Renault took over a number of formerly independent parts manufacturers and also set up in-house production of electrical components, rubber, cottonwool (for seat padding), tempered glass, and other production inputs. To end his dependence on the steel companies, Renault participated in the creation of the Union des Consommateurs de Produits Métallurgiques et Industriels (UCPMI), which acquired and operated Thyssen's Hagodange steelworks in Lorraine after 1919, and in 1930 he founded the Société des Aciers Fins de l'Est (SAFE) to produce special steels in electric furnaces and later American cold-rolled steel after UCPMI refused to invest in that new technology. Renault also installed his own gas and electric plants at Billancourt to end his dependence on the Paris power companies.

Renault did not neglect marketing, but his approach centered less on advertising and promotion than on investing in potential customers like Automobiles de Place (fleet sales of taxicabs remained important to Renault in the 1920s) and on building up the company-owned distribution and sales system. Renault was also not averse to boosting sales, as General Motors did, by offering consumer credit. However, the company's chief similarity to General Motors in the 1920s lay in its policy of product diversification. In addition to offering a full line of automobiles, Renault produced trucks, buses, and a variety of military hardware. Renault also continued to manufacture aircraft engines, which eventually drew the company into aircraft production (see below). All these activities were sufficiently remunerative that they kept Renault's total sales and profits at a level comparable to Citroën's, even though Citroën's output of automobiles substantially exceeded Renault's by the end of the 1920s.[23]

The third member of France's Big Three, Peugeot, did not enjoy the wartime expansion of Renault, Citroën, or Berliet, and it came out of the war with significantly fewer financial resources. Peugeot still had the foremost production man in the French automobile industry in Ernest Mattern, but the company's conservative president, Robert Peugeot, rejected Mattern's recommendation to move quickly into the mass production of a Ford-style small car. Instead, Peugeot continued to turn out a full line of prewar models that lacked popular appeal. Because of this decision and difficulties in converting to peacetime production, the company's sales stagnated in 1919–1921, and Mattern left to join Citroën in 1922. Under a new general manager, Lucien Rosengart, Peugeot finally managed to boost its production after 1923, and Mattern's successor as technical director, Philippe Girardet, put in place a sophisticated accounting system that greatly improved production management and cost control over the long term. But in the short run, Peugeot continued to fall behind Citroën and Renault.

At this juncture, the younger generation of Peugeots took control, ousted Rosengart, and brought in a new managing director, Maurice Jordan, who committed the company to the production of a limited line of small cars at an expanded and modernized assembly plant at Sochaux. As part of this new strategy, bicycle manufacturing was spun off into a separate company. Just as important, Jordan brought Ernest Mattern back in 1928 to oversee the refurbishing of the Sochaux plant and the launching of the new models. The Peugeot 201, introduced in 1929, was an instant success, and in 1930 Peugeot's sales rose to within 5,000 units of Renault's, a striking turnaround from five years earlier, when Peugeot sold just 16,676 cars (compared to 44,836 for Renault and 61,487 for Citroën). Peugeot still lacked the marketing brio and technological daring of Citroën and the broad diversified strength of Renault, but its newfound production efficiency and strong collective management, plus a popular line of cars, kept it solidly in third place in the French auto industry in the early 1930s.[24]

The onset of the Great Depression interrupted the expansion of the

French automobile industry in the late twenties and precipitated the industry's sharpest contraction since the beginning of World War I. Whereas France's truck and automobile production had increased five-fold between 1920 and 1929, it declined 35 percent between 1929 and 1935. This decline was particularly hard on the small companies that were already finding it difficult to keep up with France's Big Three in technology and production efficiency. The number of French car-makers, which had already fallen from 156 in 1924 to 90 in 1929, declined to only 20 in the early 1930s. By 1935, just ten of the twenty largest French auto manufacturers in 1913 were still in business.[25] By contrast, two of the three largest French companies navigated the early thirties relatively easily, thereby reinforcing and accelerating the process of concentration that had begun in the postwar decade.

In the early 1930s, both Renault and Peugeot had recently upgraded their production facilities and were financially sound thanks to record sales in 1929 and 1930. Peugeot capitalized on the success of its model 201 by introducing the larger 301 and 401 in the early thirties, and it followed the 01 series with the equally successful 02 series, starting with the 402 in 1935. Renault also introduced new models in the early thirties, but it mainly responded to the Depression by intensifying its rationalization efforts and by increasing its investments in collateral industries such as aircraft and military equipment. In spite of high-profile labor problems at Billancourt in 1936–1938, Renault was in a good position to expand its auto and truck production as demand recovered in the late thirties.

In contrast to the caution displayed by Peugeot and Renault in the early thirties, André Citroën pursued headlong expansion as the Depression deepened, and this ultimately drove his firm to financial collapse. Citroën had never been good at containing costs, and it was only under pressure from the investment bank Lazard Frères, which had gained three seats on Citroën's board when the company went public in 1924, that he had instituted a cost-reduction program in the late 1920s. In 1929, however, Citroën succeeded in ousting the Lazard representatives, and, in the words of Schweitzer and Sabates, "in place of safe and sane management, Citroën returned to his old ways: novelty at all cost and all power to the *patron*."[26] Stung by the unexpected success of Peugeot in 1929–1930, Citroën disregarded the 33 percent decline in his company's sales in 1930–1932 and plunged into debt to build a unified assembly line and to increase capacity at the Quai Javel plant. Additional debt was taken on to launch Citroën's most ambitious car yet, the Traction-Avant, which featured front-wheel drive, torsion bar suspension, and other innovations. But in late 1934, before the Traction-Avant could have an impact on the company's financial performance, Citroën defaulted on a 62 million franc interest payment and had to declare bankruptcy. Following protracted negotiations among the company's chief creditors and shareholders—Paribas, Lazard Frères, and Michelin—Citroën was forced out, and the company was reorganized with Pierre Michelin as president. Already in declining health, André Citroën died in July 1935.

The stunning collapse of Citroën in 1934–1935 again made Renault France's largest automaker, but Automobiles Citroën rebounded in 1937–1938 thanks to the sound management of the Michelins and burgeoning sales of the Traction-Avant. The late thirties also witnessed the emergence of a fourth major French auto company, Simca, which was launched in 1936 by Fiat's French sales director, Henri Pigozzi, to make a French version of the Fiat Topolino, the kind of small car that the Big Three had been unwilling and unable to produce. The surprisingly buoyant demand for automobiles in France and Europe in the years leading up to World War II allowed all four of France's leading auto companies to increase sales and revenues, and all four ranked among France's twenty-five largest industrial firms in the late 1930s. By then, the related industries of tire and rubber, aviation, and petroleum had also given rise to large-scale enterprises.

Tire and Rubber

The early automobiles would have remained slow and unreliable, and even more prone to breakdown than they already were, had it not been for the introduction of pneumatic tires that greatly reduced the vibrations associated with traditional solid tires. In 1888, Harvey du Cros founded the Dunlop Rubber Company in Dublin to manufacture a pneumatic bicycle tire invented by a Scots veterinarian, J-B Dunlop, and within a year this tire had come into widespread use in Great Britain. In 1893, the French bicycle maker, Adolphe Clément, founded the Société Française des Pneus Dunlop to manufacture Dunlop tires under license, but production began only in 1896 after the French firm had been taken over by British Dunlop. After World War I, the French Dunlop company moved into the production of automobile and bus tires at a converted munitions plant in Montluçon, and by the end of the 1930s it had gained a 30 percent share of the French automobile tire market.[27]

Two other foreign tire and rubber companies—Continental of Hanover, Germany, and B. F. Goodrich of Akron, Ohio—also established marketing and manufacturing subsidiaries in France in the early 1900s. Continental's plant at Clichy was sequestered during World War I and was eventually sold to the Société Industrielle des Téléphones, but B. F. Goodrich continued to operate in France into the post–World War II era as part owner of Kléber-Colombes.[28] Meanwhile, Raymond Bergougnan, a maker of rubber stamps in Clermont-Ferrand, had introduced the Gaulois brand of bicycle tires as early as 1889 and had moved into the manufacture of auto and truck tires during and after World War I using technology licensed from the Americans. In the 1930s, Bergougnan et Cie was still the second largest French tire and rubber company and ranked among the one hundred largest publicly held French industrial firms, but by then it had long been overshadowed by Michelin et Cie, which had emerged as the dominant French tire company in the 1890s and a leader in the world industry after 1900.[29]

The Michelin Tire Company traces its origins to a firm founded in Clermont-Ferrand in the 1830s by two cousins, Edouard Daubrée and Aristide Barbier, to refine sugar and to construct refining equipment. Because they had access to early rubber-making technology, Daubrée and Barbier also made balls and other rubber products as a sideline. After the death of the founders, the Daubrée-Barbier enterprise languished under the direction of the family notary until 1886 when André Michelin, a grandson of Barbier, took control. André was already fully occupied with a successful metal construction business in Paris, so he convinced his younger brother Edouard, an aspiring artist also living in Paris, to return to Clermont-Ferrand to direct the family firm, which was relaunched as Edouard Michelin et Cie in 1889. Edouard proceeded to sell off all parts of the business except its rubber fabrication plant, which at the time was mainly devoted to making brake pads for carriages. As the story goes, Edouard was introduced to the new pneumatic bicycle tires when an English tourist stopped in Clermont-Ferrand to have his Dunlop tire repaired (a laborious process because the Dunlop tires had to be glued to the rims). Edouard and his workers set about developing a bicycle tire that was easy to remove and repair, resulting in the *démontable,* a tire with an inner tube that did not have to be glued to the rim to be airtight. The tire created a sensation when introduced at the Paris-Brest bicycle race of 1894, and within months Michelin had emerged as the leading maker of bicycle tires in the world despite a legal battle with Dunlop over patent infringement. Company revenues that had amounted to only 450,000 francs in 1891 jumped to 2 million francs in 1895, and André Michelin soon gave up his metal business to become the firm's commercial director in Paris, while Edouard continued as production director in Clermont-Ferrand.[30]

To capitalize on the success of their bicycle tires, the Michelins turned at once to designing and producing pneumatic tires for carriages and automobiles (a challenging project, given the much greater weight that auto tires would have to bear). They introduced their first automobile tire in the Paris-Bordeaux road race of 1895, and the next year they signed contracts with two leading automakers, De Dion-Bouton and Bollée, to install Michelin *pneus* on their new cars. By plowing back profits from the sale of bicycle tires, the Michelins were able to quadruple the size of their production facilities in Clermont-Ferrand between 1895 and 1898, which put them in position to benefit fully from the coming takeoff of French auto production. They continued to make technical improvements in existing products and periodically introduced new products (such as the anti-skid, steel-studded Semelle auto tire in 1906). They also skillfully promoted their name and products in numerous ways, including the distribution of Michelin guidebooks and maps and the creation of one of the world's most recognizable corporate symbols (Bibendum, the Michelin tire man).[31] Through these actions, the Michelins were able to sustain an almost geometric growth in the value of their sales, from 5.8 million francs in 1899 to 100 million in 1910. In the process, what had been a small family firm as late as 1900 soon took on the attributes of a modern big business. The number of employees rose from less than 700 in 1898 to 10,000 by 1910. While ownership remained concentrated in the Michelin family and ultimate authority remained vested in André and Edouard Michelin, the company developed a sizable managerial hierarchy and a well-delineated, departmentalized organizational structure. The company integrated backward into the production of raw materials (rubber, tire cord) and diversified into the production of rims, valves, and other components of auto and truck wheels. It also went multinational, with plants in Karlsruhe, Germany, Stoke-on-Trent, United Kingdom, Turin, Italy (to supply Fiat), and Milltown, New York.[32]

In the years immediately preceding World War I, Michelin began to lose its leading position in tire and rubber technology to the fast-rising American companies, especially Goodyear, Firestone, and Goodrich. Thanks to research at the Akron Rubber Institute, the Americans made revolutionary advances in the strength and durability of tire rubber that Michelin neither duplicated nor adopted. To make matters worse, the Michelin brothers increasingly diverted their attention and resources to aviation between 1908 and 1914. During World War I, Michelin expanded its tire and rubber production to meet the needs of the French military, but it also devoted an entire factory to the building of Bréguet bombers. In the process, Michelin surrendered most of the world market for tires beyond Europe to the Americans and fell further behind in tire technology.

After the war, Michelin et Cie again focused exclusively on manufacturing tires and, thanks to the expansion of French auto production, enjoyed rising sales through the 1920s. The introduction of a better tire-mounting system by Dunlop in 1927 rendered the Michelin design obsolete. That, coupled with the dramatic contraction of overseas markets after 1929, threatened to permanently undermine Michelin's position, but the company responded constructively to these new challenges. In the 1930s, Michelin launched a massive reequipment of its French factories that incorporated American mass-production techniques. It also adopted the Dunlop tire-mounting system and began to reassert its leadership in product design, notably by introducing the use of steel cord in tire bodies, which foreshadowed its revolutionary development of the steel-belted radial tire after World War II. Although Michelin closed its Milltown, New York, plant in 1929—thereby abandoning the American market for thirty years—it set up new production in Spain, Belgium, Czechoslovakia, and Argentina to get around the trade barriers that had undercut its exports after 1929. By 1936, Michelin had recovered its position in the world tire market and, with 27,000 employees and assets of 1,037 million francs, had reconfirmed its status as one of France's largest manufacturing firms.[33] After Michelin's virtual takeover of Citroën in 1935, the Michelin-Citroën combine came to represent the largest concentration of industrial assets in France, and one of the largest in Europe, at the end of the 1930s. By then, Michelin already possessed the financial and organizational resources that would allow it to play leading roles in both the tire and rubber and automobile industries worldwide in the second half of the twentieth century.

Aircraft and Aircraft Engines

As in the automobile industry, the French took the lead in the development of the aircraft industry in Europe, and there were close technological and personal connections between the two industries in their infancy. Many of the leading figures in the French auto industry were enthusiasts for and promoters of aeronautics, including Albert De Dion, Louis Renault, and André Michelin, and many of the French aviation pioneers got their start in the automobile industry (including Louis Blériot, who started out making acetylene headlights and other accessories for automobiles before founding the S.A. Blériot-Aéronautique in 1909). Heavier-than-air flight depended not only on the design and construction of aircraft but also on the development of powerful yet lightweight gasoline engines. Not surprisingly, most of these engines were at first supplied by automobile manufacturers, such as De Dion-Bouton, Panhard et Levassor, Peugeot, and Renault. Nor is it surprising that the two companies that came to dominate the design and production of aircraft engines in France before and during World War I—Moteurs Gnôme and Hispano-Suiza—started out making automobile engines.

In addition to making airplane engines, Renault and other automakers also dabbled in aircraft construction (as did the Michelins) in the early years of the industry. However, because of the great differences between the design and construction of airplanes and automobiles, aircraft manufacturing rapidly became the purview of specialized companies founded by aviators and aviation enthusiasts in the years preceding World War I. In addition to Blériot, these firms included Ateliers d'Aviation Bréguet, founded by Louis Bréguet, scion of the distinguished industrial family, and Nieuport-Astra, founded by Henri Deutsch de la Meurthe, an important petroleum merchant who had earlier played a major role in the development of the dirigible.[34]

From the beginning, the military provided the only significant market for aircraft in France. In 1911–1913, the early aircraft makers competed fiercely for the contracts to build the few dozen reconnaissance airplanes that the French army and navy were authorized to buy. The outbreak of World War I, however, brought about a revolutionary expansion of the role of the airplane in warfare and almost overnight turned aircraft manufacturing into a major industry. Between 1914 and 1918, the number of aircraft manufacturers in France doubled, from fifteen to twenty-nine, and the productive capacity of the industry increased at least fivefold, as its annual output went from 5,111 aircraft and 8,091 engines in 1915 to 22,000 aircraft and 40,000 engines in 1918. By the end of the war, France had produced 52,000 airplanes and 91,000 airplane engines, more than any other country.[35]

Lacking its own facilities for aircraft production, the French military had to purchase all its aircraft from private companies during the war. However, to avoid dependence on a few large suppliers, it took pains to spread orders among as many producers as possible. Even in the case of aircraft engines, where the military used a limited number of models, it refused to buy all units of a given model from the company that had developed it and instead required that company to share the order with subcontractors. Thus, of the 35,000 Hispano-Suiza engines purchased by the French Air Force in 1914–1918, only one in twelve was manufactured by the Hispano-Suiza Company. Similarly, although Nieuport, Bréguet, and SPAD (Société pour l'Aviation et ses Derivés, a subsidiary of Blériot) designed the leading models of French fighters and bombers, they had to share the production of those airplanes with many other companies. As a result, a company like Blériot grew enormously during the war, going from a payroll of a few hundred in 1914 to 3,000 in 1918, but it did not grow as much as it would have if the French government had allowed greater concentration in aircraft production. In 1918 none of the largest aircraft companies was as large as the leading automobile companies.

The end of World War I dramatically reduced government expenditures for aircraft, and the postwar development of civil and commercial aviation failed to fill the resultant gap, despite the hopes of aviation enthusiasts. Throughout the 1920s, combined military and civilian demand for aircraft remained significantly below the wartime levels: French aircraft makers had been turning out 2,400 airplanes per month in 1918, but total French output of airplanes was only 800–1,000 per year ten years later. This contraction in demand, coupled with the rapid evolution of aircraft design, kept any one aircraft maker from attaining the scale of production achieved by companies like Renault, Citroën, and Michelin. Rather than consolidating the positions they had acquired during the war, Blériot-SPAD, Bréguet, and Nieuport-Astra were hard-pressed just to survive in the face of fierce competition from start-up companies armed with new technology and political connections.

Because rapid changes in the design of military aircraft kept companies from setting up long production runs of single models in the 1920s and 1930s, the real profits in the airframe industry were to be found not in production but in the design and licensing of prototypes. The men who understood this best and consequently enjoyed the greatest success in the French aircraft industry in the interwar years were Henri Potez and Marcel Bloch. Potez and Bloch had first entered the aircraft business in 1917–1918 as subcontractors (Bloch's initial experience was in organizing Paris furniture makers to produce airplane propellers). During the postwar contraction in military aircraft procurement, Bloch returned to the furniture business while Potez built limited numbers of small fighters and trainers at a factory in his hometown, Albert (Somme). When the Air Ministry set up a particularly generous system of payments for prototypes in 1929, Bloch and Potez assembled a brilliant team of engineers and quickly became France's foremost designers of military aircraft, for which they reaped handsome royalties and licensing fees. Eventually Potez and Bloch cobbled together a manufacturing company out of the remnants of failed or failing aircraft companies, but they never committed their full resources to production. Instead, they made a killing in 1936 when the Popular Front government took over their factories as part of the nationalization of French military aircraft production. At the same time, they parlayed their connections with the Popular Front into appointments to head the two largest state companies created by the nationalization: the Société Nationale des Constructions Aéronautiques Sud-Ouest (SNCASO), headed by Bloch, and SNCAN (Aviation-Nord), headed by Potez. These positions allowed them to promote the adoption of their own designs and thus assured the survival of their private design company (which was not nationalized) within the structure of an ostensibly state-owned industry. The pinnacle of Marcel Bloch's career, however, came after World War II, when he emerged from internment to found France's leading private aviation company under his *nom de guerre,* Marcel Dassault.[36]

In large part because of the long-standing policy of the French government to discourage concentration among the suppliers of military aircraft, the largest companies to emerge in the French aviation industry in the interwar years were found not in the design and production of airframes but in the manufacture of engines. Automobile manufacturers had made the first airplane engines, and they continued to produce aircraft engines for the military during World War I. However, as the government orders fell off after 1918 and as the technology became more sophisticated, most French automakers dropped out of the aircraft engine business. By the early 1920s, only four automakers still produced aircraft engines—Renault, Lorraine-Dietrich, Hispano-Suiza, and Salmson—along with the one true specialist in aircraft engines, Gnôme et Rhône.

Renault built more aircraft engines than any other French company except Gnôme et Rhône during World War I, and this remained an important part of Renault's business after 1918. In the late 1920s, Renault did attempt unsuccessfully to develop a high-performance military aircraft engine to compete with Pratt and Whitney of the United States, but mostly it continued to produce small engines for civilian aircraft. In the 1930s, Renault took over the Caudron Aircraft Company in order to develop a line of "personal" airplanes that would serve as a captive market for its engines, but the collapse of the general aviation sector in France during the Depression undermined this venture, and Renault wrote off the entire investment in 1937.

Lorraine-Dietrich suffered a similar decline. The French branch of the Alsatian locomotive manufacturer had entered automobile production in 1908 using the Lorraine-Dietrich brand name, and in 1914 it had started making aircraft engines under patents confiscated from Daimler by the French government. Lorraine-Dietrich continued to make engines for military aircraft after the war, but with only limited success. In the early 1930s it was taken over by Potez and Bloch and renamed the Société des Moteurs et Automobiles Lorraine (SMAL). In 1936, SMAL abandoned auto production, and its remaining aircraft engine factory was nationalized.

Hispano-Suiza was founded in Barcelona in 1908 to manufacture and market a luxury sports car designed by a brilliant young Swiss engineer, Marc Birkigt. The popularity of the Hispano-Suiza in France led the company to set up a factory in Paris in 1911 that, after the outbreak of war in 1914, concentrated on building a highly regarded V8 aircraft engine designed by Birkigt. At the end of the war, the Société Française Hispano-Suiza was spun off as an independent company under the control of Birkigt and Swiss bankers and continued to manufacture sports cars and high-powered engines for military and commercial aircraft. The company narrowly avoided nationalization in 1936 by putting its aircraft engine production under a French-controlled subsidiary, the Société d'Exploitation des Moteurs Hispano-Suiza, headed by the French technocrat Raoul Dautry. Although this company continued to produce engines for both military and commercial aircraft in the late 1930s, it was overshadowed by Gnôme et Rhône, which emerged as the largest and strongest company in the French aviation industry in the course of the thirties.

The history of Gnôme et Rhône represents one of the greatest success—and comeback—stories in the annals of twentieth-century French business. Louis Seguin, a grandson of the French railroad pioneer Marc Seguin, founded Moteurs Gnôme in 1905 to manufacture automobile engines. When the auto business slumped in 1907, Seguin introduced a seven-cylinder, air-cooled rotary engine that dominated the early market for airplane engines and propelled Moteurs Gnôme from a 240,000 franc loss in 1908 to a profit of 8 million francs in 1913. Soon, however, another new company, Société des Moteurs Le Rhône, introduced an even better rotary engine, designed by Louis Verdet. In self-defense, Gnôme merged with Rhône in 1914—just in time to benefit from the adoption of the Rhône engine for most of France's fighter aircraft.

By the end of the war, Gnôme et Rhône was the largest manufacturer of aircraft engines in the world. However, the postwar drought in military orders and the company's rapid loss of technical leadership almost ruined it. In the early 1920s, Gnôme et Rhône engines were no longer competitive because limitations inherent in the rotary design kept them from achieving the 300+ horsepower demanded by the military, so military orders increasingly went to Lorraine-Dietrich and Hispano-Suiza. Meanwhile, the industrialist-financier Lazare Weiller and his associates had taken control of the company and had started to move it into motorcycles and automobile components. When this attempt at diversification failed, Weiller turned the company over to his son Paul-Louis Weiller, an engineer and much-decorated wartime reconnaissance pilot. The younger Weiller pushed Gnôme et Rhône back into aircraft engine production by acquiring the European and world rights to the Jupiter engine developed by Bristol Aircraft in England. Improvements in the Jupiter engine allowed the company to reclaim a dominant place in the market for military and commercial aircraft engines by the end of the 1920s. In the early 1930s, Gnôme et Rhône introduced two new lines of engines, including a 1,000-horsepower military engine for the Potez-Bloch fighters that soon became the backbone of the French air force. While other aircraft engine makers retrenched, Gnôme et Rhône's sales soared, from 80 million francs in 1934 to 440 million by 1938. Its assets rose accordingly, from a modest 131 million francs in 1931 to 303 million in 1936, which catapulted it into the ranks of the top fifty French manufacturing firms. Eventually, Gnôme et Rhône was nationalized and formed the basis for SNECMA, France's "national champion" in the world aircraft engine industry in the second half of the twentieth century.[37]

Petroleum

The technological, corporate, and personal linkages that tied together the automobile, tire, and aircraft industries in France by and large did not extend to the petroleum industry. To be sure, a leading French oilman, Henri Deutsch de la Meurthe, played a leading role in the early development of the aeronautical industry, but for the most part the French petroleum industry was founded and developed by men and companies unconnected to the automobile and its allied industries. Yet, more than in many other countries, the rise of oil consumption in France depended on the development of motorized transportation. Whereas petroleum refining emerged as a major industry in the United States in the late 1800s in response to demand for lamp oil, fuel oil, and lubricants, the French petroleum industry remained small and rudimentary before 1900 (although not as small and rudimentary as often portrayed). The great expansion of French petroleum—and the emergence of world-class French oil and gas companies—came after World War II, but the foundations of the French industry were laid in the early twentieth century in response to the rise of the automobile and to the growing importance of motorized warfare on land, on sea, and in the air. By the mid-1930s, France had a partially state-owned national oil company, the Compagnie Française des Petroles (CFP), playing a major role in the development of Middle East oil, and oil refining had emerged as an important industry in France. It therefore seems appropriate to look at the French petroleum industry to conclude our examination of the cluster of industries and large companies that arose with the advent of the internal combustion engine.

The Birth of the French Oil Industry, 1860s–1914

Within a few years of the drilling of the first American oil well at Titusville, Pennsylvania, in 1859, various French vegetable oil merchants, who had been refining lamp oil from rapeseed (colza), began importing American crude petroleum after they discovered that they could extract kerosene from petroleum using the same methods used in the refining of rapeseed. Among these vegetable-oil-refiners-turned-petroleum-refiners were Alexandre Deutsch de la Meurthe and Fenaille et Despeaux, who had operated refineries near Paris since the 1840s; Paix et Cie, which operated a refinery near Douai in the department of the Nord; and Charles and Henri Desmarais, scions of a family of Paris jewelers, who had entered the vegetable oil business in 1861.

Because French import duties were initially the same on refined and crude petroleum, these early French oilmen soon realized that it was more profitable to import American refined oil than to bother with refining American crude. In July 1871, however, the National Assembly of the newly founded Third Republic voted to raise import duties on refined petroleum well above those on crude, thereby giving the French oil merchants a strong incentive to continue to operate refineries and to set up new ones.[38] To eliminate the cost of losing up to 20 percent of their imported crude oil in the refining process, the French oilmen worked out an understanding by which their American suppliers agreed to send them partially refined petroleum that retained just enough impurities to qualify as crude oil under French customs regulations (this came to be known as "French crude"). The French importers carried out a second refining process to remove the remaining impurities and to separate the imported oil into its various components, and they then distributed the final products—mostly kerosene—in fifty-liter drums and five-liter cans to grocery stores and other retail outlets.

Although the French oil companies constructed refineries that were much smaller and less expensive than those being constructed in the United States, the required investment in storage facilities, transportation, and packaging was large enough that only two dozen French companies entered the business in the 1870s. In fact, most of the production and sale of petroleum products continued to be controlled by four early entrants—Deutsch de la Meurthe, Fenaille et Despeaux, Paix, and Desmarais Frères—along with a few well-financed newcomers such as Lille-Bonnières, a joint-stock company founded by Belgian capitalists in 1877 to operate refineries at Lille and Bonnières.[39] The nature and extent of these firms' operations are best seen in the case of Desmarais Frères, the company for which we have the most information.

While continuing to operate rapeseed refineries at Gonfreville and Harfleur near Le Havre, the Desmarais brothers set up their first petroleum refinery at Colombes near Paris in 1871 and began marketing kerosene under the Astralene label. In the late 1870s they added depots for crude oil at Le Havre and Blaye (near Bordeaux) and subsequently built refineries at both locations. Their Le Havre refinery employed 200 workers and processed 15,000 tons of crude oil per year, mostly between September and February, when the demand for lamp oil was at its peak. In addition, Desmarais began marketing France's first motor fuel, Oriflamme, in 1885. By the 1890s, they had acquired a fleet of river barges that delivered crude oil in bulk to their refineries and moved the refined oil to fourteen distribution centers around the country, where it was packaged in five-liter cans and delivered by wagon to retailers.[40]

Lacking sources of crude oil that they could exploit directly, the French refiners soon faced the threat of being either forced out of the business or turned into dependencies of the Standard Oil Company as the latter established virtual monopoly control over the American petroleum industry. In the early 1880s, Standard started selling refined oil in France at such low prices that, even with the high French tariff, the French refiners could not compete. They responded by forming a syndicate that managed to boycott Standard crude oil long enough to force Standard to negotiate a new understanding. Under its terms, the French refiners agreed to buy 90 percent of their *American* crude from Standard, and Standard agreed to stop competing with the French companies for sales of refined petroleum in France.[41]

It became apparent that the French had gotten the better of the deal with Standard—obtaining Standard's withdrawal from the French retail market in return for a non-exclusive agreement to buy Standard crude oil—when the opening of new oil fields in Russia, Rumania, and Austrian Galicia gave the French refiners the opportunity to integrate backward into crude oil production and to end their dependency on Standard. The move into crude oil production was led by Alexandre Deutsch de la Meurthe and his sons Henri and Emile. In 1879 the Deutsches wanted to expand into Spain, which, like France, had just placed a high import duty on refined oil to help create a domestic refining industry, and they convinced the Paris Rothschilds to finance their new refinery at Seville. The success of the Seville refinery persuaded the Rothschilds to back another Deutsch de la Meurthe refinery, at Fiume to serve the Austrian Empire. The need to assure steady supplies of crude oil for the Seville and Fiume refineries in turn took the Rothschilds and Deutsches to the Russian Caucasus, where in 1886 they founded the Société Commerciale de Naphte Caspienne et de la Mer Noire (or BNITO, from its Russian initials). As Russian oil production took off and as exports from Russia rose to the level of American exports (roughly 1.4 million tons in 1900), BNITO came to rival Standard as a force in the world oil market.[42]

The success of the Rothschilds and Deutsches in the Russian Caucasus inspired similar undertakings by other French oil companies. For example, Desmarais Frères joined with Fenaille et Despeaux, Paix, Lille-Bonnières, and the Raffineries du Pétrole du Nord (founded in 1891 to build and operate a refinery at Wasquehal near Lille) to create Aquila Franco-Romana, through which the group bought and exported Rumanian crude oil and later refined oil at Ploesti. The same consortium also acquired holdings in the Galician oil field in the Austrian Empire. These initiatives gave the French companies additional leverage in their dealings with Standard Oil and also helped them weather a radical shift in French oil policy after 1900.

In 1903, the French parliament, responding to pressure from the domestic alcohol and vegetable oil producers, raised duties on imported crude oil in such a way as to nullify the protection of domestic oil refining that had been established in 1871. Had such an alteration in the rules of the game occurred twenty years earlier, it might have destroyed the French oil industry in its infancy. By the early 1900s, however, the French oil companies were so entrenched in distribution and marketing that they were able to survive a drastic reduction in domestic refining capacity. Indeed, the ultimate effect of the change in tariff policy was simply to accelerate a restructuring of the industry that was already under way.

By 1900, the demand in France for refined petroleum was shifting from kerosene for lamps to gasoline for motors. But the French refineries built in the 1870s and 1880s were rudimentary distilleries that could extract only fifteen tons of naturally occurring gasoline from every one hundred tons of imported crude oil. So imports of refined oil—mainly gasoline—were already on the rise before 1903. The French companies knew before 1903 that they were going to have to build newfangled "cracking" plants, which primarily produced gasoline, to replace their obsolete refineries. The tariff law simply assured that these refineries would be built abroad, near the French oil companies' foreign sources of crude oil, rather than in France. Thus in 1904, Desmarais Frères and its partners began constructing what the historians of Desmarais called "the best equipped refinery in Europe" at Limanowa in Galicia. Also in 1904, another group of French capitalists joined with representatives of the German Discontogesellschaft to found the Société Industrielle des Pétroles to process Rumanian crude oil at new refineries at Rouen and Cette and to buy a one-third interest in a Rumanian refinery. In this way, the French maintained a foothold in oil refining even as most domestic refineries were being shut down between 1900 and 1908.[43]

Although much smaller than its counterparts in the United States, Britain, Germany, and Russia, the French oil industry remained expansive and profitable on the eve of World War I. Lille-Bonnières, for example, saw its profits rise from 225,700 francs in 1900 to 1.28 million francs in 1913. After a shaky start, the profits of the Société Industrielle des Petroles (SIP) rose even faster, from 33,000 francs in 1907–1908 to 2,170,000 in 1912–1913, and the company's stock became a hot item on the Paris Bourse, with the price of a share rising from a subpar 420 francs in 1911 to 845 francs by the end of 1913.[44] But perhaps the most encouraging development for French oil in the prewar years came in 1911, when the Rothschilds and Deutsch de la Meurthe merged BNITO into Royal Dutch Shell in return for 40 percent of the shares in this new combine, putting them in a position to play an even larger role in the expanding world oil industry in the years ahead.

French Oil Comes of Age, 1914–1934

As in other belligerent countries, oil consumption soared in France between 1914 and 1918 as motor vehicles, aircraft, and oil-powered naval vessels became indispensable elements in the prolonged fighting. However, this did little to foster a restructuring or even an expansion of the French oil industry. By 1914, the distribution of oil in France had long been controlled by the infamous Cartel of Ten that the Turkish oil baron Calouste Gulbenkian once famously denounced as "a monopolistic association of grocers."[45] At the beginning of the war, this group contracted to supply petroleum products to the French armed forces, and this arrangement remained in effect throughout the war even after oil imports were put under a government purchasing agency, the Consortium Pétrolier Français, in 1917.[46] What did change between 1914 and 1918 was the source of French oil imports. The closing of the Dardanelles by the Turks deprived the French importers of their Russian and Rumanian oil supplies, and Austria's participation in the war as a German ally cut off Galician supplies. As a result, France became more dependent than ever on American oil and particularly dependent on the leading offspring of the break-up of Standard Oil in 1912, Standard of New Jersey (later Exxon).

The real crisis for the French oil industry came not during the war but in the year following the armistice, when Jersey Standard imposed an embargo on oil shipments to France in response to supposed French favoritism toward Royal Dutch Shell and in response to the Anglo-French agreement (made official at the San Remo Conference in 1920) to give France (and perhaps Royal Dutch Shell) Germany's 25 percent stake in the Turkish Petroleum Company and to exclude the Americans from the Mesopotamian oil field. The Jersey Standard boycott, coupled with the victory of the conservative Bloc National in the parliamentary elections of 1919 and the formation of the Poincaré government in 1920, brought about the demise of the French government's control of oil imports, opened up the petroleum market in France, and ushered in a decade of unprecedented change and upheaval in French oil.[47]

Four related developments dominated the French oil industry in the 1920s: (1) a huge increase in oil consumption, accompanied by a complete overhaul in the physical facilities for distributing and marketing refined petroleum in France; (2) the invasion of the French market by foreign companies and a rash of mergers and acquisitions that reduced the ranks of independent companies and consolidated control of the industry in a few very large corporations; (3) a long, unsuccessful effort to salvage France's investment in oil production and refining in Rumania, Russia, and Galicia, and a much more successful effort to develop a new source of crude oil in the Middle East; and (4) a government-backed effort to resurrect and develop a refining industry on French soil. The first two developments are best examined together.

The consumption of petroleum in France, as measured by imports, increased tenfold in the 1920s.[48] This increase sprang in part from the belated conversion of most warships and commercial vessels from coal to fuel oil and from the increasing use of petroleum-based lubricants in heavy industrial machinery. But it was above all driven by the growth in vehicular traffic, as the number of automobiles in France rose sevenfold, from 156,872 in 1920 to 1,100,000 in 1930.[49] The increase in consumption was in turn closely bound up with the decision by major foreign oil companies—especially Standard of New Jersey and Anglo-Persian—to move into direct distribution of refinery products in France. Taking advantage of the free-market orientation of the Poincaré government, Jersey Standard created a new French subsidiary, L'Economique, in March 1920 to market its petroleum products in France. In April 1920, L'Economique contracted to supply petroleum to La Pétroléenne (formerly Fenaille et Despeaux). Three years later, it absorbed La Pétroléenne and proceeded to build a new distribution system based on hundreds of American-style "Eco" service stations that were supplied by company-owned fleets of tanker cars and trucks. L'Economique also absorbed Standard's old marketing subsidiary, Bedford Petroleum, as well as A. André et Fils, the leading French lubricating oil importer, and the Compagnie Générale des Pétroles of Marseille. By 1927, 85 percent of Jersey Standard's oil exports to France went to its own subsidiaries.[50]

The emerging British giant, Anglo-Persian, also moved into the direct marketing of petroleum in France in the 1920s. While Jersey Standard emphasized the marketing of gasoline and lubricating oil to the general public through a network of service stations, Anglo-Persian initially concentrated on selling heavy fuel oils to French railroads, steamship lines, manufacturers, and the French navy through a new subsidiary, the Société Générale des Huiles et Pétroles (SGHP). The SGHP set up fueling stations for the British Peninsular & Oriental Steamship Company at Le Havre and Marseille and acquired its own fleet of tankers. It then absorbed the petroleum assets of two members of the Cartel of Ten, Lesieur and Paix (including Paix's refinery at Courchelettes, which the SGHP rebuilt and expanded to supply fuel oil to its customers in northern France). By 1927, the SGHP had become the largest seller of fuel oils in France. It had also followed Jersey Standard into the retail marketing of gasoline with a string of BP filling stations. (British Petroleum, founded before 1914 by the German-dominated European Petroleum Union to distribute oil in the United Kingdom, was taken over by the British government during World War I and ceded to Anglo-Persian, which eventually adopted the name.)[51] Royal Dutch Shell also moved into oil refining and marketing in France after 1920 by absorbing two other members of the Cartel of Ten, Raffineurs du Midi and Deutsch de la Meurthe. The latter's distribution company, Pétroles Jupiter, subsequently became the basis of Royal Dutch Shell's retail system in France.[52]

The wave of mergers and acquisitions in the early 1920s left just three members of the old French oil cartel independent: Desmarais Frères, Société Industrielle des Pétroles, and Lille-Bonnières-Colombes. For all intents and purposes, however, the last two had become the marketing arms of American companies (Lille-Bonnières-Colombes for Atlantic Refining and SIP for Sinclair Oil).[53] So, as things turned out, the only major French firm that attempted to compete in the domestic market with Jersey Standard, Anglo-Persian, and Royal Dutch Shell as an independent after 1920 was Desmarais Frères. Under the leadership of Robert Cayrol, Desmarais invested 120 million francs in 10,000 gasoline pumps and 300 tank trucks and set up its own chain of filling stations in 1925. At the same time, Desmarais moved to end its dependence on Jersey Standard for its supply of refined petroleum by investing in the new French production company, Compagnie Française des Pétroles.[54]

As the distribution and marketing of refined petroleum in France increasingly fell into the hands of the foreign-owned multinationals, the survival of an independent French oil industry came to depend on how the French government handled its great windfall, the acquisition of Germany's 25 percent share of the Turkish Petroleum Company (TPC), which held exclusive rights to the as yet undeveloped Mesopotamian oil fields located in the new British protectorate of Iraq. In 1923, the Poincaré government decided to assign the French holdings in the TPC (later renamed the Iraq Petroleum Company) to a private company created expressly for that purpose, the Compagnie Française des Pétroles (CFP). To placate Jersey Standard and Royal Dutch Shell, both of which had maneuvered furiously between 1920 and 1923 to control the French stake in Mesopotamia, Poincaré allowed each to purchase significant shares of the new firm. Jersey Standard and its ally Paribas and their dependents ended up with 27 percent of the shares of the CFP, and Royal Dutch Shell came away with 8 percent, while Petrofina, the new Franco-Belgian company created by the Banque de l'Union Parisienne, acquired a 15 percent stake; Desmarais Frères and other French independents held 20–25 percent.[55]

Jersey Standard apparently intended to use its position in the CFP to block or at least slow down the development of Mesopotamian oil to prevent a world glut at a time when American production was increasing rapidly, thanks to the uncontrolled development of the east Texas oil field, and Russian oil, by then in the hands of the Bolsheviks, had become something of a wild card in the international market. Jersey Standard also intended to use the CFP against Royal Dutch Shell (according to Gregory Nowell, the CFP "was the joint revenge of Standard Oil and the Banque de Paris et des Pays-Bas for Royal Dutch Shell's ambition to corner the French market").[56] This plan seemed to benefit from the appointment as chairman of the CFP of Ernest Mercier, who was not only playing a leading role in the French electrical industry as head of the Messine Group but also heading the Omnium International des Pétroles, which administered the Rumanian oil holdings of Paribas. Nowell characterizes Mercier as a tool of Jersey Standard and Paribas, but in truth Mercier tended to follow the lead of those such as Robert Cayrol of Desmarais, who saw the CFP as the means to end French oil dependence on Jersey Standard, Anglo-Persian, and the other multinational oil companies by developing France's own sources of crude oil.[57] Indeed, under Mercier, the CFP pushed the IPC to move forward with the exploration and exploitation of the Mesopotamian field. In 1927, oil was discovered near Mosul in northern Iraq, and the IPC soon set up drilling operations and started planning pipelines to move the crude oil to the Mediterranean coast. In 1934, two pipelines were opened that together promised to deliver 4 million tons of crude oil yearly, one-fourth of which (about 1 million tons) would go to the CFP. By then, changes in French oil policy had made it clear that the CFP would not simply be a middleman, selling crude oil to established refining companies, but would itself be a major oil refiner.[58]

In 1928, as a counterpart to efforts by the multinationals to stabilize the world oil market, notably through the "As Is" Agreement among Standard, Anglo-Persian, and Royal Dutch Shell locking in their respective shares of world production and pegging world prices to American prices, the French parliament established a system of import quotas based on the most recent five years' experience of companies already operating in France. This served two purposes: to block Petrofina's plan to flood the French market with oil purchased from the Soviets and to give assurances to companies already in France that any new investments in refining capacity would not be undercut by massive new imports of gasoline and other refinery products. At the same time, another French law reinstated the tariff protection on refined oil that the 1903 legislation had all but eliminated, thereby giving those holding import licenses an incentive to import crude oil to be refined locally rather than refined oil. Together, these laws represented a new commitment by the French government (again headed by Poincaré) to establish French energy independence and to create a world-class refining industry on French soil.

Against this backdrop, the CFP moved immediately to set up a new subsidiary, the Compagnie Française de Raffinage (CFR), to construct two modern refineries to process the CFP's anticipated share of Iraq oil. When French banks balked at financing this venture, Poincaré agreed to put sufficient government funds into the CFP to raise its capital by one-third (and to give the government a one-quarter ownership of the company). With this backing, the first CFR refinery (with an annual capacity of 900,000 tons) opened at Gonfreville near Le Havre in 1933. A second refinery (capacity of 400,000 tons) opened at Martigues on the Mediterranean coast two years later. Meanwhile, other companies quickly followed the CFP's lead. Royal Dutch Shell built refineries at Pauillac (Gironde) and Petit-Couronne (Rouen); a consortium of Jersey Standard, Atlantic, and Gulf built France's largest refinery (with a capacity of 1 million tons a year) near Le Havre; other refineries were constructed on the Mediterranean coast, the lower

Seine, and at various locations on the Atlantic coast by Socony, the SGHP, the Compagnie Générale des Pétroles, Pechelbronn, and Petrofina. Moreover, Saint-Gobain, in the first major foray by a leading French chemical company into petrochemicals, built a huge but ultimately under-utilized refinery on the Etang de Berre (later sold to Shell).[59]

Between 1928 and 1938, France went from having only one modern oil refinery (the SGHP's Courchelette refinery) with an annual capacity of 300,000 tons to fifteen refineries with a total capacity of 7.8 million tons a year. According to Edgar Faure, France's actual output of refined oil rose from perhaps 100,000 tons in 1927 to 6.3 million by 1938—a massive increase. Indeed, the following figures on France's imports of crude and refined oil (in thousands of tons) provide eloquent testimony to the revolutionary growth and restructuring of the industry after 1928:[60]

Year	Crude	Refined	Total
1928	188	2,867	3,055
1931	450	3,724	4,174
1933	2,799	3,018	5,817
1936	6,018	1,485	7,503
1938	6,968	1,177	8,145

As a result of the transformation of the French oil industry in the twenty years following World War I—and especially the development of a modern refining sector—a cohort of large oil companies took a place in the ranks of big business in France alongside the big steel, electrical, chemical, and automotive companies. In terms of assets, Standard-France and the CFP were among the ten largest industrial firms in France by 1936. The SGHP, Raffineries des Pétroles du Nord (Petrofina), the Société Industrielle des Pétroles, and probably Desmarais Frères and Shell-France were among the top fifty industrial firms. Through a combination of private enterprise and state support, France had gained a presence in yet another new industry from which, as late as 1914, it had looked as if it would be excluded.

CHAPTER FIFTEEN

Chemicals and Materials

Industrial chemicals and materials constituted the fourth industry—along with steel, electricity, and motor transport—that experienced great technological and organizational change and the concomitant rise of large-scale corporate enterprise in the late nineteenth and early twentieth centuries. In this immense and varied industry, the years between 1880 and 1930 brought the continued growth of established firms making old products—inorganic acids and alkalis, organic dyestuffs and pharmaceuticals, glass and cement—as well as the birth of new firms making new products such as electrochemicals, electrometals, and cellulose-based artificial fibers.[1] Of course, as time went on, the distinction between the "old" and "new" sectors began to blur as firms in one sector ventured into the other. Moreover, companies in both sectors increasingly exhibited a tendency to get big, either because the interconnectedness of their products and processes predisposed them to pursue economies of scope or because price competition pushed them to seek economies of scale to cut costs or to eliminate competition. Whatever the cause, the trend toward bigness in chemicals and materials culminated in the 1920s in the birth of multiproduct, multinational giants in Germany (IG Farben), Great Britain (Imperial Chemicals), and the United States (Allied Chemicals, Du Pont).[2]

The production of chemicals and materials did not grow as fast in France as in the other major industrialized countries from the 1880s to the 1930s, so the relative decline of the French chemical industry evident by the late nineteenth century continued into the twentieth century. But the French continued to have their strengths and successes. France had been among the leading European producers of heavy chemicals—soda, sulfuric acid, phosphates—at the end of the nineteenth century, and it remained a leader in this sector down to World War II.[3] In addition, France greatly expanded its production of coal-based synthetic dyes in the 1920s, which allowed it to reduce its long-standing dependence on the Germans and Swiss in that sector. Most importantly, France fully participated in the rise of the fastest-growing new industries—electrochemicals, aluminum, industrial gases, artificial fibers—while strengthening its position in the old but expanding sector of cement and building materials. These developments did not lead to the creation of a French giant comparable to IG Farben, Imperial Chemicals, or Du Pont, but they did, by the 1930s, give France eight or nine very large chemical and materials firms that ranked among the three or four largest European producers in their sector and also ranked among the fifty largest industrial enterprises in France. A dozen other French chemical firms ranked among the top one hundred French industrial firms.[4] From this small population of leading firms, this chapter singles out and focuses on the seven that best illustrate the development of the chemicals and materials industries in France in the era of the Second Industrial Revolution: Saint-Gobain, Air Liquide, Rhône-Poulenc, Lafarge, Pechiney, Ugine, and Kuhlmann (between 1966 and 1971 these last three merged into a single giant firm, P.U.K., that is now known simply as Pechiney). Each firm or its successor played a major role in the European and world economies in the second half of the twentieth century.

The Survival and Transformation of Two Established Powers: Saint-Gobain and Kuhlmann

The production of heavy industrial chemicals—particularly inorganic acids and alkalis—had driven the growth of the French chemical industry throughout the nineteenth century and remained the single largest sector of the industry in the early twentieth century.[5] After 1900, however, this sector increasingly developed on two tracks: One involved the continued and expanded production of traditional products (acids, alkalis, phosphates); the other involved developing new products and processes (the electrolytic production of chlorine and light metals, gas liquefaction, nitrates for fertilizer and high explosives). Of the three largest French chemical firms at the beginning of the twentieth century, Pechiney most wholeheartedly embraced the latter track, eventually abandoning the production of acids and alkalis and staking its future on the new electrochemicals and electrometals, especially aluminum. By contrast, Saint-Gobain and Kuhlmann dedicated most of their resources to the traditional products, but they too eventually realized that staying on top required changing with the times, and both moved into new products and processes after World War I.

At the beginning of the twentieth century, Saint-Gobain remained a uniquely bicephalous corporation that derived a third of its revenue from the manufacture of flat glass and two-thirds of its revenue from heavy chemicals, especially sulfuric acid and superphosphate fertilizer. Saint-Gobain spent the years 1900–1913 fine-tuning these established businesses by mechanizing the production of plate glass, substituting the catalytic or contact process for the old lead-chamber process in making sulfuric acid, and developing new sources of phosphoric ores in North Africa. It also moved back into soda production on a limited scale with a new ammonia-process plant at Varangéville, and it took tentative steps into the production of nitrogen and celluloid. However, only in response to the effects of invasion and occupation in 1914–1918 did Saint-Gobain fundamentally reassess its traditional ways of doing business.[6]

The destruction of virtually all of Saint-Gobain's production facilities in the department of the Aisne during World War I forced the company to rethink and modernize its approach to making glass. Accordingly, Saint-Gobain constructed a new glassworks at Thourotte, where it adopted the new continuous process technology developed by Pilkington in Great Britain. It also set up its first true research laboratory, which soon proved its worth by developing Securit safety glass for automobiles, which would account for 28 percent of its plate glass sales by the 1930s. When sales of traditional forms of plate glass fell in the early 1920s, Saint-Gobain started producing common flat glass (verre à vitre, or window glass), which at that time accounted for 70 percent of all flat glass sales in France. To do this, it acquired rights to the Fourcault process, brought all Fourcault glass manufacturers in France into a cartel, and then negotiated a market-sharing agreement with companies using the rival processes of the American firm Libby-Owens to give the Fourcault group 70 percent of the French market. At the same time, Saint-Gobain moved into bottle manufacturing by taking over several regional bottle works and by building its own automated bottle plant in the Nord. It then divided the domestic market with the bottlemakers grouped around Souchon-Nouvesel (see Chapter 9). In the 1930s, Saint-Gobain began making fiberglass using equipment and technology developed by Owens-Corning in the United States, thereby laying the foundations for its strong thrust into the building materials industry after World War II.

The policy of diversification that preserved and strengthened Saint-Gobain's position in the glass industry in the 1920s and 1930s was less successful in chemicals. Saint-Gobain did not create a research laboratory to develop new chemical products until 1936. Until then, it clung to the "fertilizer strategy" that had served it so well since the 1890s. Saint-Gobain continued to be the leading French producer of superphosphates in the 1920s, but by then demand for superphosphates was leveling off as interest turned to potassium and nitrate fertilizers. Saint-Gobain found it hard to break into these new areas, in part because the French government vested control of the Haber-Bosch process for ammonia synthesis—seen as the key to large-scale, low-cost production of nitrates—in a state company, the Office National Industriel de l'Azote (ONIA). Saint-Gobain did join with Air Liquide to exploit an alternative to the Haber-Bosch process, but that remained a relatively small operation and was more Air Liquide's than Saint-Gobain's (see below). Saint-Gobain also set up plants to make ammonium sulfate using older technology, and it launched a joint venture with the Mines d'Aniche to convert coke-oven gases into a nitrogen-potassium mixture *(potazote)*, but these at best gave Saint-Gobain a secondary position in nitrate production. As nitrates increasingly dominated the fertilizer market, Saint-Gobain found that its share of total fertilizer sales in France fell from 26 percent in 1913 to only 13 percent in 1939. Saint-Gobain continued to increase its production of sulfuric acid, but, with superphosphate production stagnant, it was forced to sell more and more of its sulfuric acid in the open market at low prices.

To offset the slow growth of its heavy chemicals business, Saint-Gobain started producing the cellulose used in the manufacture of paper and artificial fibers. In 1924, it launched the Société Cellulose du Pin as a joint venture with the Comptoir des Textiles Artificiels (CTA) and the Navarre Paper Company to extract cellulose from the pine trees of the Landes in southwestern France. However, the new company's mixed-use factory employed an untested technology that failed to produce either cellulose suitable for making rayon or wood pulp suitable for paper. Disaster was averted only by revamping the factory to make brown paper packaging. Eventually, Saint-Gobain and CTA succeeded in producing cellulose for rayon tire cord and cellophane with an improved technology, but this production began in earnest only after World War II.

Saint-Gobain had an even more expensive setback when it tried to move into petroleum refining. In 1928, Saint-Gobain joined in the creation of the Compagnie des Produits Chimiques et Raffineries de Berre (PCRB) to build a large oil refinery on the Mediterranean coast when it was unclear whether the new Compagnie Française des Pétroles was going to set up its own refinery on French soil. Ultimately, as we saw in Chapter 14, the CFP did create a refining subsidiary that had privileged access to the French share of Iraqi crude oil. So when the PCRB refinery went on line in 1931, it had to buy its crude oil on the open market at disadvantageous prices. Moreover, it lacked good outlets for its refinery products since the oil companies that controlled oil and gas distribution in France had their own sources of supply. For these reasons, the PCRB never prospered and only served as a drag on Saint-Gobain's financial performance throughout the 1930s. The chemical and glass giant ended up selling its majority holding in PCRB to Shell in 1948.

Despite its mixed record in the years following World War I, Saint-Gobain saw its assets increase almost 100 percent in real terms between 1913 and 1930, a rate of growth substantially below that of small companies exploiting new technologies like Air Liquide but quite respectable when compared to established industrial corporations in chemicals, steel, and electricals inside and outside of France.[7] Saint-Gobain remained the largest French firm in chemicals and glass and France's third largest manufacturing enterprise (after Wendel and Citroën) in the early 1930s.

On the eve of World War I, the Manufactures des Produits Chimiques du Nord–Etablissements Kuhlmann was France's largest producer of a wide range of inorganic chemicals (including chlorine, nitric acid, and sulfates), and it was second to Saint-Gobain in the production of superphosphates.[8] Most of this production was concentrated in plants in the Nord and in Belgium that were lost or destroyed in the German invasion of 1914. But like the steel companies of northern France, this apparent disaster turned out to be a blessing in disguise. With government backing, Kuhlmann built or acquired nine new plants in the unoccupied part of France between 1914 and 1918, giving it a truly national scope for the first time. Most important were a new sulfuric acid plant near Marseille, built at government expense, and a fertilizer plant at L'Estaque, formerly owned by Peñarroya. Kuhlmann also set up its first real research laboratory at Levallois. As a result of these initiatives, Kuhlmann was a much larger company in 1918 than it had been four years before in spite of losing its biggest chemical factories.

After the war, Kuhlmann recovered and rebuilt its three great plants in the department of the Nord (Loos, Madeleine, and Wattrelos), while also rationalizing and expanding production at the plants acquired during the war, in order to maintain and strengthen its position in sulfuric acid and superphosphate production. At the same time, Kuhlmann moved into new industries. In cooperation with Coignet of Lyon, it started producing bonemeal, gelatin, and adhesives, and through a joint venture with the Gillets' Progil, it started making cellulose for the rayon industry. More importantly, Kuhlmann moved into *carbochimie* through a series of joint ventures with the large coal companies of the Nord, which were making heavy investments in ovens to convert coal into coke for the steel industry. These new subsidiaries—Anzin-Kuhlmann, Courrières-Kuhlmann, Marles-Kuhlmann, and the Société Ammonia (owned jointly with the Mines de Lens)—used waste gases from the coking ovens to make hydrogen, methanol, ethylene, and especially ammonia, which gave Kuhlmann a position in the increasingly important nitrogen industry by the end of the 1920s. Most important for the company's long-term growth and profitability, however, was its move into synthetic dyestuffs.

As we saw earlier, German and Swiss companies dominated the production of both dye intermediaries and finished dyes in France by the beginning of the twentieth century. Indeed, as of 1913 only two French companies made intermediaries as well as finished dyes, and French-owned companies accounted for only one-fourth of the 9,000 tons of finished dyes consumed by the French textile industry annually.[9] But all this changed with the coming of war. To replace dyestuffs no longer imported from Germany, the French government underwrote expanded production of dye intermediaries at the Saint-Denis plant of Poirrier et Dalsace and at the sequestered plants of Hoechst and BASF; it then sent some of these intermediaries to Switzerland in exchange for finished dyes. To increase domestic production of finished dyes, the French government backed the creation of two new companies, the Compagnie Française de Produits Chimiques and Matières Colorantes de Saint-Clair du Rhône. When these companies proved unable to meet French needs, the government sponsored a larger and more ambitious enterprise, the Compagnie Nationale de Matières Chimiques et de Produits Chimiques (CNMC), which assumed control of sequestered German assets and set up new plants at Oissel and Villers Saint-Paul (Creil). The CNMC began operations in 1919 by producing synthetic indigo for French military uniforms. By 1922, after it had gained access to German dye patents under the terms of the Treaty of Versailles, the company was turning out 6,000 tons of 600 different dyes.[10]

When German chemical companies cut off dye shipments to France in 1923 in retaliation for the French occupation of the Ruhr, the future of dye production in France suddenly looked even brighter, and Kuhlmann seized the moment to take control of the CNMC (in which it had been a shareholder from the beginning) and several smaller dyeworks, including Saint-Clair du Rhône. Almost overnight, Kuhlmann gained control of 70 percent of French synthetic dye production and a substantial share of domestic production of dye intermediaries. Although the new dyestuffs division of Kuhlmann succeeded in replicating the new dyes introduced by the Germans and Swiss, it focused principally on mass-producing the dyes in greatest demand, especially synthetic indigo, which accounted for 4,200 of the 9,900 tons of dyes produced by the company in 1926–1927.[11] Kuhlmann also entered into market-sharing agreements with the Germans, Swiss, and British to assure its control of the French domestic and colonial markets. As a result, dye imports into France fell from a level of 6,000 tons a year in 1920 to 1,200 tons a year by 1930, and French production jumped to 17,000 tons by 1930. Thanks to the new businesses that Kuhlmann developed during and after World War I, especially in dyestuffs, the company's assets rose some 500 percent between 1913 and 1930, and Kuhlmann acquired the product mix and production capabilities that would keep it at the forefront of the French and European chemicals industries for the next forty years.[12] Even more impressive, however, were the achievements of Kuhlmann's old rival, Pechiney, which largely abandoned the old chemicals industry of the nineteenth century and assumed leadership in the new electrochemical and electrometallurgical industries in the early twentieth century.

Electrochemicals and Electrometals: Ugine and Pechiney

Between the mid-1880s and 1913, a wave of inventions and innovations revolutionized the chemicals and materials industry in France and the world by introducing entirely new products and making possible the large-scale, low-cost production of products previously in limited supply. Among these innovations, perhaps the most important involved the use of electrolysis in making chemicals and metals. These included the Hall-Héroult process for refining aluminum, the Gall-Montlaur and Corbin processes for the synthesis of chlorates, and the Castner-Keller process for making chlorine and caustic soda. Also important were the use of the electric arc furnace in the production of carbides, ferro-alloys, and metallic elements and the Linde and Claude processes for air liquefaction and the production of hydrogen, oxygen, and nitrogen. Finally, there was the revolution in the production of nitrogen compounds, which began with the Birkeland-Eyde process for synthesizing nitric acid from atmospheric nitrogen and hydrogen and culminated in the Haber-Bosch process for the high-pressure synthesis of ammonia from nitrogen and hydrogen.[13]

In France, the development of these products and processes tended to be undertaken not by the established chemical companies but by start-ups expressly created to exploit newly patented technologies. Indeed, the wide-open nature of the new chemicals industry in France encouraged the proliferation of new firms, each jockeying to gain a dominant position in a segment of the industry and to use that as a springboard for expansion into other segments. But, as so often happens in industrial history, the age of the start-ups soon gave way to a period of consolidation. In France, this progression led to three companies controlling much of the new chemicals industry by the 1930s: Pechiney and SECEM-AEU (Ugine) in electrochemicals and electro-metallurgy and Air Liquide in industrial gases and nitrogen. In this section, we look at the rise of the first two; the story of Air Liquide is told in the next section.

What eventually became the Société d'Electrochimie, d'Electro-Métallurgie et des Aciéries Electriques d'Ugine (SECEM et AEU)— "Ugine" for short—had its origins in the founding of the Société d'Electrochimie (SEC) in 1889 to produce potassium chlorate, a key ingredient in matches, using the electrolytic process invented by Henri Gall and Armand de Villardy, comte de Montlaur. With financial backing from the Swiss dynamo maker Cuenod-Sautter, the SEC constructed a hydroelectric plant and factory at Vallorbe in the Swiss Alps that turned out 400 tons of chlorates in its first year of operation, 1890–1891. In 1894 it opened a comparable facility in France at Pré-mont on the Arc River in the department of Savoie. The next year the SEC negotiated a market-sharing agreement with Pechiney and Saint-

Gobain, both of which continued to make potassium chlorate by traditional chemical methods. That agreement gave SEC a virtual monopoly in the Swiss market and one-third of the French market for potassium chlorate, but it also precluded further expansion of chlorate production for the time being. Having momentarily saturated the market for chlorates, the SEC faced for the first time what would become a recurring challenge for all electrochemical companies: finding new chemicals to produce in order to keep expensive hydroelectric plants operating at an efficient and profitable level.[14]

The Société d'Electrochimie's efforts to diversify began in 1895 when it acquired the rights to Henri Moissan's technique of synthesizing calcium carbide in an electric furnace. Calcium carbide was a new product of enormous potential that would soon give rise to three new industries: acetylene, synthetic abrasives, and cyanamids. After Henry Gall demonstrated the viability of the new technology in tests at Vallorbe and launched commercial production of calcium carbide at Prémont, the SEC created a subsidiary, the Société des Carbures Métalliques (SCM), to undertake large-scale production at two new plants. When these plants went on line in the early 1900s, they made the SEC the world's largest manufacturer of calcium carbide. Although the SEC eschewed forward integration from carbides to acetylene, it did move into the electrolytic or electrothermic production of calcium cyanamid and other chemicals, including sodium, sodium cyanide, calcium, hydrofluoric acid, and potassium permanganate. Most importantly, when the Hall and Héroult patents expired in 1907, it began producing aluminum at Prémont and alumina, the raw material for aluminum, at a plant near Marseille. In 1911, when it joined the new aluminum cartel Aluminium Français, the SEC accounted for 6 percent of France's annual output of the metal.

The outbreak of war with Germany in 1914 caused a number of problems for the Société d'Electrochimie. France lacked its own sources of potassium salts, so the cutting off of imports of potassium chloride from Germany disrupted its production of potassium chlorate. Moreover, Henry Gall's Alsatian origins and the company's complex ties with German and Swiss companies put the SEC under a legal cloud and led to Gall being prosecuted for trading with the enemy in the fall of 1914 (he was acquitted). However, none of this kept the company from receiving large orders for war matériel from 1915 onward. As part of the government's crash program to increase the domestic output of chlorine—much in demand for poison gas and other applications—

the SEC was encouraged to take over La Volta, a financially troubled manufacturer of chlorine and caustic soda. This was the first of a series of mergers and acquisitions that transformed the SEC over the next seven years. In 1919, the company absorbed its subsidiary in carbide production, the SCM, and merged with an important maker of ferro-alloys, Jacques Barut's Société Electrométallurgique du Giffre. In the process, the company's capital was doubled, and it changed its name to the Société d'Electrochimie et d'Electrométallurgie (SECEM). In 1921 the company moved even more decisively into electrometallurgy by merging with the Société des Forges et Aciers Electriques Paul Girod (Ugine) and becoming SECEM et AEU (AEU stands for Aciéries Electriques d'Ugine).

The origins of the Aciéries Electriques d'Ugine went back to the turn of the century, when a brilliant young Swiss metallurgical scientist, Paul Girod, invented and patented an electric furnace to produce ferro-alloys. In 1903, Girod founded a Swiss joint-stock company to license the Girod furnace to steelmakers worldwide and to construct a plant at Ugine in the French Alps to produce ferro-alloys. Ugine was perhaps the largest and most advanced electrical steelworks in the world when it opened its doors, but it failed to turn a profit in its first three years. In 1908, Girod transferred Ugine to a new French company, the Compagnie des Forges et Aciéries Electriques Paul Girod, and moved it into the production of special steels for tools and ball bearings. When sales remained sluggish, Girod sold electric power to cover his fixed costs. Even so, the company was on the verge of bankruptcy in early 1914 and was saved only by the outbreak of the war.[15]

Paul Girod became a French citizen in early 1914, just in time to make Ugine eligible to manufacture armor plate, armor-piercing shells, and other munitions for the French government when war broke out. By mid-1915, Ugine was producing 55 percent of the alloy steel employed in French armories. The resulting profits made Girod a wealthy man and allowed Girod's French firm to pay off its debts and buy up the shares of its Swiss mother firm, the S.A. Electro-Métallurgique Procédés Paul Girod. But in 1918, the wartime boom gave way to a peacetime bust, and soon Girod's company was once again in serious financial trouble. It was at this point that Henri Gall stepped in and engineered a takeover of Ugine by SECEM. As a result of the merger, Paul Girod became a vice president of the new firm, SECEM et AEU, but he soon clashed with Gall and left to create a new electrical steelworks in the Italian Alps with the support of Benito Mussolini. Jacques

Barut thereafter ran Ugine as a virtually autonomous division of the larger company.

Through the remainder of the twenties and into the thirties, SECEM et AEU (by then known as Ugine) sought to establish strong positions in three rather distinct industries: power and light, steelmaking, and electrochemicals. By the end of World War I, the company was already a major producer of hydroelectricity, and Henry Gall, as managing director, devoted much of his time and effort until his death in 1930 to enlarging the firm's electrical output. That output continued to increase through the 1930s so that, by the time the French power and light industry was nationalized in 1946, Ugine accounted for one-tenth of France's total kilowattage. Meanwhile, the metallurgical division of the company, centered on the Ugine plant, expanded its production of special steels, started making steel tubes for the petroleum refining industry, and introduced a new process for making stainless steel that was subsequently licensed by U.S. Steel and Bethlehem Steel.[16] The chemical division continued to manufacture its prewar mix of products, as well as products introduced during the war (such as chlorine, magnesium, and hydrogen peroxide). In the 1930s, one subsidiary opened the largest carbide furnace in Europe at Lannemezan, while another moved into the production of acetone. SECEM et AEU also continued to produce a certain amount of alumina and aluminum, the only French firm other than Pechiney to do so.[17]

Overall, however, the verdict on Ugine after World War I is mixed. On the one hand, it survived the tumultuous early years of the electrochemical and electrometallurgical industries and established itself as a national leader in specialty steel and in several product areas in chemicals. By the early 1930s, it was the fifth largest chemical company in France and ranked among the fifty largest manufacturing companies in France. On the other hand, it was only one-third the size of Pechiney in 1930 (one-half its size in 1936) and clearly took a backseat to that company in size, influence, and long-term significance.

The Société Anonyme des Produits Chimiques d'Alais et de Camargue (PCAC or, later, Pechiney) was the only old-line French chemical company to maintain and improve its standing in the industry between the 1890s and 1930s by refocusing its resources on electrometallurgy and electrochemistry, but it took this path only after newer, more adventuresome firms had shown the viability of the new technology. As we saw in Chapter 8, PCAC spent most of the 1880s and 1890s seeking new markets for its output of salt and sulfuric acid after the advent of the Solvay ammonia process had made it impossible to continue operating its Leblanc sodaworks. In contrast to Saint-Gobain and Kuhlmann, which responded to a similar challenge by moving into the production of superphosphate fertilizers, PCAC diverted its output of sulfuric acid into the production of caustic soda for the soap industry and copper sulfate for the winegrowers. Meanwhile, it found a ready market for the sea salt it produced at Salins de Giraud in a nearby Solvay sodaworks, it continued to produce chlorine and potassium chlorate by established methods, and it remained the world's only producer of aluminum until 1889.

In 1886 the managing director of PCAC, A. R. Pechiney, made two decisions that might well have proven fatal for the company's long-term development. First, he chose not to purchase and implement the electrolytic process for making chlorates patented by his employee, Henri Gall; and second, he decided not to acquire the rights to Paul Héroult's electrolytic process for refining aluminum. Of course, both processes were soon acquired and applied by other companies—the Gall-Montlaur process by the Société d'Electochimie (SEC) and the Héroult process by a new Swiss-backed company, the Société d'Electrométallurgie Française (SEMF). It took SEC with its electrolytic production twenty years to drive Pechiney completely out of the chlorate business. However, when SEMF began producing aluminum electrolytically at Froges in 1889, aluminum prices fell 50 percent, and PCAC had no choice but to close down its old-style chemical production of aluminum almost immediately. With no domestic competition, SEMF proceeded to build three additional plants, each one larger than its predecessor, and to steadily increase its output of aluminum from 309 tons in 1890 to 784 tons in 1900 and to 4,240 tons by 1910. On the eve of World War I, SEMF was the second largest aluminum refiner in the world (after the Pittsburgh Reduction Company, the future Alcoa).[18]

To his credit, A. R. Pechiney quickly recognized his error in refusing to buy the Héroult process and in 1897 acquired Calypso, an aluminum plant recently built on the Arc River near Saint-Jean-de-Maurienne to exploit the Hall process, the American counterpart of the Héroult process. Although it produced only 19 tons of aluminum in its first year, the Calypso plant gradually increased its output to 670 tons by 1905. However, it was Adrien Badin, who joined the company as principal engineer in 1900 and succeeded Pechiney as managing director seven years later, who finally committed PCAC to truly large-scale production of aluminum after 1905. This involved acquiring bauxite mines, adopting the more efficient Bayer process for producing alumina, enlarging the Calypso plant and adding a second reduction plant at Saint-Jean-de-Maurienne, and converting to the Héroult process when it became available. As a result, Pechiney's aluminum output rose to 1,563 tons by 1907 and 2,666 tons by 1910, four times the level in 1905 but still substantially below SEMF's.

To complicate matters further for Pechiney, three other firms began refining aluminum in France after the Héroult and Hall patents expired: the Société d'Electrochimie at Prémont, the Société des Forces Motrices et des Usines de l'Arve (SARV) at Chedde, and SARV's offshoot, the Société des Produits Electrométallurgiques des Pyrénées at Auzat. By 1910, total French aluminum output approached 9,000 tons, one-fifth of the world total (which turned out to be France's all-time highest share of world production). However, because supply continued to exceed demand worldwide and the price continued to fall, none of the French aluminum producers was reaping much profit. To correct this, Badin and other industry executives came together in 1911 to form a cartel, L'Aluminium Français, which in turn negotiated market-sharing, price-fixing agreements with the other major producers in Europe and North America. Aluminium Français also served as the vehicle through which the French producers launched the Southern Aluminum Company, an ambitious effort to break into the American market by building and operating the world's largest reduction plant on the Yadkin River in North Carolina.[19]

The outbreak of war in 1914 disrupted the plans to supply French capital and French bauxite to the Southern Aluminum Company, and in 1916 the plant was sold to Alcoa. Meanwhile, Pechiney turned to producing war matériel such as phenol, a key intermediary in the manufacture of explosives, as well as ammonium nitrate, chlorine, and various electrochemicals (cyanamids, sodium and potassium chlorate, ammonium perchlorate). Indeed, as the war dragged on, Pechiney increasingly moved into electrochemicals while continuing to strengthen its position in aluminum. To this end, it absorbed the Société des Produits Electrométallurgiques des Pyrénées in 1914 and the Société des Forces Motrices et des Usines de l'Arve in 1916. SARV had been founded in 1895 to build a power plant at Chedde on the Arve River and to produce chlorates with an electrolytic process invented by Paul Corbin, son-in-law of Armand Lederlin of Les Blanchisseries et Teintureries de Thaon. While perfecting its production of chlorates, SARV-

Chedde began producing a new high explosive, cheddite, and then added aluminum production when the Héroult process fell into the public domain. (Chedde was able to diversify so broadly and so quickly because it produced the cheapest electrical power in France.) When Pechiney took control of SARV in 1916, the Chedde plant was dedicated exclusively to the production of chlorates and perchlorates and expanded rapidly, with its workforce rising from 200 in 1914 to 1,372 by 1917.[20]

Pechiney emerged from World War I much enlarged and more diversified, but it immediately faced two challenges. The first involved major changes in corporate leadership following the unexpected death of Adrien Badin at age forty-five in 1917 and the passing of the company's longtime chairman, Emile Guimet, in 1918. The new chairman was Gabriel Cordier, a leading executive in both the railroad and electrical industries, who had joined the Pechiney board only in 1916. Under Cordier, the direction of operations was divided between Emile Boyoud, longtime director of the Calypso plant, and Louis Marlio, a high-ranking state engineer who had been brought into the company by Badin in 1916 for his political connections. These executives had to deal with a second challenge, the postwar collapse of demand for aluminum and munitions that left the company sitting on large unsold inventories (Chedde, for example, had 10,000 tons of chlorates in its warehouses). This crisis provided the final impetus for a long-contemplated merger between Pechiney and SEMF that was finalized in 1921.[21] The resulting company, known officially as Alais, Froges, et Camargue (unofficially as Pechiney), controlled 90 percent of French aluminum capacity along with substantial production capacity in electrochemicals. Reflecting the dominant role of Pechiney in the new company, Cordier assumed the chairmanship, and Emile Vielhomme, the former chairman of SEMF, became vice-chairman. The managing director of SEMF, Jacques Level, joined Boyoud and Marlio in a triumvirate of chief operating officers.

At first, retrenchment was the order of the day for Alais, Froges, et Camargue (AFC). In its first year, it cut its workforce by 60 percent, from 6,525 to only 2,380, but as economic conditions improved in the course of the twenties, and especially as the growth in automobile production raised the demand for aluminum, the company increased capacity at existing aluminum plants and added two new plants. As a result, its output of aluminum rose from 13,000 tons in 1923 to over 25,000 tons by 1929.[22] The 1920s also brought increased diversification in electrochemicals, especially in the production of chlorine derivatives, nitrogen compounds, magnesium, and aluminum alloys. By the early 1930s, AFC had solidified its position as France's largest producer of electrochemicals and as one of the world's leading makers of aluminum, and it had also become a major producer of electrical power (accounting for one-eighth of French electrical output). As of 1936, AFC (Pechiney) was France's fourth largest industrial enterprise (with assets exceeded only by Wendel, Saint-Gobain, and the Compagnie Française des Pétroles) and one of a handful of French companies that were major powers in their industries beyond France.

Industrial Gases: The Rise of Air Liquide

The synthesis of calcium carbide in Moissan's electric furnace proved to be a crucial breakthrough in the development of several new chemicals. One was cyanamid. Another was acetylene. The French were particularly interested in the latter. Their efforts to manufacture and utilize acetylene led to a series of inventions that culminated in the birth of an important new industry, industrial gases, and the rise of the company that came to dominate this new industry worldwide in the second half of the twentieth century, Air Liquide.

Whereas many of the key innovations in French electrochemistry and electrometallurgy occurred in the Southeast and made Lyon and Grenoble centers for these industries, the chain of inventions that led from calcium carbide to acetylene to Air Liquide was largely the work of scientists and engineers based in Paris and associated with the Paris electrical industry. In addition to Henri Moissan, these included Hippolyte Fontaine, a leading authority on dynamos and electric motors and editor of the influential *Revue Industrielle;* the Le Chatelier brothers—Henry, Louis, and André—each of whom would play an important role in the launching of the acetylene industry in France;[23] and especially Georges Claude, a young engineer employed by Thomson-Houston who became the "indispensable man" in the development of gas technology and in the founding of Air Liquide.

In 1892, Henri Moissan discovered how to generate acetylene by dissolving calcium carbide in water, and three years later Henri Le Chatelier demonstrated that a mixture of acetylene and pure oxygen produced the hottest and brightest flame yet known to man. Le Chatelier and his associates (who included Georges Claude's patron at Thomson-Houston, the Lettish engineer Abdank-Abakanowicz) immediately set out to manufacture acetylene in commercial quantities, but they were stymied by acetylene's annoying habit of exploding spontaneously when stored in steel tanks. So they brought in Claude to find a way to stabilize and store acetylene. He did this by dissolving acetylene in acetone and then combining this solution with charcoal (following the model of Alfred Nobel, who stabilized nitroglycerine by combining it with kieselguhr). To bring Claude's system to market, the Compagnie Française de l'Acetylène Dissous was founded in 1896, with Hippolyte Fontaine as president and Abdank and Le Chatelier as directors.[24]

Initially, everyone thought the market for acetylene would be in mobile lighting systems for trains and road vehicles, but the invention of the oxyacetylene welding torch opened a potentially much larger market, provided that a cheap source of oxygen—and a convenient way to store it—could be found. To this end a *société en participation* was formed in 1899 to support research that Claude was already conducting after hours and on weekends to find a commercially viable method of liquefying air and separating it into liquid oxygen and liquid nitrogen. The head of the group backing this research was Paul Delorme, a former classmate of Claude's and a fellow engineer for Thomson-Houston.

Before Claude had completed his research, he was beaten to the punch by the German pioneer in refrigeration and ice-making technology, Carl von Linde, who succeeded in liquefying air on a commercial scale in 1901. Linde's system, which involved the single expansion of compressed air through a needle valve, was soon brought to market in the United States by the Linde Air Products Company, later a part of Union Carbide. Claude persevered, however, since his line of inquiry promised to produce liquid air more economically than the Linde system once a method of lubricating a moving piston at low temperatures could be found. Discovery of that lubricant in petroleum ether allowed Claude to demonstrate his system to his backers on May 26, 1902—one day before they planned to meet to dissolve their partnership. By the end of June 1902, Claude had built a working apparatus that could produce twenty-five pounds of liquid air per hour.[25]

Delorme and the other backers were sufficiently convinced of the practicality and superiority of Claude's air liquefaction method that in the fall of 1902 they founded a joint-stock company, Air Liquide, with Delorme as president, to commercialize it.[26] In cooperation with its sister company, the Compagnie Française de l'Acetylène Dissous, Air

Liquide opened its first air liquefaction plant in June 1903 at Boulogne-sur-Seine, adjacent to Claude's laboratory. That same year André Le Chatelier founded the Société d'Acetylène Dissous du Sud-Est to exploit the Claude process in the south of France and to develop the technology and equipment for steel welding (primarily for the underwater repair of steamships). In 1904, Air Liquide launched the Compagnie des Gaz Comprimés to make canisters for storing and shipping industrial gases and to produce those gases at a plant in Lyon. Meanwhile, Claude proceeded to the next phase of research, designing a machine to separate liquid air into oxygen and nitrogen. This work consumed two years and required an investment of 500,000 francs by Air Liquide, but by 1904 Claude had developed a separation system that offered significant efficiencies over the comparable Linde system, which had been on the market since 1902. Air Liquide soon started producing liquid oxygen and nitrogen, and by 1907 profits from its various operations were sufficient for the company to declare its first dividend.[27]

Between 1906 and 1913, the nominal capital of Air Liquide rose from 1 million francs to 11 million, and its assets increased even more, from 614,000 francs to over 23 million, making Air Liquide France's eighth largest chemical company and its seventy-sixth largest publicly held industrial enterprise on the eve of World War I.[28] This rapid growth reflected progress on three fronts: perfection of the technology and development of nationwide production in Air Liquide's core businesses (industrial gas and welding equipment), the implantation of these businesses outside of France, and the development of additional products and processes. These years also witnessed the emergence of an approach to organizational development that would distinguish Air Liquide's entire history: undertaking initial geographical expansion or product diversification through joint ventures or legally separate subsidiaries and later absorbing the most successful of these into the mother company while continuing to operate in related fields (for example, acetylene production and welding services) through sister companies with which Air Liquide shared top management. In effect, from its earliest years Air Liquide was creating an industrial group.

To sustain the growth of Air Liquide's core businesses, Georges Claude continued to improve his processes for air liquefaction and separation between 1906 and 1913. These improvements were incorporated in a line of compact, highly efficient machines that could produce up to 20 cubic meters of oxygen and 400 cubic meters of nitrogen per hour at 99.7 percent purity. With these machines, Air Liquide manufactured and bottled gas at six plants in France. The company then marketed this gas through its subsidiary, Gaz Comprimé. Air Liquide also furnished machines to foreign subsidiaries and independent gas producers. Meanwhile, the production of acetylene remained the purview of Air Liquide's sister companies, Acetylène Dissous and Acetylène Dissous du Sud-Est.[29] In 1909, the creation of yet another sister company, Soudure Autogène Française, headed by André Le Chatelier, consolidated the welding services end of the business.

Armed with proprietary technology that had few rivals worldwide, Air Liquide moved quickly into foreign markets. This entailed the creation of wholly owned or majority-owned subsidiaries in Belgium and Italy and the signing of licensing agreements with firms in England, Germany, Austria, Russia, Spain, Sweden, Greece, and Turkey. Beyond Europe, Air Liquide founded a Canadian subsidiary in 1910, and it launched the Groupe Air Liquide en Extrême-Orient, which set up plants in Saigon in 1910 and Kobé, Japan, in 1911.[30] In 1914–1915, Air Liquide set out to establish a presence in the United States, the world's largest market for oxyacetylene welding, through a joint venture with Percy Rockefeller's American Oxygen Company. That led to the creation of the Air Reduction Company, which, with Union Carbide, became one of the prime movers in the American industrial gas industry in the 1920s.[31]

Air Liquide also took early steps toward product and process diversification in the years before World War I. The company entered the refrigeration equipment business with contracts to equip the refrigerator ships of Chargeurs Réunis and the Compagnie Générale Transatlantique, and it participated in a joint venture with a Belgian company, Société d'Ougrée-Marahaye, to utilize liquid oxygen in the smelting of pig iron. Air Liquide also began producing hydrogen peroxide at its Lyon plant, and it financed Georges Claude's research on the industrial production of rare gases, mainly neon and argon. This research led to the invention of neon lighting, which created a sensation in 1910 when it was first used to illuminate the facade of the Grand Palais for the Paris Auto Show.[32]

The mobilization of August 1914 initially disrupted Air Liquide's operations, but the company came to benefit greatly from World War I as demand burgeoned for oxygen and nitrogen for use in the manufacture of war matériel (nitrogen-based explosives) and hospital supplies (hydrogen peroxide). Accordingly, Air Liquide quadrupled the size of its Boulogne-sur-Seine plant and built three additional plants for industrial gases. It also started producing liquid chlorine at La Grande-Paroisse, on the Seine southeast of Paris, in a plant that the French government had recently seized from the German pharmaceutical company Merck.[33] Although it came out of the war with greatly increased manufacturing capacity, Air Liquide did not suffer from the overcapacity that plagued many other war suppliers. On the contrary, the continued growth of oxyacetylene welding and the proliferating industrial applications of oxygen and nitrogen after the war seemed to render Air Liquide recession-proof.

In the early 1920s, Air Liquide continued to expand its core businesses while streamlining its operations through mergers, notably with Acetylène Dissous in 1923.[34] The company also continued to develop new products, the most important of which was synthetic ammonia. Working at his laboratory at La Grande-Paroisse in 1917, Georges Claude had developed an alternative to the Haber process for the synthesis of ammonia from nitrogen and hydrogen gas. To exploit this new Claude process, Air Liquide launched the Société Chimique de la Grande-Paroisse (SCGP) in 1918 as a fifty-fifty joint venture with Saint-Gobain. Encouraged by the initial results, the two partners decided in 1919 to bring ammonia production at La Grande-Paroisse up to a world-class scale, necessitating an increase in SCGP's capital from 14 to 34 million francs. They also moved into the American market with the founding of Lazote Inc., a joint venture between SCGP and Du Pont.[35]

By the end of the 1920s, Air Liquide's social capital had risen to 88 million francs and its assets amounted to more than 500 million francs, making it France's fourth largest chemical company and placing it among France's top twenty-five publicly held industrial enterprises. By 1930, Air Liquide was operating thirty-two oxygen plants and twenty-six acetylene plants in France, and its Champigny plant (formerly part of Acetylène Dissous) remained a leading developer and manufacturer of welding equipment. Meanwhile, Air Liquide continued to strengthen its position beyond France. To its existing subsidiaries in Canada, Belgium, North Africa, and East Asia, it added a new one in Southeast Europe. In the United States, it deepened its relationship with Du Pont by exchanging its shares in Lazote for shares in Du Pont, while Du Pont continued to license the Claude ammonia process. In 1930 Air Liquide also participated in the founding of Claude Lumière, which reinforced the company's stake in yet another high-tech growth area, neon lighting, and helped sustain it through the ups and downs of the Great Depression.[36]

Pharmaceuticals and Artificial Fibers: The Making of Rhône-Poulenc

In contrast to the dramatic rise of Air Liquide in the field of industrial gases, no genuinely world-class big business appeared in France in the area of pharmaceuticals and artificial fibers between 1900 and 1930. However, Rhône-Poulenc did emerge as the clear leader in France in both areas. Although at best a mid-size firm by European standards, Rhône-Poulenc was vying with Kuhlmann by the end of the 1930s to become France's largest pure chemical company (in contrast to Pechiney and Saint-Gobain, which continued to mix chemical production with other specialties). More importantly, Rhône-Poulenc had put in place by 1939 the technical and organizational resources that would enable it to become France's leading chemical manufacturer after World War II and a bona fide power in the world chemical industry by the end of the twentieth century.[37]

The origins of Rhône-Poulenc lay in the success of two firms whose early history we examined in Chapter 8: Poulenc Frères and Gilliard, Monnet, et Cartier (later renamed Usines du Rhône). By the 1890s, Poulenc Frères was well established as the leading French supplier of fine chemicals to pharmacists and research scientists and a leading seller of photographic supplies (the operative words here being "supplier" and "seller," since Poulenc Frères still did not manufacture most of the goods it sold). The company continued to be run by the sons of the founder Etienne Poulenc even after it became a *société anonyme*, Etablissements Poulenc Frères (EPF), in 1900. Through the 1890s and into the 1900s, Poulenc Frères grew steadily by adding the production of colors for glass and ceramics and by developing and marketing pharmaceuticals such as Stovaine, one of the first synthetic anesthetics.[38]

In contrast to the steady progress of Poulenc Frères, the history of Usines du Rhône was punctuated by crisis and upheaval in the twenty-five years preceding World War I. In the late 1880s, the company was still run by two of the founders, Prosper Monnet and Jean-Marie Cartier, along with the heirs of the third founder Marc Gilliard; and it still concentrated on making synthetic dyes and related products (phenol, methyl chlorate, resorcinol), as it had since its founding in the 1860s.

In the 1890s, however, in the face of growing competition from German dyemakers, the company moved into new product lines—saccharin, vanillin and other artificial flavorings, and especially pharmaceuticals such as salicylic acid, antipyrine, ethyl chloride, and antidiphtheria serum—but it soon discovered it lacked sufficient financial resources to support this diversification. To raise additional capital, the company became a *société anonyme* in 1895 under the name Société Chimique des Usines du Rhône (SCUR), but Monnet and Cartier remained in charge. The renamed company continued to expand its operations in the late 1890s, integrating backward into the production of dye intermediaries amd establishing overseas subsidiaries (the Saccharin Company in Great Britain, Crown Manufacturing in the United States), but a heavy investment in the production of a new synthetic indigo dye produced heavy losses when BASF introduced a lower-cost competitor.

In the early 1900s, the company's chief creditor, the Société Générale, forced out Monnet and Cartier and brought in Eugène-Henri Boyer from the electrical industry as the new chairman and two new technical directors, Nicolas Grillet and Joseph Koetschet. The new management team moved quickly to pare down SCUR's product line by getting out of dyestuffs and by focusing on the products with the greatest money-making potential, including saccharin, vanillin, cellulose acetate, aspirin (introduced in France in 1908 under the brand name Rhodine), and scents and flavorings (its most lucrative product in the early 1900s was the Lance Parfum Rodo, a squeeze-bottle perfume applicator popular in Brazil during Carnaval). After suffering a decline in business from 1895 to 1906, Usines du Rhône enjoyed growing sales and renewed profitability in the eight years leading up to the war.

As happened with almost all French chemical companies, the outbreak of war in 1914 proved to be a boon for both Poulenc Frères and the Usines du Rhône. Poulenc Frères received government contracts to make both poison gas and antidotes for poison gas, and it found a profitable niche producing German goods that were no longer available in France and Great Britain, such as the antisyphilitics salvarsan and neo-salvarsan. As a result, Poulenc Frères saw its workforce grow from 500 to 2,000 and its sales increase from 15.7 million francs to almost 36 million francs between 1914 and 1916. Usines du Rhône, however, enjoyed even greater wartime expansion (its sales jumped from 5.6 million francs in 1914 to 121.6 million francs in 1916) by filling huge government orders for phenol, chlorine, and a particularly nasty poison gas, yperite, and by increasing its output of saccharin to offset sugar shortages resulting from the disruption of sugar beet cultivation in the north of France.

At the end of the war, Poulenc Frères saw its sales drop by one-fourth, but it soon recovered by resuming production of well-established products like lithium, bromine, and bismuth and by adding new products such as vanillin, caffeine, citric acid, and glucose. Usines du Rhône, however, faced a much greater postwar challenge. With the canceling of munitions contracts, its sales fell by 75 percent, and it had to scramble to find viable replacements. Ultimately it found its answer in the production of cellulose acetate, which offered an entrée into the rising field of artificial fibers. Indeed, no strategic decision was more important for the long-term development of Rhône-Poulenc than its decision to begin making artificial silk (rayon), the first of the man-made fibers that would become so important for the textile industry over the course of the twentieth century.

The artificial silk industry was born in 1884 when Comte Hilaire Bernigaud de Chardonnet patented a method of drawing liquified nitrocellulose through spinnerets to form silk-like filaments. Chardonnet then founded a company that began producing this artificial silk in 1892. At about the same time, German scientists came up with a second form of artificial silk, made by dissolving cellulose in cuprammonium hydroxide, which a German company, the Vereinigte Glanzstoff Fabriken (VGF), began producing in 1899. Meanwhile, British scientists developed a third form of artificial silk, viscose, by treating cellulose with caustic soda and carbon bisulfide, and British entrepreneurs set up the British Viscoid Company to produce it in commercial quantities.[39]

While Chardonnet's version of artificial silk continued to dominate the French market for man-made fibers in the early 1900s, several firms introduced the newer forms to France. In 1902, the Société La Soie Artificielle began making cuprammonium silk at a plant in Givet (Ardennes) under a license from VGF. In 1904, Joseph Gillet et Fils, the leading makers of natural dyestuffs in Lyon, founded another company to manufacture cuprammonium silk, La Soie Artificielle d'Izieux. The same year, Ernest Carnot, son of the assassinated president of the Third Republic, Sadi Carnot, launched the Société Française de Viscose (SFV) with the support of the German licensees of the British viscose process. A second French viscose company, the Société Ardechoise pour la Fabrication de la Soie Viscose, was founded in 1905.[40]

Because both the nitrocellulose and cuprammonium forms of artificial silk were expensive to make and enjoyed little price advantage over natural silk, industry observers expected viscose to emerge as the dominant form of artificial silk, but efficient production of viscose proved difficult to achieve even as the number of would-be manufacturers multiplied. In 1904, Courtaulds, the leading British silk manufacturer, finally succeeded in setting up large-scale production of viscose at Coventry using technology developed by Carnot's SFV, and it soon moved into the world's largest potential market for artificial fiber, the United States, through the creation of American Viscose. Meanwhile in continental Europe, the proliferation of new viscose companies plus the movement of cuprammonium silk makers into viscose production prompted efforts to form cartels to pool technology and curtail ruinous price competition. In France, the Carnots and Gillets brought the various cuprammonium and viscose manufacturers together in the Comptoir des Textiles Artificiels (CTA) in 1911 to manage the production and marketing of all artificial fibers. However, on the eve of World War I, the French were producing only 2,900 tons of rayon annually, about one-tenth of the world total. World production of viscose rayon took off after the war, but in the highly cartelized French sector of the industry, ouput of rayon remained flat, and that presented a golden opportunity to the Usines du Rhône (SCUR).[41]

In the early 1920s, SCUR was already France's leading producer of cellulose acetate, which would soon emerge as the fourth form of rayon. The company had started making cellulose acetate in 1910 as feedstock for non-flammable movie film. With the outbreak of World War I, it discovered a much larger market for cellulose acetate, as the chief ingredient in the "dope" used to stiffen the fabric covering of aircraft. By 1917, however, it was clear that aircraft production would plummet at the end of the war, so SCUR launched the Société Générale du Rhodoïd to find alternative uses for cellulose acetate. By 1921, Rhodoïd's researchers had discovered how to recover the acetone used to dissolve cellulose acetate, which was the key breakthrough in making the production of acetate fiber economically viable. This quickly caught the eye of Edmond Gillet and Alfred Bernheim of CTA, and in April 1922 CTA and SCUR launched a fifty-fifty joint venture, the Société pour la Fabrication de la Soie Artificielle Rhodiaseta (changed later to Rhodiaceta), to produce and market acetate fiber in France and abroad. SCUR agreed to supply its technical know-how plus the necessary chemical feedstocks to the cellulose acetate plant to be built by Rhodiaceta, and it agreed to spin the cellulose acetate into filaments at its Roussillon plant.

When the Rhodiaceta plant finally opened at Lyon-Vaise in 1928, French production of acetate fibers took off, and SCUR and Rhodiaceta moved quickly to set up similar production in Germany, Austria, Italy, Czechoslovakia, Switzerland, and Brazil. To enter the U.S. market, Rhodiaceta licensed Du Pont to make acetate fibers in return for 28 percent of the profits (CTA had previously licensed Du Pont to make viscose fibers, and Du Pont was also producing the sheet form of viscose under license from the French patent holder, La Cellophane). Rhodiaceta and Du Pont also agreed to share the results of future research, which led to Rhodiaceta becoming the French licensee for Du Pont's nylon in the late 1930s. The enormous growth of Rhodiaceta after World War II on the strength of its production of nylon and other Du Pont fibers and materials, would, more than anything else, account for Rhône-Poulenc's great success in the second half of the twentieth century.[42]

Meanwhile, as Rhodiaceta's operations were taking off in 1928, SCUR's managers turned to strengthening the company's position in its core businesses, chemicals and pharmaceuticals. One way to do this was through a friendly merger with Etablissements Poulenc Frères. In the wake of the grand consolidation of the German and British chemicals industries through the creation of IG Farben and Imperial Chemicals, French politicians had become interested in consolidating the highly fragmented French chemical industry as a matter of national security. When attempts to bring about a merger of Kuhlmann and Saint-Gobain foundered in 1926, attention turned to the possibility of the EPF-SCUR merger.[43] After two years of negotiations, it was agreed that SCUR would acquire EPF and that the new company would be named the Société des Usines Chimiques Rhône-Poulenc (SCURP). The chairman of SCUR, Eugène Boyer, assumed the chairmanship of the new company, and Nicolas Grillet of SCUR and Georges Roché of Poulenc became its managing directors.[44]

The new directors of Rhône-Poulenc moved quickly to streamline operations by closing marginal plants and concentrating production at three sites: Roussillon for heavy chemicals, Saint-Fons (Lyon) for fine chemicals, and Vitry-sur-Seine for pharmaceuticals. In the process, the workforce of Rhône-Poulenc was cut dramatically, from 4,497 in 1928 to 2,760 by 1933. Beyond these efforts at rationalization, the success of Rhône-Poulenc in its first decade can be traced to four policies:

(1) emphasizing the company's strengths in pharmaceuticals and artificial fibers, (2) setting up a pharmaceutical research laboratory at Vitry and developing new high-value products such as sulfanamides, antispasmodics, antihistamines, and vasodilators, (3) further enhancing its position in the domestic chemicals and pharmaceuticals markets through cross-licensing arrangements with foreign companies like IG Farben, Hoffmann La Roche, and Du Pont, and (4) continuing to develop artificial fibers through Rhodiaceta.[45] As a result of these policies, Rhône-Poulenc enjoyed rising revenues and profits in the 1930s and saw its position in the French chemicals industry advance relative to other firms. Although its assets were only half of Kuhlmann's in 1936, Rhône-Poulenc had surpassed Kuhlmann in total revenues by 1938, according to Jean-Pierre Daviet.[46] As World War II approached, the company already had in place the policies and structures that would allow it to play a much larger role in the European and world chemical industries in the postwar era.

Big Cement: Lafarge and Its Rivals

The fifth area within the sprawling French chemicals and materials industry that gave rise to very large firms in the early twentieth century was the manufacturing of cement and related building materials. Since antiquity, masons had known how to mix water, clay, and lime to form mortars to bind together bricks, stones, or tiles that, once dried, remained largely impervious to moisture and the elements (in other words, the setting and drying process was somehow irreversible). However, the modern cement industry developed from two products introduced in the late eighteenth and early nineteenth centuries that went far beyond traditional mortars. The first was hydraulic lime—a limestone-based cement that could set and dry underwater and could thus be used to construct the foundations of bridges, docks, and seaside fortifications. Hydraulic lime was in fact a special case of a larger category that the French called *ciments naturels,* cements based on naturally occurring forms of lime and clay that require little processing. The second and ultimately more significant product was what the British called Portland cement and the French called *ciment artificiel*—a manufactured cement produced by "burning" a precise combination of lime and clay minerals to the point of vitrification. Portland cement shared hydraulic lime's attribute of setting underwater, but it was much stronger in a variety of applications and became the key ingredient in

modern concrete, the mixture of cement and crushed stone that provides a cheap and versatile substitute for quarried building stones.

Manufacturing the various kinds of natural and artificial cements
was a low-tech enterprise compared to making pharmaceuticals, industrial gases, dyestuffs, and aluminum, but it proved to be just as
important economically in the nineteenth and twentieth centuries. In
France, lime burning and cement making first emerged as a major industry in response to the great public works projects of the Second
Empire (Markovitch estimates that French cement production tripled
between the early 1850s and early 1870s). The industry continued to
grow in the 1870s and 1880s but at a slower rate as structural iron
increasingly dominated public works construction. However, in the ensuing decades, when structural steel began to replace structural iron,
the high cost of steel prompted French engineering and construction
companies to turn to the new technology of reinforced concrete, and
this became the building material of choice in France for the great
infrastructure projects of the early twentieth century (hydroelectric
dams, roads and bridges, harbor and port expansions) and for the reconstruction following World War I. As a result, cement production
doubled in France between 1900 and 1920 and doubled again between
the early 1920s and early 1930s.[47]

In France, as elsewhere, the cement industry had always been highly
fragmented, and a certain amount of France's growing output of cement in the early twentieth century continued to be divided among
dozens of small-scale companies exploiting local deposits of stone and
clay to serve local builders. At the same time, several French cement
companies managed to break out of the confines of their local markets
and to establish regional dominance. Some of these then expanded into
the French colonies, other European countries, and parts of North and
South America, paralleling the international expansion of French construction companies.[48] Through continued internal growth and mergers
and acquisitions, a few of these firms became leaders in the European
and world cement industries in the twentieth century.

As of 1930, the largest French cement company, in terms of balance-
sheet assets, was Poliet et Chausson. It was founded in 1901 as a joint-
stock company to bring together the many small producers of cement,
gypsum, and plaster in the Paris region, and it grew rapidly in the
1920s by developing new products, by modernizing its production facilities, and by acquiring additional plants through mergers (by 1930
it operated thirty-five in all). Its output of cement rose from 100,000

tons in 1915 to 1.1 million tons by 1928.[49] Poliet et Chausson eventually combined with and adopted the name of another large cement firm, Ciment Français, which had been founded in Boulogne in the 1840s by Charles Demarle and Emile Dupont to produce Portland cement. The building boom of the 1850s and 1860s brought orders from the French railroads, the City of Paris, and various ports, and the output of Demarle and Dupont's firm rose from 50 tons in 1846 to 7,750 tons in 1860 and 91,850 tons in 1880. In 1881, the successors to Demarle and Dupont merged with another Portland cement maker to create the Société des Ciments Français et des Ciments Portland de Boulogne-sur-Mer et de Devres (Ciments Français, for short). This company expanded throughout France in the early twentieth century, but its center of gravity remained in Boulogne and the north of France.[50]

Long before Poliet et Chausson consolidated cement production in the Paris region and Ciments Français emerged in the Pas-de-Calais, France's most important cement maker, the S.A. Chaux et Ciments de la Farge et du Teil, had established itself in the south of France. The origins of the Lafarge Company go back to 1749, when the Pavin family took over the Lafarge estate, situated on the Rhône River near Montélimar, where the renowned *chaux du Teil* used in building bridges across southern France had been produced since the Middle Ages. However, the Pavins showed little interest in lime production until 1830, when the overthrow of Charles X prompted Auguste Pavin de Lafarge, the royal tax receiver for Lyon, and his sons to retire from government service and to devote themselves to managing their estates. The eldest son, Léon, a graduate of the Ecole Polytechnique, took charge of the limekilns of Teil and expanded them to produce much-sought-after hydraulic lime in the 1830s, and this production was continued in the 1840s by another engineer, Félix Gueyrard. When Gueyrard gave up his lease on the Lafarge lime and cement works in 1848, Léon's younger brother Edouard assumed control, beginning a period of direct family administration that continued uninterrupted until 1960.

The Pavin de Lafarge Company was operating twenty limekilns with an annual output of 50,000 tons by 1864 when it signed its "contract of the century" to supply 110,000 tons of hydraulic lime for construction of the jetties of Port Saïd. At about the same time, the company started selling its own version of Portland cement along with color glazes, polychrome mosaic tiles, and other specialized building materials that spread the Lafarge name throughout France and continental Europe. The development of a *ciment blanc* for the facade of the New York Stock Exchange helped to open the American market in the 1870s. In the 1880s, control of the Lafarge Company passed to the next generation, with Joseph Pavin de Lafarge succeeding his father, Edouard, as president (a position he would hold until the 1930s). Under Joseph, the company first grew horizontally by absorbing dozens of small local cement works in different parts of France and North Africa, and then it consolidated and upgraded its production facilities and increased its total output fivefold, to 800,000 tons a year in the early 1900s. This made Lafarge, in the estimation of the company historian, "undoubtedly the world's largest lime-burner" on the eve of World War I.[51]

The expansion begun before the war continued in the 1920s as Lafarge, by then a *société anonyme,* built or acquired new cement works at Sète, Fos-sur-Mer, and Angoulême (the last purported to be the most advanced in France) and set up a company with the Wendels at Thionville in Lorraine to convert iron slag into building materials. As of 1930, Poliet et Chausson may have been larger than Lafarge in terms of balance-sheet assets (308 million francs to 269 million francs), but Lafarge remained France's largest cement manufacturer, with an output of 1.7 million tons, twice the level of 1913.[52] Just as importantly, Lafarge was continuing to expand overseas, both in the French Empire (with the founding of a subsidiary in Morocco to match those in Algeria, Tunisia, and Indochina) and in Europe, Japan, and the United States. This expansion continued into the 1930s, with the company moving into plaster and gypsum production around Paris and acquiring France's fourth largest cement maker, the Compagnie Nouvelle de Ciments Boulonnais. By World War II, the company had already established the leading position in the production and marketing of cement in France, Europe, and overseas that it would maintain and enhance in the postwar era. By the 1990s, following mergers with Canada Cement, General Portland, and the Belgian coal and chemical giant Coppée, Lafarge was second only to Saint-Gobain in France and Europe in building materials and second in the world in cement production.[53]

In spite of the great diversity in their products and operations, the largest French manufacturers of chemicals and materials—and for that matter the large industrial firms presented in the earlier chapters in Part

III—shared many common attributes and similarities in how they rose to prominence in the early twentieth century. Behind most of these firms stood entrepreneurs or entrepreneurial families of unusual talent that, in an era of rapid technological progress, was often coupled with great technical expertise. One need only think of the Pavins de Lafarge, the Le Chateliers, Henri Gall, Georges Claude, Adrien Badin, Lazare Weiller, Louis Renault, André Citroën, and Pierre Azaria. Other common threads in these industrial success stories were the role played by banks—particularly the new industrial investment banks such as Paribas, the Banque de l'Afrique du Sud, and Franco-Suisse—and the way each of these firms used a combination of the four classic growth strategies—horizontal combination, vertical integration, product diversification, and geographical expansion—to achieve its size and market dominance. In addition, thanks to the legal environment in France, the problems of industrial finance, and the need to develop multiple technologies, it was not uncommon for these firms to eschew the American model of a single unified corporate structure and instead to develop as less tightly controlled industrial groups, often with the aid of holding companies (Air Liquide, Pechiney, the CGE, and the big steel companies come to mind). Finally, whatever growth strategies and organizational structures they adopted, all of these firms were acquiring to a greater or lesser degree the organizational capabilities that Alfred Chandler has identified as indispensable for the success of modern industrial enterprises. This was part of a larger story—the rise of managerial capitalism—that is the focus of the final chapter.

CHAPTER SIXTEEN

The New World of
Managerial Capitalism

In the early decades of the twentieth century, a cohort of business enterprises emerged in France that were distinctly larger and more complex than the leading enterprises of the previous century. Many of these arose in the industries of the Second Industrial Revolution—steel, electrical manufacturing and generation, automobiles and aircraft, tire and rubber, petroleum refining, and industrial chemicals and materials. There were also very large firms in older sectors of the economy—in food processing, textiles, ship construction, retailing, banking—and of course in the transportation sector, where the trunk line railroad companies remained in the 1920s, as they had been since the 1850s, France's largest business enterprises.[1]

By the 1920s, all these firms faced problems of administration, co-ordination, and control rarely faced by even the largest firms of the nineteenth century. These problems arose in part because of the companies' sheer size and in part because they were trying to do more things than their predecessors, and things that were inherently more difficult. Some industrial firms were manufacturing products of unprecedented complexity, and some were doing so on a much larger scale. Some firms were diversifying their product lines, some were combining the manufacture of finished goods with the production of raw materials or semi-finished goods, and some were doing all this plus integrating forward into distribution. Many firms, both industrial and commercial, were seeking to operate on a much broader geographical scale than ever before. Companies were employing not just more workers but also many more kinds of workers. Central offices that once had been simple affairs—the boss plus a few clerks and accountants—were becoming collections of departments and services employing hundreds of white-collar workers in multistory headquarters to provide staff support to the firm's line operations.

To make matters worse—or at least more complicated—companies in the early twentieth century were under pressure to do whatever they did more efficiently and cost-effectively. This was partly the result of rising competition in both domestic and foreign markets and partly a matter of ideology. The quest for efficiency was in the air in France as elsewhere by the early 1900s. On the eve of World War I, French executives discovered Frederick W. Taylor and "scientific management"; soon they would discover Henry Ford and Fordism, while one of their own, Henri Fayol of the Commentry-Fourchambault-Decazeville Steel Company, was emerging as an influential proponent of improving business performance through more rational organization. By the 1920s, the first wave of business consultants was arriving from America to tell French businessmen what they were doing wrong and how to correct it.[2]

For all these reasons, managing the large business firm in France was becoming a formidable undertaking in the early twentieth century. Firms were constructing more complex organizational structures (often necessitating the drawing up of formal organization charts) and recruiting professional engineers and other college-educated personnel to staff their emerging managerial hierarchies. In the process, more and more firms—even some that remained under the control of the founder or his family—were moving from what Alfred Chandler calls "family" or "entrepreneurial capitalism" to "managerial capitalism." In doing so, the foremost among them were acquiring the organizational capabilities that would allow them to survive the political and economic turbulence of the 1930s and 1940s and to play leading roles in the European and global economies of the second half of the twentieth century.

To conclude the story of the emergence of modern business enterprise in France, this chapter examines the new world of managerial capitalism that took shape in the executive suites and on the factory floors of France's largest industrial firms from the 1890s to the 1930s. It begins with the railroads which, in France as in the United States, faced the challenges of bigness as early as the 1850s and responded by setting up the most complex managerial systems to be found in French business at the turn of the twentieth century. It then turns to the analogous developments in France's largest manufacturing firms. Throughout, the discussion focuses on three defining themes: the creation of complex organizational structures; the growing role of professional managers in the formulation and implementation of corporate policies and strategies; and the new problems and challenges in the management of industrial enterprises that made the recourse to professional managers and complex organizations necessary.

Managing the Railroads

In France, as in the United States, the rise of managerial capitalism began with the building of the railroads in the second third of the nineteenth century. As we saw earlier, the French railroad system was largely controlled by six regional trunk carriers by the 1880s. One of these, the Western, was subsequently nationalized and became the basis for the state rail system in the early 1900s. However, the other five trunk lines remained in private hands and continued to be by far the largest private business enterprises in France until they too were nationalized in 1937. As of 1929, the largest railroad company, the Paris-Lyon-Méditerranée (P-L-M), possessed balance-sheet assets of 18.6 billion francs (twelve times the assets of the largest French manufacturing firm, Wendel Steel) and employed over 115,000 people (three and a half times the number employed by Wendel).

In France as elsewhere, managing railroads posed unprecedented challenges not just because railroads employed so many people but also because they combined so many disparate activities: the building and maintenance of hundreds of kilometers of track and hundreds of stations spread over a wide area; the operation and maintenance of thousands of pieces of rolling stock (locomotives, tenders, passenger and freight cars); and the coordination of complex flows of people and merchandise, not only within a company's own system but also into and out of that system. To manage and coordinate all these activities, the French railroad companies pioneered the business policies and practices that came to distinguish managerial capitalism from personal capitalism, including the separation of ownership and control, the vesting of operational authority in a hierarchy of professional managers, and the development of highly articulated, departmentalized organizations with clear lines of authority from top to bottom as well as explicit mechanisms, embodied in written rules and regulations, for carrying out and coordinating their myriad activities.

In the French railroad companies, as in all limited-liability joint-stock companies, supreme administrative authority was vested in a board of directors elected by the shareholders (or, more precisely, by those among them who owned enough shares—typically twenty to forty— to qualify to attend the annual shareholders' meeting). The full boards of French railroads met frequently to deal with matters of policy (as often as once a week, in the case of the P-L-M), but the supervisory function of the directors was mainly exercised through standing committees. At the Northern Railroad, for example, the Audit Committee (Commission de Comptabilité) examined all accounts, and the Comité de Direction received weekly reports from department heads and made all major personnel decisions. Yet there was only so much that committees of directors meeting weekly could accomplish. Consequently, the directors had to delegate the responsibility for day-to-day operations to salaried executives. In the centralized structure adopted by French railroads, the key executive was the *directeur-général,* an all-powerful figure answerable only to the board, who appointed and supervised the department heads and stood at the apex of an extensive managerial pyramid.

Bankers and financiers—especially those descended from the founders—continued to dominate the boards of directors of the French railroads.[3] However, the position of *directeur-général* and other high positions in the management hierarchy were filled mostly by professional engineers, especially graduates of the Ecole Polytechnique and the chief *écoles d'application,* the Ecole des Ponts et Chaussées (Roads and Bridges) and the Ecole des Mines. These included Paulin Talabot, the founding *directeur-général* of the P-L-M, and his successors Gustave Noblemaire and Léon Mauris as well as the early general directors of the Paris-Orléans (Charles Didier), Southern (Alexandre Surell), and Western (Adolphe Jullien). Jules Pétiet, who was the top salaried executive of the Northern Railroad in the 1860s and 1870s, was something of an anomaly in that he was a civil engineer trained at the Ecole Centrale des Arts et Manufactures, but he was succeeded by Albert Sartiaux, a product of the Polytechnique and Ponts et Chaussées. Overall, *centraliens* constituted the largest group in railroad management in France in the nineteenth century, but two out of three of the top positions (*directeur-général* and chief engineer) were held by *polytechniciens.* Meanwhile, most of the lower level management positions, such as station manager, shop foreman, and chief mechanic, were held by *gadz'arts,* graduates of the provincial *écoles des arts et métiers.* But they too shared the engineering ethos and mentality that provided much of the cohesiveness in the managerial hierarchies of the French railroads.[4]

Running the railroads, of course, depended on more than the common background and esprit de corps of the engineers who occupied the managerial ranks. It also required the development of clear lines of authority and well-defined operational policies and organizational structures. At the time of their founding, the French railroad companies adopted the centralized functional model of administration that the British railroads had pioneered (and which most American railroads also adopted), and they continued to use this model with modifications throughout their histories. In its earliest versions, this model divided the operations of the railroads among four departments, each headed by a director or chief engineer who answered to the *directeur-général*. There was one staff department, the Service Centrale, that handled such functions as accounting, correspondence, legal affairs, and personnel administration for the entire company; and there were three line departments: Exploitation (Traffic), Traction et Matériel, and Voie et Travaux (Way and Works).[5]

Over time, this rudimentary organization evolved into something considerably more complex, as can be seen in the history of the P-L-M. By the early 1900s, the P-L-M had moved from four basic departments to five; these became six in the 1920s, when Traction et Matériel was replaced by three separate departments (Traction, Matériel, and Approvisionnements). At the same time, the central staff department, Services Généraux, was expanded to provide a larger array of statistics and accounting data to the top managers and to provide additional support services to corporate headquarters. For example, an office of tourism was set up in the 1920s to plan a campaign to promote rail travel by the general public (until then promotion and publicity by French railroads had amounted to little more than placing travel posters—albeit very artistic ones—in train stations).[6]

In the 1920s, as earlier, the most important service at the P-L-M and all other railroads was Exploitation, which was responsible for both getting business and moving passengers and freight. It employed fully one-half of the railroad's total workforce. Within the Service de l'Exploitation, there were both staff offices that provided accounting, legal services, and technical support for the department and the line organization, consisting of twelve geographical divisions headed by inspectors to whom both station and train personnel answered. The Services du Matériel et de la Traction (a single department in 1910, separate departments in 1926) handled the maintenance and repair of locomotives, rolling stock, and all other equipment, as well as the administration of all depots. The Service des Approvisionnements (Purchasing)—a subdivision within Matériel et Traction in 1910, a separate department in 1926—provided fuel and other supplies to the other operating departments. The Service de la Voie maintained the tracks in twelve arrondissements. However, because the latter did not correspond to the geographical sections in Exploitation or Traction, it proved difficult to decentralize management at the P-L-M through a multidivisional organization. Indeed, as in other highly centralized railroads, such as the New York Central in the United States, effective oversight of operations at the P-L-M was possible only at the top of the administrtive chain of command, in the office of the *directeur-général*. Consequently, that executive continued to exercise enormous power throughout the history of the company.[7]

By the beginning of the twentieth century, the French railroad companies had created the most elaborate organizational structures and embodied the most advanced form of managerial capitalism in France, but they were not alone in moving in that direction. Within the transportation sector, the major French steam navigation companies faced many of the same operational challenges faced by the railroads, including getting and scheduling freight and passenger traffic and maintaining equipment and infrastructure, and they responded by setting up hierarchies of managers to oversee and coordinate these activities.[8] The large deposit banks, with their branch networks and multiple services, were also becoming increasingly managerial and hierarchical by the early 1900s. In the commercial sector, the big Paris department stores, long run as family enterprises, began to establish management hierarchies by the 1920s as they integrated backward into production and moved toward multiple store retailing.[9] But the enterprises that faced managerial challenges most similar to those faced by the railroad companies in the early 1900s were the big manufacturing firms that were operating technically sophisticated multiunit production facilities, were sometimes developing multiple product lines, and were integrating backward into the production of raw materials and (in some cases) forward into distribution and sales. How these firms addressed the growing complexity of their operations is our next subject.

Managing the Large Industrial Enterprise

The organizational history of France's large manufacturing firms has been less studied than the organizational history of the French railroads, but a reading of the available company histories and industrial studies suggests that these firms tended to deal with their growing size and complexity as the railroads did, by developing hierarchical organizations based on functional departments supervised by salaried managers drawn mainly from the engineering profession. Some industrial firms also made use of the holding company model, administering their various activities through a network of subsidiaries rather than through a unified corporate structure.

Building Organizations

By the early years of the twentieth century, almost all large industrial enterprises—even those that were still closely held by a single person or a single family—had become *sociétés anonymes* and were thus, at least in theory, being run by a board of directors elected by the shareholders. As in the case of the railroads, these boards met as often as once a week to review the company's performance and to set corporate policy, but they necessarily delegated the supervision of day-to-day operations (and often much of the strategic planning) to either a managing director *(administrateur-délégué),* who had much the same status and authority as the *gerant* in the old *sociétés en commandite,* or to a salaried *directeur-général* who, like his counterpart in the railroad companies, played the role of the modern COO. In some companies, the positions of chairman of the board *(président)* and *directeur-général* were eventually combined in the *président-directeur-général* (PDG), the French version of the modern CEO.

The *administrateur-délégué* (AD) or *directeur-général* (DG) presided over a managerial pyramid in which policies made by the board of directors, or committees of the board, and by the *direction générale* (the DG or AD and his top advisers) were communicated to the directors of the functional or product-based departments, who then oversaw implementation of those policies by the operating units under their supervision. At the same time, of course, the operational data on which all decision-making depended was being communicated up the chain of command from the factory floor and sales offices to the department heads and then in summary form to corporate headquarters. As in the case of large firms elsewhere, the organizational structures of the big

French manufacturing firms differentiated between line and staff functions—that is, between the making and selling of the company's products (the line functions) and the various support (staff) functions such as accounting, correspondence, legal and governmental affairs, and personnel. Consequently, shadowing the chain-of-command within the line organization was a second chain-of-command through which corporate officers communicated policy in support areas to the administrative offices at each level of operations. For example, the chief accountant would make policy for and oversee the activities of the accountants and bookkeepers spread through the organization. Of course, how this centralized functional model of corporate governance was set up in practice evolved over time and varied by industry and company.

At Schneider et Cie, for example, the chairman *(président)* in the 1870s, Henri Schneider, divided the company's operations into two *services*—the Service Productif, which included mines, blast furnaces, steelworks, and other manufacturing facilities; and the Service de Bureau, which comprised accounting, legal affairs, personnel, and other staff functions. By the early 1900s, this simple bipolar organization had been replaced by a more articulated structure based on four departments—Sales, Personnel, Finance and Accounting, and Production (Exploitation). In 1913, Eugène Schneider II further refined this organization by setting up four staff departments and a single line department (Exploitation) made up of four divisions: Mines and Metallurgy, Mechanical and Electrical Construction, Artillery, and Naval Construction (an additional area of production—public works construction—was set up as a semi-independent Service Technique that answered directly to the *directeur-général*). The most important thing about the 1913 reorganization was that Sales no longer constituted a separate department. Instead, sales offices were attached to each of the product divisions under Exploitation, foreshadowing the later transformation of product divisions into autonomous profit centers in American multidivisional companies.[10]

At the Marine-Homécourt Steel Company, another early form of multidivisional organization took shape after 1900 when the longtime *directeur-général*, Adrien de Montgolfier, and his successor, Claudius Magnin, brought the company's widely dispersed production facilities together in four regional groups. Under a group director answering to the DG, each group combined a particular area of production (such as crude steel at Homécourt and artillery components at Saint-Chamond) with its own sales office, laboratories, and support services. In the estimation of a research team from the Crédit Lyonnais that evaluated the company in 1908, "these diverse groups [were] entirely independent from one another both technically and commercially and could be treated as so many distinct businesses"—not a good thing, in their view, because it meant poor coordination and redundant management (too many engineers!).[11]

In the French chemical industry, the product lines were more extensive than in the steel industry, but the organizational structure of the French chemical companies tended to be simpler and generally adhered to the classic centralized functional model. Pechiney divided its operations into three functional services in the pre–World War I era. The Service Commercial handled all sales; the Service d'Exploitation oversaw manufacturing operations; and the Secrétariat-Général in Paris supervised administrative services. After its reorganization in 1905–1906, the Usines du Rhône had two operating divisions: Services Commerciaux, headquartered in Paris, and Production, centered in Lyon. At Saint-Gobain, the board of directors finally stopped trying to micromanage the company's operations at its twice weekly meetings and in 1900 gave full authority over ongoing operations to three DGs—one supervising the production and sale of glass, one supervising chemical production, and one supervising chemical sales. Despite this administrative asymmetry, Saint-Gobain continued to operate as two companies—one for glass and one for chemicals—with each organized around the functional division of production and sales.[12]

The elaboration and refinement of centralized, departmentalized administrative structures continued at France's leading industrial firms through the era of World War I and into the 1920s, but increasingly this represented only half the story of organizational development. In fast-growing industries like steel, chemicals, electricals, and automobiles, companies that were diversifying their product lines and/or integrating backward into raw materials production or forward into distribution and marketing increasingly found that they could do these things most easily by creating or acquiring subsidiaries that were only partially integrated into the mother company's administrative system. The holding company model—already common in the electrical industry by 1900—became increasingly common in all industries by the 1920s. As a result, companies came to acquire dual structures that allowed them to manage some activities through a centralized administrative hierarchy and others through a network of partially or wholly owned subsidiaries. A classic example of this arrangement is found in the Compagnie Générale d'Electricité (CGE). On one level, the CGE in the 1920s was a centrally managed manufacturing enterprise that operated six metals processing plants and four equipment manufacturing plants. On another level, it was, in the words of a Crédit Lyonnais analyst, "un omnium des valeurs industrielles" (a holding company that participated in a broad array of other companies).[13]

Marine-Homécourt, Aciéries de Longwy, and many other top iron and steel companies followed the electrical companies into forming groups in the 1920s, notably by coming together to share control of the former German iron- and steelworks in Lorraine, Luxembourg, and the Sarre and by acquiring subsidiaries inside and outside the steel industry. Schneider acquired extensive holdings in heavy industry in central Europe, mainly through the creation of the Union Européenne Industrielle et Financière. In chemicals and aluminum, Pechiney, following its merger with SEMF in 1921, developed along two tracks: The domestic manufacturing and sales operations of Pechiney and SEMF were integrated into a single organization under the *vice-président-délégué*, Jacques Level, while the *administrateur-délégué*, Louis Marlio, presided over various subsidiaries plus Aluminium Français, which not only handled international sales of Pechiney aluminum but also served as a holding company for yet more subsidiaries. In the automobile industry, the production and sale of automobiles, engines, and machine tools at the Société Anonyme des Usines de Renault (SAUR) were managed through a typical centralized organizational structure (although Louis Renault, emulating his hero Henry Ford, long avoided drawing up an organizational chart for the company). At the same time, SAUR became the center of a large industrial group through its investments in two steel companies (UCPMI and SAFE), various makers of automobile parts and components, a consumer credit company, the leading taxicab company (Automobiles de Place), and an airplane company (Avions Caudron).[14]

In some cases, subsidiaries were eventually folded into the mother company and placed under its central administrative system. This occurred at Air Liquide, as we saw in Chapter 15. In other cases, there was partial administrative integration, as happened at Pechiney in the 1930s when the accounting systems and other headquarters operations of the various subsidiaries were merged with those of the mother company. Even when the connection between the mother companies and the subsidiaries seemed confined to the sharing of common directors, the flow of paper—operational reports coming into headquarters, policy directives going out—provided a means for the mother company to monitor and manage the subsidiaries. The absence of unified organizational charts did not preclude a measure centralized control and direction.

Professionalizing Management

No matter how France's largest industrial firms arranged the boxes on their organizational charts, they still needed to fill the boxes with competent personnel. Even in companies wholly owned by a single *patron* or family, where positions at the top were reserved for members of the family, those people were increasingly expected to have appropriate training and expertise by the 1900s. In the words of Maurice Lévy-Leboyer, "the privilege of birth, when not accompanied by a diploma, no longer allowed one to rise up the corporate ladder."[15] In companies where ownership was fragmented and where bankers and other representatives of outside interests dominated the board of directors, there was an even stronger tendency to bring in professional managers chosen on the basis of merit to run the company. At the same time, all industrial companies more and more were filling positions in middle and lower management with people who had formal education in technical or scientific fields.

The new professional top and middle managers in French industry had varied backgrounds, but few were the product of schools of business or management. Prior to World War II, the closest thing in France to an American-style, university-level business school was the Ecole des Hautes Etudes Commerciales (HEC), founded in 1881 by the Paris Chamber of Commerce. The HEC, however, mainly offered training in foreign languages, international law, and accounting to prepare the sons of the bourgeoisie to represent French companies abroad. A few HEC graduates made their way to the top of the management pyramid in major French industrial firms by the 1920s, including Samuel Guillelmon at Renault. Later, when companies expanded their sales and product promotion organizations in response to the business downturn in the 1930s, they hired more HEC graduates. This happened in the new French oil refining industry: Between 1929 and 1939, Desmarais Frères hired sixteen "HECs," Jupiter (Shell) hired eleven, and the Compagnie Industrielle des Pétroles hired fourteen. Companies in consumer chemicals (L'Oréal, Salins du Midi) also brought in HECs to manage commercial operations.[16] But in heavy industry, and especially in the industries of the Second Industrial Revolution, the new managerial personnel came mainly from schools of engineering. Indeed, when we speak of the professionalization of French industrial management in this era, we mean above all the increasing presence of college-educated engineers in positions of responsibility.

Just like the railroads, the large industrial firms started recruiting state engineers educated at the Ecole Polytechnique, the Ecole des Mines, and the Ecole des Ponts et Chaussées to oversee technical operations as early as the 1820s. Starting in the 1830s, they recruited even more civil engineers trained at the Ecole Centrale des Arts et Manufactures. By the 1860s and 1870s, they were also hiring people trained at the various schools of engineering being set up outside of Paris, including the *écoles des arts et métiers*, the Ecole Centrale Lyonnaise, the Ecole des Hautes Etudes Industrielles (HEI) of the Institut Catholique in Lille, and the provincial *écoles des mines,* especially the one in Saint-Etienne. The growing need for specialists in chemistry and electricity at the end of the nineteenth century led to the founding of the Ecole de Physique et de Chimie Industrielle de Paris (EPCI) in 1881 and the creation of various private and public schools of electrical engineering, including the Ecole Supérieure d'Electricité (Supér-Elec) in Paris and the Institut Electrotechnique de Grenoble. Graduates of all these schools were beginning to show up in the ranks of middle and top management at France's leading high-tech companies by the early 1900s. Pride of place, however, continued to go to the graduates of the Ecole Polytechnique.

In the nineteenth century, *polytechniciens* had typically started out in state service and then moved at mid-career into high-level positions in private industry as technical directors or even as full-fledged *directeurs-généraux* (often after an intermediate stop at a railroad). By the 1900s, however, it was not uncommon for *polytechniciens* and even products of the elite graduate schools (Mines, Ponts et Chaussées) to begin their careers in private industry, as graduates of the Ecole Centrale and the provincial engineering schools did. As a result, the number of *polytechniciens* employed in private industry rose from 1,700 in 1905 to 3,600 (one-half of the available pool) by the 1920s. Of course, at whatever stage of their careers they entered the private sector, *polytechniciens* and graduates of the *grandes écoles* could expect to start higher on the corporate ladder and to rise higher than the graduates of the less prestigious engineering schools. Indeed, as more *polytechniciens* joined private industrial firms, they tended to crowd other engineers out of the top positions (of all engineers running companies in 1939, 62 percent were *polytechniciens,* up from only 32 percent in 1912). However, the incidence of engineers in industrial management and the incidence of graduates of particular schools in the top management of the leading firms varied from industry to industry and firm to firm.[17]

In the early twentieth century, the French industry (other than the railroads) that was most dominated by engineers from the elite schools was the electrical industry. Engineers trained at the Ecole Polytechnique and the Ponts et Chaussées had been prominent in the founding of the industry, and as of the 1920s they held most of the top management positions at the leading firms. These included Albert Petsche and Ernest Mercier at SLEE and UDE, Gabriel Cordier at EELM, Louis Loucheur and Alexandre Giros at Loire et Centre and EENF, and Auguste Detoeuf at Alsthom. Pierre Azaria, *administrateur-délégué* of the CGE, was a rare *centralien* among the top executives of the industry. But school affiliation was less important than ability and experience in managing electrical companies, and all these top executives drew widely from the engineering profession in putting together their management teams. Pierre Azaria was especially successful in assembling a diverse team of engineer-managers around the turn of the century who stayed with the CGE over the next thirty or forty years and eventually succeeded to top management positions.[18]

In the iron and steel industries, professional engineers, especially those trained at the Ecole des Mines and Ecole des Ponts et Chaussées, had played prominent roles in founding and managing the leading joint-stock companies in the early nineteenth century (for example, Etienne Cabrol at Decazeville and Léon Talabot at Denain-Anzin), but as late as the 1890s it was still possible to rise to top management positions in these companies without engineering training (witness the rise of two accountants, Alexandre Dreux and Ernest Nahan, to the top jobs at the Aciéries de Longwy and Aciéries de Micheville). After 1900, however, the management of the big steel companies was increasingly dominated by professional engineers, especially those who had served in the Corps des Mines, where they had worked with forgemasters in defining mining concessions or in enforcing government regulations. Among the members of the Corps des Mines who ended up running steel companies were Paul Nicou, who succeeded Nahan as DG at Micheville, Léon Levy at Châtillon-Commentry, Jean Bichelonne at Senelle-Maubeuge, François Villain and Ernest Cuvelette at Nord-Est, and Théodore Laurent at Marine-Homécourt.[19]

Although study at the Ecole Polytechnique and the Ecole des Mines, followed by service in the Corps des Mines or at the railroads, constituted the "royal road" to the position of managing director or president of a leading steel company, it was not the only path to the top. A number of top iron and steel officials came out of the provincial engineering schools, including Xavier Rogé and Camille Cavallier of Pont à Mousson, who were graduates of the Châlons *arts et métiers,* and Claudius Magnin of Marine-Homécourt, a product of the Ecole des Mines de Saint-Etienne.[20] Reliance on the provincial engineering schools was a matter of policy at Schneider et Cie. The Schneiders occasionally recruited graduates of the Paris *grandes écoles* for special purposes, but they developed most of their engineering talent in-house. Sons of Le Creusot employees who showed promise in the company primary school would be funneled into special preparatory classes and then sent to the Ecole des Arts et Métiers d'Aix, which by the end of the nineteenth century served essentially as the Schneiders' private engineering school. Upon graduation, these new engineers were hired by Le Creusot and usually stayed there for their whole career.[21]

Saint-Gobain recruited production managers for both the glass and chemicals divisions from the Ecole Polytechnique and the Ecole Centrale as early as the 1830s, and this practice continued over the ensuing century. In the 1920s, the glass division was directed by a *centralien,* Lucien Delloye, who recruited other *centraliens* to staff the central office and to serve as inspectors and troubleshooters in the various glassworks (which were usually run by non-engineers). The chemicals division was directed by Edmond Delage, a *polytechnicien* and former member of the Corps des Mines who had come to Saint-Gobain by way of the Western Railroad; like Delloye, he proceeded to staff his management hierarchy with other engineers, mostly *centraliens.*[22] At Pechiney, the movement of professional engineers into management began in 1900 with three critical hires: Adrien Badin, a graduate of the Ecole des Mines de Saint-Etienne, as chief engineer; Emile Boyoud, a *centralien* and a former student of Henri Moissan, as *chef de fabrication*; and the *polytechnicien* Paul Vittenet as Pechiney's assistant and later director of the company's central offices in Paris. Twenty years later, following the death of Badin and the merger with SEMF, three other engineer-executives of national stature—Gabriel Cordier, Jacques Level, and Louis Marlio—were running Pechiney along with Boyoud. And in 1927, when the company adopted a more coherent departmentalized structure, a new cohort of engineer-managers was hired to fill key positions.[23]

In comparison to the steel, chemicals, and electrical industries, the French automobile industry remained less the domain of the professional engineer and more a refuge for autodidacts, reflecting the background of the leading automakers. Louis Renault had been denied admission to the Ecole Centrale, and Marius Berliet was a self-taught mechanic of modest social origins. Both put a premium on on-the-job training and generally avoided college-educated engineers. The Peugeots did hire college-trained engineers, but only those from provincial schools who were willing to work their way up from the factory floor (such as Ernest Mattern, a graduate of the Châlons *arts et métiers* who started out at Peugeot in 1906 as a foremen at the Lille plant). Not surprisingly, the carmakers who did recruit from the Ecole Polytechnique and other *grandes écoles*—Gabriel Delaunay-Belleville, Gabriel Voisin, and André Citroën—were themselves *polytechniciens*. Citroën was unique among French automakers in his willingness to hire large numbers of *polytechniciens* and *centraliens* directly out of school even when he did not have a defined slot for them. By 1934, Citroën employed twenty-five *centraliens* and twenty-one *polytechniciens*, including a number of his classmates from the Polytechnique class of 1898, whom he put in key management positions. He also brought in *gadz'arts* engineers, including Louis Guillot, an expert on assembly lines, who became the company's production director.[24]

In sum, by the 1920s the administration of France's leading industrial firms was increasingly in the hands of college-educated engineers who had made it into the top positions in their companies on the basis of merit—or on the basis of those proxies for merit, diplomas and "credentials"—rather than on the basis of personal or family connections. However, there was still little sense among them that they represented the advance guard of a new *managerial* profession. Most continued to view themselves as engineers, not as managers, and most continued to draw their sense of identity from membership in professional organizations such as the Société des Ingénieurs Civils and even more from school affiliations (the alumni associations of the Ecole Polytechnique and Ecole Centrale were especially assiduous in cultivating a sense of identity and esprit de corps among their *anciens élèves*). Only in the 1950s and 1960s did the French really start viewing "le management" as a true profession. Even so, it is easy to see now, with the aid of hindsight, that the profession of industrial management was already taking shape in France in the early decades of the twentieth century as the engineer-managers at the leading industrial firms worked out solutions to the problems presented by the size and complexity of their companies' operations.

Coping with Complexity

In many ways, managing large industrial firms in the early twentieth century was not much different from managing them in the nineteenth. Executives still had to mobilize large amounts of money to support current operations and finance new plant and equipment. They still had to master all the ins and outs of the production process and deal with the various aspects of labor management. Like their predecessors, they still had to manage the firm's relations with suppliers and customers, government officials, and other industrialists. Yet, as firms grew in size and as their operations became more complex, all these tasks became more demanding and more time-consuming, necessitating the hiring of additional personnel and even the creation of new offices or departments at headquarters. Accounting operations in particular expanded greatly in the early 1900s, not only because of the increased size of firms but also because advances in accounting practices, especially in cost accounting, required the collection and analysis of much more data than ever before.[25] But what presented the biggest administrative challenges and required the biggest commitment of administrative assets was the setting up of much more complex production systems and expanding from manufacturing into distribution and marketing. It was mainly to cope with the complexity of these new marketing and manufacturing operations that France's largest firms expanded their management hierarchies and in general became more managerial between 1900 and 1930.

The makers of producer goods such as steel, aluminum, and bulk chemicals had long managed to avoid setting up extensive sales organizations, in part because they sold to a relatively small number of industrial customers and in part because they had been able to form common selling agencies *(comptoirs)* that also served as cartels guaranteeing a fixed share of the market to each member. Cartelization continued to be a major goal for these companies during and after World War I, but they increasingly found that the introduction of new products, the changing state of supply and demand for existing products, and the inability of marketing agreements to cover all situations and to eliminate all competition at home and abroad forced them to develop more direct means of stimulating demand and acquiring customers. For example, as the growth of municipal water systems slowed in the 1920s, France's leading maker of iron pipe, Pont à Mousson, began to lobby for greater expenditures on sewers and water systems. As the company's managing director Marcel Paul explained, "it is not so much a question of declaring our cast-iron pipe the best in the world; it is a question of creating a movement in favor of hygiene and water, a question of creating needs and customers."[26] At the same time, Pont à Mousson started expanding its Service Commercial, and by the mid-thirties it had fifteen full-fledged sales offices in France and the French colonies and supported sales representatives in eighty-nine foreign countries.[27] Meanwhile, the big steel companies, plagued by excess capacity after the takeover of the German steelworks in Lorraine in 1918, discovered that the old *comptoirs* no longer sufficed to assure the sale of their output. Marine-Homécourt and its partners in the MarMichPont group thus set up a marketing subsidiary, DAVUM, and the Aciéries de Longwy followed suit with the creation of Longovica. Pechiney continued to sell its aluminum through Aluminium Français (virtually a wholly-owned subsidiary following the PCAC-SEMF merger), but to promote the sale of its chemical products in an increasingly competitive market, it relied on its own commercial service, which came to include in-house market research and advertising offices as well as a global network of sales offices.[28]

Forward integration into distribution and sales was even more important for companies in the automotive industry, which, uniquely among the new industries of the early twentieth century, depended mainly on the general retail market. Before World War I, Renault, Peugeot, and the other French automakers had sold most of their cars and trucks through non-exclusive franchised dealers. As they shifted toward true mass production after 1918, however, they saw the need to expand and to take firmer control of their channels of distribution. Renault went from a network of 94 dealers in 1914 to 1,165 dealers by 1929. Starting from scratch in 1919, Citroën put together a network of 400 dealers by 1926 (unlike dealers for other companies, these were exclusive dealers who agreed to sell only Citroëns). Renault, Peugeot, and Citroën also created subsidiaries to offer consumer credit so that people could buy cars on the installment plan. By the early 1930s, Renault and Citroën were substituting company-owned and operated retail outlets for franchised dealerships (Renault operated thirty-one of these by 1929; Citroën had twenty by 1934).[29] Building up extensive commercial divisions also involved, in the case of Citroën, hiring in-house publicity and advertising people. Indeed, the only company in the French automotive industry that put more resources into publicity and promotion was the tire manufacturer Michelin.[30]

Although sales and marketing were becoming more important for France's largest industrial firms by the early 1930s, the management of sales still took a backseat to production management, especially at firms that aspired to mass produce complex machinery. The latter included the makers of aircraft, automobiles, and electrical equipment. The aircraft and aviation engine manufacturers like Bréguet, Blériot, and Gnôme et Rhône had to deal with the imperatives of mass production mainly in time of war or impending war, in 1914–1918 and again after 1938. The electrical manufacturers faced a more sustained challenge as France undertook to build a national system of electric power generation and distribution, but only part of their production involved new production methods. Thomson-Houston, CGE, and Alsthom mass-produced some matériel (cable, insulators, light bulbs), but they also built dynamos, steam turbines, transformers, and other large components to order using traditional craft methods. So in the end it was the automakers that faced the biggest challenges in production management. To build the thousands of cars and trucks needed to satisfy the burgeoning demand for motor vehicles in France after World War I, these companies had to figure out how to manufacture some 12,000 to 15,000 parts and components in large numbers and to exacting standards (to allow for interchangeability). They also had to learn how to assemble these parts quickly and efficiently into a finished product that could be sold at a low enough price to attract a middle-class clientele. To accomplish this, the major French auto companies were putting more thought and effort into production management than were companies in other French industries in the interwar years. Therefore, the auto industry provides the best place to observe how French industrial firms were coping with complexity in production in the first three decades of the twentieth century.

Before World War I, the French automobile industry was a craft industry in which hundreds of skilled workers used general-purpose machine tools to fabricate the various parts that were then fitted together by hand by teams of assemblers to produce automobiles one at a time. In that context, the key to success was finding ways to reduce the cost of labor, and it was with that in mind that Louis Renault and other early automakers turned to the emerging discipline of scientific management associated with the American engineer Frederick W. Taylor. Taylor contended that existing systems of production based on skilled labor could be made more productive and less costly through careful planning of the overall production process, through intensive analysis of each stage in production—especially using time-and-motion studies to determine the one best way to do each job—and through adoption of incentive pay systems using differential piece rates based on a standard hourly or daily output for each worker in the system. In other words, for Taylor lowering production costs was a matter of improving the flow of materials through the plant, improving the way each job was done, and above all forcing or enticing each worker to put forth greater effort.[31]

Taylorism was first brought to the attention of French industrialists in 1904, when the influential industrial scientist Henry Le Chatelier published accounts of Taylor's early experiments in the *Revue Métallurgique*. Le Chatelier later arranged for the publication of a French translation of Taylor's *Principles of Scientific Management* in 1912. By then, Ernest Mattern was already using some Taylorist techniques at Peugeot's Lille plant, although Mattern had probably not yet read Taylor.[32] But Taylorism really came to the fore in France in December 1912 when Louis Renault abruptly sent time-and-motion analysts into his Billancourt plant, provoking a walk-out and launching a long, sustained controversy over OST (*organisation scientifique du travail*) that pitted organized labor against big business.[33] Despite this inauspicious beginning, elements of scientific management—especially centralized production planning and scheduling, job design based on time and motion studies, and incentive pay programs—gradually spread through the French automobile industry and eventually into much of the rest of French industry, including coal, steel, machinery manufacturing, railroad maintenance, ship construction, and even textiles.[34] But of even greater importance was the shift from Taylorism to Fordism—from efforts to make the craft system more productive to the adoption of a new system of mass production based on the moving assembly line, the substitution of semi-skilled for skilled workers, and the replacement of general-purpose with dedicated machinery. In France as elsewhere, this transition was first made in the auto industry.

By 1913, Louis Renault, André Citroën, and Ernest Mattern were making plans to follow Ford into the mass production of automobiles. However, as we saw in Chapter 14, the outbreak of World War I determined that they first applied Fordist techniques to the production of munitions and military hardware. After the war, it was Citroën who made the first and largest commitment to the mass production of automobiles by setting up a moving assembly line at his Quai Javel plant in 1921. In 1924, that plant was expanded and reorganized around two assembly lines, one for chassis on the ground floor and one for auto bodies on the second floor, with the two converging at the end. In 1933 Citroën rebuilt the Javel plant yet again to bring all assembly operations for two car models together under one roof. By then, Renault had also moved into assembly-line auto production at its new Ile de Seguin plant, and Peugeot had followed suit at its expanded Sochaux plant. Many of the second-tier French automakers also set up assembly lines, including the machine-gun manufacturer Hotchkiss, and Berliet continued to use assembly-line methods to produce trucks at his Venissieux plant, still the largest automotive factory in France.[35]

French automobile assembly lines never attained the speed and efficiency found in American ones, partly because the French lagged in the development of completely interchangeable parts and partly because the refusal by the big steel companies to adopt quality standards created chronic issues of quality control for the automakers (problems that were only partially solved when the auto companies integrated backward into steel production). Even so, the adoption of the moving assembly line and related mass-production technologies brought about a huge increase in French automobile output. Just as important, as Aimée Moutet has emphasized, it imparted a whole new logic to auto production that pushed firms toward continuous manufacturing at all levels (versus stop-and-go batch production), forced them to coordinate separate production processes more closely, and necessitated the creation of an array of new support services and supervisory positions. At Citroën, fully one-third of the 30,000-person workforce was employed in non-production positions by 1929. Louis Renault, ever vigilant to minimize the number of "non-productive" employees in his organization, managed to keep the percent of support personnel lower than Citroën, yet by 1932 even Renault employed 2,500 white-collar workers, constituting about 8 percent of his total workforce.[36]

One of the largest staff departments at Renault, Citroën, and the other car companies was the *bureau d'études*, where scores of engineers and draftsmen designed the thousands of individual parts that went into each car model, built and tested prototypes, and resolved basic issues about materials and costs. At Citroën, the engineering department employed 440 by the early 1930s, while Renault's Service d'Etudes employed 348, including no less than fourteen grades of designers and draftsmen.[37] Even larger at each company was the *service de fabrication,* which employed hundreds of production engineers, time-and-motion analysts, work preparers, and inspectors to implement the production plans that came out of the *bureau d'études.* At Renault, the Service de Fabrication employed 530, making it second in size only to the Service Commercial among the service departments.

Closely tied to the design and implementation of production plans was the management of human resources. This fell under the purview of personnel departments, which were growing in size, complexity, and importance at the French auto companies in the 1920s. For example, when Ernest Mattern moved from Peugeot to Citroën in 1922, he created a "manpower service" *(service de main d'oeuvre)* that not only centralized hiring for all Citroën plants but also determined the tasks assigned to each job, what wage would be paid, and even which jobs were necessary and which could be eliminated. While Renault used limited psychological and physiological testing in hiring workers (mainly to keep clumsy people out of high-risk jobs), Mattern's manpower service ran all applicants through a gauntlet of tests that included tests of vision, hand-eye coordination, and muscular strength. Once hired, Citroën workers were regularly evaluated on their job performance quantitatively. Those who fell below 70 on a 100-point scale were fired; those who rated 90 or above got a raise or promotion.[38]

Notwithstanding all the attention paid to personnel matters, the chief source of productivity gains in the era of Ford-style mass production was the substitution of machinery for labor, which entailed a massive increase in fixed assets and fixed costs. As always, substituting fixed capital for labor was a gamble that paid off only if factories operated at or near full capacity. For the French auto companies, this strategy worked well in the late 1920s, but it became problematical with the economic downturn of the early 1930s. With profits depending more and more on the ability of companies to stimulate sales and to control costs, the thirties found all French automakers adopting budgeting systems tied to sales forecasts. For example, on the advice of the American management consultant Wallace Clark, the leading purveyor of budget control systems in France, Renault set up a Service d'Estimation in 1931 that forecast sales for the following year, drew up a production plan and company budget on the basis of that forecast, and then tracked adherence to the budget by each department. Budgeting and cost control thereafter became routine activities at Renault and other auto manufacturers, as did efforts to eliminate waste and to improve quality. At Michelin, a new Service des Economies, which employed law students to identify waste and inefficiency in each department, soon became the arbiter of all new expenditures. This system was transferred to Citroën when the Michelins took control in 1935.[39]

The move toward Ford-style mass production and toward more extensive and complex systems of production management was not limited to the auto industry in interwar France. By the 1930s, assembly lines and all they entailed were beginning to appear in electrical manufacturing, in metallurgical manufacturing, in food processing and canning, in the manufacture of shoes and watches, and even in the repair and maintenance of railroad cars. Similarly, the various staff functions needed to support mass production—including planning and scheduling, personnel management, analytical cost accounting, and sales forecasting—were appearing in these industries, although not to the degree found in the auto industry. Although mass production was as yet neither as widespread nor as well managed in France as it was in the United States, the efforts to move toward mass production had served to introduce the principles and institutions of managerial capitalism at a number of large French manufacturing firms in the 1920s and 1930s. In the years ahead, these firms would increasingly set the tone and agenda for business in France and would serve as the vehicles for France's drive toward economic modernity during the "thirty glorious years" following World War II.

France on the Verge

In spite of the rapid growth of certain of its industries between 1900 and 1930—notably steel, aluminum, electricals, automobiles, organic chemicals, and industrial gases—France's gross domestic product was still only three-fourths of Germany's or Great Britain's and only one-seventh of the United States' on the eve of the Great Depression. Accordingly, analysts and observers inside and outside French business, preoccupied with national strength in the wake of World War I, were less interested in celebrating France's recent achievements than in calling attention to its continuing deficiencies. Indeed, during the interwar years, as Richard Kuisel has shown, the French engaged in the most searching critique of their country's economic performance and prospects since the time of the Saint-Simonians in the early nineteenth century.[1]

We now know, of course, that France had come farther and was in comparatively better shape by 1930 than most people realized at the time. Even as the Depression took hold and deepened in the 1930s, France stood on the threshold of extraordinary economic advances. Following the hiatus of World War II and its immediate aftermath, France experienced its greatest sustained economic expansion in history during the 1950s and 1960s. In spite of various setbacks that greatly reduced the rate of growth in the 1970s and 1980s, the forward momentum imparted to its economy in the "thirty glorious years" allowed France to surpass Great Britain, close the gap with Germany and the United States, and secure its position as the second largest economy in Europe and fourth largest in the world by the close of the twentieth century.[2] Just as striking was the newfound prominence of France's leading industrial and commercial firms. As of 1990, France's twenty-seven largest industrial firms ranked among the one hundred largest firms in Europe, and twelve French firms ranked among the hundred largest firms in the world (see Table 8).[3]

The path that France followed to economic success and prominence

Table 8. The thirty largest French industrial firms in 1990

France	Rank in Europe	World	Company	Industry	Turnover (in millions of FF)
1	12	28	Elf-Aquitaine	petrochemicals	175,479
2	14	31	Renault	automobiles	163,620
3	15	32	PSA (Peugeot)	automobiles	159,976
4	20	40	Alcatel-Alsthom	electricals	144,053
5	22	45	Total	petroleum	128,445
6	25	54	Général des Eaux	diversified	116,822
7	29	70	Usinor-Sacilor	steel	97,308
8	36	81	Rhône-Poulenc	chemicals	78,810
9	39	84	Pechiney	aluminum	76,869
10	42	89	Thomson	electricals	75,228
11	43	94	Lyonnaise des Eaux	construction	70,679
12	45	99	Saint-Gobain	materials	69,076
13	53		Michelin	tires	62,736
14			Bouygues	construction	56,727
15	56		BSN Danone	food	52,897
16	59		Schneider	electricals	49,884
17			GEC-Alsthom	electricals	48,487
18			Beghin-Say	food	37,671
19	81		Aérospatiale	aerospace	35,237
20	82		Bull	electronics	34,580
21	90		Lafarge-Coppée	cement	32,543
22	93		Arnault	diversified	30,396
23	95		L'Oréal	cosmetics	30,359
24	96		Hachette	publishing	30,047
25	97		CEA Industrie	nuclear	29,712
26			Financière Agache	textiles	29,076
27	98		Air Liquide	industrial gas	28,914
28			SAE	construction	26,906
29			CarnaudMetalBox	packaging	24,415
30			Matra	electronics	24,347

Source: Expansion (November–December 1991).

in the late twentieth century was a circuitous one. The French economy of 1990 was not simply an enlarged version of its 1930 economy, nor were France's largest companies in 1990 simply larger versions of what they had been sixty years before. France's leading enterprises and the French economy as a whole underwent enormous changes in the intervening years. Six areas of change were particularly important:

1. *Technological innovation: The "Third Industrial Revolution."* Much of the economic growth experienced by France and the other developed countries after World War II sprang from science-based industrial research and development—often financed by national governments rather than by private firms—which gave rise to new lines of products and whole new industries. Economic historians are increasingly calling this the Third Industrial Revolution, to distinguish it from the Second Industrial Revolution of 1880–1930 and the First Industrial Revolution of 1760–1870. Although the French did not distinguish themselves in the highest profile new industry—computers and electronics—they did fully participate in other new fields associated with the Third Industrial Revolution, including telecommunications, nuclear energy, aerospace, and pharmaceuticals and biotechnology.

2. *Nationalization.* Three times in the twentieth century the French government took control of all or part of major industries, starting with the takeover of the Banque de France, the armaments industry, and the railroads by the Popular Front government of 1936–1937. The second wave came at the end of World War II, when the new Fourth Republic assumed control of coal, gas, and electrical generation and distribution; the Paris Metro, Air France, and the largest steamship companies; the four largest commercial banks (including the Crédit Lyonnais and the Société Générale) and the four largest insurance companies; and the aircraft maker Gnôme et Rhône (renamed SNECMA) and the Renault Automobile Company. The third wave came under the presidency of François Mitterrand in 1981–1982, when the rest of the banking sector was nationalized along with the iron and steel industries and the major electrical and chemical manufacturers, including CGE, Thomson, Pechiney, Saint-Gobain, and Rhône-Poulenc. Although many of these companies were subsequently privatized, starting with Saint-Gobain in 1986, there were still more state-owned companies in France at the end of the twentieth century than in any other historically non-communist country.

3. *Industrial restructuring and concentration.* As a by-product of the nationalizations, and more broadly as a response to the growing inter-

national competition that accompanied the formation of the European Economic Community, French commerce and industry underwent a dramatic restructuring after 1960. In declining industries and those under especially strong competitive pressures—such as textiles and metallurgy—this restructuring took the form of horizontal integration to reduce excess capacity and to eliminate obsolete facilities. In more technologically progressive industries, it involved concentrating resources and expertise that had been spread over several firms in the hands of "national champions" capable of competing on equal terms with the leading firms from other countries (this form of restructuring was especially evident in electrical equipment, telecommunications, aluminum and nonferrous metals, chemicals, automobiles, and aerospace).

4. *Multinationalization.* As the world economy became increasingly open and interconnected in the postwar period, there was a great increase in foreign direct investment and in the formation of foreign subsidiaries by French manufacturing firms. In 1995, at least seventeen of France's thirty largest industrial enterprises (listed below) were drawing half or more of their annual revenues from operations outside France.[4]

Percentage of Annual Revenues Derived Outside of France

Michelin	82	Alcatel	71	Lafarge	61
Beghin-Say	79	Usinor	68	Peugeot	58
Rhône-Poulenc	79	Aérospatiale	68	Schneider	58
Air Liquide	77	L'Oréal	66	Renault	53
CarnaudMetalBox	75	Pechiney	65	BSN Danone	50
Thomson	72	Saint-Gobain	62		

5. *Ownership and control: Groups, holdings, and hierarchies.* Much has been made of the persistence of personal or family control of France's largest commercial and industrial enterprises in the late twentieth century. The British scholars Richard Whittington and Michael Mayer have estimated that in 1993 twenty-nine of France's one hundred largest privately owned firms were under personal control (versus only sixteen of the top hundred German firms and three of the top hundred British firms). However, their definition of personal control includes instances in which executives were able to dominate by force of personality joint-stock companies with highly dispersed ownership (for example, Jean Seydoux at Chargeurs).[5] In truth, examples of con-

tinued control of large firms by families or individuals based on majority ownership became increasingly rare in France after 1960 and tended to be found in firms of recent origin where the founder was still the owner (Arnault et Associates, Sodexho). Among older companies, Michelin remained the chief example of continued personal or family control. The dominant trend after 1945, reinforced by the extensive nationalizations, was toward greater control by salaried professional managers. There was also a trend toward tying enterprises together through holding companies or through cross-investment (firms taking ownership positions in each other). Especially important was the emergence of industrial groups tied to financial institutions. At the center of one such group was Indosuez, the finance company born from Egypt's nationalization of the Suez Canal that later merged with the Banque de l'Indochine. At the center of another group was Paribas (later BNP Paribas).[6]

6. *Strategies and structures: Toward the American model?* Alfred Chandler and his followers have long been criticized for putting forth the American version of business development as a universal model to which all countries should aspire and for judging the success of other countries in terms of their movement toward American practices. The Chandlerian model of business development is usually seen as involving not only the quest for bigness and a shift from personal to professional management but also growth through diversification (both in products and markets) and adoption of the multidivisional form of organization (supposedly the optimal way to coordinate diversified operations). In the 1970s, Chandlerian analysts cited continuing low levels of diversification and divisionalization in French companies after World War II as evidence of the enduring backwardness of French business. This in turn prompted some French scholars to protest that France was being judged by inappropriate, Americentric criteria. The recent work of Whittington and Mayer, however, undercuts the early Chandlerian criticism of France while at the same time confirming the broad applicability of the Chandlerian model of development. According to Whittington and Mayer, there was a strong trend in France after 1970 toward diversification and multidivisional organization. By their calculations, the number of France's one hundred largest industrial firms adopting strategies of related or unrelated (conglomerate) diversification rose from only thirty-six in 1950 to sixty-five by 1993, and the number of top one hundred firms with multidivisional structures rose from zero in 1950 to forty-two in 1970 and seventy-five in 1993.[7] It

appears that the movement toward American business practices—which, we have seen, actually began in certain French companies in the early twentieth century—had become one of the dominant themes in French business by the closing years of the twentieth century.

From the perspective of the present study, what is especially noteworthy about the transformation of French business after 1945 is the degree to which it represented a continuation of processes and trends that had begun earlier. The nationalization of industries, for example, was hardly a new phenomenon in France in 1936. As we saw in Chapter 2, state ownership of the railroads had been contemplated from the earliest days of railroad construction; the government takeover of the rail companies began in the 1870s and proceeded by stages until the final step, the formation of the SNCF, in 1937. Nationalization of the tobacco industry and telephone service in the late nineteenth century also provided precedents for later nationalizations. By the same token, many French companies set up multinational operations well before 1945. Saint-Gobain had subsidiaries elsewhere in Europe as early as the mid-1800s, and Air Liquide had operations on four continents within a decade of its founding. The leading woolen manufacturers of Roubaix-Tourcoing had plants in the United States and Russia before 1900. The French electrical manufacturers set up subsidiaries in Spain and Italy in the early 1900s, while Schneider moved aggressively into eastern Europe in the interwar years. French oil companies participated in the exploitation of oil fields in Russia, Rumania, and the Austrian Empire long before CFP took control of France's stake in Iraq in the 1920s. As we saw in Chapter 16, the institutions and practices of managerial capitalism that would become dominant in French big business in the 1980s and 1990s—including the formation of holding companies and industrial groups, corporate governance by professional managers, and even multidivisional organization—had their beginnings in the early 1900s and even before. But perhaps the most important example of continuity in French business development from the pre-1930 era to the post-1945 era is found in the roster of France's leading firms.

Most of France's largest industrial and commercial enterprises at the end of the twentieth century were either already extant in 1930 (and already among France's largest companies) or were the products of mergers among companies extant in 1930 (sometimes accompanied by a change of name). In other words, the renovation and restructuring of French industry in the post–World War II era depended less on creating entirely new enterprises than on combining and reorganizing established ones. The chief exceptions to this were found in retailing and consumer products. Consumerism on the scale known in Britain and America by the turn of the twentieth century finally came to France in the 1960s, and this was reflected in the advent of new kinds of mass retailing—especially the *hypermarchés* of Casino, E. Leclerc, and Carrefour—and new consumer products companies such as L'Oréal, which was founded by a pharmacist to market suntan lotion in 1936 (the year French workers won paid vacations and started flocking to the beaches) but only emerged as a global leader in cosmetics and pharmaceuticals in the 1960s and 1970s. Yet even in France's new consumer economy there was room for updated versions of established companies. One of these was Pinault-Printemps-Redoute, a major retailing firm created by the merger of the Printemps-Prisunic department store chain and La Redoute, a leading mail-order house founded by a family of Roubaix wool spinners in the 1920s.

The continued importance of pre-1930 companies in the new French economy of the late twentieth century was especially evident in consumer durables and heavy industry. The automotive industry continued to be dominated by the firms that had risen to preeminence in the early 1900s, except that the Big Three of 1930—Citroën, Renault, and Peugeot—had been reduced to the Big Two after Peugeot absorbed Citroën in the 1970s. In tire and rubber, Michelin was even more dominant in France in the 1990s, than it had been in 1930; it had also become a leading player in the global tire market, along with Goodyear of the United States and Bridgestone of Japan. In petroleum, the national champion first set up in 1926—Compagnie Française des Petroles (Total)—remained one of France's two major oil companies in 1990 along with Elf-Aquitaine, a state enterprise created after 1940 to exploit newly discovered natural gas fields in southwestern France and new oil fields in Algeria and other French colonies (by 2000 the oil refining and marketing divisions of Total and Elf-Aquitaine had merged with the Belgian petroleum company Petrofina to form Total-Fina-Elf).

The French steel industry, under severe competitive pressure, underwent a complex series of mergers, downsizings, and restructurings from the late 1940s to the 1970s that gathered the old-line steel companies into two large combines, Usinor and Sacilor (the former included Denain-Anzin, Nord-Est, Longwy, and Vallourec; the latter included Wendel, Marine-Homécourt, and other Lorraine steelmakers). The Mitterrand government nationalized and merged these two firms in the

1980s in order to create a single national steel company. Another declining industry, textiles, also experienced drastic downsizing and concentration, but with less government involvement. What was left of the industry by the 1980s ended up in holding companies built around two of the leading French textile firms dating from the nineteenth century, Dollfus-Mieg and Agache.

The more technologically advanced sectors of French industry also experienced massive restructuring after World War II that nonetheless preserved the role of many established companies. In the electrical industry, the power and light companies created before 1940 were nationalized in 1946 and disappeared into a single state enterprise, Electricité de France. At the same time, the state took over the coal mining and gas companies and combined them in, respectively, Charbonnages de France and Gaz de France. A convoluted series of corporate restructurings put the assets of the electrical manufacturing and telecommunications industries into three combines built around pre-1930 firms: Alcatel-Alsthom, Thomson, and Schneider Electric. Alcatel-Alsthom, an expanded version of CGE that included Alsthom and the leading French makers of telephone and radio equipment (CIT and CSF), specialized in electrical and telecommunications equipment; Thomson, a much reworked version of Thomson-Houston, focused on consumer electricals; and Schneider Electric, the old Schneider-Le Creusot stripped of its steelworks and machinery plants, concentrated on control systems. Meanwhile, the restructuring of France's production of chemicals, nonferrous metals, and building materials also left those industries in the hands of three long-lived companies: Saint-Gobain, Pechiney, and Rhône-Poulenc. Saint-Gobain specialized in glass, fiberglass, and cardboard-based packaging; Pechiney produced aluminum and aluminum cans; and Rhône-Poulenc became the leading French producer of chemicals, artificial fibers, and pharmaceuticals. Cement continued to be dominated by the two companies that already dominated the industry in 1930, Lafarge and Poliet (the latter having merged with Ciments Français and adopted its name). Air Liquide remained in 2000, as it was in the 1930s, one of the world's leading makers of industrial gases.

The survival and continuing importance of so many long-lived industrial firms in France at the end of the twentieth century would seem to confirm a major argument in the Chandlerian literature, namely that the organizational capabilities acquired by the leading companies of the Second Industrial Revolution allowed them to maintain their industrial leadership into the era of the Third Industrial Revolution. As was noted at the beginning of this book, scholars have tended to ascribe France's postwar economic miracle to the new policies and attitudes that arose in response to the shock of defeat and occupation in 1940, coupled with postwar financial aid from the United States and the subsequent move toward European economic integration. All these things certainly contributed to France's post-1945 successes, but they would have had little permanent impact had there not been modern enterprises in place that were capable of carrying out a large-scale program of industrial renovation and expansion.

By the end of the 1930s, France's leading industrial companies had already mastered the critical production technologies and created the complex organizations that later allowed them to repair the physical damage of World War II quickly (albeit with large doses of government planning and massive outside assistance) and then to move on to developing or adapting the technologies of the Third Industrial Revolution and to serving the rapidly evolving needs of a modern consumer economy. In other words, the French economy took off after World War II in large part because French companies had acquired the necessary technical expertise, human resources, and organizational capabilities in the preceding half century. By the same token, to preserve the independence of French industry in an era of heightened global competition, the French government was able to sponsor the formation of national champions and other large firms after 1960 because the building blocks for those firms—and the people to run them—were already in place.

Although developmental economists may not like to admit it, there are few quick fixes for the economic backwardness of nations. France's economic success in the late twentieth century did not arise solely from policies and programs put in place after World War II. In many ways, the decisive steps in the modernization of the French economic system came, as they did for the American and German economies, in the years between 1890 and 1930—the era of the Second Industrial Revolution—when the seeds were sown for the later efflorescence of large-scale enterprise and managerial capitalism. But, as we have seen, the innovations of the early twentieth century depended in turn on the achievements of hundreds of entrepreneurs and state officials—not to mention the exertions of thousands of workers—over the previous hundred years. Far from being a recent construct, France's economic and business system at the beginning of the twenty-first century was the product of a convoluted and cumulative process of technological, institutional, and organizational development reaching back to the time of the French Revolution and even beyond—to the very beginnings of the French nation.

Notes
Index

Notes

Prologue

1. Alfred D. Chandler, Jr., *The Visible Hand: The Managerial Revolution in American Business* (Cambridge, Mass., 1977); and *Scale and Scope: The Dynamics of Industrial Capitalism* (Cambridge, Mass., 1990).
2. For early statements of the pessimist position, see David Landes, "French Entrepreneurship and Industrial Growth in the Nineteenth Century," *Journal of Economic History* 9 (May 1949): 45–61; and "French Business and Businessmen," in E. M. Earle, ed., *Modern France* (Princeton, 1951), 334–353. For examples of how French scholars sought to account for French economic retardation in the nineteenth century, see André Broder, "Le Commerce extérieur: L'Echec de la conquête d'une position international," in Fernand Braudel and Ernest Labrousse, eds., *Histoire économique et sociale de la France*, vol. 3, pt. 1 (Paris, 1976), 305–346; and François Caron, *An Economic History of Modern France* (New York, 1979), 35–39. For a review of the literature, see Colin Heywood, *The Development of the French Economy, 1750–1914* (Cambridge, 1992).
3. See Patrick O'Brien and Caglar Keyder, *Economic Growth in Britain and France, 1780–1914: Two Paths to the Twentieth Century* (London, 1978); and Rondo Cameron and Charles Freedeman, "French Economic Growth: A Radical Revision," *Social Science History* 7 (Winter 1983): 3–30.
4. See the various works co-authored by Charles Sabel: *Second Industrial Divide: Possibilities for Prosperity* (with Michael J. Piore) (New York, 1984); with Jonathan Zeitlin, "Historical Alternatives to Mass Production," *Past and Present* 108 (August 1985): 133–176; and *World of Possibilities: Flexibility and Mass Production in Western Industrialization* (New York, 1997).
5. See N. F. R. Crafts, "Economic Growth in France and Britain, 1830–1910: A Review of the Evidence," *Journal of Economic History* 44 (March 1984):

49–67, as well as Jean-Pierre Dormois, *L'Economie française face à la con-
currence britannique à la veille de 1914* (Paris, 1997).

6. See particularly Patrick Fridenson and André Straus, eds., *Le Capitalisme
   français, 19e–20e siècles: Blocages et dynamismes d'une croissance* (Paris,
   1987).

7. See especially *The Wheels of Commerce* (New York, 1982) and *The Perspective of the World* (New York, 1984).

8. An early but influential portrayal of France's postwar boom as a product of
   wartime shocks is found in the chapter by Charles Kindleberger in Stanley
   Hoffmann et al., *In Search of France* (Cambridge, Mass., 1963), 118–158.
   For a brief restatement of this argument that confirms its status as "con-
   ventional wisdom," see Gordon Wright, *France in Modern Times,* 5th ed.
   (New York, 1995), 435–438.

9. The best account of French industrial restructuring as a product of European
   economic integration is Claude Prêcheur, *1968: Les Industries françaises à
   l'heure du marché commun* (Paris, n.d. [1968]).

10. See Alfred D. Chandler, Jr. et al., eds., *Big Business and the Wealth of
    Nations* (Oxford, 1997).

Introduction

1. See James B. Collins, *The State in Early Modern France* (Cambridge, 1995).

2. F. H. Lawson, A. E. Anton, and L. Neville-Brown, eds., *Amos and Walter's
   Introduction to French Law,* 3rd ed. (Oxford, 1967), 26–33.

3. Fernand Braudel, *Wheels of Commerce* (New York, 1982); Braudel, *The
   Identity of France,* vol. 2 (New York, 1991), 551.

4. On the rise of Lyon, see Richard Gascon, *Grand Commerce et vie urbaine
   au XVIe siècle: Lyon et ses marchands,* 2 vols. (Paris, 1971).

5. Braudel, *The Identity of France,* vol. 2, 560–565.

6. Paul Butel, *L'Economie française au XVIIIe siècle* (Paris, 1993).

7. See Gérard Gayot, *Les Draps de Sedan, 1646–1870* (Paris, 1998).

8. Pierre Léon, "La Réponse industrielle," in Fernand Braudel and Ernest Labrousse, eds., *Histoire économique et sociale de la France,* vol. 2 (Paris,
   1970), 259.

9. For brief sketches of the leading French metallurgical enterprises of the eighteenth century, see Guy Richard, *Noblesse d'affaires au XVIIIe siècle* (Paris,
   1974), 147–172. On Babaud de la Chaussade, see P. W. Bamford, *Privilege
   and Profit: A Business Family in Eighteenth Century France* (Philadelphia,
   1988).

10. Jean-Pierre Daviet, *Une Multinationale à la française: Saint-Gobain, 1665–
    1989* (Paris, 1989), 9–56.

11. Jean Bouvier, "Vers le capitalisme bancaire: L'Expansion du crédit après
    Law," in Braudel and Labrousse, vol. 2, 301–324.

12. On French banking and finance in the eighteenth century, the fundamental
    source remains Herbert Lüthy, *La Banque protestante en France* (Paris,

1961). See also Bouvier, "Vers le capitalisme bancaire." A good brief review of the French fiscal system and the financial crisis is found in Richard Bonney, ed., *The Rise of the Fiscal State in Europe, c. 1500–1815* (Oxford, 1999), 123–176.

13. The classic discussion of the economic effects of the wars of 1792–1815 remains François Crouzet, "Wars, Blockade, and Economic Change in Europe, 1792–1815," *Journal of Economic History* 24, no. 4 (December 1964): 567–581.

14. David Landes, *The Wealth and Poverty of Nations* (New York, 1998), 3–16.

15. For an introduction to the demographic question in modern French history, see Joseph J. Spengler, *France Faces Depopulation: Postlude Edition, 1936–1967* (Durham, N.C., 1979); and Colin Dyer, *Population and Society in Twentieth Century France* (London, 1978).

1. Continuity and Change in Merchant Capitalism, 1800–1840s

1. This is Pierre Léon's estimate, based on the number paying the business license tax *(patente)*. See Fernand Braudel and Ernest Labrousse, eds., *Histoire économique et sociale de la France,* vol. 3, pt. 1 (Paris, 1976), 282.

2. On Rothschild, see Niall Ferguson, *The House of Rothschild,* vol. 1, *Money's Prophets, 1798–1848* (New York, 1998), 282; on the Mallets, see Christian Grand, *Trois siècles de banque: De Neuflize, Schlumberger, Mallet, 1667–1991* (Paris, 1991), 109.

3. Bertrand Gille, *La Banque et le crédit en France de 1815 à 1848* (Paris, 1959), 37. By contrast, Maurice Lévy-Leboyer has emphasized the chronic backwardness of French banking, especially in relation to British banking, throughout the nineteenth century. See his chapter in Braudel and Labrousse, vol. 3, pt. 1, 347–390.

4. Dale W. Tomich, *Slavery in the Circuit of Sugar: Martinique and the World Economy, 1830–1848* (Baltimore, 1990), 18.

5. Ibid., 15.

6. For an excellent brief account of the economic development of Bordeaux in the eighteenth century, see the chapters by François Crouzet in F-G Pariset, ed., *Bordeaux au XVIIIe siècle* (Bordeaux, 1968). More detailed accounts of the colonial trade are found in Paul Butel, *Les Négociants bordelais, l'Europe, et les îles au XVIIIe siècle* (Paris, 1974); and Eric Saugera, *Bordeaux, port négrier* (Paris, 1995).

7. By 1838–1842, the French colonies were producing an average of 84,000 tons of sugar per year, versus 103,000 tons in 1791 (Tomich, 15). As of 1846, the tonnage of ships carrying goods directly between Bordeaux and the sugar islands amounted to 39,300 tons, compared to 69,000 tons for Le Havre's colonial shipping, 52,700 tons for Marseille's, and 34,700 tons for Nantes' (France, Direction général des douanes, *Tableau général du commerce extérieur de la France,* 1846).

8. See Paul Butel, *Les Dynasties bordelaises* (Paris, 1991), 172–314; on the Johnstons, Yan de Siber, *Bordeaux et son négoce en vins* (Pauillac, 1985).

9. Louis Desgraves and Georges Dupeux, eds., *Bordeaux au XIXe siècle* (Bordeaux, 1969), 35–82; Butel, *Les Dynasties bordelaises*, 205–214, 221–248, 270–277; Marthe Barbance, *Vie commerciale de la route du cap Horn au XIXe siècle: L'Armement A-D Bordes et fils* (Paris, 1969).

10. Tomich, 289–291.

11. Jacques Fierain, *Les Raffineurs de sucre des ports en France, XIXe–début du XXe siècle* (New York, 1977), 66–69.

12. For figures on total tonnage of shipping, see *Tableau général du commerce de la France,* 1835, 1851.

13. On the economic history of Nantes in the eighteenth and nineteenth centuries, see the chapters by Jean Meyer and Jacques Fierain in Paul Bois, ed., *Histoire de Nantes* (Toulouse, 1977).

14. Cotton imports through Le Havre rose from less than 62,000 bales in 1818 to over 632,000 bales (89 percent of French cotton imports) by 1860. Coffee imports rose from 5,500 tons in 1820 to 25,452 tons in 1860 (virtually 100 percent of the French total). The number of people emigrating to the New World through Le Havre went from 10,000 in 1820 to 59,000 in 1847, and reached almost 97,000—the all-time high—in 1854. See Jean Legoy, *Le Peuple du Havre et son histoire*, vol. 2, pt. 2 (Saint-Etienne-du-Rouvray, 1982), 422.

15. *Journal du Havre,* quoted by Legoy.

16. For an overview of the economic development of Le Havre, see André Corvisier et al., *Histoire du Havre et de l'estuaire de la Seine* (Toulouse, 1987).

17. For a brief introduction to the history of Marseille, see Edouard Baratier et al., *Histoire de Marseille* (Toulouse, 1987). On the commerce and shipping of Marseille, see Paul Masson, *Les Bouches du Rhône: Encyclopédie départementale,* vol. 9, *Le Mouvement économique: Le Commerce* (Marseille, 1922).

18. See Masson, 353–361.

19. Roland Caty and Eliane Richard, *Armateurs marseillais au XIXe siècle,* 2nd ed. (Marseille, 1986), 27–28, 188–89.

20. A. Delavenne, *Recueil généaloqique de la bourgeoisie ancienne,* 2 vols. (Paris, 1954–1955), vol. 1, 65–67.

21. Ibid., vol. 2, 337–339; Samir Saul, *La France et l'Egypte de 1882 à 1914* (Paris, 1997), 6 n.12.

22. Caty and Richard, 271–306.

23. On the long-term development of Lyon and its region, see Pierre Léon, "La Région lyonnaise dans l'histoire économique et sociale de la France: Une Esquisse," *Revue Historique* 237 (1967): 31–62.

24. Quoted by Félix Rivet, *La Navigation à vapeur sur la Saône et la Rhône, 1783–1863* (Paris, 1962), 138, 379.

25. On Delahante, see *Dictionnaire de biographie française* [hereafter DBF], vol. 10, 643–645; and Louis Bergeron, *Les Rothschild et les autres* (Paris, 1991),

85–88. On the Banque de Lyon, see Bertrand Gille, *La Banque en France au XIXe siècle* (Geneva, 1970), 44–60.

26. Jean Bouvier, *Les Rothschild* (Paris, 1968), 50.

27. Besides the work of Christian Grand (note 2), see *Mallet Frères et Cie: 250 ans de banque* (Paris, 1963); and Romuald Szramkiewicz, *Les Régents et censeurs de la Banque de France nommés sous le Consulat et l'Empire* (Geneva, 1974), 225–234.

28. Max Gérard, *Messieurs Hottinguer, banquiers de Paris,* 2 vols. (Paris, 1968/1972).

29. The best brief account of the "assembling" of these families into the *haute banque* is found in Bergeron.

30. Ibid., 36; Henry Coston, *Dictionnaire des dynasties bourgeoises et du monde des affaires* (Paris, 1975), 593–599; Georges Albertini, *Cent Ans boulevard Haussmann: MM. Worms et Cie* (Paris, 1978).

31. Frédéric Barbier, *Finance et politique: La Dynastie des Fould* (Paris, 1991).

32. Niall Ferguson, *The House of Rothschild,* 2 vols. (New York, 1998–1999).

33. Ibid., vol. 1, 269.

34. The *particule nobiliaire* "de" was added after 1817 when Emperor Francis II made all the Rothschilds barons of the Austrian Empire.

35. Anka Muhlstein, *Baron James: The Rise of the French Rothschilds* (New York, 1984), 163–165.

36. Bergeron, 47, 53; Coston, 200–203.

37. Szramkiewicz, 207–212.

38. Ibid., 67; Coston, 176–178.

39. Bergeron, 35–36, 80–82; Coston, 518–520; Jean Lambert-Dansette, *Genèse du patronat, 1780–1880* (Paris, 1991), 377.

40. Jacques Wolff, *Les Perier: La Fortune et les pouvoirs* (Paris, 1993).

41. Gille, *La Banque et le crédit,* 251.

42. Grand, 60–70.

43. Gérard, vol. 1, 252.

44. Bertrand Gille, *Histoire de la maison Rothschild* (Geneva, 1965), vol. 1, 401–430.

45. Robert Bigo, *Les Banques françaises au cours du XIXe siècle* (Paris, 1947), 123–127.

46. The best introduction to the thought of Saint-Simon remains Frank E. Manuel, *The New World of Henri Saint-Simon* (South Bend, Ind., 1963).

47. Jean Autin, *Les Frères Pereire: Le Bonheur d'entreprendre* (Paris, 1984), 13–47.

48. Jean Lenoble, *Les Frères Talabot: Une Grande Famille d'entrepreneurs au 19e siècle* (Limoges, 1989).

49. See Georg G. Iggers, ed., *The Doctrine of Saint-Simon, an Exposition: The First Year, 1828–29* (Boston, 1958). On Emile Pereire's plan for a new bank in 1831–1832, see Rondo Cameron, *France and the Economic Development of Europe* (Princeton, N.J., 1960), 115–117. Robert B. Carlisle recounts the history of the Saint-Simonian movement and provides an invaluable guide

to the Saint-Simonian literature in *The Proffered Crown: Saint Simonianism and the Doctrine of Hope* (Baltimore, 1987).

50. See "Les Saint-simoniens et le crédit," in Gille, *La Banque en France au XIXe siècle,* 105–124.

51. Herbert Lüthy, *La Banque protestante en France,* vol. 2 (Paris, 1961), 433–438.

52. Louis Bergeron, *Banquiers, négociants, et manufacturiers parisiens du Directoire à l'Empire* (Paris, 1978), 87–120.

53. On the early operations of the Banque de France, see Bergeron, *Banquiers,* 126–133, 147–149; Gille, *La Banque et le crédit,* 77–88; Alain Plessis, *La Banque de France et ses deux cents actionnaires sous le Second Empire* (Geneva, 1982), 15–50.

54. Gille, *La Banque et le crédit,* 105–126; Plessis, *La Banque de France,* 15–50; Cameron, 113–114.

55. Michèle Ruffat et al., *L'UAP et l'histoire de l'assurance* (Paris, 1990), 44–45.

56. Georges Hamon, *Histoire générale de l'assurance en France* (Paris, 1897); Gille, *La Banque et le crédit,* 183–201; Charles E. Freedeman, *Joint-Stock Enterprise in France, 1807–1867* (Chapel Hill, 1979), 21–22, 70–73; Jacques Boudet, ed., *Le Monde des affaires en France* (Paris, 1952), 74–79.

57. Pierre Léon in Braudel and Labrousse, vol. 2, pt. 1, 241–274; Dominique Barjot, "From Tournon to Tancarville: the Contributions of French Civil Engineering to Suspension Bridge Construction, 1824–1959," *History and Technology* 6 (1988): 177–201.

58. François Caron, *Histoire des chemins de fer en France,* vol. 1, *1740–1883* (Paris, 1997), 11–78.

59. Reed G. Geiger, *Planning the French Canals: Bureaucracy, Politics, and Enterprise under the Restoration* (Newark, Del., 1994), 167.

60. Caron, 47.

61. On the evolution of French government policy on railroads, see Frank Dobbins, *Forging Industrial Policy: The United States, Britain, and France in the Railway Age* (Cambridge, 1994); and Yves Leclercq, *Le Réseau impossible: La Resistance au système des grandes compagnies et la politique économique en France, 1820–1852* (Geneva, 1987) (figures on state expenditures, p. 191).

62. On the early railroad construction in France, see the older but still useful work by Pierre Dauzet, *Le Siècle des chemins de fer en France, 1821–1938* (Paris, 1948); and especially Caron; and Georges Ribeill, *La Révolution ferroviaire: La Formation des compagnies de chemins de fer en France, 1823–1870* (Paris, 1993).

63. Figures from Jouffroy cited by Leclercq, 197, n. 59.

64. Caron, 192.

2. The Revolution in Banking and Transportation, 1850s–1870s

1. Jean Bouvier, *Un Siècle de banque française* (Paris, 1973), 196. This and all other translations from French to English are the author's unless otherwise indicated.

2. See Alain Plessis, *La Banque de France et ses deux cents actionnaires sous le Second Empire* (Geneva, 1982), 1–17.

3. Rondo Cameron, *France and the Economic Development of Europe, 1800–1914* (Princeton, N.J., 1961), 125–134; Bertrand Gille, *La Banque en France au XIXe siècle* (Geneva, 1970), 187–188.

4. Louis Bergeron, "Les Espaces du capital," in Jacques Revel, ed., *Histoire de la France*, vol. 1 (Paris, 1989), 318–325.

5. As of 1850, the Banque de France had twenty-seven branches, thanks to its takeover of departmental banks of emission that had failed in 1848. However, because a clause in the act renewing its charter in 1857 required the Banque to set up a branch in every department, its network grew to seventy-four branches by 1870. See Plessis; and Robert Bigo, *Les Banques françaises au cours du XIXe siècle* (Paris, 1947), 114–116.

6. Bergeron, 352; Alain Plessis, "Le 'Retard français': La Faute de banque? Banques locales, succursales de la Banque de France, et financement de l'économie sous le second Empire," in Patrick Fridenson and André Straus, eds., *Capitalisme français, XIXe–XXe siècles* (Paris, 1987), 199–210; and "Les Banques locales de l'essor du Second Empire à la 'crise' de la Belle Epoque," in Michel Lescure and Alan Plessis, eds. *Banques locales et banques régionales en France au XIXe siècle* (Paris, 1999), 202–236.

7. Plessis, "Les Banques locales," 226.

8. Charles Freedeman, *Joint-Stock Enterprise in France, 1807–1867* (Chapel Hill, N.C., 1979). See the Appendix, 145–177.

9. It should be noted that Laffitte had founded his Caisse Générale not as a *société anonyme* but as a *commandite par actions* that vested full liability in the company's general director and did not require approval by the Conseil d'Etat. For a discussion of the *commandite par actions* as an alternative to the *société anonyme*, see Freedeman, 47–65.

10. Cameron, 130–134; Maurice Lévy-Leboyer, "Le Crédit et la monnaie: L'Evolution institutionnelle," in Fernand Braudel and Ernest Labrousse, *Histoire économique et sociale de la France,* vol. 3, pt. 1 (Paris, 1976), 380–382.

11. Rothschild's letter is reproduced in Gille, 134.

12. Cameron, 147.

13. Freedeman, 85–92.

14. Gille, 188.

15. Hubert Bonin, "Le Comptoir national d'escompte de Paris: une Banque impériale, 1848–1940," *Revue Française d'Histoire d'Outre-mer* 78 (1991): 477–497.

16. Guy Beaujouan and Edmond Lebée, "La Fondation du Crédit industriel et commercial," *Histoire des Entreprises* 6 (November 1960): 5–40.

17. Edouard Lebée, "Le Groupe des banques affiliées au Crédit industriel et commercial: Ses Origines et son développement," *Histoire des Entreprises,* (May 1961), 5–40. On the Société Marseillaise de CIC, see Michel Lescure, "Banques régionales et croissance économique au XIXe siècle: L'Exemple de la Société marseillaise de crédit," in Lescure and Plessis, 293–322.

18. On the founding of the Banque de l'Indochine, see Yasuo Gonjo, *Banque coloniale ou banque d'affaires: La Banque de l'Indochine sous la IIIe République* (Paris, 1993); and Marc Meuleau, *Des Pionniers en Extrême-Orient: Histoire de la Banque de l'Indochine, 1875–1975* (Paris, 1990).

19. Jean Bouvier, *Le Crédit Lyonnais de 1863 à 1882* (Paris, 1961; reprinted in 3 vols., 1999).

20. See the commemorative volume, *SG: Société Générale, 1864–1964* (Paris, 1964); and two long chapters in Bertrand Gille, *La Banque en France au XIXe siècle.*

21. Eric Bussière, *Paribas, Europe, and the World, 1872–1992* (Antwerp, 1992), 19–57.

22. Lévy-Leboyer, 408–409.

23. On this concept, see Jean Bouvier in *Histoire économique et sociale de la France,* vol. 4, pt. 1, 187ff.

24. By the mid-1840s, the state engineers of the Ponts et Chaussées were beginning to realize that they had greatly underestimated the cost of railroad construction. For example, the cost of building the 133 kilometer line from Paris to Orléans, first estimated at 22 million francs, turned out to be 60 million francs. By the early 1850s, the engineer Auguste Perdonnet calculated that the first installment of French railroads had cost on average 375,000 francs per kilometer, versus 270,000 francs per kilometer for railroads in Belgium, 235,000 in Germany, and 95,000 in the United States. So the 1,860 kilometers of railroads that had been built in France by 1848 cost some 740 million francs. See Georges Ribeill, *La Révolution ferroviaire: La Formation des compagnies de chemins de fer en France, 1823–1870* (Paris, 1993), 434–435, n. 23 and 24.

25. Jean Villain, *Le Réseau du Nord: Ses Origines, son rôle, son activité* (Lille, 1932).

26. These points and much of what follows are from François Caron, *Histoire des chemins de fer en France,* vol. 1, *1740–1883* (Paris, 1997); and Ribeill. Also useful are Pierre Dauzet, *Le Siècle des chemins de fer en France, 1821–1938* (Paris, 1948); and Louis Girard, *La Politique des travaux publics sous le Second Empire* (Paris, 1952).

27. Caron, 202.

28. This figure is given by Jean Lenoble, *Les Frères Talabot: Une Grande Famille d'entrepreneurs au 19e siècle* (Limoges, 1989), 199.

29. For this phase of the story, see Robert B. Carlisle, "Les Chemins de fer, les Rothschild, et les saint-simoniens," *Economies et Sociétés* 5 (1971): 647–676.

30. Xavier Daumalin and Marcel Coudurie, *Vapeur et révolution industrielle à Marseille* (Marseille, 1997), 208.

31. The creation of the P-L-M was part of the protracted contest between the Pereires and the Rothschild-Talabot group for control of the railroads of southeast France, Switzerland, Austria, and northern Italy. It was only when Talabot acquired the Bourbonnais line, allowing him to connect his Lyon-Marseille line to Paris without using the Paris-Lyon, that Auguste Dassier of the Paris-Lyon accepted the merger that formed the P-L-M. See Cameron, 241–247.

32. See François Caron, *Histoire de l'exploitation d'un grand réseau: La Compagnie du chemin de fer du Nord, 1846–1937* (Paris, 1973), 73–88.

33. On the railroad conventions of 1859, see Girard, 191–208.

34. Alfred de Foville, *La Transformation des moyens de transport et ses conséquences économiques et sociales* (Paris, 1880), 93.

35. According to Foville (287), throughout the period of rapid growth of French foreign trade in the middle decades of the nineteenth century, the value of goods moving through France's ports remained twice as large as the value of goods moving in and out of France via the railroads. For example, the value of imports by sea averaged 2,827 million francs a year in 1867–1876 versus 1,434 million francs for overland imports.

36. See Roland Caty and Eliane Richard, *Armateurs marseillais au XIXe siècle*, 2nd ed. (Marseille, 1986), 61–66.

37. In 1850, the British steamer fleet consisted of more than 1,100 ships weighing 168,000 tons, compared to 126 ships weighing 14,000 tons in the French fleet. By 1900, this disparity had widened and the German fleet had also surpassed the French:

	France	Germany	United Kingdom
Ships	1,272	1,390	9,208
Tonnage	528,002	1,319,000	7,208,000

B.R. Mitchell, *European Historical Statistics* (New York, 1975), 615–618.

38. Caty and Richard (74–85) provide a good short account of the early years of the Messageries Maritimes. The definitive history of the company is Paul Bois, *Le Grand Siècle des Messageries Maritimes* (Marseille, 1991).

39. The Messageries Maritimes accounted for one-half of the steamer tonnage operating out of Marseille and one-third of all French steamer tonnage in 1869. By 1900, only four companies operated more tonnage: British India, Hamburg America, Peninsular & Oriental, and Norddeutscher Lloyd. See Yves Guyot and Arthur Raffalovich, *Dictionnaire du commerce, de l'industrie, de la banque*, 2 vols. (Paris, 1901), vol. 1, 941–942.

40. The main source on the history of the CGT remains Marthe Barbance, *Histoire de la Compagnie générale transatlantique* (Paris, 1955). A good account of the neo-slave trade is found in Jean Legoy, *Le Peuple du Havre et son histoire*, vol. 2, pt. 2, *Du négoce à l'industrie, 1800–1914* (St-Etienne du Rouvray, 1982), 250–253.

41. Bernard Bernadac, *Histoire de la Compagnie de Navigation Mixte et des relations France-Afrique du Nord, 1850–1969* (Marseille, 1985).
42. Caty and Richard, 71–74.
43. Michael S. Smith, "Unlikely Success: Chargeurs Réunis and the Marine Transport Business in France, 1872–1914," *Entreprises et Histoire* 6 (September 1994): 11–28.
44. For a discussion of the problem of French competitiveness in the marine transport business in the late nineteenth century, see Smith.
45. Albert Charles, "La Modernisation du port de Bordeaux sous le Second Empire," *Revue Historique de Bordeaux* n.s. 11 (1962): 25–49.
46. On the modernization of Le Havre's port, see Legoy, 181–187. On Le Havre's later problems, see Jules Charles-Roux, "La Grande Navigation et les ports français," *Revue des Deux Mondes* (March 15, 1907), 332–347.
47. René Barruey, *Le Port modern de Marseille, du dock au conteneur, 1844–1974* (Marseille, 1994).
48. There are numerous accounts of the building of the Suez Canal, all of which draw heavily on de Lesseps' own account. See, for example, John Marlowe, *World Ditch: The Making of the Suez Canal* (New York, 1964); and more recently, Ghislain de Diesbach, *Ferdinand de Lesseps* (Paris, 1998). Hubert Bonin has written a history of the Suez Company that emphasizes the post-nationalization period: *Suez, du canal à la finance, 1858–1987* (Paris, 1987). The best study of the Suez Company in the late nineteenth century is found in Samir Saul, *La France et l'Egypte de 1882 à 1914* (Paris, 1997), 225–294.

3. The New World of Financial and Commerical Capitalism, 1870s–1900s

1. Yves Breton et al., eds., *La Longue Stagnation en France: L'Autre Grande Dépression, 1873–1897* (Paris, 1997), 225–234. For a more pessimistic assessment of French banking in this era, see the chapter by André Gueslin in Youssef Cassis, ed., *Finance and Financiers in European History, 1880–1960* (Cambridge, 1992), 63–92.
2. By 1901, among all French banks publishing balance sheets, the four biggest banks accounted for 66 percent of total assets, 72 percent of deposits and current accounts, 71 percent of discounting (commercial portfolio), and 54 percent of profits. See the chapter by Jean Bouvier in Fernand Braudel and Ernest Labrousse, eds., *Histoire économique et sociale de la France*, vol. 4, pt. 1 (Paris, 1979), 172.
3. Figures presented by Maurice Lévy-Leboyer indicate that, in terms of total capital and total deposits, the Crédit Lyonnais was twice as large as the Société Générale and perhaps four times as large as either the CIC or the Comptoir d'Escompte in the 1890s (Braudel and Labrousse, *Histoire économique et sociale*, vol. 3, pt. 1, 461).
4. Youssef Cassis, *Big Business: The European Experience in the Twentieth Century* (Oxford, 1997), 240–243, 247.

5. René Girault, *Emprunts russes et investissements français en Russie, 1887–1914* (Paris, 1973), 325.

6. Samir Saul, *La France et l'Egypte de 1882 à 1914* (Paris, 1997).

7. Lévy-Leboyer, 461.

8. Jacques Dagneau, *Les Agences régionales de Crédit Lyonnais, 1870–1914* (New York, 1977).

9. On the "copper affair" see Lévy-Leboyer, 459–462; and M. A. Abrams, "The French Copper Syndicate, 1887–1889," *Journal of Economic and Business History* 4 (1932): 409–428. On the post-1889 history of the Comptoir d'Escompte, see Hubert Bonin, "Le Comptoir Nationale d'Escompte de Paris dans l'entre-deux-guerres," in Ministère de l'économie, des finances, et du budget, *Etudes et documents,* vol. 4 (1992), 225–382.

10. See *SG: Société Générale, 1864–1964* (Paris, 1964); and John P. McKay, *Pioneers for Profit: Foreign Entrepreneurship and Russian Industrialization, 1885–1913* (Chicago, 1970), 65–67.

11. Eric Bussière, *Paribas, Europe, and the World, 1872–1992* (Antwerp, 1992), 59–81.

12. On the history of the Banque de l'Indochine, see Marc Meuleau, *Des Pionniers en Extrême-Orient: Histoire de la Banque de l'Indochine, 1875–1975* (Paris, 1990); and Yasuo Gonjo, *Banque coloniale ou banque d'affaires: La Banque de l'Indochine sous la IIIe République* (Paris, 1993).

13. See Niall Ferguson, *The House of Rothschild,* vol. 2 (New York, 1998), 505. By comparison, Jacques Dagneau has estimated that the total capital of the Crédit Lyonnais was 438 million francs in 1900 (Dagneau).

14. Jean Bouvier in *Histoire économique et sociale,* vol. 4, pt. 1, 172.

15. Ferguson, 382.

16. John McKay, "The House of Rothschild (Paris) as a Multinational Industrial Enterprise, 1875–1914," in Alice Teichova et al., eds., *Multinational Enterprise in Historical Perspective* (Cambridge, 1987), 74–86.

17. Max Gérard, *Messieurs Hottinguer, banquiers à Paris,* vol. 2 (Paris, 1972); Hubert Bonin, *La Banque de l'Union parisienne, 1874/1904–1974* (Paris, 2001), 19, 44–72.

18. See Hubert Bonin, *La Banque de l'Union Parisienne,* 7–17; and " 'Blue Angels,' 'Venture Capital,' and 'Whales': Networks Financing the Take-off of the Second Industrial Revolution in France, 1890s–1920s," at *http://www.thebhc.org/publications/BEHonline/2004/Bonin.pdf.*

19. Louis Bergeron, "L'Espace du capital," in Jacques Revel, ed., *Histoire de la France,* vol. 1 (Paris, 1989), 361–362; Hubert Bonin, *Histoire de banque: Crédit du Nord, 1848–1998* (Paris, 1998), 28–57.

20. Christophe Lastécouères, "Jules Gommès ou la troisième signature d'une région: La Plus Grande Banque locale de Bayonne face à l'installation des sociétés de crédit, 1880–1914," in Michel Lescure and Alain Plessis, eds., *Banques locales et banques régionales en France au XIXe siècle* (Paris, 1999), 81–126.

21. See Jean-Marie Moine, "Banque locale et financement de l'industrialisation:

La Banque Thomas et la sidérurgie du bassin de Longwy, 1863–1907," in Lescure and Plessis, 127–172.

22. Lescure and Plessis, 231–232; Henri Morsel, ed., *Rhône-Alpes, terre d'industries à la Belle Epoque* (Paris, 1998), 37, 240, 425.

23. Michel Lescure, "Banque régionale et croissance économique au XIXe siècle: L'Exemple de la Société marseillaise de crédit," in Lescure and Plessis, 293–322.

24. See Bouvier in *Histoire économique et sociale*, vol. 4, pt. 1, 173.

25. There were also merchants who specialized in the domestic phase of the trade in each of these commodities, but they have left surprisingly few traces for the historian to study.

26. Claude Fohlen, *L'Industrie textile au temps du Second Empire* (Paris, 1956), 127–131; Jean Legoy, *Le Peuple du Havre et son histoire*, vol. 2, *Du Négoce à l'industrie, 1800–1914* (Saint-Etienne-du-Rouvray, 1982), 255–257.

27. Alston Hill Garside, *Cotton Goes to Market* (New York, 1935), 119–120.

28. On the rise of futures markets, see Garside, 130–169.

29. A case in point was the Siegfried brothers, who came to Le Havre as agents for the Alsatian cotton industry in the 1850s. During the American Civil War, the eldest brother, Jules, went to Bombay and made a fortune by setting up the importation of Indian cotton to replace American cotton. After the war the Siegfrieds opened an office in New Orleans, but thereafter they gradually withdrew from the cotton trade. Jules entered public life and moved to Paris. The second brother, Jacques, joined the board of the Comptoir d'Escompte and made a career in banking. The youngest brother, Ernest, stayed in Le Havre and continued to play a limited role in the cotton trade, but his son Georges also went into banking, eventually serving as director of the Crédit Commercial de France in the 1920s. The Siegfrieds seemed to understand that one big score in the cotton trade was all any family could hope for, so they took their winnings and moved on. See André Siegfried, *Mes Souvenirs de la IIIe République: Mon Père et son temps, Jules Siegfried, 1836–1922* (Paris, 1946).

30. The best source on the rise of the wool market of Roubaix-Tourcoing is M. Mussault, *Histoire du marché à terme sur laines peignées de Roubaix-Tourcoing* (Paris, 1909). On the wool trade more generally, see Fernand Maurette, *Les Grands Marchés des matières premières* (Paris, 1922), 65–90.

31. On the Lyon silk trade see Pierre Cayez, *Crises et croissance de l'industrie lyonnaise, 1850–1900* (Paris, 1980), 23–52; and Giovanni Federico, *An Economic History of the Silk Industry* (Cambridge, 1997), 153–156.

32. Coal, of course, was produced domestically in France as well as imported, and there were domestic coal merchants who acted as middlemen between domestic coal mining companies and various consumers of coal in the nineteenth century. Among these was the Dehaynin family, best known for Félix Dehaynin's invention of the coal briquette that became widely used as fuel by railroads and steamship lines. However, historians have done little

work on these domestic coal merchants, so the focus here is on the coal importers.

33. Georges Albertini, *Cent Ans boulevard Haussmann: Worms et Cie* (Paris, 1978).

34. Many of these trading companies were associated with France's new colonies in sub-Saharan Africa and Southeast Asia. The most important was the Compagnie Française de l'Afrique Occidentale (CFAO), which grew out of the commerce in oil seeds between West Africa and Marseille that was pioneered by Auguste Verminck from the 1840s to the 1880s. See Chapter 11 and Hubert Bonin, *C.F.A.O., cent ans de compétition* (Paris, 1987).

35. See Pierre Léon, "L'Epanouissement d'un marché national," in Braudel and Labrousse, eds., *Histoire économique et sociale de la France,* vol. 2, pt. 1, 284–285.

36. Léon, 285.

37. Louis Bergeron, "Permanences et renouvellement du patronat," in Yves Lequin et al., *Histoire des français, XIXe–XXe siècles* (Paris, 1983), vol. 2, 250.

38. Louis André, *Machines à papier: Innovation et transformations de l'industrie papetière en France, 1798–1860* (Paris, 1996), 398–402.

39. Gustave Roy, *Souvenirs, 1823–1906* (Nancy, 1906); and Roy file in Archives Nationales (hereafter cited as AN) F^{12}5262.

40. The rise of public warehouses (*magasins généraux*) that offered storage facilities—and later credit—independent of the wholesale merchants provided another way that manufacturers could circumvent the *négociants-commissionnaires.* The City of Paris began creating such public warehouses in the commercial district on the Right Bank in the 1830s and 1840s, and in the 1850s private warehouses were built adjacent to the new belt-line railroad (Chemin de Fer de Ceinture) that was created to transfer freight from one trunk line to another and that soon became the heart of the capital's rail-based distribution system. In 1860, the Crédit Mobilier merged these warehouses into a single company, the Compagnie des Entrepôts et Magasins Généraux, which later took over warehouses elsewhere in France and became a major force in wholesaling and distribution at the national level. In *Paris, la ville, 1852–1870* (Paris, 1977), 486–524, Jeanne Gaillard presents the story of the founding of the Entrepôts et Magasins Généraux as a battle between Saint-Simonian financiers and the old merchant elite of Paris for control of the French marketing system in the railroad age.

41. Claude Fohlen, *L'Industrie textile au temps du Second Empire* (Paris, 1956), 126–157; and *Une Affaire de famille au XIXe siècle: Mequillet-Noblot* (Paris, 1955), 54–59, 70–71, 91–92, 105–107.

42. Pierre Lamard, *Histoire d'un capital familial au XIXe siècle* (Belfort, 1988), 131, 150, 178–184.

43. See André Gueslin, *L'Invention de l'économie sociale* (Paris, 1987); and Ellen Furlough, *Consumer Cooperation in France: The Politics of Consumption* (Ithaca, N.Y., 1991).

44. On the "prehistory" of mass retailing in Paris, see Bernard Marrey, *Les Grands Magasins des origines à 1939* (Paris, 1979), 9–41.

45. Quote in Marrey, 48. Besides Marrey, see the biography of Renouard in Veronique Bourienne, "Boucicault, Chauchard, et les autres: Fondateurs et fondation des premiers grands magasins parisiens," in *Paris et Ile-de-France* 40 (1989): 326–332.

46. On Boucicault and the Bon Marché, see Marrey and Bourienne, and especially Michael B. Miller, *The Bon Marché: Bourgeois Culture and the Department Store, 1869–1930* (Princeton, N.J., 1981).

47. The article by Veronique Bourienne provides a guide to the literature on these stores and summarizes what is known about the founding of each, which is often surprisingly little.

48. Philip Nord, *Paris Shopkeepers and the Politics of Resentment* (Princeton, 1986), 61.

49. While cash operations were crucial, it should be noted that, in their never-ending search for competitive advantage, some department stores resorted to offering consumer credit at the end of the nineteenth century. The leader in this trend was Georges Dufayel, who in the 1870s took over the Etablissements Crespin, the pioneer in "subscription sales" (in return for regular installment payments, customers received coupons or tokens good for merchandise at participating stores). Dufayel used the Crespin system in launching the Grand Magasin Dufayel in 1892. He also ran a huge consumer credit organization that attracted 3.5 million clients by 1904. Among the participating stores was Samaritaine, although it later set up its own consumer credit company, La Semeuse. Dufayel's store and credit business declined rapidly after his death in 1916, but others soon took up the practices of consumer credit and installment buying. See Bourienne, 289–297; and Theodore Zeldin, *France, 1848–1945: Taste and Corruption* (Oxford, 1980), 280.

50. On the Magasins Réunis and other provincial department stores, see Marrey, 41–55, 191–198. Another chain of department stores originated in Paris with a *magasin de nouveautés* founded by the Gompel brothers on the Boulevard Voltaire in 1893. In 1898 they launched a joint stock company, Paris-France, that over the next twelve years created a chain of some 100 stores under the name Dames de France. See the Paris-France file in AN 65 AQ T142; and Pierre Moride, *Les Maisons à succursales multiples en France et à l'étranger* (Paris, 1913), 102–111.

51. Moride, 71–95.

52. On Félix Potin, see Georges d'Avenel, *Le Mécanisme de la vie moderne*, 5th ed., vol. 1 (Paris, 1908), 155–218; and Jacques Boudet, ed., *Le Monde des affaires en France* (Paris, 1952), 616–619. On the Reims grocers, see Moride, 102–111, and Bergeron, "Permanence et renouvellement," 269–271. On Casino, see Michelle Zancarini Fournel, "A l'origine de la grande distribution, le succursalisme: Casino, Saint-Etienne, 1898–1948," *Entreprises et Histoire* 4 (November 1993): 27–39.

II. The Flowering of Industrial Capitalism

1. Whitney Walton, *France at the Crystal Palace: Bourgeois Taste and Artisan Manufacture in the Nineteenth Century* (Berkeley, 1992).
2. The social origins of the early French industrial capitalists have not been studied as systematically as the origins of the British factory masters, but see Louis Bergeron, *Les Capitalistes en France, 1780–1914* (Paris, 1978); and "Permanences et renouvellement du patronat," in Yves Lequin, ed., *Histoire des Français, XIX–XXe siècles*, vol. 2 (Paris, 1983), 153–292. Also see Jean Lambert-Dansette, *La Genèse du patronat, 1780–1880* (Paris, 1991).
3. For an example of how the history of modern industrial enterprise can be told in terms of these four growth strategies, see Alfred D. Chandler, Jr., *Scale and Scope* (Cambridge, Mass., 1990).

4. Textile Capitalism

1. The persistence of hand-loom weaving serves as an indicator of this phenomenon. According to government statistics (*Annuaire Statistique,* vol. 13 [1890], 240–243), as of 1887 there were still some 28,000 hand looms in use in the French cotton industry (versus 73,000 power looms); 25,000 hand looms in woolens production (versus 45,000 power looms); and 21,000 hand looms in linen, jute, and hemp production (versus only 18,000 power looms). See Didier Terrier, *Les Deux Ages de la proto-industrie: Les Tisserands du Cambrésis et du Saint-Quentinois, 1730–1880* (Paris, 1996); and Tessie P. Liu, *The Weaver's Knot: The Contradictions of Class Struggle and Family Solidarity in Western France, 1750–1914* (Ithaca, N.Y., 1994).
2. Charles Ballot, *L'Introduction du machinisme dans l'industrie française* (Lille/Paris, 1923; reprint, Geneva, 1978), 43.
3. See Serge Chassagne, *Oberkampf, un entrepreneur capitaliste au siècle des lumières* (Paris, 1980); Sidney D. Chapman and Serge Chassagne, *European Textile Printers in the 18th Century: A Study of Peel and Oberkampf* (London, 1981); and especially the published version of his doctoral thesis, Serge Chassagne, *Le Coton et ses patrons: France, 1760–1840* (Paris, 1991).
4. Chassagne, *Le Coton,* 75–93.
5. Chapman and Chassagne, 44. In 1805, probably his firm's best year, Oberkampf printed over 1.7 million ells of cloth, of which 1 million were printed on the cylindrical presses (Louis Bergeron, *Banquiers, négociants, et manufacturiers parisiens du Directoire à l'Empire* [Paris, 1978], 224).
6. In 1813, there were fifty-two *filatures* employing 5,000 workers to operate some 744 jennies with 150,000 spindles (all powered by horses or by hand) in the department of the Seine. The largest works, with over 20,000 spindles, belonged to Richard-Lenoir (Bergeron, 205, 214).
7. Romuald Sramkiewicz, *Les Régents et censeurs de la Banque de France nommés sous le Consulat et l'Empire* (Geneva, 1974), 60–75; *Histoire documentaire de l'industrie de Mulhouse et de ses environs au XIXe siècle,* 2 vols. (Mulhouse, 1902), vol. 1, 414.

8. Jean-Pierre Chaline, *Les Bourgeois de Rouen: Une Elite Urbaine au XIXe siècle* (Paris, 1982), 102–107. On Holker, see Chassagne, *Le Coton,* 181–199.

9. Quoted by Chaline, 73.

10. Norman mills typically had 10,000 to 25,000 spindles before 1840 (the largest, belonging to Fauquet-Lemaître, had 36,000). The steam-powered mills built after 1860 had 50,000 to 75,000 spindles (Claude Fohlen, *L'Industrie textile en France sous le Second Empire* [Paris, 1956], 196–197). Whereas Rouen and its vicinity hosted 191 spinning mills in 1859, this number was down to 98 by 1889 and 54 by 1910, although the total spindlage of the industry rose between 1860 and 1910 (J. Levainville, *Rouen: Etude d'une agglomeration urbaine* [Paris, 1913], 217).

11. On the Keittingers, see Chaline, 102–106. Chaline also discusses the Rouen branch of the Fauquet family and provides a genealogy (Table 6), but the main source on the Fauquets of Bolbec is Chassagne, *Le Coton,* 568–574. On the issue of dynasties, see Chaline's contribution to a special issue of *Mouvement Social:* "Les industriels normands: un patriciat sans dynasties?" (July–Septembre 1985), 43–56.

12. Geneviève Dufresne, "Une Dynastie d'industriels du coton: Les Waddington, 1792–1957," *Entreprises et Histoire* 9 (1995): 71–92.

13. The Compagnie Française du Télégraphe de Paris à New York laid and operated a cable from Brest to Cape Cod before going broke in 1895 and merging with another French cable company to form the Compagnie Française des Câbles Télégraphiques. The full story of the PQ is related by Pascal Griset in *Entreprises, technologie et souverainété: Les Télécommunications transatlantiques de la France, XIX–XXe siècles* (Paris, 1996), 59–124.

14. On the career of Pouyer-Quertier and his firm, see Chaline, *Les Bourgeois de Rouen,* 114–117; and Dominique Barjot et al., *Les Patrons du Second Empire: Anjou, Normandie, Maine* (Paris/Le Mans, 1991), 54.

15. Levainville, 264.

16. On the early development of Alsatian cloth printing, see Henry Laufenberger and Pierre Pflimlin, *L'Industrie de Mulhouse,* vol. 2 of *Cours d'économie alsacienne* (Paris, 1932), 3–10; André Brandt, "Les Origines de l'industrie de Mulhouse," in *Bulletin de la Société Industrielle de Mulhouse,* 1946 (3–4), 9–23; J-M Schmitt, "The Origins of the Textile Industry in Alsace: The Beginning of the Manufacture of Printed Cloth at Wesserling, 1762–1802," *Textile History* 13, 1 (May 1982): 99–110; Geoffrey Ellis, *Napoleon's Continental Blockade: The Case of Alsace* (Oxford, 1981), 188ff.; and Michel Hau, *L'Industrialisation de l'Alsace* (Strasbourg, 1987), 366–367.

17. Hau, 75–88.

18. See, for example, Max Dollfus, *Histoire et généalogie de la famille Dollfus de Mulhouse* (Mulhouse, 1909); Edouard Sitzmann, *Dictionnaire biographique des hommes célèbres de l'Alsace,* 2 vols. (Rixheim, 1910); A. Delavenne, *Recueil généalogique de la bourgeoisie ancienne;* 2 vols. (Paris, 1954–1955); Camille Schlumberger and Charles Spoerry, *Tableaux généalogiques*

de la famille Schlumberger, 2 vols. (Paris, 1953–1956); and the family trees in Hau, 464–480.

19. Hau, 80–88, 348–363; *Histoire documentaire,* vol. 1, 445–448.

20. Hau, 467–470 and passim; *Histoire documentaire,* vol. 1, 405–408.

21. Hau, 472–474 and passim; Sitzmann, vol. 2, 690–692; Henri Coston, *Dictionnaire des dynasties bourgeoises et du monde des affaires* (Paris, 1975), 498–500; M. A. Calame et al., *Regards sur la société contemporaine: Trois familles industrielles d'Alsace* (Strasbourg, 1989), 123–213. On Schlumberger Ltd., see Ken Auletta, *The Art of Corporate Success* (New York, 1984).

22. Georges Poull, *L'Industrie textile vosgienne, 1765–1981* (Rupt-sur-Moselle, 1982), 9–25.

23. Poull, 25–55; A. Lederlin et al., *Monographie de l'industrie cotonnière* (Epinal, 1905); Henry Boucher, "L'Industrie et commerce," in Léon Louis, ed., *Le Département des Vosges* (Epinal, 1889), 191–228.

24. The chief sponsor of the bill, Jules Méline, was a deputy for the Vosges and was tied directly to the cotton industry through his in-laws, the Bluches. As for the impact of tariff policy, one example must suffice: The decision to incorporate Madagascar into the customs regime of metropolitan France (taken in 1897 when Méline was prime minister) gave French cotton manufacturers such dominance in that market that exports of cotton cloth from the Vosges to Madagascar increased from 19,000 kilograms in 1897 to 620,000 kilograms in 1899 (Poull, 50).

25. Poull, 187–190, 211–232, 249–252, 256–260, 329–334, 353–360; R. B. Forrester, *The Cotton Industry of France* (Manchester, 1921), 1–22.

26. Claude Ferry, *Les Blanchisseries et teintureries de Thaon, 1872–1914* (Nancy, 1991), 237.

27. Poull, 55–86.

28. Jean Lambert-Dansette, *Origines et evolution d'une bourgeoisie: Quelques familles du patronat textile de Lille-Armentières, 1789–1914* (Lille, 1954), 153–156.

29. Paul Mairet, *La Crise de l'industrie cotonnière, 1901–1905* (Dijon, 1906), 27.

30. In an important article on Roubaix, David Landes attributed the division to the long-standing contempt of the older and larger Lille for its smaller upstart neighbors and attributed the dynamism of Roubaix entrepreneurs to a psychological need to compensate for their "inferiority" vis-à-vis the Lillois ("Religion and Enterprise: The Case of the French Textile Industry," in Edward C. Carter II et al., *Enterprise and Entrepreneurs in 19th and 20th Century France* [Baltimore, 1976], 41–86). Landes also took the opportunity to dismiss any causal link between business success and Protestantism, pointing out that the textile dynasties of the Nord were as fervently Catholic as those of Alsace were Protestant (it is possible, however, that the common characteristic of these two communities—strong religious faith—*does* account in part for their success).

31. Lambert-Dansette, 161n; Frédéric Barbier et al., *Le Patronat du Nord sous le Second Empire: Une Approche prosopographique* (Geneva, 1989), 365; Michael S. Smith, *Tariff Reform in France, 1860–1900* (Ithaca, N.Y., 1980), 136; Michel Battiau, *Les Industries textiles de la Région Nord-Pas de Calais* (Paris, 1976), 446–468.

32. Pierre Deyon, "La Ville et les hommes du XIXe siècle," in Louis Trenard et al., *Histoire de Roubaix* (Dunkerque, 1984), 290–293; Barbier, *Patronat du Nord*, 315–319; Maurice Daumas, *L'Archéologie industrielle en France* (Paris, 1980), 290–293.

33. Based on cotton consumption figures in B. R. Mitchell, *European Historical Statistics, 1750–1970* (New York, 1975), 427–428; and value added estimates in T. J. Markovitch, "L'Industrie française de 1789 à 1914," *Cahiers de l'ISEA*, AF6, June 1966, Table 3.

34. Based on Markovitch, Table 4.

35. Ibid., Table 3.

36. Charles Ballot, *L'Introduction du machinisme*, 233–240.

37. Lambert-Dansette, 113–150; Alfred Aftalion, "Les Kartells dans la région du nord de la France: Les Kartells à formes simples dans les filatures de coton et de lin, 1899–1907," *Revue Economique International* 4 (1908): 144–165.

   The value of French linen thread production fell from an average of 388 million francs per year in 1865–1874 to 170 million francs per year in 1895–1904; the value of France's annual output of linen cloth fell from 514 million francs to 180 million francs over the same interval (Markovitch, table 3).

38. On the Agaches, see Barbier, *Patronat du Nord*, 75–80; and Louis Bergeron, "Permanences et renouvellement du patronat," in Yves Lequin, ed., *Histoire des Français, XIX–XXe siècles*, vol. 2 (Paris, 1983), 174–175. On Agache-Willot, see Benôit Boussement and Jean-Claude Rabier, *Le Dossier Agache-Willot, un capitalisme à contre-courant* (Paris, 1983).

39. Markovitch, table 3; Mitchell, 443–445.

40. *Annuaire statistique de la France*, vol. 1 (1878), 374–375.

41. Daumas, cited in n.32, 106–117. The quotation from Young is on page 115.

42. Christopher C. Johnson, *The Life and Death of Industrial Languedoc, 1700–1920* (New York, 1995), 19.

43. Louis Bergeron, "Douglas, Ternaux, Cockerill: Aux Origines de la mécanisation de l'industrie lainière en France," *Revue Historique* 247 (1972): 67–80. At the height of the First Empire, Ternaux owned three plants in and around Sedan (his hometown), one near Verviers, two in Louviers (to which he added the Decretôt plant in 1810), and several in Reims, plus sales offices in Paris, Genoa, and Livorno. By 1819 he controlled upwards of one hundred plants, agencies, and offices and employed directly or indirectly 20,000 persons. See Charles Ballot, *L'Introduction du machinisme*, 195–208; and L. M. Lomüller, *Guillaume Ternaux, 1763–1833, créateur de la première integration industrielle française* (Paris, 1978).

44. Georges Causse, "L'Industrie lainière rémoise à l'époque napoléonienne,"

Revue d'histoire moderne et contemporaine 17 (June–September 1970): 574–593.

45. On the unraveling of Ternaux's empire, see Lomüller, 303–316.

46. Maurice Lévy-Leboyer, *Les Banques européennes et l'industrialisation internationale dans la première moitié du XIXe siècle* (Paris, 1964), 121–129.

47. Johnson, 30.

48. The Vitalis family firm employed 368; the firm created by the merger of the Teisserenc and Calvet firms employed 258. According to Johnson (69), these were the fifteenth and twenty-fourth largest woolens firms in France as of 1849.

49. Johnson, 35–39.

50. This ranking comes from a list compiled by the National Assembly in 1849 and reproduced in Johnson, 69. On Mazamet, see Rémy Cazals, *Les Révolutions industrielles à Mazamet, 1750–1900* (Paris, 1983), 69–89, 104–123.

51. Katrina Honeyman and Jordan Goodman, *Technology and Enterprise: Isaac Holden and the Mechanization of Woolcombing in France, 1848–1914* (Brookfield, Vt., 1986).

52. David Gordon, *Merchants and Capitalists: Industrialization and Provincial Politics in Mid-Nineteenth Century France* (Tuscaloosa, Ala., 1985), 17–18, 57–57, 62–65; Claude Fohlen, *L'Industrie textile*, 329ff.

53. Trenard, 123–134.

54. As noted earlier, Isaac Holden et Cie remained the largest woolcomber in France in the late nineteenth century, but its Croix facility had always been an English enclave, known locally as "Holden City," which was integrated more closely with the Holden enterprise in Bradford than with the rest of Roubaix industry. After World War I, when their Reims and Croix plants were heavily damaged, the Holden clan gradually retreated from France. Honeyman and Goodman, 69–74, 99–101.

55. *Trenard*, 171–212; Battiau, 87, 177–200; Bergeron, "Permanences et renouvellement du patronat," 162–164.

56. Bergeron, "Permanences et renouvellement du patronat," 167–171.

57. Jean-Claude Daumas, "Les Etablissements Blin et Blin d'Elbeuf à la fin du XIXe siècle: Capital familiale, industrialisme, et paternalisme dans un secteur en déclin," *Entreprises et Histoire* 6 (September 1994): 87–108.

58. Cazals, 165–209.

59. On the traditional organization of the Lyon silk industry, see Robert Bezucha, *The Lyon Uprising of 1834* (Cambridge, Mass., 1974), 1–47.

60. The Jacquard loom doubled the productivity of the *canuts* since it could be operated by one person (versus the two needed to operate the traditional loom), but its height meant that it could be set up only in new buildings with especially high ceilings that were being built specifically to accommodate the machine in the suburbs.

61. Yves Lequin, *Les Ouvriers de la région lyonnaise, 1848–1914*, vol. 1, *La Formation de la classe ouvrière régionale* (Lyon, 1977), 27–36.

62. Maurice Daumas, 324.

63. Ibid., 330–340. On Bonnet's plant, see Pierre Cayez, *Métiers jacquard et hauts fourneaux: Aux Origines de l'industrie lyonnaise* (Lyon, 1978), 163.

64. Proponents of mechanization had hailed Sauvagère as the wave of the future in the 1820s. See Alain Cottereau, "The Fate of Collective Manufactures in the Industrial World: The Silk Industries of Lyons and London, 1800–1850," in Charles Sabel and Jonathan Zeitlin, eds., *World of Possibilities: Flexibility and Mass Production in Western Industrialization* (Cambridge, 1997), 75–152.

65. Quoted by France and Philippe Bouchardeau, *Histoire de la chambre de commerce de Valence*, vol. 1 (Grenoble, 1981), 38.

66. Cayez, 177. Cottereau (n. 64) makes much of the success of non-industrialized production in silk before 1850 while ignoring the post-1850 transformation of the industry. The account here rejects this either/or approach, emphasizing that, even before 1850, the Lyonnais silk industry combined industrial and non-industrial elements.

67. George J. Sheridan, Jr., *The Social and Economic Foundations of Association Among the Silk Weavers of Lyon, 1852–1870* (New York, 1981), 211–219.

68. According to François Robert, *Les Archives d'entreprise en Rhône-Alpes aux XIXe–XXe siècles, Guide documentaire* (Lyon, 1993), vol. 1, 334, the Société J. B. Martin was "among the most important in the textile industry" from 1850 to 1890. It consisted of a *moulinage* of 20,000 spindles and a weaving plant of 600 power looms at Tarare and a dyeworks at Roanne. The company also had a network of subcontractors in Lorraine employing an additional 700 looms.

69. Pierre Cayez, *Crises et croissance de l'industrie lyonnaise, 1850–1900* (Paris, 1980), 87. See his list of the major enterprises, 66–67, 78, 86.

70. Giovanni Federico, *An Economic History of the Silk Industry, 1830–1930* (Cambridge, 1997), 226.

71. According to Federico (55), this expanded Italian silk throwing was financed and controlled by French *marchands de soie*. There was also a trend toward eliminating silk throwing altogether, sending reeled silk directly to the weavers. This could be done only with the highest-quality silk, but the savings in processing costs made it worthwhile. By 1900, perhaps one-fifth of all silk woven in and around Lyon had not been thrown.

72. Charles Sabel and Jonathan Zeitlin, "Historical Alternatives to Mass Production: Politics, Markets, and Technology in 19th Century Industrialization," *Past and Present* 108 (August 1985): 133–174.

73. Federico, 62; Emile Levasseur, *Questions ouvrières et industrielles en France sous la Troisième République* (Paris, 1907), 112–115.

74. According to Michel Laferrère (*Lyon, ville industrielle* [Paris, 1960], 217), rayon comprised 90 percent of the fibers used in the Lyonnais textile industry by 1937.

75. Markovitch's figures indicate that the total value of textile production increased fourfold between the post-Napoleonic decade and the pre–World War I decade (Table 4).

76. Lévy-Leboyer, 469.

77. This kind of specialization is at the heart of an important ongoing debate over the necessity of big business in the modern world and the future course of American industrialization. In addition to the works of Sabel and Zeitlin already cited, see Charles F. Sabel and Michael J. Piore, *The Second Divide* (New York, 1984); and more recently Philip Scranton, *Endless Novelty: Specialty Production and American Industrialization, 1885–1925* (Princeton, N.J., 1997).

78. Bergeron, "Permanence et renouvellements," 153–194.

5. The Capitalism of Coal

1. The 33 million metric tons of coal produced by France in 1900 was approximately one-fifth the amount produced in the German Empire, one-seventh the amount produced in Britain, and one-eighth the amount produced in the United States. See figures in B. R. Mitchell, *European Historical Statistics, 1750–1970* (New York, 1975), 362; and Mitchell, *International Historical Statistics: Americas and Australasia* (New York, 1983), 400.

2. In the early twentieth century, France's two largest coal-mining companies, Anzin and Lens, were the biggest industrial companies in France in terms of employment (with 16,393 and 16,319 employees, respectively). By comparison, Britain's three largest independent coal companies in terms of employment were Powell Duffrin (14,779), Lambton (13,905), and Fife (13,853). The largest independent German coal company, Harpener Bergbau, employed 26,000. On the French and German companies, see Youssef Cassis, *Big Business: The European Experience in the Twentieth Century* (Oxford, 1997), 242, 245; on the British companies, see Roy Church, *The History of the British Coal Industry*, vol. 3 (Oxford, 1986), 400.

3. Production and consumption figures are found in Dominique Barjot, ed., *L'Energie aux XIXe et XXe siècles* (Paris, 1991), 110.

4. For a detailed picture of coal-mining politics from the 1770s to the 1820s, see Gwynne Lewis, *The Advent of Modern Capitalism in France, 1770–1840: The Contribution of Pierre-François Tubeuf* (Oxford, 1993).

5. Guy Richard, *La Noblesse d'affaires au XVIIIe siècle* (Paris, 1975), 185–196.

6. Richard; Reed G. Geiger, *The Anzin Coal Company, 1800–1830* (Newark, Del., 1975), 20–22; Marcel Gillet, *Les Charbonnages du nord de la France au XIXe siècle* (Paris, 1973), 25–30.

7. Geiger, 22–29; Gillet, 31–35. Adding to the effects of war was the Law of July 28, 1791, which reaffirmed the rights of landowners to the subsoil and invalidated many royal concessions, leading to a new wave of disputes and to de facto fragmentation of concessions among various claimants. See Lewis, 115–211.

8. Anzin's average annual output, 1841–1850, was 680,000 tons at a time when total French annual output averaged around 4 million tons. For the full story on Anzin's development in this era, see Geiger.

9. Gillet, 36–51.

10. Marius Sutet, "Jules Chagot, fondateur de la Compagnie des mines de Blanzy, 1801–1877," *Actes du Congrès national des sociétés savantes* (1964), vol. 2, 807–816; Bertrand Gille, *Recherches sur la formation de la grande entreprise capitaliste* (Paris, 1959), 56–65; 72–85.

11. Marius Dargaud, "Les Structures sociales, économiques, et financières des sociétés métallurgiques de Commentry," *Actes du Congrès national des sociétés savantes* (1961), 385–404.

12. Lewis.

13. Gille, 96–104; Robert R. Locke, *Les Fonderies et forges d'Alais* (Paris, 1978), 11–65; Jean-Michel Gaillard, "La Naissance d'une entreprise industrielle au XIXe siècle: La Compagnie des mines de la Grand'combe," *Mines et mineurs en Languedoc-Roussillon* (Montpellier, 1977), 191–200.

14. Donald Reid, *The Miners of Decazeville* (Cambridge, Mass., 1985), 9–23.

15. Rolande Trempé, *Les Mineurs de Carmaux, 1848–1914,* 2 vols. (Paris, 1971), vol. 1, 21–51.

16. Christopher Johnson, *The Life and Death of Industrial Languedoc* (Oxford, 1995), 16–17, 154–175.

17. Quoted by L-J Gras, *Histoire économique générale des mines de la Loire* (Saint-Etienne, 1922), 207–208.

18. Ibid., 201–295.

19. Pierre Guillaume, *La Compagnie de la Loire, 1846–1854* (Paris, 1966), 25–38; Gille, 113–121.

20. Guillaume, 157–225.

21. Gillet, 59–64, 85–116; Frédéric Barbier, *Le Patronat du Nord sous le Second Empire* (Paris, 1989), 95–98, 145–163.

22. Barjot, 103–111.

23. Julien Turgan, *Les Grands Usines, Etudes industrielles en France et à l'étranger*, 20 vols. (Paris, 1860–1895), vol. 15 (1883–1884).

24. Bertrand Gille, *La Sidérurgie française au XIXe siècle* (Geneva, 1968), 295.

25. Marc Simard, "Situation économique de l'entreprise et rapports de production: Le Cas de la Compagnie d'Anzin, 1860–1894," *Revue du Nord* 65 (July 1983): 581–602.

26. See the pessimistic assessment of the company by the Crédit Lyonnais in 1899 in Henri Morsel, ed., *Rhône-Alpes, terre d'industrie à la Belle Epoque, 1899–1914* (Paris, 1998), 63–90.

27. Gras, 730–752, 797–820.

28. Johnson, 230–235.

29. Reid, 50–52, 115.

30. Trempé, vol. 1, 55–65.

31. George J. Lamb, "Coal Mining in France, 1873–1895," Ph.D. diss., University of Illinois, 1976, 358–400; Lucien Delpeuch, "Evolution d'une entreprise familiale: La Société des houillères de Blanzy-Montceau (Jules Chagot et Cie), 1856–1900," *Information Historique* (April 1972), 59–69;

Lucien Peyronnard, *Le Charbon de Blanzy: La Famille Chagot et Montceau-les-mines* (Le Creusot, 1981), vol. 2.

6. The Capitalism of Iron and Steel

1. As David Landes explains in *The Unbound Prometheus* (New York, 1968), 89–92, 249, steel is a particularly strong form of iron that results when the carbon content is between 0.1 and 2 percent. By contrast, pig iron, the product of the smelting of iron ore, which when reheated and poured into molds becomes cast iron, has a carbon content between 2.5 and 4 percent. It is strong but brittle and cannot hold up under repeated pounding as steel can. Wrought iron, the product of the refining of pig iron, is almost pure, with a carbon content of less than 0.1 percent. It is malleable and much more versatile than cast iron but not as strong as steel.

2. See the figures for pig iron and crude steel production in B. R. Mitchell, *European Historical Statistics, 1750–1970* (New York, 1975), 391–404.

3. In traditional French practice, iron was extracted from ore using charcoal either in a "catalan" forge or in the *forge comtoise*. In the catalan forge, wrought iron was obtained directly from ore, without passing through a pig iron stage, by slowly heating the ore in direct contact with the charcoal. This required high-grade ore and lots of charcoal and was found mainly in the Pyrenees at the outset of the nineteenth century. The more sophisticated *forge comtoise*—so named for its prevalence in the province of Franche-Comté in eastern France—involved a two-step process in which ore was first smelted in a *haut-fourneau* (blast furnace) to yield *fonte* (pig iron) which was then refined into *fer* (wrought iron) in a *feu d'affinerie* (refining furnace). It produced good results even with poor quality iron and was more widely distributed.

4. The English started using partially combusted coal (coke) in the smelting of iron ore in the early 1700s, and after Cort's invention of puddling and rolling technology in the 1760s, they also used coal to refine pig iron into wrought iron. The fully evolved "English metallurgy" thus used what the French called the *forge à l'anglaise* in a three- or four-step process that started with the smelting of iron ore with coke, followed by the refining of the resulting pig iron in direct contact with coke in a "fining forge" or *mazérie* to produce *fonte mazée*, which could then be cast into various forms or further refined into wrought iron through puddling and rolling. Puddling meant reheating the pig iron in a reverbatory furnace fueled by coal to remove excess carbon and other impurities. A rolling mill *(laminoir)* subsequently squeezed out the slag and shaped the iron into bars, rails, and sheets. Because a larger quantity of iron could be produced for a given input of fuel and labor with the English forge, the new metallurgy enjoyed a competitive advantage over the old metallurgy. It was of course also more capital intensive: Setting up a *forge à l'anglaise* cost 500,000 to 700,000 francs at the outset of the nineteenth century.

5. Denis Woronoff, *L'Industrie sidérurique en France pendant la Revolution et l'Empire* (Paris, 1984), 315–368.

6. Gille and others believe that, because the twenty-five year head start that the British iron industry gained during the years of the Revolution and Empire gave it such a competitive advantage over the infant French industry, the latter would never have survived in an open market. See Bertrand Gille, *La Sidérurgie française au XIXe siècle* (Geneva, 1968), 46.

7. See Serge Benoit, "Croissance de la sidérurgie et essor de la construction métallique urbaine au siècle dernier: Le Cas de Châtillon-Commentry," in Frédéric Seitz, ed., *Architecture et métal en France, 19e–20e siècles* (Paris, 1994), 99–129.

8. Gille, *Sidérurgie,* 189.

9. Ibid., 45–78.

10. René Sedillot, *La Maison Wendel de 1704 à nos jours* (Paris, 1958), 128.

11. Gille, *Sidérurgie,* 52.

12. Ibid., 189.

13. The best sources on the early years of Le Creusot are by Agnès d'Angio: "La Création et les débuts de la société Schneider Frères et Cie, 1836–1945, ou l'expérience de la gérance à deux," in Jacques Marseille, ed., *Créateurs et créations d'entreprises de la révolution industrielle à nos jours* (Paris, 2000), 613–647; and *Schneider et Cie et les travaux publics* (Paris, 1995), 41–47. See also two older works: Joseph-Antoine Roy, *Histoire de la famille Schneider et Le Creusot* (Paris, 1962); and J-B Silly [Bertrand Gille], "La Reprise du Creusot, 1836–1848," *Revue d'Histoire des Mines et de la Métallurgie,* vol. 1, no. 2 (1969): 233–278.

14. On the matter of ownership, see Angio, *Schneider et Cie,* 44.

15. On the early years of Decazeville, see Donald Reid, *The Miners of Decazeville* (Cambridge, Mass., 1985), 9–20; on Alais, see Robert R. Locke, *Les Fonderies et forges d'Alais à l'époque des premières chemins de fer, 1829–1874* (Paris, 1978).

16. According to André Thuillier (*Economie et société nivernaises au début du XIXe siècle* [Paris, 1974]), the purpose of Martin's enterprise was "to furnish to the forge the machines and castings that it needed and to utilize the surplus pig iron produced by the company's blast furnaces" (294). Among the things it made for the general market were wagon wheels, iron bedsteads, cylinders for rolling mills, bridge pilings, and even roof supports for Chartres Cathedral (Paris, Exposition des produits de l'industrie française en 1839, Rapport du jury central, vol. 1, 354–406).

17. For the whole story of Fourchambault, see Guy Thuillier, *Georges Dufaud et les débuts du grand capitalisme dans la métallurgie en Nivernais au XIXe siècle* (Paris, 1959).

18. Gille, *Sidérurgie,* 47.

19. Ibid., 155.

20. Marius Dargaud, "Les Structures sociales, économiques, et financières des

sociétés métallurgiques de Commentry," *Actes du Congrès des sociétés savantes,* 1961, 385–420.

21. Benoit.

22. See Gille, *Recherches sur la formation de la grande entreprise capitaliste* (Paris, 1959), 98–99, 113; and Jean Lenoble, *Les Frères Talabot* (Limoges, 1989), 79ff. On the founders of Denain, see Frédéric Barbier, ed., *Le Patronat du Nord sous le Second Empire* (Geneva, 1989), 215–220, 355–358, 361–365. On Montataire, see the Martellière dossier in Archives Nationales (hereafter cited as AN) F¹²5203.

23. Pierre Cayez, *Metiers jacquards et hauts fourneaux: Aux origines de l'industrie lyonnaise* (Lyon, 1978), 237.

24. Gille, *Sidérurgie,* 158.

25. Cayez, 332–336.

26. L-J Gras, *Histoire économique de la métallurgie de la Loire* (Saint-Etienne, 1908), 1–68.

27. Ibid., 224; AN F¹²5169.

28. Julien Turgan, *Les Grands Usines,* 20 vols. (Paris, 1860–1895), vol. 4 (1865), 193.

29. "Rapport du mission" (December 1908) in Crédit Lyonnais, Etudes financières, DEEF 21068 (653–656); Gras, 203–240. On the casting for the *Eylau,* see the 1855 report in AN 65AQ K135.

30. Emile Martin and his son worked together on this new process at a plant at Sireuil (Charentes), which Emile purchased in 1858 after leaving Fourchambault. Pierre Martin took out a series of patents on the new process in 1864–1865 and then formed a new company, Société des Aciers Martin, to commercialize the process. See André Thuillier, *Economie et société nivernaises,* 291–321.

31. Although praised in Turgan's *Grands usines* (vol. 3 [1863], 257–272), the Saint-Seurin plant did not thrive, and Jackson soon transferred his Bessemer equipment to Imphy, acquired from Commentry-Fourchambault in 1862 at a time when that firm's president, Stephane Mony, was de-emphasizing metallurgy in favor of marketing coal. The Imphy enterprise failed in 1869, however, and soon ended up back in Mony's hands (by then Mony had seen the necessity for Commentry-Fourchambault to move into steel). See Guy Thuillier, *Georges Dufaud,* 105.

32. François Caron sees the railroad companies as instrumental in the adoption of the new steelmaking technology in the 1860s. He points out that, initially, fully 83 percent of the new steel went into rails ("French Railroad Investment, 1850–1914," in Rondo Cameron, ed., *Essays in French Economic History* [Homewood, Ill., 1970], 330).

33. The Wendels set up two Bessemer converters at Hayange in the 1860s, Le Creusot installed Siemens-Martin hearths in 1867 and two Bessemer converters in 1870, Denain-Anzin added both Bessemer and Siemens-Martin production in 1872, and Châtillon-Commentry set up a Bessemer converter at a new plant at Beaucaire (Bouches-du-Rhône) in 1873.

34. Gille, *Sidérurgie,* 233–279 (quotation from page 261).

35. On Mokta-el-Hadid, see David Prochaska, *Making Algeria French: French Colonialism in Bône, 1870–1920* (Cambridge, 1990), 62–94. For the broader developments, see Pierre Cayez, *Crises et croissance de l'industrie lyonnaise, 1850–1890* (Lyon, 1980), 195–202; and Gille, *Sidérurgie,* 233–279.

36. Comité des Forges de France, *La Sidérurgie française, 1864–1914* (Paris, n.d.), 147.

37. Gille, *Sidérurgie,* 164, 189.

38. Locke, 92–93. Terrenoire did set up Martin steel production at Alais in 1875, but this turned out to be one of many disastrous moves that led to the failure of Terrenoire by 1887.

39. Reid, 9–23, 49–71.

40. Philippe Jobert et al., *Les Patrons du Second Empire,* vol. 2, *Bourgogne* (Paris, 1991), 57–62, 69–72.

41. Ibid., 138–144.

42. Jean-Luc Mayaud et al., *Les Patrons du Second Empire,* vol. 3, *Franche-Comté* (Paris, 1991), 89–94, 130–136, 143–148 (quotation from page 143).

43. Mayaud, 76–78; M. A. Calame et al., *Regards sur la société contemporaine: Trois Familles industrielles d'Alsace* (Strasbourg, 1989), 89–93.

44. Ibid., 152–158 (quotation from page 157).

45. Jean-François Belhoste, *Histoire des forges d'Allevard des origines à 1970* (Grenoble, 1982).

46. See Gille, "Les plus grandes sociétés métallurgiques en 1881," in *Sidrurgie,* 295. Gille lists the ten largest metallurgical firms in terms of capital in 1881 as Le Creusot, Fourchambault, Franche-Comté, Châtillon-Commentry, Marine, L'Horme, Denain-Anzin, Terrenoire, Alais, and Decazeville.

7. Hardware, Machinery, and Construction

1. Claude-Isabelle Brelot and Jean-Luc Mayaud, *L'Industrie en sabots: La Taillanderie de Nans-sous-Sainte-Anne (Doubs)* (Paris, 1982).

2. Julien Turgan, *Les grands usines,* 20 vols. (Paris, 1860–1895), vol. 12 (1881), 1–90.

3. Ibid., vol. 17 (1882), fascicule 328.

4. Henri Junger, *Dictionnaire biographique des grands négociants et industriels* (Paris, 1902), 29.

5. See Charles Sabel and Jonathan Zeitlin, "Historical Alternatives to Mass Production," *Past and Present* (August 1985), 133–176; and Michael Piore and Charles Sabel, *The Second Industrial Divide* (New York, 1984).

6. Emile Levasseur, *Questions ouvrières et industrielles en France sous la Troisième République* (Paris, 1907), 52.

7. L-J Gras, *Histoire de l'armurerie stéphanoise* (Saint-Étienne, 1905), 240–255. According to Paul Passama (*L'Integration du travail: Formes nouvelles de la concentration industrielle* [Paris, 1910], 38), the Manufacture Français

d'Armes employed 3,000 and had 15 million francs in sales in 1908, mostly catalogue sales to hunters.

8. Michael Hanagan, *The Logic of Solidarity* (Champaign-Urbana, Ill. 1980), 196; L-J Gras, *Essai sur l'histoire de la quincaillerie et la petite métallurgie à Saint-Etienne* (Saint-Etienne, 1904), 115, 143–144, 152.

9. See Pierre Lamard, *De la Forge à la société holding: Veillard-Migeon et Cie, 1796–1996* (Paris, 1996).

10. On the development of Swiss watchmaking and the role of the Japys in it, see David S. Landes, *Revolution in Time: Clocks and the Making of the Modern World* (Cambridge, Mass., 1983), 260–263.

11. This and what follows is based primarily on Pierre Lamard, *Histoire d'un capital familiale au XIXe siècle: Le Capital Japy, 1777–1910* (Belfort, 1988).

12. Ibid., 282.

13. This and what follows comes mainly from René Sédillot, *Peugeot, de la crinoline à la 404* (Paris, 1960).

14. Paris, Exposition des produits de l'industrie française en 1839, Rapport du jury central, vol. 1, pt. 2 (Paris, 1839), 233–279.

15. Ibid., vol. 2, 34. On the development of the textile machinery industry of Alsace and the role of the British in it, see Michel Hau, *L'Industrialisation de l'Alsace, 1803–1939* (Strasbourg, 1987), 98–101; and W. O. Henderson, *Britain and Industrial Europe, 1750–1870,* 3rd ed. (Leicester, 1972), 28–29. As David Pinkney points out in *The Decisive Years in France, 1840–47* (Princeton, N.J., 1985), 29, the manufacture of textile machinery had become part of metallurgical manufacturing by the 1840s, as iron replaced wood as the main raw material for these machines (a 200-spindle spinning machine required six tons of iron, while a mechanical loom used 2,600 pounds of iron).

16. Jacques Payen, *Capital et machine à vapeur au XVIIIe siècle: Les Frères Périer et l'introduction en France de la machine à vapeur de Watt* (Paris, 1969), 99–166.

17. James M. Edmonson, *From Mécanicien to Ingénieur: Technical Education and the Machine Building Industry in Nineteenth Century France* (New York, 1987), 102.

18. Ibid., 102–129.

19. François Bouchayer, *Les Pionniers de la houille blanche et de l'électricité* (Paris, 1954), 17–50.

20. Serge Benoit, Genevieve Dufresne, and Gerard Emptoz, "Une Production de pointe dans une entreprise innovante: Les Turbines Fontaine au temps des fondateurs de la Maison de Chartres, 1837–1873," in Bruno Belhoste et al., *Le Moteur hydraulique en France au XIXe siècle* (Paris, 1990), 151–317.

21. Brenier developed high-pressure turbines to power the new paper mills being founded near Grenoble in the 1860s (see Chapter 9). He was succeeded by his son-in-law André Neyret and Neyret's partner Charles Beylier. They later merged with Piccart-Pictet of Geneva to form Neyrpic, which remained the leading French turbine manufacturer through much of the twentieth century,

becoming a division of the electrical giant Alsthom in the 1960s. See Bouchayer, 33–42; and Henri Morsel and Jean-François Parent, *Les Industries de la région grenobloise* (Grenoble, 1991), 157, 166, 171–173.

22. Turgan, vol. 2 (1863), 1–64; Emmanuel Chadeau, *L'Economie du risque: Les Entrepreneurs, 1850–1980* (Paris, 1988), 23–32; Frédéric Barbier et al., *Le Patronat du Nord sous le Second Empire* (Geneva, 1989), 104–110.

23. Jacques Payen, "La Position de la France dans l'industrie européenne des machines à vapeur durant la seconde moitié du XIXe siècle," *History and Technology* 1 (1984): 198.

24. Turgan, vol. 2 (1863).

25. Edmonson, 166.

26. Arthur Louis Dunham, *The Industrial Revolution in France, 1815–1848* (New York, 1955), 251–252.

27. Paris, Exposition Universelle International de 1900, Rapport du Jury International, Groupe IV, classes 19 and 20.

28. Edmonson, 428ff.

29. François Caron, "French Railroad Investment, 1850–1914," in Rondo Cameron, ed., *Essays in French Economic History* (Homewood, Ill., 1970), 315–340.

30. François Crouzet, "Essor, declin, et renaissance de l'industrie française des locomotives, 1838–1914," *Revue d'Histoire Economique et Sociale* 55, nos. 1–2 (1977): 112–210; and Jacques Payen, *La Machine locomotive en France des origines au milieu de XIXe siècle* (Paris, 1988).

31. Dunham, 440; Henderson, 62.

32. Production figures are from Crouzet, 202; on Cail in 1863, see Turgan, vol. 2 (1863), 1–64.

33. On the early history of Graffenstaden, see Hau, 102–103; and Paul Leuilliot, *L'Alsace au début du XIXe siècle, 1815–1830*, vol. 2 (Paris, 1960), 332–333.

34. See Anne Burnel, "La Société de construction des Batignolles des origines à 1939," *Culture Technique* 26 (1992): 65–71.

35. François Crouzet, "When the Railroads Were Built: A French Engineering Firm During the 'Great Depression' and After," in Sheila Marriner, ed., *Business and Businessmen: Studies in Business, Economic, and Accounting History* (Liverpool, 1978), 105–139; and Joseph Dubois, "L'Usine de Fives-Lille et la construction ferroviaire française au XIXe siècle," *Revue du Nord* (April–June 1985): 517–526.

36. Crouzet, "Essor, declin, et renaissance."

37. Michel Laferrère, *Lyon, ville industrielle* (Lyon, 1960), 271ff.; Pierre Cayez, *Métiers jacquard et hauts fourneaux: Aux origines de l'industrie lyonnaise* (Lyon, 1978), 315–317.

38. Guy Richard, "De la sidérurgie à la métallurgie de transformation: L'Entreprise de Dietrich de Niederbronn de 1685 à 1939," *Actes du 88e Congrès national des sociétés savantes*, 1963, 508–525; Hau, 101–103, 376–378.

39. Caron, *Histoire de l'exploitation d'un grand réseau: La Compagnie du Chemin de Fer du Nord, 1846–1937* (Paris, 1973), 299–300.
40. Caron, "French Railroad Investment," 335–338; Burnel.
41. Crouzet, "When the Railroads Were Built."
42. See Agnes d'Angio, *Schneider et Cie et les travaux public, 1895–1949* (Paris, 1995), 41–66.
43. According to Barjot, "at the international level, a form of division of labor was taking shape, sharing the spoils between the British and the French; to the former, the world at large—to the latter, Europe; to the former, the railways—to the latter, the bridges and tunnels." ("An Opportunity Seized Early: French Entrepreneurs in the Export Market for Major Public Works, 1857–1914," in Wolfram Fischer, ed., *The Emergence of the World Economy*, vol. 2 [Wiesbaden, 1986], 489). Among Barjot's other works, see especially *Travaux publics de France: Un Siècle d'entrepreneurs et d'entreprises, 1883–1992* (Paris, 1993), 15–68.
44. Henri Loyrette, *Gustave Eiffel* (New York, 1984), based on the Eiffel papers at the Musée d'Orsay and the Archives Nationales.
45. Yet another area of metallurgical construction that emerged in the nineteenth century was the building of iron-hulled steamships. This was largely independent of the established French shipbuilding industry that centered on wood sailcraft, and it was undertaken initially at shipyards owned by the new steam navigation companies (La Ciotat of Messageries Maritimes, Penhoët of the Compagnie Générale Transatlantique). However, by the end of the nineteenth century, this industry supported a number of large, ostensibly independent joint-stock companies, including the Forges et Chantiers de la Méditerranée, the Ateliers et Chantiers de la Loire, and the Chantiers et Ateliers de Saint-Nazaire (the CGT's Penhoët shipyard spun off as a separate company).

8. The Capitalism of Chemicals

1. Lavoisier and his followers introduced modern chemical nomenclature in the 1780s, but the chemical industry was slow to adopt it (along with much of the rest of the emerging science of chemistry). Consequently, terms such as "oil of vitriol" and "aqua fortis" (hydrochloric acid) continued in usage for some time. The chemistry behind the manufacture of even useful products was often only dimly understood. In many cases, it was not until the end of the nineteenth century that the underlying chemical reactions were identified and portrayed in standard chemical notation. For clarity's sake, however, this account will use modern chemical names throughout, even though that may be technically anachronistic.
2. John Graham Smith, *The Origins and Early Development of the Heavy Chemical Industry in France* (Oxford, 1979), 1–191.
3. Ibid.
4. See Ibid., 192–306. Also, on Malétra, J-P Chaline, *Les Bourgeois de Rouen*

(Paris, 1982), 118–119; and on Kestner, Marc Drouot, André Rohmer, and Nicolas Stoskopf, *La Fabrique de produits chimiques, Thann et Mulhouse* (Strasbourg, 1991).

5. Jean-Pierre Daviet, *Un Destin international: La Compagnie de Saint-Gobain de 1830 à 1939* (Paris, 1988), 1–210; and Daviet, *Une Multinationale à la française: Saint-Gobain, 1665–1989* (Paris, 1989), 84–134.

6. Michel Laferrère, *Lyon, ville industrielle* (Paris, 1960), 475–485; and Laferrère, "La Rôle de la chimie dans l'industrialisation de Lyon au XIXe siècle," in Pierre Léon et al., *L'Industrialisation en Europe au XIXe siècle* (Paris, 1972), 393–400.

7. Jean-Etienne Léger, *Une Grande entreprise dans la chimie française: Kuhlmann, 1825–1982* (Paris, 1988), 15–38; André Thépot, "Frédéric Kuhlmann, industriel et notable du Nord, 1803–1881," *Revue du Nord* (April–June 1985), 527–546; Paul Baud, *L'Industrie chimique en France* (Paris, 1932), 260–262; and L. F. Haber, *The Chemical Industry in the Nineteenth Century* (Oxford, 1958), 110.

8. In 1869, the Salindres plant processed 2,000 tons of bauxite to produce two tons of aluminum. Twenty years later, in the last year of the Sainte-Claire Deville process, it produced only three tons.

9. C-J Gignoux, *Histoire d'une entreprise française: Pechiney* (Paris, 1955), 9–40.

10. Fred Aftalion, *A History of the International Chemical Industry* (Philadelphia, 1991), 57–58.

11. Paris, Exposition Universelle Internationale de 1900, Rapports du Jury International, Groupe XIV, classe 87 (hereafter cited as 1900 Exposition, Chemical Industry), pt. 1, 13–23.

12. Baud, 267.

13. Daviet, *Une Multinationale*, 141–148; *Un Destin international*, 285–295, 321–340.

14. 1900 Exposition, Chemical Industry, pt. 1, 40.

15. Gignoux, 41–90.

16. On Coignet, see Association Française pour l'Avancement des Sciences, *Lyon, 1906–1926* (Lyon, 1926), 456–457; Laferrère, "Le Rôle de la chimie"; and Pierre Cayez, *Metiers jacquard et hauts-fourneaux: Aux origines de l'industrie lyonnaise* (Lyon, 1978), 340. On the match monopoly, Bonnie Gordon, *Phossy Jaw and the French Match Workers* (New York, 1989), 25–28. On the other firms, see 1900 Exposition, Chemical Industry, pt. 1, 23–53, 330–331, 397.

17. 1900 Exposition, Chemical Industry, pt. 2, 16.

18. Aftalion, 76; Cayez, 340.

19. Marcel Peyrenet, *Le Dynastie des Gillet* (Paris, 1978); 1900 Exposition, Chemical Industry, pt. 2, 12–30.

20. Anthony Travis, *The Rainbow Makers: The Origins of the Synthetic Dyestuff Industry in Western Europe* (Bethlehem, Pa., 1993), 31–66.

21. In addition to Travis, the best sources on aniline red and the rise and fall

of La Fuchsine include Jean Bouvier, *Le Crédit Lyonnais, 1863 à 1882*, vol. 2 (Paris, 1960), 374–381; Pierre Cayez, *Crise et croissance de l'industrie lyonnaise, 1850–1890* (Paris, 1980), 226–231; and Henk Van Den Belt, "Why Monopoly Failed: The Rise and Fall of Société La Fuchsine," *British Journal of the History of Science* 25 (1992): 45–63.

22. In this, the Meissonnier firm was not alone. In Le Havre, Oeschger et Cie, founded in 1846, continued to make logwood dyes such as *hématene,* an extract of campeche wood, at the end of the century. Another Le Havre firm, Ernest Dubosc et Cie, pioneered the exploitation of the quebracho tree from South America as a source of tannins while also developing a black dye from campeche wood *(chrysohématene)* for the silk industry. See 1900 Exposition, Chemical Industry, pt. 2, 12–30.

23. Claude Ferry, *Les Blanchisseries et teintureries de Thaon, 1872–1914* (Nancy, 1991), 35.

24. Haber, 109.

25. Archives Nationales (hereafter AN) 65AQ P297; Julien Turgan, *Les Grands Usines*, 20 vols. (Paris, 1860–1895), vol. 9 (1870), 281–320; Charles Mallet, *Dictionnaire encyclopédique des notabilités contemporains* (Paris, 1894), 8–10; 1900 Exposition, Chemical Industry, pt. 2, 18–26.

26. Pierre Cayez, *Rhône-Poulenc, 1895–1975* (Paris, 1988), 12–26; 1900 Exposition, Chemical Industry, pt. 2, 26–29.

27. R. Koehler, "Industrie photographique," in Association Française pour l'Avant des Sciences, *Lyon en 1906* (Lyon, 1906), 371–383.

28. Erik Bergengren, *Alfred Nobel: The Man and His Work* (Edinburgh, 1962), 51–70; Jean-Marie Moine, *Les Barons de fer* (Nancy, 1989), 68–69.

29. See Armand Galliot, "75 Ans d'activité d'un holding: La Société Centrale de Dynamite, 1887–1962," in AN 65AQ P312[1].

30. Bergengren, 85ff.

31. Jean-Yves Mollier, *Le Scandale de Panama* (Paris, 1991), 368.

32. Galliot.

33. Lenard R. Berlanstein, *Big Business and Industrial Conflict in Nineteenth Century France: A Social History of the Paris Gas Company* (Berkeley, 1991), 131–190.

9. The Capitalism of Glass, Paper, and Print

1. According to T. J. Markovitch ("L'Industrie française de 1789 à 1914," *Cahiers de l'INSEA*, AF6 [June 1966]), France's production of glass rose tenfold in the nineteenth century, from 42,800 tons per year in 1803–1812 to 441,200 tons per year in 1905–1913.

2. The Nord's share of total French glass output rose from 12 percent to 25 percent between 1820 and 1860. By the latter date, it accounted for fully 80 percent of the window glass and 30 percent of the plate glass produced in France. The Loire accounted for 10–13 percent of French glass production by the 1860s, while the next largest departments in glass—the Aisne, Meurthe, and Rhône—accounted for less than 5 percent each. See J-B

Daviet, "De la Première à la seconde industrialisation: Les Maîtres de verreries du département du Nord au XIXe siècle," *Revue du Nord* (April–June 1985), 461–483.

3. Of Daviet's many publications on Saint-Gobain, the most important is the published version of his doctoral thesis: *Un Destin international: La Compagnie de Saint-Gobain de 1830 à 1939* (Paris, 1988). This provided the basis for an overall history of the firm, *Une Multinational à la française* (Paris, 1989). The discussion that follows is based mainly on the latter.

4. Daviet, *Une Multinational*, 72.

5. Ibid., 78.

6. Archives Nationales (hereafter cited as AN) 65 AQ S257; Daviet, *Un Destin international*, 282, 302.

7. Daviet, *Un Destin international*, 318–319.

8. Julien Turgan, *Les Grands Usines*, 20 vols. (Paris, 1880–1895), vol. 3 (1863), 273–320.

9. See Françoise Birck, "Entre le patronage et l'organisation industrielle: Les Cristalleries de Baccarat dans le dernier quart du XIXe siècle," *Genèses* 2 (December 1990): 29–55.

10. Joan W. Scott, *The Glassworkers of Carmaux* (Cambridge, Mass., 1985), 74–77.

11. See Scott for a discussion of the labor unrest at Carmaux that followed the reorganization of production in the 1880s.

12. See Martine Capelle and Pierre Labasse, *Le Feu d'action: Histoire des Verreries Souchon-Neuvesel* (Paris, 1994).

13. Michael Hanagan, *The Logic of Solidarity: Artisans and Industrial Workers in Three French Towns, 1871–1914* (Champaign-Urbana, Ill., 1980), 96; and the Crédit Lyonnais report of 1906, in Henri Morsel, ed., *Rhône-Alpes, terre d'industrie à la Belle Epoque* (Paris, 1998), 127–137.

14. Pierre Cayez, "Structure et stratégie de groupe: Le Cas de la société Souchon-Neuvesel, 1900–1940," in *Entreprises et entrepreneurs, XIX–XXe siècles* (Paris, 1980), 132–148; and Capelle and Labasse, 1–38.

15. Jean Merley et al., *Histoire d'une entreprise forezienne: La Verrerie BSN de Veauche* (Saint-Etienne, 1983) (quotation "entirely emancipated" on page 55).

16. Merley; and Capelle and Labasse.

17. Louis André, *Machines à papier: Innovation et transformations de l'industrie papetière en France, 1798–1860* (Paris, 1996), 34–35, 117–118.

18. French paper production increased by a factor of 33 or 46, depending on which figures one uses. Markovitch estimates that France's average annual paper production rose from 14,000 tons in 1802–1814 to 650,000 tons in 1905–1912 (Table de Base XVIII–XIX). Jacques Boudet, ed., *Le Monde des affaires en France* (Paris, 1952), 204, estimates that it rose from 20,000 tons in 1800 to 700,000 tons in 1913, while André indicates that production rose from 18,000 tons in 1810 to 600,000 in 1908.

19. Markovitch's figures suggest that cardboard and packaging accounted for 50 percent of the total tonnage of French paper production by the 1900s, versus only 15 percent at the outset of the nineteenth century.

20. André, 55–80. See also Charles Coulton Gillispie, *Science and Polity in France at the End of the Old Regime* (Princeton, N.J., 1980), 444–459; *The Montgolfier Brothers and the Invention of Aviation, 1783–84* (Princeton, N.J., 1983), 7–10; and Leonard N. Rosenband, *Papermaking in Eighteenth Century France: Management, Labor, and Revolution at the Montgolfier Mill, 1761–1805* (Baltimore, 2000), 8–21.

21. André, 81–114.

22. See André for the definitive account of the development of the French paper industry, 1800–1860.

23. Turgan, vol. 1, 145–208. On the earlier history of Essonnes, see André, 168–216.

24. For the history of the Montgolfier enterprise in the nineteenth century see (in addition to André) Léon Rostaing, *La Famille de Montgolfier, ses alliances, ses descendants* (Lyon, 1910).

25. On the rag trade and the growing scarcity of rags circa 1860, see Turgan, vol. 1, 157.

26. Boudet, 197–204; Frédéric Barbier, "L'Introduction des techniques," in Roger Chartier and Henri-Jean Martin, eds., *Histoire de l'édition française,* vol. 3 (Paris, 1990), 53–56; Richard D. Hills, *Papermaking in Britain, 1488–1988* (London, 1988), 119–176.

27. Barbier, 55–56.

28. Alain Plessis, *Regents et gouverneurs de la Banque de France sous le Second Empire* (Geneva, 1985), 130–135.

29. See Paris, Exposition Universelle Internationale de, 1900, Rapports du Jury International, groupe XIV, classe 88 (hereafter 1900 Exposition, Paper), 31; Raoul Blanchard, "L'Industrie de la papeterie dans le Sud-est de la France," *Revue de Géographie Alpine* 14 (1926): 168.

30. Henri Coston, *Dictionnaire des dynasties bourgeoises et du monde des affaires* (Paris, 1975), 167–170.

31. Jean-Marie Borgis, *Moulin-Vieux: Histoire d'une papeterie dauphinoise, 1869–1989* (Grenoble, 1991), 13–24; Henri Morsel and Jean-François Parent, *Les Industries de la région grenobloise* (Grenoble, 1991), 75–88.

32. Borgis, 1–24; François Bouchayer, *Les Pionniers de la houille blanche et de l'électricité* (Paris, 1954), 1–50.

33. Blanchard, 182. The figures come from 1900 Exposition, Paper, 91; and Morsel and Parent, 96. See also Bouchayer, 20–32.

34. 1900 Exposition, Paper, 88.

35. André, 412.

36. According to jury reports at the 1900 World's Fair (1900 Exposition, Paper, 67–108), there were still 395 paper mills in operation in France in 1900, compared to 700 at the beginning of the century.

37. Barbier, 123. The newspaper circulation estimates come from Claude Bellanger et al., *Histoire générale de la presse française,* 3 vols. (Paris, 1969), vol. 2, 18; and from Michael B. Palmer, *Des Petits Journaux aux grandes agences: Naissance du journalisme moderne* (Paris, 1983), 328. Markovitch estimates that the amount of paper consumed by the press and book publishers rose from 2,000 tons a year in 1815–1824 to over 200,000 tons a year in 1905–1913 (Markovitch, Tables de Base, XVIII–XIX).

38. On the technological evolution of printing, see Barbier, 51–66; Bellanger, vol. 2, 13–28, and vol. 4, 61–132; and James Moran, *Printing Presses: History and Development from the Fifteenth Century to Modern Times* (Berkeley, 1973), 107, 140, 193, 199.

39. Frédéric Barbier, *Patronat du Nord sous le Second Empire* (Geneva, 1989), 145–53; and in Chartier and Martin, vol. 3, 67–91; Coston, 165–166.

40. *Dictionnaire de biographie francaise* (hereafter cited as DBF), vol. 5, 1520–1521. The dates in the title notwithstanding, Frédéric Barbier's *Trois Cents Ans de librairie et d'imprimerie: Berger-Levrault, 1676–1976* (Paris, 1981) ends in 1830.

41. Boudet, 438; Chartier and Martin, vol. 3, 85–86; Jean-Yves Mollier, *L'Argent et les lettres: Histoire du capitalisme d'édition, 1880–1920* (Paris, 1988), 51–80.

42. Carla Hesse, "Economic Upheavals in Publishing," in Robert Darnton and Daniel Roche, eds., *Revolution in Print: The Press in France, 1775–1800* (Berkeley, 1989), 69–97.

43. DBF, vol. 13, 1; Mollier, 81–102; Albert George, *The Didot Family and the Progress of Printing* (Syracuse, 1961).

44. Mollier, 127.

45. Turgan, vol. 4 (1865), 289.

46. DBF, vol. 8, 183; Chartier and Martin, vol. 3, 573.

47. The story of Paul Dupont et Cie is told in detail in Mollier, 121–150 (quotation—"deplorable"—on page 148).

48. For this and the following paragraphs, see Jean Mistler, *La Librairie Hachette de 1826 à nos jours* (Paris, 1964). Also DBF, vol. 14, 466–474; Boudet, 684–688; Chartier and Martin, vol. 3, 202–207; and Mollier, 171–198. The best source on Hachette is now Jean-Yves Mollier, *Louis Hachette* (Paris, 2000).

49. This information and the rest that follows on the French newspapers is drawn from Bellanger, vols. 2 and 3; as well as from Boudet, 420–435; and Palmer. For comic relief, see also the irreverent (and inaccurate) discussion of "press magnates" in Theodore Zeldin, *France, 1848–1945: Taste and Corruption* (Oxford, 1980), 178–192.

50. In addition to the works cited above, see Francine Amaury, *Histoire du plus grand quotidien de la IIIe République: Le Petit Parisien, 1876–1944,* 2 vols. (Paris, 1972); and Micheline Dupuy, *Un Homme, un journal: Jean Dupuy, 1844–1919* (Paris, 1959).

10. Industrial Capitalism and Consumer Goods

1. See, for example, Susan Strasser, *Satisfaction Guaranteed: The Making of the American Mass Market* (New York, 1989).
2. Computed from figures in T. J. Markovitch, "L'Industrie française de 1789 à 1914," *Cahiers de l'INSEA* AF6 (June 1966).
3. Louis Bergeron, "Une Nouvelle forme de capitalisme: Le Négoce et l'industrie des grands produits de consommation en France au XIXe siècle," in Paul Bairoch, ed., *Passages des économies traditionnelles aux sociétés industrielles* (Geneva, 1985), 195–210.
4. This system was developed in the United States by Oliver Evans in the late eighteenth century. The British engineer Henry Maudsley was instrumental in bringing it to continental Europe in the first half of the nineteenth century, so in France it was sometimes called the "Anglo-American" system. See the description of it as it was applied at the Saint-Maur mill in 1860 in Julien Turgan, *Les Grands Usines,* 20 vols. (Paris, 1860–1895), vol. 1 (1860), 49–64. See also Marcel Arpin, *Historique de la meunerie et de la boulangerie depuis les temps préhistoriques à l'année 1914,* vol. 1 (Paris, 1948), 198–202.
5. For a detailed description of the Corbeil plant, see Maurice Daumas, *L'Archéologie industrielle en France* (Paris, 1980), 224–228.
6. With the 150 tons milled daily at Le Havre, the total daily output of the Grands Moulins de Corbeil was 500 tons (Paris, Exposition Universelle International de 1900, Rapport du Jury International [hereafter 1900 Exposition], Groupe X, classe 56).
7. Louis Bergeron, "Permanence et renouvellement du patronat," in Yves Leguin, ed., *Histoire des Français, XIX–XXe siècles* (Paris, 1983), vol. 2, 242; and "Une Nouvelle forme de capitalisme."
8. 1900 Exposition, Groupe X, classe 56, 173. On the Lyon pasta industry see Pierre Cayez, *Crises et croissance de l'industrie lyonnaise* (Lyon, 1980), 314; and Silvano Serventi and François Sabban, *Pasta: The Story of a Universal Food* (New York, 2002), 176–184.
9. Jacques Boudet, ed., *Le Monde des affaires en France* (Paris, 1952), 239.
10. The machinery introduced by Huntley and Palmers in the 1840s included steam-powered mixing machines, reciprocal and cylindrical cutters, and a system of rails to move the dough and finished biscuits within the plant. See T.A.B. Corley, *Quaker Enterprise in Biscuits: Huntley and Palmers of Reading, 1822–1972* (London, 1972), 45–55.
11. For a selection of this promotional art, see Georges Herscher, *L'Art et les biscuits: La Publicité de la firme Lefevre-Utile de 1897 à 1914* (Paris, 1978).
12. Jean-Louis Kerouantan, *LU, une usine à Nantes* (Nantes, 1989). Although as late as 1914 Huntley and Palmers had still not adopted the new automated equipment that the American manufacturers and Lefevre-Utile were using by 1900, it remained four times the size of LU, with almost 5,000 employees and an annual output of over 24,000 tons (Corley, 304, 309).

13. Figures presented by Markovitch (Table de Base XXI) indicate that yearly per capita consumption of bread in France rose from 221 kilograms in 1815–1824 to 294 kilograms in 1885–1894 and then began a steady decline that has continued to the present.

14. By contrast, per capita consumption of sugar in Great Britain, already 7 kilograms per year in the 1820s, rose to 40 kilograms by 1899. Other large consumers of sugar were the Americans (30 kilograms per head per year in the 1890s), the Swiss (as high as 25 kilograms per head in 1889), and the Danes (22 kilograms per head in 1892). See Jules Hélot, *Le Sucre de betterave en France de 1800 à 1900* (Cambrai, 1900), 211.

15. These figures are from Jacques Fierain, *Les Raffineries de sucre des ports en France, XIXe-début du XXe siècles* (New York, 1977), 116–118, 197–205.

16. There were some 500 such *fabriques* in France in the late 1830s, around 350 in the 1890s. Some 37 of these were *usines centrales* that processed beet juice piped in from a number of crushing mills *(râperies)* in the surrounding area (Hélot, 175, 208). Among the largest was at Villenoy-les-Meaux in the Seine-et-Marne, which employed 500–600 workers in high season (mid-October to mid-January) to process juice from fourteen *râperies* brought in through 114 kilometers of pipelines. Philippe Bernard, *Economie et sociologie de la Seine-et-Marne, 1850–1950* (Paris, 1953), 111.

17. Overall refining costs fell from 40 francs per 100 kilograms of refined sugar in 1800 to 10 francs per 100 kilograms in 1860. On the technological changes and their economic impact, see Fierain, 18–38; and Dale Tomich, *Slavery in the Circuit of Sugar: Martinique and the World Economy, 1830–1848* (Baltimore, 1990), 191–204.

18. Unless otherwise noted, the discussion of the sugar industry of Nantes—and that of Marseille following—is based on Fierain.

19. Archives Nationales (hereafter cited as AN) F¹²5159.

20. Fierain, 245.

21. The average yearly production of beet sugar in France rose from 102,260 tons in 1856–1860 to 189,300 tons in 1866–1870 and 300,000 tons by the late 1870s.

22. On this important venture, see Samir Saul, *La France et l'Egypte de 1882 à 1914* (Paris, 1997), 375–476.

23. Crédit Lyonnais, Etudes financières, DEEF 24006; Joseph Valynseele, *Les Say et leurs alliances* (Paris, 1971), 208, 347; Fierain, 125.

24. Fierain, 191. There is no history of the Lebaudy firm, but some information can be gleaned from Bertrand Gille, *Recherches sur la formation de la grande entreprise capitaliste* (Paris, 1959), 123; and Henri Coston, *Dictionnaire des dynasties bourgeoises et du monde des affaires* (Paris, 1975), 343–345.

25. Coston, 537–539.

26. See Louis Bergeron, "Permanence et renouvellement du patronat"; and the entry on Crespel-Dellisse in Frédéric Barbier, *Le Patronat du Nord sous le Second Empire* (Geneva, 1989), 129–134.

27. Barbier, 85–88; Coston, 50–52.
28. Even more than sugar, chocolate and confectionery was a growth industry in the nineteenth century. While the consumption of sugar was rising twentyfold in France in this period, the consumption of cocoa, chocolate, and confectionery rose thirty-eight–fold, according to Markovitch's estimates.
29. Turgan, vol. 14 (1882) and vol. 13 (1880).
30. This information and what follows is drawn mainly from Bernard Marrey, *Un Capitalisme idéel* (Paris, 1984).
31. See J. Othick, "The Cocoa and Chocolate Industry in the Nineteenth Century," in Derek Oddy and Derek Miller, eds., *The Making of the Modern British Diet* (London, 1976), 77–90; and Turgan, vol. 7 (1867), 97–128.
32. On the development of Noisiel as an industrial site and as a company town, see Daumas, 302; and John S. Gardner, "Noisiel-sur-Marne and the *ville industrielle* in France," in Gardner, ed., *The Company Town: Architecture and Society in the Early Industrial Age* (New York, 1992), 43–74.
33. Markovitch, Table de Base XV (Corps gras).
34. Paul Masson et al., *Les Bouches du Rhône: Encyclopédie départementale,* vol. 8, *Le Mouvement économique: L'Industrie* (Marseille, 1926), 446–463.
35. 1900 Exposition, groupe 14, classe 87, 363; Masson.
36. Masson.
37. Identified on the basis of the jury reports for the 1900 Exposition and Masson.
38. By the 1890s, Jules Charles-Roux sat in the Chamber of Deputies for the Bouches-du-Rhône, was president of the Compagnie Générale Transatlantique and vice president of the Compagnie Universelle de Suez, and served on the boards of the Banque de France and myriad other companies. Jean Jolly et al., *Dictionnaire des parlementaires français* (Paris, 1960–), vol. 8, 2922.
39. 1900 Exposition, groupe 14, classe 87, 337–337, 356–370; Masson, 258; Turgan, vol. 2, 65–128.
40. 1900 Exposition, groupe 14, classe 87, 368–369; on Maurel et Prom, see Boudet, 489; and Louis Desgraves and Georges Dupeux, *Bordeaux au XIXe siècle* (Bordeaux, 1969), 390.
41. Masson, 412–432.
42. Masson, 432–446; Louis Pierrein, *Industries traditionnelles du port de Marseille: Le Cycle des sucres et des oléagineux, 1870–1958* (Marseille, 1975), 217.
43. Pierrein, 219–221.
44. Masson, 432–446; Pierrein, 221. With the financial help of various Marseille banks, the CSCOA was relaunched in 1887 as the Compagnie Française de l'Afrique Occidentale (CFAO) under the direction of Verminck's son-in-law, Frédéric Bohn. The CFAO soon became one of the most successful firms operating in French West Africa but remained a trading company that avoided forward integration into processing and manufacture,

in contrast to Verminck and Maurel et Prom of Bordeaux. See Hubert Bonin, *CFAO, cent ans de competition* (Paris, 1987).

45. AN 65 AQ R545 (Société des Etablissements Verminck).

46. Pierrein, 220.

47. Masson, 460; Pierrein; 1900 Exposition, groupe 14, classe 87, 360–62.

48. Whitney Walton, *France at the Crystal Palace: Bourgeois Taste and Artisan Manufacture in the Nineteenth Century* (Berkeley, 1992); Leora Auslander, "The Creation of Value and the Production of Good Taste: The Social Life of Furniture in Paris, 1860–1914," Ph.D. diss., Brown University, 1988; revised version published as *Taste and Power: Furnishing Modern France* (Berkeley, 1996).

49. François Faraut, *Histoire de la Belle Jardinière* (Paris, 1987).

50. Faraut, 68–99.

51. Turgan, vol. 13 (1880).

52. Henri Junger, *Dictionnaire biographique des grands négociants et industriels* (Paris, 1902); Paul Passama, *L'Integration du travail: Formes nouvelles de concentration industrielle* (Paris, 1910), 100.

53. Alfred Aftalion, *Le Developpement de la fabrique et le travail à domicile dans les industries de l'habillement* (Lille, 1906), 78.

54. François Bassieux, *L'Industrie de la chaussure en France* (Paris, 1908), 23. Because the French army demanded that its boots be hand sewn, Godillot only used sewing machines for foreign orders. There was a similar mixture of hand and machine production at Chaussures F. Pinet, which in the 1870s employed 700–800 workers at its Rue de Paradis plant in Paris to make women's shoes. See Turgan, vol. 13 (1880).

55. See Ross Thomson, *The Path to Mechanized Shoe Production in the United States* (Chapel Hill, 1989).

56. Aftalion, 51.

57. Aftalion (57) described the Pressoir et Premartin plant without naming it. The name comes from Lenard Berlanstein, *The Working People of Paris, 1871–1914* (Baltimore, 1984), 219, n.52. On the Monteux factory, see John M. Merriman, *The Red City: Limoges and the French Nineteenth Century* (New York, 1985), 169, 215, 222.

58. Henri Morsel and Jean-François Parent, *Les Industries de la région grenobloise* (Grenoble, 1991), 25.

59. Morsel and Parent, 31–32.

60. 1900 Exposition, groupe XIV, 177.

61. Turgan, vol. 1 (1860), 273–232. See also Walton, 154; and especially Marc de Ferrière le Vayer, "Christofle: A Family Firm," in Y. Cassis et al., eds., *Management and Business in Britain and France: The Age of the Corporate Economy* (Oxford, 1995), 74–87.

62. See particularly Henri Clouzot and Charles Follot, *Histoire du papier peint en France* (Paris, 1935).

63. Markovitch, Table de Base IX.

64. This and what follows depend heavily on Camille Grellier, *L'Industrie de la porcelaine en Limousin: Ses Origines, son évolution* (Paris, 1908).

65. Jean d'Albis, "Histoire de la fabrique Haviland de 1842 à 1925," *Bulletin de la Société archéologique et historique du Limousin* 96 (1969): 193–225.
66. Merriman, 81.
67. Grellier, 257.
68. Albis, 215–221.

11. The New World of Industrial Capitalism

1. Michel Hau found that, with few exceptions, the industrial firms launched in the Bas-Rhin in 1801 required only 10,000 to 50,000 francs. See Hau, *L'Industrialisation de l'Alsace, 1800–1939* (Strasbourg, 1987), 328.
2. Serge Chassagne, *Le Coton et ses patrons: France, 1760–1840* (Paris, 1991), 456–478. See also Hau, 327–331.
3. Jacques Fierain, *Les Raffineries de sucre des ports en France* (New York, 1977), 36–37; Louis André, *Machines à paper: Innovation et transformations de l'industrie papetière en France, 1798–1860* (Paris, 1996), 178; Pierre Léon, in Fernand Braudel and Ernest Labrousse, eds., *Histoire économique et sociale de la France,* vol. 3, pt. 2 (Paris, 1976), 520.
4. Braudel and Labrousse, vol. 3, pt. 1, 365.
5. Figures on capitalization of a large sample of firms are found in Chassagne and Hau (cotton), André (paper), and Fierain (sugar). On the metallurgical firms, see the studies by Bertrand Gille collected in *La Sidérurgie française au XIXe siècle* (Geneva, 1968).
6. According to Adeline Daumard et al., *Les Fortunes françaises au XIXe siècle* (Paris, 1973), table 2, 194, only one in twenty of the small number of people leaving estates in 1820 left ones worth 100,000 francs or more.
7. Claude Fohlen, *Une Affaire de famille au XIXe siècle: Les Mequillet-Noblot* (Paris, 1955). Alain Plessis has pointed out that even the Mequillet-Noblot enterprise was not entirely self-financed but depended on bank credit to maintain its working capital in periods of slack sales. See Alain Plessis, "Le Financement des entreprises," in M. Lévy-Leboyer, ed., *Histoire de la France industrielle* (Paris, 1996), 136.
8. Patrick Verley, *Entreprises et entrepreneurs du XVIIIe siècle au début du XXe siècle* (Paris, 1994), 78.
9. See Charles E. Freedeman, *Joint-Stock Enterprise in France, 1807–1867* (Chapel Hill, 1979); and also the discussions in Plessis, Hau, and André.
10. See the studies of the Saglios and Renouard de Bussière in M. A. Calame et al., *Regards sur la société contemporaine: Trois familles industrielles d'Alsace* (Strasbourg, 1989). See also Pierre Cayez, *Métiers jacquard et hauts fourneaux: Aux Origines de l'industrie lyonnaise* (Lyon, 1977), 252–263; Plessis, 146; and Louis Bergeron, *Les Rothschild et les autres* (Paris, 1991).
11. Plessis, 143–144.
12. See Yannick Lemarchand, "The Dark Side of the Result: Self-Financing and Accounting Choices Within Nineteenth Century French Industry," in Yannick Lemarchand and R. H. Parker, eds., *Accounting in France/La Comptabilité en France* (New York, 1996), 127–149.

13. André, 187–188; J-B Daviet, *Un Destin international: Saint-Gobain de 1830 à 1939* (Paris, 1988), 120–121; Laurent Batsch, "Le 'Décollage' de Schneider, 1837–1875: Stratégie industrielle et politique financière," *Entreprises et Histoire* 18 (June 1998): 23–56.

14. Batsch, 37.

15. Gille, 211–279.

16. Paulin Talabot of Denain-Anzin and Eugène Schneider of Le Creusot took part in the founding of the Société Générale, while every member of the initial board of directors of the Crédit Lyonnais was also on the board of a major iron or steel company, including the bank's president, Henri Germain (Châtillon-Commentry), Alexandre Jullien (Terrenoire), Henry Darcy (Hauts-Fourneaux de Marseille), and Alfred Deseilligny (Le Creusot). See Gille, 186–188.

17. Several French industrial managers wrote treatises that helped to spread the techniques of cost accounting to a larger professional audience, notably Pierre-Antoine Godard-Desmarest, the long-time head of Baccarat (1822–1839), who published his *Traité générale et sommaire de la comptabilité commerciale* in 1827; and C-A Guilbault, one-time executive at the Vierzon metalworks and *chef de comptabilité* at the Forges et Chantiers de la Méditerranée, who published a widely consulted two-volume text on industrial accounting and administration in 1865.

   On the development of French accounting literature, see Trevor Boyns et al., *The Birth of Industrial Accounting in France and Britain* (New York, 1997), 83–95.

18. Marc Nikitin, "Setting Up an Industrial Accounting System at Saint-Gobain, 1820–1880," *Accounting Historians Journal* 17, no. 2 (1990): 73–93, reprinted in Lemarchand and Parker, 198–213; "The Birth of Industrial Accounting in France: The Role of Pierre-Antoine Godard-Desmarest (1767–1850) as Strategist, Industrialist, and Accountant at the Baccarat Crystal Works," *Accounting, Business, and Financial History* 6, no. 1 (1996), 93–100; Nikitin, "Comptabilité et analyse financière à Decazeville dans les années 1830," *Entreprises et Histoire* 13 (December 1996): 53–66.

19. Boyns, 175–205.

20. See P. L. Cottrell, *Industrial Finance, 1830–1914: The Finance and Organisation of English Manufacturing Industry* (London, 1980); and Michael Collins, *Banks and Industrial Finance in Britain, 1800–1939* (London, 1991).

21. According to François Caron (*An Economic History of Modern France* [New York, 1979], 165–166), "plants employing more than 500 people accounted for 86 and 80 percent, respectively, of the labor force in mining and metallurgy" by 1900. Caron's analysis was based on the 1906 industrial census that classified workers by *établissement*, not by firm. An *établissement* is a single center of operations, such as a mine, mill, or warehouse. Many firms were made up of several *établissements,* so his figures do not

strictly speak to firm size. This is a common problem for historians working from the French census figures.

According to industry census data, there were 3,200 firms with 50 to 500 employees and 133 with more than 500 in France in the 1840s, and by 1896 there were over 8,000 *établissements* with 50–500 employees and 472 with more than 500, of which 13 employed more than 5,000 (France, Direction du travail, *Résultats statistiques du recensement des industries et professions du 29 mars 1896,* vol. 4 [Paris, 1901], 198ff.).

22. At Anzin, the turnover averaged 15 percent a year, 1898–1913, but could go as high 33 percent in a given year (Odette Hardy-Hémery, *De la Croissance à la desindustrialisation: Un Siècle dans le Valenciennois* [Paris, 1984], 31). Similar rates were experienced at Carmaux, which had the additional problem of strong seasonal fluctuations as peasant-miners left the pits to plant and harvest crops. See Rolande Trempé, *Les Mineurs de Carmaux, 1848–1914,* vol. 1 (Toulouse, 1971), 147–149.

23. Such recruitment schemes were at best stopgaps. Carmaux continued to find the great majority of its workers within a twenty-five-kilometer radius. Trempé, vol. 1, 156–169.

24. According to Michelle Perrot, there were probably 15,000 English workers in France by the 1820s. See Michelle Perrot, "The Three Ages of Industrial Discipline in Nineteenth Century France," in John M. Merriman, ed., *Consciousness and Class Experience in Nineteenth Century Europe* (New York, 1979), 159.

25. Hau, 320–322.

26. Chantal George, "L'Economie sociale au Creusot: Patronage ou paternalisme?" in *Les Schneider, Le Creusot* (Paris, 1995), 318–331. More generally, see Peter N. Stearns, *Paths to Authority: The Middle Class and the Industrial Labor Force in France, 1820–1848* (Urbana, Ill., 1978).

27. Michel Hau has calculated that 29 percent of the employees of the Dollfus-Mieg Company in Alsace were *qualifié* in 1848 (482 of 1,655), but only 18.8 percent (438 of 2,324) were skilled in 1898. See *L'Industrialisation de l'Alsace,* 314.

28. Stearns, 91.

29. Maurice Lévy-Leboyer, "Hierarchical Structure, Rewards, and Incentives in a Large Corporation: The Early Managerial Experience of Saint-Gobain, 1872–1912," in Norbert Horn and Jurgen Kocka, eds., *Law and the Formation of the Big Enterprises in the Nineteenth and Early Twentieth Centuries* (Göttingen, 1979), 451–480.

30. Donald Reid, "Industrial Paternalism: Discourse and Practice in Nineteenth Century French Mining and Metallurgy," *Comparative Studies in Society and History* 27 (1985): 579ff.; George.

31. René Sedillot, *La Maison Wendel de 1704 à nos jours* (Paris, 1958), 190–197. Yves Lequin, *Les Ouvriers de la région lyonnaise, 1848–1914,* 2 vols. (Lyon, 1977), vol. 2, 113–114.

32. Trempé, vol. 1, 262.

33. Hardy-Hémery, 38–46.

34. Claude Ferry, *Les Blanchisseries et teintureries de Thaon, 1872–1914* (Nancy, 1991), 150ff.

35. Lequin, vol. 2, 114–115.

36. In addition to the previously cited articles by Perrot, Reid, and George, see Gérard Noiriel, "Du 'Patronage' au 'paternalisme': La Restructuration des formes de domination de la main-oeuvre ouvrière dans l'industrie métallurgique française," *Mouvement Social* 144 (July–September 1988): 17–36; and Gerald Friedman, "The Decline of Paternalism and the Making of the Employer Class: France, 1870–1914," in Sanford Jacoby, ed., *Masters to Managers* (New York, 1991), 153–172.

37. See Perrot.

38. Pierre Laroque, *Les Rapports entre patrons et ouvriers* (Paris, 1938), 34–100.

39. The collection of these rules in the Bibliothèque Nationale has been catalogued by Anne Biroleau and Alain Cottereau, *Les Reglements d'ateliers, 1798–1936* (Paris, 1984).

40. Chassagne, 489–492.

41. Reproduced in Joseph-Antoine Roy, *Histoire de la famille Schneider et du Creusot* (Paris, 1962), 100–103.

42. Alfred D. Chandler, Jr., *The Visible Hand: The Managerial Revolution in American Business* (Cambridge, Mass., 1977), 67–72.

43. Patrice Bourdelais, "Des Représentations aux réalitiés: Les Contremaîtres du Creusot, 1850–1900," in Yves Lequin et al., *L'Usine et le bureau* (Lyon, 1990), 151–166.

44. For the overall evolution of strike activity in France, see Edward Shorter and Charles Tilly, *Strikes in France, 1830–1968* (Cambridge, 1974); and especially Michelle Perrot, *Les Ouvriers en grève: France, 1871–1890*, 2 vols. (Paris, 1974).

45. Sanford Elwitt, *The Making of the Third Republic: Class and Politics in France, 1868–1884* (Baton Rouge, 1975); David M. Gordon, *Merchants and Capitalists: Industrialization and Provincial Politics in Mid-Nineteenth Century France* (Tuscaloosa, 1985).

46. Judith E. Vichniac, *The Management of Labor: The British and French Iron and Steel Industries, 1860–1918* (Greenwich, Conn., 1990), 102–109.

47. The Union des Compagnies Houillères was a spin-off of another patronal association, the Comité des Houillères du Nord et du Pas-de-Calais. In 1891, the government forced the Comité to sign the Convention of Arras, an historic collective bargaining agreement with the miners' union, by threatening to withdraw the troops guarding the mines during a strike. Thereupon, the Comité dissolved so as not to be forced into serving as a permanent collective bargaining agent for the coal companies. See Marcel Gillet, *Les Charbonnages du nord de la France au XIXe siècle* (Paris, 1973), 163–169.

48. There are several standard accounts of French tariff politics in the early nineteenth century, including Shepard Bancroft Clough, *France: A History of National Economics, 1789–1939* (New York, 1939); and Frank A.

Haight, *A History of French Commercial Policies* (New York, 1941). Both of these drew on the older work by Auguste Arnauné, *Le Commerce extérieur et les tarifs de douane* (Paris, 1911).

49. See Roger Priouret, *Origines du patronat français* (Paris, 1963), 57–90; and Bertrand Gille, *Recherches sur la formation de la grande entreprise capitaliste* (Paris, 1959), 129–162.

50. Arthur Louis Dunham, *The Anglo-French Treaty of Commerce of 1860 and the Progress of the Industrial Revolution in France* (Ann Arbor, 1930).

51. Michael S. Smith, "Free Trade versus Protection in the Early Third Republic: Economic Interests, Tariff Policy, and the Making of the Republican Synthesis," *French Historical Studies* 10, no. 2 (Fall 1977): 293–314.

52. Michael Stephen Smith, *Tariff Reform in France: The Politics of Economic Interest, 1860–1900* (Ithaca, N.Y., 1980); and Eugene O. Golob, *The Méline Tariff* (New York, 1944).

53. Smith, *Tariff Reform*, 204–229.

54. The railroad executives sought an across-the-board increase in imports to increase traffic on their lines but also favored freer importation of specific products—coal, iron rails, and railroad equipment—to lower their operating costs and to end their dependence on national producers of these necessary supplies (Smith, *Tariff Reform*, 32–33).

55. The basic documentation on the Freycinet Plan and the Conventions of 1883 is found in Alfred Picard, *Les Chemins de fer français*, 6 vols. (Paris, 1884). See also Veron Duverger, *Le Régime des chemins de fer français devant le parlement, 1871–1887* (Paris, 1887); Richard von Kaufmann, *La Politique française en matière de chemins de fer* (Paris, 1900); Réné Thevenez, *Législation des chemins de fer et des tramways* (Paris, 1909); and Kimon Doukas, *The French State and the Railroads* (New York, 1945). The best short account of the complex railroad politics of this period is found in François Caron, *Histoire des chemins de fer en France,* vol. 1 (Paris, 1997), 419–536.

56. See the letters in Archives Nationales (hereafter cited as AN) F^{12} 4835.

57. Chambre de Commerce de Paris, *Avis exprimés pendant les années 1881 et 1882* (Paris, 1882), 28–41.

58. François Caron, *Histoire de l'exploitation d'un grand réseau: La Compagnie du chemin de fer du Nord, 1846–1937* (Paris, 1973), 266–268.

59. Journal Officiel, Documents Parlementaires, Chambre des Députés, session of July 30, 1883, 278–281.

60. Caron, *Histoire de l'exploitation d'un grand réseau,* 367.

61. See note 59.

62. For the evolution of French jurisprudence in this area, see François Caron, "Ententes and stratégies d'achat dans la France du XIXe siècle," *Revue : Française de Gestion* (September–October 1988): 127–133; and Charles E. Freedeman, "Cartels and the Law in France before 1914," *French Historical Studies* 15, no. 2 (Spring 1988): 462–478.

The last great antitrust prosecution was of the calcium carbide cartel in

1915; the acquittal in this case ushered in the heyday of French cartelization in the 1920s. See Robert O. Paxton, "The Calcium Carbide Case and the Decriminalization of Industrial Ententes in France, 1915–1926," in Patrick Fridenson, ed., *The French Home Front, 1914–1918* (Providence, 1992), 153–180.

63. J-B Daviet, *Un Destin international: Saint-Gobain de 1830 à 1939* (Paris, 1988), 341–359; and "Trade Associations and Agreements and Controlled Competition in France, 1830–1930," in H. Yamazaki and M. Miyamoto, eds., *Trade Associations in Business History* (Tokyo, 1988), 269–295.

64. Bertrand Gille, "Esquisse d'une histoire du syndicalisme patronal dans l'industrie sidérurgique française," *Revue d'Histoire de la Sidérurgie* 5, no. 3 (July–September 1964): 209–250.

65. Robert Pinot, "L'Organisation syndicale de la sidérurgie française," in Comité des Forges de France, *La Sidérurgie française, 1864–1914* (Paris, n.d.), 439–470.

66. Charles E. Freedeman, *The Triumph of Corporate Capitalism in France, 1867–1914* (Rochester, 1993), 116.

67. Ibid., 119. On the Comptoir de Longwy and its imitators, see also P. Obrin, *Le Comptoir métallurgique de Longwy* (Paris, 1908); and Jean-Marie Moine, *Les Barons de fer: Les Maîtres de forge en Lorraine* (Nancy, 1989), 193–200. The best discussion in English of *ententes* and cartels in French iron and steel is Michael J. Rust, "Business and Politics in the Third Republic: The Comité des Forges and the French Steel Industry, 1896–1914," Ph.D. diss., Princeton University, 1973.

68. Gillet, 220–302.

69. Alfred Aftalion, "Les Kartells dans la région du nord de la France: Les Kartells à formes simples dans les filatures de coton et de lin, 1899–1907," *Revue Economique International* 4, no. 1 (January 1908): 107–165.

III. The Second Industrial Revolution and the Beginnings of Managerial Capitalism, 1880s–1930

1. See Chandler's contributions to *Big Business and the Wealth of Nations,* edited by Alfred D. Chandler, Jr., Franco Amatori, and Takashi Hikino (Cambridge, 1997).

2. On the last point see Leslie Hannah, "Marshall's 'Trees' and Global 'Forests': Were 'Giant Redwoods' Different?" in Naomi Lamoreaux, Daniel M. G. Raff, and Peter Temin, eds., *Learning by Doing in Markets, Firms, and Countries* (Chicago, 1999), 253–294. For a selection of criticisms of the Chandler paradigm, plus citations of other critiques—and critiques of the critiques—see the Colloquium on *Scale and Scope* in the *Business History Review* 64, no. 4 (Winter 1990): 690–758; and the special issue of the *Business History Review* on Chandler (vol. 71, no. 2 [Summer 1997]). See also the various works of Philip Scranton, especially *Endless Novelty: Specialty Production and American Industrialization, 1865–1925* (Princeton,

N.J., 1997); and a special issue of *Business History* on the family firm (vol. 35 [October 1993]).
3. Maurice Lévy-Leboyer, ed., *Histoire de la France industrielle* (Paris, 1997).
4. Youssef Cassis, *Big Business: The European Experience in the Twentieth Century* (Oxford, 1997), 242–244, 252–254. Inexplicably, Cassis did not include on his lists France's largest firms in terms of assets and probably in terms of employees—the railroads—which were old companies but did fit the Chandlerian paradigm.
5. These thirty-seven firms all qualified as big businesses by German (if not American) standards. With assets of 300 million francs or more in 1930, each would have ranked among the top sixty-five manufacturing firms in Germany in 1930, according to the figures in *Scale and Scope*, 705–713.

12. Big Steel

1. See John P. McKay, *Pioneers for Profit* (Chicago, 1971).
2. According to Bertrand Gille, the top ten metallurgical firms in France accounted for 52 percent of total output in 1869, versus 13 percent in 1845 (Gille, *La Sidérurgie française au XIXe siècle* [Geneva, 1968], 191).
3. On the complex train of events that led to the creation of the first Thomas steel mills in France, see Claude Beaud, "Schneider, de Wendel, et les brevets Thomas: Le Tournant technique de la sidérurgie française, 1879–1880," *Cahiers d'Histoire* 20 (1975): 363–378; and Jean-Marie Moine, *Les Barons de fer* (Nancy, 1989), 56–60.
4. The Meurthe-et-Moselle's share of French pig iron production went from 21 percent in 1875 to 69 percent in 1912, and its share of steel production went from less than one-half of 1 percent in 1875 to almost 50 percent in 1912, when the department accounted for nearly three-fourths of the Thomas steel made in France. Comité des Forges de France, *La sidérurgie française, 1864–1914* (Paris, n.d.) (hereafter cited as CFF), 167; *Annuaire statistique de la France* 1 (1878): 360–363.
5. Michael S. Smith, "Putting France in the Chandlerian Framework: France's 100 Largest Industrial Firms in 1913," *Business History Review* 72, no. 1 (Spring 1998): 57–58.
6. For example, the revenues of Marine Steel, one of the two or three largest metallurgical firms in France in both 1870 and 1913, went from 20 million francs in 1874 to 104 million in 1912–13. See the annual reports in Archives Nationales (hereafter cited as AN) 65 AQ K135.
7. Claude Prêcheur, *La Sidérurgie française* (Paris, 1963), 100. See also CCF, 257–259; and Paris, Exposition Universelle Internationale de 1900, Rapports du Jury International, Groupe XI, classe 64 [hereafter cited as Paris Exposition 1900], 33–36.
8. CFF, 254–256; Paris Exposition 1900, 37–38; *Les Assemblées Générales* (hereafter cited as AG), 1913, 1877, 1939.
9. CFF, 259–261; Raymond Poidevin, *Les Relations économiques et financières*

entre la France et l'Allemagne de 1898 à 1914 (Paris, 1969), 731–736; John F. Godfrey, *Capitalism at War: Industrial Policy and Bureaucracy in France, 1914–1918* (New York, 1987), 239–256; Prêcheur, 21.

10. According to Pierre Fritsch (*Les Wendel, rois de l'acier français* [Paris, 1976], 91ff.), the Thiers-Bismarck agreement putting the Wendels' holdings in Germany came in spite of direct appeals by Robert de Wendel and Theodore de Gargan to Bismarck in Berlin and by Robert de Wendel's wife to Thiers in Paris. Thiers apparently did not like the Wendels because of their loyalty to the Bourbon dynasty and their cooperation with Napoleon III. He also thought that the loss of Lorraine iron would be more than compensated for by the development of iron deposits in Normandy.

11. In 1869, the French departments of the Moselle and the Meurthe produced 410,430 tons of pig iron (30.4 percent of the French total) and 142,367 tons of iron (16 percent of the French total). In 1872, the part of those departments retained by France—combined in the new department of the Meurthe-et-Moselle—produced 224,202 tons of pig iron (18.4 percent of the French total) and only 8,058 tons of iron (less than 1 percent of the French total). CFF, 173–174.

12. Fritsch, 91–107; René Sedillot, *La Maison de Wendel de 1704 à nos jours* (Paris, 1958), 229–237.

13. Fritsch; Sedillot. The figures for production in 1913 come from the thesis of François Roth as cited by Jean-Noël Jeanneney, *François de Wendel en République* (Paris, 1976), 17.

14. Moine, 162; Jeanneney, 17; Claude Prêcheur, *La Lorraine Sidérurgique* (Paris, 1959), 257. It should be noted that, if the Wendels' three plants—Joeuf, Hayange, and Moyeuvre—are viewed as a single enterprise, which indeed they were in spite of their separation by an international frontier, the total iron and steel production of their firm outstripped that of any other French firm and exceeded the production of all but a few German firms.

15. See the Dreux dossier in AN F¹²8577. Another factor in the turnaround of Longwy, it should be noted, was the French government's decision to restrict temporary admission of foreign pig iron as of 1888, which particularly worked to the benefit of the pig iron producers of the Meurthe-et-Moselle. See Michael S. Smith, *Tariff Reform in France, 1860–1900* (Ithaca, N.Y., 1980), 218–219.

16. On the career of Alexandre Dreux, see Moine, 80–82 and passim. On the technical development of the Aciéries de Longwy, see Paris Exposition 1900, 17–18. For the production figures, see Prêcheur, *Lorraine*, 257.

17. Moine, 61–62, 66–67, 82.

18. Moine, 53–54, 69; Prêcheur, *Lorraine*, 257.

19. Moine, 436, n. 102.

20. Annual report in AG, 1913, 2355.

21. CFF, 206–209; Odette Hardy-Hémery, "Croissance et marché en sidérurgie: Les Avatars des Forges et Aciéries du Nord-Est, 1817–1948," in Patrick Fridenson and André Straus, eds., *Le Capitalisme français* (Paris, 1987), 119–133; Moine, 76.

22. L-J Gras, *Histoire économique de la métallurgie de la Loire* (Saint-Etienne, 1908), 318–324. On the politics of protection and Jullien's role in it, see Smith, *Tariff Reform*.

23. CFF, 192–208; Odette Hardy-Hémery, *De la croissance à la désindustrialisation: Un Siècle dans le Valenciennois* (Paris, 1984), 78.

24. Donald Reid, "Fayol, Experience to Theory," *Journal of Management History* 1, no. 3 (1995): 21–36; and *The Miners of Decazeville* (Cambridge, Mass., 1985), 121–122.

25. CFF, 274.

26. CFF, 273–275; AG, 1913, 707–712.

27. Gras, 283–382; CFF, 262; Paris Exposition 1900, 209–211; AN 65 AQ K381 (on Holtzer). On the Compagnie des Fonderies, Forges, et Aciéries de Saint-Etienne, see the book of that title by Daniel Colson (Saint-Etienne, 1998). On Firminy in France, see the 1906 Crédit Lyonnais report in Henri Morsel, ed., *Rhône-Alpes, terre d'industries à la Belle Epoque* (Paris, 1998), 91–125. On Firminy in Poland, see McKay, 340–349.

28. Although Le Creusot integrated forward into construction, the only major construction company to integrate backward into steelmaking was SFCM-Cail, which was building its own steel mill in the Nord and participating in Thyssen's Caen project on the eve of World War I.

29. This account of the early years of Marine Steel is based on the 1908 "Rapport de mission" in the Crédit Lyonnais Archives, Etudes Financières (hereafter cited as CL-EF) DEEF 21068, which is also the source of the quotation.

30. Ibid.

31. See the annual reports in AN 65 AQ K136$^{1-2}$, and Prêcheur, *Lorraine,* 257.

32. Paris Exposition, 1900 27–28, 42–44; Henri d'Ainval, *Deux siècles de sidérurgie française* (Grenoble, 1994), 183–203.

33. Claude Beaud believes that Henri Schneider made an historic mistake in taking only a minority interest in Joeuf, but it did at least give his company an assured source of cheap pig iron and crude steel for the specialized steel production later undertaken at Le Creusot. See Beaud, "Schneider, de Wendel, et les brevets Thomas."

34. On the development of Schneider et Cie, 1870–1914, see J-A Roy, *Histoire de la famille Schneider et Le Creusot* (Paris, 1962), 65–103; the various articles of Claude Beaud, including "La Stratégie de l'investissement dans la société Schneider et Cie, 1894–1914," in *Entreprises et Entrepreneurs, XIX– XXe siècles* (Paris, 1983), 118–131; the articles in *Les Schneider, Le Creusot: Une Famille, une entreprise, une ville* (Paris, 1995); and Paris Exposition 1900, 40–42, 148–150.

35. Agnes d'Angio, *Schneider et Cie et les travaux publics, 1895–1949* (Paris, 1995), 67–108.

36. For the convoluted story of the development of steel armor in this era, see Thomas J. Misa, *A Nation of Steel* (Baltimore, 1995), 95–131.

37. Claude Beaud, "Les Schneider, marchands de canons, 1870–1914," *Histoire, Economie, Société* 14 (1995): 107–131; Beaud, "De L'Expansion internationale à la multinationale: Schneider en Russie, 1896–1914," *Histoire,*

Economie, Société 4 (1985): 575–602; Beaud, "Investments and Profits of the Multinational Schneider Group, 1894–1943," in Alice Teichova et al., eds., *Multinational Enterprise in Historical Perspective* (Cambridge, Mass., 1987), 87–102.

38. Paris Exposition 1900, 185.
39. Ibid., 179–187.
40. Ibid., 179.
41. Carol Kent, "Camille Cavallier and Pont à Mousson: An Industrialist of the Third Republic," Ph.D. diss., Oxford University, 1972; Moine, 84–86.
42. Roger Martin in Maurice Lévy-Leboyer, ed., *Histoire de la France industrielle* (Paris, 1996), 330.
43. The production figures are from Prêcheur, *Lorraine*, 257; and Paris Exposition 1900, 179–181. In general, see *Pont à Mousson à cent ans* (Nancy, 1957); Kent; and Martin.
44. On the Société Française des Métaux, see the statutes and annual reports in AN 65 AQ K56[1]. On Rouart et Cie, see Paris Exposition 1900, 310–311, and Groupe V, classe 55, 100.
45. AN 65 AQ K284; Paris Exposition 1900, 312–318; Hardy-Hemery, *De la croissance,* 79; Catherine Omnès, "Structures capitalistes et stratégies de croissance: Vallourec et l'industrie de tube d'acier, 1880–1978," in *Entreprises et entrepreneurs XIX–XIXe siècles* (Paris, 1983), 164–183.
46. AN 65 AQ K217; Paris Exposition 1900, 311; Omnès.
47. Paris Exposition 1900, 312–314; Omnès; AG, 1913, 1505–1508.
48. Paris Exposition 1900, 24–25.
49. Paris Exposition 1900, Groupe XI, classe 65, 548; CFF, 262.
50. Paris Exposition 1900, Groupe XI, classe 65, 549.
51. Paris Exposition 1900 38; CFF, 261; AN 65 AQ K36; AG, 1913, 2177.
52. See Eric Bussière, "The Evaluation of Structures in the Iron and Steel Industry in France, Belgium, and Luxembourg: National and International Aspects, 1900–1939," in Etsuo Abe and Yoshitaka Suzuki, eds., *Changing Patterns of Industrial Rivalry* (Tokyo, 1990), 141–162.
53. Moine, 166–167.
54. The unpublished dissertation by Michael Rust ("Business and Politics in the Third Republic: The Comité des Forges and the French Steel Industry, 1896–1914," Ph.D.diss., Princeton University, 1973) remains the best source on this issue.
55. Arthur Fontaine, *French Industry during the War* (New Haven, 1926), 274; B. R. Mitchell, *European Historical Statistics 1750–1970* (New York, 1975), 400.
56. To compensate for the decline of domestic production, French steel imports rose from 257,000 tons in 1914 to 2.7 million tons in 1917 (Fontaine, 277). On the wartime procurement system and the role of the Comité des Forges, see Godfrey, especially 221–238.
57. Saint-Chamond produced 25,000 artillery shells per day until the new plants of Loucheur and Citroën went on line in 1916. Thereafter, it produced 200,000 new and refitted shell casings per day while also manufacturing

75mm cannons, 155mm howitzers, and tanks. See "Les Fabrications de guerre, 1914–1918," in AN 65 AQ K136.

58. The muckraking journal *Crapouillot,* drawing on a secret parliamentary inquiry into war profiteering in the 1920s, caused a sensation in 1933 by publishing figures on the wartime profits of the steel and munitions makers. Firminy, for example, was reported to have had profits of 17 million francs in 1917 (versus 2.9 million in 1915); Saut-du-Tarn 4.7 million (up from 745,000); and Tréfileries du Havre 9.12 million (up from 3.9 million). See Godfrey, 232–233.

59. Jacques Bariéty, *Relations franco-allemands après la première guerre mondiale* (Paris, 1977), 146.

60. Hardy-Hémery, *De la croissance,* 100–102. The quotation is on page 100.

61. Duncan Burn, *The Economic History of Steelmaking, 1867–1939* (Cambridge, 1961), 410.

62. Prêcheur, *Lorraine,* 213.

63. AG, December 15, 1930, 146–151.

64. According to Hardy-Hémery, Nord-Est made little effort to coordinate and integrate the production of these diverse properties, so the expanded company was more a conglomerate than a single unified steel company ("Croissance et marché en sidérurgie").

It should also be noted that, with the sale of Pont à Vendin and the closing of its Decazeville steelworks (worn out by full-scale wartime production), Commentry-Fourchambault-Decazeville got out of steelmaking and limited itself thereafter to coal production (AG, 1930, 281).

65. Catherine Omnès, *De l'atelier au groupe industriel: Vallourec, 1882–1978* (Paris/Villeneuve d'Ascq, 1981), 111–177.

66. Claude Beaud, "The Interests of the Union Européenne in Central Europe," in Alice Teichova and P. L. Cottrell, eds., *International Business and Central Europe, 1918–1939* (New York, 1983), 375–398; and Paul Harold Segal, *The French State and French Private Investment in Czechoslovakia, 1918–1938* (New York, 1987), 100–144.

67. See Prêcheur, *La Sidérurgie française,* 67ff.; Prêcheur, *Lorraine,* 208–228; and Bariéty, 145–146.

68. Bussière, 156–157.

69. On the intense negotiations and politicking relative to coal and iron flows between France and Germany, 1919–1923, see Bariéty; and M. Brélet, *La Crise de la métallurgie: La Politique économique et sociale du Comité des forges* (Paris, 1923), 104–113.

70. An additional factor in the success of French steel after 1924 was the devaluation of the franc and the stabilization of the German mark, which gave the French a distinct price advantage in foreign markets. As a result, French steel exports burgeoned to 3.8 million tons in 1925, making France the world's leading steel exporter. The continued strength of French exports, especially to Belgium and Great Britain, would be a key factor in the success of the industry in the late 1920s. See Charles Gide and William Oualid, *Le Bilan de la guerre pour la France* (Paris, 1931), 228.

71. Matthias Kipping, "Inter-Firm Relations and Industrial Policy: The French and German Steel Producers and Users in the 20th Century," *Business History* 38, no. 1 (January 1996): 1–25.

72. The reorganization of German steel after 1926 is nicely summarized in Alfred D. Chandler, Jr., *Scale and Scope: The Dynamics of Industrial Capitalism* (Cambridge, Mass., 1990), 550–558.

73. Kipping.

74. Prêcheur, *Lorraine,* 212–213.

75. See the commemorative volume, no author, *Théodore Laurent, 1865–1953: L'Industriel, l'homme* (Paris, 1955).

76. On the negotiations, see Charles S. Maier, *Recasting Bourgeois Europe* (Princeton, N.J., 1975), 516–541.

77. Report on Marine-Homécourt of November 1923, CL-EF, DEEF 50702.

78. For a critical assessment of Marine-Homécourt's activities in the interwar period, see Eric Bussière, "Stratégies industrielles et structures de management dans la sidérurgie française: Le Cas de Marine-Homécourt dans l'entre-deux-guerres," *Revue Historique* (July–September 1988), 27–52.

79. AG, December 15, 1930, 146–151.

80. Omnès, *De l'atelier au groupe industriel,* 129–147.

81. Mitchell, 395, 400.

82. The combined output of pig iron in France, Luxembourg, and the Saar in 1930 was 14.4 million tons (compared to 9.7 million tons in Germany), and combined steel output was 13.6 million tons (versus 12.5 million in Germany). Mitchell, 395–405.

83. When the effect of wartime and postwar devaluation of the franc is removed by converting asset values in 1913 and 1930 to U.S. dollars (five francs to the dollar in 1913, 25.5 francs to the dollar in 1930), the mean assets of the ten largest French iron and steel companies rose from $17.25 million in 1913 to $27.75 million in 1930.

13. The Electrical Industry

1. For example, France had only 2,000 kilometers of electric tramways in 1902 when there were already 3,400 kilometers of electric tramways in Germany, 3,600 in the United Kingdom, and 48,000 in the United States.

2. Although per capita consumption in the country as a whole still lagged behind consumption in other industrialized countries in the 1930s, Paris had drawn abreast of New York, London, and Berlin by then, and the consumption rates in the industrial regions of the North, Northeast, and Southeast were comparable to those in other industrial regions of Europe.

3. This overview draws on the critical but grudgingly optimistic assessment by Maurice Lévy-Leboyer in "Le système électrique en France, 1880–1940," *Revue Française de Gestion* (September–October 1988), 88–99.

   With François Caron, Henri Morsel, and Fabienne Cardot, Lévy-Leboyer directed a great collective effort in the 1980s to research and write the history of electricity and the electrical industry in modern France. Some of this research was presented in a series of colloquia sponsored by the Association pour l'Histoire de l'Electricité en France, but it mainly appeared in the massive *Histoire générale de l'électricité en France* published in Paris by Fayard in three large volumes (equal to ten 300-page volumes) between 1991 and 1996. The present chapter depends heavily on the first two volumes of this work, directed respectively by Caron and Cardot and Lévy-Leboyer and Morsel, hereafter cited as HGEF, I and HGEF, II. If no other source is cited for a particular passage, the reader can assume that it relied on this source.

4. For the story of electric traction in France, especially its financial aspects, the best source remains John P. McKay, *Tramways and Trolleys: The Rise of Urban Mass Transport in Europe* (Princeton, N.J., 1976), 125–162.

5. Of the thirty-five power plants in France rated at 2,000 horsepower or more in 1906, twenty-one were general-purpose plants that accounted for two-thirds of the country's power and light capacity. Fourteen plants served the traction industry. HGEF, I, 572.

6. These companies were the Société d'Eclairage et de Force par Electricité, the Compagnie Parisienne de l'Air Comprimé, the Société Continentale Edison, and three companies named for the sectors they controlled: Place Clichy, Champs-Elysées, and Rive Gauche.

7. HGEF, I, 562–566; Alain Beltran, "Stratégies et développement d'un secteur de banlieue: Nord-Lumière (Le Triphasé) de 1898 au début des années 20," in Fabienne Cardot, ed., *La France des électriciens, 1800–1980* (Paris, 1985), 93–110.

8. HGEF, I, 579–582, 608–610.

9. A fifth holding company that merits mention was Continental Edison, founded in 1882 to promote the Edison power and light system in France. In 1888, it won the concession to supply electricity in the north-central sector of Paris. After the creation of the CPDE in 1907, however, it survived mainly as a holding company for small local electric companies in western and central France.

10. Report of May 1903 on CGE, Crédit Lyonnais Archives, Etudes Financieres (hereafter cited as CL-EF), DEEF 23814.

11. Jacques Marseille et al., *Alcatel-Alsthom, Histoire de la Compagnie Générale d'Electricité* (Paris, 1991), 33–69.

12. Ibid.

13. HGEF, I, 640–646.

14. HGEF, I, 589–591; 652–655 (quotation appears on page 591).

15. Eric Bussière, *Paribas, Europe, and the World, 1872–1992* (Antwerp, 1992), 78.

16. See the discussion by Henri Morsel in HGEF, I, 637–640; and in the introduction to Henri Morsel, ed., *Rhône-Alpes, terre d'industries à la Belle Epoque, 1899–1914* (Paris, 1998), 227–238.

17. Florent Guillain was a civil engineer with the Ministry of Public Works who entered parliament as deputy for the Nord in 1893 and rose quickly, be-

coming colonial minister in 1898 and later vice president of the Chamber of Deputies. His combination of technical expertise and political prominence gave him entrée to corporate boardrooms. In addition to becoming chairman of CFTH in 1902, Guillain also became chairman of the steel giant Marine-Homécourt, a director of the P-L-M Railroad and the Suez Company, and a censor of the Banque de France. In the decade before World War I, he was one of the most influential industrialists in France, serving as president of both the Comité des Forges and the Union des Syndicats de l'Electricité. See *Dictionnaire de biographie française*, 20 vols. (Paris, 1933–2004) (hereafter cited as DBF), vol. 17, 125–126.

18. The discussion of the manufacturing activities of Thomson-Houston and other French electrical companies depends on the work of Pierre Lanthier, both his chapter in HGEF, I, 671–726; and his unpublished doctoral thesis, "Les Constructions électriques en France: Financement et stratégies de six groupes industriels internationaux de 1880 à 1940," Université de Paris-Nanterre, 1988.

19. Marseille, 62–92; Jules Rapp, "Aux Origines de la Compagnie Générale d'Electricité," *Bulletin d'Histoire de l'Electricité* (December 1985), 103ff.; CL-EF, DEEF 23814, 27130.

20. Michel Laferrère, *Lyon, ville industrielle* (Paris, 1960), 311ff.

21. Emmanuel Chadeau, *L'Economie du risque: Les Entrepreneurs, 1850–1980* (Paris, 1988), 250–264; and "Produire pour les électriciens: Les Tréfileries et Laminoirs du Havre de 1897 à 1930," in Fabienne Cardot, ed., *Des Entreprises pour produire de l'électricité* (Paris, 1988), 285–303.

22. *La Belle Histoire de la CEM* (Paris, 1950), in Archives Nationales (hereafter cited as AN) 65 AQ M118[1]; René Bidard, "La Compagnie Electro-Mécanique au cours du temps," in Cardot, *Des Entreprises pour produire,* 215–246.

23. *Les Assemblées Générales* (hereafter cited as AG) 1913, 1185; Lanthier in HGEF, I, 715–716; Guy Tournois, "Jeumont-Schneider: Qui es-tu? D'Où viens-tu?" in Cardot, *Des Entreprises pour produire,* 247–268.

24. Even though the French government established a National Coal Bureau in 1916 with the power to set price controls on coal, the price of domestically produced coal rose fourfold and the price of imported coal rose sixfold between 1914 and 1918.

25. The following overview of the electrical industry in the 1920s relies heavily on "Panorama de l'électrification, de la Grande Guerre à la nationalisation," in HGEF, II, 27–134.

26. While thermal production in France doubled from 1923 to 1930 and then leveled off, the production of hydroelectric power continued to increase, from 3,700 million kilowatt-hours in 1923 to 7,545 million in 1930 and to over 9,000 million in 1935, when hydroelectric output exceeded thermal output in France for the first time.

27. The dominant French firm in wireless and radio in the 1920s was the Compagnie Générale de Télégraphe Sans Fils, founded in 1919 with the backing of the Compagnie Française des Câbles Télégraphiques. The Compagnie

Sans Fils served as a holding company that organized France's activities in wireless telegraphy, radio manufacturing, and radio broadcasting (via Radio-France). However, compared to what the Americans, British, and Germans were doing, French activity in these areas remained modest until after World War II. See HGEF, II, 1078–1081; and Pascal Griset, *Entreprise, technologie, et souveraineté: Les Télécommunications transatlantiques de la France* (Paris, 1996).

28. AG, 1930, 503; HGEF, II, 1119–1121, 1135–1146.

29. HGEF, II, 700–715; Alain Beltran, "L'Energie électrique dans la région parisienne entre 1878 et 1946," Thèse du Doctorat d'état, Université de Paris-Sorbonne, 1995, 497–521. On Mercier and the Messine Group, see also Richard F. Kuisel, *Ernest Mercier, French Technocrat* (Berkeley, 1967), 8–21.

30. HGEF, II, 754–763.

31. CFTH eventually acquired an 80 percent share in Compagnie des Lampes and dominated the French lightbulb market with its Mazda brand. See P. Lemaigre-Voreaux, "L'Industrie de lampes électriques en France de 1881 à nos jours," in Monique Trédé, ed., *Electricité et électrification dans le monde* (Paris, 1990), 499–506.

32. Lanthier, "Les Constructions électriques en France," 668–682; Louis Carpentier, "L'Essor d'une entreprise de construction électrique et mécanique au XXe siècle: L'Alsthom," in Cardot, *Des Entreprises pour produire*, 269–274.

33. Marseille, 100–143.

34. Chadeau, "Produire pour les électriciens," 285–303.

35. Bidard, 215–246; *La Belle Histoire de la CEM*; HGEF, II, 1054–1056.

36. Marseille, 138.

14. The Automobile and Its Allies

1. The best account of the origins of the automobile industry is still found in Jean-Pierre Bardou et al., *The Automobile Revolution* (Chapel Hill, 1982), 1–24. See also James M. Laux, *The European Automobile Industry* (New York, 1992), 1–7.

2. James M. Laux, *In First Gear: The French Automobile Industry to 1914* (Montreal, 1976), 52–54; René Sedillot, *Peugeot, de la crinoline à la 404* (Paris, 1960), 73–93; Alain Jemain, *Les Peugeot: Vertiges et secrets d'une dynastie* (Paris, 1987), 18–36.

3. Laux, *In First Gear*, 14–20, 26–29.

4. According to Laux (*In First Gear*, 71–72), French automakers sold 7,200 cars abroad in 1903 compared to 6,900 at home.

5. Laux, *In First Gear*, 42–51, 139–41; Patrick Fridenson, *Histoire des usines Renault, 1898–1939* (Paris, 1972), 43–64.

6. Louis Hatry, *Louis Renault, patron absolu* (Paris, 1982).

7. Fridenson, 65–79.

8. Michel Laferrère, *Lyon, ville industrielle* (Paris, 1960), 361–399.

9. Laux, *In First Gear,* 103–107.
10. Ibid., 215.
11. On the reorganization of Peugeot, see Sedillot, 93–112; and Jemain, 37–44. On Mattern, see Yves Cohen, "Ernest Mattern chez Peugeot, 1906–1918, ou comment peut-on être taylorien," in Maurice Montmollin and Oliver Pastré, eds., *Le Taylorisme* (Paris, 1984), 115–126; and "Inventivité et compétitivité: L'Interchangeabilité des pièces face à la crise de la machine-outil en France autour de 1900," *Entreprises et Histoire* 5 (1994): 53–72. On Peugeot's production and revenues, see Laux, *In First Gear,* 215.
12. Compare the assets (millions of francs) and workforces of the following in 1910–1913 (figures drawn from Michael S. Smith, "Putting France in the Chandlerian Framework: France's 100 Largest Industrial Firms in 1913," *Business History Review* 72 (Spring 1998): 46–85; and Youssef Cassis, *Big Business: The European Experience in the Twentieth Century* (Oxford, 1997), 242–243:

	Assets	Workers
Saint-Gobain	136.0	11,540
Thomson-Houston	135.3	4,000
Marine-Homécourt	120.1	13,200
Schneider	110.0	15,000
Longwy	96.0	7,000
CGE	88.0	6,000
Renault	?	3,300
Peugeot	63.1	2,425
De Dion–Bouton	24.6	2,700

13. Bardou et al., 74.
14. See David A. Hounshell, *From the American System to Mass Production, 1800–1932* (Baltimore, 1984).
15. On the problems of introducing interchangeability and mass production into the French auto industry, see Cohen, "Inventitivité"; "Modernization of Production in the French Automobile Industry Between the Wars: A Photographic Essay," *Business History Review* 65 (1991): 754–780; and "Calibres, tolérances, hiérarchies et doigtés: L'Art de l'interchangeabilité dans l'automobile à l'exemple de Peugeot, 1910–1940," in Claudine Fontanon, ed., *Histoire de la mécanique appliquée* (Paris, 1998), 161–189.
16. Fridenson, 98–119.
17. On Berliet, see Laferrère, 378–380; on Peugeot, see Jemain, 45–52; and Sedillot, 113–120.
18. On the early career of André Citroën, see three works authored or co-authored by Sylvie Schweitzer: *Des Engrenages à la chaine: Les Usines Citroën, 1915–1935* (Lyon, 1982); with Fabien Sabates, *André Citroën, les chevrons de la gloire* (Paris, 1980); and a biography, *André Citroën* (Paris, 1992).

19. Fridenson, citing a report of the Ministry of Commerce, 119.

20. Laferrère, 380–386.

21. For a clear statement of the marketing perspective on the Ford–General Motors rivalry, see Thomas McCraw and Richard Tedlow, "Henry Ford, Alfred Sloan, and the Three Phases of Marketing," in Thomas K. McCraw et al., *Creating Modern Capitalism* (Cambridge, Mass., 1997), 266–300.

22. Schweitzer, *Des Engrenages,* 20–44. The quotation on Saint-Ouen is on page 32.

23. Between 1926 and 1930, Citroën built 50 percent more cars than Renault—380,000 versus 245,000—according to figures presented in Daniel Henri, "Comptes, mécomptes, et redressement d'une gestion industrielle: Les Automobiles Peugeot de 1919 à 1930," *Revue d'Histoire Moderne et Contemporaine* (January–March 1985), 35, 43. For Renault's strategies in the 1920s and for a comparative analysis of the performance of Renault and Citroën, see Fridenson, 157–191.

24. This account of Peugeot in the 1920s relies heavily on Henri.

25. These included Renault, Peugeot, Berliet, Panhard et Levassor, Delahaye, Unic, Chenard et Walcker, Delaunay-Belleville, and Rochet-Schneider. In addition, the British Darracq Company had spun off a French Darracq company in 1915, and the latter was still producing cars under the Talbot label in the 1930s. Delage automobiles were still being made in small numbers by Delahaye. However, Delahaye, Berliet, and Unic were mainly producing trucks and other heavy vehicles (like fire engines) by the 1930s.

26. Schweitzer and Sabates, 388.

27. See Pierre Couderc, *Dunlop-Montluçon, 75 ans d'histoire partagée* (Premilhat, 1996).

28. On Continental, see Daniel Bordet et al., *Pneu Continental: Le Temps des pionniers, 1890–1920* (Paris, 1996); on B. F. Goodrich, see Mansel G. Blackford and Austin Kerr, *BFGoodrich, Tradition and Transformation, 1870–1995* (Columbus, 1996), 105, 131–132, 225–226.

29. On Bergougnan and the early French tire industry, see Jacques Boudet, ed., *Le Monde des affaires en France* (Paris, 1952), 223–225.

30. The best sources on the early business history of Michelin are Alain Jemain, *Michelin, un siècle de secrets* (Paris, 1982); and the chapter by Lionel Dumond in André Gueslin et al., *Michelin, les hommes du pneu: Les Ouvriers Michelin à Clermont-Ferrand de 1889 à 1940* (Paris, 1993), 9–72.

31. See Olivier Darmon, *Le Grand Siècle de Bibendum* (Paris, 1997); and Stephen L. Harp, *Marketing Michelin: Advertising and Cultural Identity in Twentieth Century France* (Baltimore, 2001), 15–53.

32. In addition to Dumond and Jemain, see the materials in Archives Nationales (hereafter cited as AN) 65 AQ O 525.

33. Figures on assets and workforces in the 1930s are from Cassis, 253; and Bruce Kogut, "Evolution of the Large Firm in France in Comparative Perspective," *Entreprises et Histoire* 19 (October 1998): 143ff.

34. The authoritative study of the early French aviation industry is Emmanuel

Chadeau, *L'Industrie aéronautique en France, 1900–1950* (Paris, 1987). It is the principal source for this section.

35. By comparison, the United Kingdom produced 41,000–52,000 aircraft engines in 1914–1918, Germany 40,000, and the United States (in 1917–1918) 32,420. See James M. Laux, "Gnôme et Rhône, an Aviation Engine Firm in the First World War," in Patrick Fridenson, ed., *The French Home Front, 1914–1918* (Providence, 1992), 135–152.

36. On Potez and Bloch and the nationalization of the French airframe industry, see Chadeau, 224–270.

37. On the development of Gnôme et Rhône, see Laux, "Gnôme et Rhône"; and Chadeau, 276–300.

38. The ostensible reason for the new tariff was to control a dangerous substance in the aftermath of the suppression of the Paris Commune in May 1871, when *les pétroleuses*—women wielding early versions of Molotov cocktails—supposedly caused the fires that gutted central Paris. According to Gregory P. Nowell, however, the real reason for the tariff was to protect the French shale oil industry, which was nonetheless soon marginalized by the growth of imported petroleum. See Nowell's "Realpolitik vs. Transnational Rent-Seeking: French Mercantilism and the Development of the World Oil Cartel, 1860–1939," Ph.D. diss., Massachusetts Institute of Technology, 1988, for the best account of the early French oil industry. An abridged and revised version of this work was published as *Mercantile States and the World Oil Cartel, 1900–1939* (Ithaca, N.Y., 1994).

39. Lille-Bonnières merged in 1909 with the Société des Huiles Minerales de Colombes, a distributor of imported petroleum founded in 1869, and was renamed Lille-Bonnières-Colombes. See AN 65 AQ O 80.

40. *Desmarais Frères, un siècle d'industrie française de petrôle, 1896–1961* (Paris, 1961).

41. See Robert André, *L'Industrie et le commerce du petrôle en France* (Paris, 1910), 107–110.

42. See Bertrand Gille, "Capitaux français et pétroles russes, 1884–1894," *Histoire des Entreprises* 12 (November 1963): 9–94; and John P. McKay, "The House of Rothschild (Paris) as a Multinational Industrial Enterprise, 1875–1914," in Alice Teichova et al., eds., *Multinational Enterprise in Historical Perspective* (Cambridge, 1987), 74–86. It should be noted that the Nobel brothers were the largest producers and distributors of Russian oil, but they concentrated on the Russian domestic market.

43. The best sources on prewar developments in French oil remain the study by Robert André and the history of Desmarais Frères (n.40). See also Nowell, *Mercantile States,* 45–53.

44. For Lille-Bonnières, see *La France économique et financière,* October 18, 1913 (clipping in AN 65 AQ O 80). For the SIP, see various clippings in AN 65 AQ O 36.

45. Quoted by, among others, R. W. Ferrier in "French Oil Policy, 1917–1930: The Interaction Between the State and Private Interests," in D. C. Coleman and Peter Mathias, eds., *Enterprise and History* (Cambridge, 1984), 243.

As of 1914, the Cartel of Ten consisted of Desmarais Frères, Fenaille et Despeaux, Fils de Deutsch de la Meurthe, Société Industrielle des Pétroles, Raffineurs du Midi, Lille-Bonnières-Colombes, Paix et Cie, G. Lésieur et Cie, Raffineries du Pétrole du Nord, and Compagnie Générale des Pétroles. An eleventh company, A. André et Fils, was included for lubricating oil. According to Edgar Faure (*La Politique française du pétrole* [Paris, 1938], 58), 60 percent of the market was controlled by the top three firms: Fenaille et Despeaux, Desmarais, and Deutsch de la Meurthe.

46. See Ferrier, 237–262.

47. The most authoritative account of the complex oil politics following World War I is found in Nowell, *Mercantile States*, 80–148.

48. B. R. Mitchell (*European Historical Statistics 1750–1970* [New York, 1975], 418, 423 n.11), citing Markovitch, estimates France's imports as 352,000 tons per year in 1920–1924; by 1930, these imports were up to 3,857,000 tons, consisting of 460,000 tons of crude oil and 3,397,000 tons of refined oil.

49. J. Morice, *La Demande d'automobiles en France* (Paris, 1957), cited by Fridenson, 159.

50. G. S. Gibb and E. H. Knowlton, *The History of Standard Oil Company (New Jersey)*, vol. 2, *The Resurgent Years, 1911–1927* (New York, 1956), 507ff.

51. Joseph Huré, *De la Naissance de la SGHP à la SFBP d'aujourd'hui* (Paris, 1971).

52. Faure, 78.

53. AN 65 AQ O 36 and 65 AQ O 80. The tenth member of the Cartel of Ten, Raffineries des Pétroles du Nord, was absorbed by Petrofina of Belgium. There were also two smaller French independents, Pechelbronn (an Alsatian company repatriated after 1918) and the Société des Carburants. See Faure, 78.

54. *Desmarais Frères.*

55. Nowell, 177.

56. Ibid., 218.

57. Cayrol sat on the board of directors of the CFP from its founding and later served as vice-chairman of both the CFP and its refining subsidiary, the CFR.

58. On the founding and early years of the CFP, see Nowell, 170–183; and Richard F. Kuisel, *Ernest Mercier, French Technocrat* (Berkeley, 1967), 21–44. While the French oil companies pursued the development of new crude oil production in the Middle East through the CFP, they retained holdings in Rumania and Galicia (part of Poland after 1918), which they hoped to revive. One of the chief French firms in East Europe was the Société Française des Pétroles de Silva Plana. Its chief asset was the Limonowa complex in Galicia, and the company was still controlled by the oilmen who had created Limonowa before the war. The problem for Silva Plana and other companies in the region was declining production and rising costs. In 1929, Limonowa produced only 77,000 tons of crude oil, of which it refined 57,000 tons, mostly for local consumption (only 3 percent of this oil was

exported to France). According to figures presented at the annual meeting of Royal Dutch Shell shareholders in 1930, the Soviet Union accounted for only 7 percent of world production in 1929, Rumania 2 percent, and Poland less than that (*Les Assemblées Générales*, 1930, 1362). Thus, after 1920 East Europe was no longer a viable alternative to the United States as a source of crude oil for France, as it had been before 1914.

59. See Georges de Gasquet, *L'Industrie française de raffinage du pétrole: Evolution et structure* (Aix-en-Provence, 1957).

60. Adopted from Mitchell, 418.

15. Chemicals and Materials

1. The increase in the production of heavy chemicals in Europe was reflected in the tripling of the output of sulfuric acid between 1900 and 1938, from 2.9 million tons to 9.3 million tons. The rise of the electrochemical and electrometallurgical industries is illustrated by the increase in aluminum production in Europe, from 4,000 tons in 1900 to 130,000 tons in 1930 and 375,000 tons in 1939. The production of artificial fibers rose even faster, from 12,000 tons in 1913 to 126,600 tons in 1929 and 471,000 tons in 1939. See B. R. Mitchell, *European Historical Statistics, 1750–1970* (New York, 1975), 454, 460–462; and Sterling Brubaker, *Trends in the World Aluminum Industry* (Baltimore, 1967), 35–39.

2. The story of the rise of these great chemical combines is succinctly told in Alfred D. Chandler, Jr., *Scale and Scope: The Dynamics of Industrial Capitalism* (Cambridge, Mass., 1990), 170–187, 356–365, 563–586.

3. France doubled its output of sulfuric acid in 1900–1930 and remained the third largest producer in Europe even as the number of European countries producing sulfuric acid rose from eight to twenty (Mitchell, 460–462).

4. The following list of France's twenty largest chemicals and materials companies in the 1930s is drawn primarily from a list of France's 200 largest industrial enterprises in 1936 in Bruce Kogut, "Evolution of the Large Firm in France in Comparative Perspective," *Entreprises et Histoire* 19 (October 1998): 143ff. The firms with assets of 300 million francs or more ranked in the top 50 industrial firms in France; those with assets of 130 million francs or more ranked in the top 100.

Company	Assets, 1936 (in millions of francs)
Saint-Gobain	1,432
Alais, Froges, et Camargue (Pechiney)	1,151
Kuhlmann	887
Ugine	556
Gillet-Thaon	552
Air Liquide	496
Rhône-Poulenc	407

Poliet et Chausson	321
Chaux et Ciments Lafarge (assets in 1930)	269
Bozel-Malétra	193
Glace et Verres Spéciaux du Nord	189
Société Chimique de la Grande-Paroisse	175
Société Lyonnaise des Textiles	162
Ciments Français	152
Matières Colorantes de Saint-Denis	148
Société Nationale de la Viscose	142
Société de la Viscose Française	140
Produits Chimiques et d'Engrais d'Auby	130
Givet-Izieux	129

5. According to the calculations of T. J. Markovitch ("L'Industrie française de 1789 à 1914," *Cahiers de l'INSEA* AF6, June 1966, Table 3), the production of sulfuric acid, soda, and phosphates accounted for one-third of the value added by the entire French chemical industry in 1905–1913 and still accounted for 30 percent of the value added in 1924–1934.
6. This account of Saint-Gobain's evolution in 1900–1930s depends on Jean-Pierre Daviet, *Une Multinationale à la française: Saint-Gobain, 1665–1989* (Paris, 1989); and *Un Destin international: La Compagnie de Saint-Gobain de 1830 à 1939* (Paris, 1988).
7. In order to assess the change in asset values of Saint-Gobain and other companies between 1913 and 1929–1930, one must compensate for the currency depreciation associated with World War I and for the impact of mergers and acquisitions. To compensate for currency depreciation, the franc and mark figures below have been converted to dollar values at the 1913 and 1930 exchange rates. To take mergers into account, the 1913 figures are those of the main constituents of the later firm. Thus the assets listed for Pechiney in 1913 are those of both Alais et Camargue and SEMF (Froges); those for IG Farben are the assets of the seven companies that came together in 1925: Bayer, Hoechst, BASF, AGFA, Greisheim-Elektron, Casella, and Kalli und Weiler. Assets are in millions of dollars.

Country	Company	Assets in 1913	Assets in 1929–1930	Increase (in percent)
France	Saint-Gobain	27.2	53.2	96
	Pechiney	18.8	42.3	125
	Rhône-Poulenc	4.6	10.7	133
	Air Liquide	3.5	20.1	474
	Marine-Homécourt	24.0	28.3	18
	Schneider	22.0	28.6	30
	Longwy	19.2	37.3	94
	TLH	11.6	46.3	299

Germany	Deutsche Solvay	27.5	32.0	16
	IG Farben	117.5	498.0	324
United States	Owens-Illinois	25.0	46.0	84
	PPG	38.7	100.0	158
	Allied Chemical	182.0	402.0	122
	Du Pont	263.0	618.0	135

8. Kuhlmann's output of superphosphates rose from 55,000 tons in 1900 to 220,000 tons in 1913, while its output of all chemicals rose from 200,000 tons to 530,000 tons. See L. F. Haber, *The Chemical Industry, 1900–1930* (Oxford, 1971), 154; and Jean-Etienne Léger, *Une Grande Entreprise dans la chimie française: Kuhlmann, 1825–1982* (Paris, 1988), 37–53.

9. William F. Ogburn and William Jaffe, *The Economic Development of Postwar France* (New York, 1929), 462–467.

10. Haber, 194–195.

11. Archives Nationales (hereafter cited as AN) 65 AQ P183.

12. For the history of Kuhlmann in the twentieth century, see Léger, 57–100.

13. Haber, 76–97.

14. The principal source for this account of the early years of the SEC is *Mémorial de la Société d'Electro-Chimie, 1889–1964* (Lyon, 1991). It also draws on the documents in AN 65 AQ K373 and P117.

15. On the beginnings of the Girod enterprises, see the documents in AN 65 AQ K97; Henri Morsel, ed., *Rhône-Alpes, terre d'industries à la Belle Epoque* (Grenoble, 1998); and Marie-Françoise Bal, *Ugine au XXe siècle: Itineraire d'une ville industrielle* (Grenoble, 1993).

16. Annual reports for 1929 and 1930 in *Les Assemblées Générales* (hereafter cited as AG), 1929, 977–980; 1930, 1277.

17. *Mémorial de la Société d'Electro-Chimie.*

18. There is no history of SEMF, but the story of its beginnings can be pieced together from the following: François Bouchayer, *Les Pionniers de la houille blanche et de l'électricité* (Paris, 1954), 55–66; C-J Gignoux, *Histoire d'une entreprise française (Pechiney)* (Paris, 1955), 65–118; Paul Morel et al., *Histoire technique de la production d'aluminium* (Grenoble, 1991), 32–64; Philippe Mioche, *L'Alumine à Gardanne de 1893 à nos jours* (Grenoble, 1995), 17–28.

19. On Pechiney's reentry into aluminum and the complex story of the French aluminum industry before World War I, see the sources in the previous note, plus two unpublished French doctoral dissertations: Florence Hachez-Leroy, "L'Aluminium Français, instrument d'une stratégie de groupe, 1911–1960" (Université de Paris IV, 1995); and Ludovic Cailluet, "Stratégies, structures d'organisation, et pratiques de gestion de Pechiney des années 1880 à 1971" (Université de Lyon II, 1995).

20. On SARV and Chedde, see Bouchayer, 67–78; and Ludovic Cailluet, *Chedde, un siècle d'industrie au pays du Mont-Blanc* (Grenoble, 1997).

21. According to Ludovic Cailluet ("Stratégies, structures," 138), this merger

was mainly the work of TLH, CGE, and other aluminum-consuming companies that had taken control of SEMF in 1917.

22. These and other company-level figures for aluminum production come from Morel, 76.

23. The Le Chateliers were one of the most distinguished families in French science and engineering. Their father, Louis L. P. Le Chatelier (1815–1873), played key roles in the building of the Chemin de Fer du Nord and in the founding of the French aluminum industry. Henry Le Chatelier (1850–1936) was professor of applied chemistry at the Ecole des Mines and the Collège de France and made the key discoveries that underlay the development of the oxyacetylene welding torch. André Le Chatelier (1861–1929) was an engineer with the Genie Maritime whose studies of the use of alloy steels in traction underlay the new science of rheology. Louis Le Chatelier (1853–1928) was a civil engineer involved in the planning of the Paris Metro who went on to direct the Etablissements Cail and the Hauts-Fourneaux et Aciéries de Caen. Louis Le Chatelier's grandson Robert (b. 1930) later served as CEO of Ugine. See François Le Chatelier, *Louis Le Chatelier, Elisabeth Durand, leurs ascendants, leur descendants* (Nancy, 1973).

24. Claude, *Ma Vie et mes inventions* (Paris, 1957), chapter 5; Le Chatelier, 157–169.

25. For Claude's own description of his air liquefaction and separation system, see Georges Claude, *Liquid Air, Oxygen, Nitrogen* (London, 1913).

26. Delorme remained *président-directeur-général* of Air Liquide until 1945, when he was succeeded by his son Jean Delorme, who headed the firm until 1967.

27. See *Cinquantenaire de la Société L'Air Liquide, octobre 1902–octobre 1952* (Paris, 1952) in AN 65 AQ P4^1. The preceding account of the company's founding as well as the account of the company's subsequent history relies heavily on this source.

28. These rankings are from Michael S. Smith, "Putting France in the Chandlerian Framework: France's 100 Largest Industrial Firms in 1913," *Business History Review* 72, no. 1 (Spring 1998): 57.

29. In addition to producing acetylene in southern France, Acetylène Dissous du Sud-Est developed and marketed welding equipment, especially for shipbuilding and repair, and set up repair facilities adjacent to the shipyards of Marseille, and also in the port of Saigon to serve the shipyards of Messageries Maritimes through a joint subsidiary with Air Liquide, the Société d'Oxygène et d'Acetylène d'Extrême-Orient. See *Cinquantenaire* in AN 65 AQ P4^1.

30. See the 1913 report in the Crédit Lyonnais Archives, Etudes Financières (hereafter cited as CL-EF), DEEF 30212, 3937; and the March 1962 issue of *La Cryogène* in AN 65 AQ P4^2.

31. See William Haynes, *The American Chemical Industry*, vol. 6 (New York, 1949), 5–8. The details of Air Liquide's involvement in the Air Reduction Company are sketchy. All officers of Air Reduction were Americans, but

Air Liquide documents imply that it was represented on the board. Confidential reports in the Crédit Lyonnais files indicate that Air Liquide continued to have a significant financial stake in Air Reduction through the 1920s, and Air Liquide's 1930 annual report, in a section devoted to international operations, noted that Air Reduction was "in excellent condition" (AG, 1930, 1045).

32. The Claude Neon Lighting Company, in which Air Liquide participated, became a leader in electrical signage. See Claude, *Ma Vie*, chapter 7; and Wiebe E. Bijker, *Of Bicycles, Bakelite, and Bulbs: Toward a Theory of Sociotechnical Change* (Cambridge, Mass., 1995), 213–218.

33. Renaud de Rochebrune and Jean-Claude Hazera, *Les Patrons sous l'Occupation* (Paris, 1995), 251.

34. Acetylène Dissous du Sud-Est remained nominally independent, but at the death of its founder, André Le Chatelier, in 1929 it too was merged into Air Liquide. The company had already absorbed Gaz Comprimé and its chief foreign subsidiaries, Air Liquide Belge and Aira Liquida Italiana, in an earlier round of mergers in 1911–1912.

35. On Lazote, see David A. Hounshell and John Kenly Smith, Jr., *Science and Corporate Strategy: Du Pont R & D, 1902–1980* (Cambridge, 1988), 183–189.

36. AG, 1929, 846–850; AG, 1930, 1044–1048.

37. By the mid-1990s, Rhône-Poulenc was Europe's fifth largest chemical company with fifty-five plants in France, fifty elsewhere in Europe, one hundred outside Europe, and 83,000 employees worldwide. Among its specialties, it ranked first in the world in vaccines and analgesics, second in intermediate polymers for the textile and automobile industries, and third in veterinary products. See Jean-Michel Béhar, *Guide des grandes entreprises* (Paris, 1995), 227–233.

38. This section draws heavily on Pierre Cayez, *Rhône-Poulenc, 1895–1975* (Paris, 1988).

39. For a concise account of the beginnings of the rayon industry, see D. C. Coleman, *Courtaulds: An Economic and Social History*, vol. 2 (Oxford, 1969), 1–24.

40. See Bloch-Pimentel, "Notice sur la soie artificielle, 1902," in AN 65 AQ H283; as well as 65 AQ H151 (on Izieux); and 65 AQ H284 on the Chardonnet company.

41. Coleman, 76–104.

42. Cayez, 95–106.

43. Jean-Pierre Daviet, "An Impossible Merger? The French Chemical Industry in the 1920s," in Y. Cassis, F. Crouzet, and T. Gourvish, eds., *Management and Business in Britain and France* (Oxford, 1995), 171–190.

44. Cayez, 107–112.

45. Ibid., 113–140.

46. Daviet, "Impossible Merger." According to Kogut, the assets of Kuhlmann in 1936 were 887 million francs, and the assets of Rhône-Poulenc were 407 million.

47. These estimates are based on figures on the growth of the French cement industry in Markovitch, Table de Base XI.

48. See Dominique Barjot, *Travaux publics de France: Un Siècle d'entrepreneurs et d'entreprises, 1883–1992* (Paris, 1993), 53–66.

49. AG, 1929, 593–598; Jacques Boudet, ed., *Le Monde des affaires en France* (Paris, 1952), 167–170.

50. G. Baire, "Notice sur la Société des ciments français de Boulogne-sur-mer, 1899," in AN 65 AQ S52; and AG, 1929, 1239.

51. For this quotation and the early history of Lafarge, see Léon Dubois, *Lafarge-Coppée, 150 ans d'industrie* (Paris, 1988), 1–33 (quotation on page 33). See also the documents in AN 65 AQ S198.

52. AG, 1930.

53. See Béhar, 151; and Dubois.

16. The New World of Managerial Capitalism

1. For recent efforts to identify and rank France's largest firms, see Youssef Cassis, *Big Business: The European Experience in the Twentieth Century* (Oxford, 1997); Michael S. Smith, "Putting France in the Chandlerian Framework: France's 100 Largest Industrial Firms in 1913," *Business History Review* 72, no. 1 (Spring 1998): 46–85; and Bruce Kogut, "Evolution of the Large Firm in France in Comparative Perspective," *Entreprises et Histoire* 19 (October 1998), 136–148.

2. See Patrick Fridenson, "Un Tournant taylorien de la société française, 1904–1918," *Annales* 42 (September–October 1987): 1031–60; and the works of Aimée Moutet, especially *Les Logiques de l'entreprise: La Rationalisation dans l'industrie française de l'entre-deux-guerres* (Paris, 1997).

3. The Northern Railroad remained the "Rothschild railroad," with Alphonse de Rothschild succeeding his father James as chairman of the board in 1868 and being succeeded in turn by his son Edouard in 1906. The banking families that remained prominent on the board of the P-L-M from its founding into the early 1900s included the Mallets, Hottinguers, Neuflizes, Mirabauds, and (again) the Rothschilds. On the shareholders and directors of the Northern Railroad, see François Caron, *Histoire de l'exploitation d'un grand réseau: La Compagnie du chemin de fer du Nord, 1846–1937* (Paris, 1973), 275ff. On the board membership of the P-L-M, see the annual reports in Archives Nationales (hereafter cited as AN) 77 AQ 158–163; and *Les Assemblées Générales*.

4. On the role of engineers in railroad administration, see François Caron, *Histoire des chemins de fer en France*, vol. 1 (Paris, 1997), 256–280; and Georges Ribeill, *La Révolution ferroviaire* (Paris, 1993), 299–334. On the role of the Arts et Métiers engineers, see C. R. Day, *Education for the Industrial World: The Ecoles d'Arts et Métiers and the Rise of French Industrial Engineering* (Cambridge, Mass., 1987), 220–221.

5. On the organizational structure of the early railroads, see Caron, *Histoire des chemins de fer*, 256–280; and Ribeill, 193–246.

6. Marc Martin discusses the "politique publicitaire parsimonieuse" of French railroads in *Trois siècles de publicité en France* (Paris, 1992), 127. On French railroad posters, see Florence Camard et al., *Le Train à l'affiche* (Paris, 1989).

7. On the organization and operations of the P-L-M, see Ray Morris, *Railroad Administration* (New York, 1910), 296, especially the foldout organization chart; and the 1926 report of the Credit Lyonnais (Crédit Lyonnais Archives, Etudes Financières [hereafter cited as CL-EF] DEEF 29248, 1586–12). See also Albert Meinadier, *La Compagnie des chemins de fer de Paris à Lyon et à la Méditerranée* (Paris, 1908).

8. At Messageries Maritimes, for example, the managing director supervised the central office directly but depended on subordinates to run the branch offices and repair facilities located in the company's home ports and in various ports of call around the world. The captains of the company's sixty-two ocean liners, each with a crew of a hundred or more, represented an additional level of middle management. See Paul Bois, *Le Grand Siècle des Messageries Maritimes* (Marseille, 1991), 65–66 and passim.

9. See in particular the experience of Au Printemps under Gustave and Pierre Laguionie, discussed by Marc Meuleau in "Les HEC et l'évolution du management en France, 1881–années 1980," Thèse du Doctorat, Université de Paris X, 1992, vol. 4, 1087–1155.

10. See Daijiro Fujimura, "Schneider et Cie et son plan d'organisation administrative de 1913: Analyse et interpretation," *Histoire, Economie, et Société* 10, no. 2 (1991): 269–276; Alain Dewerpe, "Travailler chez Schneider," in *Les Schneider, Le Creusot* (Paris, 1995), 181–183; and Agnès d'Angio, *Schneider et Cie et les travaux publics, 1895–1949* (Paris, 1995), 122–125.

11. "Rapport de mission, 1908," in CL-EF DEEF 21068.

12. On the organization of Pechiney, see Ludovic Cailluet, "Stratégies, structures d'organisation, et pratiques de gestion de Pechiney des années 1880 à 1971," Thèse du Doctorat, Université de Lyon II, 1995, 101. On Usines du Rhône, see Pierre Cayez, *Rhône-Poulenc* (Paris, 1988), 41, 51; on Saint-Gobain, see Jean-Pierre Daviet, *Un Destin international: La Compagnie de Saint-Gobain de 1830 à 1939* (Paris, 1988), 238–251.

13. Report of April 1926 on CGE, CL-EF DEEF 23814.

14. Cailluet; Claude Beaud, "Investments and Profits of the Multinational Schneider Group, 1894–1943," in Alice Teichova et al., *Multinational Enterprise in Historical Perspective* (Cambridge, 1987), 87–102; Patrick Fridenson, *Histoire des Usines de Renault* (Paris, 1972).

15. Maurice Lévy-Leboyer, ed., *Le Patronat de la seconde industrialisation* (Paris, 1979), 167.

16. Meuleau, "Les HEC," vol. 3, "Vers une nouvelle gestion de l'entreprise."

17. The figures are drawn from Maurice Lévy-Leboyer, "Le Patronat français, 1912–1973," in *Le Patronat de la seconde industrialisation*, 137–188. See also the other contributions to that volume; and André Grelon, "The

Training and Career Structures of Engineers in France, 1880–1939," in Robert Fox and Anna Guagnini, eds., *Education, Technology, and Industrial Performance in Europe, 1850–1939* (Cambridge, 1993), 42–64.

18. See Pierre Lanthier, "Les Dirigeants des grandes entreprises électriques en France, 1911–1973," in Lévy-Leboyer, *Le Patronat de la seconde industrialisation,* 101–136; and Jacques Marseille et al., *Alcatel-Alsthom* (Paris, 1992).

19. Jean-Marie Moine, *Les Barons du fer* (Nancy, 1989), 89–96.

20. Moine, 83–89.

21. Claude Beaud, "Les ingénieurs du Creusot à travers quelques destins du milieu du XIXe siècle au milieu du XXe," in André Thépot, ed., *L'Ingénieur dans la société française* (Paris, 1985), 51–60.

22. Daviet, 252–262.

23. Cailluet, 76–115, 206–263.

24. Sylvie Schweitzer, *André Citroën* (Paris, 1992), 85–90.

25. On the development of accounting in France in the early twentieth century, see Jean-Pierre Daviet, "Les Problèmes de gestion: Marketing et gestion financière," in Maurice Lévy-Leboyer, ed., *Histoire de la France industrielle* (Paris, 1996), 254–273.

26. Quoted by Jean Bouvier in reviewing Alain Baudant, *Pont à Mousson, 1918–1939,* in *Annales* (January–February 1982), 156.

27. Alain Baudant, "Propriété, direction, et idéologie de l'entreprise: Pont à Mousson, 1919–1939," *Entreprises et Entrepreneurs, XIX–XXe siècles* (Paris, 1983), 269–289.

28. Cailluet, 280–297.

29. Patrick Fridenson, "French Automobile Marketing, 1890–1970," in Akio Okochi and K. Shimokawa, eds., *Development of Mass Marketing* (Tokyo, 1981), 127–154.

30. See Stephen L. Harp, *Marketing Michelin: Advertising and Cultural Identity in 20th Century France* (Baltimore, 2001).

31. The standard work on Taylorism remains Daniel Nelson, *Frederick W. Taylor and the Rise of Scientific Management* (Madison, Wis., 1980).

32. Yves Cohen, "Ernest Mattern chez Peugeot (1906–1918) ou comment peut-on être taylorien?" in Maurice de Montmollin and Olivier Pastré, eds., *Le Taylorisme* (Paris, 1984), 115–118.

33. Fridenson, *Histoire,* 70–79.

34. There is a large and growing literature on the French experience with scientific management. See in particular George C. Humphreys, *Taylorism in France, 1904–1920* (New York, 1986); and Moutet.

35. On the development of mass production in the automobile industry, see Moutet, 111–136; Fridenson, "The Coming of the Assembly Line to Europe," in W. Krohn, E. T. Layton, and P. Weingart, eds., *The Dynamics of Science and Technology* [Sociology of the Sciences, vol. 2, 1978], 159–175; Sylvie Schweitzer, *Des Engrenages à la chaîne: Les Usines de Citroën* (Lyon, 1982); and Yves Cohen, "The Modernization of Production in the French

Automobile Industry Between the Wars: A Photographic Essay," *Business History Review* 65 (Winter 1991): 754–780.

36. Fridenson, *Histoire,* 323–328.

37. Jean-Pierre Poitou, *Le Cerveau de l'usine: Histoire des bureaux d'études Renault de l'origine à 1980* (Aix-en-Provence, 1988), 60–61.

38. Schweitzer, *Des Engrenages,* 62–63.

39. Moutet, 259–302.

Conclusion: France on the Verge

1. Richard F. Kuisel, *Capitalism and the State in Modern France: Renovation and Economic Management in the Twentieth Century* (Cambridge, 1981), chapters 3 and 4.

2. In 1990 the gross domestic product (GDP) of these countries (in billions of dollars) was as follows: United States, $3,535; United Kingdom, $691; Federal Republic of Germany, $998; France, $835. The unification of Germany raised its GDP 50 percent above France's by 2001, but the per capita GDP of the two countries remained comparable ($26,570 in Germany and $24,210 in France).

3. While France had twelve firms in the top hundred in the world in 1990, none of these firms ranked in the top twenty-five. How it stacked up against other leading industrial countries is shown below:

	France	*Germany*	*Japan*	*UK*	*USA*
Firms ranked in top 25	0	4	4	4	10
Firms ranked in top 100	12	12	16	9	33

4. Tabulation adapted from Jean-Michel Béhar, *Guide des grandes entreprises* (Paris, 1995), 301.

5. Richard Whittington and Michael Mayer, *The European Corporation: Strategy, Structure, and Social Science* (Oxford, 2000), 108.

6. On the formation of industrial groups in the 1960s and 1970s, see François Morin, *La Structure financière du capitalisme français* (Paris, 1974); and Patrick Allard et al., *Dictionnaire des groupes industriels et financièrs en France* (Paris, 1978).

7. Whittington and Mayer, 128–134, 163–168.

Index

Accounting, 301–303, 481–482
Acetylene, 440, 446–447
Aciéries de France, 337–338; assets of, 334t
Aciéries de Longwy, 336, 341–342, 360, 362–363, 368–369, 489; assets of, 334t, 370t
Aciéries de Micheville, 342, 362; assets of, 334t, 370t
Aciéries de Saint-Etienne, 195
Aciéries du Nord et de la Lorraine, 364, 370t
Aciéries et Forges de la Lorette, 195
Adant process, 271
Administrateur-délégué, 467–468, 470
Administration: centralized functional model of, 470; decentralized multidivisional model of, 487–488; holding company model of, 469–470
AEG. See Allgemeine Elektricitäts Gesellschaft
Agache, Edouard, 146–147, 228
Agache-Willot, 146, 490
Aircraft engine industry, 417, 419–421, 478
Aircraft industry, 416–419
Air France, 485
Air Liquide, 435, 436, 446–451, 486t, 488, 490
Air Reduction Company, 449
Alais, Froges, et Camargue. See Pechiney

Alais, Mines, Forges, et Fonderies d', 166–167, 183, 192; assets of, 334t, 370t
Algeria, 191–192
Allard Law (1791), 24
Allcard et Buddicom, 212
Allevard, 107, 196, 363
Allgemeine Elektricitäts Gesellschaft (AEG), 373, 382, 398t
Alluard Frères, 292
Alsace: cotton industry of, 133, 137–140; machinery industry of, 207–208, 209, 212, 214
Alsthom, 395, 398t, 490
Aluminium Français, 444
Aluminum, 225–226, 228, 439, 443–446; European production of, 552n1
Aluminum Company of America (Alcoa), 444
American System of Manufacture, 404–405
Ancy-le-Franc, 185
André et Fils, 427
Anglo-French Treaty of Commerce (1860). See Trade treaties
Anglo-German Trust, 234–235
Anglo-Persian Oil Company, 427–428, 430
Aniche, Mines d', 165, 435
Antilles trade, 16–17, 38
Anzin, Mines d', 163–165, 168–169, 171–172, 311

Aquila Franco-Romana, 424
Arlés-Dufour, François, 57, 75, 155
Arnavon et Cie, 282
Artificial fiber, 435–436, 453–456
Assembly lines, 404–405, 409, 412, 480
Assurances Générales, 61
Ateliers de Constructions Electriques du
   Nord et de l'Est (ACENE), 383, 385,
   397
Atlantic Refining Company, 430–431
Aubrives et Villerupt, Société
   Métallurgique d', 334t, 352
Audincourt, Forges d', 184–185
Automobile industry, 400–413; budgeting
   in, 481; personnel management in, 481;
   professional managers in, 475; sales
   management in, 477–478. See also
   specific companies

Baccarat, Cristallerie de, 242, 301
Balguerie-Stuttenberg, Pierre, 38
Bamberger, Henri, 78
Banking and finance, 21–23, 58–60, 71–
   80, 97–108. See also Haute banque;
   specific banks
Banks, joint –stock, 32, 34–35, 38, 71, 97–
   101
Banks, private. See Haute banque
Banque de France, 23, 32, 34, 49–50, 53,
   54–55, 59–60, 69, 73, 102, 105, 106
Banque de l'Indochine, 75, 100, 487
Banque de l'Union Parisienne, 104, 105,
   429
Banque de Lyon, 47–48
Banque de Marseille, 45
Banque de Paris et des Pays-Bas (Paribas),
   78–79, 100, 343, 429, 487
Banque Devilder, 106
Banque du Havre, 41
Banque Gommès, 106
Banque Impériale Ottomane, 104
Banque Royale, 22
Banque Thomas, 106–107
Banque Verley Decroix, 106
Barbe, Paul, 234–235
Barbier et Cie, 202
Bartholony, François, 51, 65, 85
Barton et Guestier, 38
Basse-Loire, Usines Métallurgiques de,
   334t, 338, 355
Batignolles, Société des Constructions de,
   213, 215

Bazar de l'Hôtel de Ville, 122–123
Bazin family, 44
Beaucaire fair, 116, 118
Becquey, François, 63
Beet sugar, 275–279. See also Sugar
   refining
Beghin, Raffineries et Sucreries, 278
Béhic, Armand, 90
Belgium: banking in, 71; coal imported
   from, 114; glass manufacture in, 241;
   trade treaty with, 313–314
Belle Jardinière, 121, 286–287
Bergasse family, 44, 45, 275
Berger-Levrault, 256–257
Bergès, Aristide, 252
Bergougnan et Cie, 414
Berliet Automobile Company, 405–407,
   549n25
Bessand family, 287
Bessemer process, 177–178, 189–190,
   192, 337
Besson, Edouard, 90
Bethmann family, 38
Béthune, Mines de, 170
Bicycle industry, 206, 401, 404, 413–415
Bidermann, Jacques, 54
Billancourt, 401–403, 405
Birkeland-Eyde process, 439
Bischoffsheim family, 78
Biscuits, 268–269
Blanchet Frères et Kléber, 251, 253, 299
Blanchisseries et teintureries de Thaon
   (BTT), 141–142
Blanzy, Mines de, 163, 165, 175
Blériot-Aeronautique, 417
Blin et Blin, 152
Blount, Edouard, 77, 85
BNITO (Société de Napthe Caspienne et
   de la Mer Noire), 424, 426
Boigues, Louis, 182, 183–184
Bon Marché, 121–123, 125, 287
Bordeaux, 17, 36–39, 70, 93, 272, 283
Bottle industry, 242–245
Boucicault, Aristide, 121–122, 124
Bourdon, Frances, 182
Boussois (Compagnie Réunis de Glace et
   Verres Spéciaux de la Nord de la
   France), 241
Braudel, Fernand, 6, 14–15
Breadstuffs, 268–269
Bréguet, Ateliers d'Aviation, 417, 418
British Petroleum, 428

British Viscoid, 453
Brown-Boveri, 384–385, 397
Business education, 471–476
Butel, Paul, 17

Cail, J.F., 210, 273. *See also* Derosne et
    Cail; Société Française des
    Constructions Mécaniques
Caisse d'Escompte, 58
Caisse de Comptes Courantes, 59
Caisse de Dépôts et Consignations, 107
Caisse Générale du Commerce et de
    l'Industrie, 71
Calcium carbide, 439, 440; cartel for,
    538n62
Calla family, 208, 209
Campionnot, Pierre-Joseph, 194
Canals and waterways: financing of, 63
Candle making, 285
Canson family, 248–249, 253
Caribbean colonies: French acquisition of,
    16–17; Great Britain's occupation of, 36
Carmaux, Mines de, 167, 174, 304, 306
Carnaud (J.J. Carnaud et Forges de Basse-
    Indre), 334t, 355, 370t, 486t
Carnot family, 453
Carret et Fils, 268
Cartel of Ten, 426, 428
Cartels, 320–323, 366, 368, 444
Casimir-Périer, Jean, 173
Cassis, Youssef, 97, 328
Caudron Aviation Company, 420
Cellulose du Pin, 435
Cement industry, 456–459
Chagot family, 165, 175
Chain stores, 125–126
Chaix, Napoleon, 259
Chandler, Alfred D., Jr., 2, 8, 309, 325–
    328, 358, 487
Chandlerian paradigm, 327–328, 487–
    488, 490–491
Chantiers et Ateliers de la Gironde, 351
Chantiers de la Buire, 214
Chappée et Fils, 352
Charbonnages de Beeringen, 357
Charbonnages de France, 490
Chargeurs Réunis, 92, 486
Charles-Roux (Canaple), 282
Charles-Roux, Jules, 91, 282
Châtillon-Commentry, 175, 184–186, 301,
    349, 360; assets of, 334t, 370t
Chaussade, Badaud de la, 20

Chedde, 444–445
Chemical production, growth of, 435–436
Chemicals industry, 219–236, 432–456;
    assets of largest companies in, 552n4,
    553n7; cartels in, 320–321;
    management of, 469. *See also* Dyes;
    Electrochemical Industry;
    Pharmaceutical Industry; specific
    companies
Chemin de fer de l'Est. *See* Eastern
    Railroad
Chemin de fer du l'Ouest. *See* Western
    Railroad
Chemin de fer du Midi. *See* Southern
    Railroad
Chemin de fer du Nord. *See* Northern
    Railroad
Chevalier, Michel, 57
Chocolate and confectionery, 279–280
Christofle et Cie, 290
Church, Edward, 46–47
Ciments Boulonnais, 459
Ciments Français, 458, 490
Cirages Françaises, Société Générale des,
    334t, 355
Citroën (André Citroën et Cie), 360, 406,
    408–410, 412–413, 416, 475, 477–478,
    480, 481, 482, 489
Claude, Georges, 446–447, 448, 450
Claude Lumière, 450–451
Clermont-Ferrand, 414–415
Clothing industry, 286–288
Cloth printing and dyeing, 132–133, 134–
    135, 137–140
Coal industry, 161–176; cartels in, 322;
    impact of World War I on, 386–387;
    labor relations in 303–304, 306, 308;
    largest companies in, 172t;
    nationalization of, 490
Coal trade, 114–115
Cognacq, Ernest, 122
Coignet et Cie, 229, 437
Au Coin de Rue, 121, 123
Colbert, Jean-Baptiste, 14, 16, 19, 21, 45
Colonial trade, 16–17, 36–37, 39–40, 42
Comité des Forges, 321, 360, 364
Comité Française de Filature de Coton,
    323
Commentry-Fourchambault, 165–166,
    174, 183–184, 334t, 344–345, 353. *See
    also* Decazeville
Commercial Code of 1808, 298

Commercial Code of 1810, 319–320

Compagnie de la Loire, 169, 173

Compagnie des Compteurs, 375, 396–397

Compagnie des Indes, 20, 24, 54

Compagnie Electro-Mécanique (CEM), 384–385, 397

Compagnie Française de l'Acetylène Dissous, 447–448

Compagnie Française de l'Afrique Occidentale (CFAO), 507n34, 531n44

Compagnie Française de Raffinage, 430–431

Compagnie Française des Pétroles (CFP), 422, 427, 429–430, 488, 489

Compagnie Française du Télégraphe de Paris à New York, 510n13

Compagnie Française pour l'Exploitation des Produits Thomson-Houston (CFTH). See Thomson-Houston

Compagnie Générale de Distribution d'Energie Electrique (CGDEE), 376–377

Compagnie Générale d'Electricité (CGE), 379–380, 383, 395–396, 398t, 470, 473, 485, 490

Compagnie Générale des Eaux, 103

Compagnie Générale de Télégraphe Sans Fils, 490, 546n27

Compagnie Générale de Traction, 375–376

Compagnie Générale Française des Tramways, 391

Compagnie Générale Transatlantique (CGT), 89–90, 93

Compagnie Nationale des Matières Colorantes et des Produits Chimiques, 438

Compagnie Parisienne de Distribution de l'Electricité (CPDE), 378–379, 391

Compagnie Réunis de Glace et Verres Spéciaux de la Nord de la France. See Boussois

Compagnie Royale d'Assurances, 61

Compagnie Universelle du Canal Maritime de Suez, 94

Companies, legal forms of, 298, 302–303

Comptoir de l'Industrie Cotonnière, 142

Comptoir de Longwy, 321–322

Comptoir de Quincailleries Réunis de l'Est, 119

Comptoir d'Escompte de Paris, 69–70, 74–75, 99

Comptoir des Textiles Artificiels, 435, 454

Conseil d'Etat, 71, 72, 74, 164

Construction industry, 215–217

Consumerism, 238–239, 265–266

Continental Edison, 545n9

Continental System, 133, 137, 147, 313

Continental Tire Company, 413–414

Copper industry, 99, 103, 352

Corbin, Antoine, 125

Corporate officers, types of, 467–468

Cottin, Joseph-Daniel, 132

Cotton industry, 19–20, 132–144; cartels in, 323; labor relations in, 305, 306; machinery for, 207–208. See also Cloth Printing and Dyeing

Cotton trade, 41, 55–56, 109–111, 506n29

Courrières, Mines de, 170

Courtaulds, 454

Crédit Commerciale du Havre, 41

Crédit du Nord, 70, 106

Crédit Foncier de France, 72

Crédit Foncier Egyptien, 99

Crédit Industriel et Commercial (CIC), 75, 76, 98–100

Crédit Lyonnais, 48, 75–77, 97–98, 99, 105–106, 113, 391–392, 485

Crédit Mobilier, 32, 72–74, 77, 84–85, 101

Crespin sales system, 508n49

Cronier, Ernest, 277

Cruse, Herman, 38

Crystal, 242

Cuenod-Sautter, 439

Darblay family, 248, 250–251, 267

Darcy, Henry, 175

Darcy, Hugues, 185, 192

Darmstadter Bank, 73

Darracq Automobile Company, 403, 404, 549n25

Dassier, Auguste, 84

Daubrée et Barbier, 414

Davillier family, 54, 133

DAVUM (Compagnie des Depôts et Agences de Ventes d'Usines Métallurgiques), 368

Decazeville (Houillères et Fonderies de l'Aveyron), 167, 174, 183, 193, 301, 306, 345

Declaration of the Rights of Man and the Citizen (1789), 23–24

De Dion-Bouton, 401, 404

Delahante, Adrien, 47, 78
Delahaye Automobile Company, 404, 549n25
Delmas-Viljeux, 89
Demachy, Charles, 54
Denain-Anzin, 186, 301, 334t, 344, 356, 362, 370t, 489
Department stores, 121–125, 508n49
Deposit banks. *See* Banking and finance; Banks, joint-stock
Depression (1870s and 1880s), 136, 174, 238
Depression (1930s), 411–412, 483
Derosne et Cail, 210, 213, 215–216, 271, 277. *See also* Société Française des Constructions Mécaniques
Desandrouin, Jacques, 163
Desmarais Frères, 423, 424, 425, 428
Desmoulins et Droulers, 149
Deutsch de la Meurthe, Fils de, 422, 424, 426
Didot family, 246, 247, 257–258
Dietrich family, 214–215. *See also* Lorraine-Dietrich
Directeur-général, 464, 465, 467–468
Docks et Entrepôts de Marseille, 93–94
Docks Rémois, 126
Dollfus-Mieg et Cie (DMC), 139, 143, 490
Dombasle, Alexandre Mathieu de, 200–201
Dorizon, Louis, 99
Dreux, Alexandre, 341–342, 369
Dreyfus Frères, 99
Droulers-Agache, 145–146
Dufaud, Georges, 183–184
Dufayel, Georges, 508n49
Dunkirk, 112, 268
Dunlop Rubber Company (Société Française des Pneus), 413, 414–415, 416
Du Pont, 432, 450, 456
Dupont, Mayer, 342–343
Dupont, Paul, 258–259
Dupuy de Lôme, Henry, 90
Dutilleul, Ernest, 78
Dyes, 229–233, 437–438

Eastern Railroad (Chemin de Fer de l'Est), 85, 319
Ecole Centrale des Arts et Manufactures, 472, 474; students of, 252, 464
Ecole Centrale Lyonnaise, 472

Ecole des Hautes Etudes Commerciales, 471–472
Ecole des Mines, 367, 464, 473
Ecole des Ponts et Chaussées, 464, 472, 473
Ecole Polytechnique, 472, 473, 474; students of, 57–58, 367, 406, 464
Ecoles des arts et métiers, 464, 472
Eichthal, Adolphe d', 91
Eiffel, Etablissements, 217
Eiffel, Gustave, 122, 198, 216–217
Eiffel Tower, 198, 217
Elbeuf, 137, 151, 152
Electrical equipment industry, 382–385, 386, 394–399, 469, 490; largest firms in, 390t; mass production in, 478
Electrical industry (power and light), 376–382, 386–389, 391–393; largest firms in, 390t
Electricité de France, 393–394
Electric traction industry, 374–376; largest firms in, 390t
Electrochemical industry, 438–446
Electrometallurgy industry, 396, 441–442, 443–446
Elf-Aquitaine, 489
Empain Group, 375–376, 378, 385, 390
Energie Electrique de la Basse-Isère, 368
Energie Electrique du Littorale Méditerranéen, 381
Energie Electrique du Nord de la France, 381
Energie Industrielle, 393
Enfantin, Prosper, 57, 94
Engineers, as industrial managers, 472–476
Entrepôts et Magasins Généraux, Compagnie des, 407n40
Entrepreneurship, 6–7
Escaut-Meuse, 334t, 354, 370t
Essonnes, Papeteries d' (Darblay et Beranger), 246, 247, 248, 250–251, 267
Etablissements Métallurgiques de la Gironde, 367
Etienne family, 272–273
European Economic Community, 7–8, 486
Explosives, 234–235, 445

Fabre, Cyprien, 44, 45, 89
Farben, IG, 432, 456
Farm machinery, 199–201
Fauquet family, 135

Fenaille et Despeaux, 422, 423, 424, 427, 551n45
Firearms, 201–202, 211
Firmin-Didot, Société, 258
Firminy, Aciéries et Forges de, 188, 346, 360; assets of, 334t, 370t
Firminy-Roche la Molière, Mines de, 168, 174
Fiscal systems, development of, 13
Fives-Lille, Compagnie de, 213, 215–216
Flour mills, 266–269
Fontaine et Brault, 209
Force et Lumière, Société Générale de, 382
Fordism, 408–410, 479–482
Ford Motor Company, 402, 404–405, 407–408
Forges de Franche-Comté, Société des, 195
Forges et Aciéries Electrique Paul Girod, Compagnie de, 441–442
Fougerolles, 216
Fould family, 52, 65, 92, 342–343
Fourchambault. See Commentry-Fourchambault
Fournier et Cie, 285
Foville, Alfred de, 87
Fraissinet et Cie, 43, 89
Fraissinet, Marc-Constantin, 44, 89
Franchising, 125–126
François I (king of France), 16
Franco-Suisse (Société Franco-Suisse pour l'Industrie Electrique), 381–382
French government:, 12–13, 23–30; banking policies of, 72–74; promotion of steam navigation by, 43, 89–90; railroad policies of, 64–66, 81–83, 316–319; road-building activities of, 62; sugar export policies of, 270, 272, 273; trade policy of, 313–316
French Revolution, 23–27; trade of Lyon disrupted by, 45–46; trade of Marseille disrupted by, 42; woolens industry influenced by, 147–148
Frèrejean family, 186–187
Freycinet Plan (1878), 317, 335, 344
Fuchsine, Société de la, 76–77, 231, 233
Futures exchanges, 110–113

Gagneau, Henri: work rules of, 308
Gall, Henry, 441–442
Gall-Montlaur process, 439, 440

Gallois, Charles, 121
Garnier-Pagès, Louis-Antoine, 81
Gases: oxygen and nitrogen, 446–451; poison, 452–453
Gay-Lussac, Joseph, 223–224
Gaz de France, 490
Géliot, Henri, 142
General Electric Company, 375, 394, 398t
General Motors, 407–408
Germain, Henri, 75–76, 98, 185, 192, 231
Germany: annexation of Alsace-Lorraine by, 139, 140, 214, 339–343; automobile industry in, 400–401; big business in, 327–329; Bordeaux wine trade with, 37; cartels of, 322; dye industry of, 231–232; dye patents of, 438; economic development of, compared to France, 4, 5; electrical industry in, 372–373, 398t; paper industry of, 249–250; petroleum refining industry in, 426, 429; porcelain manufacture in, 291–292, 293; steam navigation of, 93, 503n37; steel industry of, 339–340, 356, 363–366, 371t
Gillet family, 142, 230, 453
Gilliard, Monnet, et Cartier. See Usines du Rhône
Girod, Paul. See Forges et Aciéries Electrique Paul Girod
Giros, Alexander, 381
Glass industry, 237–245, 434–435; cartels in, 320–321
Glove making, 288–289
Gnôme et Rhône, 417, 420–421, 485
Godard-Desmarest, Pierre-Antoine, 242, 301
Godillot, Alexis, 287, 288
Goodrich, B.F., 414
Gorcy, Société Métallurgique de, 353
Goudchaux family, 115
Goulet-Turpin, 126
Government. See French government
Graffenstaden, Société de, 139–140, 213
Graissessac, Mines de, 167–168, 174
Grammont, 384, 396
Grand Central Railroad, 83, 85
Grand'combe, Mines de, 166–167, 169, 174–175, 306
Grande Huilerie Bordelaise, 283
Grande-Paroisse, Société Chimique de la, 450

Grandes Ecoles: formation of, 29; recruitment from, 472–476. *See also* specific schools
Grand Magasin Dufayel, 508n49
Grand Magasin du Louvre, 122, 124
Grand Moulin de Corbeil, 267
Grand Moulin de Nancy, 267
Grands magasins. See Department stores
Grandval, Joseph, 274
Great Britain: accounting, 302–303; coal exports of, 115; cotton industry in, 132, 134–135, 140–141; deposit banking in, 71, 75, 76; economic development of, versus France's , 3–4, 5, 26–27; factory production in, 128, 132; glass industry in, 239; iron production in, 178–179, 181–182, 517n4; machinery production in, 206–207, 208–209; paper industry of, 247; petroleum refining industry in, 427–428; printing industry of, 255; steam navigation of, 93, 503n37; wine trade with, 37
Grocery stores, 125–126
Gros, François, 133
Guadaloupe, 16, 36
Guestier, Daniel, 38
Gueugnon, Forges de, 194
Guinon, Marnas, et Bonnet, 230

Haber-Bosch process, 435, 439
Hachette et Cie, 260–261
Hall-Héroult process, 439
Hardware industry, 199–206
Harvey process, 348, 351
Haussmann, Baron, 72
Haute banque, 32, 48–56, 101–105. *See also* names of specific bankers
Hauts-Fourneaux de la Chiers, 370t, 396
Hauts-Fourneaux de Marseille, Compagnie des, 192
Hauts-Fourneaux et Aciéries de Caen, 334t, 338–339, 356
Hauts-Fourneaux et Forges de la Côte d'Or, 193
Haut-Fourneaux, Forges, et Aciéries de la Marine et des Chemins de Fer, Compagnie de. *See* Marine-Homécourt
Haviland et Cie, 292–293
Le Havre, 40–41, 93, 109–111, 272, 423, 428
Hayange. *See* Wendel et Cie
Heilmann woolcomber, 150

Hennebont, Forges et Aciéries d', 355
Hentsch, Edouard, 78
Heywood, John, 140–141
Hispano-Suiza, 417, 418, 420
Holden et Cie, 149, 513n54
Holding companies, 487
Holker, John, 20, 132, 135
Holtzer et Cie, 188, 195, 346; assets of, 334t
Horme, Fonderies et Forges de l', 214
Hottinguer family, 41, 50–51, 101, 104
Houlès-Cormouls, 149, 152–153
Huntley and Palmers, 268
Hydroelectric power. *See* electrical industry
Hypermarchés, 489

Imperial Chemicals, 432
Imphy, 519n31
Imprimeries Paul Dupont, Société Nouvelle des (SNPD), 259
Incorporation Law of May 1863, 76
Indiennes, 132–134
Indosuez, 487
Industrial finance, 296–303
Industrial firms: largest in 1936, 329–330t; largest in 1990, 484t. *See also* specific industries
Industrial gases, 446–451
Industrial paternalism, 306
Insurance industry, 41, 60–62, 102–103
International Telephone and Telegraph, 394–395
Iraq Petroleum Company, 426–427, 429–430
Iron and steel industry, 20, 177–197, 332–371, 489–490; cartels in, 321–322, 366; cost accounting in, 301–302; cost of plant and equipment in, 296–297; financing of, 298–301; organizational structure in, 468–469, 470; professional managers in, 473–474; protection of, 313, 315; recruiting workers in, 305–306; sales organization in, 476–477; work rules in, 308–309. *See also* specific companies

Jackson Frères, 187–188, 190
Jacquard loom, 148
Jaluzot, Jules, 122
Japy Frères, 118–119, 202–205
Javel Chemical Works, 220

Jay, Louise, 122
Jeumont. *See* Ateliers de Constructions
    Électriques du Nord et de l'Est
Jobert-Lucas, Pierre, 147, 150
Joeuf. *See* Wendel et Cie
Johnston family, 37–38
Journal, Le, 262–263
Journal de Lille, 256
July Monarchy, 148, 164, 259

Kay, John, 132
Keittinger family, 135
Keyder, Caglar, 3–4
Kléber-Colombes, 414
Knutange, Société Métallurgique de, 364
Koechlin, André, et Cie, 139–140, 207–
    208, 212, 214. *See also* Société
    Alsacienne de Constructions
    Mécaniques
Koechlin family, 139
Kuhlmann (SA de Manufacture des
    Produits Chimiques du Nord), 225,
    228, 436–438, 456
Kuhn Loeb, 100
Kuisel, Richard, 483

Labor relations, in industry, 303–312
Labor unions, 311–312
Laederich family, 142
Lafarge (SA Chaux et Ciments de la Farge
    et du Teil), 458–459, 486t, 490
Laffitte, Jacques, 53–54, 58, 60, 61, 62–
    63, 85
Latin Trust, 234–235
Laurent, Théodore, 367–368
Law codes, 12–13, 25–26
Law, John, 22, 71
Lawton family, 38
Lazard Frères, 412
Lebaudy family, 277
Le Blan, Julien, 145
Leblanc soda, 18, 221–222, 223–227, 228
Le Chapelier Law (1791), 24
Le Chatelier family, 446–448, 479,
    555n23
Le Creusot, 20, 54, 165, 178, 180–181.
    See also Schneider et Cie
Lefevre-Utile, 268–269
Legrand, Victor, 64
Lens, Mines de, 170, 345, 363
Le Quellec et Bordes, 38
Lesieur et Cie, 431
Lesseps, Ferdinand de, 94, 235

Lille: automobile industry in, 403–404,
    405; clothing industry in, 287–288;
    chemical industry in, 225; cotton
    industry in, 142, 143; linen industry in,
    145; printing and publishing industry
    in, 256; railroad equipment industry in,
    213–214
Lille-Bonnières-Colombes, 423, 425,
    550n39
Limoges, porcelain industry of, 292–293
Linde Air Products, 447
Linde process, 439, 447
Linen industry, 145–146, 323
Lister-Holden woolcomber, 149
Lodève, woolen and worsted industry of,
    148
Loire, department of the: coal industry of,
    168–169, 173–174; glass manufacture
    in, 238, 244–245; iron and steel
    industry of, 173, 186–189, 345–346,
    346–349, 367
Loire et Centre, Compagnie
    Hydroélectrique de la, 381
London, 49, 103
Lorraine-Dietrich (Société Lorraine des
    Anciens Etablissements de Dietrich),
    214–215, 405, 420
Lorraine ironfields, 20, 178, 181, 191,
    336, 339–343, 363–366
Loucheur, Louis, 381
Louis XI (king of France), 15
Louvroil, Société Française pour la
    Fabrication des Tubes de, 334t, 354,
    370t
Lumière Frères, 233–234
de Luze family, 38
Lyon, 15–16, 45–48, 75–77, 113–114,
    153–154, 156–158, 186–187, 229–231,
    233–234. *See also* Usines du Rhône

Magasins généraux, 507n40
Magasins Réunis, 125, 508n50
Magnin, Claudius, 347, 349, 367, 468
Magnin, Joseph, 193
Malétra, 222, 229
Mallet family, 50, 55, 61, 102
Mame et Cie, 257
Management: personnel, 481–482;
    production, 479–481;
    professionalization of, 471–476;
    railroad, 463–466; sales, 476–479;
    structures, 467–471, 487–488. *See also*
    labor relations

Managerial capitalism, 461–463, 488
Managerial hierarchies, 464–465, 467–468, 471–475
Manby and Wilson, 182, 184, 209
Mannesmann process, 354
Manufacture Française d'Armes et Cycles, 202
Marais et de Sainte-Marie, Papeteries de, 248, 253
Marchéville, Daguin, et Cie, 227
Marine-Homécourt (Compagnie des Hauts-Fourneaux, Forges, et Aciéries de la Marine et des Chemins de Fer), 183, 188–189, 190, 213, 300–301, 346–349, 360–361, 362, 363, 364, 367–368, 468–469, 489; assets of, 334t, 370t
MarMichPont, 353, 367–368
Marmont, Auguste-Louis Viesse de, 184
Marrel Frères, 188, 345–346
Marseille, 16, 17, 24, 42–45, 90, 92, 93–94, 273–275, 281–285
Marsilly, Commines de, 171–173
Martenot, J-B, 185
Martin family, 165–166, 189, 519n30
Martin, J.B., et Cie, 514n68
Martinique, 16, 36
Massif Central, coal industry of, 162–163, 166–168, 173–175
Le Matin, 262–263
Mattern, Ernest, 404, 409, 411
Matussière, Amable, 251–252
Maurel et Prom, 38, 89
Mayer, Michael, 486, 487
Mazamet, woolen and worsted industry of, 148–149, 152–153
Méline, Jules, 511n24
Méline Tariff (1892), 135, 141–142, 315, 323
Menier et Cie, 279–280
Mequillet-Noblot, 118, 297–298
Merchant-manufacturers, 18–19
Mercier, Ernest, 392, 429
Messageries Générales, 62–63
Messageries Maritimes, 89–90, 92, 93
Messageries Nationales (Royales), 62–63, 89–90
Messine Group, 391–392
Metal Box, 355
Metallurgy industry. See Aluminum; Copper industry; Electrometallurgy industry; Iron and steel industry
Métaux, Société Française des, 354
Meurthe-et-Moselle, department of the:

cartels in, 321–322; farm implements in, 200–201; iron and steel industry of, 336, 339–343, 348–349, 353, 362–363, 366–369
Michaud et Cie, 281
Michelin, André, 414–415
Michelin et Cie, 414–416, 486t, 487, 489
Michelin, Pierre, 413
Michel-Schmidt, Maurice, 350
Mineral water industry, 243, 245
Mines de la Loire, Société des, 169, 172t, 173
Mining laws (1810), 164, 168
Mirabaud family, 55
Mitterrand, François, 485, 489
Moissan, Henri, 446–447
Mokta-el-Hadid Mining Company, 92, 191–192
Montambert-La Beraudière, Mines de, 169, 173–174
Montataire, Forges et Fonderies de, 186, 355; assets, 334t
Montbard-Aulnoye, Société Métallurgique de, 354–355, 360
Montbéliard, pays de, 203–206
Montgolfier, Adrien de, 347, 348, 468
Montgolfier family: paper enterprises of, 246, 248–249, 252–253; worker benefits from, 306
Mony, Stephane, 185, 345
Morny, Comte Charles de, 75, 83
Morris, Frank, 133
Mors Automobile Company, 406, 408–409
Motte family, 143–144, 151
Moyeuvre. See Wendel et Cie
Mulhouse: cloth printing at, 137–140; cotton exchange of, 116; machinery industry of, 207–208
Mulhouse-Thann Railroad, 139
Multinationalization, 486
Munitions industry: firms of, 345–346, 351, 354–355; impact of World War I on, 359–360, 387, 452–453

Nantes, 39–40, 268–269, 272–273, 283
Napoleon I, 46, 49–51, 133, 137, 147, 257, 313
Napoleon III (Louis-Napoleon Bonaparte), 32, 67–68, 71, 73, 82–83, 94, 169, 314
Napoleonic Code, 26, 61, 307
National, Le, 57, 255
Nationalization, 485, 488

Navarre Paper Company, 435
Navigation Mixte, Compagnie de, 92
Négociants-commissionnaires, 117–118, 507n40
Neon lighting, 449
Newspapers, printing and publishing of, 255, 261–264
New York Cotton Exchange, 110–111
Neyrand Frères et Thiollière, 202
Neyrpic, 521n21
Nobel Française, Société de, 234–235
Nord, department of the: automobile production in 403–404, 405; cartels in, 322–323; chemical production in, 225; cotton industry of, 142–144; electrical industry in, 381, 385, 386, 395, 397; flour milling in, 267–268; glass industry of, 241–242, 245; iron and steel industry of, 186, 190, 343, 344, 346, 349, 354, 362; linen industry of, 145; petroleum industry in, 422, 423, 424, 428; printing industry in, 256; railroad equipment industry in, 213–214; sugar refining in, 278–279
Nord-Est (Forges et Aciéries du Nord et de l'Est), 343, 363; assets of, 334t, 370t, 489
Nord-Lumière, 378, 392
Norsk Hydro, Paribas investment in, 100
Northern Railroad (Chemin de Fer du Nord), 65, 80, 81–82, 85–86, 88, 319, 464
La Nouvelle Société Houillères et Fonderies de l'Aveyron. *See* Decazeville
Nouvelles Verreries de Givors. *See* Souchon-Nouvesel et Cie

Oberkampf, Christophe, 20, 132–133
O'Brien, Patrick, 3–4
Office National Industriel de l'Azote (ONIA), 435
Omnium International des Pétroles, 429
L'Oréal, 486t, 489
Oriflamme, 423
Ouest-Lumière, 381
Ouillins, Ateliers et Forges d', 212, 213

Paix et Cie, 422, 423, 428, 551n45
Pallot Frères, 202
Palotte, Jacques, 185
Panama Company, 217, 235
Panhard et Levassor, 401, 405, 549n25

Paper industry, 117, 246–254
Paquet, Nicolas, et Cie, 89
Parent, Basile, 213
Paribas. *See* Banque de Paris et des Pays-Bas
Paris: as business center, 48–62; clothing industry in, 286–289; electrical system of, 377–379, 391–392; home furnishings production in, 290–291; retail trade in, 120–125; sugar refining at, 272, 276–277; transportation system of, 64–65, 376, 389–391. *See also* Automobile industry; Banking and finance, Railroads
Paris-France, 508n50
Paris Gas Company, 235–236, 378
Paris-Lyon-Méditerranée Railroad (P-L-M), 47, 83–84, 88, 319, 465–466
Paris Metro (Compagnie de Chemin de Fer Métropolitain de Paris), 376, 378, 389–390, 485
Paris-Orléans Railroad (P-O), 65, 81, 83,174
Paris-Saint Germain Railroad, 64–65
Parissot, Pierre, 286
Pas-de-Calais, department of the: cartels in, 322; cement industry of, 458; coal mines of, 165, 169, 171, 306, 322
Pasta, 268
Pastré family, 44
Pauwels et Cie, 217
Pavin family, 458–459
Pechelbronn, 431, 551n53
Pechiney (Alais, Froges, et Camargue), 225–226, 228, 442–446, 470, 474, 485, 486t, 490
Peñarroya, 103
Perdonnet, Auguste, 502n24
Pereire family, 38–39, 57, 64–65, 72–73, 83, 84–85, 91, 124
Périer family, 54–55, 173
Permezel, Léon, 157
Perregaux, Laffitte et Cie, 53–54
Perret-Olivier, 224
Personnel management, 481–482
Petit Journal, Le, 262–263, 264
Petit Parisien, Le, 263, 264
Les Petits-fils de François de Wendel, 340. *See also* Wendel et Cie
Petits Fils de Léonard Danel, SA des, 256
Petrofina, 429, 431, 489
La Petroleénne, 427

Pétroles du Nord, Raffineries des, 424, 431
Pétroles Jupiter, 428
Petroleum industry, 103–104, 421–431
Petsche, Albert, 392, 394–395
Peugeot, Armand, 206, 401, 403–404
Peugeot family, 205–206
Peugeot, Société Anonyme des Automobiles et Cycles, 206, 403–404, 406, 411, 412, 486t, 489
Pharmaceuticals industry, 229, 452, 455–456
Phénix group, 61
Philibert Frères, 200
Photographic plates, 233–234
Pila, Ulysse, 113
Pilkington Brothers, 241
Pinault-Printemps-Redoute, 489
Plant and equipment, cost of, 296–297
Plant size, 534n21
Poincaré, Raymond, 365–366, 427, 429
Poirrier et Dalsace (SA des Matières Colorantes et Produits Chimiques de Saint-Denis), 232–233, 318
Poliet et Chausson, 457–458, 459
Polytechniciens, 464, 472–473, 475
Pompey, Hauts-Fourneaux, Forges et Aciéres de, 334t, 342–343, 370t
Pont à Mousson, Hauts-Fourneaux et Fonderies de, 334t, 353–354, 370t
Pont à Vendin, Société Métallurgique de, 345, 356
Porcelain industry, 291–293
Potez-Bloch Aircraft Company, 418–419
Potin, Félix, 125–126
Poulenc Frères, 229, 451, 452–453, 455. *See also* Rhône-Poulenc
Pouyer-Quertier, Augustin-Thomas, 136
Président-directeur-général, 467–468
Presse, La, 255, 262
Au Printemps, 122
Printing and publishing industry, 254–264
Prioux, Louis-Stanislaus, 118
Production management, 479–481
Produits Chimiques et Raffineries de Berre, Compagnie de, 431, 436
Professionalization of management, 471–476
Proto-industry, 18–21, 131; farm implements, 199–200; woolens, 146–147
Prouvost et Cie, 151

Public warehouses. *See Magasins généraux*
Publishing. *See* Printing and publishing

Quai Javel, 406, 409, 412

Raffinerie du Chatenay, 273
Raffineries de la Méditerranée, 274–275
Raffineries de Saint-Louis, 275
Railroad Act of 1842, 64, 212
Railroad equipment industry, 211–215
Railroads, 31–32, 63–66, 67, 72–73, 80–88, 139–140; coal industry and, 164, 166, 174, 175; government policy toward, 63–64, 82–83, 86–87, 316–319; iron and steel industry and, 179–180, 181, 182, 186–187, 188–189, 193, 199; management of, 102–103, 463–466; printing industry and, 259, 261. *See also* specific railroad companies
Rambourg, Nicolas, 185, 240
Rayon, 436, 453–456
Recquignies, Forges de, 363, 369, 370t
Refrigeration equipment, 354, 447
Reims: grocery chains in, 126; woolen and worsted industry of, 112, 147, 150
Renard Frères et Franc, 230–231
Renault (SA des Usines de Renault), 360, 401–403, 404, 405, 407–408, 410–411, 412, 419–420, 485, 486t, 489; administrative organization of, 470, 480–481; assembly line at, 479–480; engineers and, 475; scientific management at, 479; sales forecasting at, 481; sales organization of, 477
Renouard, Romain, 121, 123
Retail trade, 119–126
Réunion, Ile de la, 39, 270
Reveillon, J-B, 209–291
Rhodiaceta, 454–455
Rhône-Poulenc, 451–456, 485, 486t, 490. *See also* Poulenc Frères; Usines du Rhône
Richarme Frères, 244–245
Risler et Dixon, 207–208
Rive-de-Gier: bottle making at, 244; coal mines of, 168, 169, 173; steelmaking at, 188–189, 348
Roads, 62–67
Robais, Jesse van, 19
Rocca-Tassy-Roux, 284–285
Rochebelle, Mines de, 166
Roman, Jacques, 133

Rombas, Société Lorraine des Aciéries de, 364, 370t
Rosario, Port of, 350
Rostand family, 43–44, 90, 274–275
Rothschild family, 52–53, 55–56, 424
Rothschild, James de, 34, 52–53; in banking, 72–73, 74, 77, 101; in insurance, 61; railroads and, 65, 83, 84, 85–86
Rouart, Henri, et Cie, 354
Roubaix-Tourcoing: cotton spinning in, 142–143; woolcombing at, 149–151; woolens and worsted industry of, 143, 151, 488; wool trade of, 112–113
Rouen, 19–20, 115, 116, 134, 137, 222, 229
Rousseau process, 271
Royal-Dutch Shell, 104, 115, 426, 428–430
Roy, Gustave, 118
Ruel, Xavier, 123
Russia: French bankers in, 98, 99; petroleum refining in, 103–104, 424, 429

Sacilor, 489
SAFE. See Société des Aciers Fins de l'Est
Saint-Chamond, 188–189, 361
Saint-Domingue (Hispaniola), 16
Sainte-Claire Deville process, 226
Sainte-Clothide, Verrerie de, 243
Saint-Etienne: arms industry, 201–202; coal industry, 168–169; forges near, 186–187; grocery chains in, 126; railroads constructed in, 64
Saint-Galmier, Société de la Verrerie de (Veauche), 245
Saint-Gobain, 20–21, 223–224, 227–228, 238–242, 299, 301–302, 305, 434–436, 469, 474, 485, 486t, 488, 489
Saint-Quirin, Verrerie de, 239–240, 241
Saint-Simonians, 57–58, 71, 87–88, 94, 191–192, 483
Sales management, 476–479
Salins de Giraud, 225
La Samaritaine, 122
Samuel, Marcus, 104, 115
Saulnes, Marc Raty et Cie, Hauts-Fourneaux de, 334t
Saut-du-Tarn, Forges de, 186
SAUTS. See Société des Aciéries et Usines à Tubes de la Sarre

Savings banks, 107–108
Say, Raffineries et Sucreries, 272–273, 276–277
Say's Law, 129
Scale and Scope (Chandler), 2, 325, 358
Schaken, Pierre, 213
Schlumberger family, 140, 207
Schmaltzer, J-J, 138–139
Schneider et Cie, 165, 182–183, 212, 336, 350–351, 486t, 488, 490; assets of, 334t, 370t; finances of, 300, 301; labor relations at, 305–306, 308, 309, 311–312; management structure of, 486; recruitment of managers by, 474. See also Le Creusot
Schumpeter, Joseph, 6
Schÿler family, 38
Scrive-Labbe, Antoine, 145
Second Industrial Revolution, 8, 325, 326–327, 328–330, 485, 491
Secretan, Eugène, 99
Sedan, woolen and worsted industry of, 19, 147
Séguin, Louis, 420–421
Séguin, Marc, 62, 212
Seillière family, 54, 182
Seligmann, Aron-Elias, 53
Senelle-Maubeuge, Société Métallurgique de, 334t, 342, 370t
Sharp and Roberts, 139, 208
Shoes: chain stores for, 125; manufacture of, 287–288
Siècle, Le, 262
Siegfried brothers, 506n29
Siemens-Martin process, 178, 189–191, 192, 195, 337–339, 345–346
Silk, artificial. See Rayon
Silk industry, 45–46, 113–114, 153–158
Silk trade, 15–16, 113–114
Silva Plana, Société Française des Pétroles de, 551n58
Silverplate industry, 290
Simca, 413
Slave trade, 36, 37, 39, 109
Soap industry, 280–283
Sochaux automobile plant, 406
Société Alsacienne de Constructions Mécaniques (SACM), 140, 214, 394–395
Société anonyme (SA): characteristics of, 298; management structure of, 467–468
Société à responsibilité limité (SARL), 76

Société Centrale des Dynamite, 234–235

Société d'Electrochimie, 439–441

Société d'Electrochimie, d'Electro-Métallurgie et des Aciéres Electriques d'Ugine (SECEM et AEU), 439, 441–442

Société d'Electrométallurgie Française (Froges). *See* Pechiney

Société de Napthe Caspienne et de la Mer Noire. *See* BNITO

Société des Aciéries et Usines à Tubes de la Sarre (SAUTS), 365, 369, 370t

Société des Aciers Fins de l'Est (SAFE), 410

Société des Aciers Martin, 519n30

Société des Forces Motrices et des Usines de l'Arve (SARV), 444

Société des Métaux, 99

Société en commandite: characteristics of, 298; management structure of, 467–468

Société Française des Constructions Mécaniques (Anciens Etablissements Cail), 339. *See also* Cail, J.F.; Derosne et Cail

Société Française des Pneus. *See* Dunlop Rubber Company

Société Française du Crédit Mobilier, 73

Société Franco-Suisse pour l'Industrie Électrique. *See* Franco-Suisse

Société Générale, 77–78, 79, 99, 100, 101, 452, 485

Société Générale des Huiles et Pétroles (SGHP), 428

Société Générale des Verreries de la Loire et du Rhône, 244

Société Générale de Transports Maritimes à Vapeur (SGTMV), 92, 191–192

Société Industrielle des Pétroles, 425–426

Société Lorraine Minière et Métallurgique (SLMM), 365, 368–369, 370t

Société Lyonnaise des Eaux et de l'Eclairage (SLEE), 391–392

Société Marseillaise de Crédit (SMC), 75, 107

Société Nancienne de Crédit Industriel, 106

Société Nationale des Chemins de Fer (SNCF), 83, 488

Société pour l'Aviation et ses Dérivés (SPAD), 418

Solages family, 167

Solvay et Cie, 226–227

Sommier family, 277

Souchon-Nouvesel et Cie, 244–245, 435

Soult, Marshal, 57–58, 148–149, 166

Sous-Comptoir de l'Industrie et du Commerce, 75

Southern Aluminum Company, 444

Southern Railroad (Chemin de Fer du Midi), 85, 88

SPAD. *See* Société pour l'Aviation et ses Dérivés

Sprague system, 375

Standard Oil Company, 424

Standard Oil Company of New Jersey, 426–428, 429–430

Steam engines: manufacture of, 208–209, 211

Steam navigation, 43–44, 46–47, 88–93, 503n37. *See also* specific steam navigation companies

Steel industry. *See* Iron and steel industry

Steffen process, 271

Strasbourg-Basel Railroad, 85, 139

Strikes, 173, 310–312

Sud-Lumière, 378

Suez Canal, 89, 94, 115, 487

Sugar refining, 37, 39–40, 42, 269–279; plant and equipment cost for, 296. *See also* specific refining companies

Sugar trade, 16–17, 36, 270, 272, 273, 276

Sulfuric acid, 220, 224, 227

Superphosphates, 227–228, 435, 436–437

Taffin, Pierre, 163

Talabot, Léon, 186

Talabot, Paulin, 57–58, 65, 75, 77, 464; coal enterprises of, 166; Marseille port plan of, 93–94; railroads of, 83, 84, 191–192; Suez Canal plans of, 94

Talvende Frères et Douault, 283

Tariff policy, 135, 141–142, 179, 206, 313–316. *See also* Trade treaties

Taylorism (scientific management), 404, 409, 478–479

Ternaux, Guillaume, 147

Terrenoire, La Voulte, et Bessegès, Forges et Fonderies de, 183, 186–187, 300, 344

Terre-Rouge, Société Métallurgique de, 364

Textile industry, 18–20, 131–160. *See also* specific textile industries

Textile trade, 116–119

Texunion, 142

Third Industrial Revolution, 8, 327, 485, 491

Thiriez et Cie, 143

"Thirty Glorious Years," 3, 7–8, 331, 483–484

Thomas-Gilchrist process, 178, 191, 336; financing adoption of, 106–107; firms using, 338–343, 348, 349, 363–365

Thomson-Houston, 374–376, 382–383, 394–395, 398t, 486t, 490

Thoreau, Paul, 193

Thyssen, August, 338–339

Tinplate, 355

Tire and rubber industry, 413–416

Tocqueville, Alexis de, 26, 29

Tomich, Dale, 35–36, 39

Tool and machinery production, 206–209, 211, 216–217. See also railroad equipment industry

Tourcoing. See Roubaix-Tourcoing

Trade treaties: with Belgium, 313–314; with England (1860), 74, 189, 222, 276, 426–427

Tramways, 375–377, 390–391

Transportation. See Canals and waterways; Railroads; Roads; Steam navigation

Treaty of Utrecht (1713), 163

Treaty of Versailles, 364, 365

Tréfileries et Laminoirs du Havre (TLH), 384, 396–397, 398t

Trefousse, Goguenheim, et Cie, 290

Le Triphasé, 378, 392

Aux Trois Quartiers, 121

Trudaine, Daniel-Charles, 132

Tubes de Valenciennes, 357–358

Turbine manufacture, 209, 383–385

Turkish Petroleum Company. See Iraq Petroleum Company

Ugine. See Société d'Electrochimie, d'Electro-Métallurgie, et des Aciéries Electriques d'Ugine

Union Carbide, 447, 449

Union d'Electricité, 392

Union des Compagnies Houillères, 536n47

Union des Consommateurs de Produits Métallurgiques et Industrielles (UCPMI), 364, 370t, 410

Union des Producteurs d'Electricité des Pyrenées-Orientales (UPEPO), 389

Union Européene Industrielle et Financière (UEIF), 363, 470

Union Générale, crash of, 317

United States: automobile industry in, 404–405, 407–408; cotton production in, 109–110, 506n29; electrical industry in, 372–373, 398t; petroleum refining industry in, 422–423, 424, 426–427; steel industry in, 326, 328, 356; tire and rubber industry in, 415–416; wood-pulping process of, 249–250

Usines du Rhône, Société Chimique des, 233, 451–452, 454–455, 469. See also Rhône-Poulenc

Usinor, 489, 486t

Usquin, Philippe, 167–168

Vallourec, 363, 489

Vegetable oil refining, 280–281, 283–285

Venissieux automobile plant, 406

Verdié et Cie. See Firminy, Aciéries et Forges de

Vereinigte Glanzstoff Fabriken, 453

Vereinigte Stahlwerke, 366

Verminck, Etablissements, 284

Veuve Pastré, 44

Veuve Perrin et Fils, 289

Vidalon, Papeteries de, 248–249, 253

Videau, Paul, 121–122

Vignal, Jean, 92

A La Ville de Paris, 121

Visible Hand, The (Chandler), 2

Vosges, department of the: cotton industry of, 140–142

Waddington family, 135–136

Wallpaper industry, 290–291

Watch industry, 118–119, 203–204

Wendel et Cie, 20, 180–181, 306, 336, 339–341, 349, 359, 362, 364, 366–367, 368, 489; assets of, 334t, 370t

Wendel, Ignace de, 180–182

Wesserling, 133

Western Railroad (Chemin de Fer de l'Ouest), 85

Westinghouse, 351, 384, 397, 398t

Whittington, Richard, 486, 487

Wholesale trade, 108–119

Wilkinson, William, 20, 181–182

Wine trade, 36–38

Wolf-Lanmüller process, 188

Woolen and worsted industry, 19, 112, 146–153; works rules in, 308

Wool trade, 112–113

Workers, industrial, 18–19, 303–312. *See also* Personnel management

World War I: aircraft industry influenced by, 417–421; automobile industry influenced by, 405–413; chemicals industry influenced by, 435–438, 440–442, 444–445; coal industry influenced by, 386–387; electrical industry influenced by, 360, 386–397; glass industry influenced by, 434–435; iron and steel industry influenced by, 359–371, 370t; linen industry influenced by, 146; munitions industry influenced by, 359–361, 381, 451–452; reconstruction after, 359–371; tire and rubber industry influenced by, 416

World War II: electrical industry after, 393–394; French industry after, 483–490

Worms et Cie, 114, 115

Worms, Hypolite, 51, 114–115

Zuber, Jean, 291